CLASSICAL AND ROMANTIC PERFORMING PRACTICE 1750–1900

D0223116

CLASSICAL AND ROMANTIC PERFORMING PRACTICE 1750–1900

CLIVE BROWN

OXFORD

UNIVERSITY PRESS

OXFORD

UNIVERSITY PRESS

Oxford   New York
Auckland   Bangkok   Buenos Aires   Chennai
Dar es Salaam   Delhi   Hong Kong   Istanbul   Karachi   Kolkata
Kuala Lumpur   Madrid   Melbourne   Mexico City   Mumbai   Nairobi
São Paulo   Shanghai   Taipei   Tokyo   Toronto

Library of Congress Cataloging-in-Publication Data
Brown, Clive, 1947–
Classical and Romantic performing practive 1750–1900 / Clive Brown.
xiii, 662 p. : ill. ; cm.
Includes bibliographical references (p. [633]–644) and index.
ISBN 0-19-816165-4; 0-19-516665-5 (pbk.)
1. Performance practice (Music)—18th century.
2. Performance practice (Music)—19th century. I. Title.
ML457 .B76 1999
781.4'3'09033—dc21   97-050572

1 3 5 7 9 10 8 6 4 2

Printed in the United States of America
on acid-free paper

To Dorothea, who will not read this book, but without whose encouragement it would never have been finished

PREFACE

This is the book we have been waiting for. One of the joys of the last thirty years has been the forging of links between performers and scholars. Such links have already produced exciting results, and information on performing practice has been piling up for the sixteenth, seventeenth, and eighteenth centuries. The nineteenth century, however, has been largely a closed book, assumed, perhaps dangerously, to be part of a received 'tradition'. Just how wrong that tradition can sometimes be Clive Brown now shows us in awe-inspiring detail.

From the vantage point of the new Millennium, the history of twentieth-century music will perhaps seem to have been as much about the rediscovery of the past as about the music of its present. And that's not a bad thing. In a sense, this century has had three avant-gardes. The first, of course, was the great new works written in it. The second was a huge store of medieval and Baroque music recovered from near-extinction and brought to a delighted public. The third avant-garde grew out of the necessary serious thought about how such unknown music should be performed. It led naturally to a reappraisal of the music of the eighteenth and nineteenth centuries, which we thought we already 'knew'.

It is easy to forget that before 1800 there was simply no historical musical repertoire at all. Yesterday's music was as dead as yesterday's newspapers. As a repertoire began to develop from the time of Beethoven's symphonies, the chosen old works that were included in it were naturally treated as 'contemporary' music and modernized accordingly. But this modernization process couldn't continue indefinitely. By 1950, the irrationality of playing Bach as if it were Beethoven, and Beethoven as if it were Wagner, began to be intolerable to many of us. The potential hollowness of unrevised 'tradition' began to ring false. The historical movement that resulted was not an aberration; it was simply a revolution waiting to happen, when the elastic of that tradition was stretched to breaking-point. Unless we are going to play only brand-new music, we simply *have* to understand and value the past. And a relationship with that past needs to be founded on truth as well as sympathy, concern as well as exploitation, information as well as guesswork.

By the time this book has become a classic tool of eighteenth- and nine-teenth-century performing practice, it will be hard to believe that there were once musical professionals whose fear of the kind of knowledge it contains urged them to scorn the historical movement. It will be hard to explain that such 'flat-earthers' called an informed approach to music 'flummery', 'exoticism', or 'learning to play out of tune'. What these faint-hearted folk were afraid of was a loss of artistic freedom, a withdrawal of that power which performers had more and more taken over during the early part of the twentieth century. And yet, of course, music has always been a shared activity between creator and performer. You don't lose power by knowing things.

Power-hungry performers have a free hand once a composer is dead—especially if he is 200 years dead. What the historical movement has tried to do is to give that composer back his share in the proceedings. 'Tradition' and mysterious illumination from teachers can easily assume the mighty shadow of truth. But sharing the stage with a composer and his age isn't really frightening or restricting at all. It is liberating and creatively inspiring.

The thrill of that discovery, the recreation not just of unknown music of the past but of music we thought we knew all about, has been central to the musical lives of many thousands of listeners and performers ('flat-earthers' apart) for the last thirty years. During exciting years of pioneering with the London Classical Players, I have been fortunate to have learnt much from Clive Brown about nineteenth-century peforming style. Many of our landmark recordings (Beethoven, Berlioz, Brahms, Bruckner) were made with his advice and encouragement. Now he brings all this information to the public for the first time.

It is, of course, a never-ending quest, never fulfilled and by definition unfinishable. One of Dr Brown's great strengths is his acknowledgement of weakness. As he says in his own introduction: 'in most cases the effect envisaged by a composer or theorist can only be guessed at'. Yes, but guessing which is informed by everything one can find out has at least a chance of catching those intimate perfumes of the past that many of us seek.

Of course there is no 'authenticity'. Of course we don't know all the answers. Even if we did, it wouldn't make us perfect performers. Music-making must always involve guesses and inspirations, creative hunches and improvised strategies, above all, instinct and imagination. But if we don't have all the answers, the least we can do is to set out on our journey with the right questions. These questions, and indeed many of the possible answers, Clive Brown gives us in wonderful profusion. I cannot recommend this book too highly.

Roger Norrington

July 1997

Acknowledgements

This book is the result of more than ten years research; but it owes nearly as much to practical collaboration and informal discussion with scholars and practising musicians as to my own archival work. To list all those who have contributed ideas or forced me to re-examine my own interpretations of the evidence, or simply whose published work in this field, though not directly referred to in the book, has provided a starting point for my investigation is impossible. I hope those to whom I have not directly referred will pardon me.

My interest in the study of performing practice, and its relationship with scholarly editing, was stimulated in the early 1980s by Christopher Hogwood's invitation to advise the Academy of Ancient Music on the texts for their recordings of Beethoven Symphonies. In the next few years I enjoyed a fruitful exchange of ideas with Roy Goodman, Caroline Brown and other musicians associated with the Hanover Band, though the exigencies of the professional world made it difficult to put many of these ideas into practice to any great extent. I also had the great good fortune of getting to know Roger Norrington, whose enthusiasm prompts him not only to address the spirit of the music, but also to respond boldly to historical evidence about performing styles and techniques. He has not been afraid to experiment with radically different approaches to performing well-known works, often in the teeth of resistance from players who were, understandably, reluctant to attempt unfamiliar techniques in the limited time allowed for professional concerts and recordings.

The book that has finally emerged from these experiences and my own archival research has benefited greatly from many other practical experiments and academic exchanges. I cannot fail to mention the following, whose contributions have been more than incidental (though some of them may scarcely be aware of this): Robert Bottone, Duncan Druce, Angela East, Geoffrey Govier, Peter Hanson (and the other members of the Eroica Quartet), John Holloway, Yuki Konii, Colin Lawson, Harry Lyth, Hugh Macdonald, Richard Maunder, Rudolf Riedel, David Rowland, Simon Standage, Judith Tarling, and Elizabeth Wallfisch. In addition I am grateful to the following archives and their librarians or curators for friendly assistance in consulting collections, making source material available, providing microfilm, or giving permission for reproductions: Bayerische Staatsbibliothek, Munich; Bibliothèque Nationale, Paris; Bodleian Library, Oxford; The British Library, London; Conservatorio di musica Luigi Cherubini, Florence; Fürst Turn und Taxis Hofbibliothek, Regensburg; Gesellschaft der Musikfreunde, Vienna; Hessische Landes- und Hochschulbibliothek, Darmstadt; Library of Congress, Washington; Museo Donizettiano, Bergamo; New York Public Library; Öster-reichische Nationalbibliothek, Vienna; Sächsische Landesbibiliothek Dresden; Staatsbibliothek zu Berlin; Stadt- und Landesbibliothek, Vienna.

I am grateful to the Leverhulme Trust for the award of a research grant during the early stages of my research in 1987–8 and to Bretton Hall, College of the University of Leeds, for allowing me a term's release from teaching in 1995, which allowed me to finish writing the book. I should like to thank Bruce Phillips at OUP for encouraging me and prodding me to complete the book, and Helen Foster for helpful assistance in seeing it through the press. Finally, I am indebted to Nina Platts for tireless and good humoured assistance in checking proofs and preparing an index.

Contents

✧

INTRODUCTION

A comprehensive study of Classical and Romantic performing practice would require many volumes and many different authors. An adequate synthesis of the considerable body of recent secondary literature alone would fill more space than the present volume; it would also, perhaps, omit matters considered here. The purpose of this book is to investigate a number of key issues that are particularly relevant to understanding the intentions, expectations, or tacit assumptions of late eighteenth-century and nineteenth-century composers, to consider the extent to which these intentions, expectations, and assumptions may be evident in their notation, and, above all, to identify some of the constantly changing conventions of performance that informed the experience and practice of composers and executants alike.

While a broad range of major issues is examined, some significant matters, such as details of playing technique on individual instruments, methods of conducting, the physical conditions of music-making, and so on, are only touched upon in conjunction with wider issues, or if there are particular insights to offer. The technical specifications of instruments and the changes that took place in these during the period, though vitally important in recreating the textures and tone colours imagined by eighteenth- and nineteenth-century composers, have only been referred to where they are directly relevant to questions of performing style. Comprehensiveness has been eschewed in favour of a more thorough investigation of chosen issues.

In another respect the present study acknowledges self-imposed restrictions. Much heat has been generated by philosophical and aesthetic debate about the ways in which theoretical knowledge of historical performing practice has been utilized in the modern concert hall and recording studio; the author's standpoint may become to some extent apparent from the content of this book, but it is not a part of the present purpose to engage directly in that debate. It may, however, be stated as his firm conviction that dogmatism is seldom, if ever, appropriate in matters of musical performance. For much of the period examined here performers' freedom to impress their own personality on the music, often through minor, and sometimes major modifications of the strict meaning of the notation, was regarded as a right which only a few composers seriously disputed. There were good performances and bad performances, but their goodness or badness was not necessarily directly related to fidelity to the composer's text or to predetermined rules in any sense that would have been recognized by the modern devotee of urtexts and tables of ornaments. The conclusions about historical performing practice that are presented here are offered, therefore, rather as a stimulus to consider a wider range of possibilities in executing and interpreting works from this fruitful period of Western music than as a performer's guide to matters of specific detail. The author acknowledges that a fine, communicative, contemporary performance may take absolutely no account of the relevant historical performing practices, and may depart radically from anything the original composer might have conceived; but he is convinced that performances can always be enriched by greater awareness of the notational and stylistic conventions familiar to the composer and by a knowledge of the range of techniques employed by the instrumentalists or vocalists for whom the music was intended.

To determine which notational practices, styles, or instruments are appropriate to which music is far from simple. The territory is vast and complex; it is also remarkably hostile to certainties. This is partly because much information about specific composers' intentions is irrecoverably lost, and partly because the very nature of musical performance has always encouraged diversity and variety of interpretation. In some respects, such as ornamentation, a preference for particular types of instrument, the size and layout of orchestras, conducting practices, string bowing and so on, there is much concrete evidence relevant to particular individuals and places. Yet the gap between documentary evidence of this kind and a reliable aural conception of how musicians of the period might have made the music sound is very difficult to bridge. It is precisely the finer nuances of performance, which are so little susceptible to verbal explanation, that make all the difference between one style of performance and another; and that elusive quality 'good taste' does not seem to have been as susceptible to universal laws as some aestheticians would like to believe. In most cases the effect envisaged by a composer or theorist can only be guessed at, until, for the music of the late nineteenth century, the additional resource of gramophone recording became available. The existence of recordings from the early 1900s provides a salutary lesson for students of performing practice, for the aural evidence often reveals things that are startlingly different from anything that might confidently have been adduced from the documentary evidence alone. For earlier periods there are clues that this or that procedure may be more appropriate to the music of one composer while a different approach may be more suitable for that of another, but inevitably much remains highly speculative. We know, for instance, that equal temperament was vying for supremacy with various forms of unequal temperament during the closing decades of the eighteenth century, but have little firm evidence about whether Mozart, Haydn, or Beethoven expected the use of one or the other for their keyboard music, or indeed whether they regarded this as a matter of any significance for the achievement of the effects they intended.

In the matter of notation there are enormous areas of uncertainty, where we are confronted by symbols that meant one thing to one composer and something else to another, or even where a symbol has various meanings within the opus of a single composer. This is notoriously true of many ornament signs, but it is equally true of accent, dynamic, articulation, and phrasing marks. On the other hand there are symbols that are, or appear to be, distinct in form but synonymous in meaning. In printed music there is seldom any doubt about the identity of the symbol employed by the engraver, but in manuscript it is frequently unclear whether one symbol or another is intended. This is often the case, for instance, with dots and strokes used as articulation marks, turn, trill, and mordent signs, 'hairpin' diminuendo or accent marks, and many others. Though a large number of these problems are resistant to clear solutions, there are nevertheless many cases in which significant details of practices appropriate to particular composers and periods can be discovered, and these can help us to go beyond the notation to catch a glimpse of that which was taken for granted by well-trained musicians of the period. We are sometimes able to reach a high degree of certainty that such and such a symbol or form of notation had a precise meaning for a particular composer; but cases in which this kind of thing is possible are perhaps less common than some scholars and executants would like to imagine.

It is also extremely difficult to draw a line between those aspects of a composition where composers envisaged more or less strict adherence to the notation and those where they would have admitted, or indeed required, some degree of deviation from its apparently literal meaning. The eighteenth-century practice of extensive improvised ornamentation of a melodic line survived, albeit in an increasingly circumscribed form, well into the nineteenth century, especially in opera; and there were many less obtrusive types of ornamentation, such as the addition of appoggiaturas, vibrato, portamento, and the arpeggiation of chords on keyboard instruments, which either followed well-understood principles or were regarded as a legitimate area of interpretative freedom. Notation in the pre-computer era, even in the hands of so fastidious a composer as Elgar, could not by any means contain all the information that would have fixed the composer's conception with scientific exactness, nor would many composers of the Classical and Romantic periods have wished to exercise such despotic control over performance of their music. However precisely composers tried to convey their wishes, there was always the expectation, and sometimes the requirement, that the fine performer would depart from strict observance of the notation by employing some degree of rhythmic distortion, expressive phrasing, supplementary dynamics, and accentuation, along with other elements that have, to a greater or lesser extent, always been a feature of musicianly performance.

Having approached as closely as possible an understanding of what the composer envisaged, therefore, we will still be left with a broad area in which the interpretative skill of the performer would have been expected to operate. Many composers are known to have valued a considerable degree of interpretative freedom on the part of the performer. Indeed, to a large extent the core of the music remains undisturbed by differences of taste and temperament among accomplished musicians even when these result in performances that would have seemed unfamiliar to the composer. It is almost axiomatic that attempting self-consciously to preserve the stylistic peculiarities of past generations or particular performers, even where such things are theoretically reproducible (for instance, by slavish imitation of old recordings), is a path towards creative stagnation. But to regard all investigation of the relationship between a composer's notation and the artistic assumptions that may lie behind it as irrelevant to performance of the music is as perverse and one-sided as to quest for the chimera of authenticity. There can be little dispute that the more performers understand about the possible implications of the notation before them the more likely they are to render the music with intelligence, insight, and stylistic conviction; yet it is remarkable how little emphasis is placed on this approach in the vast majority of conservatoires, colleges, and universities.

Understanding the notation is not merely a matter of having an uncorrupted text of the composer's most complete version of a work. Although, in most cases, it is likely to be desirable to take an urtext as a starting-point, too great a reliance on such 'pure' texts creates its own dangers. The publication of *durchgesehene kritische Gesamtausgaben* (revised critical complete editions) in the second half of the nineteenth century sowed the seeds of a tendency which has achieved its full flowering in the second half of the twentieth century. Despite the counter-currents of heavily edited 'classics' from Ferdinand David and Hugo Riemann in the nineteenth century to Carl Flesch, Arthur Schnabel, and many others in the twentieth century, the cult of the urtext has grown slowly but steadily until many modern musicians, including advocates of period performance, have invested these editions with a mysterious, almost sacrosanct quality, as if the more literally the notes, phrasings, dynamics, and so on, which constitute the composer's latest ascertainable version of the work, are rendered, the closer the performance will be to the ideal imagined by the composer. Research into Baroque performing practice has led to a general recognition that this is not true of music from that period, yet there are still many professional musicians who believe that, from the Classical period onwards, different criteria should be applied: not a slur more nor less, a crescendo or diminuendo only if specified, one staccato note to be rendered differently from another only if the composer's writing appears to distinguish between a dot or a stroke, and so on. This picture may caricature the devotee of the urtext, but it hints at a widespread tendency to regard the relationship between notation and performance in a somewhat naïve light. Equally misguided is the attitude of many modern performers who, while acknowledging that eighteenth-century music requires different stylistic criteria from that of, say, Stravinsky or Britten, believe that from the early nineteenth century onwards an essentially undifferentiated and wholly modern approach is entirely appropriate. With respect to vibrato, for instance, the widely held notion that only a discreet and selective use is appropriate to eighteenth-century music, while nineteenth-century music, because of its increasingly 'Romantic' content, must have been characterized by a more vibrant tone quality, may actually be the reverse of the truth.

The present study aims to investigate the infinitely complex and fascinating relationship between notation and performance. The search will supply few unequivocal answers. If the following pages are more full of 'might have been' and 'seem to have' than readers seeking the solution to particular interpretative or notational problems would like, they may nevertheless find that faint rays of light will have been shed on some areas, and that the range of uncertainty has, at least, been narrowed; even if they consider some of the arguments presented here unconvincing, they may, perhaps, be stimulated to see things that they had previously taken for granted from a new angle. It is certainly not the purpose of this book to attempt to describe or prescribe an 'authentic' way of playing Classical and Romantic music; such an aim would patently be absurd. This is a critical examination of a number of central aspects of the subject, which it is hoped may provide another perspective on matters that have been the object of scholarly discussion, alert students to key issues, and stimulate performers to reappraise their approach to a familiar repertoire. The weight of evidence suggests that, throughout much of the period, a rather different relationship existed between performer and composer from that which obtains today. The almost reverential manner in which we tackle the Classical and Romantic repertoire, attempting to sublimate ourselves to the intentions of the 'great composer' by as literal a rendition of the received text as possible, owes much to mid- and late-nineteenth-century ideas, or rather, perhaps, to a misunderstanding of them. Wagner's writings were in this, as in so many other things, extraordinarily influential. He once insisted that, in performing a composer's work the executant musician should 'add nothing to it nor take anything away; he is to be *your second self*'.[1] This certainly represented a reaction against some

---

[1] 'Der Virtuos und der Künstler', *Gesammelte Schriften und Dichtungen*, 10 vols. 2nd edn. (Leipzig, 1887–8), i. 172 .

of the extreme manifestations of artistic licence, particularly prevalent in opera, by a composer who wished to exercise greater control over the performance of his music; but to interpret it, along with similar statements by other important nineteenth century musicians, as demanding slavishly literal rendition of the notation would be unhistorical; such comments can only be understood in the context of the notational and performing conventions of their day. In general, there may well be scope for a more adventurous approach to the interpretation of late- eighteenth-century and nineteenth-century notation, in which modern performers attempt to regain some of the free, creative spirit that the most accomplished Classical and Romantic musicians brought to the performance of the music of their own day.

I

ACCENTUATION IN THEORY

Accentuation is perhaps the most basic of the principal determinants of style in performance, yet it is among the least thoroughly investigated and understood aspects of historical performing practice. Here, as elsewhere, misconceptions about the standpoint of theorists and the practice of performers abound. There is a widely held notion that performance in the Classical period was characterized by a more rigid observance of hierarchical metrical accentuation than in either the Baroque or the Romantic. This view has been propounded in its most unsophisticated form by Fritz Rothschild[1] on the basis of examples given by Johann Abraham Peter Schulz and other eighteenth-century authors, without taking into account the vast corpus of theoretical writing that qualifies these early attempts at a scientific analysis of musical procedures. An insufficiently critical acceptance of such statements may have tended to encourage somewhat rigid and inexpressive performances of late eighteenth-century music. In addition, the paucity or absence of accent markings in eighteenth-century scores and their increasing frequency in nineteenth-century music has tended to engender a false idea among non-specialists that differentiated accentuation for structural or expressive purposes became more prevalent with the passage of time. There is no good reason to believe that this is the case. The proliferation of performance instructions in late eighteenth-century and nineteenth-century music is not necessarily evidence that the devices they specify were being more often employed than before; it is likelier to be an indication that composers increasingly came to regard individual patterns of expressive accentuation as integral to the character of particular pieces of music, and no longer wished to entrust this vital ingredient of expression entirely to the experience or whim of the performer. The more comprehensive notation of accents that developed during the nineteenth century, however, generated its own

---

[1] *The Lost Tradition: Musical Performance in the Time of Mozart and Beethoven* (London, 1961).

problems. The meaning of signs and written instructions varied from time to time, place to place and composer to composer, leading to confusion about their significance that has persisted to the present day.

Categories of Accentuation

Throughout most of this period accents were seen as falling into several basic categories. At a fundamental, almost subliminal, level was the accentuation connected with the metrical structure of the music, which was integral to the relationship between melodic figuration and harmony change, and the positioning of dissonance and resolution; this was variously known as grammatical or metric accent, or, in England, simply as accent. Superimposed upon this basic framework was a level of accentuation that was designated rhetorical, oratorical, or expressive accent or, by some English writers, emphasis.[2] A number of theorists further subdivided this type of accentuation. Heinrich Christoph Koch described two kinds of expressive accent, which he called oratorical and pathetic, the latter being an intensified version of the former. Some theorists seem to have regarded accentuation whose function was to define the extent and subdivision of musical phrases (here referred to as structural accent) as a distinct category,[3] but it is not always possible to see where the dividing line between this and expressive accent occurs. The majority of writers made no firm distinction between accentuation that emphasized phrase structure or rhythmic features, thus clarifying the rhetorical meaning of the music, and accentuation that was essential to its emotional content (since phrase structure and rhythm are inextricably linked with expression), yet it seems clear that this sort of notion lay behind the tripartite division of Koch and others.

Similar analyses of functionally different types of accentuation continued to be made in the following century, modified, however, in response to changes in musical style. Mathis Lussy broadly adhered to a three-part categorization, identifying metric, rhythmic, and pathetic accentuation, as counterparts to instinct, intelligence, and emotion respectively. Yet by the time Lussy wrote, there were, as he put it, 'certain modern theoreticians' who rejected the idea of the metric accent as such.[4] Perhaps the most radical rejection of the received notion of metrical accent came from Hugo Riemann, who arrived at the view that it was almost entirely irrelevant to the accentuation demanded by particular musical phrases. In an essay in 1883 he regretted that the old grammatical accent system had been constantly reproduced, even in his own earlier writ-

---

[2] e.g. by John Wall Callcott, *A Musical Grammar* (London, 1806) and John Jousse, *The Theory and Practice of the Violin* (London, 1811).

[3] This type of accentuation was described by, among others, Schulz, Türk, and later Fink and Lussy.

[4] *Le Rhythme musical, son origine, sa fonction et son accentuation* (Paris, 1883), 33.

ings, and wished to replace it with a crescendo–diminuendo system related to phrase structure.[5] Riemann's theories, which seem to have been strongly influenced by nineteenth-century practice, enjoyed considerable prestige in the late nineteenth century and, in some quarters, well into the twentieth century, but they did not displace the concept of metrical accent in conventional theory teaching.

Metrical Accent

Between the middle of the eighteenth century and the end of the nineteenth, the majority of theorists was broadly agreed about the nature and function of metrical accent. Analyses of this type of accentuation took a number of forms, and the terminology employed is diverse; but (apart from a few differences discussed below) there was broad agreement about the arrangement of accented and unaccented beats in most species of metre. Fundamental to the system, and still expounded in conventional modern theory teaching, was the age-old concept of rhythmic arrangement by twos and threes, where, in duple metres, the beats are alternately accented and unaccented and, in triple metres, the first of each group of three beats receives a greater degree of metrical accent than the others. These principles were also seen to operate in subsequent subdivisions of the beat, thus producing patterns of duple or triple grouping in smaller note values. From the various permutations of twos and threes all the commonly used metres were derived.

While the fundamental patterns of alternation of strong and weak were generally agreed, however, there was rather more diversity of opinion with respect to the relative degree of strength or weakness each beat should receive. Many writers of practical instruction manuals contented themselves merely with explaining how strong and weak beats were distributed in different metres, without making any distinction between greater or lesser accentuation of strong beats according to their position in the bar. More theoretically minded authors went further, elaborating a hierarchical system in which some accented beats received more stress than others. The precise pattern of this differentiated accentuation was determined by the metre. In the early 1770s J. A. P. Schulz explained it thus:

Duple [even] time has two principal time-units, the first of which is long, the second short: [Ex. 1.1(*a*)] If, however, these notes are divided into smaller values, such as crotchets in Alla breve time, for example, the first note of the second time-unit receives more emphasis and the crotchets themselves behave like time-units [Ex. 1.1(*b*)]

[5] Carl Wilhelm Julius Hugo Riemann, 'Der Ausdruck in der Musik', *Sammlung musikalische Vorträge*, i, no. 50 (Leipzig, 1883), 47.

Ex. 1.1. Sulzer, *Allgemeine Theorie*, 1st edn., ii. 1136–7

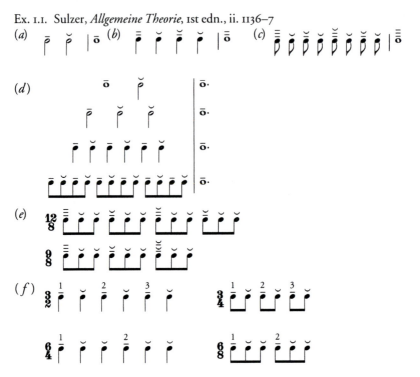

If the bar is divided into still smaller values such as quavers, each of these will have a different degree of emphasis. E.g.: [Ex. 1.1(*c*)]

This last example shows clearly the difference between the long and the short notes in duple time . . .

In triple [uneven] time the unequal value of notes is illustrated by the following example: [Ex. 1.1(*d*)]

How to play these notes in respect of their different weights and the accents placed upon them will easily be understood from what has been said about duple time . . .

In fast movements, or in time signatures where the number of notes can be divided by three, such as 12/8 or 6/4 and in all similar cases, the first note of three is invariably emphasized thus –∪∪, and the emphasis on other time-units depends on whether they are even or uneven. E.g.: [Ex. 1.1(*e*)]

After what has been said of the inner value of time-units, surely no proof is required to show that, as regards accentuation, 6/4 is essentially different from 3/2, and 6/8 from 3/4, despite the fact that both metres contain the same number of identical note values. The following table will show the difference clearly: [Ex. 1.1(*f*)] [6]

---

[6] In Johann Georg Sulzer, ed., *Allgemeine Theorie der schönen Künste*, 1st edn. (Leipzig, 1771–4), ii. 1136–7.

Similar hierarchical principles were constantly reiterated during the nineteenth century, though not wholly unchallenged. Adolph Bernhard Marx mused in 1854:

> we may content ourselves with merely marking the greater divisions (parts, sections, phrases) or we may proceed to define in detail the bars and members of the bar, distinguishing the more important with stronger accents.
>
> It may be asked how far this detailed accentuation is to be carried? In my 'Theory of Composition' I have already drawn attention to the charm that rests in this 'play of the accents,' and also to the danger of producing a fragmentary effect by obtrusion of subordinate features. This danger can easily be illustrated to the eye by a variegated accentuation, such as: [Ex. 1.2]
>
> Where is the medium between an undefined and an exaggerated accentuation?[7]

Ex. 1.2. Marx, *The Music of the Nineteenth Century*, 260

Hugo Riemann, however, was apparently, the first theorist fundamentally to question the relevance of hierarchical metrical accent to musical performance.

However, as the most penetrating expositions make clear, the system was not, in practice, so neatly logical as certain writers would have liked to make it. Not all the ways in which composers used common time (c), for instance, could be reconciled with a single conception of that metre in relation to its tempo giusto (see Chapter 8) and accentual characteristics. In addition, Schulz and Kirnberger, together with other theorists, some of whom were probably influenced by their approach[8] and others of whom were not,[9] insisted that there was an important distinction between a true quadruple metre and one which was merely derived from two bars of duple metre with the bar-line removed. Schulz explained that the true c (*Viervierteltakt*) was accented as in: Ex. 1.3(*a*) not Ex. 1.3(*b*), the latter accentuation belonging properly only to

---

[7] *The Music of the Nineteenth Century and its Culture*, trans. August Heinrich Wehrhan (London, 1854), 260.

[8] e.g. Daniel Gottlob Türk, *Klavierschule oder Anweisung zum Klavierspielen für Lehrer und Lernende mit kritischen Anmerkungen* (Leipzig and Halle, 1789); 2nd rev. edn. (Leipzig and Halle, 1802), and, in England, August Frederic Christopher Kollmann, *An Essay on Musical Harmony* (London, 1796), 73. Kollmann was certainly influenced by Johann Philipp Kirnberger, *Die Kunst des reinen Satzes in der Musik*, i (Berlin and Königsberg, 1771), ii (Berlin and Königsberg, 1776–9), trans. as *The Art of Strict Musical Composition* (New Haven, 1982): he quotes him on p. 77.

[9] e.g. François-Joseph Gossec, Joseph Agus, Charles-Simon Catel, and Luigi Cherubini, *Principes élémentaires de musique arrêtés par les membres du Conservatoire, suivis de solfèges* (Paris, ?1798–1802) and other French writers.

Ex. 1.3. Sulzer, *Allgemeine Theorie*, 1st edn., ii. 1136–7

the **c** that resulted from two bars of combined 2/4 (*zusammengesetzter Vierviertteltakt*).[10] Some writers, though, regarded this distinction as dubious. Leopold Mozart categorized all even time as duple and all uneven as triple, regarding the division of even time into four crotchets as essentially a means of making 'the even time-measure more comprehensible to the pupil', adding: 'That even time be mostly only duple, a good composer must know best himself.'[11] Half a century later Callcott too argued that, notwithstanding the notion (held by some French and German musicians) that common time was a simple rather than compound measure there were really no grounds for recognizing quadruple metres as in any essential way different from duple ones; he took the view that **c** was only distinguished from 2/4 'by the omission of the alternate Bar'.[12] Callcott even seems to have questioned the value of establishing a hierarchy among the accented notes within the bar, being content merely to recognize the normal distribution of accents on the first note of groups of two and three; in this respect he stands closer to the practical approach of many authors of instrumental methods.

In fact, it is clear that even those writers who attempted the most extensive classifications of the differences between the various types of metre were conscious that, in practice, many factors modified the strict operation of these rules. Tempo, above all, was crucial in determining the frequency and weight of metrical accents. Callcott observed: 'every species of measure may be subdivided by Accents, according to the degree of quickness in which it is performed'.[13] Even Schulz, having detailed the difference between a genuine **c** metre and one that really consisted of combined bars of 2/4, admitted that 'in performance, especially in slow pieces, it [genuine 4/4] is often confounded with the combined [type] and divided into two parts, each of two crotchets.'[14] And later in the nineteenth century Adolf Bernhard Marx articulated a generally held view when he made the observation that speed determines the extent to which a hierarchy of accents is intelligible.[15]

In the early part of the period there were also some rather basic disagreements about the metrical accentuation of triple time. A considerable number of important eighteenth-century and early nineteenth-century writers main-

[10] In Sulzer, *Allgemeine Theorie*, ii. 1135. Kollmann repeated this in his *Essay*, 72.

[11] *Versuch einer gründlichen Violinschule* (Augsburg, 1756), trans. Editha Knocker as *A Treatise on the Fundamental Principles of Violin Playing* (Oxford, 1948), I, ii, §4.

[12] *Musical Grammar*, 257.   [13] Ibid. 44.

[14] In Sulzer, *Allgemeine Theorie*, ii. 1135.

[15] *Allgemeine Musiklehre* (Leipzig, 1839)), trans. A. H. Wehrhan as *A Universal School of Music* (London, 1853), 113.

Ex. 1.4. Löhlein, *Anweisung zum Violinspielen,* 53

tained that in certain triple metres the third beat was emphasized more than the second. Schulz's example of accentuation in 9/8 (Ex. 1.1(*e*)) shows that he regarded this to be the case in that metre too. Johann Peter Milchmeyer asserted that 'in a three-four metre, the first and third crotchets are the strong beats and the second the weak beat', but he cautioned that in 3/8 only the first beat received the emphasis.[16] Georg Simon Löhlein also seems to have regarded a stress on the third beat in 3/4 as normal,[17] giving the example shown in Ex. 1.4; while Jean Jacques Rousseau[18] and François Henri Joseph Castil-Blaze,[19] among French authors, and Charles Burney[20] and Callcott,[21] among English ones, maintained a similar position. Burney, however, qualified his observation that in triple time 'the *first* and *last* are accented, the *second* unaccented' with the comment: 'if the *third* note in triple time is accented in serious music, it is always less forcibly marked than the first'. Türk, while apparently recognizing a subsidiary stress on the third beat as normal, remarked, perhaps thinking of such pieces as polaccas and chaconnes, that 'in a few cases the second is internally long and thereby the third is short'.[22] In a similar manner, the authors of the Paris Conservatoire's *Principes élémentaires de musique* recognized the possibility of a metrical accent occurring on either or neither of the last two beats.[23]

It seems likely that such conceptions of triple metre were related partly to the old practice of beating time in triple metre with an uneven tactus (a two-beat downbeat followed by a one-beat upbeat) and partly, perhaps, to its association with particular dance types in which those sorts of accentuation were characteristic. Towards the end of the eighteenth century, as the uneven tactus disappeared and the relationship between art music and dance music weakened, the idea that the third beat in triple metres might have a regular metrical accent seems largely to have died out. The new orthodoxy was that the third beat in triple metres required the least metrical accent. Around 1840 François Habeneck stated that 'In a bar with three beats, the first beat is always strong, the second is sometimes strong and sometimes weak. The third beat is always

[16] *Die wahre Art das Pianoforte zu Spielen* (Dresden, 1797), 7.
[17] *Anweisung zum Violinspielen* (Leipzig and Züllichau, 1774), 53.
[18] *Dictionnaire de musique* (Paris, 1768). [19] *Dictionnaire de musique moderne* (Paris, 1821).
[20] In Abraham Rees, *Cyclopaedia* (London, 1819), art. 'Accent'.
[21] *Musical Grammar,* 41. [22] *Klavierschule,* I, §55.
[23] Gossec et al., *Principes,* 44.

weak.'[24] The proposition that the natural metrical accentuation of triple metres was strong–weak–weaker is found in many nineteenth-century German sources: Gottfried Wilhelm Fink described it thus in 1837,[25] and Moritz Hauptmann's almost metaphysical analysis of metre and rhythm in his highly respected treatise *Die Natur der Harmonik und der Metrik* (1853) led him to propose this scheme as an essential aspect of triple metre.[26] Hauptmann's approach may well have been responsible for the similar views expressed by Arrey von Dommer (1865)[27] and Hauptmann's pupil Oscar Paul (1873).[28] Dommer's description of the third beat in 3/4 as 'completely accentless, completely upbeat' certainly indicates a very different concept of triple metre from that which had been widely held at the beginning of the century.

In reality, much in the more elaborate expositions of metrical accentuation had scant relevance to practical music-making, since such things as different varieties of common time or differently accented triple metres were not prescribed for the performer by the time signatures composers gave to their works; they were, at best, only recognizable from the nature of particular pieces of music. It is this fact that seems to be acknowledged when, in its discussion of triple time, the *Principes élémentaires de musique* stated that in 3/4 an accent may fall on the second or third beat 'through the nature of the melody'.[29] As implied by differences of opinion among theorists and complaints about the casualness of composers in choosing the correct metre, much depended, in practice, on the knowledge and stylistic sensitivity of the performer, which was acquired far less from awareness of theoretical writings than from direct musical experience. In this respect the borderline between metrical and structural accent becomes blurred.

While the performer was ideally expected to be aware of the metrical scheme that provided the framework for the composer's musical ideas, it was nevertheless acknowledged by many writers throughout the period that it was unnecessary, indeed inartistic, to make purely metrical accentuation obtrude upon the listener's perceptions, except in special cases (for example dances and marches) where distinct accentual patterns were an essential feature of the genre. Elsewhere, the metrical accentuation was generally expected to be conveyed to the listener by the melodic and harmonic structure of the music, without any necessity for the performer to contribute an obvious accent. Referring to the accents that fall on the strong beats, Johann Friedrich Schubert commented in 1804: 'These require no accentuation on the part of the singer, since they accent

---

[24] *Méthode* (Paris, c.1840), 109.

[25] In Gustav Schilling, ed., *Encyclopädie der gesammten musikalischen Wissenschaften* (Stuttgart, 1835–8), art. 'Accent'.

[26] (Leipzig, 1853).   [27] *Musikalisches Lexicon* (Heidelberg, 1865), art. 'Accent'.

[28] *Handlexikon der Tonkunst* (Leipzig, 1873), art. 'Accent'.

[29] Gossec et al., *Principes*, 44.

themselves through their inner strength.'[30] (However, it may be noted that some thirty years later G. W. Fink, though he warned in general against excessive stressing of metrical accents, made quite the opposite point about accents in singing, saying: 'The metrical accents in vocal compositions, where they generally coincide with the long syllables [of the text] should least of all be neglected.')[31]

The necessity of subordinating metrical accent to the accentuation required by the shape of the phrase and the expressive content of the music was often stressed by writers throughout the period. In England in 1770 John Holden, having remarked that 'In the performance of music, there is a certain emphasis, or accent laid on the beginning of every measure, which distinguishes one species of time from another', observed: 'There is no occasion to make the beginning, or emphatical part of the measure, always stronger, or louder than the rest, though it is sometimes best to do so.'[32] And Johann Friedrich Reichardt cautioned his reader against interpreting Quantz's instructions for metrical accentuation too literally:

Also, it would be extremely faulty if the accentuation of the notes—about which Herr Quantz says so much—were always to be marked with a particular pressure of the bow. This [accentuation] is nothing more than the slightest weight, with which anyone with a correct feeling for the beat plays, which, of his own accord, without thinking about it, he will give to the stronger beats, just as children on their coloured fiddles already give it to the notes on which, if left to themselves, they will stamp with their foot. If the child does not get this right he should not learn music.[33]

At the beginning of the nineteenth century Heinrich Christoph Koch referred similarly to the metrical accent as an 'almost unnoticeable stress',[34] and Gottfried Weber, a musician of a younger generation, made much the same point almost twenty years later when he cautioned that 'What is said of the heavy and light parts of the bar is not to be understood as that a so-called heavy or strong part of the bar must really in all cases be delivered more heavily and strongly (more *forte*) than the so-called light or weak part; we here speak rather of an internal weight.'[35]

Johann Nepomuk Hummel's description of metrical accent, too, seems to emphasize the essentially notional quality of strong and weak beats, rather than suggesting that the performer will automatically deliver them more strongly:

[30] *Neue Singe-Schule oder gründliche und vollständige Anweisung zur Singkunst* (Leipzig, [1804]), 134.

[31] In Schilling, *Encyclopädie*, art. 'Accent', i. 36.

[32] *An Essay towards a Rational System of Music* (Glasgow, 1770), 32.

[33] *Ueber die Pflichten des Ripien-Violinisten* (Berlin and Leipzig, 1776), 8–9.

[34] *Musikalisches Lexikon* (Frankfurt-am-Main, 1802), art. 'Accent'.

[35] *Versuch einer geordneten Theorie der Tonkunst* (Mainz, 1817–21), trans. J. F. Warner as *Theory of Musical Composition* (London, 1846) i. 90.

The parts of the bar are divided into accented and unaccented. By the former are to be understood those parts upon which our feelings naturally bestow a certain degree of weight or stress. The latter pass by our ear, as it were, and, in comparison with the former, appear light and unimportant.[36]

However, during the Galant and Classical periods there seems to have been a significant distinction between melody and accompaniment with respect to metrical accentuation. It arises from the characteristic textures of this music, in which accompanying parts and bass were so often given regular patterns of repeated notes, the so-called *Trommelbass*. As with so much else in the study of performing practice, it is important to distinguish here between the conventions that applied primarily to solo performance and those that were germane to ensemble or accompaniment. The metrical structure of the music, seen from the point of view of the composer, is intimately connected with such things as phrase structure, the rate of harmonic change, and the fullness or lightness of texture at any given point. To a large extent these factors will, as J. F. Schubert remarked, cause the strong beats of the metre to 'accent themselves through their inner strength'; and this probably lay behind Hummel's comments. But many writers pointed out that when instrumentalists played repeated patterns of accompaniment figures, they had to ensure that the accents were placed strictly in accordance with the music's metre unless this were expressly countermanded by the composer's markings. Thus Johann Joachim Quantz advised the cellist that 'If in a Presto that must be played in a very lively fashion several quavers or other short notes appear upon the same pitch, the first in each measure may be stressed by pressure on the bow'.[37] And Leopold Mozart gave a similar example of an 'ordinary accompaniment to an aria or concert piece, where for the most part only quavers or semiquavers appear' (Ex. 1.5).[38] In these types of accompaniment it would clearly be out of place either to make absolutely no kind of metrical accent or to place the stronger accents on metrically weaker beats, except in special circumstances, or where the composer has indicated something particular. It may well be the case that rhythmic or expressive accent

Ex. 1.5. L. Mozart, *Versuch*, XII, §9

---

[36] *Ausführliche theoretisch-practische Anweisung zum Piano-Forte-Spiel* (Vienna, 1828), trans. as *A Complete Theoretical and Practical Course of Instructions, on the Art of Playing the Piano Forte* (London, 1828), i. 59.

[37] *Versuch einer Anweisung die Flöte traversiere zu spielen* (Berlin, 1752), trans. Edward R. Reilly as *On Playing the Flute* (London, 1966), XVII, 4, §9.

[38] *Versuch*, XII, §9.

in the melody will contrast with the metrical accentuation of the accompaniment. From time to time, however, the accompanying parts will also have melodic material and will then be likely to make freer use of nonmetrical accent, in accordance with the general principles discussed below. In more intricately textured works, such as string quartets, all parts in the ensemble may alternate between the observance of metrical accentuation in accompaniment figures and the application of expressive accents in melodic passages. As is evident from later nineteenth-century discussions of accentuation, this type of differentiation weakened during the Romantic period when, in many types of music the distinction between melody and accompaniment became less clear-cut.

Before looking at the factors that were seen to modify the principles of metrical accentuation, it may be useful to note one particular situation in which, during the Classical period, it was felt by many to be specially undesirable that the hierarchy of strong and weak beats should be emphasized by the solo performer. This was in passagework with relatively fast-moving equal notes. Koch observed that in this case the metrical accent 'must be so finely modulated that it is barely perceptible, otherwise a tasteless and limping style of performance results'.[39] Burney considered that in 'very rapid divisions, ascending or descending the scale in notes of equal length, no regard is had to accents'.[40] And Milchmeyer similarly instructed that 'in a run of several bars the ear should not be able to distinguish any strong or weak beat from the beginning to the end'; though, apparently contradicting himself, he added that 'in triplets and in upwards and downwards passages of four, six, and eight notes in both hands one mostly strikes the first notes a little more strongly and in passages of four semiquavers, or in slow tempo of two quavers, one changes the finger on the first note very often in order to give the melody its true accent'.[41] J. F. Schubert commented: 'In passagework it is difficult to prescribe where the accents have their proper place; this must be entirely a matter of feeling and taste',[42] and Bernhard Heinrich Romberg, discussing accentuation in his 1840 cello school, made a similar point when he observed that in rapid passages 'it is only requisite to make a few notes here and there, prominent, in order to deprive the passage of its otherwise monotonous effect'.[43] Hummel, Carl Czerny, and Manuel García were among those who gave illustrative examples of this kind of selective accentuation; García explained that the accent '(according to the artist's instinct) is placed on any one sound selected in passages of equal notes. This is done to avoid monotony' (Ex. 1.6).[44] As in other

---

[39] *Musikalisches Lexikon*, art. 'Accent'.   [40] In Rees, *Cyclopaedia*, art. 'Accent'.
[41] *Die wahre Art*, 7.   [42] *Neue Singe-Schule*, 134.
[43] *Méthode de violoncelle* (Berlin, 1840), trans. as *A Complete Theoretical and Practical School for the Violoncello* (London, 1840), 129.
[44] Hummel, *A Complete*, iii. 61; Czerny, *Vollständige theoretisch-practische Pianoforte-Schule* op. 500, 3 vols. (Vienna, 1839), iii. 9; trans. as *Complete Theoretical and Practical Piano Forte School* op. 500, 3

Ex. 1.6. (*a*) Hummel, *A Complete*, iii. 61; (*b*) Czerny, *Vollständige . . . Pianoforte-Schule*, iii. 9; (*c*) García, *New Treatise*, 52

(*a*)

(*b*)

(*c*)

Rossini *Biancha e Fallero*

Cie - lo   il mio   lab - broins   pi   -   -   -   -   ra

vols. (London, [1839]); vol. iv, *Die Kunst des Vortrags der älteren und neueren Klavierkompositionen* (Vienna, 1846), trans. as *The Art of Playing the Ancient and Modern Piano Works* (London, [1846]); García, *Traité complet de l'art du chant* (Paris, 1840), trans. and enlarged as *García's New Treatise on the Art of Singing* (London, 1894), 52.

aspects of accentuation, however, tempo was seen as important in determining the frequency with which accents were appropriate in passagework.

Structural and Expressive Accents

After considering metrical accentuation, Koch continued with a discussion of what he called oratorical accentuation. He began his treatment of the subject with an analogy between the nature and purpose of accentuation in speech and music which is typical for the period:

Just as in speech, particularly if the speaker speaks with feeling, certain syllables of the words are marked by a special emphasis, by which the content of the speech is mainly made clear to the listener, so in the performance of a melody which has a definite feeling it is necessary to execute certain notes with a conspicuous manner of performance if the feeling which it contains is to be clearly expressed.[45]

Like other theorists of his time Koch observed that these expressive accents, which he divided into oratorical and pathetic (apparently making a distinction only of degree rather than kind between them), are much more evident in performance than the metrical accents, and, this time using an analogy with painting, he continued: 'They are at the same time the highest lights and impressions of the tone-picture, and in performance the ear will be made aware of the more definite meaning of the melody through these accents.' He further remarked:

They are distinguished from the metrical accent not only through the above-mentioned more prominent performance, but also through the fact that they are not confined to any specific part of the bar, but are merely contained in the ideal concept of the composer, which he has portrayed in notes, from which the taste of the performer must discover it. Of this type are the accents with which the notes marked * in the following extract must be performed if the melody is not to sound as lame and insignificant as that of many a schoolboy's monotonous recitation of his catechism [Ex. 1.7].

These accents represent a larger-scale structural feature of the music than that defined by metrical accentuation. In the given example, Koch's accents come exclusively on metrically strong beats, because this is required by a melody of that type, though the oratorical accents could be less regularly distributed if the melody so required. Koch's failure to differentiate clearly between the accentuation necessary to articulate the phrase structure and that required to bring out the emotional content of the music reflects the widely prevalent view of the time, that music was fundamentally a language whose principal purpose, like that of poetry, was to express something more than the mundane material of common speech; the intelligible delivery of a phrase and its emotional weight, therefore, were inseparable.

---

[45] *Musikalisches Lexikon*, art. 'Accent'; see also Türk, *Klavierschule*, VI, §12, Hummel, *A Complete*, iii. 55.

Ex. 1.7. Koch, *Musikalisches Lexikon*

Other late eighteenth-century and nineteenth-century writers seem to have been more acutely conscious of a distinction in function between structural and expressive accentuation (and articulation), but the recognition that the latter types of accentuation should operate at a significantly more obtrusive level than metrical accentuation appears to have been general. In the 1830s G. W. Fink wrote: 'A too-symmetrical and scrupulously regular, mechanical beat introduces a stiffness into the performance which equates with crudeness. As a rule, therefore, the metrical accents should not be applied anything like so sharply and strongly as the rhythmical and above all the sectional accents [*Einschnittsaccente*[46]] of the rhythmic segments.'[47] And in a similar vein Arrey von Dommer observed in 1865:

A correct oratorical accentuation must always fundamentally be a correct metrical one, despite many liberties for the sake of the particular expression. Yet it reaches beyond the simple regularity of the metrical accentual pattern, appears already as a higher artistic freedom and is a more essential part of expressive performance. One can deliver a passage with absolutely correct metrical accentuation and still play very stiffly and vapidly if the animation through oratorical accentuation is lacking.[48]

Thus, the harmonic and melodic structure of a well-written piece could be seen as virtually sufficient in itself to convey the metrical pattern of the composition to the listener so long as performers were responsive to that pattern in their choice of accentuation; there was no need for the metrical regularity of the music to be stressed. Only those notes that were important for the shape of a phrase or the expressive content of a melody were expected to receive a distinct emphasis. Although individual structural and expressive accents would often occur on metrically strong beats, the accentual pattern of a melody in performance would rarely, if ever, conform exactly with the theoretical hierarchy of

---

[46] The term *Einschnitt*, frequently employed by musical theorists of this period, has no entirely satisfactory English equivalent. The word means literally a cut, incision, or notch and was used in this context to describe the notional or real articulations which separate the 'phrases' in a musical 'sentence'.

[47] In Schilling, *Encyclopädie*, art. 'Accent', i. 36.   [48] *Musikalisches Lexicon*, art. 'Accent'.

beats, for the accentual relationships required by the phrase structure would generally override the small-scale metrical patterns with, for instance, a greater emphasis on the strong beat of one bar than another, or more stress on the second half of a 2/4 or 4/4 bar than on the first. Frequently, too, the expression might require more accent on so-called weak beats than on strong ones. Türk qualified his explanation of metrical accent with the observation that the initial note of each section of melody 'must be given an even more marked emphasis than an ordinary strong beat'[49] and added that even among these more prominently stressed beats there should be a hierarchy according to whether they were the beginning of a main section or only a unit within the larger phrase. He illustrated his meaning with an example (Ex. 1.8), observing: 'The greater the number of crosses the greater the emphasis; the o indicates that the upbeat quaver is unstressed in relation to the following note.'

Ex. 1.8. Türk, *Klavierschule*, VI, §14

Türk's concern that the upbeat should not be stressed in this context would undoubtedly have been endorsed by other theorists; but there were circumstances in which, even if nothing were indicated by the composer, some eighteenth-century musicians might have thought it appropriate to accent a note that would normally be seen as an upbeat. Quantz, for instance, had advised that 'in gay and quick pieces the last quaver of each half bar must be stressed with the bow'[50] and gave an example in which such a treatment was to be recommended (Ex. 1.9). Leopold Mozart, too, advocated a similar procedure 'in lively pieces . . . to make the performance right merry'[51] (Ex. 1. 10).

It is questionable whether, in practice, Türk would have expected the performer literally to apply the predominantly diminuendo pattern of phrasing indicated in Ex. 1.8, to other melodies any more than he would have anticipated slavish adherence to the theoretical hierarchy of metrically stronger and weaker beats in the bar (except perhaps in repeated accompaniment figures).

---

[49] *Klavierschule*, VI, §14.   [50] *Versuch*, XVII, 2, §8.   [51] Ibid., XII, §13.

Ex. 1.9. Quantz, *Versuch*, XVII, 2, §8

Ex. 1.10. L. Mozart, *Versuch*, XII, §13

His example certainly cannot be taken to prove that, as a general principle, late eighteenth- and early nineteenth-century melodies were expected, either absolutely or relatively, to have the most prominent accent on the first strong beat of each major melodic segment. Yet it seems possible that 'downbeat' rather than 'upbeat' treatment of the first part of a phrase was regarded as normal in the majority of cases at that period. A generation later it was still possible for August Ludwig Crelle to state that 'as a rule the musical unit begins powerfully and importantly, the middle continues moderately and evenly and the end speeds up and becomes less powerful'.[52]

Examples from other sources suggest, however, that even if Türk's illustration and Crelle's advice represented the most usual approach to the accentual shaping of a melody (in the absence of contrary markings by the composer) during the late Classical period, it would have been neither unknown nor considered unmusical for a performer to shape an unmarked melody differently; it is precisely this latitude that blurs the distinction between structural and expressive accentuation. In the case of Türk's example, for instance, the expressive impact of the melody could be changed by giving it the dynamic shape shown in Ex. 1.11, with its implications of a quite different accentuation.

Ex. 1.11.

A careful eighteenth-century composer, for instance Mozart, might mark such accentuation where he regarded a particularly emphatic rendition of it as vital to the expression (Ex. 1.12), but the absence of such a marking in the music of his less meticulous contemporaries, or even of Mozart himself, may not necessarily be an indication that this type of treatment would be contrary to the composer's conception. The melodies shown in Ex. 1.13, for instance, may well

[52] *Einiges über musikalischen Ausdruck und Vortrag* (Berlin, 1823).

Ex. 1.12. Mozart, Violin Sonata K. 454/ii

Ex. 1.13. (*a*) Mozart, Symphony in D K. 504/ii; (*b*) Haydn, String Quartet op. 55/2/ii; (*c*) Beethoven, String Quartet op. 18/6/ii

have elicited an 'upbeat' accentual pattern from some contemporary performers although the composer did not mark it. This is most likely to have been the case where there is an increase of harmonic tension (dissonance) at the beginning of the second bar. Theoretical support for this type of approach is provided by Hummel, who gave several examples in his piano method where he considered such accentuation appropriate (Ex. 1.14; + indicates a slight accent, ^ a more emphatic one).

It must always be borne in mind that the overwhelmingly prevalent eighteenth-century view was that details of this kind could generally be left to

Ex. 1.14. Hummel, *A Complete*, iii. 56–9

the taste of performers, whose treatment of a melody would be determined by their response to such internal musical signals as harmony, melodic shape, and so on (as discussed further below). On the other hand, it is conceivable that the modern performer's instinct to apply this sort of upbeat treatment to passages in eighteenth-century music where no dynamic instructions are given may be the anachronistic product of musical conditioning by a tradition that only became established during the course of the nineteenth century.

In short, there was general agreement during the Classical period that, within broadly defined parameters, fine and knowledgeable performers would accent a melody according to their perception of its particular character rather than rigidly emphasizing the metrical accent indicated by the time signature. Consequently, rather more flexibility is likely to have been approved in practice than the stricter theorists seem to imply. Türk cited two musical examples to show that 12/8 and 6/8 are essentially different and that a piece of music appropriate to the one cannot properly be written in the other (Ex. 1.15).[53] But his examples also illustrate that even if they were 'incorrectly' written in the other

[53] *Klavierschule*, I, §59.

Ex. 1.15. Türk, *Klavierschule*, I, 4, §59

(*a*)

(*b*)

metre, the skilful player, responding to the nature of the melody, the texture and harmonic structure of the music, and so on, would almost certainly seize upon the sense of the piece and give it an appropriate accentuation and phrasing. Many composers were clearly felt by their more theoretically minded contemporaries to reflect too little on the metre in which their conceptions could best be expressed. Nevertheless, it can scarcely be doubted that thoughtful composers strove hard to find the metre that most closely fitted the predominant accentual characteristics of their ideas. Instances of the same theme notated in different metres in Beethoven's sketchbooks may well reflect his search for the most appropriate pattern and intensity of metrical stress for a particular idea. A similar motive may also lie behind the rescoring of whole movements in different metres by, for example, Mozart and Mendelssohn.[54]

The continuing elaboration and systemization of a hierarchy of metrical accent appropriate to each metre, in a stream of nineteenth-century theoretical works, especially by German authors, seems distinctly at odds with the increasingly free approach of the more experimental musicians of that period, but such theoretical elaborations were, to a considerable extent, the result of a desire to endow *Musikwissenschaft* with the dignity of a historico-scientific discipline. Indeed, there were few nineteenth-century theorists who did not acknowledge, at least in parentheses, that the rigid hierarchy of metrical accent was overridden in practice by the requirements of the particular musical context. It seems probable that while, with minor modifications, theoretical understanding of metrical and structural accentuation during the period as a whole remained constant, practical application of that theory diverged ever further from it, in line with developing musical aesthetics. Just as the music of the late eighteenth century and early nineteenth century was characterized, in general, by distinct and regular rhythmic patterns, so the coincidence of metrical and structural accentuation was correspondingly more frequent, and

---

[54] See below, Ch. 8.

there was often a rhythmic counterpoint of metrically accented accompaniment figures with more freely accented melodic lines.

This situation is nicely summed up by J. A. P. Schulz's treatment of the subject, which could in many respects have come from a traditional theorist at any point during the period. It is worth quoting at length for the clarity with which it highlights the complexity of the interaction between the varying types of accentuation.

The accents of the melody must be made apparent. The notes which fall on the strong beats of the bar will be reckoned first among these. Of these the first note of the bar receives the most prominent pressure, so that the feeling of the beat is constantly sustained, without which no one will understand the melody. After the first beat of the bar the other strong beats of the bar are marked, but less strongly. Hereby, however, the distinction which the phrase divisions make between the beats must be well observed. The first note of a bar which is only a part of a phrase cannot be so strongly marked as when it begins the phrase or when it is the principal note of a phrase. Those who do not observe this, but constantly mark the first note of the bar with equal strength in every piece, ruin the whole piece; for by this, since they are in this respect too clear, they damage the clarity of the whole, in that they are thereby prevented from marking the phrase divisions appropriately, which is of the greatest importance. This will become clearer from what follows. The weak beats will only be marked when a new phrase begins on them, as will be shown hereafter.

Secondly, those notes in every phrase which require a particular emphasis are reckoned among the accents. As in speech many words merely serve to connect, or depend upon the principal word of the phrase, which the speaker pronounces without noticeably raising his voice, so that he might be able to make the principal word all the more audible: so also in every melodic phrase there are principal and auxiliary notes which should be well distinguished from one another in performance. Often, and particularly in pieces which have a single type of note throughout, the principal notes coincide with the aforementioned accents of the bar. In such pieces, however, where there is greater variety of melody, the principal notes almost always stand out from the ordinary notes and should be marked with particular emphasis. They can be recognized by the fact that they are in general longer or higher than the preceding and immediately following notes; or that they are raised or lowered by a ♯ or ♭ which is foreign to the prevailing key; or that they are free clashing dissonances; or that they prepare a dissonance which is tied to them; they fall mostly on the strong beats of the bar except when a new phrase division begins with them, or when the composer in order to make himself more emphatic decides on a syncopation and allows it to come in a beat too early; in such cases they also occur on the weak beat of the bar, and in the latter case are most easily recognizable by their added length, as in the fifth and sixth bars of the following example: [Ex. 1.16] All notes marked + are so many main notes of this phrase, that should be performed far more emphatically than the rest.

. . .

This may be sufficient to make those who wish to perform a piece clearly aware of the accents in it. One can easily grasp that their observation gives performance, apart from clarity, a great light and shade, especially if a differentiation of emphasis is also made between the main notes, in that one always requires more or less emphasis than another, like the main words in speech. Through this occurs the fine shadings of strong and weak

Ex. 1.16. Sulzer, *Allgemeine Theorie*, 2nd edn., iv. 701

which the great virtuosos know how to bring into their performance. But to say where and how this ought to happen is so difficult, and for those who do not have their own experience and a fine sensitivity so inadequate, that we regard it as superfluous to dwell further upon it.[55]

During the course of the nineteenth century a number of important composers strove to produce music in which accentuation was liberated from what they saw as the restrictions of metre; in such music, structural and expressive accentuation occurred with increasing frequency on beats that were metrically weak, and the distinction between free melody and metrically more regular accompaniment became far less common. Symptomatic of this attitude is Liszt's comment, in the preface to the collected edition of his symphonic poems, that he wished to 'see an end to mechanical, fragmented up and down playing, tied to the bar-line, which is still the rule in many places and can only acknowledge as appropriate the phrase-based style of performance, with the prominence of special accents and the rounding off of melodic and rhythmic shading [*den periodische Vortrag, mit dem Hervortreten der besonderen Accente und der Abrundung der melodischen und rhythmischen Nuancierung*]'.[56] His statement is not essentially in conflict with the opinion expressed by earlier writers, at least with regard to melody, but taken in conjunction with the style of much of his music and that of the mature Wagner, for instance, it becomes clear that it embodies a substantial difference in practice. Even in the music of composers closer to the Classical tradition such as Schumann and Brahms, there is evidence of a conscious attempt to escape the fetters of an over-rigid rhythmic structure; this was undoubtedly, to some extent, a conscious reaction to the conventional rhythm that underlay much early Romantic music, by composers such as Spohr, Weber, Marschner, and Mendelssohn, which sometimes contrasted awkwardly with their increasingly expressive harmonic idiom. A similar tendency can be seen in the approach to phrasing that is apparent in many mid- to late nineteenth-century editions of earlier music, such as Ferdinand David's *Die höhe Schule des Violinspiels* and Hugo Riemann's

---

[55] In Sulzer, *Allgemeine Theorie*, 2nd edn. iv. 702–3.
[56] *Liszts Symphonische Dichtungen für grosses Orchester*, 3 vols. (Leipzig, Breitkopf & Härtel, [*c*.1856]), i. 1.

editions of the Classics, or in discussions of phrasing by later nineteenth-century writers such as Mathis Lussy. It seems as if these musicians frequently envisaged structural and expressive accentuation as running contrary to the metrical accentuation where, in many cases, earlier musicians may have seen them as coinciding.

2

ACCENTUATION IN PRACTICE

In his discussion of oratorical accentuation Koch had observed that although the notation of his day was 'complete and precise' in showing pitch and duration, the things 'by which the spirit of the piece must be made palpable in performance can never fully be represented by signs'. Nevertheless, he took the view that since it is an 'established thing that the lively representation of the melody of a piece of music depends for the most part on the correct performance of the oratorical and pathetic accents',[1] a more sophisticated system for prescribing which notes should be accented and in what degree would be highly desirable. He did not believe that his contemporaries were anything like careful enough in marking the accentuation they required in their music. In this he was entirely in agreement with Türk, who, in his *Sechs leichte Klaviersonaten* of 1783, had made use of a sign (^) to indicate accentuation where he felt that it was not necessarily obvious. Türk remarked: 'I still believe that the accent which is so essential to good execution can, in certain cases, be as little left to the discretion of the performer as, for example, the extempore use of *forte* and *piano* or of one of the essential ornaments.'[2]

Discussion of the subject by Koch, Türk, and others of their contemporaries makes it abundantly clear that the relative scarcity of instructions for accent in eighteenth-century music carries no implication that expressive accents were not envisaged where they are not specifically marked. As with much else in the music of that period, even the more painstaking composers only indicated the music's most prominent and essential features, and many seem to have neglected even to do that; thus it was left to the executant to supply most of the accentuation necessary for a fine and tasteful performance. Despite the vastly increased use of various forms of accent markings by composers of succeeding

---

[1] *Musikalisches Lexikon*, art. 'Accent'.   [2] *Klavierschule*, VI, §16.

generations,[3] accomplished nineteenth-century performers would still have been expected to contribute much in the matter of accentuation and phrasing beyond what was indicated by the composer. In the section on performance in his *Violinschule* Louis Spohr, for instance, distinguished between a 'correct style' and a 'fine style'; the former required a minute observance of all the composer's performance markings, but the performer was expected to achieve the latter through 'additions of his own', among which were 'the accentuation and separation of musical phrases'.[4] To a greater or lesser extent Spohr's identification of the requirements for a fine style remains valid for all conventionally notated music, and, despite the greatly expanded use of accent marks, many of the situations in which a discrete level of unmarked accentuation was expected to be introduced in late eighteenth-century music have parallels in much nineteenth-century music, especially that of composers such as Mendelssohn and Brahms, whose instincts were more firmly rooted in the Classical tradition.

Specific examples illustrating tasteful accentuation in theory and instruction books provide many indications of the circumstances in which eighteenth- and nineteenth-century musicians felt that accents should occur, even where none were indicated. But as well as giving guidance for the placement of metrical and structural accents through specific examples, various theorists catalogued general circumstances in which, unless the composer specified something different, the performer generally needed to employ a structural or expressive accent. The following pages examine some of the factors that might imply accent in the music of this period.

Indications of Accent

Slurred Groups

During the eighteenth century and for much of the nineteenth there was a strong association between accentuation and the beginning of slurred groups of notes. Despite the unqualified endorsement of this practice by many theorists, however, the association was clearly not quite as obligatory as it sometimes appears from their writings, even in the eighteenth century. As is often the case, theorists tended to reiterate rules that were expounded by earlier authors, whether or not these accurately represented the notational habits of their contemporaries. Although some degree of accentuation at the beginning of slurred groups will frequently be appropriate in late eighteenth-century music and fairly often, too, in nineteenth-century music, there will be many situations in which the slurs have no such implications, for composers had

---

[3] See Ch. 3.
[4] (Vienna, [1832]), trans. John Bishop as *Louis Spohr's Celebrated Violin School* (London, [1843]), 181, 182.

already begun to use this symbol in a number of quite different ways during the second half of the eighteenth century.[5]

Authors of eighteenth-century and early-nineteenth-century treatises were broadly agreed about the execution of slurred groups, but individual treatments of the matter reveal some interesting differences of detail. Leopold Mozart taught that 'if in a musical composition two, three, four, and even more notes be bound together by the half-circle [slur] . . . the first of such united notes must be somewhat more strongly stressed, but the remainder slurred on to it quite smoothly and more and more quietly'.[6] The musical examples which precede this statement consist of a four-bar passage repeated thirty-four times with different patterns of slurred and separate notes, and with slurs beginning frequently on metrically weak beats. He later insisted that a degree of lengthening was integral to this accentuation.[7] In Löhlein's 1774 *Anweisung zum Violinspielen*, the first explanation of the slur says simply that the notes so marked must be 'performed in one bowstroke and softly connected to each other'.[8] But when explaining patterns of stress in a melody, by means of an underlaid text, he observed: 'when two notes come on one syllable . . . both notes will be played in one bowstroke, but the first receives a special pressure, because the syllable will be enunciated on it, and the other, as it were, melts into it [*die andere gleichsam obenein gehet*].'[9]

Many writers, especially in the earlier part of the period (when very long slurs were extremely rare), considered this type of accented and nuanced execution appropriate to slurred groups of any length. The Löhlein–Witthauer *Clavier-Schule*, for instance, referred without reservation to slurred groups 'of which the first note always receives a somewhat stronger pressure';[10] and Türk gave examples of up to eight notes in a slur for which he instructed that 'the note over which the slur begins, will be very lightly (hardly noticeably) accented'.[11] Those Classical writers who made a distinction based on the length of the slurred group, generally taught that, as a rule, groups of up to three or four notes should certainly be treated in this manner whereas longer slurred groups might not be. Asioli merely instructed that in groups of three or four slurred notes: 'The accent is given to the first; the others are played with an equal degree of force.'[12] In keyboard playing Frédéric Kalkbrenner, like Hummel, Czerny, and Moscheles, similarly taught that 'Three or four slurred notes can only be performed on the Piano by leaning on the first and

---

[5] For more extensive and general discussion of the range of meanings of slurs, see Ch. 6.

[6] *Versuch*, VII, 1, §20.   [7] See below, 'Agogic Accent'.   [8] p. 32.   [9] p. 53.

[10] Löhlein, *Clavier-Schule, oder kurze und gründliche Anweisung zur Melodie und Harmonie* (Leipzig and Züllichau, 1765), 5th edn., ed. Johann Georg Witthauer (Leipzig, 1791), 18.

[11] *Klavierschule*, VI, §38. Türk's instruction was repeated verbatim thirty years later in Friedrich Starke's *Wiener Pianoforte-Schule* (Vienna, 1819), i. 13.

[12] Bonifazio Asioli, *Principj elementari di musica* (Milan, 1809), trans. and ed. John Jousse (London, [1825]), 108.

shortening the last'[13] (Ex. 2.1); and Crelle in 1823 graphically illustrated the accentual element in slurred pairs by instructing that the first note should be forte and the second pianissimo.[14] It was in the context of piano playing that Brahms and Joachim discussed this aspect of performance in 1879, though rather with respect to articulation at the end of the slur than to accent at the beginning.[15] In 1858 the violinist Charles de Bériot recommended a small accent at the beginning of slurred groups, but no break between them.[16] But all these generalized instructions might, as their authors would undoubtedly have been the first to acknowledge, be overridden by particular musical circumstances.

Ex. 2.1. Kalkbrenner, *Méthode*, 12

Slurs that begin on metrically weak beats will often imply a displacement of accent. Milchmeyer, making no qualification about the length of slurs, observed: 'in the legato style, finally, everything hangs on the slurs and the expression which the composer wished to give to the piece; here one very often makes the weak beat strong and changes the fingers on it.'[17] Türk had also given examples of slurs beginning on weak beats, where he required a 'gentle accent', though none of his examples exceeded four notes (Ex. 2.2).[18] Philip Anthony Corri, too, expounded the general proposition that the first note of a slur, even, as he observed, were it to occur on a weak beat, would require emphasis.[19]

The association of accent with the beginning of a slur continued in theory books throughout the nineteenth century, even when composers were making much greater use of explicit accent and dynamic markings. But the association became increasingly out of touch with composers' practices, for a distinction between the symbol as an indication for legato and as a sign for the accentuation and phrasing of short figures was rarely made with clarity either by composers or theorists. Nevertheless, Mathis Lussy could still maintain without

[13] *Méthode pour apprendre le piano-forte à l'aide du guide mains* op. 108 (Paris, 1831), trans. as *Complete Course of Instruction for the Piano Forte* (London, [c.1835]), 12.

[14] *Einiges*, 93.   [15] See Ch. 6 below.   [16] *Méthode de violon* (Mainz, [1858]), 90.

[17] *Die wahre Art*, 8.   [18] *Klavierschule*, VI, §38.

[19] *L'anima di musica* (London, 1810), 72.

Ex. 2.2. Türk, *Klavierschule*, VI, §38

qualification in 1883 that 'Every time a slur [*coulé*] begins on the last note of a bar, of a beat, it is strong. Every time the end of a slur comes on the first note of a bar, of a beat, it is weak.'[20] The contemporaneous Mendel–Reissmann *Lexikon* was more cautious about implying an inevitable link between the beginning of a slur and accent; it gives the example shown in Ex. 2.3, commenting that it 'shows a shift of the accent, which is indicated by the phrasing slur and also for greater certainty by sf and ➤'.[21] Many other practical and theoretical considerations indicate that, in nineteenth-century music especially, the application of accent to the beginning of a slur, however discreet, is by no means always appropriate.

Ex. 2.3. Mendel and Reissmann, *Musikalisches Conversations-Lexikon*, 14

The weight of late eighteenth- and early nineteenth-century authority behind the idea that the first note of a short slurred group should receive greater accent and that the subsequent notes under the slur should diminuendo need not be considered to exclude other possibilities in particular circumstances. Asioli, for instance, extending the principle that ascending phrases increase in volume and descending phrases decrease in volume, instructed that in slurred ascending passages one should 'begin the passage piano and reinforce the sound to forte'.[22] (This does not, of course, necessarily exclude a slight emphasis on the first note in relation to the one immediately following.) A more important ambiguity in the slur–emphasis relationship occurs with string bowing. Here the principal accentuation or dynamic high point of the phrase may not always be intended to coincide with the beginning of the slur; this was particularly the case in works by string-playing composers. Sometimes, even in eighteenth-century music, a composer would take care to indicate the disparity between the slurring (bowing) and the accentuation, as did Vogler in his melodrama *Lampedo* (Ex. 2.4). With less fastidious composers it will be rash to assume a coincidence of slur beginning and accent as a matter of course, even

[20] *Le Rhythme musical*, 33.
[21] Hermann Mendel and August Reissmann, *Musikalisches Conversations-Lexikon* (Berlin, 1882), 14.
[22] *A Compendious Musical Grammar*, 108.

Ex. 2.4. Vogler, *Lampedo*, MS in Heissische Landes- und Hochschulbibliothek, Darmstadt, mus. ms. 1097, fo. 33ᵛ; pub. in fac. in the series *German Opera 1770–1800* (New York and London, Garland, 1986)

where no alternative is indicated. This is increasingly true of nineteenth-century music, though at least from the 1830s careful composers would seldom have left such things to chance.[23] However, there are many problematic cases in music from the period of transition between the earlier use of the slur predominantly to articulate short figures and its later widespread employment as a less specialized indication for legato. Even in the case of short slurs in string music, especially when the composer was a string player, there may well be a tension between the slur as bowing instruction and the slur as an indication for an accent-diminuendo delivery. Justus Johann Friedrich Dotzauer, in his *Violoncell-Schule*, for instance, cautioned the student to make an accent within a slur where this was necessary to maintain the integrity of the metre, observing, with respect to Ex. 2.5: 'On account of the metre the third of the slurred notes must be somewhat staccato [*muss . . . etwas abgestossen werden*], otherwise it could easily give the effect of triplets.'[24]

Ex. 2.5. Dotzauer, *Violoncell-Schule*, 33

Only in the case of slurred pairs were musicians more or less agreed throughout the period that a distinctive treatment was called for, and it was solely with respect to paired notes that Franklin Taylor in the 1880s unreservedly employed the term 'slur', observing: 'When two notes of equal length in quick or moderately quick tempo are joined together by a curved line they are said to be *slurred*,

---

[23] See Ch. 3, esp. Ex. 3.63.

[24] *Violoncell-Schule für den ersten Unterricht* (Vienna, [*c*.1836]), 18. It is noteworthy here that he evidently uses the term *abgestossen* (staccato) primarily in its sense of accent, since a simple shortening of the third note would have the opposite consequence of enhancing the triplet effect.

and in playing them a considerable stress is laid on the first of the two, while the second is not only weaker, but is made shorter than it is written, as though followed by a rest.'[25] But even where only two notes were joined in this way he remarked that there were exceptions, writing: 'When the curved line is drawn over two notes of considerable length, or in slow tempo, it is not a slur, but merely a sign of legato' (Ex. 2.6(*a*)), and in contrast to earlier writers such as Kalkbrenner and Czerny he remarked that the sign indicated legato rather than a slur 'if it covers a group of three or more notes', except where it is extended to 'end upon an accented note, then an effect analogous to the slur is intended' (Ex. 2.6(*b*)).[26]

Ex. 2.6. Taylor, 'Phrasing', in Grove, *Dictionary*

(*a*)

(*b*)

Another exception to the accentuation of the beginning of slurred pairs, at least in some musicians' practice, seems to have been the performance of 'scotch snap' figures, where a number of writers mention that the accent should occur on the second note of each pair. In his discussion of musical accent Pietro Lichtenthal gave the illustration shown in Ex. 2.7.[27] Similarly Justin Heinrich Knecht, after discussing the accentuation of long–short dotted figures, remarked: 'if, however, the dot stands after the second note of a figure of two notes or after the second and fourth notes of a figure of four notes, so the accent and the weight fall on the second and fourth notes; on the other hand the first and third notes are quickly dispatched, as follows' (Ex. 2.8).[28] Though Knecht shows no slurs these are implicit, being normally understood to be present in such figures. In contrast, however, Türk, echoing C. P. E. Bach, stated that in

Ex. 2.7. Lichtenthal, *Dizionario*, art. 'Accento musicale'

[25] In 'Phrasing', in George Grove, ed., *A Dictionary of Music and Musicians*, ii. 706 ff. (He is here referring to piano music. For further discussion of the articulation of slurred pairs see Ch. 6 below.)

[26] 'Phrasing', in Grove, *Dictionary*, ii. 707.

[27] *Dizionario e bibliographia della musica* (Milan, 1826), art. 'Accento musicale'.

[28] *Knechts allgemeiner musikalischer Katechismus* (Biberach, 1803), 4th edn. (Freiburg, 1816), 34.

Ex. 2.8. Knecht, *Katechismus*, 34

these figures: 'The first (short) note, of course, is to be accented but the emphasis should be only a very gentle one';[29] while J. F. Schubert felt that a very slight
accent on the first note might sometimes be appropriate, but that neither note
of the figure should be especially accented, and he particularly warned against
making the first note of the pair significantly shorter than its notated length (as
some theorists advised) or articulating markedly between the pairs.[30] A further
exception was, in some musicians' opinions, where there were rising two-note
figures, particularly rising semitone appoggiaturas, which were considered to
require a crescendo treatment.

Dissonance and Chromatic Notes

One of the chief reasons for stressing an appoggiatura was its dissonance. There
was a widely held view in the eighteenth century that all dissonances implied a
special degree of emphasis. Quantz advised strengthening chromatic notes,
explaining that the degree of accent was determined by the intensity of the
dissonance; and he detailed three classes of dissonance, according to the intensity of accent required.[31] Leopold Mozart was among the musicians who
instructed that accentuation was required on a dissonant note or on one that
prepares a dissonant interval, and on a chromatic note or a melody note that
occurs over chromatic harmony.[32] Similar advice was repeated by J. F. Schubert
in 1804; he observed that notes belonging to a foreign tonality should be
accented, so long as they were not too short (Ex. 2.9), and he added: 'the more
foreign or distant the tonality, the more emphasis the note which prepares or

Ex. 2.9. Schubert, *Neue Singe-Schule*, 133

---

[29] Türk, *Klavierschule*, VI, §48; Bach, *Versuch über die wahre Art das Clavier zu spielen* (Berlin, 1753), i.
III, §24. Various other matters connected with this kind of figure are considered in Ch. 6 below.

[30] *Neue Singe-Schule*, 132.   [31] *Versuch*, XVII, 2, §14 and XVII, 6, §14.

[32] Ibid., XII, §8.

makes evident the tonality must receive'.[33] Türk made much the same points about dissonances, notes preparing a dissonance, or chromatic notes that required accentuation, but having stated that the harder a dissonance is, or the more dissonant notes there are in a chord, 'the stronger must one strike the harmony', he very sensibly cautioned: 'But this rule cannot and ought not always be followed to the letter, because too many changes might then ensue'.[34]

The association of dissonance and accent continued throughout the nineteenth century. Frédéric Kalkbrenner required that 'all notes foreign to the key and those which bear an accidental should be well marked'.[35] Bernhard Romberg, having instructed that a descending scale should diminish in volume, added: 'But if, in the descending scale, a note should occur at the end which does not belong to the key in which the music is written, this note will require a stronger accent, and there are very few cases in which it will not be made a prominent feature of the passage'.[36] A musician of the next generation, Manuel García, also insisted on accenting dissonances in singing, stating: 'The stress, too, should always be laid on notes which, requiring nice and delicate intonation, are difficult to seize,—such, for instance, as dissonancies [*sic*]'.[37]

Pitch

Just as a dissonance was to be emphasized because, by its very nature, it gave prominence to the beat on which it occurred, so a particularly high or low note, especially if it were separated by a considerable interval from the preceding note, was likely to require a more forceful delivery. Thus, Leopold Mozart advised accenting particularly high or low notes following a leap. He also suggested emphasizing high notes in lively pieces, even on a weak beat, but cautioned against doing so in slow or sad ones[38] (see above, Ex. 1.10). Türk and J. F. Schubert gave similar advice (Ex. 2.10).[39] Kalkbrenner and Henri Herz seem to reflect a general opinion in suggesting that the highest note of an ascending phrase or phrase unit should be played louder than its neighbours, and that, whereas an isolated low note might be played loudly, one that came at the end of a descending phrase would normally be very gently delivered unless the composer specified the contrary or unless, as Romberg implied, some other factor, such as dissonant harmony, also exerted an influence.[40]

---

[33] *Neue Singe-Schule*, 133.   [34] *Klavierschule*, VI, §32.   [35] *Complete Course*, 12.
[36] *Méthode*, 128.   [37] *New Treatise*, 52.   [38] *Versuch*, XII, §13.
[39] Türk, *Klavierschule*, VI, §15; Schubert, *Neue Singe-Schule*, 133.
[40] Kalkbrenner, *Complete Course*, 12; Herz, *Méthode complète de piano* op. 100 (Mainze and Anvers, 1838), 32.

Ex. 2.10. (*a*) Türk, *Klavierschule*, VI, 2, §15; (*b*) Schubert, *Neue Singe-Schule*, 133

(*a*)

(*b*)

Length

Similar principles were applied to long and short notes within a phrase. According to Leopold Mozart, a note distinguished from its neighbours by greater length would be emphatic.[41] Kirnberger stated simply 'Longer note values are always performed with more weight and emphasis than shorter ones'.[42] Philip Corri observed: 'Emphasis should be generally placed on the longest and highest note of a sentence, and a note that is dotted among equal notes' (Ex. 2.11).[43] Hummel likewise commented: 'If after a short note occupying the accented time of the measure, a longer note should succeed on the unaccented time, the latter usually requires an emphasis',[44] while Czerny insisted that, in general, long notes be strongly accented.[45] Later in the century Lussy continued to promulgate this notion, commenting that a long note that follows several shorter ones 'acquires great force'.[46]

Ex. 2.11. P. A. Corri, *L'anima di musica*, 72

Syncopation

The rule of accenting individual syncopated notes that occur in an otherwise unsyncopated melody seems closely related to the principle that long notes should be more emphatic than short ones. The degree of emphasis appropriate to a particular syncopated note would, of course, depend on its length, prominence or function.

---

[41] Mozart, *Versuch*, XII, §8.

[42] *Die Kunst des reinen Satzes*, ii, 4, §116; trans. David Beach and Jurgen Thym (New Haven and London, 1982), 384.

[43] *L'anima di musica*, 72.   [44] *A Complete*, iii. 54 n.   [45] *Pianoforte School*, iii. 21.

[46] *Traité de l'expression musicale: Accents, nuances et mouvements dans la musique vocale et instrumentale* (Paris, 1874), 6th edn. (Paris, 1892), trans. M. E. von Glehn as *Musical Expression* (London, [c.1885]), 129–30. (For the implications of the term 'vibrato' in such contexts see below, Ch. 14, esp. pp. 518 ff.)

Syncopation was, however, often described as a displacement of the metrical accent. John Jousse expressed the conventional view, commenting: 'When syncopated notes happen the Emphasis lays on them contrary to the Rules of Accent'.[47] Knecht was more explicit: 'Although its first half comes on a weak part of the bar, one commonly gives [the beginning of] a syncopated note a stronger emphasis than its second half which comes on a strong part of the bar, even if there is no accent sign above or below it.'[48] Leopold Mozart, from the practical viewpoint, advised the violinist that in playing a given passage that included a syncopation (Ex. 2.12) 'You must not forget to attack the middle note rather more strongly with the up stroke; and to slur the third note smoothly on to it with a gradual fading away of the tone'.[49] In the context of tempo rubato (see below, Ch. 11), therefore, where syncopation might continue for some time, the metrical accent in the melody could be at odds with that of its accompaniment for a considerable period.

Ex. 2.12. L. Mozart, *Versuch*, IV, §23

Yet, although most authorities seem to have been in agreement about the accentuation of syncopated notes, a few authors suggested that, in certain circumstances at least, syncopated notes might receive the accent on the part of the note that occurred on the normal metrical strong beat. In the original edition of his *Violinschule* Leopold Mozart unreservedly condemned this practice. Discussing ties, he gave the following example shown in Ex. 2.13 and commented:

It is bad enough that people exist who flatter themselves greatly on their art and who yet cannot play a minim, yea, hardly a crotchet without dividing it into two parts. If one wished to have two notes, one would certainly write them down. Such notes must be attacked strongly and, with a gradual dying away, be sustained without after-pressure; just as the sound of a bell, when struck sharply, by degrees dies away.[50]

And in his consideration of performance style in general he returned to the point, observing: 'the notes which are divided by the bar-line must never be

Ex. 2.13. L. Mozart, *Versuch*, I, 3, §18

---

[47] *Theory and Practice of the Violin*, 43. See also Callcott, *Musical Grammar*, 44.
[48] *Katechismus*, 28.   [49] *Versuch*, IV, §23.   [50] Ibid. I, 3, §18 n.

separated; neither must the division be marked by an accent but must be merely attacked and quietly sustained; not otherwise than if it stood at the beginning of a crotchet.'[51] He illustrated the point with the example shown in Ex. 2.14. But in his 1787 revision of the book he added an additional footnote to one passage of syncopation (Ex. 2.15): 'This is the only case in which it is customary to mark the division of the notes by a perceptible after-pressure of the bow. That is to say: when several such notes follow each other in a quick tempo.'[52]

Ex. 2.14. L. Mozart, *Versuch*, XII, §16

Ex. 2.15. L. Mozart, *Versuch*, IV, §27

down up and so on, continuously.

J. A. P. Schulz also appears to recommend this kind of treatment for isolated syncopations, commenting on one of his examples (see above, Ex. 1.16): 'The syncopated notes in the seventh bar are certainly not real main notes; but one only wanted to show here that one has to perform such notes like main notes, namely firmly and emphatically, and the second half of them will be strengthened with a jerk in order to make the strong beat of the bar felt.'[53]

Some early nineteenth-century authors also seem to suggest this as a legitimate way of performing syncopation. Romberg illustrated something of this kind; giving advice for performing the passage in Ex. 2.16(*a*) he remarked that it might be played as if notated as in Ex. 2.16(*b*) (the staccato marks under the tie imply accent, as was common in German usage (see below, pp. 98 ff.)), and he instructed that 'in playing the third and fifth quavers a slight jerk be given to the bow'.[54] Baillot, too, described a similar treatment of syncopation (Ex. 2.17) as the first of three principal styles of performing such figures, commenting

Ex. 2.16. Romberg, *A Complete*, 42

(*a*)

(*b*)

---

[51] *Versuch*, XII, §16.
[53] In Sulzer, *Allgemeine Theorie*, 2nd edn. iv, 703.
[52] Ibid. IV, §27 (1787 edn. footnote).
[54] *A Complete*, 42.

Ex. 2.17. Baillot, *L'Art du violon*, 135

that one made it 'By swelling the note and accelerating the speed of the bow right up to the end of the note, but lightly'.[55]

Such approaches to the performance of syncopation are at odds with modern orthodoxy, which, like Leopold Mozart's earlier handling of the subject, stresses that it is always bad style to accent the second half of the note. It is possible, however, despite Mozart's explicit prohibition of that practice, that in the eighteenth and nineteenth centuries there was a greater tendency to press on the second half of an isolated syncopation when dissonance occurred at that point; and Baillot's and Romberg's discussions of the subject indicate that (except in keyboard playing, where such an effect was impossible) this kind of treatment may not infrequently have been made a feature of the passage.

Beaming

Beaming may sometimes have served, to a certain extent, to indicate phrase groupings and therefore accent,[56] especially in passages of unslurred notes or within a general legato context. It was, however, a very uncertain way of showing accent or phrasing, since only quavers and faster note values have beams, and in many contexts there is little scope for modifying the beaming from conventional groupings. Nevertheless, there are many occasions where Classical and Romantic composers seem to have used this device with the deliberate intention of showing where the accents or phrase divisions were to fall. This

[55] Pierre Marie François de Sales Baillot, *L'Art du violon: Nouvelle méthode* (Paris, 1834), 135–7.

[56] See e.g. music example i) on p. 355 of Türk's *Klavierschule*, where both slurring and beaming from weak- to strong-beat quavers are used.

notational practice was described and illustrated by Schulz as a means favoured by some composers for indicating where the phrase divisions should fall (see Ex. 4.4 below). In many cases such peculiarities of notation have been ironed out in later editions, even so-called critical editions.

There were, however, various reasons that might induce a composer to use this type of notation. J. C. Bach commonly separated the first of a group of quavers to indicate the notes to which a forte followed by a piano was intended to apply, for instance in *Lucio Silla* (Ex. 2.18); and this practice seems to have been followed by many of his contemporaries. In such cases the meaning was precisely opposite to that of the breaks in beaming that indicated the end of one phrase and the beginning of another, since it made the note following the interruption in the beaming weaker rather than stronger than the separated note.

Ex. 2.18. J. C. Bach, *Lucio Silla*, Act II, Scene vii, pub. in *The Collected Works of Johann Christian Bach*, viii (New York and London, Garland 1986)

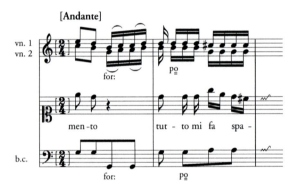

A number of early nineteenth-century writers explicitly acknowledged that the first note of groups that are beamed together contrary to the usual conventions should receive an accent. J. W. Callcott gave an example from Haydn to illustrate how a composer might employ this device (Ex. 2.19).[57] Beethoven used modified beaming on many occasions where it evidently has implications for both accent and phrasing (Ex. 2.20); but there are other occasions where inconsistency of notation (caused partly by a conflict between convenient shorthand and intentionally irregular beaming) confuses the issue. In the first movement of the Fifth Symphony, for instance, the separation of the three-note figure (Ex. 2.21(*a*)) from the first note of the bar does not always seem to be significant, though at times it certainly is (Ex. 2.21(*b*)).

Weber often used irregular beaming to clarify phrasing. Sometimes this implied accent on the first note of a beamed group, as when he beamed pairs of

[57]   *Musical Grammar*, 44; also in Jousse, *Theory and Practice of the Violin*, 43.

Ex. 2.19. Callcott, *Musical Grammar*, 44

Ex. 2.20. Beethoven: (*a*) *Chorfantasie* op. 80; (*b*) String Quartet op. 132/v

(*a*) Marcia assai vivace

(*b*)

[Allegro appassionato]

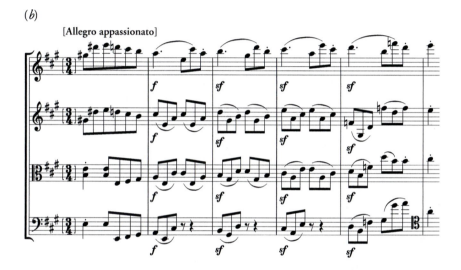

notes contrary to the normal notational convention, or sometimes it merely showed where a phrase should be articulated, particularly when accompanying voices (Ex. 2.22). Schubert, too, seems to have considered abnormal beaming to be of significance. In the autograph of the Andante of his String Trio D. 581, for instance, he clearly began by writing separate quavers in the viola and cello parts but then, having altered the first occurrences, subsequently wrote them with a beam from metrically weak to strong beats. In bars 14–15 of the cello part he even wrote the beam across the bar-line. That Schubert wanted to reinforce the irregular accentuation is suggested by the simultaneously occurring accents in the violin melody in bars 5 and 6 (Ex. 2.23). Among later composers who used modified beaming, sometimes across a bar-line, with evident implications of accent and phrasing were Schumann, Brahms, and Tchaikovsky (Ex. 2.24). The example from Tchaikovsky is particularly interesting because it shows how, in the string parts, the slurring seems to have limited implications of phrasing, for the change from fours to pairs, as comparison with the

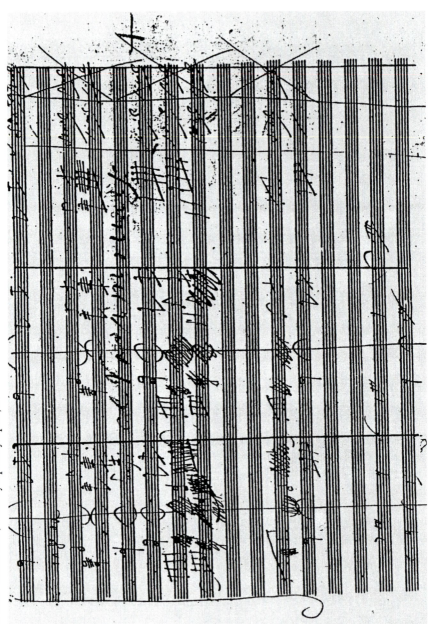

Ex. 2.21. Beethoven, Fifth Symphony op. 67/i

(a)

(*b*)

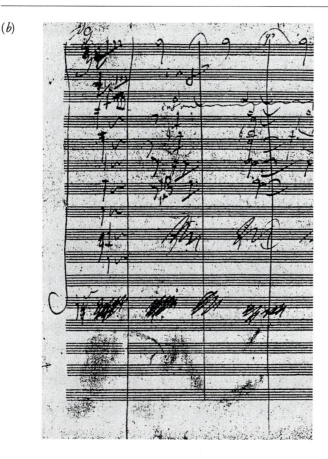

Ex. 2.22. Weber, Mass in E flat J. 224, Credo

flutes suggests, is merely to permit the players to use more bow for the crescendo.

In the early nineteenth century August Eberhardt Müller linked the beaming of triplets in threes and sextuplets in sixes with their accentuation, saying that in triplets 'the first of the three notes is gently accented while in sextuplets

Ex. 2.23. Schubert, String Trio D. 581/ii

only the first of six notes' receives an accent (Ex. 2.25).[58] Gottfried Weber, on the other hand, somewhat pedantically insisting on the metrical accentuation of sextuplets, instructed that they should be accented in groups of two notes. (Ex. 2.26)[59]

Final Notes

The rule that musical units should generally begin powerfully and progressively decline in force, was outlined by Crelle, as mentioned earlier, and many other musicians of the period. The majority view implies that in most contexts the final note of a phrase, though receiving the appropriate metrical accent, would be unlikely to have an expressive accent. But an occasional dissenting opinion can be found; Kalkbrenner, for instance, observed that 'the first and last notes of a passage should be more energetic than the rest'.[60] Hummel's examples of appropriate accentuation show some final notes gently accented, some more forcibly accented and some without any particular accent.[61]

[58] *A. E. Müller's Klavier- und Fortepiano Schule* (Jena, 1804), 16. This book is an expanded edition of Löhlein's *Klavierschule.*

[59] *Theory,* i. 90.   [60] *A New Method,* 12.   [61] *A Complete,* III, 54–9.

Ex. 2.24. (*a*) Schumann, Piano Quintet op. 44/i; (*b*) Brahms, String Quartet op. 51/2/i; (*c*) Tchaikovsky, *Symphonie pathétique* op. 74/i

(*a*)

(*b*)

Ex. 2.24. *cont. (c)*

Ex. 2.25. Müller, *Klavier und Fortepiano Schule*, 16

Ex. 2.26. G. Weber, *Theory of Composition*, i. 90

There seems to have been one important exception to the principle enunciated by Crelle and others, and it may have been quite widespread. Philip Corri, writing about keyboard playing, agreed with the majority view when he noted that 'the final note of a phrase [is] never to be played with emphasis unless marked'; but he added: 'N.B. this rule is quite reversed in singing as the last note should be sung with firmness and sustained long'.[62] Here he was echoing an aspect of the teaching of his father, Domenico Corri,[63] and, perhaps a principle of the eighteenth-century Italian school.

Other Factors

Other criteria for the performer to apply emphasis where none was specifically notated were given by musical writers throughout the period; each author had slightly different advice to offer, sometimes of a generalized nature and sometimes applied to particular examples. Manuel García recommended that the first note of every repetition of a similar figure should be distinguished by greater weight (Ex. 2.27); he felt that this was particularly applicable to passages of dotted notes (Ex. 2.28) and that in certain circumstances the short note of the figure, too, should be accented (Ex. 2.29). He also suggested that use might be made of the so-called contra-tempo (Ex. 2.30).[64] J. F. Schubert had given

---

[62] *L'anima di musica*, 73.   [63] *The Singer's Preceptor* (London, 1810).   [64] *New Treatise*, 52–4.

Ex. 2.27. García, *New Treatise*, 52

Ex. 2.28. García, *New Treatise*, 52

Ex. 2.29. García, *New Treatise*, 54

Ex. 2.30. García, *New Treatise*, 52

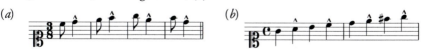

similar counsel a couple of generations earlier, remarking: 'In very special cases the notes which fall on the weak beat [may be accented].' He gave two examples (Ex. 2.31), but added: 'In the case of (b) one would do well to observe that the notes marked with ∧ must only receive a gentle emphasis, otherwise the melody could easily become bizarre. One always does better not to accent notes of this kind if one cannot rely on one's taste or if they are not specifically marked *f* or *pf* [poco forte] by the composer.'[65] Schubert also made another point, which he regarded as relevant to some of the vocal music of his period; he noted that whereas the principal rule for singers was to take account of the words in accenting the melody, there were cases where the composer had evidently

Ex. 2.31. Schubert, *Neue Singe-Schule*, 134

---

[65] *Neue Singe-Schule*, 134.

subordinated the words to the melody, and in these cases the singer should take care to adapt his accentuation to the melody rather than the words.

Types of Accent and their Realization

There were a number of ways in which accents would have been realized in performance during this period, and the sort of accentuation that would have been regarded as appropriate to particular contexts is often difficult to determine. As Koch remarked: 'the manner in which the emphasis of these notes is brought out is really easier to feel than to describe'; but he went on to identify the principal aspects of accentuation, including the statement that it 'consists partly in a certain emphatic lingering, whereby it appears as if one remains a moment longer on such an accented note than its specific duration requires'.[66]

Agogic Accent

The question of what Koch meant by lingering is related to the vexed problem of inequality, and the extent to which related procedures may have been applied during this period. It is important to distinguish, however, between:

1. 'inequality' as a specific term for a technique applied to specific note values, or types of passages, in particular circumstances, as occurred in French and French-influenced music;
2. the rendition of certain notes in performance, according to well-established conventions, with different values from the written ones, for example, dotted rhythms and some triplet patterns;[67] and
3. a more or less obvious deviation from notated values that may have been applied from time to time by performers, following the dictates of their own taste, for expressive purposes.

The last of these encompasses what Riemann designated the agogic accent, but is also directly related to the matter of rubato in its various meanings.[68]

There are numerous references to what Koch described as 'emphatic lingering' in the literature of the period 1750–1900. But before examining more closely what may have been implied by these references it is necessary to consider the German terminology, in which 'internally long' (*innerlich lang*) and 'internally short' (*innerlich kurz*) were used for strong and weak beats respectively. There has been a degree of uncertainty and confusion about whether the nomenclature implied a real chronometric lengthening of the notes that fell on these beats. It seems clear, however, that, for the most part, the terminology (which derives from that of poetry) is not to be understood as indicating that

---

[66] *Musikalisches Lexikon*, art. 'Accent'.   [67] See Ch. 16, 'The Variable Dot'.   [68] See Ch. 11.

all strong beats, which were by definition internally long, would have been expected to be lengthened in duration, even to a minimal degree, although this may easily be inferred from some mid-eighteenth-century treatments of the subject, such as Friedrich Wilhelm Marpurg's.[69] Koch, whose use of the terminology is very similar to Marpurg's, was at pains to explain that he did not consider 'long' in this context to mean actually of longer duration; in his *Versuch einer Anleitung zur Composition*, commenting on the relationship between stressed and unstressed in pairs of consecutively sounded notes, he observed: 'one of them will be perceived by the hearing as longer (that is really to say, with more emphasis), and that therefore it expresses more inner worth than the other'.[70] In the early nineteenth century, Gottfried Weber adopted a more explicit terminology for his discussion of metrical accentuation, seemingly to avoid the ambiguity of earlier expressions, writing of internal weight rather than length.[71]

It is, nevertheless, undoubtedly true that in the middle of the eighteenth century a form of unequal performance similar to, but almost certainly less pronounced than the French *notes inégales* was current among some German and Italian musicians. Quantz made detailed recommendations about lengthening notes that, according to the rules of metrical accent, fall on the internally long beats; though, as in the French tradition, this was limited to specific circumstances.[72] He regarded the procedure as appropriate to 'the quickest notes in every piece of moderate tempo, or even in the Adagio' and instructs that this stressing and lengthening must be given to the first, third, fifth, and seventh note of each figure (assuming the figure starts on the beat). Exceptions to this rule occur if the notes have staccato marks, if several notes are repeated at the same pitch, if more than two notes come under a slur, or in quaver passagework in a gigue. In the case of passagework that is too quick to permit unequal execution (i.e. very fast passagework in instrumental music and moderately fast passagework in vocal music), the first of each group of four notes was to receive this treatment. Quantz's account does not make it clear how pronounced a lengthening he required, though he stated that it should not be as much as if the note were dotted. There seem to be no direct rejections of this aspect of Quantz's teaching in the three or four decades during which his book remained a respected source of authority, unless we take J. F. Reichardt's caution against constantly marking 'the accentuation of the notes—of which Herr Quantz says so much'[73] as a criticism of his approach. Nevertheless, since other German writers failed to reiterate Quantz's instructions, it seems probable that his highly stylized description of the technique, tied rather to metrical than expressive accent, does not accurately represent normal practice in Germany even at

[69] *Kritische Briefe über die Tonkunst* (Berlin, 1760–4) i. 99 (letter 13, §2).
[70] *Versuch einer Anleitung zur Composition* (Rudolstadt and Leipzig, 1782–93), ii. 273.
[71] *Theory*, i. 90.   [72] *Versuch*, XI, §12.   [73] *Ueber die Pflichten*, 28.

the time the book was published, and that, by the 1770s at any rate, few musicians would have been employing the type of unequal performance he described.

Yet, while there is no suggestion that any form of inequality was employed as a matter of rule in the late eighteenth century or the nineteenth century, there are indications that some performers were in the habit of spontaneously converting patterns of equal notes into dotted patterns. Whether this occurred through carelessness similar to that implied by Türk when he complained that the phrase marked *a*) in Ex. 2.32 often came out as one of the three versions marked *b*),[74] or whether as a conscious modification of the notated patterns is uncertain. Manuel García, for instance, felt it necessary to comment after explaining the desirability of strongly accenting dotted notes: 'Much as we acknowledge the necessity of strongly pointing [over-dotting] the above examples [see Ex. 2.28 above], and others of a similar character, we reprobate the habit of pointing [dotting] notes of equal value.'[75]

Ex. 2.32. Türk, *Klavierschule*, I, §63

Leopold Mozart, whose *Violinschule* was published only four years after the appearance of Quantz's book, gives a rather different account of where and how he wished the performer to lengthen notes. He agreed with Quantz about the necessity for stressing the metrically strong beat and about lengthening and stressing the first note of slurred pairs, but rather than prescribing this for the fastest notes in a piece he stated that it should be applied to crotchets or quavers in 2/2 and 3/2, quavers or semiquavers in 4/4, 2/4, and 3/4, and semiquavers in 3/8 and 6/8 (though this may have been intended to indicate the same thing as Quantz's instructions). However, Mozart said nothing about lengthening separate notes. His description also gives the impression that the lengthening he required was to be subtler and less obtrusive than Quantz's, but the first sentence of the following extract makes it clear that, where slurs were concerned, he regarded a degree of lengthening as obligatory in a tasteful performance:

The first of two, three, four, or even more notes, slurred together, must *at all times* [my italics] be stressed more strongly and sustained a little longer; but those following must diminish in tone and be slurred on somewhat later. But this must be carried out with such good judgement that the bar-length is not altered in the smallest degree. The slight sustaining of

---

[74] *Klavierschule*, I, §63.   [75] *New Treatise*, 54.

the first note must not only be made agreeable to the ear by a nice apportioning of the slightly hurried notes slurred on to it, but must even be made truly pleasant to the listener.[76]

A few years later, Löhlein, in the accompanying explanation to one of the practice pieces in his violin treatise, which contained slurred pairs on adjacent notes (Ex. 2.33), instructed the pupil: 'The first of the slurred notes receives a special pressure and is sustained somewhat longer than the notation requires; the other is delivered more weakly and shorter; the third and fourth are played with a short staccato in the middle of the bow.'[77] This instruction was retained in later editions, including the fourth of 1797, which was extensively revised by J. F. Reichardt. From other evidence it seems likely that there was a fairly widespread tendency to apply agogic accent to slurred pairs throughout the eighteenth century.

Ex. 2.33. Löhlein, *Anweisung zum Violinspielen*, 79

By no means all discussions of accentuation in the second half of the eighteenth century are as explicit as those of Quantz and Mozart with respect to the circumstances in which lengthening should occur. Indeed, many musicians seem to have regarded agogic accent as a resource that performers might introduce at their own discrimination. Thus, comparison of Domenico Corri's version of J. C. Bach's 'Nel partir bell' idol mio' with the original published edition reveals instances where slurred pairs that Bach originally notated with equal note values become dotted, but also others where this is not so (see Ex. 12.7 below).

Towards the end of the century and in the early years of the nineteenth century, writers, while continuing to insist that the technique of lingering on accented notes was an essential aspect of expressive performance, treated the matter in a generally freer manner; it was no longer to be applied by rule, but rather according to the individual performer's creative conception. In this respect, attitudes reflect changing musical aesthetics and the notions of Romantic individualism found in the writings of Jean Paul Richter, Wackenroder, E. T. A. Hoffmann, and others. It is typical of this freer attitude that J. F. Schubert in his 1804 *Neue Singe-Schule*, having discussed various situations in which expressive accentuation is appropriate, added: 'It is still to be noted about the notes which should be accented, that from time to time they are also dwelt on longer'.[78] Elsewhere in the book, however, he advised:

---

[76] *Versuch*, VII, 2, §5.   [77] *Anweisung*, 79.   [78] p. 134.

It is to be observed of the accented notes that they must be performed emphatically with strength and receive an imperceptibly longer value than their specified one; but the correct tempo or specified duration of a bar may not be altered. The worth over and above its proper value which the emphasized beat receives is taken from the following beat (in a few cases also from the preceding). Also, in particularly emotional passages the equality of the beat will often be restored only in the following bar.[79]

Some twenty years later Crelle implied the possibility of lengthening as a concomitant of accent in a rather roundabout way when he observed that all accented notes 'do not hurry'.[80] (His recommendations also contain more explicit advice for rhythmic flexibility, which will be considered below.) García, discussing tempo rubato, explicitly linked the practice of lingering with accentuation. He observed: 'This prolongation is usually conceded to appoggiaturas, to notes placed on long syllables, and those which are naturally salient in the harmony. In all such cases, the time lost must be regained by accelerating other notes. This is a good method for giving colour and variety to melodies'[81] (Ex. 2.34). After his discussion of accentuation in general, he commented: 'We may likewise observe, that both accent and prolongation follow nearly similar laws.'[82]

Ex. 2.34. García, *New Treatise*, 51

The ability to employ agogic accentuation effectively, where appropriate, continued to be regarded throughout the nineteenth century as an essential aspect of more advanced artistry. Arrey von Dommer put forward the standard view when he stated that correct accentuation involves

a freer treatment of the simple metrical accents in respect of the accentuation of the beats, and in addition there may be deviations from the strict regularity of tempo in that single notes that are to be particularly emphatically brought out may well be held a little bit longer; others that have to be subordinated may well be somewhat shortened.[83]

---

[79] p. 102.   [80] *Einiges*, 61.   [81] *New Treatise*, 51.   [82] Ibid. 52.
[83] *Musikalisches Lexikon*, 16.

Some revealing examples of this type of agogic accentuation may be found in the meticulously annotated text of Rode's Seventh Violin Concerto given by Spohr in the section on advanced performance in his *Violinschule*. Comparison with the original notation shows that whereas in his verbal commentary Spohr sometimes recommended lingering on one musically more important note among a group of equal-length notes, he also occasionally specified lengthening by altering the note values of Rode's original text.[84] In almost all of the many examples of lingering specified in Spohr's commentary the player is required, in accordance with the conventions of tempo rubato at that time,[85] to regain the time lost on the emphasized note from the following ones.

Later in the nineteenth century, Hugo Riemann, who used an elaborate system of signs to indicate performance instructions as precisely as possible in his editions and pedagogical material, adopted the sign ∧ to mark agogic accents, where he required 'a slight lingering on the note'[86] (Ex. 2.35). Telling instances of this kind of emphatic lingering in practice can be heard on a number of early recordings by older artists. Those made by the great violinist Joseph Joachim in 1903, four years before his death, confirm his contemporary reputation as a master of rhythmic subtlety; the nature of his departures from the strict letter of the notation in this respect are particularly revealing (see below, Ch. 12 and Ex. 12.12).

Percussive Accent

The percussive element in accentuation is infinitely variable, from a powerful explosive attack to the slightest hint of emphasis. In mid-eighteenth-century music any of these degrees of accentuation may be appropriate, even where the composer has not marked an accent, though in later music the more powerful accents will very seldom be appropriate unless indicated. The quality of the attack is substantially conditioned by the nature of the medium; a vocal accent, depending to a considerable extent on the pronunciation of consonants, is quite different from the accent of a pianist on the one hand or a violinist on the other. Nevertheless, the intensity of the attack will be principally related to the character of the music. Charles de Bériot wrote informatively on this in the mid-nineteenth century. Like many musicians of his and earlier generations he believed that instrumentalists should seek to emulate the human voice as closely as their instrument permitted. He commented:

We cannot repeat too often that the performer will not be perfect until he can reproduce the accents of song in their most delicate forms.

By the song we mean not only the music, but also the poem of which it is the brilliant ornamentation—without which the melody would be nothing more than a vocal exercise.

---

[84] See below, Ch. 12 and Ex. 12.10.   [85] See Ch. 11 below.

[86] *New Pianoforte-School/Neue Klavierschule* (London, [1897–1910]), pt. I. 17.

Ex. 2.35. (*a*) Schubert, *Moments musicaux* op. 94 no. 1 (Brunswick, Litolff, [*c.*1890]); (*b*) and (*c*) Haydn, Piano Sonata No. 39/ii (Hob. XVI: 47) (London, Augener, [*c.*1930])

It is then of the highest importance for the singer to articulate clearly the words which he undertakes to interpret.

The clearness of the pronunciation depends entirely on the degree of force given to the consonants which begin each syllable. It is by means of this little percussion, in which the consonant seems to chase the vowel, that the singer makes himself understood even with a bass voice by the most distant of his auditors in a large room. It is well understood that the degree of intensity of this pronunciation should be in harmony with the spirit of the piece.

Having discussed the accentuation appropriate to various types of dramatic music, he continued:

These are the varied and diverse shades of expression which the violinist should render, giving to his bow a soft pronunciation for calm and serene music, and employing it with graduated force in passionate music. This accentuation gives to the instrument the prestige of words: we say that the violin speaks in the hands of the master. . . .

But just so much as pronunciation is in itself a precious quality, so much does it degenerate if employed in a systematic manner. It is for the good taste of the artist to use these means with discernment, and in such a way as to vary the effect: avoiding on the one hand too much softness, on the other too much power.[87]

He then proceeded to give a series of 'Examples of shading' showing 'Utterances of the bow from the softest sounds to the most energetic' with four examples which he considered required successively greater percussive accent. He used a wedge, indicating the attack and decay of the sound, to mark the appropriate place for the accents to be applied. (Ex. 2.36).[88]

Bériot's comments applied largely to accents that had not been specified by the composer. Where composers did mark accents, they used a range of instructions that attempted to show different types and degrees. These are considered in the next chapter; but the piecemeal growth of a vocabulary of accent

Ex. 2.36. Bériot, *Méthode*, iii. 221

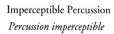

---

[87] *Méthode*, iii. 219–20.   [88] Ibid. 221.

Ex. 2.36. *cont.*

markings and instructions, as well as the varying usages of different composers, often makes it difficult to be certain what is implied without a close study of their individual practices.

3

THE NOTATION OF ACCENTS
AND DYNAMICS

಍಍಍

In the middle of the eighteenth century expressive accentuation and dynamic nuance was left largely to the discretion of the performer. As a rule, composers indicated only the most important dynamic contrasts and accents in their music. J. A. P. Schulz remarked in 1771 that dynamic marks 'are often put there only so that very crude improprieties may not be committed . . . they would, if they were really adequate, often have to be put under every note of a piece'.[1] For the effectiveness of their music in this respect, composers relied on performers' taste and experience in applying generally understood principles of phrasing and accent. To a great extent, therefore, stylish accentuation and dynamic shading during the late eighteenth century depended on the executant's recognition of the phrase structure of the music, its character, and so on. Even in the middle years of the eighteenth century this was seen to present considerable difficulties for the average performer; it was felt to be so subtle and variable that, as Schulz had implied, it could only effectively be learned from observing great musicians.[2]

The markings employed in mid-eighteenth-century music to indicate the contrasts and accents that composers regarded as essential were few and, as a rule, sparingly introduced. These instructions might encompass 'fortissimo', 'forte', 'poco forte', 'mezzo forte', 'piano', 'pianissimo', and from time to time, composers who were especially concerned to achieve a quite specific effect, such as Gluck, might employ less common terms like 'piano assai'[3] where something particularly arresting was required (Ex. 3.1). The additional dynamic shading and accentuation supplied by performers, partly in accor-

---

[1] In Sulzer, *Allgemeine Theorie*, 2nd edn. iv. 709.   [2] Ibid. (quoted in Ch. 1 above, n. 55).
[3] e.g. in the Vienna MS of Gluck's *Semiramide reconosciuta*, Österreichische Nationalbibliothek, Cod. mus. 17.793, repr. in *Italian Opera 1640–1770* (New York, Garland, 1982).

Ex. 3.1. Gluck, *Semiramide riconosciuta*, Österreichische Nationalbibliothek, Vienna, Cod. mu. 17.793, pub. in fac. in the series *Italian Opera 1640–1750* (New York and London, Garland, 1982)

dance with established conventions and partly according to their individual tastes, was an important element in the criteria by which, in the case of solo parts, their quality as artists would be judged. In orchestral playing, too, the ideal was certainly a well-controlled and aptly nuanced performance, but since this demanded uniformity of expression among all the players it necessitated control by the director if, in addition to the observance of the composer's usually scanty dynamic markings, anything other than the phrasing-off of appoggiaturas and the application of similar simple and universally accepted conventions were expected. Thus markings were even more necessary here than in solo music. J. F. Reichardt's discussion of crescendo and diminuendo in the orchestra illustrates the growing feeling, in the last quarter of the eighteenth century, that composers needed to specify their requirements more fully. He observed:

> If the composer wants to have it absolutely precisely performed he will do well to include all these different gradations exactly under the notes where they should occur . . . Or he must come to an understanding with his orchestra on particular occasions, namely that every whole or half bar should become to a degree brighter or darker, or whatever may be agreed. From time to time, however, precise specification will nevertheless be necessary so that one player does not get louder more quickly than another. The composer may, therefore, merely write *pp.* in the first bar, in the second *cresc.* and in the ninth *ff*.; in any case he may also add the sign ⎯⎯⎯⎯◁ and the orchestra will make the second bar *p.* the third *poco p.* the fourth *rinf.* the fifth *poco f.* the sixth *mf.* the seventh *più f.* the eighth *f.* and the ninth *ff*.[4]

---

[4]   *Ueber die Pflichten*, 65–7.

Reichardt's assumption that performances would commonly be under the composer's direct control also hints at one reason why such markings were relatively infrequent in mid-eighteenth-century music, which was seldom written with a view to publication. In practice, very few composers in the 1770s or 1780s took the sort of care with their scores that Reichardt recommended, and very few orchestras seem to have achieved his ideal. This is reflected in his comments about 'loud and soft and their various nuances', where he remarked:

This is, for our feelings, what the attractive force of the moon is for the sea: it will just as surely cause ebb and flow in us. The majority of orchestras only recognize and practise *forte* and *piano* without bothering about the finer degrees or the shading of the whole. That is to say they paint the wall black and white: it is all very well if it is beautiful white and beautiful black, but what does it say? It is difficult, extraordinarily difficult, to get a whole orchestra to do that which already gives a single virtuoso much trouble. But it is certainly possible: one hears this in Mannheim, one has heard it in Stuttgart.[5]

The idea that orchestras were only just learning to produce effective dynamic contrasts at that time is supported by Christian Gottlob Neefe's report of 1783 that Kapellmeister Mattioli in Bonn 'was the first to introduce accentuation, instrumental declamation, careful attention to forte and piano, all the degrees of light and shade in the orchestra of this place'.[6] Reichardt's treatment of the subject also implies that matters were not helped by confusion about the meaning of some of the terms employed at this period. He stated that such markings as *m.v.* (mezza voce) and *f.v.* (fatto voce—occasionally used as a synonym for 'mezza voce') were sometimes taken to mean the same as *mf* (mezzo forte) and sometimes even the same as *fz.* (forzato).[7] He might have added to his list *pf*. When this marking stood for 'poco forte', as proposed by Türk, and still occasionally used by Brahms (for instance in the second movement of his C minor Piano Trio), it indicated a dynamic level between *f* and *mf*; but it might easily be confused with *pf* standing for 'più forte', for example, in Galuppi's *L'Olimpiade*, where a crescendo is shown in something approaching Reichardt's manner by *f—pf—fortissimo* (Ex. 3.2).

Ex. 3.2. Galuppi, *L'Olimpiade*, Act I, Scene i

⁵ Ibid. 59.   ⁶ *Magazin der Musik*, 1 (1783), 377.   ⁷ Ibid. 68.

The situation was further complicated by the fact that some of the same terms might be employed to indicate either an absolute dynamic level, an accent or a dynamic nuance. 'Rinforzando', for instance, was sometimes synonymous with 'crescendo', sometimes designated an accent on a single note and seems sometimes to have indicated an emphatic style of performance for a phrase or passage. And, as Reichardt's remarks and Gallupi's practice suggest, a composer might use a sequence of apparently abrupt dynamic levels to indicate a smooth crescendo or diminuendo. Terms such as 'smorzando', 'morendo', 'calando', 'decrescendo', 'diminuendo', might be used as synonyms or they might have particular and specific connotations; 'calando', for example, could be synonymous with 'decrescendo' and 'diminuendo', but it could also imply a slackening of tempo as well as a decrease in volume. Despite the pioneering example of a few composers, it was not until the last decade or so of the eighteenth century that the convention of indicating a gradual increase or decrease of volume by terms such as 'cresc.' or 'dim.', or by 'hairpins', became commonplace.

Rapid diversification of musical style in the late eighteenth century and early nineteenth century progressively weakened the relationship between, on the one hand, clearly recognizable categories of music or conventions of notation, and, on the other, particular types of accentuation and dynamic shading. Schulz had already complained about this with respect to so-called 'heavy and light' performance styles in the 1770s.[8] Many composers, especially in the German sphere of influence, came increasingly to regard accentuation and dynamic nuance as integral to the individuality of their conceptions and were unwilling to entrust this merely to the performer's instinct. During the nineteenth century there was a proliferation of markings, designed to show finer grades or types of accents and dynamic effects, and performance instructions of all kinds were used ever more freely.

Pierre Baillot, from the vantage point of the fourth decade of the nineteenth century, was well aware of the consequences attendant on the development of a more individualistic, expressive, dramatic style in composition during the second half of the eighteenth century; he was also conscious that concomitantly with the growing reliance on notated dynamic and accentual detail came a decreasing awareness of the conventions that had conditioned such things in earlier music. He remarked:

This tendency towards the dramatic style was to give rise to the need to increase the number of signs and to notate every inflection in order to correspond as closely as possible to the wishes of the composer. This is what modern composers have done and this is what makes music written before this era much more difficult to perform and interpret well: we stress this point in order that students may not be in any way discouraged at the prospect of the

---

[8] See Ch. 16.

large number of works where the absence of signs makes an appeal to their intelligence which is bound to turn out to their advantage if they will only take the trouble to deepen their studies.[9]

Italian Terms and Abbreviations as Accents

The following discussion of individual terms and signs looks at theoretical explanations and at different ways in which they were used in the music of the period. A cross section of examples is cited, illustrating differences in usage, but there is no attempt at a comprehensive examination of the practices of individual composers.

Forte (f, for; ff, etc.)

Although *f* was most commonly used to indicate an absolute dynamic level, applying not just to single notes but to a whole passage, it was often used during the second half of the eighteenth century to identify notes that required a particular accent. The implications of this marking must, at first, have been wider than they later became, when other instructions for accent had come into use. Where, as was often the case in the mid-eighteenth century, *f* was the only accent instruction employed by the composer, it would have had to be deduced from the musical context whether it implied a sharp, heavy, moderate, light, rapidly decaying, or more sustained accent. In scores where other accent indications do not occur, *f* may well have been used to designate the kind of accent that would later have been indicated by *sf*. This is suggested by the two versions of Gluck's *Orfeo ed Euridice*. In the 1762 version the overture has *f* on the first beats of bars 6–10, while at the same place in the 1773 version the marking is *sf*. A third alternative is found in Rellstab's contemporary piano score of the work, which has *rf* here (Ex. 3.3).

Where it was used in conjunction with other accent markings, *f* may be presumed generally to have had a more specific meaning. *Sf, fz, rf, mfp, fp,* and *ffp,* as well as several graphic signs, were increasingly employed to indicate accents that might once have been implied by *f*. Sometimes, as in Salieri's *Der Rauchfangkehrer, ff* might even be used as an accent within a forte dynamic (Ex. 3.4). Where a composer used a range of accent markings, *f* alone, in a forte context, may have implied a weighty but not sharp execution, though there does not seem to be explicit theoretical support for such an assumption. Some composers may also have used *f,* instead of *sf,* when the forte was meant to continue beyond the initial rapid attack, especially those who employed *sf* in piano passages without any implication of a forte continuation.[10]

---

[9] *L'Art du violon*, 162.   [10] See p. 75 below, 'Sforzando'.

Ex. 3.3. Gluck, *Orfeo ed Euridice,* overture: (*a*) 1762; (*b*) 1773; (*c*) Rellstab

Ex. 3.4. Salieri, *Der Rauchfangkehrer,* Act II, no. 7, autograph in Österreichische Nationalbibliothek, Vienna Mus. Hs. 16.611; pub. in fac. in the series *German Opera 1770–1800* (New York and London, Garland, 1986)

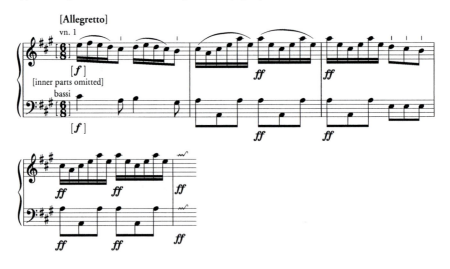

It is less common to find *f* used primarily to indicate accentuation after the widespread adoption of *sf* and *fz,* but some nineteenth-century writers continued to list it specifically as an accent marking, and it is sometimes encountered in this sense in nineteenth-century music, particularly the music of composers who employed a wide range of accent markings. Schumann, for instance, used a series of *f*s, apparently to ensure an equally weighty performance of successive chords in his Violin Sonata op. 105 (Ex. 3.5), perhaps recalling such instances as the succession of *ff*s in the first movement of Beethoven's

Ex. 3.5. Schumann, Violin Sonata op. 105/i

Violin Sonata in C minor op. 30 no. 2 or a weighty cadence in the String Quartet op. 59 no. 3 (Ex. 3.6). Beethoven occasionally used *f* with accent connotations in his early works (Ex. 3.7); in compositions of his middle and

Ex. 3.6. Beethoven: (*a*) Violin Sonata op. 30/2/i; (*b*) String Quartet op. 59/3/i

Ex. 3.7. Beethoven, String Quartet op. 18/5/iii

especially of his last period, where he sought to define expressive nuances with ever greater precision, he used it more often, seemingly to obtain an emphatic but less explosive execution than would have been elicited by *sf*, for example in the finales of the string quartets op. 127 and op. 131 or the first movement of op. 130 (Ex. 3.8). In this type of usage, too, Schumann followed Beethoven (Ex. 3.9). Another explanation of repeated 'forte' markings in some circumstances (Ex. 3.10) may have been that they were needed to prevent the normal diminuendo effect implied by the phrase structure, or to counteract the strong–weak relationships arising from the music's metrical framework. This seems likely to

Ex. 3.8. Beethoven: (*a*) String Quartet op. 127/iv; (*b*) String Quartet op. 131/vii; (*c*) String Quartet op. 130/i

Ex. 3.9. Schumann, Violin Sonata op. 121/ii

Ex. 3.10. Beethoven, String Quartet op. 18/4/iv

have been a factor in William Sterndale Bennett's frequent use of repeated *f*s in his overture *The Naiads* (Ex. 3.11).

A rather idiosyncratic use of *f* within forte or even fortissimo contexts can occasionally be found in some of Weber's music, where it seems rather to have dynamic than accentual implications. In his E flat Mass J. 224, for instance, he frequently used this means, especially in contrapuntal passages, apparently to advise the singer or instrumentalist that at that point their line should be particularly prominent. Instances of this kind should prompt the performer to consider whether, when an isolated *f* or *ff* occurs, it implies an accent or is merely a reminder of the prevailing dynamic.

Ex. 3.11. Bennett, *The Naiads*

Forte-piano (*fp*, *for:po:*, *ffp*, *mfp*)

The marking *fp* is likewise susceptible of different interpretations in eighteenth- and nineteenth-century music depending on the other accent markings employed. Where a composer did not use the marking *sfp* or *fzp*, the dynamic and accentual implications of *fp* may range from a sharp and powerful accent to a relatively gentle emphasis. A forte sustained for a definite length of time and followed by a sudden piano may sometimes be intended by *fp*, or it may require a forte followed by an immediate decrease of volume; in the latter case the piano may, perhaps, be either sudden or gradual.

Many composers juxtaposed 'forte' and 'piano' to show that a single beat or a group of notes should be played forte, perhaps with a diminuendo, before returning to piano, but not to indicate a short, sharp accent. Others undoubtedly saw *fp* as a means of indicating an accent within piano passages, where *f* alone could easily be confused with a dynamic marking that applied to the whole of the following passage. On occasion composers (for example J. C. Bach[11]) made the meaning of an *fp* clearer by the manner in which they beamed the notes. The same notational device was still used in the nineteenth century, for instance by Weber (Ex. 3.12). Among those who appear to have regarded *fp* primarily as a means of indicating a rapidly decaying accent was

---

[11] See Ex. 2.18.

Ex. 3.12. Weber, *Der Freischütz*, Act I, 'Introduzione'

Haydn; he asked that 'the first attack of the *forte* be of the shortest possible duration, in such a way that the *forte* seems to disappear almost immediately'.[12] Such an interpretation would seem appropriate for many occurrences of the instruction in Haydn's music for wind or strings, for instance in the first movement of his String Quartet op. 17 no. 4 (Ex. 3.13).

Some late eighteenth-century composers seem to have used *fp* in both these ways, and the difference is sometimes evident from the way the *f* and *p* are written, though it is impossible to tell this from most printed editions. In Mozart's autographs the distinction between the two usages is generally made clear (though not entirely consistently) by his manners of writing. Where the 'forte' and the 'piano' are intended to apply to separate beats or notes he usually wrote *f: p:*, and where he intended a forte followed rapidly by piano, *fp:* (Ex. 3.14). An

---

[12] Cited in Sandra Rosenblum, *Performance Practices in Classic Piano Music* (Bloomington, Ind., and Indianapolis, 1988), 86 (from Karl Geiringer, *Joseph Haydn* (Potsdam, 1932), plate facing 114; I have not, however, been able to trace this ref.).

Ex. 3.13. Haydn, String Quartet op. 17/4/i

Ex. 3.14. (*a*) Mozart, String Quartet K. 575/i; (*b*) iii

(*a*)

Ex. 3.14. *cont.* (*b*)

Ex. 3.15. Mozart, *Don Giovanni*, Act II, Scene vii

interesting use of *fp* by Mozart occurs in *Don Giovanni* (Ex. 3.15), where the combination of a staccato mark with *fp* seems clearly intended to indicate that the 'forte' applies only to the first note of a group of quavers. The staccato mark together with *fp* in the violins may be intended to clarify the extent and nature of the attack while the staccato mark alone in the violas and cellos seems to specify a similar, perhaps lighter accent.

A few eighteenth-century composers sought greater precision in the degree of accentuation by using *mfp* for a less powerful accent. Mozart used it fairly often, and it is also found in Salieri's music (Ex. 3.16). Whether Salieri, for instance, saw these markings essentially as accents, with a rapid decay of sound, however, is less clear. In the autograph of *Der Rauchfangkehrer*, *mfp* and *fp* are employed in several ways: Ex. 3.16 seems to suggest a fast decay after the initial accent, while Ex. 3.17 implies a diminuendo. Some composers, for instance Beethoven and Schubert, might specify a louder attack with *ffp*. Examples of even greater specificity, together with the use of dynamic markings such as *fff* and *ppp*, or sometimes as many as four or five *f*s and *p*s, are encountered with growing frequency in later nineteenth-century music.

Ex. 3.16. Salieri, *Der Rauchfangkehrer*, Act I, no. 1

Ex. 3.17. Salieri, *Der Rauchfangkehrer*, Act I, no. 5

As a wider range of accent markings was adopted by composers, anxious to designate different types and degrees of accentuation, it would seem logical that *fp* should have been employed primarily to designate a rapid falling-away of sound after the initial loudness, but probably without a sharp accent. This was certainly the way Meyerbeer made use of it. A footnote in the score of *Les Huguenots* echoes Haydn's instruction of more than sixty years earlier: 'Each note marked *fp* should be sounded loudly only at the first instant, then dying away afterwards.'[13] However, the fact that Meyerbeer felt it necessary to specify

---

[13] 1st edn. (Paris, Schlesinger, 1836), 100.

this interpretation of the marking indicates that such a usage may not have been universal even towards the middle of the nineteenth century. In fact, among Meyerbeer's contemporaries, there seems often to have been a degree of unclarity about the effect indicated by *fp*. Instances in Spohr's *Faust* indicate that he may have envisaged a more gradual decrease of volume than that required by Meyerbeer (Ex. 3.18). The same conclusion may be drawn from some of Schumann's uses of the marking, as in the Trio op. 80, where, if the violin is to correspond with the piano, an abrupt decrease in dynamic would hardly be appropriate (Ex. 3.19).

Ex. 3.18. Spohr, *Faust*, no. 5

Ex. 3.19. Schumann, Piano Trio op. 80/i

It is also probable that *fp* may sometimes have been seen as little different from, or synonymous with, *sf*/*fz* or *sfp*. In Schumann's First Symphony, though *sf* occurs quite frequently, there is no use of *sfp*; here, *fp* seems to supply its function. Schumann's subsequent symphonies use both markings freely, but the distinction is not always clear, as, for example, in his Third Symphony (Ex. 3.20), where *sfp* and *fp* are used simultaneously. Comparison of the first and second versions of Schumann's D minor Symphony (1841 and 1851) suggests a change in his practice (assuming that he did not require a different effect in 1851); in the fifth bar of the first movement, for example, the earlier version has *fp* where the later one has *sfp* and *sf*> (Ex. 3.21). Schumann's older contemporary Spohr also mixed *fp* and *fzp* in a similar manner. In *Faust*, where he did not employ *fzp*, Spohr often used *fz* and *fp* simultaneously in different parts, the former on notes followed by rests and the latter to specify the ensuing piano in a continuing part (Ex. 3.22). Mendelssohn's casual employment of *sfp* and *fp* in the Scherzo of his D minor Piano Trio, and elsewhere, certainly suggests that he did not see a very significant distinction between the two markings (Ex. 3.23).

At times *fp* was used, apparently, without any particular implication of accent, simply to obtain an abrupt decrease of volume at the end of a loud passage, for instance by Liszt and Brahms (Ex. 3.24).

Sforzando (sforzato, forzato, forzando, sf, sfz, fz, sfp, fzp)

The abbreviations *sf*, *sfz*, and *fz*, standing for 'sforzando', 'sforzato', and 'forzando' or 'forzato', were overwhelmingly regarded as synonymous, and most composers habitually employed only one or the other. Mozart, Cherubini, Beethoven, Mendelssohn, Liszt, Schumann, Berlioz, Wagner, and Brahms are among those who used *sf* or *sfz*; Haydn, Spohr, Schubert, Chopin, Dvořák and others employed *fz*. Because of the vagaries of engravers and typesetters, however, this distinction is not always apparent, in original or later printed editions. Although many writers explicitly stated that the two terms and their abbreviations were intended to convey the same thing,[14] a small number of musicians, or perhaps only theorists, acknowledged subtle distinctions between these various terms and their abbreviations; but their conclusions, considered below, are often contradictory and are likely to be of dubious relevance to composers' usages. No major composers appear to have used both markings concurrently or with differentiated meanings.

Where a composer employed both *f* and *sf*/*fz* as accents, the latter will generally have implied, as the meaning of the Italian word suggests, the sharper attack; however, it seems clear that *sf*/*fz* was sometimes intended to signify a

[14] e.g. Muzio Clementi, *Introduction to the Art of Playing on the Pianoforte* (London, 1801), 9; Dotzauer, *Violoncell-Schule*, 13.

Ex. 3.20. Schumann, Third Symphony op. 97/i

Ex. 3.21. Schumann, Fourth Symphony op. 120/i (1851 version)

Ex. 3.22. Spohr, *Faust*, no. 7

Ex. 3.23. Mendelssohn, Piano Trio op. 49/ii

relatively light accent within a piano context, whereas *fp* in piano passages is more likely, in almost all cases, to indicate a stronger dynamic contrast. In some instances *sf/fz* occurring in a piano dynamic was evidently meant to obtain a powerful accent followed by a forte continuation, whereas in others, particularly where a composer did not make use of *sfp*, an immediate return to the prevailing dynamic after an *sf/fz* in a piano passage will have been envisaged. Examples of the former can be found in Haydn (Ex. 3.25), though often when he used *fz* in piano sections he seems not to have wanted a forte continuation. This may be particularly true of his later works (Ex. 3.26). Haydn, unlike Mozart, never adopted *fzp* (*sfp*) as a regular marking to show whether or not a return to the prevailing dynamic was required.

Mozart was quite systematic in this respect as in so many others. When he wanted an *sf* within piano, he generally cautioned the performer to return to the original dynamic by writing *sfp*, as a comparison of his use of *sfp* in piano and *sf* in forte sections indicates (Ex. 3.27). Other composers of the late eighteenth century, for example Piccinni and Sacchini, had also adopted this practice. Beethoven, however, though he sometimes used *sfp* to clarify his intention, often used *sf* in quiet music, particularly in earlier works, where he undoubtedly intended an immediate return to piano (Ex. 3.28). At this stage he only seems to have used *sfp* if the previous marking was 'forte' and he required an abrupt decrease to piano after the *sf* (Ex. 3.29). By the time of the op. 59 quartets he had begun to mark *sfp* regularly in piano passages or to indicate the position and extent of the decrescendo by means of a 'hairpin' (Ex. 3.30). Other composers appear quite consciously to have used fairly complex combinations of these markings, choosing a variety of accent and dynamic instructions, and notation for different instruments or voices, in order to obtain the desired effect. Cherubini, who rarely left any ambiguity about the dynamic consequences of his *sf* markings in his late period, shows particular fastidiousness in this respect (Ex. 3.31).

Ex. 3.24. (*a*) Liszt, *Eine Faust Symphonie*, i, 'Faust' (strings); (*b*) Brahms, Second Symphony op. 73/i

(*a*)

Ex. 3.24. *cont.* (*b*)

Ex. 3.25. Haydn, String Quartet op. 17/4/i

Ex. 3.26. Haydn, String Quartet op. 76/5/i

Ex. 3.27.   Mozart, String Quartet K. 589/iv

With respect to the weight of accent implied by *sf,* some composers' practices may well have been in conflict with the opinion of many of the theorists.
Koch observed that the composer 'only uses *sf* in cases where the note should
be heavily accented, not with the gentler kind of accent';[15] and Milchmeyer
remarked: '*forzato, fz* as strong as possible, or as strong as the instrument will
take'.[16] There seem also to have been some musicians who considered *fz* a
slighter accent than *sfz.* Karl Gollmick registered this lack of agreement when
he observed '*forzando . . .* if one takes it as meaning the same thing as *sfz* it is
redundant. If one takes it as less intense, so the newer sign ^ perfectly performs
its function.'[17] The frequency with which individual composers used this
accent marking, as well as the repertoire of other accent markings that they
employed, will be a clue to the type of accent they wished to indicate by *sf*/*fz.*
Sandra Rosenblum argues that Beethoven's very frequent employment of *sf* in
all sorts of dynamic context suggests that it, together with *sfp,* is a relative
accent, its intensity dependent on the prevailing dynamic, whereas *ffp, fp,* and
mfp indicate absolute dynamic levels.[18] This may be so; yet, as far as the present
author is aware, the interpretation of *sf* as a very light accent in the music of
Beethoven or his contemporaries, even within piano contexts, is unsupported
by any theoretical discussion of *sf* in that period. In Beethoven's case there is no
reliable evidence from the composer himself or from his contemporaries to
determine whether he intended his *sf*s to denote frequent explosive accents
(which may well be thought to fit his musical personality), leaving the lighter
phrasing accents that he might have indicated with > (though he rarely did so)

---

[15]   *Musikalisches Lexikon,* art. 'Accent'.   [16]   *Die wahre Art,* 53.

[17]   *Kritische Terminologie* (Frankfurt-am-Main, 1833), 3.

[18]   *Performance Practices,* 87. For a helpful discussion of particular problems relating to these types of
accent on the fortepiano and the modern piano see ibid. 83 ff.

Ex. 3.28. Beethoven, String Quartet op. 18/4/i

Ex. 3.29. Beethoven, String Quartet op. 18/4/ii

Ex. 3.30. Beethoven, String Quartet op. 59/1/i

Ex. 3.31. Cherubini, Requiem in C minor, 'Pie Jesu'

to the performer, or whether his *sf*s were meant to cover the whole range of accents from the slightest to the most powerful.[19]

Cherubini certainly seems to have considered that *sf* indicated an absolute dynamic level and to have feared that it might, in some contexts, elicit too strong an accent from performers. In the scherzo of his First String Quartet, for instance, he used the direction *mz. sf* (mezzo sforzando) in piano passages (Ex. 3.32). Schubert, too, may have regarded *sf* as, to a degree, representing an absolute dynamic level, or at least as belonging within a restricted dynamic range, for he not only employed > very regularly as an accent sign but also used both *sf* and *sff*, implying a graduated scale, with *sf* as a middle ranking accent. Spohr, however, used *fz* to some extent as a relative dynamic marking, as a passage from the autograph of his String Quartet op. 82 no. 2 indicates (Ex. 3.33). In the forte the first violin's (and viola's) *fz* seems likely to have been relative to the other instruments' *f*, and in the piano to their presumably less powerful >. A similar intention to elicit an accent relative to the prevailing piano dynamic seems likely in Ex. 3.34.

Ex. 3.32. Cherubini, String Quartet no. 1/iii

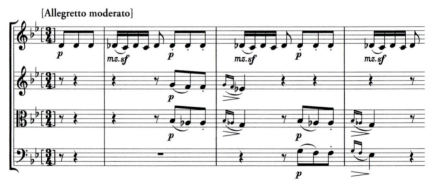

Schumann also used *sf* quite often but, since he utilized an even more extended range of accent markings with considerable subtlety, it is probable that his intentions were more narrowly conceived although they were undoubtedly not consistent throughout his career. Schumann's *sf* seems, for the most part to be a fairly powerful accent; he was sparing of its use in piano passages, where *fp*, >, and <> are more common. Brahms availed himself of *sf* much less frequently, which suggests that he regarded it as an especially weighty and significant accent to call on in particular circumstances. A few important nineteenth-century composers, including Weber, Meyerbeer, and Verdi,

---

[19] But see below for Beethoven's use of *rf*.

Ex. 3.33. Spohr, String Quartet op. 82/2/iv

Ex. 3.34. Spohr, *Faust*, no. 5

employed *sf* or *fz* even more rarely, apparently preferring the accent mark > as an exact equivalent.[20]

Rinforzando (rinforzato, rf, rfz, rinf, rfp)

In scores of the 1760s and 1770s 'rinforzando' is not infrequently found in contexts that show it to be essentially synonymous with 'crescendo'; but perhaps, as discussions of the term by some theorists suggest, it may have been used to indicate a more intense increase in volume than 'crescendo' or 'crescendo il forte'. Both 'crescendo (il forte)' and 'rinforzando' were sometimes used in the same work, for instance by Jommelli. It seems likely that Jommelli's terminology was not merely casual; the musical contexts in which these terms are used by him in *L'Olimpiade* suggest that 'rinforzando' was intended to signal a particularly rapid and powerful crescendo, or perhaps an exceptionally forceful

---

[20] See below, 'The Accent Hairpin'.

delivery of the group of notes to which it applied. (Ex. 3.35). In the following decades 'rinforzando' (or its variants and abbreviations) was often applied to short groups of notes where an increased intensity, rather than a normal crescendo, seems to have been required. This may have remained a factor in its use as an accent on a single note by some composers, implying a less explosive accent than *sf* where both markings are used in the same piece; but in many cases it seems probable that *rf* was simply regarded as indicating the same kind of accent as *sf* (e.g. in Rellstab's keyboard arrangement of Gluck's *Orfeo*, referred to above). Reichardt observed in 1776 that 'rinforzato' (*rf.*) 'should signify nothing more than a small pressure, an accent, on the note on which it stands'.[21] It seems likely to have been in this sense that Piccinni, for example, used the marking in a passage from his opera *Catone in Utica* (Ex. 3.36). Just after the turn of the century, however, A. E. Müller, having defined *rf* (rinforzando) as 'reinforced' (*verstärkt*) and *sfz* or *fz* (sforzato/forzato) as 'very strong' (*sehr stark*), added in a footnote:

Rinforzando and *sforzato* are different less in the degree than in the kind of strength with which the note is delivered: the former signifies a gradual strengthening of one and the same note, the latter a sudden accentuation of it. Most composers, however, do not make a sufficiently precise distinction in their writing.[22]

Of course, such a distinction was merely theoretical for pianists who could not actually make a single-note crescendo; though the use of this type of impracti-

Ex. 3.35. Jommelli, *L'Olimpiade*, Act I, Scene i, in *Recueil des opéra[s] composés par Nicolas Jomelli à la cour du Sérenissime duc de Wirtemberg* (Stuttgart, 1783)

Ex. 3.36. Piccinni, *Catone in Utica*, Act II, Scene viii, MS score in British Library, London, Add. 30792–4; pub. in the series *Italian Opera 1640–1770* (New York and London, Garland 1978)

---

[21] *Ueber die Pflichten*, 68.   [22] *Klavier- und Fortepiano Schule*, 29.

cable marking may have been seen as having a 'psychological' effect on the player. Beethoven and Schumann certainly employed similarly impossible markings in their piano music, but, as every sensitive pianist knows, these notes would be struck quite differently if they had any other marking (Ex. 3.37).

Ex. 3.37. Schumann, Piano Trio op. 80/iii

[In mässiger Bewegung]

An account by J. H. Knecht, almost exactly contemporary with Müller's, gives a rather different definition of the two terms. According to Knecht 'Rinforzando . . . strengthened, only applies to any note to which one should give a strong emphasis' (he made no mention of a crescendo element), while 'sforzato . . ., strengthened with decision, also applies to a single note, to which one must give a decisive but only briefly lasting emphasis'.[23] On the other hand, as implied by Müller's definition, some authorities saw rinforzando merely as a less powerful accent than sforzato, and thus Koch complained:

> Various composers mark the notes which should be accented with the word *rinforzato* (strengthened), which is shown in abbreviated form as *rf*. Who will not have noticed, however, that the notes thus marked are for the most part accented too strongly and stridently and that one mixes up the *rf* as an abbreviation for *rinforzato* with the *sf* as an abbreviation for the word *sforzato* (exploded), which the composer only uses in cases where the note should be heavily accented, not with the gentler kind of accent which is under discussion here.[24]

Franz Joseph Fröhlich, too, viewed the distinction between the two terms as one of degree rather than kind, giving the following definitions: '*sf, sforzato, sforz, forzando*, exploded, seize the note strongly, *rinforzando, rfz*, less'.[25]

Although some theorists continued to advance the notion that 'rinforzando', strictly speaking, indicated a crescendo, there was general acceptance by the

[23] *Katechismus*, 50.   [24] *Musikalisches Lexikon*, art. 'Accent'.
[25] *Vollständige theoretisch-praktische Musikschule* (Bonn, 1810–11), i. 50.

middle years of the nineteenth century that this was not how composers actually used it. Schilling's *Encyclopädie*, in the 1830s, having defined 'rinforzando' as
literally meaning crescendo, followed Koch in stating that it required 'only a
gentle pressure or accent of the note', while *sf* called for 'a very strong' one;[26] but
elsewhere in the *Encyclopädie* it is asserted that *rf* was often used as synonymous
with *sf*, and that 'in recent time *rinforzando* is used almost more than *sforzando*
for this short *forte*'.[27] At about the same time, Karl Gollmick acknowledged that
opinion was divided, commenting: '*rinforzando, rinforzato, rf, rinf*... Over the
significance of *rinf* there hangs the greatest doubt', but cited Milchmeyer's
much earlier definition in support of the explanation: 'continuously lively,
strong, as it were holding a lively conversation—for which we still have no suitable sign—corresponds most nearly with it.'[28]

An English writer, J. F. Danneley, attempted in 1825 to make a distinction
between 'rinforzando' and 'rinforzato'. He regarded the former as indicating
'strengthening of sound' and remarked of the latter: 'strengthened; it is thus
abbreviated R.F. and is placed over such notes as should be forcibly accented'.[29]
Curious though it may seem, Hugo Riemann, who is hardly likely to have
known Danneley's *Dictionary*, echoed this distinction more than half a century
later, defining rinforzando as a strong crescendo and rinforzato as 'strengthened', further observing that it was 'almost identical with *forte assai*, an energetic *forte*'.[30] But since composers rarely provided more than *rf* or *rinf*, these
distinctions remain in the realm of pure theory; to have determined which of
them might most closely suit the passage in question, performers would have
had to rely on knowledge of the composer's practice or, failing that, on the context and their own instincts. What these efforts to refine the terminology may
indicate, however, is an attempt to reconcile the evidently conflicting usages of
rf throughout the nineteenth century.

A few examples may illustrate composers' employment of this term. The
definition supported by Milchmeyer, Gollmick, and others (Riemann's rinforzato) as indicating a forceful delivery of a group of notes, but not necessarily a progressive crescendo on those notes, seems to fit many examples in
Haydn and Beethoven. In Haydn's String Quartet op. 71 no. 2 *rf* is used
apparently to emphasize the function of the last two notes as an upbeat to the
returning theme (Ex. 3.38). In Beethoven it often seems to be used to counteract the performer's natural tendency to diminuendo in what would otherwise
be weak parts of the phrase, or it may, perhaps, be seen as an instruction to
emphasize or strongly crescendo the phrase in question: the marking often
comes just before an abrupt piano (Ex. 3.39). Sometimes, however, particularly
in his late music, Beethoven used *rf* as an accent on a single note (Ex. 3.40(*a*)),

---

[26] Vol. vi. 362.   [27] Vol. vi. 8.   [28] *Kritische Terminologie*, 3.
[29] *Dictionary of Music* (London, 1825).   [30] *Musik-Lexikon* (Leipzig, 1882), 772.

Ex. 3.38. Haydn, String Quartet op. 71/2/iv

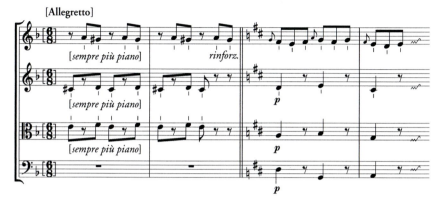

though at times the marking may be seen as an intensification of a crescendo. The fact that in some instances he certainly did not mean to indicate a progressive strengthening is clearly demonstrated by his use of *rf* in the String Quartet op. 132 (Ex. 3.40(*b*)). In such cases it seems plausible that, in accordance with the views of Koch and Fröhlich, he desired a less forceful accent than would have been elicited by *sf*. Inconsistencies abound, however (whether

Ex. 3.39. Beethoven: (*a*) Violin Sonata op. 24/i; (*b*) Piano Sonata op. 26/i; (*c*) String Quartet op. 135/iii

(*a*)

(*b*)

Ex. 3.39. *cont.* (c)

on the part of composers, copyists, or engravers). In the first edition of Beethoven's Piano Trio op. 1 no. 3, for example, the piano has *sf* while the cello, simultaneously, has *rf* (Ex. 3.41). Cherubini, on the other hand, clearly continued to use *rinf* to signify a powerful crescendo, somewhat in the manner of Jomelli. It often occurs in his music in the final bars of a passage that has earlier been marked 'cresc', evidently to ensure that the increase of volume continues (and intensifies) right up to the point of arrival at fortissimo. Typical examples of this may be found in the 'Dies irae' of his C minor Requiem and in his overture to *Anacreon*.

Ex. 3.40. Beethoven: (*a*) String Quartet op. 127/ii; (*b*) String Quartet op. 132/iii
(*a*)

Among later nineteenth-century composers who used the term fairly frequently was Liszt. His employment of 'rinforz' in, for instance, his *Années de pèlerinage* (Ex. 3.42(*a*)) seems plausibly to be in Milchmeyer's and Gollmick's sense of 'continuously lively, strong'; and his use of the term in his *Faust-Symphonie* suggests a similar interpretation (Ex. 3.42(*b*)). Brahms's use of the marking is ambiguous and may have changed with time. It occurs in the Serenade op. 11 (where, however, there is no use of *sf*), apparently as an accent applying to a single note. In the Serenade op. 16 and some later works both markings occur in contexts that suggest that Brahms may have intended *rf* to be a less powerful accent than *sf*. This appears also to be the case in the 1854 version of the Trio op. 8, where it occurs several times (Ex. 3.43); but it is conspicuous by its absence from the 1891 revision of the trio. At least one early occurrence of the marking in Brahms's works seems to accord with Liszt's use of it in the *Années de pèlerinage* (Ex. 3.44). In works of the 1880s and 1890s Brahms scarcely if ever employed it.

Ex. 3.41. Beethoven, Piano Trio op. 1/3/iii

Ex. 3.42. Liszt: (*a*) *Années de pèlerinage, Troisième année*, no. 7, 'Sursum corda'; (*b*) *Eine Faust-Symphonie*, ii, 'Gretchen'

(*a*)

(*b*)

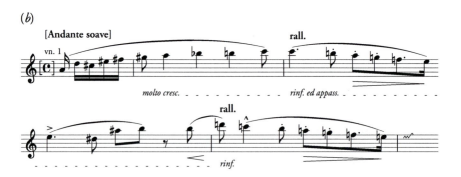

Ex. 3.43. Brahms, Piano Trio op. 8/iii (1854 version)

Signs as Accent Markings

Signs designating various types of accent, proposed and to a limited extent used by such composer-performers as Veracini and Geminiani in the earlier part of the eighteenth century, failed to gain currency. It was not until the last decades of that century that a significant number of composers began to adopt this means of specifying accents. During the nineteenth century a growing number of signs began to be used alongside the established Italian terms and their abbreviations; but here too there were many ambiguities, and scrutiny of particular composers' practices reveals considerable divergence of usage. With the introduction of a wider range of such markings the problem of understanding the conventions for applying accentuation and dynamic nuance where none was marked was largely superseded by the problem of recognizing what a particular composer intended to convey by his various performance instructions.

Ex. 3.44. Brahms, Serenade op. 16/v

The number of signs introduced during the last few decades of the eighteenth century and the first half of the nineteenth century was considerable. A glance at treatises published during this period reveals a mixture of signs that became widely adopted and others that failed to gain acceptance and are seldom encountered in music of the period. The accent signs proposed and employed during these years reflect the growing preoccupation of composers and theorists with conveying ever finer levels of expressiveness to the performer. As suggested in Chapter I, it was accepted in the eighteenth century that the metrical accentuation was often overridden by the accentuation necessitated by the shape and character of a particular melody (rhythmic accentuation), and many theorists stressed that recognition of the accentual character of a melody was vital to musical performance. Musicians working under the composer's direction and experienced artists might not find this problematic; the average musician was more dependent on notational guidance.

While late eighteenth-century composers began to acknowledge the desirability of specifying rhythmic and expressive accentuation more precisely, some musicians considered the problem of finding a means of indicating the desired pattern of emphasis in a melody. Since this was generally seen as necessitating a degree of accent less powerful than would have been suggested by such markings as *fp*, *sf*, or *fz*, a number of graphic signs and instructions were proposed and employed. Most of these either failed altogether to gain currency or, after a period of sporadic use, achieved more widespread acceptance, though often with significantly different implications than those originally envisaged. Reichardt proposed ▸ to indicate where a stress should fall. He considered that it should 'merely signify that a note, whether alone or with several in one bowstroke, should be brought out with a somewhat stronger pressure of the bow. Its form shows, at the same time, the increase of pressure. This has the same effect as a small light point in painting' [Ex. 3.45].[31] But in neither Reichardt's own scores nor those of other musicians does this sign seem to have been adopted in practice, despite Koch's sponsorship of it in his widely read *Lexikon*.[32] Domenico Corri's use, in his *A Select Collection*, of a similar sign ◂ above a note, to show that 'particular strength is to be given to it',[33] was probably independent of Reichardt. Türk proposed ^ to denote an accent less intense than would have been implied by *sf*. He described it in his 1789

Ex. 3.45. Reichardt, *Ueber die Pflichten*, 82

[31] *Ueber die Pflichten*, 81.   [32] *Musikalisches Lexikon*, art. 'Accent'.
[33] 3 vols. (Edinburgh, [*c.*1782]), i. 8.

Klavierschule,[34] explaining that he had already used it in his *Sechs leichte Klaviersonaten* of 1783. G. F. Wolf adopted this sign as a 'gentle accent' in the third edition of his *Unterricht*, published the same year as Türk's treatise,[35] and it was also used by J. F. Schubert in his *Singe-Schule* of 1804.[36] A generation later Hummel, perhaps influenced by Türk, used ∧ and + in his piano method (Türk had also used + as a sign for marking rhythmic accents[37]), explaining the former as a more pronounced accent than the latter.[38] The sign ∧ was not, however, used to any extent by composers at this stage, although an inverted form (∨) was used occasionally as an accent sign by Haydn in his later years. An example can be found in the autograph of the String Quartet op. 77 no. 1, though it is not entirely clear what kind of accent the sign was meant to convey and whether it was derived from Türk's sign (Ex. 3.46). At about the same time the short diminuendo sign (>) was also beginning to be used by a number of composers, including Haydn, as a means of specifying accentuation. However, before the general adoption of any of these various accent signs, the staccato mark (either stroke, dot, or wedge, but most commonly stroke) was often used not only to indicate separation but also to indicate accent.

Ex. 3.46. Haydn, String Quartet op. 77/1/ii

The Staccato Mark as Accent (𝅘𝅥 • ꓼ)

The accent element in staccato was discussed by theorists at an early stage, but the staccato mark's dual function was never clearly differentiated. Sometimes the mark seems to have been used merely to shorten a note, sometimes to indicate both shortening and emphasis and sometimes, apparently, to indicate primarily accent.[39] This agglomeration of functions was acknowledged in Johann Gottfried Walther's early eighteenth-century consideration of the term, in which he derived the word's two alternative forms, *staccato* and *stoccato*, from different roots. He observed:

---

[34] VI, §§15 ff.
[35] *Kurzer aber deutlicher Unterricht im Klavierspiel* (Göttingen, 1783).   [36] pp. 133 ff.
[37] See Ex. 1.8.   [38] *A Complete*, iii. 54.
[39] For further discussion of these signs as articulation, rather than accent marks, see Ch. 6.

Staccato or Stoccato is almost synonymous with spiccato, indicating that the bowstrokes must be short without dragging and well separated from each other.[40] The first derives from staccare, separate [*entkleben*], detach [*ablösen*], and this word from taccare, stick [*kleben*] and dis[taccare]; or better from attaccare, attach [*anhängen*], stick to [*ankleben*], and instead of the syllable at-, dis-, or s- signify ent-[kleben]. The second [of these terms] however derives from stocco, a stick [*Stock*], and means pushed [*gestossen*], not pulled [*nicht gezogen*].[41]

Johann Friedrich Agricola's 1757 revised version of Tosi's treatise on singing used the staccato mark unequivocally as a sign for accent without any implication of separation, instructing the pupil that a clear marking of the beat was necessary 'not only for the sake of clarity but also for the steady maintenance of an even tempo',[42] and illustrated this with an example (Ex. 3.47(*a*)). So, too, did Leopold Mozart (Ex. 3.47(*b*)).[43] But such uses of a single isolated stroke to indicate accent may sometimes be in danger of being confused with the diametrically opposite usage, alluded to by Schulz and Türk, where the stroke signified only the shortening necessary at the end of a musical phrase to separate it from the following one, in which case the note would generally be performed very lightly.[44]

Ex. 3.47. (*a*) Agricola, *Anleitung zur Singkunst*, 129, trans. Baird as *Introduction to the Art of Singing*, 155; (*b*) L. Mozart, *Versuch*, VI, §8

---

[40] See below, Ch. 7 for discussion of the various implications of *spiccato*.

[41] *Musicalisches Lexicon* (Leipzig, 1732), art. 'Staccato'.

[42] *Anleitung zur Singkunst* (Berlin, 1757), trans. and ed. Julianne C. Baird as *Introduction to the Art of Singing* (Cambridge, 1995), 155.

[43] *Versuch*, VI, §8. [44] See Exx. 4.7 and 6.15.

Reference to the accent properties of the staccato mark can be found in many eighteenth- and nineteenth-century sources. In 1808 G. W. Fink, discussing metrical accentual relationships, having observed that a note on a weak beat must act as an anacrusis to the following strong beat, qualified this by saying 'unless the composer has not expressly prevented this by a dot over the note or by means of rests'.[45] Thomas Busby observed in his *Dictionary* that vertical strokes signify that notes 'are to be played in a short, distinct, and pointed manner'.[46] He also commented that a dot, too, 'when stationed over a note, implies that such a note is to be played in a strong and striking manner'.[47] Where a distinction was made between the dot and the stroke it was predominantly the latter that was seen by the majority of early nineteenth-century German musicians as inherently having the more pronounced accent function. Knecht, echoing G. J. Vogler, instructed that notes with strokes should be delivered with 'long and sharp' staccato (*lang und scharf abgestossen*) and that those with dots should be played 'short and daintily' (*kurz und niedlich abgestupft*).[48] At least one French string method, the Paris Conservatoire's *Méthode de violoncelle*, approached Knecht's view, for after describing staccato in general terms as 'hammered' (*martelé*), it continued 'If the sign [for staccato] is lengthened a little above the note in this manner [Ex. 3.48] one lengthens the bow a little more; but if it only has dots, one makes the bowstroke very short and far enough from the bridge that the sound is round and that the staccato [*martellement*] is gentle to the ear.'[49] Fröhlich referred to strokes as indicating 'the more powerful staccato' (*der kräftigere Stoß*) and dots as indicating 'the gentler' one (*der gelindere*).[50] In the *Violinschule* of Mendelssohn's and Schumann's colleague Ferdinand David, accented martelé bowstrokes were associated with staccato strokes, while staccato dots were used to indicate the lighter springing staccato bowstroke.[51] This interpretation was followed by many German authors. Louis Schubert stated in his *Violinschule* that the stroke should be played with 'a degree of accent much stronger than the dot'.[52] Among other writers who echoed David's usage, not necessarily referring to string playing, were Arrey von Dommer, who noted that the wedge-shaped, pointed staccato

Ex. 3.48. Baillot et al., *Méthode de violoncelle*, 128

[45] *Allgemeine musikalische Zeitung*, 11 (1808–9), 229.   [46] *A Complete Dictionary of Music*, 52.

[47] Ibid. 60.   [48] *Katechismus*, 48.

[49] Pierre Marie François de Sales Baillot, Jean Henri Levasseur, Charles-Simon Catel, and Charles-Nicolas Baudiot, *Méthode de violoncelle du Conservatoire* (Paris, 1804), 128.

[50] *Musikschule*, iii. 49.   [51] (Leipzig, 1863), esp. 37 ff.

[52] *Violinschule nach modernen Principien* op. 50 (Brunswick, [1883]), ii. 34.

mark indicated 'the real short and sharp staccato' (*das eigentliche kurze und scharfe staccato*) while the dot signified 'a gentler, rounder, less pointed staccato' (*ein weicheres, runderes, weniger spitzes Abstossen*);[53] Mendel and Reissmann, observing that staccato was indicated by dots or strokes, commented: 'These latter commonly serve as a sharpening' (*Verschärfung*);[54] Riemann remarked: 'When staccato dots are distinguished in two forms, namely • and ı, the ı indicates a sharp, the • a light staccato.'[55] In the pedagogic tradition of German violin playing the influential Joachim and Moser *Violinschule* of 1905 also lent authority to that interpretation. In England this notation was adopted, for instance, by J. M. Fleming in his *Practical Violin School* of 1886.[56]

In France, however, a rather different view of the two forms of staccato mark became normal during the nineteenth century despite the treatment of staccato in the 1804 *Méthode de violoncelle*. From at least Baillot's *L'Art du violon* (1834) onwards, the French seem generally to have regarded the stroke (wedge) as not only shorter, but also lighter than the dot. Such an interpretation is suggested by many mid-nineteenth-century references, for example the definition of 'Piqué' in the *Dictionnaire de musique* endorsed by Halévy in 1854, which commented that such passages were marked with strokes (*point allongé*) and that these notes were to be 'equally marked by dry and detached strokes of the tongue or bow'.[57] In *L'Art du violon* Baillot used the dot to indicate sharply accented martelé, where the bow remains in contact with the string, and strokes (wedges) for light, bouncing bowstrokes.[58] And Emile Sauret, among other French string players, followed him in associating the dot with martelé.[59] The description of the two marks in the early twentieth-century *Encyclopédie de la musique et dictionnaire du Conservatoire* reflects French use of them (though the association of the dot with martelé is not explicit), indicating the strength with which a disparity between French and German practice persisted; there, the stroke (*point allongé*) was described as betokening that the note 'ought to be separated, struck very lightly, almost dryly' and as 'depriving the note of three-quarters of its value'; whereas the dot (*point rond*) meant that 'these notes ought to be lightly quitted, however, in a less short, less dry manner than with the stroke'.[60]

Outside France Baillot's system rather than David's was also adopted by a number of influential pedagogues. The Viennese violinist Jacob Dont, for instance, used dots to designate a martelé bowstroke (*gehämmert*) and strokes

---

[53] *Musikalisches Lexicon*, art. 'Absotssen'.   [54] *Musikalisches Conversations-Lexicon*, i. 608.

[55] *New Pianoforte School/Neue Klavierschule*, 17.

[56] *The Practical Violin School for Home Students* (London, 1886), 249, 251.

[57] Escudier (frères), *Dictionnaire de musique théorique et historique* (Paris, 1854), ii. 127.

[58] Esp. pp. 92 ff.

[59] *Gradus ad Parnassum du violiniste* op. 36 (Leipzig, [*c*.1890]), 5.

[60] Albert Lavignac and Lionel de la Laurencie, *Encyclopédie de la musique et dictionnaire du Conservatoire* (Paris, 1920–31), pt. 2 'Technique-esthetique-pédagogie', 335.

(wedges) to signify that notes should be played with a springing bow (*mit springendem Bogen*) in his 1874 edition of exercises from Spohr's *Violinschule*;[61] and the Czech violinist Otakar Ševčík made a similar use of these signs in his extremely influential teaching material, thus helping to perpetuate the confusion to the present day.[62]

Many eighteenth- and nineteenth-century German composers employed the staccato mark in contexts where its principal purpose seems to have been accentual.[63] An example from Mozart's *Don Giovanni* where ı is used in conjunction with *fp* has been cited above (Ex. 3.15). In the final movement of his Symphony no. 41 the bold staccato strokes over the tied semibreves in the viola and bass (Ex. 3.49) may merely have been intended to ensure that the players did not assume that ties were meant to continue throughout the whole passage, but they may also suggest an accent at the beginning of each new note. (A slight

Ex. 3.49. Mozart, Symphony no. 41 K. 551/iv

---

[61] *Zwölf Uebungen aus der Violinschule von L. Spohr mit Anmerkungen, Ergänzungen des Fingersatzes der Bogen-Stricharten und der Tonschattierungszeichen* (Vienna, 1874).

[62] *Schule der Violine-Technik* op. 1 (Leipzig, 1881), *Schule der Bogentechnik* op. 2 (Leipzig, 1895), etc.

[63] The question where and when a distinction between dots and strokes was intended in 18th- and early 19th-c. music is addressed in Ch. 6.

separation between notes would also be appropriate, but the staccato mark, in this context, can hardly indicate anything like the conventional reduction of the note length by a half or even a quarter of its value.) In the music of Mozart's pupil Süssmayr, too, staccato marks seem sometimes to be used essentially as accents (Ex. 3.50). And Beethoven's Piano Sonata op. 53 contains a passage in which staccato marks could scarcely have been intended to signify anything other than accents (Ex. 3.51).[64] Another instructive example of Beethoven's use of staccato marks as accents occurs in the Trio section of the Scherzo of his Septet (Ex. 3.52); acknowledging their accent function together with a degree of shortening the editor of the Peters edition of the score (*c.*1870) gave them as ∧.

Ex. 3.50. Süssmayr, *Der Spiegel von Arcadien*, no. 50, MS score in Staatsbibliothek zu Berlin, mus. ms. 21 533; pub. in fac. in the series *German Opera 1770–1800* (New York and London, Garland, 1986)

Ex. 3.51. Beethoven, Piano Sonata op. 53/iii

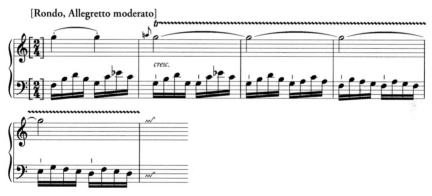

Ex. 3.52. Beethoven, Septet op. 20/iv

---

[64] Rosenblum, *Performance Practices*, 183 cites this passage as an example of staccato marks used as accents, but she seems to put rather too much weight on the theoretical distinctions between dot and stroke and, apparently confusing the form with the function, remarks: 'where composers seem to have intended an accent or a metrically accented note, the printed sign should be a stroke or a wedge'.

Where nineteenth-century German composers used both types of staccato mark, the stroke seems generally to have been intended as much to indicate accent as to specify shortening. G. F. Kogel, the nineteenth-century editor of Marschner's *Hans Heiling*, explained that Marschner used the staccato stroke to designate 'notes that ought, with short, powerful bowstrokes, to be most especially strongly (*sfz*) made to stand out'.[65] A similar type of execution appears to be implied by Schumann's use of strokes (printed as wedges), for instance in the first movement of his 'Rhenish' Symphony, where a particular passage is always marked in this way (Ex. 3.53), while only dots are used for staccato in the rest of the symphony. The autograph of 'Reiterstück' from Schumann's *Album für die Jugend* provides a good example of the composer's use of I together with ∧ and · as a graduated series of accent/articulation marks in keyboard writing (Ex. 3.54).

Ex. 3.53. Schumann, Third Symphony op. 97/i

Brahms also made a distinction between dots and strokes, and although Kogel (writing in the 1880s) considered that the stroke as used by Marschner was 'an obsolete form of notation', Brahms, who was quite conservative in his attitude towards notation, seems clearly to have associated strokes with this kind of sharp, accented staccato (Ex. 3.55).[66] Dvořák, too, made use of them in a similar way (Ex. 3.56). Amongst other composers who certainly used the stroke and the dot in this manner was Wagner, at least in some of his late works.[67] His orthography in the autographs is often unclear, nor does it always correspond with the earliest printed editions, but where Wagner is known to have overseen the publication of a work (i.e. in the case of his later operas), it may be conjectured that some of the differences result from alterations at proof stage. Among more recent composers, Schönberg seems to have inherited this tradition, for he explained in the preface to his Serenade op. 24: 'In the marking of the short notes a distinction is here made between hard, heavy, staccatoed and light, elastic, thrown (spiccato) ones. The former are marked with I ▾, the latter by ··.'[68] Elgar, too, evidently considered the stroke to have accentual qualities, to judge by passages such as Ex. 3.57.

---

[65] Full score (Leipzig, Peters, *c.*1880), preface.
[67] But see Ch. 6.

[66] See below, Ch. 6, p. 218 and Ex. 6.20.
[68] (Copenhagen and Leipzig, W. Hansen, 1924).

Ex. 3.54. Schumann, *Album für die Jugend*, 'Reiterstück'

(*a*)

(*b*)

Ex. 3.55. Brahms: (*a*) First Symphony op. 68/i; (*b*) Clarinet Quintet op. 115/i

(*a*)

(*b*)

Ex. 3.56. Dvořák, String Quartet op. 80/iv

Ex. 3.57. Elgar, First Symphony op. 55/ii

The Accent Hairpin (> or ▷)

Apart from the staccato stroke, the earliest accent sign to be widely and perma-
nently accepted was >, which seems to have developed from the sign for diminuendo shortly after that had become current. The signs < and > as graphic
illustrations of crescendo and diminuendo only began to be regularly used
from about the 1760s, though something similar had been proposed by Italian
composers, such as G. A. Piani and Francesco Veracini several decades earlier.
By the 1780s > was also being employed by many composers as an accent sign.
Mozart, however, had little interest in using it either as an accent sign or as an
indication for diminuendo, and it is found very rarely in his compositions.
Haydn began to utilize it in works of the 1790s, including the op. 71 and op. 74
string quartets, but did not employ it particularly often. Beethoven used it
sparingly in his earlier works, and even in later compositions it is far less common than *sf.* Other late eighteenth- and early nineteenth-century composers
adopted the sign more extensively, either as a synonym for the type of effect

which many of their contemporaries would have indicated by *sf* or *fz*, or as a slighter accent than implied by these markings. Early and frequent use of the sign, as both diminuendo and accent, can be found in G. J. Vogler's music; it is also commonly encountered in the music of Vogler's pupils Weber and Meyerbeer. The sign occurs frequently, too, in music by Cherubini, Süssmayr, Spohr, Rossini, and Schubert. For almost all composers born after 1800 it was an absolutely standard sign.

Occurrences of the sign in the music of the period, however, reveal a number of problematic aspects of its usage. Among the most difficult to determine is the extent to which, in particular instances, it might be purely accentual (i.e. indicating an emphasis that gives the note a degree more prominence than its unmarked neighbours), where it denotes merely diminuendo (requiring no more than a decrease in volume from the previously prevailing dynamic), or where it signifies a combination of both these things. The difficulty is compounded by ambiguous orthography on the part of composers and, where autographs are not to hand, the evident unreliability of many early editions.

Beethoven's employment of this sign usually suggests that he saw it literally as a short diminuendo 'hairpin', and he appears quite deliberately to have used it primarily as a dynamic nuance; in Ex. 3.58(*a*) it is evidently intended to reinforce the conventional accent-diminuendo treatment of appoggiaturas. In works of his early and middle periods, it is difficult to find clear examples where he might have intended it to apply to a single note as an accent. Indeed, there is little to suggest that Beethoven ever really associated this sign specifically with accent, though the successive 'hairpins' in the *Chorfantasie* and in Ex. 3.58(*b*) imply at least a small degree of accent as well as the diminuendo phrasing appropriate to this figure. In the String Quartet op. 131, where > occurs quite often over single notes, it usually seems meant to indicate a rapid diminuendo rather than an accent; only near the beginning of the 'Adagio ma non troppo e semplice' in the fourth movement may Beethoven have envisaged it as an accent sign (Ex. 3.59(*a*)). Presumably, since he freely used *sf* and not infrequently *rf*, it was meant to indicate the lightest degree of expressive weight. It is questionable whether the use of the sign in the Vivace of op. 135 indicates an accent or merely a diminuendo (Ex. 3.59(*b*)).

The problems of distinguishing between > as accent, as accent plus diminuendo, and purely as diminuendo continued well into the nineteenth century. This was exacerbated in the case of composers, such as Schubert, Bellini, and others, who often wrote large 'hairpins' in contexts that suggest a rapidly decaying accent rather than a gradual diminuendo. In Schubert's case a relationship between the size of the 'hairpin' and the intensity of the accent, perhaps resulting from the subconscious reflection of his feelings in his handwriting, often appears plausible, though it would be injudicious to press that hypothesis too far. It is interesting to note that the meaning of this sign remained a matter of

Ex. 3.58. Beethoven: (*a*) *Chorfantasie* op. 80; (*b*) Piano Trio op. 97/i
(*a*)

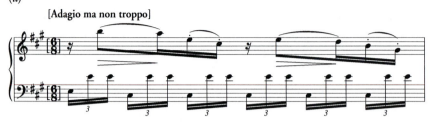

(*b*)

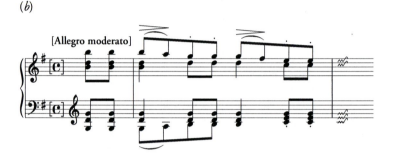

some uncertainty as late as 1841, when a writer in the *Allgemeine musikalische Zeitung* felt it necessary to explain that it need not always mean diminuendo, but could often mean simply accent. He commented: 'Very frequently *decrescendo* signs (>) occur even on short notes, by which, however, the composer only wishes to show that the notes should be performed more markedly. That this is so is shown by the use of this sign also in quiet passages.'[69]

Wagner's notation of the sign usually leaves no doubt about its accent meaning, and when he also required a distinct diminuendo he would ensure this by using both the short and long versions of the sign (Ex. 3.60). In works up to about 1880 Brahms also made his intentions absolutely clear in such circumstances by his manner of combining > with a longer diminuendo sign (Ex. 3.61). In the works of his last period, however, although Brahms continued to use the short form of the sign to denote an accent, such double signs are rare; but, as Paul Mies has persuasively argued,[70] the diminuendo and accent meanings appear often to be subsumed in the same long version of the sign. (Ex. 3.62).

[69] Anon, 'Einiges über die Pflichten des Violoncellisten als Orchesterspieler und Accompagnateur' *Allgemeine musikalische Zeitung*, 43 (1841), 133.
[70] 'Ueber ein besonderes Akzentzeichen bei Johannes Brahms', in Georg Reichert and Martin Just, eds., *Bericht über den internationalen musikwissenschaftlichen Kongress Kassel 1962* (Kassel, 1963), 215–17.

Ex. 3.59. Beethoven: (*a*) String Quartet op. 131/iv; (*b*) String Quartet op. 135/ii

(*a*)

(*b*)

Ex. 3.60. Wagner, *Parsifal*, Act III, rehearsal numbers 255–6

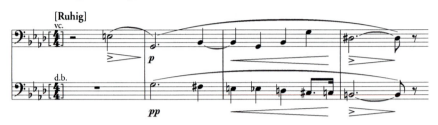

Ex. 3.61. Brahms, Piano Sonata op. 1/i

The other major question about this sign is what type of accent it might imply; in particular, whether it calls for a slighter accent than *sf* or *rf*, or whether it is synonymous with one or other of them. Haydn certainly seems, sometimes at least, to have thought of it as synonymous with *fz*, for instance in the Finale of Symphony no. 104, where the two markings appear to be interchangeable (Ex. 3.63). In the music of Vogler and his pupils Weber and Meyerbeer > seems fairly consistently to have been used as a graphic equivalent of *sf*/*fz*. It is listed as such by one of their contemporaries, the cellist J. J. Dotzauer (a leading member of Weber's orchestra in Dresden), who considered it to be merely an abbreviation for 'rinforzando' or 'sforzando' occurring over a

Ex. 3.63. Haydn, Symphony no. 104/iv

single note. For Dotzauer, all of these directions simply meant that the note should be strengthened (*verstärkt*) to an unspecified degree.[71] Vogler seems to have preferred to use > rather than *sf*, and from passages in his Singspiel *Der Kaufmann von Smyrna*, for example, it looks as though he intended it to represent a substantial accent with a rapid decay of sound, since it occurs in conjunction with *f* and *p* (Ex. 3.64). Although Weber did not entirely avoid *fz* he employed it rarely, but not apparently as a more powerful accent; its occasional appearances in *Der Freischütz* are often in conjunction with > in circumstances that make it highly improbable that a distinction between the two accent markings was intended. Weber certainly used > purely as an accent, even when the sign, as so often with Schubert, was boldly written and might be thought to be a diminuendo 'hairpin'. The use of > exclusively to mean an accent is nicely illustrated by an instance of his use of it in the score of *Der Freischütz* (Ex. 3.65). In Meyerbeer's case the correspondence between *sf* and > is confirmed, in *Les Huguenots* for instance, by his occasionally supplementing > with an

---

[71] *Violoncell-Schule*, 13.

Ex. 3.64. Vogler, *Der Kaufmann von Smyrna*, no. 7, MS score in Hessische Landes- und Hochschulbibliothek, Darmstadt, mus. ms. 1090; pub. in fac. in the series *German Opera 1770–1800* (New York and London, Garland, 1986)

Ex. 3.65. Weber, *Der Freischütz*, no. 15

instruction such as *poco sf* or *dolce sfz*. These are the only occasions in *Les Huguenots* where he used the term *sfz*; it never occurs alone (Ex. 3.66). However, Meyerbeer often combined > with another marking, such as *fp* or even ∧ , and the intention of the sign in such circumstances is not always clear. Verdi is among later nineteenth-century composers who preferred to use > rather than *sf*; it appears in all sorts of context, but seems often to suggest a quite powerful accent.

In the music of these composers > probably indicates an accent of variable strength, from a full-blooded sforzando to a gentle emphasis, depending on the context and on any other qualifying expressions. Many composers, on the other hand, apparently regarded > as having a more restricted meaning in this respect, and quite definitely as specifying a level of accent inferior to *sf*. The largest body of opinion in the first half of the nineteenth century regarded it as indicating one of the slightest degrees of accent. Philip Corri used > in his pianoforte method to mark the notes on which the expressive stress, which according to English usage he calls emphasis, should fall in a melody.[72] And

---

[72] *L'anima di musica*, 72.

Ex. 3.66. Meyerbeer, *Les Huguenots*, no. 18

Hummel, apparently equating > and ∧ (at least in terms of strength), observed that 'The *mark of emphasis* (∧ or >) is used both in *piano* and *forte* passages; it, in a slight degree, distinguishes from the rest, the note over which it stands.'[73] Both these musicians, however, saw it as appropriate to any dynamic. Later theorists increasingly considered it to be more appropriate in piano passages than in forte ones. Karl Gollmick observed: 'The sign > means only an accent on [the note] and belongs more to a gentler style of performance.'[74] Wagner on one occasion referred to > in Weber's *Der Freischütz* as indicating the 'merest sigh'.[75] Wagner's use of this accent sign in his own operas suggests that this may have been how he envisaged its execution, though, as so often in his pronouncements about the performance of earlier composers' music, he may not have been entirely correct about Weber's intention.

Schubert, who often employed *sf*, and sometimes *sff*, and who used > very frequently, undoubtedly intended the latter marking primarily to designate where the expressive stress in the melody should fall. Sometimes he reinforced

[73] *A Complete*, i. 67.   [74] *Kritische Terminologie*, 4.
[75] 'Ueber das Dirigiren', in *Gesammelte Schriften*, viii. 297.

Ex. 3.67.   Schubert: (*a*) Piano Trio D. 898/ii; (*b*) Symphony in B minor D. 759/ii
(*a*)

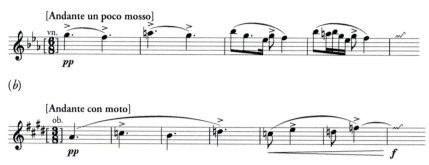

(*b*)

the message of the slurring with > and sometimes he overrode it (Ex. 3.67). The basic meaning of this sign for Schubert is tellingly illustrated by instances in *Alfonso und Estrella* where > and <> in the orchestral parts are evidently intended to support the lightest of (unmarked) emphases in the vocal line and to add subtle contrasting accentuation (Ex. 3.68). Such passages imply that, for Schubert, > corresponded with the normal degree of emphasis that a good singer would naturally give to the stressed syllables of the text or to musically important notes.

Spohr's use of the accent in his Concertante for violin, cello, and orchestra WoO. 11 (1803) suggests that in his early works he saw it, like Weber and Meyerbeer, as an accent mark that was relative to the prevailing dynamic and that could signify anything from a light emphasis to a fairly powerful accent; it

Ex. 3.68.   Schubert, *Alfonso und Estrella*, no. 11

occurs not only in piano contexts, but also simultaneously with *fp* in parts doubled at the octave and even with *fz* (Ex. 3.69; on the first occurrence of passage (*b*) he used *fz* in all parts except timpani). In later works Spohr apparently saw it more as a lighter accent, often with a quite distinct element of diminuendo (see Ex. 3.33 above).

Ex. 3.69. Spohr, Concertante WoO. 11
(*a*)

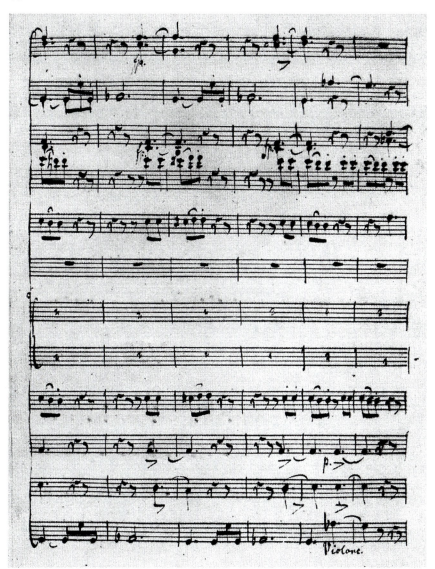

Ex. 3.69. *cont.* (*b*)

By the second half of the nineteenth century the acceptance of other signs
into common usage tended to fix > towards the middle of a wider hierarchy of
accents; but its meaning remained quite variable. The systematic discussion of
accents in the *Encyclopédie de la musique et dictionnaire du Conservatoire* supports its position as a middle ranking accent. It categorized > as necessitating 'a

stronger attack followed immediately by a diminution of tone',[76] and – was given as a gentler degree of accent. Yet Riemann perpetuated the notion of the equivalence of > and *sf*, commenting: 'A > over a note requires a stronger tone (accent, sforzato).'[77] Much depends on the number of different accent markings a composer chose to employ. In the music of Brahms, who generally scorned the newer accent signs,[78] a variety of treatments will be appropriate; in Schumann's, Wagner's, Dvořák's, and Bruckner's works and those of many of their contemporaries, however, where several of the accent signs discussed below are encountered, its meaning will be more restricted.

Another question mark over the use of this sign in the late eighteenth and early nineteenth century concerns whether any distinction was meant between the > and the ▷. On the whole this seems unlikely; but Rossini's use of the two forms (in the autograph of *La gazza ladra*, for instance) sometimes seems to hint at an apparent difference between the one as a decrescendo and the other as an accent. Like so many other notational subtleties, however, the distinction, if it were intended, appears not to have been consistently pursued, and it seems much more likely that the change in the symbol, by the omission of the inessential line, came about as a natural process of simplification, particularly when composers or copyists were writing at speed. An occasionally encountered specialized meaning of > was, when used successively (i.e. >>>>), vibrato.[79]

Le Petit Chapeau *(∧)*

The meaning of this sign[80] also varied from time to time and composer to composer. As already mentioned, it was used by Türk and Wolf in the eighteenth century to designate the notes upon which expressive stress should fall, and adopted in the instruction books of J. F. Schubert and Hummel in the early nineteenth century. In all these cases it was clearly meant to designate a relatively gentle accent, though Hummel used + to indicate an even lighter one. In 1808 G. F. Fink listed ∧ along with *f*, *sfz*, and > as one of what he designated 'nuanced expressive accents' *(nuanzirende Gefühlsaccente)*;[81] he failed to discuss the degree or type of accent implied by the sign, but since he listed it after *sfz* and > it is probable that he regarded it as slighter than those accents.

In practice, however, ∧ was scarcely employed by composers in this period. Meyerbeer seems to have been one of the earliest important composers to use it regularly, but its significance in his music is not altogether clear. In many

[76] Lavignac et al., *Encyclopédie de la musique*, pt. 2, 335.　　[77] *New Pianoforte School*, 17.

[78] See below, Ch. 6, pp. 240 f.　　[79] See Ch. 14.

[80] *Le petit chapeau* (the little hat), the name given to this accent in Lavignac et al., *Encyclopédie de la musique*.

[81] In *Allgemeine musikalische Zeitung*, 11 (1808–9), 226.

instances it appears to be a less powerful accent than >. In *Les Huguenots*, whereas > is used for *sf* and sometimes occurs with the qualification *poco sf*, ^ is, on occasion, combined with the term *dolce sf* (Ex. 3.70(*a*)). It is often found, too, in piano passages where a gentle accent seems to be implied (Ex. 3.70(*b*)). A particularly revealing instance occurs when it is used in a vocal part with the additional instruction 'mark each of the six notes but without force'[82] (Ex. 3.70(*c*)); and at a later point in the opera it occurs with the instruction 'very soft (with plaintive expression)', being superseded by > with the advent of a crescendo (Ex. 3.70(*d*)). Yet elsewhere Meyerbeer used it where a stronger accent seems called for (in *Le Prophète*, for instance, where it is found in conjunction with the instruction 'martelé'[83]); and it is difficult to see what is meant in *Les Huguenots* when a figure is first given with ^ on each note and then with both ^ and > on each note (Ex. 3.70(*e*)). It may be significant for the type of accent Meyerbeer envisaged that he very often combined it with the instruction 'tenuto', suggesting that the perceptible diminuendo effect associated with > was not, as the difference in shape implies, required. Like Meyerbeer, Verdi may have regarded ^ , which occurs sometimes in combination with slurs and sometimes alone, especially in his works from the 1860s onwards, primarily as a lighter accent than >. It seems sometimes to be intended to counter the normal tendency to phrase off the metrically weaker beats, for instance in some passages in the Requiem (Ex. 3.71(*a*)). But Verdi does not appear to have considered the difference in meaning between > and ^ to have been very pronounced, and he sometimes mixed the two signs indiscriminately, as in the 'Libera me' from the abortive *Messa per Rossini* of 1869 (Ex. 3.71(*b*)).

During the fourth and fifth decades of the nineteenth century ^ began to be more widely used. Spohr adopted it in the additional music that he wrote in 1852 for a revival of his 1813 opera *Faust*, apparently as a light accent, since it only occurs in piano and pianissimo contexts. But by that time the significance of the sign was changing; there appears to have been a growing tendency to see it as a powerful accent. Henri Herz's *A New and Complete Pianoforte School* of about 1838 had stated that ^ 'indicates, in general a degree of intensity inferior to *sf* ',[84] and Karl Gollmick, in his *Kritische Terminologie* of 1833, gave a similar definition, observing: 'The newer sign ^ requires a strong pressure on the individual note, but less harsh than *sf* ',[85] and he further observed that if one took *rf* as indicating a slighter accent than *sf* the sign ^ would signify precisely the same thing as *rf*. However, in his *Handlexikon* of 1857 Gollmick described ^ as 'the same as *sf* '.[86] Carl Czerny, in the 1840s ranked it among the stronger

---

[82] Full score (Paris, Schlesinger, [1836]), 335.

[83] Full score (Paris, Brandus and Troupenas, [1849]),739.

[84] (London, [*c.*1838]), 16. However, in the Italian edition the sign is given as > not ^.   [85] p. 4.

[86] *Handlexikon der Tonkunst* (Offenbach am Main, 1857), art. 'Accent'.

Ex. 3.70. Meyerbeer, *Les Huguenots*: (*a*) no. 5; (*b*) no. 8; (*c*) no. 12A; (*d*) no. 27; (*e*) no. 27A

(*a*)

Ex. 3.70. *cont.* (*b*)

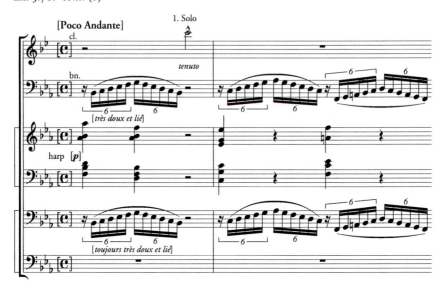

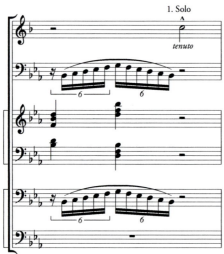

accents, stating that it 'implies a higher degree of power'.[87] Whether composers used ^ in this sense or whether they saw it as indicating a relatively gentle emphasis is evidently linked with their view of >, and those composers who used > instead of *sf* will have been likely to have favoured the lighter interpretation of ^.

[87]   *Piano Forte School: Second Supplement* (London, [*c.*1846]), 27.

Ex. 3.70. *cont.* (*c*)

(*d*)

(*e*)

Ex. 3.71. Verdi: (*a*) Requiem; (*b*) *Messa per Rossini*
(*a*)

(*b*)

For Schumann, as for Czerny, the sign normally denoted a degree of accent greater than >. This is suggested in his *Album für die Jugend*, where the piece 'Fremder Mann', which is marked *Stark und kräftig zu spielen* (to be played strongly and powerfully), has mostly ^ in forte and > in piano sections; and in 'Jägerliedchen', where both signs occur in close juxtaposition, the former seems to imply the heavier emphasis (Ex. 3.72). The sign does not appear in Schumann's First Symphony, but in the Second he used it, in conjunction with repeated *f*s, evidently to designate a weighty accent. The sign occurs more often in the Third Symphony, but in the second movement it is used, somewhat puzzlingly, over a staccato dot in a piano passage. That Schumann did not regard it as synonymous with *sf* is clearly indicated by its use in the Violin Sonata op. 121 (Ex. 3.73). Since Schumann appears not to have used *rf* as an accent mark, it seems possible that, if not always quite consistently, he was in general agreement with Gollmick's earlier opinion about the ranking, in descending order of strength, of *sf*, ^, and >. As with Meyerbeer, however, the form of the sign may also have implied a different type of accent from >.

Ex. 3.72. Schumann, *Album für die Jugend*, 'Järgerliedchen'

Ex. 3.73. Schumann, Violin Sonata op. 121/i

Berlioz's use of ^ is similarly ambiguous. Hugh Macdonald has suggested that its difference from > lies in the diminuendo element,[88] but this is not always clear, for instance when the two signs are used in fast music, in which any perceptible, or even notional diminuendo would be impossible (Ex. 3.74). Dvořák evidently intended the sign normally to be used in a forceful context; in his Violin Sonata it occurs in *ff* passages while > occurs in *f* passages (Ex. 3.75(*a*)). Its greater implication of strength for Dvořák is also suggested by a passage in his String Quartet op. 106, where the viola part is evidently meant to be more prominent than the violin (Ex. 3.75(*b*)). A revealing example of Bruckner's employment of ^ can be found in his Third Symphony, where the autograph clearly shows him using ^ over a succession of notes in the wind instruments while the strings simultaneously have a succession of down-bow signs together with the instruction *Streicher sämmtlich alles abwarts gestrichen* (all strings play

Ex. 3.74. Berlioz, *Les Troyens*, 'Danse des esclaves'

[88] 'Two Peculiarities of Berlioz's Notation', *Music & Letters*, 50 (1969), 32.

Ex. 3.75.   Dvořák: (*a*) Violin Sonata op. 57/i; (*b*) String Quartet op. 106/i

Ex. 3.76. Bruckner, Third Symphony, i, Mäßig bewegt ♩ = 66

everything down-bow); the down-bows were evidently an afterthought, as can be seen from the violin parts, where Bruckner originally wrote ^ (Ex. 3.76). The same combination of down-bow and ^, this time in the same part, occurs in Dvořák (Ex. 3.77).

The tendency of later nineteenth-century composers to employ the sign as something closer to *sf*, in line with Gollmick's later definition, is also suggested by scrutiny of Wagner's scores. His view of ^ as a powerful accent is implied by his use of it in *Siegfried* to represent 'a very strong' stroke of the anvil, while ∨ indicated 'a weaker one' and I 'a lighter stroke'.[89] In *Parsifal* Wagner employed ^ in conjunction with *sf*;[90] in *Die Walküre* the sign (inverted in the printed edition) is accompanied by the instruction *Schwer und zurückhaltend* (heavy and held back).[91] Whether this is related to Hugo Riemann's employment of ^ as an indication for agogic accent is a moot point; Riemann seems to have been isolated from other theorists in defining the difference between > and ^ as being that the latter requires 'a slight lingering on the note'.[92] The *Encyclopédie de la musique et dictionnaire du Conservatoire* expressed the orthodox view of

[89] Act I, Scene iii (Schott miniature score, 382).
[90] Rehearsal nos. 74–5 (Schott miniature score, 180).   [91] Act I, Scene i (Schott miniature score, 81).
[92] *New Pianoforte School*, 17.

Ex. 3.77. Dvořák, String Quartet op. 106/i

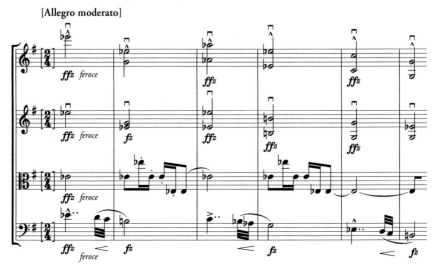

the late nineteenth century when it observed that a note marked with ^ 'should be accented, marked strongly with firmness', though (supporting Hugh Macdonald's view of its principal significance for Berlioz) the definition of > suggests that the difference between the two signs was seen less as one of power than of type, for it states that > 'demands a stronger attack [than the preceding note] followed immediately by a decrease of sonority'.[93] Curiously, perhaps, the logical interpretation of ^ (as opposed to >) as an accent without marked diminuendo, something which in any case is scarcely possible on the piano, seems seldom to be an explicit factor in its use.

The Short Messa di voce (<>)

The short crescendo-diminuendo sign, used over a single note, which derives from the *messa di voce*, is common in some nineteenth-century composers' music. From his earliest period Beethoven liked to use this expressive nuance over short phrases or long notes, and occasionally in the late works it appears in association with shorter notes where there would scarcely be time to execute a real crescendo-diminuendo (Ex. 3.78). Some of his successors, perhaps taking the hint from this usage, or from violinists such as Campagnoli or Pierre Rode, or deriving it directly from the typical eighteenth-century treatment of the *Abzug*,[94] began to employ this sign over shorter notes, purely as a type of accent. That it was seen entirely as a special kind of accent by composers such as Schumann (who used it extensively) is indicated by his use of it on the

[93] Lavignac et al., *Encyclopédie de la musique*, pt. 2, 335.   [94] See Ch. 13.

Ex. 3.78. Beethoven, String Quartet op. 135/i

Ex. 3.79. Schumann, Lied op. 101/4

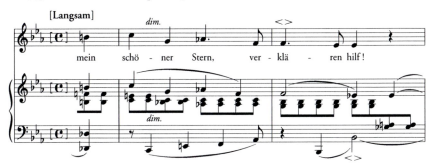

piano (Ex. 3.79; see also Ex. 3.37). It is especially characteristic of the so-called Classical-Romantic German composers, being quite common in Mendelssohn's, Brahms's, and Bruch's music, where it seems generally to require a warm but not too powerful accent, perhaps with an agogic element in some instances, and a vibrato where appropriate (Ex. 3.80(*a*)). Elgar, too used it in a similar manner in his late chamber music (Ex. 3.80(*b*) and (*c*)).[95]

The Horizontal Line (– ⊤ ∸)

The use of these signs by composers is rare before the middle of the nineteenth century, although they are mentioned in instruction books at an earlier date. Herz's piano method includes the explanation 'If the execution of a single note

---

[95] Its concomitant implications for vibrato in string playing are considered below, Ch. 14, where further examples are given. See also Clive Brown, 'Bowing Styles, Vibrato and Portamento in Nineteenth-Century Violin Playing', *Journal of the Royal Musical Association*, 113 (1988), 118–21.

Ex. 3.80. (*a*) Bruch, Violin Concerto in G minor op. 26/ii; (*b*) Elgar, Violin Sonata op. 87/i (*c*) Elgar, String Quartet op. 83/ii

(*a*)

(*b*)

(*c*)

requires to be heavily accented the sign ⸚ is employed'.[96] This sign is also listed by James Alexander Hamilton among other accent markings, but simply with the collective explanation that they all denote 'stress or marked accent on any single note or chord'.[97] Although neither author stated that the combination of dot with the line might specify not only stress, but also a degree of separation between the note so marked and the following note, this seems to be implied by its form; the dot indicates staccato yet its combination with the line suggests greater length than would be indicated by the dot alone. However, the line would also have had deep-rooted implications of stress because of its association with the sign for a strong syllable in poetry.

---

[96] *A New and Complete Pianoforte School,* 16.

[97] *A Dictionary of Two Thousand Italian, French, German, English and other Musical Terms,* 4th edn. (London, 1837), 87.

A. B. Marx, including this sign among those which indicate 'a greater degree of intensity', instructed that in this case 'the performer is, at the same time, to linger over each sound' (see Ex. 3.91);[98] and Czerny equated it with dots under a slur, especially where the notes so marked were separated by rests, observing: 'In these cases the keys must be struck with more than the usual emphasis, and the notes must be held for almost more than their usual value'.[99] Such an interpretation would nicely fit Schumann's use of it in 'Winterzeit 2', as notated in the autograph of his *Album für die Jugend* (Ex. 3.81(*a*)) or in the third movement of his 'Rhenish' Symphony, where it occurs in close juxtaposition with portato semiquavers (Ex. 3.81(*b*)). Brahms, however, among other composers, seems to have continued to employ dots and a slur, even over notes separated by rests, to indicate the type of portato illustrated in the example from Schumann's symphony. In his Horn Trio Brahms employed a more curious (?shorthand) version of the same thing, putting a slur and dot over single notes (Ex. 3.82).

Ex. 3.81. Schumann: (*a*) *Album für die Jugend,* 'Winterzeit 2'; (*b*) Third Symphony op. 97/iii

(*a*)

(*b*)

The Mendel–Reissmann *Lexikon* associated the sign with accent and a degree of sostenuto.[100] At a much later date Riemann described ⁻ as requiring '*a broad kind of playing,* but yet with, *separation of the single tones* (portato, non legato)',[101] while the *Encyclopédie* of the Paris Conservatoire described both ⁼ and ^ as instructions to 'attack the note heavily and weightily, and quit it immediately in a detached manner'.[102]

---

[98] *Universal School,* 115.

[99] *Pianoforte School,* i. 188 and iii. 24.

[100] *Musikalisches Conversations-Lexikon,* xi. 212.

[101] *New Pianoforte-School,* 17.

[102] Lavignac et al., *Encyclopédie de la musique,* pt. 2, 336.

Ex. 3.82. Brahms, Horn Trio op. 40/i

The horizontal line without a dot was used most often, in the first instance, in combination with a slur, to obviate the problem of string players interpreting dots under a slur as slurred staccato rather than portato.[103] This sign (without a slur) also occurs in Hamilton's general list of accents, with no further explanation, though its graphic design clearly implies a degree of length in the performance of notes so marked; but it was scarcely used by composers at that time. Explanations of the meaning of the sign in later instruction books differ considerably. Louis Schubert's *Violinschule* is even inconsistent between its German, French, and English versions; a literal translation of the German is 'broadly staccatoed or legato' (*breit gestoßen oder gezogen*), and the French simply reads 'broad détaché'[104] (*détaché large*), while the English has: 'played staccato with a slight emphasis on each note'.[105] Riemann and the *Encyclopédie* of the Paris Conservatoire also gave somewhat different descriptions: the former considered it to indicate that the note 'is to be held down for its full value (tenuto)',[106] and the latter that the note so marked 'ought to be pressed with more firmness than the others'.[107]

Consideration of individual examples of the use of the sign reveals some justification for all these interpretations and suggests a number of other possibilities. Liszt's employment of the horizontal line in his *Faust-Symphonie* appears to be as a tenuto instruction rather than as an accent (cautioning against matching the detached execution in the strings), though it may also have been intended to counteract the metrical accentuation and obtain equal weight on all four beats (Ex. 3.83(*a*)). Where he used it in legato passages, however, its function as an accent, implying weight without sharpness of attack, can scarcely be in doubt (Ex. 3.83(*b*) and (*c*)). Despite Liszt's example, Wagner employed this sign infrequently; indeed, many of its occurrences in his scores seem to result from additions made during publication. On at least one occa-

---

[103] See below, Ch. 6.

[104] The word *détaché* means literally separated, but in violin playing signifies extremely connected notes played in separate bows.

[105] *Violinschule nach modernen Principien*, i. 12.   [106] *New Pianoforte-School*, 17.

[107] Lavignac et al., *Encyclopédie de la musique*, pt. 2, 335.

Ex. 3.83. Liszt, *Eine Faust-Symphonie*, i, 'Faust'
(*a*)

(*b*)

(*c*)

sion he intended the sign to indicate a discrete vibrato (which also has some implication of accent[108]): Heinrich Porges noted in his account of the rehearsals for the première of the *Ring* in 1876 that at one point in Act III, Scene iii of *Siegfried* 'The strokes [lines] above the E and B of "zitternd" indicate that here Wagner wanted that gentle vibrato—not to be confused with the bad habit of tremolando—whose importance in expressive singing he often spoke of'[109] (Ex. 3.84). Elsewhere, apart from his use of the horizontal line (instead of the conventional dot) under a slur for portato, the sign may sometimes occur in Wagner's scores with a meaning similar to that envisaged by Liszt. According to transcriptions of his instructions at rehearsals of *Parsifal* he asked at one point that the quavers should be 'very sustained and held [*sehr getragen und*

---

[108] See Ch. 14, esp. pp. 518 ff.
[109] *Die Bühnenproben zu der Bayreuther Festspielen des Jahres 1876* (Chemnitz and Leipzig 1881–96), trans. Robert L. Jacobs as *Wagner Rehearsing the 'Ring'* (Cambridge, 1983), 109.

Ex. 3.84. Wagner, *Siegfried,* Act III, Scene iii

Ex. 3.85. Wagner, *Parsifal:* (*a*) rehearsal letter 45; (*b*) rehearsal letter 48
(*a*)

(*b*)

(mit Dämpf.)

gehalten], not merely slurred, a true portamento' (Ex. 3.85(*a*)); and, at a similar passage, 'very dragged [*sehr gezogen*], the quaver very clear, very distinct, the short note is the main thing' (Ex. 3.85(*b*)).[110] Here there are horizontal lines in the 1883 printed edition that are missing from the holograph score. Although they appear under slurs, it seems unlikely that Wagner intended any separation, as would have been the case with the usual portato.

In the music of many later nineteenth-century composers the horizontal line apparently had the function of indicating the slightest degree of separation and/or the slightest degree of expressive weight. There are many instances where any perceptible element of separation seems inappropriate (Ex. 3.86(*a*)). Elgar evidently considered it to some extent as indicating a very light accent, as comparison of the opening of variation XI of the Enigma Variations (Ex. 3.86(*b*)) with the passage at bar 6 suggests (Ex. 3.86(*c*)). Its accent function seems often likely, however, to have been relative rather than absolute and to have been rather to neutralize the metrical hierarchy than to give the note particular prominence. Tchaikovsky seems sometimes to imply equality of weight together with almost imperceptible articulation (emphasized by his violin bowing in Ex. 3.87(*a*)); yet on other occasions the intention appears to be to obtain an absolutely full-length note, for in the third bar of Ex. 3.87(*b*) the violins' phrasing should surely match the flute's slur, and the separated bowing was

---

[110] *Richard Wagner: Sämtliche Werke,* xxx: *Dokumente zur Entstehung und ersten Aufführung des Bühnenweihfestspiels Parsifal,* ed. Martin Geck and Egon Voss (Mainz, 1970), 174.

probably intended to allow greater power and volume. Dvořák often used this sign to indicate a lightly accented, barely detached note, especially in piano passages (Ex. 3.88(*a*)), but like Tchaikovsky and Elgar he probably used it at times to ensure that the players would give the note its full value (Ex. 3.88(*b*)). Sometimes, in the Cello Concerto for instance, there is a suggestion that he may have envisaged an element of agogic accentuation in its execution (Ex.

Ex. 3.86. Elgar, Enigma Variations op. 36: (*a*) theme; (*b*) variation XI; (*c*) variation XI
(*a*)

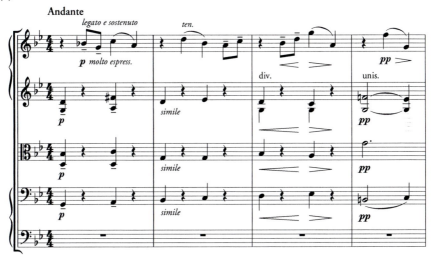

Ex. 3.86. *cont.* (c)

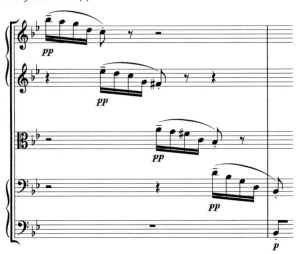

Ex. 3.87. Tchaikovsky, *Symphonie pathétique* op. 74/i
(a)

(b)

3.89). Although Brahms took a stance against adopting horizontal lines, they do appear in the Scherzo of the String Sextet op. 36, where they appear to indicate a slight weight. The theme sometimes occurs with ▬ on the weak beats, and sometimes with > (Ex. 3.90(a) and (b)). A similar interpretation of the (for Brahms) unusual employment of horizontal lines under slurs in the Second Symphony seems probable (Ex. 3.90(c)). However, Brahms's scepticism about

Ex. 3.88. Dvořák: (*a*) Violin Sonata op. 57/iii; (*b*) String Quartet op. 105/iv

(*a*)

(*b*)

the excessive employment of accent signs is indicated by his remark in a letter of 27 January 1896 to Fritz Simrock, after he had read the proofs of Dvořák's *Te Deum*: 'Do those silly accents have to stay on the stressed syllables? Nowadays one often sees that. Since the music stresses the syllables, the markings obviously make no sense whatsoever.'

Ex. 3.89. Dvořák, Cello Concerto op. 104/ii

Ex. 3.90. Brahms: (*a*) String Sextet op. 36/ii; (*b*) String Sextet op. 36/ii; (*c*) Second Symphony op. 73/i
(*a*)

(*b*)

(*c*)

The Box ☐

Among the other accent and expression signs that theorists attempted to introduce, the elongated box came closest to gaining currency, but there was not unanimity about its meaning. Herz illustrated this sign in the first quarter of the century, describing it as a graphic alternative for '*tenuto*, used when a note or chord is to be sustained'.[111] Adolf Bernhard Marx, in mid-century, regarded the same sign as indicating a greater degree of accent than dots under slurs, showing that 'the stress upon each note is to be particularly strong and marked'; and he illustrated this with Ex. 3.91.[112] This meaning was echoed in the latter part of the century in the Mendel–Reissmann *Lexikon*, where it was specified for occasions where 'the accent should be a heavier, weightier one'.[113] But like

---

[111] *A New and Complete Pianoforte School*, 16.   [112] *Universal School*, 115.
[113] *Musikalisches Conversations-Lexikon*, xi. 212.

Ex. 3.91. Marx, *Universal School*, 115

a number of other theoretical proposals, this was not adopted by composers to any significant extent.

Most of the signs discussed above are also encountered in combination with slurs. In keyboard playing and, to a large extent, in wind playing the use of a slur usually seems to have meant simply that the notes should be less distinctly separated (though in wind playing there may also have been implications for breathing). In string playing the slur is specifically a bowing instruction, but the end effect is much the same. Where such signs appear over successive notes under a slur, however, their function is as much articulation as accent, and it is as articulation marks that they are considered in Chapter 6.

4

Articulation and Phrasing

༺ེཏྟྭཊ

Just as several categories of accentuation were identified as contributing to the intended character of a piece of music, so different types and degrees of articulation were discussed by eighteenth-century and nineteenth-century musicians. Articulation could be indicated by the composer in the form of rests or by means of articulation marks; or it might be expected to be provided by performers on the basis of their experience and musicality. The functions of accentuation and articulation are broadly similar, and they are often closely linked, especially in defining musical structure. Articulation can be seen as operating principally on two levels: the structural and the expressive. At the structural level was the articulation of musical phrases and sections, while as an expressive resource, appropriate articulation of individual notes and figures was necessary to vivify a musical idea. Composers attempted, during the course of the period, to provide ever more detailed instructions for articulation in their scores, just as they did with accentuation; and, as with accents, the performer's task increasingly became one of accurately interpreting the composer's markings, rather than recognizing where it was desirable to supplement or modify the musical text. Yet even in the most carefully notated late nineteenth-century scores much still remained the responsibility of the performer.

Music was predominantly perceived throughout the period as a language, albeit a language which, like poetry, appealed more to the feelings than to the intellect. But the precision with which the language of music expressed the feelings of its creator was considered to be of great importance; Wilhelm Heinrich Wackenroder's creation, the composer Joseph Berlinger, could hope that the listener 'will feel on hearing my melodies precisely what I felt in writing them—precisely what I sought to put in them'.[1] Thus, the separation of

---

[1] *Herzensergiessungen eines kunstliebenden Klosterbruders* (Berlin, 1797), quoted in Oliver Strunk, *Source Readings in Music History* (London, 1952), 759.

phrases and sections was felt to be essential to the proper realization of a composer's musical concept, and the link between music and rhetoric was constantly cited to illustrate the importance of appropriate punctuation for the
lucid delivery of a musical discourse. Mattheson's *Vollkommene Kapellmeister* of
1739, along with other texts from the first half of the eighteenth century, had
dealt with the matter in some detail; and many subsequent discussions during
the eighteenth and nineteenth centuries employed much the same terminology. In the early 1770s Sulzer's *Allgemeine Theorie der schönen Künste* introduced its extensive consideration of the subject with the remark that 'The
phrase divisions are the commas of the melody which, as in speech, should be
made apparent by a small pause'.[2] Türk, expanding on this in 1789 with an even
closer analogy between language and music, seemed to suggest a link between
the degree of the articulation and its structural function. His account provides
a useful digest of the terms used by German theorists:

A musical sentence (a section [*Abschnitt*]), of which there can be several in a piece, would be
that which one calls a sentence in speech and would be separated from the following by a
full stop (.). A musical rhythm [*Rhythmus*] can be compared with the smaller speech unit,
which one marks with a colon (:) or semicolon (;). The phrase[*Einschnitt*[3]], as the smallest
unit, would be that which in speech will only be separated by a comma. If one wanted also
to add the caesura [*Cäsur*], one would have to compare it with the caesura of a verse (*Vers*).[4]

Baillot observed similarly in 1834: 'Notes are used in music like words in
speech; they are used to construct a phrase, to create an idea, consequently one
should use full stops and commas just as in a written text, to distinguish its sentences and their parts, and to make them easier to understand.'[5] Habeneck, a
few years later, also introduced the subject by remarking: 'In a melody, as in
speech, there are sentences [*periodes*], phrases, and figures that make up the
phrases.'[6] In much the same vein, Charles de Bériot began his discussion of
musical punctuation, in his *Méthode de violon* of 1858, with the statement: 'The
object of punctuation in music, as in literature, is to mark the necessary points
of repose: we will even add that in music punctuation is more important than
in literature because the points of repose are indicated in a more absolute way
by the strictness of the time.'[7] And in 1905 Andreas Moser could still state that
the separation and division of phrases has ' just about the same significance for
music as articulation and punctuation have for speech'.[8]

But this apparent agreement about basic principles may well mask significant differences in practice. The fact that generations of musicians have repeat-
edly emphasized the importance of musical punctuation for the proper

---

[2] Art. 'Vortrag', iv. 700.

[3] *Einschnitt*, literally a cut or incision, was often used to mean not only the division between musical
phrases or figures, but also the phrases or figures themselves.

[4] *Klavierschule*, VI, §32.   [5] *L'Art du violon*, 163.   [6] *Méthode*, 107.   [7] p. 226.

[8] Joseph Joachim and Andreas Moser, *Violinschule* (Berlin, 1905), iii. 13.

expression of a melody and that they have described that punctuation in similar terms does not mean that a musician of 1780 would have rendered it in quite the same manner as one of 1880, any more than actors or orators of different generations and traditions would have adopted the same approach to articulation in speech. Quite apart from other considerations, changes in compositional style brought in their train modified approaches to articulation, as well as to many other aspects of performance. The relationship between rules of 'correct' composition and rules of 'correct' performance, so often emphasized by eighteenth-century writers,[9] weakened in the nineteenth century as 'unfettered genius'[10] came increasingly to be seen to override prescriptive aesthetic notions. And though older music continued to be performed, indeed began to be performed more frequently as the century advanced, there seems only to have been a limited awareness of historically appropriate performance techniques; the musicians of successive generations tended to apply their own contemporary stylistic criteria to all the music in their repertoire. In particular, it seems possible that the growing emphasis on legato in both composition and performance may have led during the nineteenth century to a less distinct separation of phrases in earlier music, the articulation (where no break in continuity was indicated by the composer) being more often conveyed by accent and dynamic nuance, perhaps, than by an appreciable break in the sound. However, at every stage in this investigation it is important to bear in mind that keyboard instruments, bowed instruments, various kinds of wind instruments and the human voice all have their own mechanisms and imperatives, which affect the execution and application of articulation. The means that are available to the organist or harpsichordist to convey phrasing effectively are quite different from those available to the violinist, flautist, or singer. It is also necessary to remember that great artists will have displayed individuality just as much in this area as in others, and that any two artists of a given period may well have adopted quite distinctly personal approaches to articulating the same piece of music.

Some of the most obvious differences between periods and performing traditions will become more apparent on closer consideration; many will inevitably remain irrecoverable, for the finer details of performance that distinguish the playing and singing of the most cultivated artists are, as numerous writers pointed out, not susceptible of verbal description. These refinements certainly cannot be fully reconstructed from written accounts, however elaborate; they could only have been appreciated through hearing the artists who were felt to be the representatives of good taste in any particular period.

[9] e.g. Türk, *Klavierschule*, VI, §§23 ff.

[10] Emily Anderson, trans. and ed., *The Letters of Beethoven* (London, 1961), 1325.

The discussion of structural articulation by J. A. P. Schulz in Sulzer's *Allgemeine Theorie* provides a number of important points about general attitudes in the second half of the eighteenth century.[11] He began his consideration of the subject by affirming not only that the separation of phrases should occur in the right places but also that it should be distinctly perceptible, asserting: 'The phrase divisions should be marked in the clearest manner and correctly.' Nevertheless, it is apparent that Schulz did not regard a real break in the sound as the only method of marking the articulation, but also considered it possible to obtain the same end by a diminuendo at the end of a phrase followed by some degree of accentuation at the beginning of the new one, for he stated that it could be achieved 'either if one takes off the last note of a phrase somewhat and then comes firmly onto the first note of the following phrase; or if one allows the sound to sink somewhat and then raises it with the beginning of the new phrase.' The distinction may have been envisaged as allowing variety appropriate to different circumstances; or perhaps Schulz was thinking of the fundamental differences between various kinds of instruments: keyboard instruments incapable of dynamic accents such as organ and harpsichord, where the phrase divisions can only be made apparent by separation, clavichord and fortepiano, where subtle degrees of accentuation are also feasible but where the rate at which the sound decays is largely beyond the control of the player, and bowed instruments, wind instruments, and voice, where bow, tongue, or consonants can be used to produce many different types of articulation, and where controlled diminuendo on a single note is possible.

Unlike Türk, Schulz did not imply a direct relationship between the structural function of articulation and its degree, though he recognized the subtle variety that an experienced artist would give it according to context, noting in a footnote:

The word 'phrase' will be taken here in the widest meaning, in that the *Einschnitts* as well as the *Abschnitts* and sections of the melody will be understood by it. In performance all these divisions will be marked in the same manner; and if great players and singers really observe a shading among them, this is nevertheless so subtle and so complicated to describe that we content ourselves with the mere mention of it.

The rest of his discussion was taken up mainly with the problem of how a performer should recognize the phrase divisions. He conceded that 'If the phrase ends with a rest there is no difficulty; the phrase division [*Einschnitt*] marks itself on its own.' He also observed that it should not be a problem for the singer to mark the phrase divisions correctly, 'because he only has to govern himself by the phrase divisions of the words, above which he sings, with which the phrase division of the melody must exactly accord'; though he acknowledged that difficulties might be encountered in passagework (where the singer had to

---

[11] Art. 'Vortrag', iv. 700 ff.

deliver an extended passage to a single syllable). For instrumentalists he suggested that

The main rule which has here to be taken account of is this, that one governs oneself by the beginning of the piece. A perfectly regular piece of music observes regular phrases throughout: namely whatever beat of the bar it begins with so begin all its phrases with just the same beat. Therefore in the following pieces the notes marked with ○ are those with which the first phrase concludes, and those marked with + those with which the new phrase begins: [Ex. 4.1]

Ex. 4.1. Sulzer, *Allgemeine Theorie*, art. 'Vortrag'

Such symmetry was more characteristic of the lighter Galant style of the mid-eighteenth century than of the more emotionally charged and dramatic idioms that were associated with the development of the *empfindsamer Stil* and what has come to be known as the Viennese Classical style, where movements or sections would be likely to include a variety of contrasting and complementary figures. Recognizing this, Schulz gave an example from the beginning of a C. P. E. Bach sonata (Ex. 4.2) about which he remarked that in such music the player had to recognize phrase divisions 'from the character of the melody'. But he indicated that with each new idea, just as with the beginning of a piece, the phrasing could be deduced from the placing of the initial part of the phrase. Thus he remarked that 'it would be extremely faulty if, for example, one wanted to perform the sixth bar as if the phrase were to begin with its first note, since, in fact, the preceding ends with it, as the quaver rest of the preceding bar indicates.'

Schulz also noted that composers sometimes used modified beaming to indicate the beginnings and ends of phrases, and felt that, since it made the

Ex. 4.2. Sulzer, *Allgemeine Theorie*, art. 'Vortrag'

phrase divisions very clear, it was to be preferred to continuous beaming in doubtful cases. He observed:

If, as in the third and fourth examples [Ex. 4.3], the phrase division falls between quavers or semiquavers, which in notational practice are customarily beamed together, some composers are in the habit of separating those which belong to the preceding phrase from those with which the new one begins by the way they write them, in order to indicate the phrase division all the more clearly, namely therefore: [Ex. 4.4]

Ex. 4.3. Sulzer, *Allgemeine Theorie*, art. 'Vortrag'

Ex. 4.4. Sulzer, *Allgemeine Theorie*, art. 'Vortrag'

(This continued to be used by some composers, for instance Schumann, throughout the nineteenth century; see Ex. 4.5.)

Ex. 4.5. Schumann, Second Symphony op. 61/ii

However, observing that this type of notation could not be used with crotchets and minims, Schulz remarked that in such cases one could 'use the little stroke l over the last note of the phrase, as some now and again do'. The use of a staccato stroke for this purpose is by no means unusual in music of the period, but, as Türk was to point out, this employment of the stroke to indicate a shortened and lightened final note could easily be mistaken by less experienced players for the more common type of staccato mark, which might imply accent.

Schulz concluded his examination of this subject with some general observations on the importance of correctly articulating phrase divisions, in which he again highlighted the role of accentuation at the beginning of a figure and weakness at the end in clarifying the phrase structure of a piece. (His marking of the beginning of a phrase with +, the same sign that he had elsewhere employed to mark the notes requiring accentuation, is evidently quite deliberate.) His final paragraph shows the close link between phrasing and structural accentuation, and reinforces other writers' remarks about the subordination of purely metrical accentuation to these considerations:

It is incredible how greatly the melody becomes disfigured and unclear if the phrase divisions are incorrectly marked or indeed not marked at all. To convince oneself of this, one ought only to perform a gavotte in such a manner that the phrase divisions at the half-bar are not observed. Easy as this dance is to understand, it will by this means become unrecognizable to everyone. Here again mistakes will most frequently be made in such pieces where the phrases begin in the middle of a bar and indeed on a weak beat; because everyone is from the beginning accustomed to mark prominently only the strong beats of the bar on which the various accents of the melody fall, and to leave the weak beats entirely equal as if they were merely passing. In such cases the phrases then become torn apart through this, part of them being attached to the preceding or following, which is just as preposterous as if in a speech one wanted to make the pause before or after the comma. In the following example [Ex. 4.6], if the phrase division is marked, the melody is good in itself; if however merely the accents of the bar are marked, the melody becomes extremely flat and has the same effect as if, instead of saying: 'He is my lord; I am his squire', one wanted to say: 'He is my lord I; am his squire.'

Ex. 4.6. Sulzer, *Allgemeine Theorie*, art. 'Vortrag'

Türk, whose approach shows his intimate knowledge of this and other significant discussions of the subject, made similar points, with some qualifications. Among other things he was particularly insistent, as mentioned above, that the performer should avoid interpreting a staccato mark that was intended to show the end of a phrase as one that was designed to indicate an accent, commenting:

Necessary as it is to lift the finger at the end of a phrase, it is nevertheless faulty to perform it in such a manner that the lifting referred to is allied with a violent staccato, as in example a) [Ex. 4.7]. One hears this faulty execution very frequently when the phrase division is indicated by the usual sign for staccato, as at c). For many players have the incorrect idea that a staccato note—as one calls it in artistic language—must always be staccatoed with a certain violence. [12]

[12] *Klavierschule*, VI, §22.

Ex. 4.7. Türk, *Klavierschule*, VI, 2, §22

It should be remembered that when Türk mentioned lifting the finger, he was referring to keyboard playing. Schulz, dealing with the matter in a general way, envisaged phrase division being accomplished either through real separation or through demarcation of the phrase by means of accent and decrescendo, while Türk only mentioned the former.

Rather than using a staccato mark to indicate the shortening of the final note of a phrase, Türk proposed an alternative sign that would not give rise to such confusion and that, at the same time, would facilitate the recognition of 'the smaller, less perceptible phrase divisions' (Ex. 4.8). And he explained that he had already used this in his *Leichte Klaviersonaten* of 1783.

Ex. 4.8. Türk, *Klavierschule*, VI, 2, §22

One thing to which neither Schulz nor Türk alluded as a factor in the recognition or separation of phrases and figures was the slur, though, according to theorists, this was generally acknowledged to require not only accentuation of the initial note under the slur but also shortening of the final one; indeed, Türk specifically warned against shortening the final note under three- and four-note slurs in certain circumstances.[13] For most eighteenth-century composers the slur seems far more to have been associated with the character of a particular musical idea than with structural phrasing.

As a means of developing a good sense of phrasing Türk also recommended, together with practising dance pieces, as suggested by Schulz, the practice of songs by good composers.[14] (In this period Lieder were often printed like keyboard music on two staves with the melody doubled by the keyboard player's right hand throughout, and with the words set between the staves; keyboard players could therefore regulate their phrasing by the punctuation of the text.)

Schulz, Türk, and other eighteenth-century theorists who discussed articulation theoretically were somewhat rigid and simplistic in their approach to phrase construction. They failed almost entirely to take account of and address issues of phrase elision and other irregularities that would have disturbed the

---

[13] See Ch. 2, pp. 31 ff., 'Slurred Groups'. Also, see Ch. 6 for further discussion of slurs and their implications.

[14] *Klavierschule*, VI, §25.

symmetrical patterns of which they provided examples (though such things were touched upon from the composer's point of view by, among others, Joseph Riepel and Koch[15]). Schulz's citation of the C. P. E. Bach sonata was merely a very tentative step in that direction. None of these writers seem to have wanted to explore the circumstances in which composers (or performers) might have wished to create an artistic effect by disappointing the listener's expectations. Türk, indeed, appears to have regarded such procedures as illegitimate, for he commented at one point:

Just as it would be counterproductive if one read on continuously at the end of a phrase, so it would be erroneous if a musician carried on playing connectedly and in a single breath at a point of rest. Consequently the following manner of performance would be wholly against the musical sense: [Ex. 4.9(*a*)] instead of [Ex. 4.9(*b*)]

Ex. 4.9. Türk, *Klavierschule*, VI, 2, §19

(*a*)

(*b*)

And he observed, before going on to consider the reasons for this in greater detail, that he was convinced his comments could have 'some influence on (logically) correct performance'.[16] But if one scrutinizes the music of the best composers of the period who were most fastidious in their markings, instances of just such phrase elision, carefully indicated by the composer, are frequently encountered. In Ex. 4.10(*a*) Mozart initially ended the phrase in bar 4 in the expected way, with a slur from the *a′* to the *g♯′*, but then extended it to the *e″*, thus eliding the phrases. And in Ex. 4.10(*b*) Beethoven similarly elided the phrases with his slur in the fourth bar of the theme. The same thing is found with ever greater frequency in the nineteenth century (Ex. 4.10(*c*)) and was recommended as a device for performers by García even where nothing had been marked by the composer (see Ex. 4.26). Yet in the last quarter of the century Mathis Lussy still seemed to regard this procedure as illegitimate and even suggested that composers who indicated such things had simply got their phrasing wrong. He maintained that

It ought to be an established rule that only such notes as form a musical idea or thought, a section or a rhythm, should be connected by a slur, a curved line ⌒, or rhythmic con-

[15] Riepel, *Anfangsgründe zur musikalischen Setzkunst* (Regensburg, etc., 1752–68); Koch, *Versuch.*
[16] *Klavierschule*, VI, §19.

Ex. 4.10. (*a*) Mozart, Rondo K. 511; (*b*) Beethoven, Piano Sonata op. 31/2/iii; (*c*) Chopin, Mazurka op. 6/3

(*a*)

(*b*)

(*c*)

nection. Phrasing slurs [*liaisons rhythmiques*] should never be placed above notes belonging to two different rhythms, and should never embrace or cover the last note of one rhythm and the first of another.[17]

Türk's proposal of new signs for marking phrase divisions and expressive accents, mentioned above, typifies the growing concern, which he shared with C. P. E. Bach, J. F. Reichardt, and many other contemporaries, to find a more explicit means of indicating the articulation that, in practice, the performer had to supply on the basis of experience. Türk's 1783 sonatas had been primarily aimed at amateurs of limited accomplishments who could not be expected to possess the skill and judgement of professionals in such matters. The widening market for published music, for both professional and amateur use, was a significant factor in encouraging this development. Unfortunately, however, the carelessness of many composers and most publishers before the middle of the nineteenth century frustrated all efforts to ensure that performers might be able to rely on the accuracy of the markings in the music from which they played.

Another of Türk's contemporaries, Domenico Corri, who was not only a singer and composer (he was a pupil of Porpora), but also a publisher, was acutely conscious of the advantages of providing greater guidance in such matters for the predominantly amateur clientele at whom his publications were aimed. His *Select Collection* of vocal music was intended 'to facilitate, and at the same time to render more perfect, the performance of vocal and instrumental music',[18] and he felt that 'one of the most important articles in the execution of music (vocal music in particular) is the proper division of the PERIODS; as is

[17] *Traité de l'expression musicale*, 69.   [18] *A Select Collection*, i. 1.

evident from hearing good singers often break in upon the sense and the melody, for want of knowing how to take breath in the proper places.'[19]

In the *Select Collection* he introduced two signs for this purpose. One of these (✳), which he used in both vocal and instrumental parts, was to mark the phrase divisions of the melody; he instructed that when this was used,

a Pause is always to be made and breath taken.—The Pause to be about as long as that made by a Comma in reading, and the time taken for it to be deducted from the Note to which the mark is nearest. For example, when before the note; This [Ex. 4.11(*a*)] will be nearly equal to this [Ex. 4.11(*b*)] and when after the note, This [Ex. 4.11(*c*)] equal to this [Ex. 4.11(*d*)] NB. This is likewise applicable to Instrumental Music.

Ex. 4.11. D. Corri, *A Select Collection*, i. 8

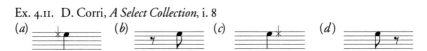

The other (⚹), which applied only to vocal parts, was to indicate points where the singer should breathe; but he should 'make the pause as imperceptible as possible', since these respirations were only 'on account of a period being too long, or when particular exertion of the voice is necessary, as before a Cadence &. &.'.[20]

Although Corri did not discuss the principles of phrase division in his introduction, his instructions in the music (in so far as the sometimes ambiguous engraving can be relied on) provide useful evidence of his practice. On the whole, his division of phrases is closely related to the harmonic and periodic structure of the music. In the instrumental parts not all the divisions that might be expected are marked (some perhaps through oversight or careless engraving), but those that are generally occur at obvious breaks in the melody. Where more than one division of the musical text would make musical sense Corri's choice is naturally determined by the vocal part, even though the instrumental part may precede it. In Giordani's 'Sento che in seno' (*Il Barone di Torre Forte*), for instance, the flute part in bars 24–32 is susceptible of being divided in several ways, but the distribution of the words in the vocal part a dozen bars later is the deciding factor (Ex. 4.12). In Paisiello's 'Ti seguirò fedele' a subsidiary articulation comes after the fourth bar in the instrumental parts, the significance of which is only clarified by the vocal entry (Ex. 4.13); and a similar thing occurs in Sacchini's 'Rasserena i tuoi bei rai' (*Enea e Lavinia*) in the third bar of the violin part (Ex. 4.14).

The positioning of Corri's first type of sign (✳) in the vocal parts is less predictable than it is in the instrumental ones; sometimes it may be suspected that the first sign has been printed where the second was intended, but elsewhere it

---

[19] *A Select Collection*, i. 2.   [20] Ibid. 3.

Ex. 4.12. D. Corri, *A Select Collection*, i. 86–7

Ex. 4.13. D. Corri, *A Select Collection*, i. 19

Ex. 4.14. D. Corri, *A Select Collection*, i. 29

is clear that he is using the former not only to mark the principal divisions, but also to indicate breaks, necessary for the articulation of the text, that are inessential to, or sometimes even contrary to, the musical sense, for example in Sacchini's 'Dolce speme' (*Rinaldo*) (Ex. 4.15). In some instances, this relationship of articulation to text means that these phrasing divisions in the same passage of music can vary within a song; thus in Geminiani's 'If ever a fond inclination' two versions of the opening melody occur (Ex. 4.16).

The *Select Collection* contains many instances where articulation is obtained by means of shortening an upbeat to a new phrase rather than by curtailing the

Ex. 4.15. D. Corri, *A Select Collection*, i. 104

Ex. 4.16. D. Corri, *A Select Collection*, ii. 5

final note of the preceding phrase. In Giordani's aria 'Sento che in seno' (Ex. 4.17), the time required for the articulation is sometimes taken from the previous note and sometimes from the following. Another good example occurs in 'The Soldier Tired' from Arne's *Artaxerxes* (Ex. 4.18). This manner of shortening upbeats for breathing was also recommended by Mary Novello later in the nineteenth century as the normal procedure for 'taking a half breath in the middle of a sentence'. She went on to say: 'the time of inhalation should be taken from the note which follows respiration, unless the musical phrase requires this note to retain its full value of duration', adding that such breaths ought to be taken before such words as 'the', 'of', 'to', and 'and'.[21] It is worth

Ex. 4.17. D. Corri, *A Select Collection*, i. 88

Ex. 4.18. D. Corri, *A Select Collection*, ii. 49

[21] *Voice and Vocal Art* (London, 1856), 11.

noting, however, that this advice seems to be contradicted in the teachings of García, Lablache, Duprez, and Novello's English contemporary John Addison.[22]

While many of Corri's indications for taking breath as imperceptibly as possible occur at places where a subsidiary articulation would make good musical sense, some are found where they might not seem so obvious. A persistent peculiarity is Corri's practice of indicating a breath immediately before a pause bar in which a cadenza is to be executed, even when this is only preceded by a single short, or even very short note. In J. C. Bach's 'Nel partir bell' idol mio' (*La clemenza di Scipione*) Corri indicates a breath after the semiquaver upbeat even though this has been preceded by a respiration (see Ex. 12.7, bar 36). Often such breaths are indicated even where the upbeat is the first syllable of a word, as in Sacchini's 'Se placar non puo quest' alma' (*Perseo*) (Ex. 4.19). Breathing in the middle of a word is also indicated between the anticipation of a note by portamento and the note itself, for instance, in Dibdin's 'Say little foolish flutt'ring thing' (*The Padlock*) (Ex. 4.20).

Ex. 4.19. D. Corri, *A Select Collection*, i. 51

Ex. 4.20. D. Corri, *A Select Collection*, ii. 22

In *The Singer's Preceptor* Corri also considered the more discreet, but nevertheless essential, articulation between words that was to some extent independent of breathing. He observed that in Handel's 'Angels ever Bright'

if the first sentence is sung without any separation of the words as written, thus [Ex. 4.21(*a*)] the effect would be the same to the Ear as if these two words 'bright and' were joined together thus 'brightand' whereas, if the word 'and' was separated from 'bright' by a break

[22] Addison, *Singing Practically Treated in a Series of Instructions* (London, 1850). See also Robert Toft, 'The Expressive Pause: Punctuation, Rests, and Breathing in England 1770–1850', *Performance Practice Review*, 7 (1994), 199–232.

Ex. 4.21. D. Corri, *The Singer's Preceptor*, 65

(*a*)

Ev - er —— bright   and   fair

(*b*)

Ev - er —— bright   and   fair

as in the following Example, it would preserve the true accent of the words, thus, [Ex. 4.21(*b*)] [. A]ll words in repetition as 'Sad sad is my breast' [']Gone gone is my rest' &c should be divided.

My song 'Beware of love' affords another instance to prove that the separating [of] words greatly conduces to effect, in the first Verse, which Koyan addresses to his Mother expressive of gratitude, the repetition of the words 'no' are sung, thus, [Ex. 4.22(*a*)]. In the second Verse, which he addresses to his Sister, conveying a sly caution with some degree of irony, the repetition of the word 'Yes' should be sung, thus, [Ex. 4.22(*b*)] and the difference of effect demonstrates the advantage produced by separation of words as above remarked; also when the letters k, th, gh &c or any harsh sounding Consonants end a word immediately followed by one beginning with similar letters, great care should be taken to divide those words.[23]

Ex. 4.22. D. Corri, *The Singer's Preceptor*, 65

(*a*)

No   no   no   no   no   Mo - ther   no ——

(*b*)

Yes   yes   yes   yes   oh   Sis - ter   yes ——

Many nineteenth-century writers of instrumental and vocal methods contented themselves with general statements about articulating phrase divisions that were not specifically marked by the composer, regarding firm rules or principles as inapplicable to such things, or at least beyond the scope of their treatise. Dotzauer opined that 'for the most part the musician must let himself be guided by his correct feelings, although, taken as a whole, there are rules about it, which are concerned with rhythm, phraseology etc.'[24] Spohr considered

---

[23] p. 65.   [24] *Violoncell-Schule*, 28.

that 'the accentuation and separation of musical phrases' were among the distinguishing features of a 'fine style' rather than a merely 'correct' one. The difference between these was, in Spohr's opinion, that the former involved 'discerning the character of the piece performed and of seizing its predominant expression and transfusing the same into performance'. And he believed that the things that elevated a correct style into a fine style were the product of 'a natural gift, which may indeed be awakened and cultivated, but can never be taught'.[25] Hummel, who took a similar view of the division between 'correct' and 'beautiful' performance,[26] did not discuss phrase division at all in his piano method, though he devoted considerable space to the distribution of expressive accents. Some ten years later Carl Czerny similarly concentrated on the role of accentuation, rather than articulation, in phrasing.[27]

To some extent, changing emphases in the discussion of articulation were connected with changing approaches to notation. Whereas the imprecision of much eighteenth-century notation often conceals places where a note at the end of a phrase was understood to require a considerably shorter duration in performance than its written length, late eighteenth-century and nineteenth-century composers increasingly tended to provide notational clues or instructions to performers that should seldom have left them in doubt about the places where the articulation that was necessary to the proper separation of musical phrases was required. A number of writers, however, considered the matter in sufficient detail to provide useful insights into their practice.

The violinist Pierre Baillot, having made the obligatory connection between music and speech, observed that the musical equivalents of punctuation marks are crotchet, quaver, and semiquaver rests, his assumption being that these will have been included by the composer; but he recognized that there were also 'light separations, silences of very short duration'[28] that were not always indicated. Like Schulz he admitted two methods of attaining them, though unlike Schulz he seems to have regarded the introduction of an actual silence as the less common means of marking the phrase divisions. He noted: 'it is necessary that the performer introduce them, when he sees the need, by allowing the final note of the section of the phrase or of the entire sentence to die away, and that, in certain cases, he even finishes that note a little before the end of its value'. However, Baillot's two examples indicate the articulations by means of rests (Ex. 4.23). Ex. 4.23(*a*), from Viotti's Violin Concerto no. 27, nicely illustrates the limitations of applying Schulz's and Türk's rule about the relationships of phrase divisions to the opening of the melody.

The remainder of Baillot's discussion of musical punctuation is concerned with the manner in which certain types of phrase ending should be executed. He made the comparison, typical of his countrymen, between the note

---

[25] *Violin School*, 181.   [26] *A Complete*, iii. 39.   [27] *Pianoforte-Schule*, iii. 5 ff.
[28] *L'Art du violon*, 163.

Ex. 4.23. Baillot, *L'Art du violon,* 163

(*a*)

(*b*)

following an appoggiatura and the mute *e* of the French language. He also commented that where a harmony note occurs on the strong beat at the end of a phrase it should be played 'neither with hardness, nor with too much softness unless it is at the end of its value, where it is necessary to allow the sound to die away to announce the end of the phrase or piece'.[29] And he made a distinction between endings that required a rallentando and a fading-away of the sound, and those where a vigorous execution with marked articulation between the final notes was needed (Ex. 4.24).

Ex. 4.24. Baillot, *L'Art du violon,* 164

(*a*)

[29] *L'Art du violon,* 164.

From the mid-nineteenth-century singer's point of view, Manuel García, like Corri, treated phrase division essentially as a matter of breathing; but this was only one of seven elements that made up what he called 'the art of phrasing' (the others being pronunciation, formation of the phrase, time, forte-piano, ornaments, and expression). In his consideration of phrase formation he made the important point that declamatory music or recitative, being musical prose, 'pays no regard to the number of bars or symmetry of cadences, or even to regularity of time' and is 'wholly influenced by prosodic accents and excitement of passion', whereas in 'melodious verse . . . there reigns a perfect regularity—required to satisfy the rhythmical instinct'. And he observed that 'a complete symmetry must be established between the different parts of the melody, and they must be enclosed within certain easily perceptible limits of duration. In this way our ear may unfailingly recognise each element of a phrase.'[30] He explained that 'Good melodies, like speeches, are divided by pauses, which are regulated . . . by the distribution and length of the several ideas composing such melodies', and having observed that the singer should inhale 'whenever rests occur simultaneously in words and melody' he remarked: 'Such rests may be introduced even where not marked by the composer, either for a better development of ideas, or to facilitate their execution.' He continued:

Breath should be taken only on the weak accents of a bar, or after the terminal note of a melodic figure; this method enables the singer to attack the next *idea* or *group* at the beginning of its value. Pauses which separate phrases and *semi-phrases*, are of longer duration than those merely separating figures or groups of notes: long rests, therefore should be selected for taking long, full breath; little rests between *figures* admit only of very short breaths, rapidly taken, and, on this account, are termed *mezzi-respiri*. These are seldom indicated, it being left to the singer to insert them when required.[31]

He illustrated this with two examples from Mozart's *Don Giovanni* (Ex. 4.25).

Sometimes, however, García noted, 'in order to increase the effect of a phrase, it is allowable to unite its different parts by suppressing pauses which separate them', and he gave an example from Donizetti's *Anna Bolena* (Ex. 4.26), but without indicating where the necessary breath would have to be taken. In cases where a similar effect was achieved by means of a portamento he instructed that the breath should be taken immediately after this had been executed, illustrating the point with passages from Rossini (Ex. 4.27). This procedure recalls Corri's indication of a breath after a portamento in Dibdin's 'Say little foolish flutt'ring thing' (Ex. 4.20 above).

In contrast to the joining of phrases for a particular effect, García noted that short figures, or even successive notes were sometimes required to be separated, not only between words but also within words, and that this could be done

---

[30] *New Treatise*, 46.   [31] Ibid. 48.

Ex. 4.25. García, *New Treatise*, 48

MOZART
Don Giovanni

Bat-ti bat-tio bel Ma-zet-to   la tua   po-ve-ra Zer-li-na, sta-rò

½R   ½R

Ma-zet-to   la tua   Zer-li-na, sta-rò

qui   co-mea gnel-li-na le tue botte ad—as-pet-tar

½R

li - na le tue

MOZART
Don Giovanni

Fin ch'han-dal vi-no cal-da la tes-ta   u-na gran fes-ta

tes-ta

fa pre pa-rar   se tro-viin piaz-za qual-che ra-gaz-za   te-co an cor quel-la

gaz-za

cer-ca me-nar   te-co an cor quel-la cer-ca me-nar,   cer-ca me-nar,

me-nar   me-nar,   me-nar,

cer-ca-me-nar,   senza al-cun or-di-ne la dan-za si-a.

me-nar,

Ex. 4.26. García, *New Treatise*, 48

DONIZETTI
Anna Bolena

Del mio pri-mi-ero a mo re ah non a-ves-si il pet - to.

a - mo - re ah

Ex. 4.27. García, *New Treatise*, 48

Allegro

ROSSINI
Gazza Ladra

Ninetta

Quan - ti con ten - ti si al - fin go -

Respire

drò _____ tut - to sor - ri - de - re

ROSSINI
Sigismondo

Qual mag - gior fe - li - ci - tà

Respire

più non _ sen - te _ le sue _ pe - - ne.

'either by breathing at each beat, or by simply quitting the sound without breathing,—which, in some cases, is indispensable'.[32] His examples include one from Meyerbeer's *Il crociato in Egitto* (Ex. 4.28).

Ex. 4.28. García, *New Treatise*, 49

While he agreed with other authorities that, in normal circumstances, breath should not be taken 'in the middle of a word, or between words intimately connected', he conceded that 'In phrases where pauses are badly arranged, an artist may sometimes be obliged to divide a word or sentence, by inhaling; but, in that case, he should disguise the act with such artifice as completely to escape detection.' Among the circumstances that favoured imperceptible breathing in the middle of a word was the occurrence of two consonants, 'especially if the second consonant be *explosive*'. And he recommended breathing through the nose on such occasions (Ex. 4.29). García considered a supplementary breath advisable before a cadenza, when this was preceded by a long note (Ex. 4.30), in which case 'a singer must avail himself of the noise made by the accompaniment to inhale'. Unlike Corri he does not seem to have regarded it as a general principle to breathe immediately before the pause note of a cadenza.

Ex. 4.29. García, *New Treatise*, 49

Another mid-nineteenth-century musician who systematically examined the subject of phrase division, the violinist and composer Charles de Bériot,

---

[32] *New Treatise*, 49.

Ex. 4.30. García, *New Treatise*, 49

had close personal connections with García, having been married to his sister, the great singer Maria Malibran. It was perhaps for that reason that Bériot approached the subject of performance style in violin playing very much by analogy with singing. In the section of his *Méthode* entitled 'De la ponctuation' Bériot began, after some general introductory remarks, in a rather elementary way, by drawing the violinist's attention to the deleterious effect of abbreviating rests (a problem for inexperienced violinists when practising without accompaniment). He then commented that

> There are, in the body of the phrase, rests of such short duration that they are not always indicated: these little points of repose are not therefore the less necessary to respiration. It is for the judgment of the artist to discern their true places, and to mark them he will let the final note expire a little before its time.

He made no attempt to lay down rules or general guidance as to where such articulation should be introduced, but he gave a series of musical examples of 'graduated punctuation in tranquil music' ranging from what he described as 'a species of religious music, vague, without order, without rhythm, without words, and so devoid of all punctuation',[33] to the opening theme of the second

---

[33] *Méthode*, 226–7.

movement of Mozart's String Quartet in D minor K. 421, in which the articulation was indicated by the composer. This was followed by one of his own *études* demonstrating 'punctuation in the energetic style', where the division of phrases and figures was again indicated throughout by rests and articulation marks.[34] A final set of examples illustrated 'breathing rests', first with music in which the composer marked the rests and then with three examples in which Bériot indicated the 'rests required for respiration' by commas (Ex. 4.31). Interestingly, the two Classical examples contain abundant articulations while the example from his own trio seems to be conceived in a much more legato

Ex. 4.31. Bériot, *Méthode*, iii. 230

34 *Méthode*, 228–9.

manner, perhaps illustrating a more developed consciousness of the stylistic difference between late eighteenth-century music and that of his own day than was common.

A further aspect of Bériot's treatment of articulation comes in the next section of the *Méthode* which is headed 'Syllabation'. Here Bériot observed:

There are rests even slighter than those we have just explained, namely those of syllabation. By this expression we mean the method of separating words and syllables to give them more force and accent in lyrical recitation.

These nuances, which are entirely in the spirit of the piece, are so delicate that they cannot be classed in the punctuation. They should be more or less marked according to the sentiment of the song.

Special schools of declamation have been established to teach us to speak well; of lyrical declamation and singing to teach us how to deliver melody. These vocal studies are great helps to the violinist, whose bow should render the accents of the soul.

In music as in literature, these little rests of syllabation cannot be written; the performer should feel them. Hence we call them the punctuation of sentiment.

The places which these little rests should occupy are indicated in the following examples by a comma. We should notice that their place is chiefly between a dotted note and the short one which follows it.[35]

All three of his examples here are operatic, though the extension to violin music of the French school at this period is not difficult to make. (Ex. 4.32)

Ex. 4.32. Bériot, *Méthode*, iii. 231
(*a*)

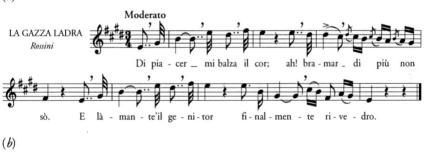

(*b*)

---

[35] Ibid. 231.

Ex. 4.32. *cont.* (*c*)

A final example, expressive rather than structural, illustrates the subtle flexibility that a musician of the mid-nineteenth century, whether singer or instrumentalist, might have been inclined to introduce into passages of equal-length notes (Ex. 4.33). Bériot's rhythmic treatment of the passage is perhaps an echo of the French tradition of unequal performance of equal-value notes, which appears, from a number of sources, to have survived in diluted form into the nineteenth century;[36] but the slight hesitation achieved by the articulation

Ex. 4.33. Bériot, *Méthode*, iii. 232
(*a*)

(*b*) Another example of Syllabation between notes of equal value

seems to be a further refinement. He remarked in his introduction to the example:

In very soft music the composers do not always mark the long and short notes, for fear that the song should take too rhythmical a form. In such cases they leave to the singer the care of marking the syllables with that infinite delicacy which lends so great a charm. Thus, for instance, if we sung with absolute equality the two quavers which begin each bar of the following Romance, our diction would be flat and cold. But if the composer had written those

[36] David Fuller, 'Notes inégales', *The New Grove Dictionary of Music and Musicians*, ed. Stanley Sadie (London, 1980), xiii. 423.

notes as dotted notes this sweet song would be too jerky in effect and would agree but little with the sentiment of its poem. It is here that a medium form is required, which the feelings alone can understand, and which no sign can express. It is sufficient for the first quaver to be a little longer than the second and that the small interval which separates them should be almost insensible.[37]

Andreas Moser (a pupil and close colleague of Joseph Joachim), born about the time Bériot's *Méthode* was published, was among late nineteenth-century musicians to consider the question of articulation at length. His treatment of stylistic issues in performance concentrated even more than those of the mid-nineteenth century on questions of how to approach the music of the past rather than that of his own day; but, despite his considerable historical knowledge,[38] his comments about performance issues in old music seem, on the whole, to reflect late nineteenth-century practices and techniques of violin playing rather than those of the periods in which the music was written.

Although he began his discussion of musical articulation with the customary reference to its relationship with speech, Moser brought his own distinct perspective to it. Having observed that a musical idea can consist of as little as two notes, he asked rhetorically how, if the two notes of the figure are not connected by a legato slur, can one tell whether they should be articulated or connected when they are not, as in the opening motif of the Allegro vivace of Beethoven's String Quartet op. 59 no. 3 (Ex. 4.34), unambiguously separated by the composer. He noted that a string player, 'who is capable of and accustomed to accomplish an unnoticeable bow change at the heel',[39] must sometimes forbear from employing this otherwise praiseworthy ability. He observed that the application of this facility in the opening of, for instance, a Handel bourée (Ex. 4.35) would result in an apparent syncopation rather than an upbeat and instructed the violinist to treat it as if a staccato dot were present. In the opening of Tartini's G major Sonata, however (Ex. 4.36), he observed that 'in keeping with the theme's gentle expression' the separation between the first two

Ex. 4.34. Joachim and Moser, *Violinschule*, iii. 13

Ex. 4.35. Joachim and Moser, *Violinschule*, iii. 13

---

[37] *Méthode*, 232.   [38] Reflected, for instance, in his *Geschichte des Violinspiels* (Berlin, 1923).
[39] Joachim and Moser, *Violinschule*, iii. 13.

Ex. 4.36. Joachim and Moser, *Violinschule*, iii. 14

notes should 'hardly, in any case not in an obtrusive manner, come to the notice of the listener'.[40] And he noted that the separation should be more or less the equivalent of a pianist playing the same key 'two or more times in succession' (presumably uninterruptedly). From this discussion of discrete separation he moved to situations in which the violinist should avoid any suggestion of articulation, citing, for instance, a passage in Spohr's Second Concerto op. 2 where 'despite the dot over the highest note in many editions, no gap should intervene between the f''' and the low b' (Ex. 4.37). He compared the performer who made a gap to an asthmatic singer, and pointed out that the phrase division (*metrische Einschnitt*) should occur where he had marked the sign ‖. He was also concerned that, through the use of a flexible wrist, the player should avoid any hint of a break between the upbeat semiquaver and the four-part chord at the beginning of the Allemand from Bach's B minor Partita for solo violin (Ex. 4.38).

Ex. 4.37. Joachim and Moser, *Violinschule*, iii. 14

Ex. 4.38. Joachim and Moser, *Violinschule*, iii. 14

After considering the degree of articulation necessary for the portato markings in the first movements of the Mendelssohn and Beethoven violin concertos, Moser referred to the articulation of slurred groups indicated by staccato marks under the last note of the group (Ex. 4.39), and remarked that such separation could be facilitated by co-ordinating the use of different strings with the divisions between the figures. He extended this point with reference to

[40] Joachim and Moser, *Violinschule*, iii. 14.

Ex. 4.39. Joachim and Moser, *Violinschule*, iii. 14

the relationship between different bowings and fingerings in the first of the Kreutzer *Études* (Ex. 4.40), where the phrasing could be reinforced by the use of the different tone colours of adjacent strings. With a couple of examples from Viotti he then illustrated the advantages of synchronizing position changes wherever possible with phrasing groups (Ex. 4.41).[41]

Ex. 4.40. Joachim and Moser, *Violinschule*, iii. 15

Ex. 4.41. Joachim and Moser, *Violinschule*, iii. 15
(*a*)

Here the fingering above is decidedly better than the one below

(*b*)

Only after reviewing these details of articulation and phrasing did he tackle the question of separating larger melodic units. He dealt first with passages in which the composer had indicated the phrase separation; referring to the opening of Beethoven's String Quartet op. 18 no. 4 (see Ex. 3.28), he observed that the staccato marks required the type of break 'which one called a "sospir" in the 17th and 18th centuries, whose length therefore was that required by a skilful singer for taking breath without disturbing the continuity of a melody as a whole'.[42] As illustration of an instance where the composer had not provided

[41] Ibid. 15.   [42] Ibid. 15.

the performer with any such guidance he chose one of his few contemporary examples, a melody by Joachim. Here the nature of late nineteenth-century practice is shown not so much by the one caesura that Moser marked as by those that he failed to indicate; the implication of his example is that the violinist would have been expected to execute all other changes of bow with the seamless legato that Moser had earlier referred to as 'a violinistic virtue that cannot be highly enough praised' (Ex. 4.42).[43] Moser, and Joachim himself, would presumably have accomplished all the other phrasing in Joachim's melody by means of dynamic nuance and accent; such an approach is verified by Joachim's own 1903 recording of his Romance in C,[44] where, although it is exquisitely phrased, there are remarkably few perceptible breaks in the sound. It is otherwise, however, in Joachim's recordings of two of the Brahms Hungarian dances, where the nature of the piece requires a much more sharply articulated performance.

Ex. 4.42. Joachim and Moser, *Violinschule*, iii. 15

Moser followed this example with a reference to occasions where a cadence-like passage lead back into a theme, as in the finale of Beethoven's Violin Concerto (Ex. 4.43), which required a 'tension rest' (*Spannungs-pause*). He

Ex. 4.43. Joachim and Moser, *Violinschule*, iii. 15

conceded, however, that there were many instances where 'musical instinct' did not suffice to decide on the phrase divisions, citing Beethoven's late quartets as especially difficult in this respect. In such circumstances, he suggested, 'only a basic insight into the rules of phrase structure and the formation of melody' could provide clarification.

---

[43] Ibid. 13.   [44] Issued on CD by Pavilion Records on Opal CD 9851 (see Ch. 12, Ex. 12.12).

As a postscript to this section of his discussion of performance matters Moser referred to orchestral bowing in a manner that again points up the difference in attitude towards vigorous passages and cantabile material. He concurred with the notion of uniform bowing in contexts where there were clear beginnings or ends of a musical phrase, but deprecated the practice in places which the 'composer conceived as sustained notes, connected phrases or long-breathed melodies'; in such circumstances he felt that the conductor should 'leave it to the individual violinist to make the bow changes as unnoticeable as possible in whatever might seem to him the best place', in order to achieve the 'illusion of a collective legato'.[45]

It will become clearer from the following consideration of the various kinds of articulation that might have been applied to individual notes and phrases, that the mid-eighteenth century's distinction between the appropriate manner of performance for an adagio and that which was required in an allegro[46] began to give way during the late eighteenth century, and succumbed entirely in the nineteenth century to a distinction between passages requiring a cantabile performance, in which phrasing was largely a matter of accentuation and dynamic nuance, and those requiring a well articulated one, where phrases and individual notes might be perceptibly separated from one another. In nineteenth-century music the performance style appropriate to particular phrases or passages was more dependent on the character the composer conceived for the individual musical idea; there was, in many respects, no longer a meaningful distinction between an allegro movement and an adagio one. Any single movement might contain everything from the most highly articulated gestures to the most lyrical and connected melody, and for this reason composers who did not want their conceptions to be misunderstood were increasingly obliged to clarify their intentions by means of signs or instructions.

[45] Joachim and Moser, *Violinschule*, iii. 16.   [46] See Ch. 10.

5

ARTICULATION AND EXPRESSION

⌒⋙✦⋘⌒

The importance that composers attached to differentiated articulation, for the intended expression of their ideas, is indicated by the early introduction and adoption of slurs and, somewhat later, articulation marks in instrumental music, where they supplied the function that was naturally provided by the words in vocal music: slurs reproduced the effect of melismas on a vowel sound, while unslurred notes corresponded with the effect of syllable change. Whether articulation marks, when these were used, were intended merely to caution the player not to slur, or whether they were meant to elicit a sharper and/or shorter staccato, similar to the explosive consonant, or whether, indeed, they might have some other significance, is among the most difficult aspects of this thorny subject. Varying theoretical accounts of the functions of dots and strokes, together with divergent usage and inconsistency on the part of composers, have inevitably caused both slurs and articulation marks to acquire a complex of meanings, some of which are only tenuously related to their principal purposes.

Before examining what composers may have wanted to convey by the use of articulation marks or slurs, however, it is necessary to determine their intentions when they left the notes without either of these markings. In some cases it is clear that, according to more or less well-understood conventions, unmarked notes were actually to be either slurred or staccato at the will of the performer. In solo parts it was often taken for granted (especially in the eighteenth century and early nineteenth century) that the performer should decide how the music would be phrased and articulated; and in orchestral parts, when singers were accompanied, it often seems to have been assumed that the phrasing in the orchestra would follow that of the vocal line. But there were undoubtedly other instances where the absence of markings is an indication for a style of performance that is neither slurred nor staccato, and it is always necessary for the performer to consider whether a specific non-legato (or indeed non-staccato) style of performance might be required.

Staccato, Legato, and Non-Legato (or 'Non-Staccato'?)

There has been a broad consensus among students of performing practice that, on the basis of a number of important sources, a more highly articulated manner of performing unmarked notes (i.e. notes without either slurs or articulation marks) was prevalent in the mid-eighteenth century than in the mid-nineteenth century. While this is likely to be broadly true, the matter is far from straightforward. Theoretical sources provide much evidence for the types of articulation available to instrumentalists and singers, and the manner in which these were to be executed. In keyboard playing this is linked with the development of the piano, and in string playing with changing designs of bow; in wind playing the evolution of the instruments themselves seems to be of less importance, but approaches to wind articulation will have been influenced by general stylistic trends. Different theoretical sources undoubtedly illuminate the differing practices of a variety of schools and traditions, and they catalogue changes over time.

Composers' usages may sometimes appear to reflect a direct and explicit connection between the notation (together with any other performance directions included in the score) and the type of execution envisaged. On the other hand, the connection between notation and execution is often unclear, and much may depend on the extent to which the composer relied on the performer's understanding of the conventions that applied to particular circumstances and contexts. This is especially important in the music of the second half of the eighteenth century, when, although theorists liked to link specific performance techniques to distinct notational practices, few composers concerned themselves with that level of detail. As Joseph Riepel remarked in his *Gründliche Erklärung der Tonordnung* (1757), after describing a sophisticated range of articulation marks that signified different kinds of execution: 'I have included the strokes and dots again only for the sake of explanation; for one does not see them in pieces of music except perhaps sometimes when it is necessary on account of clarity.'[1] Even this seems to be a rather idealistic statement, to judge from the surviving manuscript and printed material, where clarity in this respect is rarely encountered. Although nineteenth-century composers were generally more inclined to notate their required articulation with greater precision, there is still considerable scope for misunderstanding in the music of that period, especially where notes were left with neither articulation marks nor slurs.

---

[1] (Frankfurt-am-Main and Leipzig, 1757), 16.

In some instances it may seem fairly obvious that previous slurring or staccato is meant to continue, or that marking that occurs in one part should also
apply to similar figures in another. But in situations where this is not clear, the
question arises whether or not unslurred notes that the composer has left without articulation marks would have been played any differently if they did have
these markings: whether, in fact, a distinct non-legato or 'non-staccato' execution, associated with the absence of slurs or articulation marks, existed in the
period under consideration and, if it did, where it is intended and what effect
may have been envisaged. The most difficult matter may often, in fact, be to
decide whether a staccato mark really indicates a staccato execution, merely
warns against slurring, or has some other more specialized meaning (as discussed below). Here as elsewhere, contradictions abound, making it difficult to
identify any general ruling principles and adding weight to the suggestion that
a knowledge of the performing practices of the period, or those associated with
particular composers, is often more important than the actual notation, since
much that the composer regarded as obvious to the performer was not written
down, even by many later nineteenth-century composers.

Theoretical discussion of the type of performance appropriate to notes without either staccato marks or slurs occurs in a significant number of eighteenth-
century German sources. In keyboard playing C. P. E. Bach observed:

Notes that are neither detached, slurred nor fully held are sounded for half their value,
unless the abbreviation *Ten.* [*Tenuto*] (held) is written over them, in which case they must
be held fully. Crotchets and quavers in moderate and slow tempos are usually performed in
this manner, and they must not be played weakly, but with fire and a very slight accentuation.[2]

Two years later Marpurg similarly advised the keyboard player to employ a
non-legato touch unless slurring or staccato were indicated, though he seems
to have regarded this touch as less detached than Bach did, for he instructed
that 'one raises the finger from the previous key very rapidly shortly before one
touches the following note. This normal procedure, since it is always presumed, is never indicated.'[3]

Türk, too, considered a somewhat detached style of playing to be the normal
one, remarking: 'In the case of notes that should be played in the normal way,
i.e. neither staccato nor slurred, one lifts the finger from the key a little earlier
than the length of the note requires.' And he repeated Bach's comment that
Ten. would be written over them if a full-length performance were required.
However, he questioned Bach's prescription of halving the note value on the
grounds that there would not then be any appreciable difference between this

---

[2] *Versuch*, i. III, §22.
[3] *Anleitung zum Clavierspielen der schönen Ausübung der heutigen Zeit gemäss* (Berlin, 1755), 29.

touch and the staccato.[4] Türk gave the example shown in Ex. 5.1(*a*), suggesting that it would probably be played as at Ex. 5.1(*b*) or (*c*).

Ex. 5.1. Türk, *Klavierschule*, VI, 3, §40

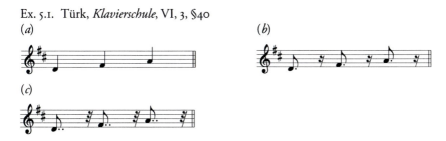

(*a*)   (*b*)

(*c*)

For the flute, Quantz had specifically limited the wind player's equivalent of the non-legato style of performance to notes of a particular value, generally the second fastest type of note in a piece, suggesting, unlike, Bach, that longer note values would be played more connectedly; there is also the implication that, presumably for technical reasons, the fastest notes would have been slurred. He instructed:

> If in an Allegro assai semiquavers are the quickest notes, the quavers must be tipped briefly for the most part, while crotchets must be played in a singing and sustained manner. But in an allegretto where semidemiquaver triplets occur, the semiquavers must be tipped briefly and the quavers played in a singing fashion.[5]

From the practical viewpoint it seems likely that some such considerations must often have applied to the fastest notes in keyboard music, where a genuinely detached style of performance is only practicable up to a certain speed. As will become apparent from examples of composers' practices, it is probable that, in some cases, fast notes in eighteenth-century string and wind parts that have neither slurs nor staccato marks would also have been intended to be played legato.

Yet there was a counter-current to the view that unmarked notes indicated a detached, quasi staccato, style of performance. At about the same time as Bach's and Marpurg's treatises, Niccolo Pasquali wrote in his *The Art of Fingering the Harpsichord*: 'The Legato is the touch that this Treatise endeavours to teach, being a general Touch fit for almost all Kinds of Passages'; and he added that all passages that have no marks for other kinds of articulation 'must be played Legato, i.e., in the usual Way'.[6] Some twenty years later Vincenzo Manfredini, writing about cantabile playing, stated that 'One must be careful not to raise the finger from the key before having played the next note.' But he added significantly: 'This rule is not only followed in this case, but on almost any occasion'.[7]

---

[4] *Klavierschule*, VI, §40.   [5] *Versuch*, XII, §22.   [6] (Edinburgh, [*c*.1758]), 26.

[7] *Regole armoniche, o sieno Precetti ragionati* (Venice, 1775), 28.

Towards the end of the eighteenth century an increasing number of authorities suggested that a legato style, rather than a non-legato or staccato one,
should be seen as the norm in keyboard playing, and that leaving the notes
unmarked was nearly or exactly the same as putting them under continuous
slurs. (In this context, it is essential to remember that long slurs indicating a
general legato were virtually unknown until after 1800.[8]) For Nicolas-Joseph
Hüllmandel in 1796 'one of the most essential rules' was that unless notes were
specified as staccato, the player should hold down a key 'til the next is struck'.[9]
Milchmeyer, at about the same time, discussed three styles of touch, like Bach,
Marpurg, and Türk, but with the important difference that his 'normal' style
was effectively legato, or, at least, as connected as the *grand détaché* of string
players of the Viotti school,[10] or the passagework of the best Italian singers of
the day:

Now I will distinguish and clearly compare the different manners of playing, which I take
to be three. I call the first the normal or natural, the second the slurred, and the third the
staccato style. In pieces by good composers, who write music as one should, all notes which
do not have a dot, stroke, or slur over them are in the natural style. To play these one lifts
the first finger off the first key when the second has been struck, the finger from the second
when the third is played, and so on. Two fingers may never be down at the same time in this
usual style of playing in a simple passage . . . The slurred style [marked by slurs] . . . requires
a soft and at the same time melting performance. All pianists should in general, according
to the requirements of the instrument, choose the slurred style, since rapped and at the same
time hacked notes certainly do not suit it; rather one should stroke it in a gentle manner.
But everything has its exceptions, so, for instance, I do not like this slurred style in runs, in
chromatic and various other kinds of passage in the bass, because the long resonance of the
stronger strings causes unpleasant sounding tones. It makes the tone of the pianoforte soft
and at the same time velvety, and by this means one can sweeten and soften the higher notes
of this instrument, which tend towards a certain hardness and dryness. All possible passages
can therefore be played in slurred style without offending the ear, but the player should only
allow himself this if the composer has marked them so. This style only requires that one
leaves the finger down somewhat longer, and on several notes [i.e. overlapping] . . . The
staccato style, in which one separates all the notes from each other, is marked with small
dots or strokes over the note, and requires a pianoforte that perfectly damps all notes, particularly the lower bass notes.[11]

By the early nineteenth century the primacy of a genuine legato as the 'normal' style of keyboard playing was firmly established. In 1801 Clementi published his opinion that 'When the composer leaves the LEGATO and STACCATO to
the performer's taste [i.e. when neither slurring nor staccato is indicated]; the
best rule is, to adhere chiefly to the LEGATO; reserving the STACCATO to give SPIRIT

---

[8] See Ch. 6, 'Slurs and Articulation'.

[9] *Principles of Music Chiefly Calculated for the Piano Forte or Harpsichord* (London, 1796), 20.

[10] See below and Ch. 7. *Grand détaché*, or even simply détaché, implied separate bows but without gaps
between the notes in the 19th c.

[11] *Die wahre Art*, 5–7.

occasionally to certain passages and to set off the HIGHER BEAUTIES of the LEGATO.'[12] And in the revised eleventh edition of his treatise he seems to have decided that even more emphatic guidance was necessary, changing the phrase 'the best rule is to adhere chiefly to the LEGATO' to the more succinct and peremptory 'let the LEGATO prevail'.

Jean Louis Adam expressed the same thing in French, in his influential Conservatoire method; apparently paraphrasing Clementi's recently published book more or less directly, he commented:

> Sometimes the author indicates the musical phrase which should be smooth, but if he abandons the choice of legato or staccato to the taste of the performer, it is best to adhere to the legato, reserving the staccato to make certain passages stand out and to make the advantages of the legato felt by means of a pleasant artistic contrast.[13]

Throughout the rest of the nineteenth century the view expressed by these writers remained the orthodox one. For instance, in Henri Herz's *A Standard Modern Preceptor for the Pianoforte* it is stated that slurs indicate 'each note being held down its full length, and till the following note is actually struck. This is called the legato style of playing, and is that which is generally used.' He further commented that 'staccato is to be used only where it is expressly indicated [by means of dots or strokes].'[14] Here there seems no longer to be any question of a non-legato touch intermediate between legato and staccato or even of a 'non-staccato'. Staccato is only to be employed where marked, and this would include every type of articulation from highly detached to virtually legato. The degree of separation or accent could be either marked by the type of signs employed, marked by additional performance directions, or entrusted to the performer's musical understanding, much in the way that a host of authors advised.[15]

The concern of mid-nineteenth-century pianists with cultivating a legato execution as the fundamental basis of their performance style finds its apogee in Sigmund Thalberg's *L'Art du chant appliqué au piano*. And at the end of the century Hugo Riemann, in his various editions of the Classics, where legato playing is particularly emphasized, reiterated the instruction that 'The legato touch should always be used, unless specially marked to the contrary',[16] thus recognizing no separate role for unmarked notes. The pedagogic aims of Riemann's editions necessitated a particularly extensive repertoire of markings to indicate a graduated series of degrees and types of articulation and accent, but by that time many composers were scarcely less meticulous.

---

[12] *Introduction*, 9.   [13] *Méthode du piano du Conservatoire* (Paris, 1804), 151.

[14] (London, [*c*.1840]), 7.

[15] e.g. C. P. E. Bach in the 1750s, Türk in the 1780s, Witthauer in the 1790s, etc.

[16] *Moments musicaux*, ed. Riemann (Brunswick, Litolff, [*c*.1890]), preface (copy in the Bodleian Library, Oxford).

A comparable, though in some respects significantly different, situation can be found in string playing. Robin Stowell summed up a generally received opinion when he referred to the 'articulated, non-legato stroke of the pre-Tourte bow' and commented that 'smooth separate bowings were only rarely used before *c.*1760'.[17] Stowell's intimate familiarity with the source material led him to give a relatively early date for the introduction of smooth, separate strokes, yet even that may be rather too late. In practice, most period instrument performers assume a fairly pronounced degree of non-legato for separately bowed notes, at least in faster tempos, in all repertoires well into the nineteenth century; but this may, in some of the contexts where it is commonly used, run counter to the expectations of the composer.

There is evidence of the use of a well-articulated bowstroke on unmarked notes, for particular repertoires and circumstances, in a number of sources. In 1776 J. F. Reichardt observed that in playing a sequence of short accompaniment notes 'one has to be aware that, if they are written without any markings, as here, they should be played short but not sharply, that is to say, the bow remains resting on the string after the note has received a short stroke' (Ex. 5.2).[18] (However, it should be noted that this description corresponds closely with instructions in other sources for the execution of notes with articulation marks.)

Ex. 5.2. Reichardt, *Ueber die Pflichten*, 23–4

Reichardt also gave a particularly detailed and lucid account of the relationship between legato bowstrokes and slow tempos, and staccato bowstrokes and fast tempos,[19] from which it is clear that the faster the speed the more detached and accented he would normally have expected the bowstrokes to be, though his account made no direct connection between these recommendations for staccato execution and the presence or absence of articulation marks. But in assessing the significance of Reichardt's advice, it is essential to bear in mind that he was writing about orchestral playing, and also, perhaps, that he was approaching the subject from a north German perspective, strongly influenced by French practice. At the time of his treatise he had just been appointed Kapellmeister to the francophile Berlin court.

There is much to suggest that there may have been significant divisions between national and regional practices in string playing in the third quarter of the eighteenth century, just as there were in keyboard playing, and that there

[17] *Violin Technique and Performance Practice in the Late-Eighteenth and Early-Nineteenth Centuries* (Cambridge, 1985), 74.

[18] *Ueber die Pflichten*, 23–4.   [19] See Ch. 10, pp. 340, 351, 367.

were widely perceived distinctions between what was appropriate in orchestral playing or accompaniment and what was allowable or desirable in solo performance. Quantz's comments on the salient characteristics of French and Italian violinists reveal both types of difference. He observed of accompaniment: 'In general it is to be noted that in the accompaniment, particularly in lively pieces, a short and articulated bowstroke, wielded in the French manner, produces a much better effect than a long and dragging Italian stroke.'[20] And he later commented:

You also find that almost all modern Italian violinists play in the same style, and that as a result they do not show up to the best advantage in comparison with their predecessors. For them the bowstroke, which, like the tongue-stroke on wind instruments, is the basis for lively musical articulation, often serves, like the wind-bag of a bagpipe, only to make the instrument sound like a hurdy-gurdy. . . . In the Allegro they consider the sawing out of a multitude of notes in a single bowstroke to be some special achievement.[21]

Quantz particularly referred to the influence of Tartini on Italian violin playing, and it is evident from many other accounts that Tartini and his disciples were specially noted not only for their use of slurring, but also for their broad and singing bowstroke, even in fast-moving notes played with separate bows.[22] Joseph Riepel's mid-eighteenth-century descriptions of a variety of separate bowstrokes, where he linked 'long and powerful strokes of the bow' to the performance of staccato notes in concertos,[23] also indicate that broader bowing was regarded as one of the characteristics of solo playing, while, as Quantz suggested, a more articulated stroke was considered appropriate to accompaniment and ensemble playing.

In singing, where the supremacy of the Italian style was unquestioned, Quantz evidently approved of a smooth and connected manner of performing relatively rapid unmarked notes. In a comment on choral singers in northern Germany he deprecated the detached manner of singing passagework that was prevalent among them, observing:

Their disagreeable, forced, and exceedingly noisy chest attacks, in which they make vigorous use of the faculty for producing the *h*, singing ha-ha-ha-ha for each note, make all the passagework sound hacked up, and are far removed from the Italian manner of executing passagework with the chest voice. They do not tie the parts of the plain air to one another sufficiently, or join them together with retarding notes [appoggiaturas]; in consequence, their execution sounds very dry and plain.[24]

There is little to suggest that this type of singing was regarded as stylish. Quantz put it down to the deficient knowledge and taste of the majority of provincial German cantors. In general, the Italian school of singing seems to have

---

[20] *Versuch*, XVII, 2, §26. [21] Ibid. XVIII, §61.

[22] For further details on the relationship between articulation, notation, and bowing styles see below.

[23] See Ch. 6. [24] *Versuch*, XVIII, §80 n.

Ex. 5.3. (*a*) Perez, *Solimano*, Act I, Scene iv, British Library, London, Add MSS 16093–94; pub. in fac. in the series *Italian Opera 1640–1770* (New York, Garland, 1978) (*b*) D. Corri, *A Select Collection*, i. 49

(*a*)

(*b*)

cultivated a genuine cantabile style of delivering every type of music. Even in fast music, separation of the notes within a syllable would have been exceptional, only to be used when specifically indicated by the composer, either by rests, or by articulation marks (Ex. 5.3). For the sake of expression, of course, it would sometimes have been considered appropriate to deliver a particular phrase in a staccato manner; but this, though occasionally marked by careful composers (Ex. 5.4), would normally have been left to the judgement of the singer.

Ex. 5.4. Perez, *Solimano*, Act I, Scene vi, British Library, London, Add MSS 16093–94; pub. in fac. in the series *Italian Opera 1640–1770* (New York, Garland, 1978)

As will become apparent from a closer consideration of string bowing styles,[25] composers' expectations in respect of different modes of articulation can only be appreciated in the light of the influences that moulded their styles,

[25] See Ch. 7.

as well as the musicians with whom they worked or for whom they wrote. Nevertheless, it is evident that there was a greater concern among instrumentalists to emulate a singing style in some quarters than in others. In view of the Italian hegemony in singing, it is not surprising that it should have been Italian musicians (and those most strongly influenced by Italy) who pre-eminently modelled their style on vocal technique.

Although nineteenth-century music tends to be much more explicitly marked in respect of legato and the various types of articulated execution, there is still considerable scope for misunderstanding a composer's intentions. In the 1820s, for instance, Dotzauer, in his discussion of performance style in general, made clear distinctions between solo playing and accompanying, and between song-like passages and others, saying that if the passage is not song-like and is not otherwise marked it should be played in a detached manner.[26] As an example he gave a passage of quavers, without articulation marks, in a moderato tempo, evidently expecting the type of stroke described in the Paris Conservatoire's violin and cello methods, where a well-extended bowing with an abrupt check between each stroke is described and its execution notated in the same way (Ex. 5.5). Yet comparison with a similar example from Spohr's *Violinschule*, which is marked with staccato strokes, provides a timely warning that all may not necessarily be as it seems at first sight, even in the nineteenth century, for Dotzauer's quavers, without staccato marks, are evidently meant to be played in a more detached style than Spohr's quavers with staccato marks (see below, Ex. 6.17).

Ex. 5.5. Dotzauer, *Méthode de violoncelle*, 56

One specific place in which late eighteenth- and early nineteenth-century musicians seem to have been specially concerned to avoid inappropriate separation was between the first and second notes of a figure where the first note was an anacrusis on a metrically weak beat. This was apparently the case even in the context of a performance style where unslurred notes were generally played in a detached manner. G. W. Fink observed in 1808:

---

[26] *Méthode de violoncelle* (Mainz, [c.1825]), 56.

The weak beats of the bar ought, according to whether they come before a strong or stronger beat, always be tied to some extent to their strong beat as an anacrusis (up-beat), as long as the composer has not specifically prevented this by a dot over the note or by rests. If, however, there is a dot over a note which occupies a weak beat, so, by means of the staccato, it acquires a somewhat greater amount of accent than it would have without it, and thus entails that the following strong beat, particularly if it is the first beat of a new bar, also receives a somewhat sharper accent, assuming that at that place the composer has not also required an exception through a *p* as an extraordinary nuancing expression mark.[27]

Fink's observation about the upbeat being tied to its strong beat is lent support by an instance in pieces written by Haydn for musical clock in the early 1790s and pinned onto the barrels of three surviving clocks by musicians closely associated with the composer. Whereas the majority of separate notes are performed shorter than their written duration, the upbeat in Hob. XIX:15, which is without staccato in the manuscript source (Elßler's *Abschrift*), is lengthened on both of the clocks that play it (Ex. 5.6).[28]

Ex. 5.6. Haydn, *Flötenuhrstück* Hob. XIX: 15

With these caveats about the limitations of relying too greatly on the presence or absence of articulation marks, it may be instructive to consider various possible interpretations of unmarked notes in music of the period.

Unmarked Notes Implying Slurs

It is difficult confidently to identify passages in eighteenth-century music where slurs, though unmarked, are appropriate. Such passages may, however,

[27] *Allgemeine musikalische Zeitung*, 11 (1808), 229.
[28] *Joseph Haydn: Werke*, XXI, ed. Sonja Gerlach and George R. Hill (Munich, 1984), 20.

be more common than is usually assumed. Many composers and copyists were evidently casual about indicating slurs in places where they felt them to be obvious; in the case of very fast notes, especially, they seem often to have marked them only very haphazardly or omitted them altogether. They seem sometimes to have considered it more important to indicate where slurring was not intended. This they might do by the addition of a few articulation marks at the beginning of a passage or by the inclusion of one of a number of terms specifying detached performance. A copyist's score of Piccinni's popular opera *La Ceccina ossia La buona figluola* provides a good example of a situation in which the inclusion of staccato marks on some notes appears to be intended to clarify the extent of an assumed slur. In Ex. 5.7(*a*), the sporadic staccato marks on the quavers in the second violin may show that this note should not be included in the slur, as, in the absence of instructions to the contrary, the players would almost certainly have inferred from the demisemiquavers; later in the aria the copyist occasionally wrote in a slur on these figures (Ex. 5.7(*b*)).

Ex. 5.7. Piccinni, *La Ceccina ossia La buona figluola*, Act I, Scene i, MS score, Conservatorio di musica Luigi Cherubini, Florence; pub. in the series *Italian Music 1640–1770* (New York and London, Garland, 1983)
(*a*)

Ex. 5.7. *cont.* (*b*)

Instances where accompanying instruments were probably meant to imitate a singer's slurring are especially common in music of this period. A couple of examples from many will illustrate this sufficiently. In a copyist's score of Umlauf's *Die schöne Schusterin*, probably connected with the 1779 Vienna production, articulation marks are employed to warn that a change of pattern occurs, but the violin seems otherwise intended to match the voice (Ex. 5.8). Here the pattern has been indicated in places, but corroboration of the composer's intention is often absent. Nevertheless, an intention for unslurred performance in passages like Ex. 5.9, from Neubauer's *Fernando und Yariko*, seems highly improbable. And in a passage from André's own edition of his Singspiel *Der Töpfer* a rare occurrence of staccato marks again provides clues (Ex. 5.10).

Mozart left much less to chance in this respect, and it may be reasonable to assume that in most of his mature compositions, except in cases of evident oversight, the absence of slurs will almost invariably indicate unslurred execution. Haydn was nowhere near so careful, especially before the 1790s; and even in the London symphonies there are many passages where his autographs only indicate slurring in a very spasmodic and general manner, leaving serious

Ex. 5.8. Umlauf, *Die schöne Schusterin*, no. 2, MS score in Österreichische
Nationalbibliothek, Vienna, Mus. HS. 16. 481; pub. in fac. in the series *German Opeera*
1770–1800 (New York and London, Garland, 1986)

Ex. 5.9. Neubauer, *Fernando und Yariko*, Act I, Scene v, printed full score (Zürich,
1788)

Ex. 5.10. André, *Der Töpfer*, [no. 4], pp. 39–40, printed full score (Offenbach,
[*c.*1773])

ambiguities. In the nineteenth century, while German composers generally became much more meticulous in such matters, there were still some whose practice was casual enough to provoke doubts about the literalness of their notation. In Weber's scores there are frequent passages where he possibly imagined slurring but failed to mark it (Ex. 5.11) and many others where a general legato is intimated by a few imprecise and sporadic slurs (Ex. 5.12). It is often, therefore, not really clear whether string players were intended to assimilate their bowing to slurs in the wind and vocal parts or whether Weber really wanted strings to play with a separate, probably broad détaché bowing, while wind and voices were slurred, for instance in several passages from the E flat Mass (Ex. 5.13). Italian composers, up to at least Verdi's earlier years, still seem often to have been content to leave much detail of this kind to the instinct or decision of performers.

Among composers who were generally careful to mark such slurring in orchestral parts, and in chamber music, there may sometimes have been a deliberate intention to abstain from prescribing details of articulation and slurring in a genuine solo part, perhaps reflecting their awareness of constantly changing performance styles, especially in string playing. A prominent example is provided by Beethoven's Violin Concerto, where the composer seems to have been content to allow Clement, or whoever else performed the work, to decide on patterns of bowing in the passagework. Performance traditions, apparently sanctioned (or at least accepted) by the composer, may be preserved in Jacob Dont's and Ferdinand David's editions of the Concerto,[29] where passages of unmarked notes receive varied bowings (Ex. 5.14). It can scarcely be doubted that Beethoven envisaged some variety of bowing where he merely wrote unmarked notes. Even where composers specified these kinds of detail, however, it is abundantly clear that the majority of nineteenth-century soloists did not feel themselves bound to follow them to the letter, and it is probable that few composers would have expected them to do so. Ferdinand David's bowings in the works of his friend and colleague Mendelssohn offer many instructive instances of the type of amplifications and modifications that are likely to have been regarded as legitimate in the mid-nineteenth century; and Brahms's correspondence with Joachim provides a revealing glimpse of the former's perception of the borderline between what was his responsibility and what was best entrusted to the executant.

---

[29] See Robin Stowell, ed., *Performing Beethoven* (Cambridge, 1994), chs. 6 and 7. Dont claimed in the preface to his edition that his father, first cellist in the Hoforchester, had often played the work with Beethoven and Clement, and had taught the concerto to his son on the basis of that experience. David, though not directly connected with Vienna, was in touch with the mainstream tradition of German violin playing of Beethoven's day.

Ex. 5.11. Weber, *Der Freischütz*, no. 3

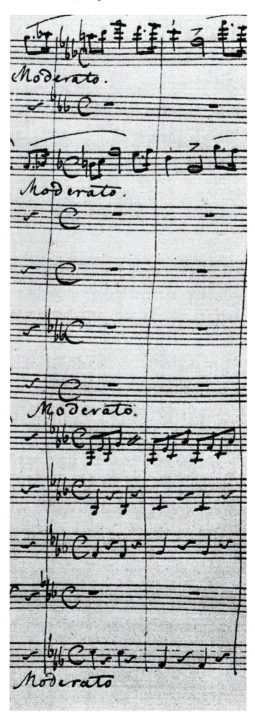

Ex. 5.12. Weber, Mass in E flat J. 224, Credo

Ex. 5.13. Weber, Mass in E flat J. 224, Gloria

Ex. 5.14. Beethoven, Violin Concerto op. 61/i: (*a*) ed. J. Dont; (*b*) ed. F. David
(*a*)

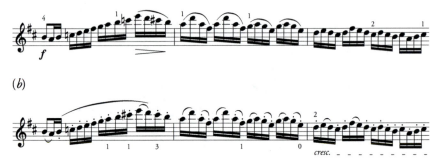

(*b*)

Sciolto and Non legato

Some eighteenth- and nineteenth-century composers took care to warn players in particular instances that where detached notes were written, they required a style of performance that was neither legato nor staccato. The term most often encountered in this context in the eighteenth century and early nineteenth century is 'sciolto' (commonly, but not always, accompanying notes without articulation marks), while in the nineteenth century 'non legato' ('non ligato') is increasingly encountered where the notes have no other markings.

'Sciolto' or its plural 'sciolte' is defined in a number of slightly different ways by writers on music. In Rees's *Cyclopaedia* Burney gave it as: 'unbound, detached, articulate. On the flute and hautbois, every note to be tongued: on the violin, tenor and bass, every note to be bowed, and cut short, as if followed by a rest of half its value.'[30] For Burney it seems essentially to have been indistinguishable from staccato, for in defining spiccato he remarked that it had 'nearly the same signification as *sciolto* and *staccato*', adding that '*sciolto* and *staccato* passages require a strong bow to every note'.[31] Other writers took a rather different view. Lichtenthal, writing in Italian, used the word as a direct opposite of 'legato',[32] while Clementi, in the revised eleventh edition of his piano method (it does not appear in the original edition) defined it as 'free, neither legato nor staccato'.[33] The term 'free' (*frei*) was also used by German authors. Koch considered it to mean: 'free, detached [*ungebunden*], therefore the notes not bound to one another or slurred, but separated and staccato [*abgestoßen*]; at the same time one also understands by it that these staccato notes should be performed with a certain freedom or with the avoidance of all kinds of hardness [*aller Arten von Härte*]'.[34] And Fröhlich, thinking of the violinist, similarly observed that *sciolto* indicated 'yet another kind of gentle stac-

---

[30] Art. 'Sciolto'.   [31] Art. 'Spiccato'.   [32] *Dizionario*, art. 'Sciolto'.

[33] *Introduction*, 11th edn. (London, 1826), 9.   [34] *Musikalisches Lexikon*, art. 'Sciolto'.

Ex. 5.15. Perez, *Solimano*, Act II, Scene xi, British Library, London, Add MSS 16093–94; pub. in fac. in the series *Italian Opera 1640–1770* (New York, Garland, 1978)

cato [*Stoß*] . . . which means free, detached. It should therefore be played with lightness, without stiffness, but especially with much flexibility of the wrist.'[35] Koch's and Fröhlich's definitions seem likely to be close to the intention behind David Perez's use of the term half a century earlier. Perez used a wide range of terms including 'staccato', battute, and 'ligato'; and 'sciolto' evidently signifies a detached execution different from staccato. In one passage in his opera *Solimano* (Ex. 5.15) Perez reinforced slurs with *lig.* [ligato], while *sciol.* [sciolto] confirmed that the absence of slurs means separate, but probably not staccato execution (as the simultaneous slurs in the wind instruments on the top two staves suggest). Another informative passage in *Solimano* indicates, perhaps, that Perez was concerned to warn the player not to slur, but did not want to induce a staccato attack (Ex. 5.16). Other characteristic occurrences of 'sciolto' come in Piccinni's *Catone in Utica*, where, although the notes also have articulation marks, 'sciolto' invariably occurs in piano or mezza voce passages, suggesting, maybe, that 'all kinds of hardness' should be avoided (Ex. 5.17). Somewhat later in the century Sacchini used 'sciolto' in a similar manner though not always in piano (Ex. 5.18). A more unusual use of the term occurs

[35] *Musikschule*, 49.

Ex. 5.16. Perez, *Solimano*, Act III, Scene vi, British Library, London, Add MSS 16093–94; pub. in fac. in the series *Italian Opera 1640–1770* (New York, Garland, 1978)

Ex. 5.17. Piccini, *Catone in Utica*: (*a*) overture; (*b*) Act II, Scene ix
(*a*)

(*b*)

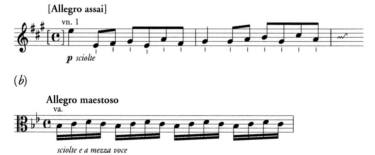

Ex. 5.18. Sacchini, *L'eroe Cinese*, Act I, Scene iv, MS score in Bayerische Staatsbibliothek, Munich, Mus. MS 543; pub. in the series *Italian Opera 1640–1770* (New York and London, Garland, 1982)

Ex. 5.19. Paisiello, *La Passione*, Pt. 2, aria 'Ai passi erranti'

Ex. 5.20. Mozart, 'Haffner' Symphony K. 385/i
(*a*)

(*b*)

in Paisiello's oratorio *La Passione* of 1782, where the phrase *sciolte stacato* [*sic*] may possibly imply something like a relaxed portato (Ex. 5.19). Mozart's untypical employment of 'sciolto' in the first movement of the 'Haffner' Symphony may, like Perez's use of it, be intended to prevent slurring but avoid staccato (Ex. 5.20).

Nineteenth-century examples can be found in music by Cherubini, Spontini, Meyerbeer, and Donizetti. Cherubini's string quartets contain several passages marked 'sciolto' or 'sciolte'. He used the direction in both piano and forte, and Fröhlich's definition would be apt in both cases (Ex. 5.21). Examples from Spontini's *La Vestale*, Meyerbeer's *Il crociato in Egitto*, and Donizetti's *Parisina* illustrate its use by younger composers (Ex. 5.22). In these examples Meyerbeer and Donizetti seem to have used 'sciolte' in Lichtenthal's sense, merely to confirm that separate notes are really intended in passages that also contain slurs.

Beethoven seems to have been among the earliest composers to make use of the instruction 'non legato' or 'non ligato', but only in his later works, where it occurs in orchestral, keyboard, and string chamber music contexts. He very often used it where a passage was preceded by similar note values with slurs. Its earliest use in the string quartets occurs at bar 20 of the first movement of op. 95, where semiquavers are to be played with separate bows (Ex. 5.23). Whether, in this context, at the extremely rapid tempo called for by Beethoven's metronome mark ($\downarrow$ = 92) the strings have much latitude for differentiating one style of detached bowing from another is a moot point; here it seems possible that it could just as well be a warning not to slur. Other examples where

Ex. 5.21. Cherubini: (*a*) String Quartet no. 2/ii; (*b*) String Quartet no. 5/iv

(*a*)

(*b*)

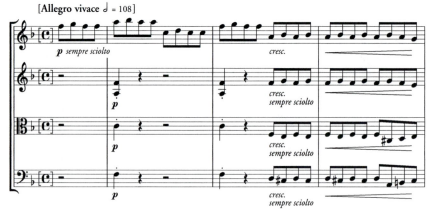

Ex. 5.22. (*a*) Spontini, *La Vestale* (Paris, Erard, [1808]), Act I, Ballet no. 1; (*b*) Meyerbeer, *Il crociato in Egitto*, no. 16 [A major, **c** Allegro agitato (Più allegro)]; (*c*) Donizetti, *Parisina*, autograph, Museo Donizettiano Bergamo; pub. in fac. in the series *Early Romantic Opera* (New York and London, 1981)

(*a*)

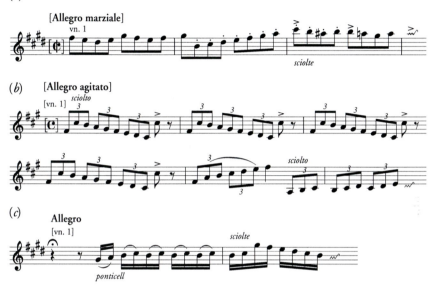

(*c*)

(*c*) Ex. 5.23. Beethoven, String Quartet op. 95/i

there is a clear intention to signal a difference from an immediately preceding passage with slurs can be found in the *Missa solemnis*, in the Piano Sonata op. III (Ex. 5.24), and at many points in the last group of string quartets. But the question arises: why did Beethoven not use staccato marks to signal that the notes were intended to be separate, as he often did in earlier works and contin-

Ex. 5.24. Beethoven: (*a*) *Missa solemnis*, Dona nobis pacem; (*b*) Piano Sonata op. 111/i

(*a*)

(*b*)

ued to do in other instances in late ones? There are very good grounds for thinking that, in the works of this period, he envisaged a specific type of performance when he either wrote 'non ligato' or (except where an earlier instruction was obviously intended to continue) left the notes without markings. The first movement of the String Quartet op. 130 is particularly revealing in this respect, for the semiquavers from bar 14 are marked 'non ligato' while those at bar 64 have staccato marks and the instruction *pp ben marcato*; and both passages return with the same markings later in the movement (Ex. 5.25). It is probable that Beethoven wanted a more connected bowstroke in the non ligato passage, and this assumption may be strengthened if the known bowing style of the violinists, for instance Joseph Boehm, with whom he worked at that time, is taken into account.[36] If this is so, it seems likely that when Beethoven used this instruction in his piano music, or when he appears intentionally to have left the notes without articulation marks or slurs (difficult though this sometimes is to identify), he meant the pianist to produce an effect similar to the broad détaché of the string player, each note receiving the emphasis of a separate bowstroke but without being shortened.

It is less likely that Beethoven made any clear distinction of this kind in earl-

---

[36] See Ch. 7.

Ex. 5.25. Beethoven, String Quartet op. 130/i

(*a*)

(*b*)

ier works, where he appears to have been more willing to use the staccato mark as a simple instruction not to slur. However, there is the possibility of an intentional distinction as early as, say, the violin sonatas op. 30, where notes in the piano part without slurs or staccato marks often correspond with separately bowed notes in the violin part; but the intention is sometimes called into question by the use of staccato marks in the violin part, as, for instance, in bar 28 of the first movement of the G major Sonata, which may merely have been meant to prevent slurring, or by the frequent absence of markings in the piano part where legato seems very likely.

As in Beethoven's late works, Schumann's use of the expression 'non legato', in the Piano Quintet, for example, implies an execution for the piano that corresponds with separate non-staccato passages in the string instruments (Ex. 5.26). In Schumann's case, considering his association with Ferdinand David and other violinists of a similar background, the association of such passages with a détaché bowing is even more persuasive. The same can be said of later nineteenth-century uses of the term, where composers were evidently

Ex. 5.26. Schumann, Piano Quintet op. 44/i

concerned to warn against legato in contexts that might otherwise lead players to slur, yet at the same time wished to avoid the danger of encouraging a staccato execution. In Liszt's *Faust-Symphonie*, the instruction appears in conjunction with a *quasi trillo* (Ex. 5.27). Max Bruch used it in his G minor Violin Concerto in a passage that would typically have received a détaché bowing, but it is necessary because of the preceding slurs (Ex. 5.28). Saint-Saëns, in his *Danse macabre* op. 40, similarly employed 'non legato' after a passage with slurs (Ex. 5.29); the requirement for a broad rather than staccato bowing in this instance is suggested by earlier passages of quavers with staccato marks that appear together with instructions such as 'staccato', 'marcatissimo', or 'leggiero'.

Ex. 5.27. Liszt, *Eine Faust-Symphonie*, i, 'Faust'

Ex. 5.28. Bruch, Violin Concerto in G minor op. 26/iii

Ex. 5.29. Saint-Saëns, *Danse macabre* op. 40

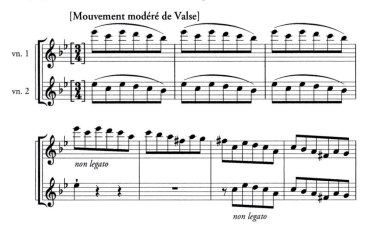

Implied Non-Legato or 'Non-Staccato'

For every late eighteenth or early nineteenth-century composer who specified 'sciolto', 'non legato', or something similar where neither slurring nor staccato was required, there were many who failed to do so; and, as implied earlier, it is frequently very uncertain where composers might have envisaged a discrete type of execution that was neither legato nor staccato, which, depending on the degree of separation, we may categorize either as non-legato or non-staccato. Schubert, when he left notes unmarked, only clarified his intentions by additional instructions such as 'staccato' or 'sempre staccato', to save writing dots continuously, or, especially in piano music, by writing 'legato' instead of continuing with slurs. He appears not to have used 'non legato' or an equivalent term. That he did, however, sometimes intend a non legato or non-staccato execution is suggested by many passages in works for piano and strings where slurring and staccato and separate notes, but not apparently staccato notes, correspond in the keyboard and string parts. There are also passages in Schubert's orchestral music, similar to the ambiguous ones in the Weber's E flat Mass (see above, Exx. 5.12 and 5.13), where slurred wind parts occur simultaneously with separately bowed string parts. But in view of Schubert's usual notational practice, the distinction was almost certainly intended; and in these cases a broad détaché bowing also seems likely (Ex. 5.30).

By the second half of the nineteenth century there is little doubt that in the vast majority of cases where a composer wrote separate notes with neither slurs nor staccato marks, these were meant to be played full-length in the manner of a détaché bowing. This is clearly what is intended by Tchaikovsky in the first movement of the Sixth Symphony, for instance, where he scored upper strings and woodwind in unison for extended passages, the wind with slurs, and the strings with separate bows (Ex. 5.31). Earlier in the movement where the strings change from passages of mixed slurs and separate bows to a passage that is again in unison with slurred woodwind, he gave the instruction 'détaché' to the

Ex. 5.30. Schubert, *Alfonso und Estrella*, Act II, no. 22

Ex. 5.31. Tchaikovsky, *Symphonie pathétique* op. 74/i

Ex. 5.32. Tchaikovsky, *Symphonie pathétique* op. 74/i

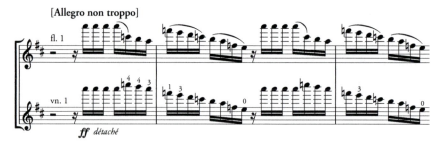

Ex. 5.33. Tchaikovsky, *Symphonie pathétique* op. 74/i

strings to ensure that they used separate bows. The choice of that particular term leaves no doubt about the style of bowing required, for by this period the technical meaning of 'détaché' in string playing was quite clear (Ex. 5.32). It seems possible that the ease with which woodwind instruments could produce a convincing staccato[37] was still associated with a greater tendency for them to do so on unslurred notes; perhaps it is significant that at another point in the first movement of the 'Pathétique' Tchaikovsky felt it necessary to give the instruction 'pesante, non staccato' to the wind, but not to the cellos and basses, who play the same figure (Ex. 5.33).

Tchaikovsky's conjunction of slurred wind, in unison with separately bowed but quasi-legato strings, will not seem at all surprising; nor, keeping in mind the dominance of the Viotti school throughout much of Europe in the early nineteenth century, would it be very hard to imagine that Schubert or Weber could have conceived a like effect in similar circumstances. And Brahms, like Tchaikovsky, evidently had a comparable intention when he wrote passages with slurred wind and separate strings, as in the last movement of the Second Symphony (Ex. 5.34). To suggest, however, that Mozart may have envisaged something similar might raise a few eyebrows. Yet this could well have been in Mozart's mind when he scored and notated a wind and string unison passage in his last symphony (Ex. 5.35). There can be little doubt that the combination of slurred wind and unslurred lower strings was deliberate, for the passage appears in both exposition and recapitulation in exactly the same guise. The violins, with their repeated notes, were certainly intended to produce a connected

Ex. 5.34. Brahms, Second Symphony op. 73/iv

sound and to have staccato or non-legato notes in the other strings seems
unlikely in this context. Such passages offer thought-provoking clues to the
expectations of late eighteenth and early nineteenth-century composers when
they left the notes unmarked.

Ex. 5.35. Mozart, Symphony no. 41 K. 551/i

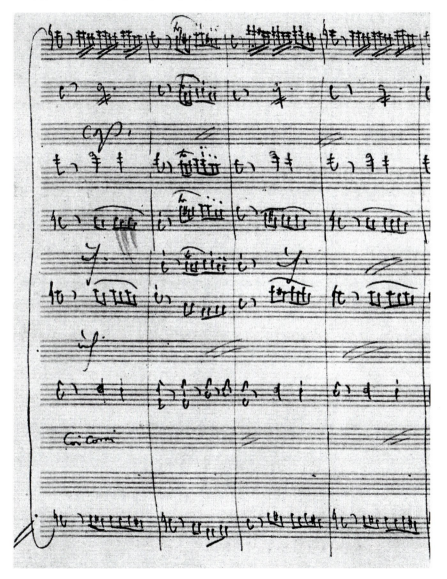

6

THE NOTATION OF ARTICULATION
AND PHRASING

Dots and Strokes as Articulation Marks

Since the late nineteenth century editors and scholars have devoted much thought to the sorts of theoretical distinctions that were historically made between various forms of articulation marks, illuminating a host of individual views, which, though fairly clear and straightforward in themselves, are frequently incompatible with one another. Theorists and authors of musical instruction books were divided between those who recognized a single staccato mark and those who advocated two forms.[1] C. P. E. Bach, whose reputation as a composer made him perhaps the most widely respected of all the eighteenth-century theorists, took the view that only one mark for unslurred staccato was necessary; but, stressing that one mark did not mean one kind of execution, he observed that the performer must execute the staccato in different ways according to the length of the note, whether it is a minim, crotchet, or quaver, whether the tempo is fast or slow, and whether the dynamic is forte or piano.[2] Bach's preference for a single staccato mark for unslurred notes was echoed by, among others, Leopold Mozart (1756), Reichardt (1776), Türk (1789), Hiller (1792), Müller (1804), and Spohr (1832).[3] Others, including Quantz (1752), Riepel (1757), Löhlein (1774), Vogler (1778), Koch (1802), Adam (1804),

---

[1] There seems no reason to distinguish between strokes and wedges; the wedge is essentially a printer's convention and, where it has any direct connection with a composer's markings, will normally represent a stroke.

[2] *Versuch,* i. III, §17.

[3] Mozart, *Versuch*; Reichardt, *Ueber die Pflichten*; Türk, *Klavierschule*; Johann Adam Hiller, *Anweisung zum Violinspielen für Schulen und Selbstunterrichte* (Leipzig, 1792); Müller, *Klavier- und Fortepiano-Schule*; Spohr, *Violinschule*.

Knecht (1803),[4] and an increasing number of nineteenth-century authorities advocated or acknowledged two signs. By the second half of the nineteenth century the recognition of two signs was more or less universal; but there was still no general agreement about precisely what they should signify. The majority of eighteenth-century and early nineteenth-century authors who described both signs favoured the stroke as the sharper and shorter of the two, yet Vogler and his admirer Knecht seem to have wanted it sharper and longer, while as late as 1837 Gustav Schilling still expressed uncertainty about the significance of the two types of staccato mark.[5] In the nineteenth century, attitudes differed somewhat according to whether the writer considered the matter primarily from the point of view of keyboard playing, string playing, or wind playing; and there were important differences between a number of French and German musicians, especially about the accent implications of the two kinds of staccato mark.[6] The most important of these disagreements will become apparent in the following pages.

The relationship of theoretical explanations to the practices of specific composers remains highly problematic. There has been little consensus even in the matter of which composers used both dots and strokes to mean different things and which used a single mark with a more variable meaning. Many eighteenth-century and early nineteenth-century manuscript scores seem at first sight to contain both markings, and patterns may apparently emerge, such as dots on a succession of notes in conjunct motion, and strokes over isolated notes or successions of disjunct notes; on closer inspection, however, discrepancies become increasingly evident, and doubt about whether a deliberate distinction between two forms of staccato mark was intended may begin to creep in, perhaps leading to the conviction that what initially appeared to be distinct dots and strokes are rather the product of writing habits or temperament.

Controversy has raged especially strongly over Mozart's practice, with vehement and sometimes intemperate advocacy on both sides of the issue. Paul Mies argued cogently in 1958 that the staccato marks on unslurred notes in Mozart's autographs, which include every stage between clear dots and long strokes, are a product of his manner of writing and are not intended to represent two distinct signs.[7] The present writer shares the opinion that, whatever their visual form, they are all simply staccato marks, and that, independently of variations in their size or shape, they mean whatever Mozart envisaged a

---

[4] Quantz, *Versuch*; Riepel, *Gründliche Erklärung*; Löhlein, *Anweisung zum Violinspielen*; Georg Joseph Vogler, *Kuhrpfälzische Tonschule* (Mannheim, 1778); Koch, *Musikalisches Lexikon*; Adam, *Méthode*; Knecht, *Katechismus*.

[5] *Encyclopädie*, art. 'Abstoßen'.   [6] See Ch. 3.

[7] 'Die Artikulationszeichen Strich und Punkt bei Wolfgang Amadeus Mozart', *Die Musikforschung*, 11 (1958), 428.

staccato mark to signify in that particular context.[8] Some scholars would also like to distinguish between dots and strokes on unslurred notes in Beethoven, but in that case the majority (including the present writer) favours a single form.[9] Here, judgement is aided by the survival of many corrected copyist's scores and parts (a resource that is, unfortunately, not available for Mozart), in which, with the exception of corrections to inaccurately notated portato (for instance in the Allegretto of the Seventh Symphony), Beethoven did not concern himself with clarifying any distinction between dots and strokes, despite many inconsistencies on the part of the copyists. In his own holographs the predominant form is the stroke, and where staccato marks over unslurred notes appear to be dots, they may in most cases equally well be interpreted as very small strokes. This is especially evident when they are compared with his staccato marks under slurs (for portato), which, like Mozart's, are invariably written as absolutely clear dots. It seems fairly certain that Beethoven's practice was in agreement with the opinion of August Eberhardt Müller, who had written in 1804 that it would be best if one used 'only the little stroke, not the dot, where the notes should be performed staccato; but used the latter only in conjunction with the slur [i.e. portato]'.[10]

Other important eighteenth- and nineteenth-century composers have received less attention in this respect. C. P. E. Bach, having advocated one form in his theoretical writings, appears to have required only one sign in his music. Haydn may, perhaps, have made a distinction between dots and strokes on unslurred notes (and even on notes under slurs[11]) in a few very late chamber works, for instance the op. 77 string quartets, where he seems to have experimented with a number of more precise notational devices, but he does not seem to have done so in earlier works. Weber may have intended to use both signs in some instances, but it is by no means clear that the apparent distinctions in most of his autographs are consequential; in *Der Freischütz*, for example, there are quite frequent cases of inconsistency (Ex. 6.1). Schubert was rather more consistent in his employment of two signs, especially in his later

    [8] For further elucidation of the present author's view, see Clive Brown, 'Dots and Strokes in Late 18th-and 19th-Century Music', *Early Music*, 21 (1993), 593–610. Other arguments against two signs are advanced by: Alfred Einstein; E. Zimmermann in Hans Albrecht, ed., *Die Bedeutung der Zeichen Keil Strich und Punkt bei Mozart* (Kassel, 1957); Robert D. Riggs, 'Articulation in Mozart's and Beethoven's Sonatas for Piano and Violin', dissertation (Harvard University, 1987). Those arguing for two distinct signs include: H. Keller, H. Unterricht, O. Jonas and A. Kreutz in *Die Bedeutung*; R. Elvers in *Neue Mozart Ausgabe* IV/13/1 (Kassel, 1961), preface, p. x (the *NMA* adopted a consistent, but very dubious policy of attempting to make a distinction between dots and strokes); Frederick Neumann, 'Dots and Strokes in Mozart', *Early Music*, 21 (1993), 429–35.

    [9] Mies argues against two marks in Beethoven in *Textkritische Untersuchungen bei Beethoven* (Munich and Duisburg, 1957); see also G. von Dadelsen, ed., *Editionsrichtlinie musikalischer Denkmäler und Gesamtausgaben* (Kassel, 1967). The present author has also taken this view in his editions of Beethoven (see the prefaces to Beethoven's *Fantasie für Klavier, Chor und Orchester* (Wiesbaden, Breitkopf & Härtel, 1992) and Beethoven's Fifth Symphony, op. 67 (Wiesbaden, Breitkopf & Härtel, 1996).

    [10] *Klavier- und Fortepiano Schule*, 27.   [11] See below.

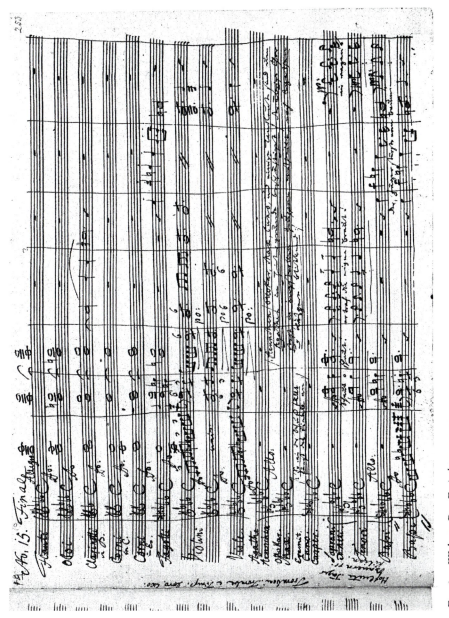

Ex. 6.1. Weber, *Der Freischütz*, no. 15

works. The orthographic distinction between thin vertical lines and staccato marks that correspond with his dots of prolongation is usually quite clear (Ex. 6.2). (The passage in Ex. 6.2(*a*) recurs with the same obvious strokes in the recapitulation, and the dotted passages are consistent throughout.) Schubert's concern to make a difference is demonstrated by a place in the autograph of *Fierrabras*, where he appears to have written dots in the cello and bass part (which was sketched first, together with the vocal parts), but subsequently changed them to strokes to match the other orchestral parts, which he added later.[12] Cherubini and Spohr were among those who appear to have shown little if any interest in using two staccato marks. It has been argued that Rossini did so, but this remains questionable, at least in all but the last operas. In *Semiramide*, for instance, many pages provide examples of an indiscriminate mixture of dots and strokes as staccato marks (Ex. 6.3). Among composers born in the eighteenth century, Meyerbeer certainly seems to have intended two signs in some works, though unlike many German composers he used the dot as his predominant staccato mark, employing strokes relatively infrequently. Marschner, too, employed both signs, apparently intentionally.[13] Never-

Ex. 6.2. Schubert, Piano Sonata in G D. 894/i
(*a*)

(*b*)

---

[12] No. 3, bar 22. It is also significant that the outer sections of this march consistently have strokes while the gentler middle section has dots throughout.

[13] See ch. 3 and n. 65 for a 19th-c. opinion on the meaning of Marschner's staccato strokes.

Ex. 6.3. Rossini, *Semiramide*, overture

theless, in almost all cases where the forms of the staccato marks range from genuine dots to smaller or larger strokes, it is very seldom wholly clear if or where composers intended a distinction between two signs.

In the music of composers born after 1800 both dots and strokes were used with increasing frequency as a means of indicating different types of staccato execution. Mendelssohn, however, still seems to have preferred a single sign. Schumann generally used dots, but wrote strokes occasionally, as did Brahms, whose deliberate intention to signify a difference between strokes and dots is attested not only in his scores, but also in a letter to Joachim of 1879.[14] Reger was also among those who undoubtedly wrote both forms of articulation mark intentionally (Ex. 6.4). But ambiguities still abounded at that time, even with composers who generally took care to make their notation as clear and informative as possible. It cannot be assumed, for example, that because composers

[14] See below.

Ex. 6.4. Reger, *Sechs Burlesquen*, no. 4

did something in one period of their lives or in particular works, the same will have been true at other times or in other instances.

Wagner's practice with respect to dots and strokes is instructive in this respect. In some early autographs he seems exclusively to have employed the dot, while in others he used the stroke (the orthography is not always easy to interpret), but there appears to be no consequential difference. In *Rienzi* and *Der fliegende Holländer*, the predominant form of staccato mark is the dot; strokes are used occasionally, but almost entirely on isolated notes, where they may have been intended to indicate an accented execution, or may simply have become a writing habit with no implications for performance. In *Tannhäuser*, however, Wagner adopted the stroke as his principal staccato mark, and dots became relatively uncommon. In later works he used dots more frequently, but the stroke remained the predominant staccato mark for the rest of his life. In the late autographs at least, there is rarely any ambiguity between the two marks, for while the strokes are clearly vertical lines, the dots tend to be elongated somewhat in a horizontal direction, as do his dots of prolongation (Ex. 6.5). In the operas of his middle period contradictions abound; in the lithographed full score of *Lohengrin* the copyist frequently wrote strokes where Wagner's autograph contains clear dots (for instance, under the slur in bar 15 of the introduction to Act III). Wagner seems, however, to have been more careful to ensure that an accurate differentiation between dots and strokes was made in the printed scores of his later operas.

Only when composers assumed real editorial control over the publication of their work did this problem finally disappear, in the generation of Elgar and Richard Strauss. But the question of what they meant remains less tractable.

Ex. 6.5. Wagner, *Siegfried Idyll*

The Functions of Staccato Marks

Both in theory and in practice, it is clear that staccato marks or other visually identical marks (whether or not a distinction was made between dots and strokes) signified a number of different things. Some of these were quite specialized and are relatively infrequently encountered outside particular repertoires. In French eighteenth-century music, for instance, dots and strokes might be used to warn against the application of inequality. Quantz, too, referred to this function of dots and strokes.[15] In such cases, the theory was that the dot merely prevented inequality and the stroke indicated both equality and staccato.[16] Since French mechanical instruments, even from the early nineteenth century, show a penchant for inequality,[17] this may be a factor worth taking into consideration in the performance of nineteenth-century French music.[18]

A particular use of the staccato mark, which is mentioned by C. P. E. Bach, can be found in the second movement of Beethoven's Violin Sonata op. 30 no. 3 in G major (and perhaps elsewhere in Beethoven's music of that period if it were to be looked for). Throughout this movement, in the autograph, Beethoven consistently placed a staccato stroke not over the first or second note on each appearance of a dotted figure first heard in bar 19, but over the dot of prolongation (Ex. 6.6); the placement is so careful and consistent in each case that it must be deliberate, for it is not characteristic of Beethoven that staccato marks regularly occur so far after the note heads to which they belong. The meaning is almost certainly ♪̣♩ , and Beethoven may possibly have derived this notation directly from the passage added in the 1787 edition of C. P. E. Bach's *Versuch* where he suggests precisely this relationship of staccato mark and dot of prolongation to signify a rest in such a figure. Bach realized the turn shown in Ex. 6.7(*a*) as Ex. 6.7(*b*), then suggested writing it as Ex. 6.7(*c*) or (*d*).[19] It may be that this notational device was used by other composers but, not being sought, has not been noticed.

The use of dots or strokes simply to indicate that the notes so marked were not to be slurred, yet not to specify a genuinely staccato execution, appears to be very common in eighteenth- and nineteenth-century music. In many scores of the period these marks are very regularly encountered in mixed figures of slurred and separate notes, even if the composer hardly ever employed them in other contexts (as was often the case in the second half of the eighteenth

---

[15] *Versuch*, XI, §12.

[16] For a very helpful discussion of the problems surrounding inequality in 18th-c. music see Fuller, 'Notes inégales'.

[17] Fuller ('Notes inégales') mentions a barrel-organ version of the overture to Mozart's *Le nozze di Figaro*.

[18] See also the reference in Bériot's *Méthode* (above, Ch. 4 n. 37).   [19] 1787 edn., i, II, 4, §24.

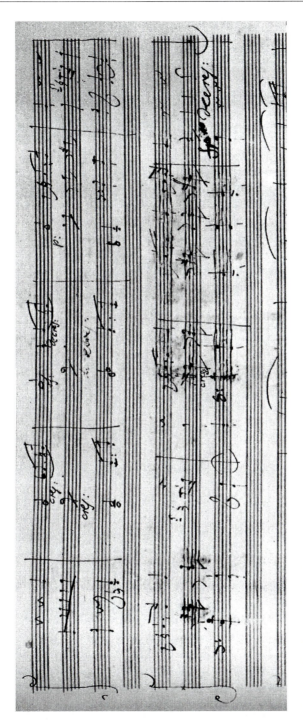

Ex. 6.6. Beethoven, Violin Sonata op. 30/3/ii

Ex. 6.7. C. P. E. Bach, *Versuch*, 1787 edn., i. II, 4, §24

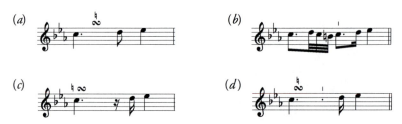

century). In such passages they are necessary to the player, as Koch observed,[20] to make clear which notes are slurred and which separate. In these circumstances the notes with articulation marks were evidently not expected to be played shorter or sharper than notes without articulation marks that occurred in close proximity to them, though whether the marked and unmarked notes were meant to be played staccato, or whether both were intended to receive some kind of non-legato execution, is often unclear. A recognition of this use of staccato marks to clarify the articulation in passages of mixed slurred and separate notes seems to lie behind a comment in Bernhard Romberg's 1840 cello method. He cautioned against misinterpreting the staccato marks in this situation, saying: 'I must here explain that whenever notes are marked to be played alternately slurred and detached, those which are to be played detached (whether marked with a dot thus ···· or dash ''''') should never be made with a close, short bow.'[21] In other words, these notes will not really be staccato in the commonly understood sense of the term, simply unslurred. Linked to this usage is the practice of including a few staccato marks at the beginning of a passage but leaving the rest without, or giving staccato marks to a figure of relatively fast-moving notes. In such instances the performer must again decide whether the composer is indicating a distinct staccato execution for the passage or merely cautioning against slurring. This applies particularly to the music of composers who did not regularly use terms like *sciolto* or *non legato* to clarify their intentions.

Recognizing the significance of a composer's notation in these situations is always difficult and seldom unambiguous. Even the most careful composers of the late eighteenth century did not always convey their intentions in this respect with absolute clarity; even in his late works Mozart sometimes wrote articulation marks on a few notes at the beginning of one or two occurrences of a figure, leaving the majority of its appearances without either slurs or staccato marks. To take one example from many: in the final movement of the String Quartet K. 575 the triplet figurations are mostly without staccato marks (Ex. 6.8(*a*)), but whether this means that they should be performed differently than

---

[20] *Musikalisches Lexikon*, art. 'Abstoßen'.   [21] *A Complete*, 35.

Ex. 6.8. Mozart, String Quartet K. 575/iv

(*a*)

(*b*)

if he had given them staccato marks throughout is uncertain. In a couple of places Mozart did supplement the notes with staccato marks, but his doing so seems principally to have been prompted by a desire to clarify the extent of a carelessly drawn slur rather than to indicate that the notes so marked required a different type of execution from others (Ex. 6.8(*b*)). It may certainly be legitimate to ask whether string players of Mozart's day, employing the types of bowstroke that were familiar to them, would have been prompted to execute notes of this speed differently if they had staccato marks than if they had not.

With most of Mozart's contemporaries, including Haydn, the difficulties posed by incomplete and ambiguous notation are far greater, since they were seemingly much more frequently content to leave many significant decisions about such performance details to the experience or *bon goût* of the executant.

In the first half of the nineteenth century, as Romberg's comment intimates, the practice of using staccato marks to clarify slurring and separation, without necessarily implying staccato execution, was remarkably persistent. The first movement of Beethoven's Fifth Symphony provides a good example of a piece in which staccato marks first appear in mixed passages of slurred and separate notes, and their lack of additional staccato meaning is shown by the fact that they occur only in the part with slurring and cease immediately the slurs finish (Ex. 6.9(*a*)). The length of the quavers and the type of accentuation they require is clearly independent of the presence or absence of staccato marks in this instance. On slower-moving notes the probability that a real staccato was intended seems greater; thus, although the staccato crotchets in Ex. 6.9(*b*)) alternate with slurred pairs, it seems likely that Beethoven wanted them to be played in a different manner from that which he would have expected if he had not given them staccato marks. This is corroborated by the continuation of the staccato marks throughout the following six bars of separate crotchets and their presence in the instruments that have crotchets followed by rests. Schumann, nearly two generations younger, can be seen to have used a similar cautionary notation from time to time. In the scherzo of the Second Symphony the first violins' theme begins without staccato marks on the semiquavers, but in bar 17, following some slurring, the first three separate notes are marked staccato (Ex. 6.10), after which the semiquavers continue as before, without staccato marks.

Ex. 6.9. Beethoven, Fifth Symphony op. 67/i
(*a*)

(*b*)

Ex. 6.10. Schumann, Second Symphony op. 61/ii

Mendelssohn's music, too, contains these patterns. An example that neatly illustrates the purpose of the staccato mark merely to confirm separation from the slur may be taken from the overture *Ruy Blas*, where an isolated staccato mark is found in the parts containing a slur, but not in the parts where there is no slur, in a passage that otherwise has no hint of staccato execution (Ex. 6.11). It also seems questionable whether the very infrequent staccato marks in the 'Con moto' section of the overture to the oratorio *Paulus* are anything but warnings not to slur; an isolated dot on a quaver is there to prevent the slur continuing over the bar-line (Ex. 6.12), while at the point where the slurring of the semiquavers ceases, a few staccato marks reinforce the absence of slurs. This practice gradually disappeared, however, in the course of the nineteenth century.

Ex. 6.11. Mendelssohn, *Ruy Blas*, overture

Ex. 6.12. Mendelssohn, *Paulus*, overture

Most theorists agreed that the staccato mark was, in general, an instruction for shortening the note. How this was to be achieved, and to what degree, depended to a considerable extent on the instrument and the musical circumstances. In string playing, shortening seems often to have been less important than the manner in which the bowstroke was made. Joseph Riepel, considering the matter from the point of view of the string player, stressed the importance of noting whether the staccato occurred in the solo part of a concerto, a melodic part in an ensemble, or an accompanying part. Riepel described staccato notes in concertos as being executed with 'long and powerful strokes of the bow', those in normal ensemble and solo playing as being 'more or less staccato' according to context, and those in accompaniments as being performed with a 'tiny width of bow'; these he marked with three different signs (|||| '''' ....), but, as mentioned above, admitted that a notational differentiation was rarely encountered in practice.[22] Leopold Mozart was less explicit about varieties of staccato, saying simply that a composer writes strokes over notes 'which he wishes to be played each with a strongly accented bowstroke and separated from one another.' (He referred to the dot only in conjunction with slurs.) Quantz made a clearer distinction than Mozart between circumstances in which the principal purpose of a staccato stroke might be to reduce the note by about half its length and those in which an accent was also required; his general rule was:

> if little strokes stand above several notes, they must sound half as long as their true value. But if a little stroke stands above only one note, after which several of lesser value follow, it indicates not only that the note must be played half as long, but also that it must at the same time be accented with pressure of the bow.[23]

In addition, however, he recognized a gentler kind of staccato in string playing (which he marked with dots) that was played 'with short strokes and in a sustained manner'.[24] Also referring to the violin Löhlein mentioned semiquavers with dots simply as being 'separated by the bowstroke in the aforementioned manner'[25] (i.e. with normal separate bows) (Ex. 6.13); but for a passage with staccato strokes he instructed: 'The crotchets over which there are strokes will be played as short as quavers, but sustained with a gentle bow somewhat longer than if they were quavers with quaver rests'[26] (Ex. 6.14). He appears to have been less concerned about the accent implications of the mark than Mozart.

Ex. 6.13. Löhlein, *Anweisung zum Violinspielen*, 33

Ex. 6.14. Löhlein, *Anweisung zum Violinspielen*, 73

²² *Gründliche Erklärung*, 15.   ²³ *Versuch*, XVII, 2, §27.   ²⁴ Ibid. 2, §12 .
²⁵ *Anweisung zum Violinspielen*, 32.   ²⁶ Ibid. 72.

For keyboard, in the second half of the eighteenth century, C. P. E. Bach instructed that staccato notes 'are always held for a little less than half their notated length',[27] while Türk considered that the finger should be lifted from the key on notes with staccato marks 'when close to half the value of the written note is past'. Conscious of the strong association between staccato and accent Türk continued: 'I should not have to mention that notes that are to be played gently can also be staccato; for all that, however, one hears some players who perform all staccato notes loud without exception, quite in conflict with the correct expression.' Echoing and expanding on Bach's opinion, he also cautioned that:

In performance of detached notes one must especially take into account the prevailing character of the composition, the tempo, the prescribed loudness and softness, etc. If the character of a piece is serious, tender, sad, etc. then the detached notes should not be played as short as in pieces of a lively, playful, etc. character. The notes that should be shortly detached, that are mixed into a melodious Adagio, should not be made as short as in an Allegro. In *forte* one can generally staccato more shortly than in *piano*. Leaping notes are, as a whole, played with a shorter staccato than intervals that progress stepwise, etc.[28]

Türk was at pains to point out, as mentioned earlier, that there were some circumstances in which a note with a staccato mark (stroke) should be shortened, but given absolutely no accent; for instance, when the stroke indicated the end of a phrase at an *Abzug* (see Ex. 4.7), or, more confusingly, when the figure ended with a metrically strong beat (Ex. 6.15).[29]

Ex. 6.15. Türk, *Klavierschule*, VI, 2, §24

There seems indeed to have been some significant lack of agreement, probably dependent on the tradition to which a writer belonged as well as the instrument concerned, about the accent element in staccato. The anonymous author of a British publication, *New Instructions for Playing the Harpsichord Pianoforte, or Organ etc.* (*c*.1790), considered that 'Staccato marks ''''' or ···· intimate the Notes must be touched very lightly with taste and spirit, keeping the

---

[27] *Versuch*, i, III, §17.

[28] *Klavierschule*, VI, 3, §36. A very similar piece of advice is given in the fifth edition of Löhlein's *Clavier-Schule*, edited and revised by Witthauer in 1791. He observed: 'How short the attack on notes that are to be staccatoed should really be cannot be determined in general, for it depends as much on the length and shortness of the notes as on the faster or slower tempo of the piece and its character. . . . It is therefore a great error, which is often committed, if all notes on which a staccato mark stands, are, without any consideration, made very short and very strong. Thereby many a piece acquires a very false and often really barbarous character' (p. 18).

[29] *Klavierschule*, VI, 2, §22.

tone off the Note not above half its natural Length.'[30] (On the organ and harpsichord, of course, any degree of percussive accent would have been impossible.) And John Erhardt Weippert's *The Pedal Harp Rotula* (1800) said simply that strokes or dots show that the notes 'must be played in a very distinct manner', giving a musical example in which half of each staccato note, of whatever length, is replaced by a rest.[31] In 1801 Clementi, in a similar vein, referred to staccato marks merely in terms of length, observing that the Italian word *staccato* denotes 'DISTINCTNESS, and SHORTNESS of sound',[32] and his explanation of the various degrees of staccato, which he designates by strokes, dots, and dots under slurs, was entirely in terms of length. Louis Adam's 1804 *Méthode*, in many respects indebted to Clementi, went a small stage further by defining these three degrees of staccato as in Ex. 6.16. This simple definition was taken up by many later nineteenth-century writers. However, as has already been mentioned in the section on accent marks, there was a growing divergence between those (predominantly keyboard players) who focused on the shortening aspect of staccato and those who emphasized its accent properties.

Ex. 6.16. Adam, *Méthode*, 154–5

Fröhlich's treatment of the execution of staccato in oboe playing, although employing the same distinctions of strokes, dots, and dots under slurs, contrasts with that of the pianists just mentioned. He observed:

On account of clarification for the student we will give a threefold specification of the types of nuances of the so-called tongue staccato [*Zungen-Stosse*]; the first, where the notes are staccatoed very short and with the greatest possible power, is notated as at a); the second, which we could call the soft staccato in contrast to the first, the hardest, in which the staccato is not executed with that force, but where, so to speak, the note receives some check during the staccato itself, is notated as at b); finally the third, yet more gently treated, with its own soft character, which almost depicts the connection between staccato and legato, is

Ex. 6.17. Fröhlich, *Musikschule*, ii. 40

---

[30] (London, [c.1790]), 4.
[31] *The Pedal Harp Rotula, and New Instructions for that Instrument* (London, [c.1800]), 5.
[32] *Introduction*, 9.   [33] *Musikschule*, ii. 40.

shown as at c). [Ex. 6.17]³³

Interestingly, Fröhlich (or rather the author from whom he pirated his material) did not acknowledge the clarinet to be capable of such a wide range of staccato attack as either oboe or bassoon, and no strokes, only dots, occur in the clarinet section of his tutor.

In fact, among German musicians, while the accent effect of staccato was more or less universally recognized, there seems to have been considerable doubt about the degree of separation required. A. B. Marx proposed a less extreme shortening of the notes than Adam, regarding the stroke as shortening a note by a half and the dot by a quarter, but cautioned that 'In both cases the exact amount of time that is to be subtracted from their original value remains undecided.' ³⁴ Marx's older contemporary Johann Daniel Andersch also seems to have felt that performers should be careful not to make too much separation, for he gave the following definition of 'Abstossen, *Staccare, Détaché*': 'Deliver the notes short and somewhat prominently, without, however, making their separation strikingly perceptible to the ear.'³⁵

In string playing the seeds of confusion over the meaning of the two signs in terms of bowstroke (therefore also of accent, length etc.) were sprouting vigorously by the 1830s;³⁶ and agreement over the significance of staccato marks in general can hardly have been helped by Spohr's employment of them in his influential *Violinschule* of 1832 (which used strokes throughout, except under slurs), for, as mentioned above, having given an exercise consisting of quavers marked with staccato strokes (Ex. 6.18), Spohr instructed the pupil:

each note receives a separate bowing. This bowing (called by the French, *détaché*) is made with a steady back-arm and as long strokes as possible, at the upper part of the bow. The notes must be perfectly equal both in power and duration, and succeed each other in such a manner, that, in changing from the down to the up-bow or the reverse, no break or chasm may be observed.³⁷

Yet, making no notational differentiation, he also used staccato strokes in passages where he specified the short, sharp, martelé bowstroke, which required both accent and separation.³⁸

Ex. 6.18. Spohr, *Violin School,* 118

³⁴ *Universal School*, 76.   ³⁵ *Musikalisches Wörterbuch* (Berlin, 1829), art. 'Abstossen'.
³⁶ See Ch. 3.   ³⁷ *Violin School,* 118.
³⁸ Particular relationships between staccato notation and string bowing are further considered in Ch. 7 below.

It is rare to encounter any direct corroboration of particular composers' usages of these signs, but a few scraps of evidence may occasionally be found; for instance, when a composer accompanied particular forms of staccato marks with explanatory instructions. Meyerbeer's use of the staccato stroke in his Parisian operas certainly seems to have approached the French view of it as light and short in contrast to a heavier and less short dot. This is strongly suggested by a passage in *Les Huguenots* where he gave staccato strokes to the piccolo and staccato dots to the bassoons; evidently not trusting his players to recognize his intentions, he added the supplementary instruction *toujours p. et très détaché* (always piano and very detached) under the piccolo part, while for the bassoons he wrote *bien marqué et détaché* (well marked and detached) (Ex. 6.19).

Ex. 6.19. Meyerbeer, *Les Huguenots*, no. 4

Another scrap of evidence that casts light on Brahms's intentions when he wrote strokes as staccato marks occurs in a letter to Joachim of 1879,[39] where he comments that instead of Joachim's suggested articulation for a figure in the last movement of his Violin Concerto op. 77 with dots under a slur (i.e. the violinist's sharply separated martelé-type staccato), he would have used staccato strokes (*scharfe Strichpunkte*) (Ex. 6.20).[40]

Ex. 6.20. Brahms, Violin Concerto op. 77/iii

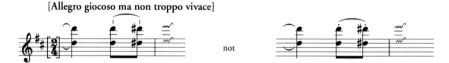

In view of the pervasive lack of consensus about and consistency in the meaning of articulation marks, however, it may seem hopeless, without firm information from composers themselves, or from sources close to them, to determine what they intended. Indeed, certainty about a composer's intentions in any given situation is only rarely to be expected. The frustratingly small

[39] Cited at length below.   [40] Brahms, *Briefwechsel* (Berlin, 1907–22), vi. 146.

amount of persuasive evidence for particular usages may, nevertheless, be valu-
ably supplemented by a consideration of composers' notational practices in
relation to prevailing attitudes to the way in which musical context affected
performance style. We cannot hope to understand the relationship between
eighteenth- and nineteenth-century notation and performance in the way that
accomplished musicians of that period, with a lifetime's experience, would
have understood it; but the more we are aware of the things that conditioned
that experience and the more prepared we are to suspend our own preconceptions about what is 'musical', the more apt we are to develop a reliable intuition
for the expectations that lay behind the notation. The inclusion of particular
forms of articulation marks in music of this period is, therefore, likely to be less
reliable as a guide to the appropriate style of delivery for a specific passage than
an understanding of the technical and stylistic characteristics of vocal and
instrumental performance with which composer and performer would have
been familiar, and an awareness of the factors that conditioned their responses
to different types and genres of music.

Musical Context as a Clue to Execution

Many clues towards achieving an appropriate style of execution may be found
in the eighteenth-century attitude towards musical context. Throughout most
of the second half of the century there was a strong connection between the
type of music and the style of execution. An adagio required a more sustained
style of performance than an andante, and an andante would not invite as
detached a performance as an allegro; a solo part would not be performed in the
same style as an accompaniment; church music, chamber music, and opera
would each require different approaches; the same music notated in 3/2 would
not elicit the same performance style as it would if it were written in 3/8, even
if it were played at the same tempo; and so on.[41] Consequently, a note, with or
without an articulation mark, would be played in very different ways in different musical contexts. The nationality and background of the performer would
also have a powerful influence on the manner of performance.

Many late eighteenth-century writers, for instance, emphasized the necessity of a detached manner of playing in faster movements and a smoother style
of performance in adagio, regardless of the speed of the individual notes. The
logical conclusion from this is, as Reichardt observed in connection with
orchestral playing,[42] that if composers wanted to go against the ruling character of a piece they would have to indicate it in some way.

---

[41] The concept of 'heavy and light' performance style, which took account of these factors, is examined
separately in Ch. 16.

[42] *Ueber die Pflichten*, 25–6. See Ch. 10 below for details of Reichardt's view of the ways in which tempo
affected the bowstroke.

Instances where such considerations appear to have been taken into account can be found in Mozart and Haydn. In *Don Giovanni* Don Ottavio's substitute aria 'Della sua pace' is an Andantino sostenuto in which players might be expected to have interpreted staccato marks with very little shortening or accent; thus in bar 16, when the music becomes more agitated, Mozart wrote not only strokes over the quavers in the bass, but also the instruction 'staccato', presumably to obtain a more sharply detached execution (Ex. 6.21). A similar use of the word 'staccato' to ensure that the notes will be significantly shortened can be seen in bar 3 of the Adagio of Haydn's Symphony no. 102. In this example Haydn's inconsistency of notation is particularly revealing: in bar 1 there are quavers with staccato marks followed by rests for all the lower strings, but in bar 3 the second violin has quavers and rests while viola, cello, and bass have crotchets with staccato marks and also the word 'staccato' (Ex. 6.22). It can hardly be doubted that Haydn wanted the same effect from all the lower strings in bar 3, and it may reasonably be assumed that it was meant to be the same as in bar 1; this being so, there are three different notations in close proximity indicating the same thing. It is surely significant that Haydn appears to have felt that staccato marks alone on the crotchets would not obtain the required shortening from the players.

The relationship between context and execution continued to be important in the nineteenth century, but changing stylistic criteria brought about some highly significant shifts of emphasis in the latter part of the eighteenth century. These were, perhaps, directly influenced by the development of the violin bow and the piano's increasing capability of producing a convincing cantabile, though both of these phenomena were themselves driven by the quest for greater sustaining power and tonal variety in instrumental performance. Comparison of Reichardt's account of the type of bowstrokes appropriate to different kinds of music with the treatment of precisely the same matter in Baillot, Rode, and Kreutzer's *Méthode de violon* (1803) and other early nineteenth-century treatises that are apparently indebted to it (for example, Bartolomeo Campagnoli's *Nouvelle méthode de la mécanique du jeu de violon*[43]) illuminates several important differences. In the *Méthode*, the basically legato treatment of the bowstroke required for adagio is extended to allegro and even presto. And in adagio the notes that are marked staccato seem to be required to be played in an even more connected manner than was suggested by Reichardt, the staccato presumably being expressed rather by accent and nuance than separation. This is quite clearly the style of playing adopted by the Viotti school

---

[43] (Leipzig, 1824). A date of *c*.1797 has conventionally been associated with an original Italian edition, but it has been impossible to trace it in any library, and there does not appear to be any reliable evidence that such an edition ever existed.

Ex. 6.21. Mozart, 'Dalla sua pace' K. 540a (substitute aria for *Don Giovanni*)

Ex. 6.22. Haydn, Symphony no. 102/ii

and its followers, whose supremacy in the first decades of the nineteenth century was virtually unchallenged.[44]

In string playing the ability to produce a seamless sound with separate bows remained a central tenet of teaching throughout the nineteenth century, as demonstrated by Moser's comments in the violin school he published, together with Joachim, in 1905. But, at the same time, other influences, from Paganini, from the Franco-Belgian school, and so on, led to the accumulation of many further techniques of bowing that widened the range of articulation of which the instrument was considered routinely to be capable. Other instruments and even the voice followed the lead of the violinists. It is well known, for instance, that the development of Liszt's transcendent technique, which depended as much on the variety of sound he was able to elicit from the instrument as from sheer virtuosity, was directly inspired by Paganini's violin playing. And, as the scores of Meyerbeer's Parisian operas indicate, the voice was often increasingly expected to accomplish quasi-instrumental effects.

[44] See Ch. 7 and, for the relationship of bowstroke to tempo, Ch. 10.

The signs available to composers for specifying articulation were too imprecise and, even where differentiated meanings were intended for dots and
strokes, too crude to do more than hint at the intended effect, and the practice
that began tentatively in the eighteenth century of providing further written
qualifications or other notational clarification became even more necessary in
the nineteenth century. The overture to *Der Freischütz* provides an interesting
example of articulation marks of the same type being used in close proximity
with apparently different meanings. In the first four bars of the Ex. 6.23
Weber probably intended the articulation marks merely to make clear that the
notes in question are unslurred; in flutes, oboes, clarinets, bassoons, and violins, bars containing mixed slurs and articulation marks are followed by a bar
of separate notes with dots in the woodwind where Weber has, in addition,
written the word 'staccato', presumably to obtain a real staccato execution in
that bar.

Since it appears that nineteenth-century string players saw no contradiction
in playing fairly fast notes in allegro movements in an essentially connected
manner, even if they had dots or strokes on them, composers of the period
needed to make their intentions clear when they wanted a short, sharp staccato.
The problem that faced eighteenth-century composers in slow movements was
thus extended to fast movements in the nineteenth century. The increasingly
frequent inclusion of words such as 'staccato', 'staccatissimo', 'leggiero', 'marcato' and so on in addition to articulation marks testifies to nineteenth-century
composers' concern to clarify their intentions. The passage from *Der Freischütz*
quoted above neatly illustrates the fact that a careful composer now needed
to specify staccato, as well as writing staccato marks, in contexts where an
eighteenth-century player would naturally have used a detached style of performance (i.e. in an allegro), but where a nineteenth-century player would tend
towards a more connected execution.

During the first half of the nineteenth century string instruments seem to
have been regarded as being incapable of an effective staccato on faster-moving
notes. The martelé is only practicable up to a certain tempo, and, especially in
Germany, bounced bowstrokes were widely resisted until well into the nineteenth century. Weber, who is known to have admired Spohr's playing, certainly seems to have been conscious of this distinction and, with his customary
sensitivity to orchestral effect, knew how to use it to good purpose. This is well
illustrated by another passage from his *Freischütz* overture (Ex. 6.24). Here the
strings have a downward scale of separate quavers which would, especially in
view of the absence of any kind of articulation marks, certainly have been
played with the détaché bowing described by Spohr; this is followed by the
scale a third higher on wind instruments where Weber has not only added staccato marks but again written the word 'staccato'. The passage is later repeated
with exactly the same markings.

Ex. 6.23. Weber, *Der Freischütz*, overture

Ex. 6.24. Weber, *Der Freischütz*, overture

Almost every important composer of the early nineteenth century can similarly be seen to have used 'staccato' or other instructions for accent, shortening,
or particular styles of performance on notes in allegro movements which a generation earlier might anyway have been expected to be played in a detached
manner. Cherubini frequently included the instruction 'staccato' with dotted
figures in allegro movements, for example in the overture to *Médée* (Ex. 6.25),

Ex. 6.25. Cherubini, *Médée*, overture

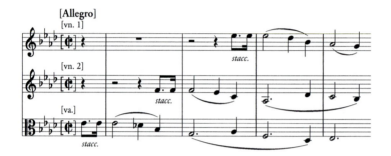

presumably to elicit the type of detached performance that Mozart had, on
occasion, taken great pains to indicate by writing rests in dotted figures in slow
movements (Ex. 6.26). Mendelssohn sometimes made an extremely interesting
juxtaposition of notes that were marked with staccato marks and others that
were shortened by means of rests (Ex. 6.27). In terms of string playing this
probably implied a slightly separated bowstroke for the former and a more pronounced separation for the latter, perhaps with an off-the-string bowstroke.
The relatively frequent occurrence of successions of semiquavers followed by
semiquaver rests in Mendelssohn's fast movements[45] seems almost certain to
have been linked with the early nineteenth-century tendency to employ con-

Ex. 6.26. Mozart, Mass in C minor, Qui tollis

---

[45] e.g. in the Scherzo of the Octet op. 20.

Ex. 6.27. Mendelssohn, String Quartet op. 13/iii

nected bowstrokes in allegro movements even where staccato marks were present.

Other Articulation Marks

In addition to the dot and stroke, later nineteenth-century composers employed other signs as articulation marks. These, like dots and strokes, have already been discussed in the context of accentuation,[46] and they are seldom without an element of accentual implication. Nevertheless, some theorists liked to see them primarily as indicating degrees and types of articulation. Towards the end of the century Riemann gave the following list of markings, some of which were in general use at the time and some of which will scarcely be encountered outside Riemann's editions. It is questionable whether his use of them corresponds with that of all the composers who employed them at that time, but, in view of Riemann's respected position, his definitions may have influenced some of his contemporaries. The list is given here as it occurs in the English version of the preface to his edition of Schubert's *Moments musicaux* op. 94 and two scherzos;[47] additional comments that only appear in the German version, or phrases that may have a slightly different significance in the German, are given in square brackets together with a literal English translation:

∧ a slight *prolongation* in the time of the note
> a *reinforcement* of the sound
− *full holding* of the note until the beginning of the next one (*legato* touch)
⨪ the note *to be held nearly the full length* and to be slightly detached from the next one (*non legato, portato*)
· the note to be more detached than ⨪ [*leichtes Absetzen*—light separation]: half *staccato*
▾ the note to be struck sharply [*scharfes Abstossen*—sharp staccato]: quite *staccato* [*wirkliches staccato*—real staccato]

[46] See Ch.3.   [47] (Brunswick, Litolff, [c.1890]); copy in the Bodleian Library, Oxford.

⌣ a light touch and *not quite legato* [(*meist nach einer Note mit* ∧) *leichtere Tongeben und unvollkommene Bindung* (*Abzug*)—(mostly after a note with ∧) lighter delivery of the note and imperfect connection (*Abzug*)]

, (comma) indicates a short [(*meist kurzen*)—(mostly short)] pause not otherwise marked, especially before the re-entering of a theme.

The last two signs are certainly confined, for the most part, to didactic works. It is interesting to note that although the implication of accent is present in Riemann's definition of the staccato stroke, his explanation of the horizontal line and the horizontal line with dot here contains no suggestion of added weight.

Slurs and Articulation

The principal meaning of the slur was to signify that the notes within it should be smoothly connected to one another, as in a vocal melisma or a figure performed by a string player in a single, continuous and even bowstroke. The slur may carry other messages about the execution of the legato phrase, which must be deduced partly from the period, background, and notational habits of the composer, and partly from the musical context. It is important, for instance, to determine whether the music is conceived in terms of strings, wind, keyboard or voice, whether it shows other evidence of having been notated with care, and so on. Since the 'natural' pre-classical bowstroke implied a degree of accent at the start, and an element of separation between strokes, there was an early tendency to see that style of performance as, to a certain extent, inherent in the notation and integral to the meaning of the slur in music for other instruments.

Slurs, or signs that are graphically indistinguishable from slurs, however, could signify a number of quite different things. In vocal music the slur might be used, in its general sense of legato, to clarify the grouping of notes on a single syllable (though this was not a consistent convention during the period); but it might also specify an audible portamento, sometimes between notes on different syllables of text.[48] Of course, the same sign often means a tie, but it may not in all instances indicate a simple prolongation of the note. One persistent curiosity of notation that certainly remained common until the generation of Berlioz and Schumann was the practice of using a two-beat note tied to a one-beat note instead of a two-beat note with a dot in feminine cadences or similar contexts (Ex. 6.28), and it seems likely that the notation was intended to warn the performers with the sustained note that they should nuance it in the normal manner required for such cadences. What Beethoven meant by his occasional use of notes that appear to be superfluously tied, most notably in the *Große Fuge* op. 133, remains questionable; but he may well have intended some-

[48] See Ch. 15.

Ex. 6.28. Sterndale Bennett, Fantasie-Overture *Paradise and the Peri* op. 42

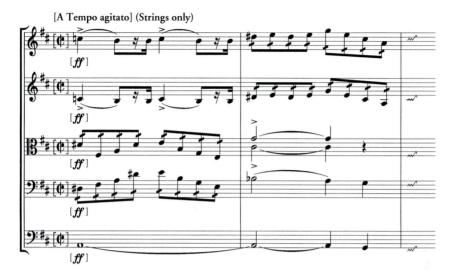

thing similar to the shortening and diminuendo applied to feminine cadences.[49] Not all notes on the same pitch that are joined in this manner are meant to be played without separation. Quite apart from disputed questions, such as whether the tied notes in the Scherzo of Beethoven's Cello Sonata op. 69 require a repetition of the second note as recommended by Czerny[50] (perhaps bearing in mind the string players' practice of emphasizing the strong beat in a syncopation[51]), it was by no means uncommon for composers to use slurs (without any other articulation mark) over groups of notes repeated at the same pitch to obtain a very connected portato, though in these cases the symbol will usually encompass more than two notes. Instances of this can be found in works as diverse as Salieri's *Der Rauchfangkehrer* and Wagner's *Parsifal*.[52] From an early stage, successive notes at the same pitch were sometimes included within a slur over a phrase or figure, thus demanding the minutest separation to articulate these as repeated notes within the general context of the legato phrase (Ex. 6.29). Furthermore, the appearance in eighteenth-century music of longer slurs than usual may occasionally be a form of shorthand for the continuation of a slurring pattern already established, for example in Galuppi's *La diavolessa* (Ex. 6.30).

[49] See Emil Platen, 'Zeitgenössische Hinweise zur Aufführungspraxis der letzten Streichquartette Beethovens', in Rudolf Klein, ed., *Beiträge '76–78: Beethoven Kolloquium 1977; Dokumentation und Aufführungspraxis* (Kassel, 1978), 100–7.

[50] And similar cases in the piano sonatas opp. 106 and 110; see Paul Badura-Skoda, 'A Tie is a Tie is a Tie', *Early Music*, 16 (1988), 84 ff.

[51] See Ch. 2 'Syncopation'.
[52] See below, 'Articulated Slurs'.

Ex. 6.29. Beethoven, Fifth Symphony op. 67/iv

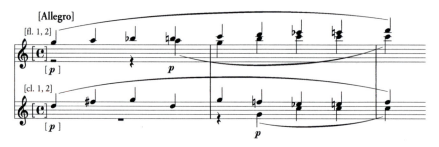

Ex. 6.30. Galuppi, *La diavolessa*, Act I, Scene ii, Österreichische Nationalbibliothek, Vienna, MS 18070; pub. in fac. in the series *Italian Opera 1640–1770* (New York and London, Garland 1978)

Apart from these primary meanings, a similar symbol could be used to designate something quite different. In Haydn's string music, for instance, it sometimes identified a passage that should be played on the same string (Ex. 6.31). It was also employed to define a triplet or other irregular grouping, often without any implications of slurring. And Berlioz, for instance, used a slur-like sign in horn parts to show the application of hand stopping without change of embouchure.[53] In French and French-influenced eighteenth-century music a long slur might indicate that the normal inequality did not apply to the notes that were encompassed by it.[54]

Ex. 6.31. Haydn, String Quartet op. 64/4/ii

[53] Macdonald, 'Two Peculiarities', 25.   [54] Fuller, 'Notes inégales', 422.

The Nuanced Slur and the Slur as Legato

In piano playing there was more or less universal agreement throughout the nineteenth century that slurred pairs should be performed approximately as described in 1804 by Adam, who observed:

> when there are only two notes connected together and when the two notes are of the same value or when the second of them has half the value of the first, it is necessary, to express this slur, in the *forte* as well as in the *piano*, to press the finger a little on the first and to lift it on the second, taking away half its value while touching the second more gently than the first. [Ex. 6.32][55]

Ex. 6.32. Adam, *Méthode*, 153

Sometimes greater shortening of the second note was recommended, for instance by Crelle, who illustrated the second of slurred pairs of semiquavers as demisemiquavers.[56] And as the opinions of Hummel, Kalkbrenner (above, Ex. 2.1), Czerny, Moscheles, and others indicate, shortening of the final note was also regarded by many nineteenth-century pianists as appropriate to longer slurred groups.

The detaching of the last note under slurs, particularly in the case of equal pairs where the first note could be seen as an appoggiatura, was known in German as the *Abzug*. This term is quite often encountered in late eighteenth- and early nineteenth-century writings, and its discussion by various writers offers a useful glimpse of some of the issues surrounding articulation in these circumstances.

Late eighteenth-century views on the performance of the *Abzug* are neatly summarized in J. F. Reichardt's treatise *Ueber die Pflichten des Ripien-Violinisten* of 1776. He observed:

> The appoggiatura of fixed duration always receives a stronger pressure of the bow than the note itself. It is erroneous, however, if the note after an appoggiatura is for this reason always taken off. One can divide *Abzuge* into the false [*uneigentliche*] and the genuine [*eigentliche*] *Abzug*. In the case of the false *Abzug*, which is appropriate to any note that has an appoggiatura, the bow carries on more weakly, or even remains stationary on the string. In the case of the genuine *Abzug*, which is appropriate to any note that has an appoggiatura and is followed by a rest, the bow is lifted completely from the strings as soon as the note has been faintly heard.

---

[55] *Méthode*, 151.   [56] *Einiges*, 93.

The lifting of the bow applies to every note that is followed by a rest, with this exception, that a note without an appoggiatura is held for its full value before the bow is lifted; a note with an appoggiatura, however,—like the last syllable in speech—will be heard as extremely short and weak, as long as a rest follows. Since this is the last, and therefore will not be obscured by any following one, it will always be heard strongly enough. In any case, the appoggiatura will cause the listener to have such a lively expectation of the following note that the smallest touch of the note is sufficient to satisfy him.[57]

This treatment of appoggiaturas became associated, to a considerable extent, with the performance of any paired notes, and to some degree with the execution of other short slurred groups. But even in the eighteenth century there were differing opinions about the niceties of performance in these circumstances.

Koch referred obliquely to Reichardt's distinction between the 'true' and 'false' *Abzug* in his discussion of the performance of appoggiaturas:

This soft slurring of the appoggiatura to its following main note is called the *Abzug*, on the execution of which the opinion of musicians is still divided. Some hold namely that, for example, on the keyboard the finger or on the violin the bow should be gently lifted after the main note; others, however, regard this as unnecessary, so long as a rest does not follow the main note.[58]

Later in the nineteenth century Johann Andreas Christian Burkhard considered that the *Abzug* was

In general the manner of handling the various refined instruments by the use of the finger for bringing out and separating the various notes; or the manner in which the principal note that follows an appoggiatura is taken off by the bow on string instruments and by the finger on keyboard instruments, by which one can distinguish the true and false *Abzug* according to whether the bow or finger is fully lifted from the string as soon as the note has been faintly heard, or goes on more weakly, or remains on the string.[59]

Other definitions of *Abzug* in the first half of the nineteenth century were given in 1827 by Andersch, who regarded *Abzug* as signifying 'A manner of performance by which one gives the strongest pressure to an appoggiatura which is attached before a main note and finishes the latter softly;'[60] and in 1840 by August Gathy, who referred to it as 'the lifting or drawing away of the bow from the string on instruments of the violin family or of the finger from the key or from the hole on keyboard or wind instruments'.[61] But by this stage the terminology seems to have had a rather more tenuous connection with contemporary practice.

There is evidence that the theoretical discussion of the 'true' and 'false' *Abzug* may be related to the manner in which these figures were notated in the

---

[57] pp. 41–3.   [58] *Musikalisches Lexikon*, art. 'Vorschlag'.
[59] *Neues vollständiges musikalisches Wörterbuch* (Ulm, 1832), art. 'Abzug'.
[60] *Musikalisches Wörterbuch*, art. 'Abzug'.
[61] *Musikalisches Conversations-Lexikon*, 2nd edn. (Leipzig, 1840), art. 'Abzug'.

eighteenth and nineteenth century. In numerous cases composers took considerable extra trouble to shorten the second note and write a rest. Instances of slurred pairs both with and without a shortened final note (indicated by either a rest or staccato mark) are legion in the works of Haydn, Mozart, Beethoven, and Schubert.

Brahms's correspondence with Joachim in 1879 provides a revealing late nineteenth-century perspective on the different attitudes towards the execution of short phrasing slurs of a pianist who was also a great composer and a violinist with considerable talent in composition. Joachim, approaching the matter from the point of view of the executant, acknowledged the difficulty of deciding whether slurs were an indication for general legato or for phrasing, observing that it was

tricky to decide with slurs where they merely mean: so and so many notes in the same bowstroke, or on the other hand, where they signify meaningful division of groups of notes, for instance: [Ex. 6.33(*a*)] could just as well sound connected, even when played with different bowstrokes, while on the piano this would have to sound approximately thus in all circumstances: [Ex. 6.33(*b*)].

Ex. 6.33.
(*a*)

(*b*)

Brahms disagreed, remarking that

the slur over several notes does not reduce the value of any of them. It signifies legato, and one makes it according to groups, phrases, or whims [*Gruppe, Periode oder Laune*]. Only over two notes does it reduce the value of the last one: [Ex. 6.34(*a*)] With longer groups of notes: [Ex. 6.34(*b*)] would be a freedom and refinement in performance, which, to be sure, is generally appropriate.

Ex. 6.34.
(*a*)

(*b*)

In other words, Brahms regarded the shortening of the last note in pairs as obligatory, whether or not a rest or staccato mark was indicated, and in a longer group as optional. There is also a suggestion that, as a composer, Brahms did not concern himself with specifying all the refinements of phrasing that he might expect the performer to contribute, for he added: 'With me such considerations are unprofitable [*unnütz*]. But you have the broom in your hand [Joachim was at that time working on the solo part of Brahms's Violin Concerto] and we have much to sweep up.'[62]

There is evidence, despite Brahms's opinion to the contrary (which may, perhaps, have owed something to his antiquarian interests), that even the distinctive execution of slurred pairs was becoming increasingly rare during the nineteenth century. Mendelssohn in 1845 felt it necessary to point out that these figures would have been given an accent-diminuendo treatment in Handel's day, implying that it was no longer automatically customary to perform them in that manner.[63]

In Brahms's music, however, there are many instances where the traditional nuanced performance of slurred pairs will certainly have been intended. In the third movement of his String Quartet op. 51 no. 1 (Ex. 6.35), this is made a feature of the music. The occurrence of slurs over a pair of conjunct descending notes in other works by Brahms often seems to call for a similar treatment, for instance in the Adagio of the Clarinet Quintet op. 115 (Ex. 6.36). In this extremely legato context physical separation is unlikely to have been envisaged, but accent-diminuendo on each pair (albeit quite discreet) may well have been. In many other cases in Brahms's string music the degree of accent in slurred pairs seems likely to have been little more than would be achieved by the bow change, for instance in the first movement of the String Quartet op. 67 (Ex. 6.37). Tempo will often be a deciding factor.

Ex. 6.35. Brahms, String Quartet op. 51/1/iii

Ex. 6.36. Brahms, Clarinet Quintet op. 115/ii

[62] *Briefwechsel*, vi. 149–53.
[63] See Nicholas Temperley, 'Berlioz and the Slur', *Music & Letters*, 50 (1969), 391.

Ex. 6.37. Brahms, String Quartet op. 67/i

The most significant cause of ambiguity in the meaning of the slur through-out the period, as the Brahms–Joachim correspondence implies, was the ten-dency to indicate sections of continuous legato with a succession of fairly short slurs (usually over a single bar), something technically necessary in string writ-ing, where the bow was only capable of slurring a limited number of notes without changing. This was also common in eighteenth-century and early nineteenth-century keyboard writing and was a cause of frequent confusion to less experienced performers. Before the end of the eighteenth century it is rare to find longer slurs than are practicable in a single bowstroke. This is the case even in wind music, where the breath can sustain a more extended unbroken phrase, or in keyboard music, where the length of a legato passage is unlimited, provided it does not (before the advent of the pedal) contain leaps that go beyond the reach of the hand. The connection between the slur and string bowing remained strong in the minds of eighteenth-century musicians; Löhlein, for instance, remarked in his *Clavier-Schule*, when explaining the use of slurs and articulation: 'The keyboard is not so perfect with respect to expres-sion as string and wind instruments. However, uniform notes can be per-formed in a variety of ways, and one can imitate some kinds of bowstrokes.'[64]

Where eighteenth-century and early nineteenth-century composers wrote a succession of shorter slurs it may not be the case that there was an intention to signify expressive accent at the beginning followed by diminuendo and short-ening of the last note for each slurred group, particularly if the slurs are over a series of whole bars or half-bars. Despite the commonly accepted eighteenth-century convention for the articulated performance of slurred figures, Türk expressly warned against their separation in circumstances such as Ex. 6.38(*a*), saying that they must not be performed as in Ex. 6.38(*b*).[65] And Czerny still felt it necessary in 1839 to state that when slurs 'are drawn over several notes, although the slurs are not continuous, but are broken into several lines, they are considered as forming but one, and no perceptible separation must take place'.[66] He added that where a composer wished a break to occur between slurs he would have to place a dot or dash over the last note under the slur.

A further problem concerned the question of whether accent or dynamic nuance (other than diminuendo) was permissible within a slur. Theoretical treatment of the subject in the early part of the period appears largely to exclude

[64] 2nd edn., 69.   [65] *Klavierschule*, VI, §§19–21.   [66] *Piano Forte School*, i. 187.

Ex. 6.38. Türk, *Klavierschule*, VI, 2: (*a*) §21; (*b*) §19

(*a*)

(*b*)

such possibilities. At the beginning of the nineteenth century Koch could still describe the slur exclusively in terms of its basic function of articulating a short phrase or figure with an even legato. He maintained that any type of accent or articulation after the first note of a slur was a contradiction of its meaning:

> It is an error in the performance of such slurs if, on string instruments, the performer accents the second, or the note which is tied to the preceding one, with a pressure of the bow or on wind instruments with a fresh pressure of breath; through such an accent the feeling of a renewed attack is to a certain extent aroused, and the real intention and effect of the slur is to a large extent lost.[67]

By the time Koch made that statement he was evidently out of touch with the practice of contemporary composers, but it is surprising how long such ideas persisted, for the much younger musician Philip Corri could still state in 1810 that 'a long slur forbids any emphasis within it'.[68]

Clearly, the longer slurs that begin to be found with increasing frequency during the early years of the nineteenth century, in the works of Beethoven, Clementi, and other composers of their generation, were intended to show that the passage as a whole should be legato, though not necessarily to forbid accentuation, dynamic shaping, or phrasing; nor were the beginnings and ends of such slurs inevitably meant to be distinguished by, respectively, accent and articulation. Even within shorter slurs, accentuation or dynamic nuance (other than the conventional diminuendo) seems often to have been envisaged, though not always indicated. This frequently applies in Beethoven's music, where articulation or accentuation within slurs is sometimes implicit, as in the opening of the Adagio espressivo of the Violin Sonata op. 96 (Ex. 6.39), or sometimes hinted at, for instance by beaming. There are, in fact, numerous situations in music of this period where an accent-diminuendo interpretation of short slurred groups may not be envisaged.

Beethoven's music provides many challenging examples of slurs that do not conform comfortably to theoretical explanations.[69] Consideration of his auto-

---

[67] *Musikalisches Lexikon*, art. 'Legato'.   [68] *L'anima di musica*, 72.

[69] For examples from his piano music see Rosenblum, *Performance Practices*, 164 f.

Ex. 6.39. Beethoven, Violin Sonata op. 96/ii

graphs together with corrected copyists' scores and parts also provides some valuable lessons in the extent to which we may rely upon the notation in the autographs as providing accurate and precise information about what he had in mind, reminding us that twentieth-century notions of accuracy and completeness can rarely be applied, even to the music of the most conscientious composers of this period. An instructive instance may be taken from the Fifth Symphony. The phrase that begins at bar 64 of the last movement makes its first appearance with viola and clarinet in unison, but with two different patterns of slurring (Ex. 6.40); in subsequent appearances of this frequently occurring phrase Beethoven predominantly drew the slur from the second note, but sometimes from the first or, ambiguously, from between the first and second notes. In the copied score and parts that Beethoven himself extensively corrected, however, the copyist almost invariably drew the slur from the first note of the figure; but although Beethoven made many changes to the copies in these bars, occasionally adding missing slurs, he did not in any instance attempt to change the beginning of the copyist's slurs from the first to the second note. Had he wanted any kind of expressive accent on the second note of the figure he would have been bound to do so. (The frequency with which this phrase occurs surely rules out oversight on the composer's part.) The conclusion that Beethoven simply intended to signify a legato execution for the whole phrase is almost inescapable. In the case of this four-note phrase, despite the ambiguity in the beginning of the slur, an accent-diminuendo treatment of the whole figure is plausible from the musical point of view, though it can by no means be certain that Beethoven did not conceive some kind of subsidiary accentuation on the metrically strong third note.

Ex. 6.40. Beethoven, Fifth Symphony op. 67/iv

Some composers, for instance Clementi and Berlioz, adopted the practice of eliding slurs in a manner that seems to suggest accentuation within a context of continuous legato. Similar occasional instances in Beethoven's music appear more likely to result from lengthening a slur to include subsequent notes. Examples where deliberate slur elision seems to be the composer's intention can occasionally be found in Clementi's music,[70] and much more consistently and consequentially in Berlioz's works.[71]

The Long Phrasing Slur

The confusion between string bowing, the employment of slurs to indicate the articulation of short figures in keyboard or wind writing, and the use of longer slurs to show the extent of a melodic phrase or simply to signify legato troubled many later nineteenth-century musicians. Their efforts to make sense of earlier composers' admittedly inconsistent practices added another layer of confusion to the situation, particularly where late nineteenth-century editions obscured the original composer's intentions by replacing short slurs on individual figures with long phrasing slurs.

It is not clear to what extent late nineteenth-century musicians were correct in believing that the slurs employed by earlier composers, particularly in keyboard music, did not adequately represent their musical intentions. It is certainly true that many composers up to and including Mendelssohn's generation were far from consistent in this respect. Yet the difficulty seems partly to have arisen from an assumption that slurs that were merely meant to specify details of legato groupings within the larger phrase were invitations to give the slurred figures a distinctly articulated execution and thus to distort the contours of the musical structure. This was clearly Karl Klindworth's motivation for modifying the slurring in his edition of Mendelssohn's *Lieder ohne Worte*, where he stated in the preface: 'Whenever it seemed desirable for the better understanding of the composer's intentions, I have added phrasing slurs, which extend the short bar-sections into melodic phrases. A comparison of the opening of no. 14 in the old with the present edition will serve to illustrate my method of procedure' (Ex. 6.41).[72] And, with reference to op. 30 no. 1 in E flat, he observed:

The new phrasing-slurs are intended to preserve the pianist from the error of rendering the melody according to the strict rules of pianoforte playing, which would require that in every group of slurred notes the first is to be accented and the last slightly shortened in value, thus dividing it from the following group. In thinking over the manner in which Mendelssohn may have intended the melody to be played I have imagined the style in which, for instance, a great violinist would render the song thus phrased. He would certainly link the last group

[70] Rosenblum, *Performance Practices*, 169 ff.   [71] See Macdonald, 'Two Peculiarities'.
[72] (London, Novello, 1898), p. iii.

Ex. 6.41. Mendelssohn, *Lieder ohne Worte*, ed. Klindworth, p. iii

of notes played with one bow to the first note of the new bow, without shortening its value, and thus he would logically connect phrase to phrase, so that the melody might appeal to our hearts in a broad and unbroken stream.[73]

Klindworth was only twenty-one years younger than Mendelssohn, and, while it is possible that his understanding of the intentions behind the composer's notation may have been incorrect in particular instances, there are no very good grounds for believing that he was fundamentally mistaken about the style in general. If one listens to Joachim's violin playing in his own Romance in C, one hears precisely the kind of performance that Klindworth wished the pianist to achieve; and there is no doubt that Joachim's musicianship was deeply affected by his early association with Mendelssohn. Whatever Mendelssohn may have intended his slurs to convey, it seems very unlikely that he expected them to be played according to what Klindworth called the 'strict rules of pianoforte playing'. Klindworth was certainly not alone among late nineteenth-century musicians in believing that the manner in which most composers employed slurs was often an inadequate guide to the realization of their intentions. Lussy, also, criticized the practice of his contemporaries in this respect.[74]

It was Hugo Riemann, however, who made the most sustained effort to find a mode of notating every aspect of phrasing with the greatest precision. He laid out his premises in detail in 1884,[75] and over the next decades made practical use of his principles in his many editions of late eighteenth-century and nineteenth-century piano music. As he remarked in the preface to his edition of Schubert's *Moments musicaux* op. 94 and two scherzos for Litolff's Verlag,

The principal difference between editions with phrasing marks, and others, is in the **use of the slur**. The curved lines or slurs used to indicate the **legato** touch (very often in an incorrect manner in Music for the Pianoforte, originating from Violin-bowing) reveal the **thematic** analysis of a musical work, the union of motives into phrases and the disjunction of phrases from each other; thus supplying a long-felt want of musical Notation, namely, an **unequivocal punctuation**; enabling the performer (even the least talented) to give a cor-

---

[73] Ibid. pp. v–vi. [74] *Le Rhythme musical,* 66 f.
[75] *Musikalische Dynamik und Agogik: Lehrbuch der musikalische Phrasierung* (Hamburg, 1884).

rect interpretation of musical thoughts. This analysis is rendered more detailed and complete by means of the following sign [Ex. 6.42(*a*)], which shews the extent of the shorter motives contained within a phrase. This sign is sometimes doubled [Ex. 6.42(*b*)], to point out the principal subdivisions of a phrase; and it is always written obliquely [Ex. 6.42(*c*)], where it falls upon a bar[line]. **This sign by no means indicates a disconnection of the phrase in performance**, but is simply intended as an analytical mark; nevertheless, the expression cannot be correct unless the sign is thoroughly understood.

Ex. 6.42.   Schubert, *Moments musicaux* op. 94 no. 1 (Brunswick, Litolff, [*c*.1890])

Klindworth's editions and those of many other late nineteenth-century and early twentieth-century editors, including Donald Francis Tovey, were profoundly affected by Riemann's examples, leading to a host of phrased editions, some of which have remained in use to the present day. The problem with such editions is that although, in general, they may not radically distort the performance style envisaged by the composer, they will always run the risk of obscuring details. In Klindworth's edition of Mendelssohn's *Lieder ohne Worte*, for example, in the fourth bar of Ex. 6.41, where Mendelssohn began a new slur on the final note of the phrase, Klindworth's version may well conceal an intentional connection between the phrase units.

Articulated Slurs

Articulation marks combined with slurs are directly derived from string-playing techniques. The simultaneous employment of these signs originally signified simply that the specified type of articulation should be produced in a single bowstroke rather than with alternate down- and up-bows. But it was not long before composers began to employ the same notations for other instruments and for vocal music, and, as with all types of notation that were widely adopted, subtle and not so subtle differences of usage between different instruments and different schools of composers and performers soon began to emerge.

Another subject addressed in Brahms's correspondence with Joachim illuminates one particular area in which, by the second half of the nineteenth century, there were fundamental and deep-rooted contradictions. Their discussion of these issues was prompted when, during work on Brahms's Violin Concerto, Joachim marked some bowings with dots under a slur which puzzled Brahms; as mentioned above, it is clear that they did not disagree on the musical effect of the passage (i.e. a sharp staccato), merely on the manner of notating it (see Ex. 6.20). Brahms wrote to Joachim:

With what right, since when and on what authority do you violinists write the sign for portamento (⌢⃛) [i.e. portato[76]] where none is intended? You mark the octave passages in the Rondo (⌢̇), and I would use sharp strokes [*scharfe Strichpunkte*] ''. Must that be so? Up to now I have not given in to the violinists with their damned horizontal lines ⌣⌣. Why should ⌢̇ mean anything different to us from what it did to Beethoven?'[77]

Joachim replied with a detailed account of the origins and meanings of these signs as he understood them and remarked that he always cautioned his pupils to take into account whether the composers were pianists or string players when deciding how to execute passages designated with dots under a slur. Joachim thought, erroneously, that a divergence of meaning only originated around 1800.[78]

In fact, the meaning of articulation marks under a slur was already a problem in the middle of the eighteenth century and has continued to cause confusion among performers. The main difficulty is to decide whether the notation indicates sharply separated notes, more gently emphasized and slightly separated, sometimes almost legato notes, or some intermediate degree of articulation, but there is the additional problem in eighteenth- and nineteenth-century string playing of whether sharp separation, if this was envisaged, was intended to be produced by a firm or bouncing bowstroke. Thus the same notation could indicate every degree of articulation, from a pulsation with hardly perceptible separation to a flying staccato. The range of meanings of dots and strokes under slurs in the mid- and later eighteenth century is well illustrated by the following examples.

In 1732 Walther, somewhat vaguely defining the 'Punctus percutiens', remarked that in instrumental and vocal music a dot over or under a note means that it is to be played staccato, but when in instrumental music (by which he obviously means string music) there is also a slur these notes are 'to be executed with a single bowstroke'. The implication here is that the notes are still to be performed staccato.[79]

Twenty-one years later, C. P. E. Bach, from the clavichord player's point of view, regarded dots under a slur as designating portato (*Tragen der Töne*). For German keyboard players of the second half of the eighteenth century, portato seems to have involved a degree of accent on each note but not perceptible

---

[76] A number of 19th-c. composers used the term 'portamento' where 'portato' would now be used. 'Portamento' is used throughout this book for the singer's legato or the audible slide between two notes that is sometimes a consequence of legato, especially in vocal music and string playing. 'Portato' is used to describe all degrees of articulation indicated by dots under slurs which are intermediate between pure legato and a sharply detached staccato. This is a well-established usage: portato notes were defined by Lichtenthal in 1826 as 'those which are marked to occur without the bow being raised from the string . . . therefore they are neither legato nor detached [*sciolto*], but almost dragged, giving to each note a little stroke of the bow' (*Dizionario*, i. 128 and fig. 122).

[77] *Briefwechsel*, vi. 146.   [78] Ibid. 148 ff.

[79] *Musicalisches Lexicon*, art. 'Punctus percutiens'.

separation. Marpurg described it in the following terms: 'When the sign for staccato and that for slurring appear together on various notes that follow one another, this signifies that the notes that are thus designated should be marked with a somewhat strong pressure of the finger and connected together as in normal procedure',[80] while a generation later Türk remarked that 'the little dots show the pressure which each key must receive, and through the slur the player will be reminded to hold on the note after the pressure until its notated value is fully expired'.[81] But when this sign was written over a single note rather than a group of notes it signified the *Bebung* (repeated pressure made without lifting the key, which affects the steadiness of pitch of the note).[82] Yet five years after the publication of C. P. E. Bach's *Versuch* Niccolo Pasquali's *The Art of Fingering the Harpsichord*, apparently leaning towards string playing practice, used dots under a slur to indicate a succession of markedly detached notes all to be played staccatissimo with the same finger.[83]

At about the same time J. F. Agricola explained the singer's portato (though he did not employ the term) in a similar manner to the keyboard portato (the text describes it as notated by 'little strokes [*Strichelchen*]' under a slur, but the accompanying musical example shows dots under a slur); he counselled that such notes 'must neither be detached nor attacked, but each note only marked by means of a gentle pressure with the chest'.[84] Very similar descriptions of the performance of portato by singers and wind instrument players were given by other writers, for instance, Johann Samuel Petri and J. B. Lasser.[85]

Quantz recognized three types of articulated slur: these were slurs alone used on notes repeated at the same pitch, dots under slurs, and strokes under slurs. The first, which he only mentioned in connection with the flute, is produced by the breath with movements of the breast; the second is produced on the flute by sharper articulation 'so to say staccato with the chest', but without tonguing, and on the violin 'with a short bowstroke and in a sustained manner' (i.e. portato); and the third, which is only mentioned in connection with the violin, is performed with completely detached strokes in a single bow.[86] Leopold Mozart described Quantz's second and third categories in a similar manner, but in addition he used strokes under a slur to indicate a bowstroke which seems to resemble the modern slurred staccato (i.e. without lifting the bow fully from

---

[80] *Anleitung zum Clavierspielen*, 29.   [81] *Klavierschule*, VI, 3, §37.

[82] *Versuch*, I, 3, §20.   [83] Lesson XVI.

[84] *Anleitung zur Singkunst*, 135. The German is 'müssen nicht abgesetzt, auch nicht gestoßen, sondern nur, und zwar jede, durch einen gelinden Druck mit der Brust markirt werden'. Julianne Baird (*Introduction to the Art of Singing by Johann Friedrich Agricola* (Cambridge, 1995), 160) translates this rather differently, interpreting the words 'nich abgesetzt, auch nicht gestoßen' as '[one must] neither separate nor detach [the notes]', omitting the implication of accent in the word 'gestoßen'.

[85] Petri, *Anleitung zur practischen Musik, vor neuangehende Sänger und Instrumentspieler*, 2nd edn. (Leipzig, 1782); Lasser, *Vollständige Anleitung zur Singkunst* (Munich, 1798).

[86] *Versuch*, VI, 1, §11 and XVII, 2, §12.

the string; for technical reasons it seems clear that when he refers to 'a quick lift of the bow', he means a release of pressure rather than raising it clear of the string).[87] It may be significant that both these authors only illustrated the portato on notes repeated at the same pitch.

Dealing specifically with violin playing, Joseph Riepel described three possible articulation marks under a slur: (a) ⌢⌣, (b) ⌢⌣, and (c) ⌢⌣. His explanation of their meaning does not tally with Quantz and Mozart. For (*a*) he seems to have envisaged a technique similar to the modern slurred staccato, where short bowstrokes, with a quick pressure and release, and the bow barely, if at all, leaving the string, produce sharply articulated notes; for (*b*) he required a longer bowstroke, with the bow somewhat raised from the string between notes; and for (*c*) he prescribed a very sustained portato for which he described the execution as follows: 'the bow is hardly raised at all, rather, it almost represents the sound of a lyre.'[88] (In practice, though, the wavy line was commonly written without a slur.)

The casualness with which composers actually used these signs quickly becomes evident on perusal of manuscript or printed music of the period. In the autograph of a symphony by Pokorny (a pupil of Riepel) dots under a slur and a wavy line can be seen being employed in close proximity, evidently to mean the same thing (Ex. 6.43).

J. F. Reichardt referred in 1776 to sharply separated notes in a single bowstroke and to the portato, but made no notational distinction; both are indicated by dots under slurs. His example of portato, however, is shown with notes repeated at the same pitch, while his sharply separated notes are shown in melodic figures. He described the portato as the 'softest' way of executing repeated notes, saying: 'one takes several notes in a bowstroke without completely joining them to one another; between every note there remains a small pause of the bow.' But he warned against connecting the notes too smoothly, since this would tend to obscure the melodic part;[89] in this he seems to be not entirely in agreement with Mozart, who required merely that the notes 'must be separated from each other by a slight pressure of the bow'.

Löhlein's *Anweisung zum Violinspielen* (1774) uses dots under a slur to indicate sharp separation, and the text makes no mention of a portato.[90] In the exercises in chapter XI, however, there seem to be several instances of what, from their context as repeated accompaniment notes at the same pitch, look like portato; these too are simply marked with dots under a slur. Löhlein also employed dots under a slur over a single note to indicate vibrato (*Bebung*) of the left hand—a violinist's counterpart to C. P. E. Bach's *Bebung* on the clavichord (see Ex. 14.20).[91] But elsewhere the same notation seems to have been

---

[87] Ibid., I, 3, §17 and VII, 1, §17.

[89] *Ueber die Pflichten*, 24, 17–18.

[91] *Anweisung zum Violinspielen*, 68–70.

[88] *Gründliche Erklärung*, 16.

[90] pp. 32–3.

Ex. 6.43. Franz Xaver Pokorny, Symphony in C, i, autograph in Fürst Thurn und Taxis Hofbibliothek, Regensburg, Pokorny 7; pub. in fac. in the series *The Symphony 1720–1840* (New York and London, 1984)

used in string music to indicate a *Bebung* with the bow, for instance in Gluck's operas, sometimes in conjunction with the instruction 'tremolando'.

In string music, portato rather than a staccato was generally indicated by the theorists for accompaniment figures where notes were repeated at the same pitch. Indeed, Giuseppe Maria Cambini suggested in about 1800 that this style of bowing should be used whenever 'piano', 'dolce', or 'piano dolce' were written, even though the composer had not specifically indicated a portato bowing; and to mark this bowstroke, Cambini used either dots or a wavy line.[92] But as the descriptions of Quantz, Mozart, and Reichardt imply, a considerable variation in pressure and separation was current.

A final example from an eighteenth-century treatise introduces the possibility of executing slurred staccato where none seems to be indicated. In his *Anweisung zum Violinspielen* of 1792 J. A. Hiller explained that if dots (without a slur) occur, 'as long as these dots should not merely be strokes, they signify a totally different kind of performance, which in artistic language is called *punto d'arco* (attack with the bow). In this case several of the notes thus marked are taken in one bowstroke and brought out shortly by a jerk of the bow'; he later added that 'the *punto d'arco* can most easily be made with the up-bow from the point of the bow up to the middle'.[93] As his music example confirms, he is referring to the staccato in a single bowstroke at a moderate tempo, which other authors designated by dots under a slur or strokes under a slur. He added that soloists can attempt this bowstroke at much faster tempos. Hiller used the notation of dots under a slur to mean portato, but seems to have meant (the passage is far from clear) that the same notation could also be used for the 'punto d'arco'; it certainly was used by others in this sense.[94]

In the eighteenth-century use of this notation there is evidently an area of uncertainty where the type of execution envisaged is on the borderline between portato and staccato. This is very clearly brought out in Koch's definition of 'Piquiren' in his 1802 *Lexikon*:

> With this expression one denotes a particular kind of bowstroke on string instruments by which many stepwise notes following on from one another are given with a very short staccato . . .; e.g. [Ex. 6.44(*a*)]
>
> One leaves the performance of running notes in a quick tempo to solo players who have particularly practised this; however, on notes which are repeated at the same pitch and performed at a moderate tempo one also uses this kind of stroke in orchestral parts; e.g. [Ex. 6.44(*b*)]

Nineteenth-century sources reveal a number of different preoccupations. Several of the markings dealt with by eighteenth-century writers became largely obsolete; the Gluck tremolando and the *Bebung* gradually disappeared

---

[92] *Nouvelle Méthode théorique et pratique pour le violon* (Paris, *c.*1800), 23.   [93] pp. 41 ff.

[94] For another, somewhat different, use of the term *punta* (*punto*) *d'arco* that seems also to have been current in the late 18th c. and early 19th c. see below, Ch. 7, 'String Bowing'.

Ex. 6.44. Koch, *Musikalisches Lexikon*, art. 'Piquiren'
(*a*)

(*b*)

from normal usage, as did the employment of the wavy line to indicate portato. In Paris, where Gluck's influence remained strong, these practices seem to have lingered longest. Spontini, who dominated Parisian grand opera during the first decade of the nineteenth century, used a wavy line in very much the same contexts as Gluck.[95] The use of the wavy line as an indication for portato was touched on by Baillot in 1834,[96] and the Gluck tremolando was referred to by Berlioz in his *Grand traité* (1843).[97] The wavy line continued to be used in string music to indicate left-hand vibrato and tremolo with separate bow-strokes, and on the piano, particularly in vocal scores of operas, to indicate the pianistic equivalent of the tremolo. The tendency of composers to use signs haphazardly and inconsistently continued as before, though the possible range of meanings shifted. For instance, while Pokorny had used the wavy line and dots under a slur to mean portato, Rossini randomly employed either the wavy line or a figure consisting of three or four diagonal strokes to mean a tremolo with separate bowstrokes (Ex. 6.45) in the manner described in the *Principes élémentaires de musique* (*c*.1800), where it was observed: 'One uses it [the wavy line] normally on a semibreve in the accompaniment parts of an obbligato recitative. The effect of the tremolo is the same as that produced by a succession of demisemiquavers on the same pitch in a fast movement. Only string instruments and timpani are able to produce the effect of the tremolo.' There follows a music example headed 'Manner of executing the tremolo' (Ex. 6.46).[98]

In piano methods the use of dots under a slur to mean portato seems to have been generally accepted at the beginning of the nineteenth century; Adam's explanation of this notation in his *Méthode du piano du Conservatoire* (1802), that it signified that each note was to be sustained for three-quarters of its value,[99] was widely repeated in other piano methods and even, somewhat anomalously, in some string methods. Singing methods and wind tutors also continued to link the notation of dots under a slur with portato, for instance the oboe method in Fröhlich's *Musikschule*, where it is described as having 'a

---

[95] For further discussion of these signs and their implications see Ch. 14.   [96] *L'Art du violon*, 137.
[97] *Grand traité d'instrumentation et d'orchestration modernes* op. 10 (Paris, 1843), 19.
[98] Gossec et al., *Principes*, i. 48.   [99] p. 155.

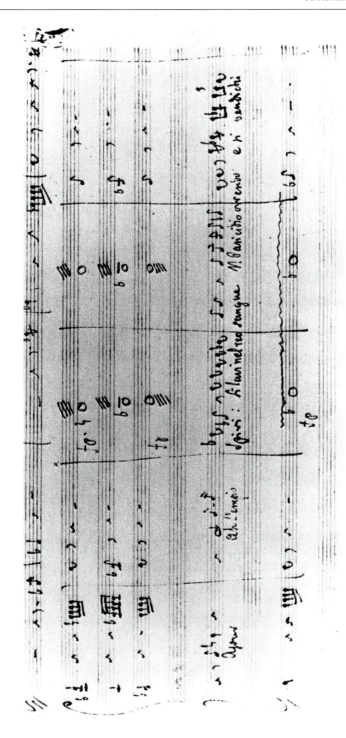

Ex. 6.45. Rossini, *Semiramide*, Act II, no. 10

Ex. 6.46. Gossec et al., *Principes*, i. 48

distinctive soft character which almost occupies the bridge between staccato and slurring'.[100] Some authorities, particularly pianists, also noted that in passages marked portato each note received a slight emphasis;[101] for violinists, such an effect is a natural outcome of the technique. Lichtenthal, borrowing an example from Francesco Pollini,[102] observed that in cantabile phrases a slightly delayed entry of each note 'contributes not a little to the expression',[103] and gave Ex. 6.47 as an illustration. Apparently related to this practice may have been a tendency for nineteenth-century keyboard players to employ a type of arpeggiation in portato passages. Moscheles, for instance, illustrates the performance of portato figures in his Studies op. 70 book I as in Ex. 6.48. As these examples imply, the possible range of subtle degrees of accentuation, pressure,

Ex. 6.47. Lichtenthal, *Dizionario*, fig. 141

[100] Vol. ii. 40.

[101] Czerny, *Pianoforte-Schule*, iii. 24; Hummel, *Anweisung*, i. 64; Starke, *Wiener Pianoforte-Schule*, i, pt. I, 13; Daniel Steibelt, *Méthode de piano* (Leipzig, [1809]), 57.

[102] *Metodo per clavicembalo* (Milan, 1811).   [103] *Dizionario*, art. 'Staccato'.

Ex. 6.48. Moscheles, *Studies for the Piano Forte . . .* op. 70, 2 vols. (London, [*c*.1843]), i. 6

and separation in the execution of portato, demanded in particular musical contexts, is undoubtedly greater than is conveyed by the instructions given by any one theorist.

In nineteenth-century string methods more fundamental ambiguity continued as strongly as ever. Fröhlich, with no apparent sense of inconsistency, used dots under a slur in the violin method section of his *Musikschule* to mean slurred staccato, having earlier used them to mean portato.[104] Dotzauer, in his *Méthode de violoncelle* of about 1825, used dots under a slur only in the context of the staccato, but in his later *Violoncell-Schule* of about 1836 he also described a springing staccato (whose use he did not, however, recommend except in rare instances) with the same notation.[105] Spohr's *Violinschule* of 1832, on the other hand, ignoring springing staccato altogether, used dots under a slur for the normal string player's slurred staccato, but also indicated, though only in passing, that phrases marked in this manner might, especially in slow movements, be executed with a more gentle detaching of the notes.[106]

The meaning of dots or strokes under slurs during the late eighteenth and early nineteenth century, therefore, is by no means clear and consistent. In keyboard music it is safe to assume, despite the contrary example from Pasquali, that in the vast majority of instances the intended execution of dots under slurs is portato; also in wind music and vocal music this notation will usually indicate portato. In string music the situation is much more complex, particularly where the composer was both a keyboard player and a string player, and with the dissemination of an increasingly sophisticated variety of bowings in the nineteenth century, the range of possible meanings became even wider. In these circumstances, the musical context considered in conjunction with what is known about a composer's background and training is the only reasonable guide to understanding the intentions behind these notations. It may be helpful at this point to consider some particular cases in which one or another interpretation seems to be required.

On at least a couple of occasions Haydn used quite distinct strokes rather than dots under slurs. One of these occurs in the autograph score of his Concertante in B flat for violin, cello, oboe, bassoon, and orchestra (1791; Hob. I:105), but his intentions are far from clear. At bars 100–1 of the first movement

---

[104] Vol. iii. 48.   [105] *Méthode de violoncelle*, 27–8; *Violoncell-Schule*, 22.
[106] *Violin School*, 115.

Ex. 6.49. Haydn, Concertante Hob. I:105

(*a*)

più lento

(*b*)

più lento

he wrote in the solo violin part (Ex. 6.49(*a*)). Since he almost invariably wrote unambiguous dots under slurs the use of strokes here seems to imply that he wanted something different from a portato bowing, and at first sight it appears likely that he imagined a sharply detached bowstroke, as indicated with this notation by Quantz, Leopold Mozart, and Riepel. But at the parallel passage in the recapitulation (bars 218–19) he gave the figure as it appears in Ex. 6.49(*b*). This leaves it uncertain whether he required a contrast the second time or whether the different notation arose simply from inadvertence and, if the latter, whether he regarded the two forms as having distinct meanings at that stage. Ten years later, in the Trio section of the Minuet of his String Quartet op. 77 no. 1, he took care to make a clear notational difference, which suggests very strongly that he was concerned to specify the difference between sharply detached notes in one bowstroke and portato. In the Eulenburg miniature score and most editions of the parts this has uniformly been printed with dots under slurs in all parts, but in the autograph Haydn clearly wrote strokes under slurs for the first violin, with its leaping figures, and dots under slurs for the repeated crotchet accompaniment of the three other parts (Ex. 6.50).

Haydn's late autographs generally show greater concern for precision in matters of articulation than his earlier ones, and it would be rash to assume, just

Ex. 6.50. Haydn, String Quartet op. 77/1/iii

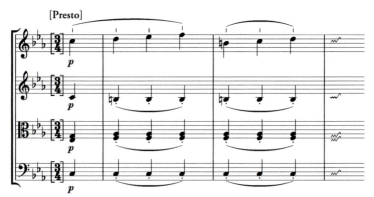

because in 1800 he used strokes under slurs to indicate staccato, that passages marked with dots under slurs in his earlier works should never be performed staccato, or indeed, since so many of his earlier autographs are missing, that the printed editions faithfully reflect the original notation. Haydn, an active violinist throughout his career, would have been conversant with the use of both notations for a slurred staccato. Nevertheless, in the vast majority of cases the musical context suggests that Haydn used dots under slurs to indicate some kind of portato; this would undoubtedly have ranged from very smooth to fairly detached, but lifted or sharply accented bowstrokes rarely seem appropriate.

Mozart, despite his father's distinction between dots and strokes under a slur, seems not to have used the latter at all. In keyboard music he undoubtedly used dots under a slur to indicate portato, and in most instances in his string music the context strongly suggests that this is also what he required there; but the possibility remains that he sometimes used this notation in string writing where he wanted a more sharply articulated bowstroke. It is evident from one of his letters that he knew and admired the slurred staccato; he described the playing of Fränzl to his father in 1777, saying: 'He has too a most beautiful clear, round tone. He never misses a note, you can hear everything. It is all clear cut. He has a beautiful staccato, played with a single bowing up or down.'[107] It is quite likely that such a staccato would have been notated with dots under a slur and it is certainly possible that Mozart might have employed the same notation for this effect. There are places where it appears probable on musical and technical grounds that this was the execution he required. One instance, about which there seems little room for doubt, occurs in the first movement of his Violin Concerto in D K. 211 (Ex. 6.51). On the other hand, there are places where modern performers commonly play a sharply detached slurred staccato but where Mozart probably imagined a more connected bowstroke, for instance, in the first movement of the String Quartet in D K. 575. At bar 66 he introduced the figure shown in Ex. 6.52(*a*). When he repeated it four bars later and on all its five subsequent appearances he wrote the bowing as in Ex. 6.52(*b*). Printed editions generally give the first bowing on all appearances of the figure, but it is arguable that the other bowing reveals Mozart's intentions more clearly.

Ex. 6.51. Mozart, Violin Concerto K. 211/i, Allegro moderato

---

[107] Emily Anderson, trans. and ed., *The Letters of Mozart and his Family*, 2nd edn. (London, 1966), 384.

Ex. 6.52. Mozart, String Quartet K. 575/i

A sharply detached bowstroke would certainly be possible with the first bowing, but the subsequent version makes this much less likely; Mozart would have been well aware that the down-bow produced a different, less crisp staccato than the up-bow. In general, musical and technical considerations suggest that Mozart used dots under slurs in his later string music to signify an equivalent of the portato that he clearly intended in his keyboard music.

Beethoven seems consistently to have meant portato by dots under a slur in keyboard, wind, and string music. This was surely the significance of his often quoted letter to Carl Holz on the importance of distinguishing between strokes and dots in copying the autograph of the A minor String Quartet;[108] the only clear and consistent differentiation in this autograph is between dots under slurs and strokes on unslurred notes. Such an interpretation of that letter is supported by Beethoven's care in correcting copyists' parts of the Seventh Symphony; in the many instances where the copyist had written ⌢, Beethoven painstakingly altered it to ⌢. Despite his often chaotic writing in other places, Beethoven invariably wrote dots under slurs with absolute clarity.

Though Beethoven almost certainly never intended his dots under slurs to indicate a staccato, the precise degree of articulation will certainly vary according to the musical context. Modern performers, especially string players, but also wind and keyboard players, often misunderstand the implication of Beethoven's dots under slurs and play them in a sharply detached manner. It is probable that this notation was already being misinterpreted by string players in the mid-nineteenth century.

Schubert, like Haydn, Mozart, and Beethoven, was a string player as well as a keyboard player. He grew up during a period when the Viotti school was rapidly gaining dominance and the slurred staccato was an essential part of every aspiring string player's technique, and it seems clear that not all the passages which he notated with dots under a slur are meant to be played portato. For instance, assuming that the first edition faithfully reflects Schubert's lost autograph, a slurred staccato execution is surely indicated in the Menuetto of

---

[108] Anderson, *The Letters of Beethoven*, iii. 1241.

Ex. 6.53. Schubert, String Quartet op. D. 353/iii

the String Quartet op. 125 no. 2 (Ex. 6.53); if this is not Schubert's notation, it merely provides evidence of the 1840 editor's practice.

When Schubert wrote dots under a slur for arpeggio or scale passages of moderate to rapid velocity it seems possible that he envisaged something on the borderline between portato and staccato, even when he gave the same notation to string and wind instruments, as in the fourth variation of the Andante of the Octet, or to violin and piano, as in the Andante of the 'Trout' Quintet (Ex. 6.54). It is possible in a passage such as this that Schubert was especially concerned to indicate the equality of accentuation (the slight emphasis on each note). A passage in the 'Trout' Quintet where a more distinct staccato may be appropriate is variation 2 of the Andantino; the combination of tempo[109] and notation (the *fp* and the separate bow for the first note on the first appearance of the figure) provide almost a *locus classicus* for slurred staccato, though a relatively relaxed rather than extremely crisp staccato would probably be best suited to the context.

Many of Schubert's string-playing associates would certainly have used dots under slurs as a notation for distinctly articulated bowstrokes, as is suggested by bowings in manuscript parts of his Sixth Symphony used by members of his circle, dating from between 1825 and 1828, where the triplet semiquavers in the second movement, given in Schubert's autograph with staccato dots, were marked (after the parts were written) to be played in groups of three or six semiquavers to the bow.[110] Composers themselves very rarely notated slurred staccato in their orchestral compositions; on occasion, though, dots under slurs were unquestionably used to specify this effect. One example occurs in the first

[109] Probably rather fast (see Ch. 10).
[110] In the collection of the Gesellschaft der Musikfreunde, Vienna.

Ex. 6.54. Schubert, Piano Quintet 'The Trout' D. 667/i

movement of Spohr's Fourth Symphony *Die Weihe der Töne* (Ex. 6.55); another is in the Allegro vivacissimo final movement of Mendelssohn's Third Symphony (Ex. 6.56).

When writing for solo strings Mendelssohn quite frequently used dots under slurs in contexts where he clearly wanted slurred staccato, and he also used the same notation for various types of slurred spiccato as well as for por-

Ex. 6.55. Spohr, Fourth Symphony *Die Weihe der Töne* op. 86/i

Ex. 6.56. Mendelssohn, Third Symphony op. 56/iv

tato. A good example of the slurred staccato is found in the Scherzo of the Octet, and this is probably also the bowing required in the last movement of his Piano Trio op. 66, dedicated to Spohr, whose performance of the slurred staccato Mendelssohn admired (Ex. 6.57). A lighter staccato or spiccato seems to have been intended in the last movement of Mendelssohn's Violin Concerto, while in the first movement of the same concerto the dots under slurs in the wind and solo violin part in the second subject clearly indicate portato (Ex. 6.58(*a*) and (*b*)). Mendelssohn's friend, the violinist Ferdinand David, marked the latter passage with lines under slurs in his edition of the concerto (Ex. 6.58(*c*)).

Even singers could sometimes be expected to execute dots under a slur as sharply articulated notes rather than as portato. An interesting example of this can be found in Meyerbeer's *Les Huguenots*, where flute and oboe have a figure of repeated semiquavers which is immediately answered by the solo soprano in inversion. Both figures are notated with dots and slurs, but Meyerbeer has indicated for the wind instruments 'appuyez chaque note' (press each note), and for the voice 'saccadé' (jerkily) (Ex. 6.59).

While most writers before the middle of the nineteenth century seem to have been relatively unconcerned by the ambiguities of notating portato, slurred staccato, springing staccato, and spiccato, the French violinist Baillot attempted greater precision. For a succession of notes played in a single rebounding bowstroke—a type of bowing discouraged by most German authorities at that time—he proposed strokes or wedges under a slur. He also observed that since dots under a slur could mean both a very smooth portato

Ex. 6.57. (*a*) Mendelssohn, Octet op. 20/iii; (*b*) Mendelssohn, Piano Trio op. 66/iv
(*a*)

(*b*)

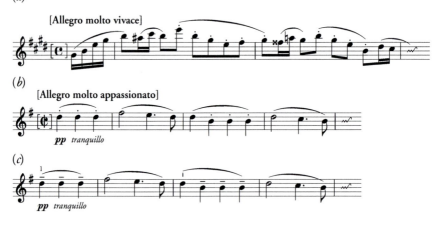

Ex. 6.58. Mendelssohn, Violin Concerto op. 64: (*a*) iii; (*b*) i; (*c*) i
(*a*)

(*b*)

(*c*)

(which he called *ondulation*) and staccato (or *détaché articulé*), two other different notations should be used. For portato he proposed a sign rather similar to the eighteenth-century wavy line, confining dots under a slur to the staccato. But rather confusingly he also repeated Adam's formula for the rendition of dots under a slur, and it is not entirely clear from Baillot's account whether he regarded *ondulation* and portato as synonymous or significantly different.[111]

[111] *L'Art du violon*, 268–70.

Ex. 6.59. Meyerbeer, *Les Huguenots*, no. 7, Andante cantabile ♩. = 69, 12/8

Later in the century there was a more widespread concern for notational precision, and a greater number of theorists and composers began to use increasingly differentiated systems. The scheme expounded in Ferdinand David's *Violinschule*, as mentioned above,[112] associated strokes or wedges with martelé bowstrokes, and dots with sautillé bowstrokes; David also employed horizontal lines for tenuto bowstrokes: strokes under slurs indicated the slurred staccato, dots under slurs indicated sautillé or spiccato in a single bowstroke, and lines under slurs indicated portato.[113] Yet the association of dots under slurs with staccato was so deeply ingrained that even David did not consistently adopt his own criteria for distinguishing between slurred staccato and slurred spiccato in his numerous editions. Other authors who were undoubtedly influenced by David's theoretical notation of articulation marks, such as Hermann Schröder,[114] followed all his distinctions except the one between slurred staccato and spiccato. In a further example of inconsistency, David often used lines under slurs for portato in his editions, but also continued to use dots under slurs where portato seems to have been intended by the composer. In this case, it is possible that some of David's apparent lack of consistency arose from the fact that he failed to recognize the composer's intention; in his edition of Beethoven's violin sonatas, for example, he sometimes used his line-under-slur notation, sometimes retained Beethoven's dots under slurs, and sometimes mixed editorial slurred staccato with Beethoven's original portato notation.

The horizontal line under a slur to indicate portato was adopted by many composers during the second half of the nineteenth century, including Wagner, Dvořák, and Bruch. Brahms, however, resisted this notation even after his correspondence with Joachim on the subject and continued to use dots under a slur solely as an indication for portato; but he did relent to some extent in at least one instance, for in the first edition of his Violin Sonata op. 108, the violin part in the score has dots under slurs for the first sixteen bars of the third movement while, for the same passage, the separate violin part has lines under slurs. Other signs used in conjunction with slurs, such as >>>> and ∧∧∧∧, or simply a slur without articulation marks used over notes repeated at the same pitch, were also employed with increasing frequency by many composers during the second half of the century in a search for ever more precise definition of the type of articulation required.

---

[112] See Ch. 3.

[113] The horizontal line under a slur has a longer history than might be suggested by the Brahms–Joachim correspondence. It was apparently used by the young Franz Berwald as early as 1818 in the Poco adagio of his G minor String Quartet (F. Berwald: *Sämtliche Werke*, xi (Kassel, 1966)).

[114] *Die Kunst des Violinspiels* (Cologne, 1887).

7

STRING BOWING

⟨❊⟩

An understanding of specific techniques of bowing, and how and where they might have been employed, can throw considerable light on attitudes towards articulation as a whole. Not only were string instruments widely regarded as the most versatile and, after the human voice, the most expressive instruments throughout most of this period, but also, because of the technical means by which the sound is produced, descriptions of the mechanism for executing the various bowings often allow a clearer notion of the aural effects that were being sought than descriptions of articulation in singing, keyboard, or wind methods. Closer scrutiny of this subject is also important for understanding eighteenth- and nineteenth-century performing practice in general because it is an area in which modern practice appears, to a considerable extent, to be sharply at odds with the historical evidence. In much of the Classical and Romantic repertoire that is still central to our experience, it is likely that most modern string players employ an anachronistic bowing style, which often produces a very different type of articulation from that envisaged by composers of the period. The principal point at issue, in this respect, is whether the widespread employment of what Carl Flesch categorizes as springing or thrown bow-strokes,[1] mainly in the middle and lower half of the bow, for passages of moderate- to fast-moving notes approximates to historical practice in the majority of circumstances in which it is currently employed.

The three basic types of bow that were current during this period were what Michel Woldemar (and, later, Fétis) described and illustrated as the 'Tartini', 'Cramer' and 'Viotti' bows (Fig. 7.1). The first, with its convex stick, corresponds with the bows illustrated in the tutors of Leopold Mozart (1756) and Löhlein (1774) as well as in many illustrations of the period up to the 1770s; for

---

[1] *The Art of Violin Playing* (London, 1924) i. 73.

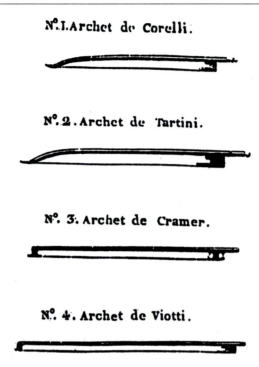

N°. I. Archet de Corelli.

N°. 2. Archet de Tartini.

N°. 3. Archet de Cramer.

N°. 4. Archet de Viotti.

FIG. 7.1. Woldemar's illustration of the types of bow that 'were in use successively since the origin of the violin' from his *Grande méthode*, 3

instance, Carmontelle's water-colour of the Mozart family in about 1764. The second, with a slightly concave stick and a more developed head, is much closer to the modern Tourte-style bow though lighter and shorter; it seems to have been in use as early as the 1750s and was probably especially characteristic of Mannheim, hence the association of this type with Wilhelm Cramer, one of the most celebrated products of that school. It seems possible, from what can be seen of the bow on Della Croce's Mozart family portrait of about 1780, that by that date Leopold was using a bow of a transitional type. During the last three decades of the eighteenth century there were many variants of this basic design in use; it is possible that the bow favoured by Viotti was one of these transitional types (as implied by Baillot's depiction of Viotti's bow as slightly shorter than a Tourte), but, whatever bow Viotti himself may have used, the 'Viotti' bow was evidently regarded by Woldemar and Fétis as identical with the model developed by François Tourte in the 1780s, which has served as the pattern for subsequent bow makers up to the present day. Woldemar (1750–1815) stated in about 1800 that the 'Cramer' bow had been 'adopted in his day by most artists and amateurs'; he added that the 'Viotti' bow 'differs little from Cramer's in respect of the head but the nut is lower and brought nearer to the button [screw], it is longer and has more hair; it is used a little slackly for playing and is almost exclusively in use today'.² Tourte bows may well have been more rapidly disseminated through Europe than has often been suggested. Violinists of the Mannheim school were almost certainly using them at the time of Woldemar's treatise, for when the Mannheim and Munich violinist Franz Eck took on Spohr as his pupil in 1803 one of the first things he did was to have him buy a new bow; according to Spohr's diary this was a genuine Tourte, which he obtained at a music shop in Hamburg. Although each of these designs of bow was particularly well adapted to certain types of strokes it does not seem to be the case that all the strokes of which they were capable were widely exploited.³

Bowstrokes are to a considerable extent conditioned by the physical characteristics of the bow, and there is no doubt that many of the changes in bowing style that came about between the middle of the eighteenth century and the end of the nineteenth century resulted, at least in part, from the development and adoption of different bow types.⁴ Strokes that are highly effective in producing a particular articulation with one design of bow may be less effective with another. But where a certain kind of bow is well adapted to produce a certain kind of stroke it does not follow that it will necessarily have been widely used in that way as soon as the design was perfected; nor, where a later design is better at producing a particular effect, would it be safe to assume that the same effect was not attempted with an earlier style of bow. One of the particular characteristics of the earlier bows was their tendency to produce a distinctly articulated effect in passages of moderate or fast notes played with separate bowstrokes. The later bows did not produce this effect so readily; the increased strength and resilience of the bow stick led to a more immediate response and a gradual minimizing of the 'small softness' at the beginning of a stroke referred to by Leopold Mozart.⁵ Together with this development went a change in the perception of the character of the normal separate bowstroke in passages at moderate to faster speeds; whereas the majority of string players of the mid-eighteenth century probably regarded separate strokes as having a naturally detached effect, there seems to have been an increasing shift towards seeing them as more or less smoothly connected, and this reached its culmination in the practices of the Viotti school in the late eighteenth century (though it had probably been typical to a considerable extent of Italian players of an earlier generation). Of course, much depended on the particular context, and there

---

² *Grande Méthode ou étude élémentaire pour le violon* (Paris, [c.1800]), 3.

³ For further information on bows and their characteristics see Stowell, *Violin Technique*, ch. 1, where, however, the meaning of the quotation from Woldemar is somewhat obscured—he translates 'il se joue un peu détendu' (it is used a little slackly for playing) as 'it looks slightly straighter when in use'.

⁴ Spohr, for instance, is reported by Alexandre Malibran to have identified a link between the instrument (bow?) and performing practices in the music of his youth.

⁵ *Versuch*, V, §3.

were many accepted ways of achieving more or less pronounced degrees of separation and smoothness. The Cramer and Tourte bows readily allowed a semi-springing stroke, using a tiny length of bow about the middle, and this became popular with certain solo players for particular types of continuous passage-work during the last decades of the eighteenth century; these bows, especially the Tourtes, were also capable of producing an effective martelé at the point, which became a characteristic bowstroke for players influenced by the Viotti school. The staccato in a single bowstroke (a series of rapid martelé-type strokes executed in the upper half of the bow), Fränzl's mastery of which Mozart praised in 1777, was widely regarded as an indispensable resource of the best players. Other kinds of lifted and rebounding strokes were certainly employed from time to time for special effects, but there is nothing in the literature of the period to suggest that springing or thrown strokes in the middle or lower half of the bow were normally used for faster-moving notes with staccato marks. In the vast majority of circumstances where this type of stroke is used today, it seems highly probable that most players of the second half of the eighteenth century and first half of the nineteenth century would have used the bow in a very different manner. In fact, although the modern bow is eminently capable of these types of stroke, it seems probable that the principal factors in the bow's evolution were a search for greater volume and power and the achievement of a more effective cantabile.

During the eighteenth century and to a considerable extent during the nineteenth century, with all these designs of bow, the upper half was much more extensively used, especially for a succession of shorter strokes, than it is in modern violin playing. Whenever the writers of string methods during the late Baroque, Galant, and Classical periods were specific about which part of the bow would normally be employed for shorter strokes, they invariably referred to the upper half, or indeed to the top quarter of the bow. Corrette in 1738 instructed that 'quavers and semiquavers are played at the tip of the bow',[6] Robert Crome in the 1740s cautioned 'take care you don't let your Bow Hand come too near the Fiddle, but rather play with the small end of the Bow, unless it be to lengthen out a long note'.[7] Reichardt in 1776 succinctly categorized the types of strokes which he recommended for different lengths of notes as follows:

First long notes, and for these observe equal strength throughout the whole of the bow, [Ex. 7.1(*a*)] then faster notes, for which one makes a stroke quickly through the whole bow; [Ex. 7.1(*b*)] then others, for which one only uses half the bow, from the middle to the point, and then those which one staccatos with the top quarter of the bow. [Ex. 7.1(*c*)] It is best if one

---

[6]   *L'École d'Orphée, méthode pour apprendre facilement à jouer du violon dans le goût françois et italien avec des principes de musique et beaucoup de leçons*, op. 18 (Paris, 1738), 7.

[7]   *Fiddle, New Modell'd* (London, [c.1750]), quoted in Edmund van der Straeten, *The Romance of the Fiddle: The Origin of the Modern Virtuoso and the Adventures of his Ancestors* (London, 1911), 204.

takes triplets for these separate bowstrokes to acquire equality in up- and down-bows. [Ex. 7.1(*d*)][8]

Ex. 7.1. Reichardt, *Ueber die Pflichten:* (*a*) and (*b*) p. 9; (*c*) and (*d*) p. 10

(*a*)

(*b*)

(*c*)

(*d*)

Generally, the shorter and more delicate the stroke, the nearer the point; thus Kirnberger specified the point of the bow for light metres, requiring well-separated bowstrokes.[9] In contexts where this sort of specially distinct but light bowstroke was required composers occasionally gave the instruction 'punta d'arco',[10] or some similar expression, apparently to obtain a lighter stroke than the ordinary detached stroke in the upper half, which might otherwise have been used. This is a fairly frequently encountered direction in orchestral scores of the second half of the eighteenth century and first half of the nineteenth century; Piccinni indicated it in *La Ceccina, ossia La buona figluola* (1760) (Ex. 7.2(*a*)), and David Perez in *Solimano* (*c*.1768) (Ex. 7.2(*b*)). Haydn requested it in his String Quartet op. 55 no. 1 (Ex. 7.2(*c*)). It was later to be required in similar contexts by Rossini in *L'Italiana in Algeri* and many other operas (Ex. 7.2(*d*)), by Weber in *Der Freischütz* (Ex. 7.2(*e*)), by Beethoven in the String Quartet op. 132 (Ex. 7.2(*f*)), by Meyerbeer in *Il crociato in Egitto* (Ex. 7.2(*g*)), and by Berlioz in the *Symphonie fantastique* (Ex. 7.2(*h*)).

In many ways the punta d'arco of the eighteenth century and early nineteenth century seems to have been the equivalent of the modern springing (sautillé or spiccato) bowstroke, which probably came into general use for passages of this type towards the middle of the nineteenth century.[11] The term 'punta d'arco' was defined thus by Lichtenthal in 1826: 'The notes marked with this expression require a particular execution, which consists of striking gently

---

[8] *Ueber die Pflichten*, 9–10.   [9] *The Art of Strict Musical Composition*, 388.

[10] *Punta d'arco, colla punta del arco* (sometimes *punto d'arco*, especially in German sources) seems normally to have been used to indicate a short detached stroke near the point of the bow.

[11] See the quotation from Schröder, *Die Kunst des Violinspiels* below and n. 24.

Ex. 7.2. (*a*) Piccinni, *La Ceccina ossia La buona figliuola*, Act I, Scene viii; (*b*) Perez, *Solimano*, Act I, Scene viii (*c*), British Library, London, Add MSS 16093–94; (*c*) Haydn, String Quartet, op. 55/1/iii; (*d*) Rossini, *Semiramide*, no. 5, autograph, p. 152; (*e*) Weber, *Der Freischütz*, no. 9, Andantino; (*f*) Beethoven, String Quartet op. 132/v; (*g*) Meyerbeer, *Il crociato in Egitto*, no. 17 (Allegretto moderato, 4 sharps, **c**); (*h*) Berlioz, *Symphonie fantastique* op. 14/i

(*a*)

(*b*)

(*c*)

(*d*)

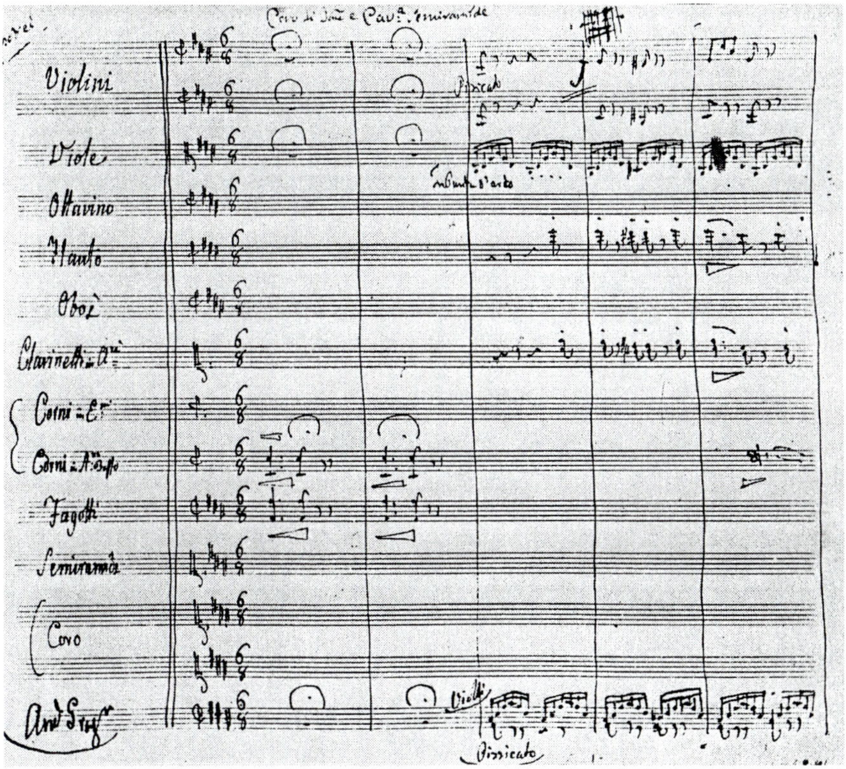

on the string with the point of the bow, thus producing a light staccato.'[12] And *Busby's Dictionary* explained punta d'arco as: 'with the end, or with a slight touch of the bow'.[13] Johann Adam Hiller seems to have understood the term differently, applying it to the staccato produced at the point of the bow by a series of short strokes in one up-bow;[14] but this would not fit most of the instances where the expression appears in eighteenth- and early nineteenth-century music.

All the passages marked 'punta d'arco' in Ex. 7.2 are places where the natural instinct of the modern player would be to use the middle or lower half of the bow with an off-the-string stroke which would now be known as spiccato; but it seems clear that this instinct did not come so naturally to eighteenth-century and even nineteenth-century players. Defining the word 'spiccato' in his

---

[12] *Dizionario*, art. 'Punta d'arco'.

[13] *Thomas Busby's Dictionary of 300 Musical Terms*, 3rd edn., rev. by J. A. Hamilton (London, [1840]), 40.

[14] *Anweisung zum Violinspielen*, 41.

Ex. 7.2. *cont.*

(*e*)

(*f*)

(*g*)

(*h*)

Dictionary of Musical Terms in the fourth decade of the nineteenth century, J. A. Hamilton wrote: 'Pointedly, distinctly. In violin music, this term implies that the notes are to be played with the point of the bow.'[15] And as late as the 1870s the anonymous author of *The Violin: How to Master it. By a Professional Player*, discussing the use of the upper half of the bow, remarked: 'All rapid music, which is bowed and not slurred, ought to be played with this part; all that is fine and delicate in violin playing is found in the upper half of the bow'; he only allowed the use of the lower half when 'the short stroke is wanted crisp, loud and noisy'.[16]

The latter type of bowing in the lower half would scarcely have been envisaged by most eighteenth- and early nineteenth-century players except as a special effect or in connection with chords and other strongly emphasized separate notes. The use of such strokes in succession, however, is described by Baillot and Charles de Bériot, and was certainly used by a few virtuosi in the first half of the nineteenth century, including Molique, Lafont, and Louis Maurer. Its widespread use by certain schools of players is implied in a review of Spohr's *Violinschule* in 1833, which criticized his failure to discuss it; the reviewer observed that the French described the bowing in question as: 'very dry (with the heel of the bow)'.[17] It is significant, however, that this painstaking reviewer, who praised the precision of Spohr's bowing instructions as a whole, did not identify any other important omission in his treatment of the subject; for Spohr's extensive catalogue of bowstrokes does not mention anything resembling thrown or springing bowings except the fouetté stroke (a special effect produced by throwing the bow forcibly onto the string at the point), though it deals with various circumstances in which there is time to produce articulation by a lifting and replacing action of the bow.

Bowings in nineteenth-century editions of the standard German chamber music repertoire frequently imply the use of the upper half of the bow in places where modern players almost always use sprung or thrown strokes in the middle or, more frequently, the lower half. Bowed editions by Ferdinand David, Joseph Joachim, Andreas Moser, and other nineteenth-century German editors clearly show that many passages that are now generally played off the string were then intended to be played in the upper half with a détaché, martelé, or slurred staccato bowstroke. How little this accords with the modern way of playing such passages will be well known to chamber music players who, when sight-reading works by Haydn, Mozart, Beethoven, Mendelssohn, Schumann, and others from these editions, have found themselves caught at the 'wrong end' of the bow by the editor's bowing. None of the above-mentioned violinist-editors rejected springing and thrown strokes entirely, though David (b. 1810)

---

[15] Art. 'Spiccato'.   [16] (Edinburgh, *c.*1880), 55.

[17] *Caecilia*, 15 (1833), 277–80. There are two printing errors in the French at this point, for it reads: 'tres rec [?sec] (du telon [?talon] de l'archet)'.

probably used them somewhat less than Joachim (b. 1831) and Moser (b. 1859); but in their editions of the Classics all were agreed in their extensive use of the upper half of the bow for many passages where the modern player's instinct would be to employ the lower half. Newer editions have reversed many of these bowings.

A few passages from David's editions of Beethoven, Schubert, and Mendelssohn will illustrate the point.[18] In the second movements of Beethoven's string quartets op. 18 no. 4 and op. 59. no. 1, the stroke envisaged by David is mostly to be made between the middle and point of the bow, probably quite close to the point (Ex. 7.3(*a*) and (*b*)), though at times he clearly

Ex. 7.3. Beethoven: (*a*) String Quartet op. 18/4/ii; (*b*) String Quartet op. 59/1/ii; (*c*) String Quartet op. 59/1/ii

(*a*)

(*b*)

[18] For details of David's Beethoven editions, see Clive Brown 'Ferdinand David's Editions of Beethoven', in Stowell, ed., *Performing Beethoven*, 121; his editions of Schubert's chamber music include the Quartet in D minor and the piano trios (Peters, Leipzig, plate no. 7127); David's edited text of Mendelssohn's string quartets was never published, but his own performing copy of the quartets (a bound volume containing all but op. 80), to which Alan Tyson kindly gave me access, contains even more bowings and fingerings than most of the published editions (see Brown, 'Bowing Styles').

requires the same effect to be produced at both ends of the bow (Ex. 7.3(*c*)). In the first movement of Mendelssohn's String Quartet op. 44 no. 3 (Ex. 7.4), David's bowing indicates that the passage of staccato quavers in this extract are to be played in the upper half, either détaché or martelé; the bowings in parentheses are from the Peters *Neu revidierte Ausgabe* and imply a thrown stroke in the lower half, which is how most violinists would now play them. A passage from David's edition of Schubert's Piano Trio op. 99 shows the use of a slurred staccato in the upper half, followed by a detached bowing near the point for the semiquavers. The Peters *Neu revidierte Ausgabe* indicates a light stroke (probably sautillé) in the middle of the bow (Ex. 7.5). And in many places in Beethoven's string music David used a slurred staccato to achieve a sharply separated effect that modern violinists would almost certainly achieve by means of a springing stroke in the middle or lower half of the bow, depending on speed and volume (Ex. 7.6). Similar examples can easily be found in editions by other nineteenth-century violinists, which, taken as a whole, depict a distinct nineteenth-century performing tradition for that repertoire in Germany. The question remains whether the bowing style revealed in these editions has any demonstrable link with the practices that would have been expected by those composers and their immediate predecessors.

Ex. 7.4. Mendelssohn, String Quartet op. 44/3/i, copy fingered and bowed in ms by F. David (kindly made available by Dr Alan Tyson)

Ex. 7.5. Schubert, Piano Trio D. 898/i: (*a*) ed. F. David; (*b*) *Neu revidierte Ausgabe* (Peters)

(*a*)

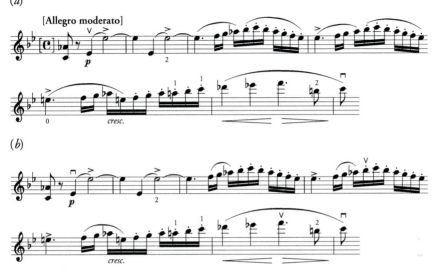

(*b*)

Ex. 7.6. Beethoven, Piano Trio op. 1/1/iv, ed. F. David

Joachim's attitude towards these kinds of bowing is revealing. As a boy Joachim studied in Vienna with Joseph Boehm, who in the 1820s had worked with Beethoven on the performance of his late string quartets and had premièred Schubert's Piano Trio op. 100 in 1828; Boehm was thus directly connected with the Viennese performance traditions of Beethoven's time, if not of Haydn's and Mozart's. When the 12-year-old Joachim went from Vienna to Leipzig he seems to have carried with him the notion that the use of springing bowstrokes in Classical compositions was unacceptable; he saw no objection, however, to their use in virtuoso music, and through the practice of Paganini's caprices he had acquired the technical facility to use them. Concerned about the propriety of employing such techniques in the Classics, he asked Mendelssohn's advice and, according to Andreas Moser, received the practical musician's reply: 'Always use it, my boy, where it is suitable, or where it sounds well.' Moser's comment on this is interesting, for it suggests that even when he came to write Joachim's biography at the end of the century, many violinists were still opposed to the use of these strokes in the Classical repertoire; he observed that Mendelssohn's influence had freed Joachim 'from certain prejudices and habits to which violinists are prone—for example, that the use of the springing bow is not permissible in Classical compositions'.[19]

The endurance of opposition to springing bowstrokes in this repertoire was undoubtedly strengthened by Spohr's powerful influence on German string playing. His objection to them was well known; Moser referred to Spohr's opinion that spiccato 'is a showy [*windbeutelige*] sort of bowstroke which is not appropriate to the dignity of Art'.[20] Spohr continued to voice his distaste for springing bowings during the latter part of his life when, largely under the influence of Paganini and Franco-Belgian violinists, they were being increasingly employed. His pupil Alexandre Malibran reported that he was horrified when violinists used springing bowings in the works of the Classical masters 'who more than all others wished to have a free, well-nourished tone'.[21] Spohr, whose musical experience stretched back to the 1790s and who became well acquainted with Beethoven during his years in Vienna (1812–15) firmly maintained that this was the 'true tradition'. Throughout his life Spohr was admired not only as a highly individual exponent of his own music and that of the Viotti school, but also as an ideal interpreter of Classical chamber music. His rejection of springing bowings in the compositions of the Viennese masters seems, therefore, to have stemmed from a genuine tradition; he did not merely apply to this repertoire, in a stylistically inappropriate manner, the broad and sonorous bowing style, derived from the Viotti school, which he required in his own music. No less an authority than Friedrich Rochlitz (b. 1769), whose encounter with Mozart in 1789 had proved a turning-point in his life, remarked in a review of Spohr's performances of string quartets by Mozart, Beethoven (op. 18), and others in 1804 how responsive his playing style was to the requirements of different composers:

> He is altogether a different person when he plays, for example, Beethoven (his darling, whom he handles exquisitely) or Mozart (his ideal) or Rode (whose grandiosity he knows so well how to assume, without any scratching and scraping in producing the necessary volume of tone), or when he plays Viotti and Galant composers: he is a different person because they are different persons. No wonder that he pleases everywhere and leaves scarcely any other wish behind than that one might keep him and listen to him always.[22]

According to Malibran, Spohr would only admit the propriety of springing bowings in a few scherzos by Beethoven, Onslow, and Mendelssohn. Onslow (1784–1853) apparently shared Spohr's opinion, for he was reported to have said

---

[19] *Joseph Joachim*, trans. Lilla Durham (London, 1901), 46.
[20] Joachim and Moser, *Violinschule*, iii. 12.
[21] *Louis Spohr* (Frankfurt-am-Main, 1860), 207–8.
[22] *Allgemeine musikalische Zeitung*, 7 (1804–5), 202–3.

about the performance of his own music: 'Ah! the miserable creatures! They bounce me too much, much too much; I almost talk myself to death with the frequent repetition of this exhortation and they always do it again and again! It is a foregone conclusion, a nail in my coffin.'[23]

Spohr's authority weighed heavily on the younger generation of German violinists; he himself taught many of them, and even those who were not his pupils, such as Joachim, revered him as a master. But Spohr's almost total rejection of springing bowings was not shared for long by many, for the influence of a newer French (Franco-Belgian) school of violin playing was already beginning to be felt in the 1830s. It is noteworthy that Henry Holmes (dedicatee of Spohr's last three violin duets), in his English edition of Spohr's *Violinschule* (1878), supplemented the section on bowing with exercises for practising sautillé, and that Spohr's own pupil David included sautillé and sauté bowing in his *Violinschule* (1863).[24] In Hermann Schröder's *Die Kunst des Violinspiels* (1887) the full range of firm and springing bowings is discussed, and when considering sautillé, which he called 'der leichte Bogen', he remarked: 'The light bow is now an indispensable bowing style for every violinist, especially those who have been formed by the newer French school'; but in a comment which suggests that Spohr was seen as the last significant representative of an older tradition of playing, he continued: 'In the old Italian and particularly in the German school up to L. Spohr, it was less used. One played passages suited to these bowstrokes on the whole with short strokes with an on-the-string bowing at the point.'[25]

Nevertheless, it is clear that springing bowings were used by some violinists in certain contexts in the eighteenth century. Spohr's diary from 1803 contains appraisals of the playing of two violinists, J. A. Fodor (1751–1828) and A. F. Tietz (?1742–1810), in which he criticized their use of a springing bow in passagework, characterizing it as the 'old method'.[26] It will be useful, therefore, to consider when, where, by whom, and in what contexts this sort of bowing might have been employed during the eighteenth century.

The origins of the type of springing bowstroke deprecated by Spohr are not difficult to determine; a number of independent sources are entirely in agreement. The discovery and introduction of the technique were credited to the celebrated Mannheim violinist Wilhelm Cramer (1746–99). Christian Daniel Friedrich Schubart in his *Ideen zu einer Ästhetik der Tonkunst*, posthumously published in 1806 but written in 1784–5, observed of Cramer: 'His bowstroke is wholly original. He does not do it like other violinists, straight down, but above and off [*gerade herunter, sondern oben hinweg*], he makes it short and

---

[23] Malibran, *Louis Spohr*, 208.
[24] The distinction is based on the degree of spring. [25] p. 72.
[26] *Louis Spohr Lebenserinnerungen*, ed. F. Göthel (Tutzing, 1968), i. 45.

extremely exact.'[27] During the last two decades of the century Cramer's bow-stroke seems to have been widely imitated, and Woldemar's *Grande méthode* (*c.*1800) identifies this technique as the *coup d'archet à la Cramer* (Ex. 7.7), noting that it is played with 'one bowstroke per note, the bow straight [upright?— *l'archet droit sur la corde*] on the string about the middle of the stick'.[28] In connection with another illustration of Cramer's style (Ex. 7.8), Woldemar gave the instruction: 'This genre requires a lot of neatness, of precision, of exactness, and the first note of the bar is usually forte.'[29] If these examples really represent the sort of passages in which Cramer himself used this bowing, it seems clear that it consisted of a series of very short bowstrokes in the middle of the bow with little pressure of the index finger, rather than the somewhat longer ones in the upper half of the bow which other violinists might have been expected to use for the same music. An admirer of Cramer's style of playing passagework wrote in 1804:

Cramer in London was the first to introduce a new, more attractive manner of playing into his concertos. Half, even whole pages full of rolling passagework were played staccato. Whereas formerly one played these fast notes with the end of the bow, now one used the middle of the bow [*Wie man vorher mit der Seite des Bogens diese geschwinden Noten abspielte,*

Ex. 7.7. Woldemar, *Grande méthode*, 47

Ex. 7.8. Woldemar, *Grande méthode*, 37

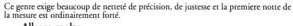

[27] (Vienna, 1806), 139.   [28] p. 47.   [29] p. 37.

so brauchte man jetzt die Mitte des Bogens]. Thereby they were made more separate, rounder, in a word, more beautiful.[30]

In another article, this kind of bowstroke was described (probably by the same writer), as being played 'with a half-bouncing bow',[31] but however neatly Cramer executed the bowstroke, it seems that many of his imitators were less successful. The writer went on to observe: 'Many, however, also ruined their previously good manner of playing after laborious effort to play with the middle of the bow, through too strong a pressure on the strings. The bow hopped here and there, and the tone became unpleasant, rough, and scratchy.'[32]

But this technique was not universally adopted. There appears to be no clear evidence of its having been used by orchestral players, and those players who did use it seem specially to have employed it in the passagework of concertos. Even in that context, many other musicians do not seem to have been so enamoured of it, and it appears already to have acquired a bad name in some quarters at an early stage. Leopold Mozart wrote to his son in 1778 giving an account of a visit to Salzburg by the violinist Janitsch. He admired many aspects of his playing, commenting especially on his 'facility and lightness of bowing' and describing it as similar to Lolli's except that he played adagio better. (The comparison of Janitsch's playing with that of Lolli is revealing, for a writer in 1799 observed of Lolli's performance in allegro: 'his was not the modern use of the bow where it is believed that effectiveness is to be found in clipped, hopping strokes and where the bow's long melting stroke, which almost outbids the beauty of the human voice, is neglected'.[33]) Leopold contrasted Janitsch's style of playing with that of other unnamed violinists, but evidently had followers of Cramer in mind, writing: 'I am no lover of rapid passages where you have to produce the notes with the half tone of the violin and, so to speak, only touch the fiddle with the bow and almost play in the air.'[34] Everything that is known of the violinists with whom the younger Mozart associated and whom he admired argues that he shared his father's preference for the broader style. This is suggested in particular by his praise for the playing of Ferdinand Fränzl[35] and by Rochlitz's comment that Mozart specially admired the playing of Johann Friedrich Eck for its tone, bowing, and command of legato; that Fränzl and Eck probably rejected the Cramer stroke entirely is suggested by what is known of their joint pupil, Eck's younger brother Franz. Franz Eck undoubtedly helped to foster the profound prejudice of his 19-year-old pupil Spohr against springing bowings during their trip to St Petersburg in 1803, since Spohr stated in his diary that one of the first things they worked on intensively was his faulty bowing technique.

[30] Anon., 'Ueber die heutige verworrene Strichbezeichnung', *Allgemeine musikalische Zeitung*, 6 (1803–4), 730.

[31] Ibid. 5 (1802–3), 665. [32] Ibid. 6 (1803–4), 730. [33] Ibid. 1 (1798–9), 579.

[34] Anderson, *The Letters of Mozart*, 455. [35] Ibid. 384.

From this and other scraps of evidence (for instance Schubart's descriptions of other violinists' styles of playing), it seems clear that Cannabich (Cramer's teacher), Eck, and other members of the Mannheim school during the 1770s and 1780s did not cultivate Cramer's style of bowing, which he almost certainly developed after he left Mannheim, at about the age of 20, during the mid-1760s. The weight of circumstantial evidence strongly supports Schröder's statement that springing bowings were little used in the late eighteenth-century Italian and German (Mannheim) schools, and these were precisely the schools most closely associated with Mozart and Haydn.

Nevertheless, the Cramer bowstroke was certainly popular with many string players, cellists as well as violinists. Jean Louis Duport, in his *Essai . . .* identified two methods of detached playing: 'the first is with strong bowing on the string, if one wants to play with full tone, the second is with a somewhat bouncing bow if one wants to perform in a flirting manner', and he instructed that the latter stroke should be made 'with the third quarter of the bow towards the point'.[36] Bernhard Romberg,[37] another of the leading cellists during the last decade of the eighteenth century and the early decades of the nineteenth, also described this type of bowing in his *Méthode de violoncelle* (1840), saying that it

may be introduced in light, easy passages, and is particularly suited to those pieces which are written in a playful style . . . For music of a higher order it is not so well adapted, and should never be used except in quick movements . . . This bowing cannot be employed in *forte* passages, since these require a greater pressure of the bow. This bowing was formerly in great repute with all Artists, who introduced it in passages of every description. It is, however, quite incompatible with a fine, broad style of playing, which fully accounts for the inferiority of their compositions.[38]

A third important cellist of the period, J. J. F. Dotzauer, omitted all mention of springing bowing in his *Méthode* of about 1825; some ten years later in his *Violoncell-Schule*, however, springing bowing is briefly mentioned, perhaps reflecting the revival of interest in this technique which occurred, in the wake of Paganini's popularity, in the middle decades of the nineteenth century.

If, as seems to be the case, springing bowings were very much peripheral to the Classical orchestral and chamber music traditions, the question remains: what kinds of bowstrokes were employed at that time in the sorts of places where they later came to be used? Also, although according to Schröder spring-

---

[36] *Essai sur le doigté du violoncelle et sur la conduite de l'archet* (Offenbach am Main, André, [*c.*1808]), 159.

[37] Romberg was associated with Beethoven in the Bonn court orchestra around 1790; his view of sautillé accords well with the idea that Beethoven may have envisaged it for a few scherzos, as Spohr suggested. (For further discussion of Romberg and Beethoven, see David Watkin, 'Beethoven's Sonatas for Piano and Cello', in Stowell, ed., *Performing Beethoven*, 89–116. Other musicians in Bonn at that time included the violinist Andreas Romberg, whose compositions reveal no suggestion of springing bowstrokes, and the cellist Joseph Reicha, who had accompanied Janitsch to Salzburg in 1778 and whose playing Leopold had rated even more highly.

[38] *A Complete*, 109.

ing strokes were an indispensable part of every violinist's technique by the last quarter of the nineteenth century, in what circumstances would they have been used in the music of mid- to late nineteenth-century composers?

Several quite distinct schools of string playing existed between about 1750 and 1880; these were distinguished from one another by a number of stylistic traits, but above all by their approach to bowing. The opposite poles in the mid-eighteenth century were represented by the French and Italian schools. As mentioned in chapter 5, the French tradition of short and well-articulated bowing was preferred by Quantz, at least for the accompaniment of lively pieces, to the 'long dragging stroke' of the Italians. This seems also to have been very much the approach recommended by Löhlein and Reichardt. In this style the bow was raised from the string for rests or to separate longer notes in faster tempos, but was normally used on the string with more or less short strokes for quicker notes. As Quantz observed:

> It was said above that the bow must be somewhat raised from the string for notes which have a little stroke over them. I only mean this to be so in the case of notes where there is sufficient time. Thus in allegro the quavers and in allegretto the semiquavers are excepted from this if many follow one another: for these must certainly be played with a very short bowstroke, but the bow will never be lifted or separated from the string. For if one wanted always to lift the bow as far as is required for the so-called *Absetzen*, there would not be enough time remaining to return it again at the right time, and notes of this sort would sound as if they were hacked or whipped.[39]

The Italian style of bowing which Quantz contrasted with the French seems to have been that associated primarily with Tartini. Schubart referred to the 'majestic sustained stroke' possessed by members of the Tartini school, and, while objecting that this 'may hinder the speed of performance and not be suited to winged passages', he admitted that it made these players 'unsurpassably good for the church style, since their bowing has just so much power and energy as is required for the true expression of the pathetic church style'.[40] Having commented favourably on Leopold Mozart's method, Schubart objected: 'however, his bowstroke is too Tartini-ish, and not suitable enough for presto'.[41] Yet earlier, he had remarked: 'He certainly leans towards the Tartini school, but he nevertheless allows the pupil more freedom in bowing than that school'.[42]

There were other important contributions to violin playing from groups and individuals during the second half of the century. The French style described by Quantz was never a model for solo playing, and the majority of soloists, even French violinists such as Pierre Gavinès (whom Viotti called 'the French Tartini'), learned much from the Italian style. The same influence was strong in Mannheim. But it is apparent that the austerity of Tartini's bowing

[39] *Versuch*, XVII, 2, §27.   [40] *Ideen*, 59.   [41] Ibid. 298.   [42] Ibid. 158.

style was modified considerably at this time; Antonio Lolli and a number of other Italian players evidently cultivated a lighter and more flexible bowing technique, though they still emphasized the singing qualities of the instrument and do not seem to have adopted the half-bouncing Cramer bowstroke.

Pugnani, though not a pupil of Tartini, was also noted for his broad and powerful bowstroke. In the hands of Pugnani's pupil Viotti this Italian style became transformed and subsumed into the Parisian school represented by Viotti's pupils and disciples, chief among whom were Rode, Kreutzer, and Baillot. Woldemar observed in 1801, after praising the excellent qualities of the Italian school, 'but it was reserved for Viotti to eclipse the glory of his predecessors and to become to some extent the leader and model of a new school'.[43] This school came so much to exercise a hegemony over European violin playing during the early decades of the nineteenth century that a writer in 1825 could say: 'It is, as is well known, distinguished by a characteristic use of the bow, and almost all present-day celebrated violin virtuosi have more or less adopted it';[44] and the English author William Gardiner commented that all violinists heard in England during recent times, except (significantly) François Cramer, the son of Wilhelm Cramer, were 'of the Viotti School'.[45]

By the time the Viotti school was recognized as dominant, however, the seeds of diversification were already beginning to sprout. Another tendency developed during the 1820s and 1830s, partly prompted by the astonishing impact of Paganini, but partly, perhaps, by a general shift in taste towards greater lightness and brilliance which was also reflected in the enormous popularity of Rossini. The principal characteristic of the newer approach was diversity of bowing, especially the employment of various bounced and thrown strokes as a fundamental element of technique rather than as occasional effects. Signs of this are already to be found in the playing and teaching of one of the leading representatives of the Viotti school, Baillot: his *L'Art du violon* of 1834 catalogues a much greater diversity of bowing techniques than is to be found in the Conservatoire method, which, together with Rode and Kreutzer, he had edited thirty years earlier. It is interesting in this context that when Baillot played in Vienna in 1809 a critic objected that his excessively varied bowing led to exaggeration.[46] The fact that the modern type of very crisp, almost percussive bounced bowings, produced in the lower half of the bow, were not part of the standard technique of the Classical and early Romantic periods is supported by the entry on staccato in Schilling's *Encyclopädie*, where it was observed:

[43] *Méthode de violon par L. Mozart redigée par Woldemar, élève de Lolli* (Paris, 1801), 1.
[44] *Cäcilia*, 2 (1825), 267.   [45] *The Music of Nature* (London, 1832), 216.
[46] *Allgemeine musikalische Zeitung*, 10 (1808–9), 603.

On string instruments, on which only notes of longer duration can be given an effective staccato, this is done by means of a short dig or jerked stroke of the bow (mostly upwards), on wind instruments, on which notes of shorter duration also admit this sort of performance, by a suppressed blast of air and a special movement with the tongue.[47]

In other words, the staccato (a series of moderate to fairly rapid notes, produced in a single bowstroke and more or less sharply articulated) was the only recognized means of achieving a succession of really detached notes; this would hardly have been the case if modern types of bounced bowing were regularly employed. Evidence of the employment of this type of stroke in places where modern players invariably use some form of bounced stroke can be found, as mentioned in Chapter 6, in manuscript parts of Schubert's Sixth Symphony used in Vienna for performances of the work during his lifetime, where the passages in the middle section of the Andante which appear simply as separate staccato notes in the autograph are bowed with dots under slurs in the parts, indicating a slurred staccato or perhaps the less detached portato. Similar use of slurred staccato where modern players would use sautillé or lower-half martelé can, as already demonstrated, be found in Ferdinand David's editions of Beethoven and Schubert. It seems too that by the 1820s the dominance of the Viotti school had largely eclipsed the memory of the Cramer sautillé (which had mainly been peculiar to aspiring virtuosos), at least in Germany. The unfamiliarity of this type of bowing to cultivated German musicians who came to maturity in the early 1800s, when the ascendancy of the Viotti school was reaching its height, is graphically illustrated by the reaction of the 42-year-old Frankfurt Kapellmeister and violinist Carl Guhr to Paganini's playing in 1829:

In *allegro maestoso* [i.e. a moderate allegro] he particularly loves a manner of bowing which materially differs in execution and effect from that taught in the Parisian violin school in *allegro maestoso*. There it is said you are to give every *staccato* note the fullest possible extension and to use half the bow in order that the whole string may vibrate properly and the tone may become round . . . But Paganini allows the bow rather to make a jumping, whipping [*springende, peitschende*] movement and uses for that purpose almost the middle of it and only so much of its length as is necessary to put the string into vibration—this bowing he employs with a half-strong sound [*halb starken Ton*], perhaps just a degree more than *mezzo forte*, but then it is of the greatest effect.[48]

Yet by the middle of the century the employment of springing bowings of various kinds was certainly becoming more widespread in Germany, both in solo and orchestral playing, and the older and newer approaches seem often to have come into conflict. A writer in 1840, discussing the lack of discipline in orchestral playing, complained:

Staccatos, for example, are so seldom performed uniformly, and it occurs to me that in this respect a firmer control on the part of the orchestra director would be appropriate. Very

---

[47] Art. 'Abstoßen.'   [48] *Ueber Paganini's Kunst die Violine zu spielen* . . . (Mainz, [1829]), 11.

often, one violinist plays light dancing figures with a springing bow while another uses a firm bow for them; this disturbs and spoils the effect.[49]

It is clear that by the 1840s an expanded repertoire of bowstrokes was beginning to be used, especially by players influenced by the most recent trends in French violin playing. Also, with the increasingly institutionalized training of string players, bowings that would previously have been the province of the virtuoso were being employed in the orchestra. The meticulously detailed scores of Meyerbeer's Parisian operas provide abundant evidence of the use of springing bowings in an orchestral context, but they also call for bowing at the point where the vast majority of modern players, left to their own instincts, would certainly not choose to use that kind of stroke (Ex. 7.9).

Ex. 7.9. Meyerbeer, *Les Huguenots*: (*a*) Act II, no. 7; (*b*) Act II, no. 9; (*c*) Act III, no. 16
(*a*)

(*b*)

(*c*)

The lesson of numerous nineteenth-century texts is, therefore, that although by the middle of the century the full range of modern bowstrokes was being taught and employed, especially in the Franco-Belgian school, the type of bowstroke that would have been considered appropriate in specific contexts was by no means the same as that which would be used by the majority of mod-

---

[49] *Neue Zeitschrift für Musik*, 31 (1849), 218.

ern players in similar circumstances. In particular, the off-string stroke for detached notes, so ubiquitous in modern violin playing, was far less frequently introduced and would generally have been seen as quite a special effect until fairly late in the century.

8

TEMPO

Historical evidence and contemporary experience demonstrate that tempo is among the most variable and contentious issues in musical performance. The majority of musicians regard it as their inalienable right to select their own tempo. To a considerable extent the exercise of choice in this, as in other interpretative matters, has been seen throughout the period as an essential part of the performing musician's creativity. John Holden put the matter nicely when he observed in 1770:

it must be acknowledged that the absolute time which ought to be allowed to different pieces, is the most undetermined matter, that we meet with, in the whole science of music. There is one insuperable difficulty, which frustrates all attempts towards regulating this particular, viz. the different humours and tastes of different persons; which are so various, that one person shall think a tune much too quick, for the intended expression, while another thinks it not quick enough.[1]

For the modern performer who wishes to approach the composer's intentions as closely as possible it is important not to misunderstand the workings of the relevant conventions and, through simple ignorance, choose a tempo radically different from that envisaged by the composer. This can all too easily happen when a term such as 'andante molto' is used by some composers to mean a faster pace than their normal andante and by others a slower one, or when the significance of ₵ for the tempo in particular cases is unrecognized. It is arguably more fundamental to the integrity of a composition that the performer should appreciate the thinking that lay behind the composer's methods of indicating tempo than that he should attempt to achieve specific chronometric tempos (however authentic) in particular cases; indeed, if this more limited end is attained the likelihood of choosing radically inappropriate speeds is greatly

---

[1] *Essay*, 36.

lessened. But, as becomes apparent on closer investigation, it is by no means easy to be confident even about the relationship of one tempo to another in many instances, especially since the tempo is indicated not merely by the Italian term prefixed to the piece, but by a complex of other related factors and conventions that differ from composer to composer, place to place, and period to period.

With the advent of the metronome in the second decade of the nineteenth century we have a mass of largely untapped information about the tempo predilections of many major and minor composers, which offers tantalizing possibilities of making better-informed judgements about differing notions of the speed implied by 'allegro', 'andante', and so on, and the other factors in the tempo equation than are possible with the limited evidence for chronometric tempos in the eighteenth century. But this evidence is by no means easy to interpret and must be approached with considerable circumspection. Early metronome marks reveal the last phase of a complicated yet, in the case of some composers, remarkably consistent method of designating tempo. Paradoxically, as will become apparent later, the availability of the metronome as a means of exactly fixing tempo may have played a part in lessening later nineteenth-century composers' concerns to indicate their wishes clearly in other ways, often making it particularly difficult to ascertain their intentions where metronome marks were not supplied. Tradition, after the lapse of a generation or more, is an extremely unreliable guide to such matters, as, for instance, a comparison of the timings of performances at Bayreuth in Wagner's lifetime with subsequent ones shows.

Choice of Tempo

Every sensitive musician is aware that the quest for historically appropriate tempos must essentially be concerned with plausible parameters rather than with precisely delineated or very narrowly defined absolute tempos. Many psychological and aesthetic factors, as well as the varying physical conditions in which performance takes place, militate against the notion that a piece of music should be rigidly bound to a single immutable tempo. As A. B. Marx observed in the 1830s: 'the same piece of music must sometimes be played somewhat faster, sometimes slower, according to the larger or more constricted space in which it is performed, according to the stronger or weaker forces employed, but particularly according to the decision of the moment.'[2] This was a view evidently shared by Marx's friend (at that time) Mendelssohn;[3] for it was reported of Mendelssohn that 'though in playing he never varied the

---

[2] Schilling, *Encyclopädie*, art. 'Tempo'.

[3] The two musicians later fell out over Mendelssohn's refusal to perform Marx's oratorio *Moses*.

tempo when once taken, he did not always take a movement at the same pace, but changed it as his mood was at the time'.[4] This may well go some way towards explaining Mendelssohn's relative reluctance to supply metronome marks for his own works.

Even where a metronome or another method of exact tempo specification had been used to fix the tempo of a particular piece of music, few theorists or composers would have disagreed with Weber's assertion, in a letter accompanying metronome marks for *Euryanthe*, that such means would at best serve to avoid 'gross blunders'[5] but are of limited value unless performers feel the rightness of the tempo within themselves. Yet many musicians, including major composers, were insistent that a well-chosen tempo is vital to the effective realization of a piece of music. Although some, like Weber, Mendelssohn, and Marx (and, later, Wagner and Brahms), showed a clear awareness of the limitations of the metronome and were wary of insisting too rigidly on a precise tempo, it cannot be assumed that most composers were happy with the idea that the performer should depart radically from their intentions in this respect, any more than they would have been with alterations to the harmony or structure of the music. For this reason a considerable number of nineteenth-century composers took great care in assigning metronome marks to their music and insisted upon their validity; in relation to *Aida*, for instance, Verdi wrote in a letter of 10 August 1871: 'take care that all the tempos be just as indicated by the metronome.'[6]

But the divergences of practice with regard to tempo in the early nineteenth century that had helped to convince many musicians of the need for the metronome were scarcely lessened by its adoption. Even where a composer's own metronome marks exist, movements have frequently been taken at radically different speeds. The quintessentially Romantic idea, encapsulated in Weber's assertion that the right tempo can only be found 'within the sensitive human breast', may be seen as characteristic of an outlook that became stronger during the course of the nineteenth century. In periods of artistic vigour (i.e. when contemporary art is powerfully in tune with the feelings of an age) the prevalent aesthetic seems to overrule any effective notion of fidelity to the wishes of the original artist. Mozart is relevant to Brahms's and Tchaikovsky's generation not so much as a late eighteenth-century composer in his own right, but rather as the symbol of a pure beauty for which they nostalgically yearn. For Wagner and his contemporaries, Beethoven's music is seen less as the expression of his own spirit and times than as an anticipation of later musical values.

---

[4] Grove, *Dictionary*, art. 'Mendelssohn', ii. 299.

[5] Friedrich Wilhelm Jähns, *Carl Maria von Weber in seinen Werken: Chronologisch-thematisches Verzeichniss seiner sämmtlichen Werken* (Berlin, 1871), 374.

[6] Franco Abbiati, *Giuseppe Verdi* (Milan, 1959), iii. 466.

Such assimilations of past music to present or localized aesthetics begin almost immediately, often indeed within the composer's lifetime. Many of Beethoven's and Schumann's metronome marks, especially those that ask for very fast tempos, were clearly not uncontroversial even among their contemporaries and close associates. An edition of Beethoven's Septet (in a quintet arrangement) published by Schlesinger at about the time of the composer's death[7] gives slower metronome marks for all the movements, and very significantly slower ones for some, than Beethoven himself had given to the work ten years earlier (see Table 8.1).

Table 8.1. Metronome Marks for Beethoven's Septet op. 20

Movement	MM Beethoven	Schlesinger
Adagio	♪ = 76	—
Allegro con brio	𝅗𝅥 = 96	𝅗𝅥 = 84
Adagio cantabile	♪ = 132	♪ = 96
Tempo di Menuetto	♩ = 120	♩ = 92
Andante	♪ = 120	♪ = 96*
Scherzo	𝅗𝅥. = 126	𝅗𝅥. = 120
Andante con moto	♪ = 76	♪ = 63
Presto	𝅗𝅥 = 112	𝅗𝅥 = 100

* The printed note value is ♩ but the speed of the demisemiquavers demonstrate that this must be a misprint.

Anton Schindler, Beethoven's amanuensis and self-declared guardian of his posthumous tradition, felt so strongly about his own notion of the proper tempos for Beethoven's music that he resorted to forging entries in the conversation books to support his view and to suggest, quite without solid foundation, that Beethoven had repudiated a considerable number of his metronome marks in later life. The story about Beethoven losing some metronome marks and replacing them with quite different ones, which is often cited as evidence that his preserved metronome marks lack authority, derives from Schindler and is not supported by any reliable evidence.[8] Schindler's claim that in the letter sent to London in 1827 with metronome marks for the Ninth Symphony 'All the tempos were different, some slower, some faster'[9] than those he gave earlier to Schott is simply untrue: only one, 66 instead of a mistaken 96 for the initial

---

[7] Copy in the British Library, London.

[8] For a recent repetition of the tale see Donington, art. 'Tempo', *New Grove Dictionary of Music and Musicians* 18 (1980), 675, where it is cited without reference to its derivation from Schindler.

[9] *Biographie von Ludwig van Beethoven* (Münster, 1840), 220.

Presto of the fourth movement, differs. In Schumann's case, discomfort with many of his fast metronome marks, even on the part of his wife, gave rise within a short time of his death to the now discredited rumour that his metronome was faulty; and Clara Schumann altered many of them in her edition of his piano works.[10]

There can be little doubt that through ignoring the implications of a composer's metronome marks, accomplished musicians have frequently committed what the composers themselves would have regarded as, in Weber's phrase, gross blunders. Yet the unquestioning acceptance of metronome marks, even if only as an approximate guide, is also injudicious; for although a composer's metronome marks (or other form of chronometric tempo marking) can give the performer an invaluable message about tempo, these markings are not without their hazards. It was all too easy for printers, engravers, copyists, or even the composers to make mistakes. Errors in the transmission of metronome marks are far from uncommon; some of these are easily recognizable, yet in numerous instances where a wrong note value or number seems highly probable, the composer's real intention remains unclear. A sizeable number of Beethoven's metronome marks are evidently printing or transcribing errors. In the case, referred to above, of ♩. = 96 instead of 66 at the beginning of the Finale of the Ninth Symphony in the list published by Schott in 1826 and in the subsequent editions, it has been possible to demonstrate the manner in which the mistake occurred.[11] Other metronome marks are so obviously incorrect that they have never caused serious problems, but a few which are almost certainly wrong have continued to mislead modern interpreters, resulting in performances that certainly fail to convey what Beethoven conceived.[12] Even a cursory glance at other composers' metronome marks quickly reveals similar mistakes: for instance the overture to Spontini's *Nurmahal* in the original edition has ♩ = 123 in the score and ♩ = 122 on the index page, but since neither of these numbers occurs on the metronome they are probably both misprints for 132.[13] And Hugh Macdonald has drawn attention to many similar problems with Berlioz's metronome marks.[14]

Nevertheless, the vast majority of metronome marks will be an accurate record of what composers or editors intended to convey at the time they gave them. Whether they are an accurate record of the tempo at which, in practice,

[10] See D. Kämper, 'Zur Frage der Metronombezeichnungen Robert Schumanns', *Archiv für Musikwissenschaft*, 21 (1964), 141; and B. Schotel, 'Schumann and the Metronome', in A. Walker, ed., *Robert Schumann: The Man and his Music* (London, 1972), 109 ff.

[11] Otto Baensch, 'Zur Neunten Symphonie', in Adolf Sandberger, ed., *Neues Beethoven-Jahrbuch* (Augsburg, 1925), 145 ff.

[12] See Clive Brown, 'Historical Performance, Metronome Marks and Tempo in Beethoven's Symphonies', *Early Music*, 19 (1991), 247 ff.

[13] Copy of full score in Bodleian Library, Oxford.

[14] 'Berlioz and the Metronome', in P. A. Bloom, ed., *Berlioz Studies* (Cambridge, 1992), 17–36.

the music was performed or directed is another question. Comparison of late nineteenth- and early twentieth-century composers' metronome marks with recorded performances which they themselves directed (for example, Elgar)[15] show that they often diverged significantly from their own instructions (and not only with respect to tempo). There is evidence that earlier composers, too, were not consistent in this matter. When Berlioz incorporated several numbers from his *Huit scènes de Faust* into *La Damnation de Faust* he gave them all slower metronome marks than before. And Saint-Saëns recalled that when he heard Berlioz conduct a performance of his *Grande messe des morts* several of the tempos were quite different from the ones printed in the score: the Moderato (♩ = 96) at the beginning of the 'Dies Irae' was more like an allegro and the Andante maestoso (♩ = 72) following, like a moderato.[16]

Notwithstanding such suggestions of variable practice, nineteenth-century anecdotes documenting composers' concerns about finding the right tempo for performances of their work abound. Where they appear to have favoured a more *laissez-faire* attitude, as in the case of Weber, Wagner (after *Tannhäuser*), or Brahms, the underlying assumption seems to have been rather that a knowledgeable musician would light upon a tempo within the range envisaged by the composer, than that any tempo, even if chosen by a sensitive artist, would do. Wagner was not giving an entirely free rein to the performer when he wrote that things would be in a sorry state 'if conductors and singers are to be dependent on metronome marks alone' and that 'they will hit upon the right tempo only when they begin to find a lively sympathy with the dramatic and musical situations and when that understanding allows them to find the tempo as though it were something that did not require any further searching on their part'.[17] He had remarked earlier that the composer's greatest concern was 'to ensure that your piece of music is heard exactly as you yourself heard it when you wrote it down: that is to say, the composer's intentions must be reproduced with conscientious fidelity so that the ideas which it contains may be conveyed to the senses undistorted and unimpaired';[18] this suggests rather that he was expecting them to find the composer's tempo (variable though that may have been in his own practice).

Weber's, Wagner's, and Brahms's expectations may not have been too unrealistic while they and the musicians who worked with them were there to provide a yardstick. However, since culture is dynamic and artistic taste is far from universal, the musicianship that results from training and experience within

---

[15] E. O. Turner, 'Tempo Variation: With Examples from Elgar', *Music & Letters*, 19 (1938), 308–23; Robert Philip, 'The Recordings of Edward Elgar (1857–1934): Authenticity and Performance Practice', *Early Music*, 12 (1984), 481–9.

[16] Camille Saint-Saëns, *Musical Memoires*, trans. E. G. Rich (London, 1921), 136–7.

[17] 'Über die Aufführung des "Tannhäuser"', *Gesammelte Schriften und Dichtungen*, v. 144.

[18] 'Der Virtuos und der Künstler', 169.

different traditions often leads to quite sharply contrasting notions of the appropriate tempo for particular compositions. The good taste and orthodoxy of one place or time may thus be the 'gross blunder' of another just as much with respect to tempo as to other aspects of performance.

It is possible to argue that such concerns are irrelevant: dead composers no longer have any rights in their music; it belongs to posterity to do with it as it will. Yet many musicians who favour radically different tempos from those indicated by metronome marks or historical evidence do not take that stance; they challenge the validity of the evidence. This is nowhere more apparent than in the case of the very rapid tempos in fast movements that seem to have been favoured by many early nineteenth-century musicians, but which have run so contrary to later taste. Various theories have been advanced to show that metronome marks are not a correct record of the tempo at which composers wanted their music to be performed. Apart from suggestions that they did not properly know how to use the machine or that their metronomes were faulty, one author has even gone so far as to advance the bizarre theory that the manner of indicating metronome markings for faster tempos up to about 1848 has been completely misunderstood, and that they should really be performed at half the speed.[19] Though this theory has attracted a few supporters,[20] it has been ably rebutted by other scholars.[21] Further unequivocal support for the rejection of such ideas can be found in a number of early accounts of how to use metronomes or pendula,[22] and perhaps most explicitly in the method initially adopted for indicating the metronomic tempos in the autograph of Schubert's opera *Alfonso und Estrella*. For instance: for a movement in ¢ the score has '160 = ♩ 2 Striche im Takt', or for a movement in 12/8 '92 = ♪ 12 Striche im Takt'.[23] More reasonable arguments, based on psychological and experiential grounds, might lead to the plausible conclusion that composers' perceptions of tempo in their imagination may have been faster than they would require in performance and that this often results in metronome marks at the upper limit of practicable tempo; but in these cases the margin of error is rarely likely to be enormous, and the metronome marks retain their validity as a guide to the composer's conception.

The important qualification in Marx's comment, quoted earlier, is 'somewhat' faster or slower. One of the fundamental problems that was explicitly

[19] Willem R. Talsma, *Wiedergeburt der Klassiker* (Innsbruck, 1980).

[20] e.g. Clemens von Gleich, 'Original Tempo-Angaben bei Mendelssohn', in H. Herrtrich and H. Schneider (eds.), *Festschrift Rudolf Elvers zum 60 Geburtstag* (Tutzing, 1985), 213 ff.

[21] e.g. Wolfgang Auhagen, 'Chronometrische Tempoangaben im 18. und 19. Jahrhundert', *Archiv für Musikwissenschaft*, 44 (1987), 40–57.

[22] e.g. Gesualdo Lanza, *The Elements of Singing* (London, [1809]) and Herz's discussion of metronome marks in *Méthode complète de piano*, 12.

[23] See *Alfonso und Estrella*, ed. Walther Dürr, *Neue Schubert Ausgabe*, II/6 (Bärenreiter, Kassel, 1993), preface, pp. vii ff.

articulated, or that underlay many musicians' comments on tempo, was the degree of deviation from the 'ideal' tempo that was possible without altering the intended impact of the music. The acceptable margins of variation cannot be exactly prescribed, but it is obvious to every accomplished musician that, while it would be inartistic to insist on a single immutable tempo for any piece of music in all circumstances, music can be performed at tempos so different from those envisaged by the composer that the character of the composition is completely altered. Thus Quantz conceded that it would 'do no harm . . . if a melancholy person, in accordance with his temperament, were to play a piece moderately fast, but still well, and if a more volatile person played it with greater liveliness';[24] yet he also stressed:

We see daily how often tempo is abused, and how frequently the very same piece is played moderately at one time, and still more quickly at another. It is well known that in many places where people play carelessly, a presto is often made an allegretto and an adagio an andante, doing the greatest injustice to the composer, who cannot always be present.[25]

Other eighteenth-century musicians were more insistent on the necessity for a composer's tempo to be adhered to within a quite narrow margin. Kirnberger, for instance, felt that only the composer was in a position to dictate the correct tempo and that 'a little degree more or less can do much damage to the effect of a piece';[26] and he suggested that for greater certainty composers should append to their pieces a note of their duration. A similar recommendation was made by Johann Adolf Scheibe in about the same period.[27] There was scarcely a German theorist of the late eighteenth century who did not stress the impor- tance of finding the right tempo. Among composers and performers Pisendel was noted for his extraordinary ability to divine a composer's tempo inten- tions,[28] and Mozart's confident mastery of everything concerning tempo is reflected in his often-quoted letters on the subject.[29] Most accomplished eighteenth-century and early nineteenth-century musicians would have been confident that they could discern a careful composer's intentions with a high degree of accuracy, but the meaning of the clues and instructions to which they were sensitive were largely forgotten during the nineteenth century and are very imperfectly understood by most performers of the late twentieth century.

---

[24] *Versuch*, XVII, 7, §55.   [25] Ibid.   [26] In Sulzer, *Allgemeine Theorie*, art. 'Bewegung'.
[27] *Ueber die musikalische Composition, erster Theil: Die Theorie der Melodie und Harmonie* (Leipzig, 1773), 299.
[28] See Türk, *Klavierschule*, I, §75.   [29] See Anderson, *The Letters of Mozart*.

Late Eighteenth-Century and Early Nineteenth-Century Tempo Conventions

During the Classical period and the early part of the Romantic period, the determination of tempo was widely acknowledged to depend on a subtle balance and relationship between a number of basic factors. The most important of these were the metre, the tempo term,[30] the note values employed in the piece, the quantity of fast notes that it contained, and the types of figuration in which these notes were used. Additional influences might include such things as the character of the piece and the genre to which it belonged, the harmonic movement, or any close relationship to a specific dance type. All these considerations were intimately related to the speed that competent composers conceived for their music or that well-trained musicians would have chosen for it. Nevertheless, it is evident that there were important variations in emphasis depending on nationality and school, and that individual composers developed their own usages, notably in the matter of metre and tempo terms.

At the beginning of the seventeenth century, tempo was theoretically determined largely by metre and the so-called principles of proportional notation. During the course of that century the system of modern time signatures began to emerge, though, as with all evolutionary processes, some elements of the older scheme were retained as anomalous features in the new. The notion of a tactus to which the various metres were related, never very consistent, was already weakening in the early years of the seventeenth century and by the beginning of the eighteenth had long ceased to provide an adequate means of indicating tempo. The tactus is still mentioned in a few late eighteenth-century treatises,[31] but by that stage it had little if any relevance for practical music.

By the middle of the eighteenth century the notion of a universal tactus had been effectively displaced by the idea that each metre had a natural rate of motion. This concept of metre seems to have been well established and generally understood in Germany and France; the Italians may have been rather more pragmatic. Few instrumental or singing methods of the period dealt with the tempo implications of metre in any depth, though many alluded to them. Leopold Mozart's account is typical of the majority of practical authors, who left the more esoteric aspects of the subject to be imparted to the student by a teacher, or expected an understanding of the refinements of tempo to be absorbed instinctively through experience: Mozart merely mentioned that the various types of metre are 'sufficient to show in some degree the natural difference between a slow and a quick melody',[32] without giving any further guid-

---

[30] The phrase 'tempo term' will be used for words like 'allegro', 'andante', etc., together with their qualifiers ('moderato', 'sostenuto', etc.) although in most cases they have connotations of expression as well as tempo.

[31] In Holden's *Essay*, for instance.   [32] *Versuch*, I, 2, §4.

ance. A few eighteenth-century theorists, however, offered more detailed expositions of contemporary thought on these matters. Perhaps the most comprehensive account was given by J. P. Kirnberger and J. A. P. Schulz in Kirnberger's *Die Kunst des reinen Satzes in der Musik* and in a number of articles in Sulzer's *Allgemeine Theorie der schönen Kunste*. Stressing the vital role of metre in determining tempo, Kirnberger observed that the composer (and, presumably, also the performer) must have 'a correct feeling for the natural tempo of every metre, or for what is called *tempo giusto*' and observed that this, like a proper feeling for accentuation and the articulation of phrases, could be attained by the study of all kinds of dance pieces, since each dance has its definite tempo which is determined by the metre and the note values employed in it.[33]

There was no universally recognized chronometric definition of these natural rates of motion of the various metres, and no precisely defined relationship between one metre and another. For eighteenth-century musicians who were intimately familiar with the speeds of the dance types closely associated with particular metres, it seems probable that this natural tempo, or tempo giusto, was not merely a nebulous concept. But in practice there was an abundance of complications. Theorists who wanted to be able to expound a clear and logical system also had to grapple with the difficulties created by the diverse uses which had been made of the most frequently employed metres. For instance, some common dances of radically different kinds, such as the minuet and the sarabande, were written in the same metre, in this case 3/4, and this led to these metres having more than one natural tempo. Some considered 3/8 as the proper metre for the minuet, but as John Holden remarked: 'we frequently write them in the triple of crotchets, which makes no material difference, because the name itself determines the quickness of the time.'[34]

Duple and quadruple metres, too, appeared in a number of different guises. According to some writers there were three different kinds of four-crotchet time (abbreviated hereafter as 4/4, although this form of the time signature was scarcely used in the eighteenth century and early nineteenth century). The large 4/4 and the common 4/4 were described by, among others, Schulz and Türk: these were usually designated by the time signature 𝄴, but both writers regarded 4/4 as the proper time signature for the former; large 4/4 (explained by some as a substitute for 4/2) required a slow tempo and contained nothing faster than quavers, while common 4/4, which could contain shorter notes, required a faster tempo. In addition Schulz insisted that a distinction should be made between the common 4/4 and the *zusammengesetzten* (put together) 4/4 (also marked with a 𝄴), each bar of which, being derived from two joined-up bars of 2/4, had a different accentuation from common 4/4 and required the character of 2/4 in its delivery. Other writers of a more practical bent

---

[33] *The Art of Strict Musical Composition*, 376.   [34] *Essay*, 40.

(particularly in England and France) ignored these theoretical distinctions, recognizing only one type of 4/4 or **C**, whose character was governed by the musical content and the tempo terms.

Another point, about which the German theorists appear not to have been entirely clear, is whether the crotchets in 2/4 were regarded as essentially livelier than those in 4/4. Neither Schulz nor Türk explicitly say so; indeed, in the case of Schulz's *zusammengesetzten* 4/4 they are exactly the same, since he says that, with regard to performance style and motion, the *zusammengesetzten* metres are identical to the simple metres from which they are derived. It follows from this, however, that common 4/4 has a character that is different from 2/4 and *zusammengesetzten* 4/4. But there seem to have been considerable differences of opinion about the relationship of 2/4 to 4/4, since many composers treated it as if it were really 4/8. Hummel's metronome marks for Mozart symphonies (e.g. the 'Linz') suggest a steadier interpretation of the crotchets in 2/4 than in 4/4; and, somewhat later, Bernhard Romberg, after listing tempo terms with what he regarded as appropriate metronome marks, added: 'When the above marks [i.e. tempo terms] occur in 2/4 time . . . the strokes of the pendulum must be rather slower than in Common or **C** time.'[35] In the music of Beethoven and Mendelssohn, metronome marks appear to bear out this view of 2/4 to some extent: compare for instance the Allegro **C** ($\downarrow$ = 80) in Beethoven's Sixth Symphony op. 68 with the Allegro 2/4 ($\downarrow$ = 126) of the String Quartet op. 59 no. 1 or the Allegro non troppo **C** ($\downarrow$ = 92) of Mendelssohn's *Erste Walpurgisnacht* op. 60 with the Vivace non troppo 2/4 ($\downarrow$ = 126) in the 'Scotch' Symphony op. 56. But in Beethoven's case, and that of other composers, the situation is complicated by a tendency to employ a type of 2/4 with four quaver beats in the bar that stands in the same relationship to **C** as **C** does to **¢**: for example, the 2/4 adagios in Beethoven's string quartets opp. 18 no. 6 and 59 no. 1 or the first and last movements of op. 18 no. 2. The treatment of 2/4 by later nineteenth-century composers continued to be variable in this respect; Schumann and Dvořák, for instance, do not seem to have regarded **C** and 2/4 as, in themselves, implying any basic difference in the speed of the crotchets in relation to the tempo term, but Dvořák quite frequently wrote movements in 4/8 which have a different character.

In doubtful cases the note values employed in the piece and its overall musical characteristics were generally expected to provide the necessary clues to decide in which of the metrical sub-types the piece belonged. Despite these complexities, the idea of a tempo giusto seems to have played an crucial part in the thinking of many eighteenth- and early nineteenth-century musicians. The tempo giusto was considered to be the speed at which a piece in a given metre, containing a certain range of note values and with a particular character, would

---

[35] *A Complete*, 110. See also Peter Williams, 'Two Case Studies in Performance Practice and the Details of Notation, 1: J. S. Bach and 2/4 Time', *Early Music*, 21 (1993), 613–22.

be performed unless made faster or slower by a specific tempo term. At the root of the system, despite all the anomalies, was the idea that, other things being equal, the smaller the denominator in the time signature (i.e. the larger the note values), the slower and heavier the pulse; thus, the same melody notated in 3/2, 3/4, and 3/8 would be performed successively faster and lighter.

But halving the note values did not imply doubling the speed. Schulz explained: 'For example, the quavers in 3/8 metre are not as long as the crotchets in 3/4, but also not as short as the quavers in the latter metre. Therefore, a piece marked vivace in 3/8 time would have a livelier tempo than it would in 3/4 time.'[36] In a similar vein, Koch observed that the same musical phrase notated in 2/2 and 2/4 (with halved note values) should be played more slowly in the former than the latter, adding: 'and therefore the note values used will, if not in the most exact manner, nevertheless to some extent fix the speed of the movement, and therefore the expression which one is accustomed to affix to every movement to designate the speed will be all the clearer.' But his following remarks may be taken as a caution against assuming that composers can be relied upon to have observed such principles consistently, for he continued: 'However, people do not take the hint in this matter that the nature of the thing gives us; if it happens from time to time, this is more accidental than intentional, for the use of these two metres in respect of the speed of movement is taken to be wholly arbitrary.'[37] And he complained that, in fact, they were often employed in a diametrically opposite manner: 2/4 for slow pieces and (evidently thinking of alla breve) 2/2 for fast ones. He regarded the former use as less excusable than the latter, since at least writing fast pieces in 2/2 had the practical advantage of requiring fewer beams to the notes.

The use of tempo terms to modify the natural rate of motion of a metre had already begun during the course of the seventeenth century. At first words like 'presto', 'adagio', 'vif', 'lent', 'brisk', 'drag', and so on seem only to have indicated a somewhat slower or faster pace than normal, but gradually a larger number of terms and an extended range of variation evolved as composers became concerned not only to determine the tempo but also to govern the expression. The Paris Conservatoire's *Principes élémentaires de musique* (c.1800) observed:

Formerly tempo was determined by the nature of the metre . . . In a word, the tempos increased in speed accordingly as the metres decreased in value. Modern music no longer observes this rule rigorously; and as at present each metre can be played at three tempos, that is to say slow tempo, moderate tempo, and fast tempo and their nuances, it follows that the silence of the metre in this matter has been replaced by terms which indicate the degree of slowness or fastness which the tempo should have.[38]

[36] In Sulzer, *Allgemeine Theorie*, 2nd edn. iv. 707.   [37] Koch, *Versuch*, ii. 292.
[38] Gossec et al., *Principes*, 43.

In his discussion of 2/4, Schulz considered the theoretical relationship between the tempo terms, the tempo giusto of a specific metre, and the note values, explaining:

It [2/4] is appropriate to all light and pleasant motions of feeling which, according to the quality of the expression, can be softened by andante or adagio or made even more lively by vivace or allegro. The particular tempo of this and all other metres is determined by these words and by the types of notes employed.[39]

Schulz's reference to 'the types of notes employed' hints at a further subtlety in the system. The relationship between larger note values and slower and heavier execution applied not only between metres with different denominators, but also within the same metre. As has already been explained, a melody notated in 2/2 which was transcribed into half note values in 2/4 would, assuming the tempo term remained constant, theoretically be performed somewhat more quickly and more lightly; similarly, if a melody were renotated with halved note values in the same metre, so that two bars of the original version became one of the new version, it too would be played faster and more lightly than before, though not twice as fast. Only if the composer reduced the tempo term, say from 'allegro con brio' to 'allegro moderato', would the music be played at the same speed. Such transference from one form of notation to another within the same metre could take place without significant alteration of the pattern of accentuation, since tempo played a large part in determining the frequency and weight of accents, though the different notation, even if the tempo remained the same, would probably have been intended to convey a somewhat different message about the style of performance.[40]

For musicians responsive to these conventions, therefore, larger note values, even within the same metre, implied slower and heavier music. An allegro in 2/4 containing a significant number of semiquavers as its fastest notes would, therefore, probably have a crotchet pulse, and this would be faster and lighter than the minim pulse of one that contained nothing faster than quavers. In that case the relationship that more commonly existed between pieces in different metres would then exist between pieces in the same metre.[41] Thus, though the crotchet pulse of an allegro containing semiquavers in 2/4 might be faster than the minim pulse of another having only quavers, the crotchets in the latter would still be faster than the crotchets in the former. But as was normally the

---

[39] In Sulzer, *Allgemeine Theorie*, 1st edn. ii. 1253.

[40] See Ch. 16, 'Heavy and Light Performance'.

[41] The recognition of which note value constitutes the pulse unit in these instances depends entirely on the nature of the music. Quantz discussed a type of adagio 3/4 which moves basically in crotchets and is performed at twice the speed of one in which there is quaver motion. A similar situation seems often to have existed with the true alla breve; it is clear that ¢ was often used when ¢ was really meant, either because a composer regarded the value of the pulse unit as obvious or through inadvertent omission of the vertical bar. The vexed question of alla breve is discussed more fully in Ch. 9 below.

case, in practice there would not be a 2 : 1 relationship. A good example of this is provided by the first movement of Beethoven's Fifth Symphony op. 67 and the last movement of his Seventh Symphony op. 92, both of which are Allegro con brio in 2/4: op. 67, with quavers as the fastest notes, has the metronome mark $\quarternote$ = 108, while op. 92, with semiquavers, has the metronome mark $\quarternote$ = 72.

The tempo terms, the metre, the note values, and the actual speed at which the music should be performed were therefore seen by theorists as necessarily interdependent elements in the system. Considerable evidence can be found to show that many composers during the century between 1750 and 1850 did not merely regard these relationships as purely theoretical. For instance, when Mozart changed the finale of his Quartet in B flat major K. 458 from ¢ (alla breve) to 2/4 with halved note values he also reduced the tempo term from 'Presto' to 'Allegro assai'; and when Mendelssohn did a similar thing with his *Sommernachtstraum* overture, changing it from ¢ in the orchestral version to C with half note values in the piano duet version, he altered the tempo term from 'Allegro di molto' to 'Allegro vivace'. An example of the same principle operating when a piece was renotated in halved note values without a change of metre is provided by a comparison of the first version of Mendelssohn's Octet with the published version. When he revised the first movement, halving the note values but keeping the metre the same (i.e. two bars of C became one), he altered the tempo term from 'Allegro molto e vivace' to 'Allegro moderato ma con fuoco'.

Another important constituent of the tempo equation was the quantity of fast-moving notes which a piece contained. After discussing the effect of metre, tempo term, and note values, Schulz went on to explain how this additional factor also exercised an influence on the speed of the pulse unit. He observed: 'If the piece is in 2/4, marked with allegro and has few or even no semiquavers, so the beat is faster than if it were filled with them; the same is true of slower tempos.'[42]

Among other factors affecting tempo, Schulz pointed out that the time units in uneven (i.e. triple) time were naturally lighter than those in the equivalent even (i.e. duple or quadruple) time; thus the crotchets in an allegro 3/4 were felt to be somewhat livelier than those in an allegro 2/4 or 4/4. John Holden made a similar point, saying 'it is generally agreed, that every mood of triple time ought to be performed something quicker, than the correspondent mood of common time'.[43] Holden also drew attention to the convention that tempo was differently perceived in different genres of music, observing that 'the real length of the measure ought to be made something more, in Church music; and often much less in Opera music'.[44] Türk similarly mentioned that church music required a 'far more moderate tempo' than 'music for the theatre or in

---

[42] In Sulzer, *Allgemeine Theorie*, 1st edn. ii. 1253.   [43] *Essay*, 36.   [44] Ibid. 27.

the so-called chamber style',[45] and he considered the same to be true of pieces that were more elaborately worked out (contrapuntal) or serious.

These views about tempo are confirmed in many eighteenth-century and early nineteenth-century sources. The following passage from J. F. Schubert's *Neue Singe-Schule* (1804), for instance, indicates that the ideas on tempo expounded by earlier writers were still seen as valid at that time, and also identifies some of the other things that were felt to have a bearing on tempo.

> The correct tempo or degree of speed cannot be determined by any heading, and can only be gathered from the inner characteristics of a composition itself. So, for instance, an allegro with semiquavers ought not to be performed as quickly as if the fastest passages are only in triplets or quavers. An allegro in church style or in an oratorio must have a slower tempo than an allegro in theatre or chamber style. An allegro where the text has a solemn content and the character of the music is exalted or pathetic must have a more serious motion than an allegro with a joyful text and lightweight music. A well-worked-out allegro with a powerful, full harmony must be performed more slowly than a hastily written allegro with trivial harmony. In an adagio in 3/8 metre the quavers will be performed more slowly than the quavers in the same tempo in 3/4 metre. . . . Differences in compositional style or manner and national taste also necessitate a faster or slower tempo.[46]

There were therefore a number of less obvious factors that could to some extent affect the choice of tempo term that, in combination with the metre and note values, a composer considered would convey the correct tempo range to the performer. Some of these will be considered further in relation to the varied and fluctuating meaning of tempo terms. Clearly the matter was of such complexity that even when this method of indicating tempo was part of the current performing tradition only the most gifted and experienced musicians will successfully have found their way through the maze of complications.

Late Eighteenth-Century Tempo

The extent to which Haydn, Mozart, and other late eighteenth-century composers were consistent in their application of the principles of tempo determination outlined above cannot be objectively assessed. It is reasonable to conclude that Haydn and Mozart were very careful to indicate the desired speed by their choice of the appropriate tempo term, in combination with the metre, note values of the piece, and other relevant factors. Yet, even if it is possible to determine the internal relationships of Haydn's or Mozart's tempo system with a fair degree of confidence,[47] there is insufficient information to do more than speculate about the absolute tempo range they might have con-

---

[45] *Klavierschule*, I, §72.   [46] p. 124.

[47] See Neal Zaslaw, 'Mozart's Tempo Conventions', *International Musicological Society Congress Report*, II (Copenhagen, 1972), 720–33.

ceived for a given tempo formula. No chronometric tempo markings by major composers of the eighteenth century are known, and the evidence provided by contemporary and retrospective accounts is frustratingly slender. There are general statements by 'ear witnesses': for instance, that Haydn and Mozart liked their allegro first movements slower than they had come to be played in the second decade of the nineteenth century, although 'both let the minuets go by quickly', while 'Haydn loved to take the finales faster than Mozart'.[48] It was also reported some seven years after Mozart's death that although he 'complained about nothing more vigorously than the bungling of his compositions in public performance—chiefly through exaggeration and rapidity of tempo' he nevertheless insisted upon a tempo, when directing his own music in Leipzig, that drove the orchestral players to the limits of their ability.[49] Perhaps the Viennese allegro was already faster in Mozart's day than the north German allegro. There is certainly evidence that in the early years of the nineteenth century there was a growing preference, in general, for faster tempos in fast movements; and there may be reason to believe that broader tempos began to be preferred in slow movements.

References to the tempo of specific pieces by late eighteenth-century composers, too, often provides only relative information. In Mozart's case, we learn, for instance, that in 1807 the first movement of a piano concerto was taken 'twice as fast' as Mozart performed it, while the Larghetto of his String Quartet K. 589 was taken 'twice as slow' as under the composer's direction.[50] (The latter reference is to a performance by the French cellist Lamarre, who may well have misunderstood the meaning of ¢ in conjunction with 'Larghetto' in the Quintet.) Gottfried Weber commented that in Paris the adagio in the overture to *Don Giovanni* was played a little slower than Mozart had directed it in Prague, while in Vienna it was performed a little faster and in Berlin nearly twice as fast, and that in all three places the allegro was given a little faster than Mozart took it.[51] Occasionally the evidence is more precise, such as the plausible assertion that 'Ach ich fühl's' from *Die Zauberflöte* was performed under Mozart at a speed in the range ♪ = *c*.138–52 (i.e. considerably faster than after his death).[52] Specific and interesting, but rather less plausible, is the list of metronome tempos given by the ageing Václav Jan Tomášek in 1839 as a supposed record of speeds taken in performances of *Don Giovanni* in Prague in

---

[48] *Allgemeine musikalische Zeitung*, 13 (1811), 737.

[49] Friedrich Rochlitz in ibid. 1 (1798–9), 84. The reliability of Rochlitz's retrospective account of Mozart's visit to Leipzig has been doubted since Jahn questioned it in his Mozart biography, but whatever licence Rochlitz may have taken in embellishing his recollections, it seems unlikely, from what is known of his profoundly moral character, that he would wilfully have invented things that were fundamentally untrue.

[50] Ibid. 9 (1806–7), 265.

[51] Ibid. 15 (1813), 306.

[52] Gottfried Weber in ibid., (1815), 247–9; also in Georg Nikolaus Nissen, *Wolfgang Amadeus Mozarts Biographie* (Leipzig, 1828), 123 f.

1791.[53] Comparison of Tomášek's marking with two other sets is interesting, for they are fairly consistent with those given in the 1822 publication of the opera by Schlesinger;[54] but both Tomášek and Schlesinger are noticeably different from the chronometric tempos for the opera given by William Crotch in about 1825: his markings show a clear preference for slower speeds, especially for the sections with faster tempo terms.[55] Hummel's metronome marks for Mozart's last six symphonies and Czerny's similar metronome marks together with some for his quartets and quintets certainly preserve an early nineteenth-century Viennese view of an appropriate tempo for these works (revealing significantly faster tempos for many movements than has been customary in the twentieth century); whether they preserve the composer's practice is more questionable.[56]

For Haydn the anecdotes and general comments are supplemented by just a few more precise pieces of information. Among the apparently most authoritative tempos are those reportedly given for Haydn's *Creation* by Salieri (who played in the first and many subsequent performances) and by Sigmund Neukomm, Haydn's pupil at the time and the arranger of the 1800 vocal score. Neukomm's, although not given until 1832, seem more likely to be closer to Haydn's intentions than the four given by Salieri in 1813.[57] In addition there are metronome marks by Czerny for the twelve London symphonies, which, however interesting, are open to the same objections as those he gave for Mozart's works. The metronome marks for Haydn's string quartets supplied by Karol Lipínski are even less likely to reflect anything but a mid-nineteenth-century view of Haydn; nevertheless, his edition contains some surprises for modern performers, particularly with respect to the tempos of the minuets and trios, which reflect a pre-Wagnerian view of these movements.[58]

The key to translating Haydn's and Mozart's tempos into chronometric ones with any degree of confidence, therefore, is missing. It is only possible to hypothesize with reasonable plausibility on the relationships between them,

[53] See Walter Gerstenberg, 'Authentische Tempi für Mozarts "Don Giovanni"?', *Mozart-Jahrbuch* (1960–1), 58–61.

[54] See Max Rudolf, 'Ein Beitrag zur Geschichte der Tempoabnahme bei Mozart', *Mozart-Jahrbuch* (1976–7), 204–24.

[55] *Don Giovanni . . . arranged for the piano forte, with an accompaniment for flute or violin . . .* (London, n.d. [*c.*1825]). The metronome marks up to 'Batti batti' are listed in Zaslaw, 'Mozart's Tempo Conventions'.

[56] For Hummel's metronome markings for Mozart symphonies, see R. Munster, 'Authentische Tempi zu den sechs letzten Sinfonien Mozarts?', *Mozart-Jahrbuch* (1962–3), 185 ff. For Czerny's metronome marks for Haydn and Mozart, see William Malloch, 'Carl Czerny's Metronome Marks for Haydn and Mozart Symphonies', *Early Music*, 16 (1988), 72–81.

[57] See Nicholas Temperley, 'Haydn's Tempos in *The Creation*', *Early Music*, 19 (1991), 235–45 and *Wiener allgemeine musikalische Zeitung*, 1 (1813), 628.

[58] *Vollständige Sammlung der Quarteten für zwei Violinen, Viola u. Violoncelle von Joseph Haydn. Neue Ausgabe. Revidirt und mit Tempobezeichnung versehen von Carl Lipinski* (Dresden, 1848–52). Copy in the British Library, London, Hirsch III. 266.

though in the case of the slower tempos the evidence is not unambiguous.[59] With many other late eighteenth-century musicians, particularly Italian composers working in Italy, there may have been less concern to define the tempo more narrowly than to put it into one of the three, or at best five, main tempo categories. Italian composers working elsewhere in Europe, particularly those involved directly or indirectly with publishing, seem to have been more careful, as performance directions and metronome marks given for their own works (admittedly composed towards the ends of their careers) by Mozart's Italian contemporaries Clementi (1752–1832) and Cherubini (1760–1842) suggest.

Beethoven's Tempo Preferences

Only in Beethoven's case does it become possible to assess with any significant degree of objectivity the extent to which a major composer of the Classical era was consistent in his handling of the theoretical eighteenth-century tempo equation, and what that meant to him in terms of absolute tempo; for Beethoven gave metronome marks, many of them admittedly retrospective, to a considerable number of important works, the earliest of which were composed around 1800. His musings on the subject of tempo, which he jotted on a draft of the *minore* section of his song 'Klage' WoO. 113 (*c.*1790), show that he was well aware of the principles that lay behind the Kirnberger–Schulz analysis of the relationship between tempo, metre, tempo term, and note values:

That which follows will be sung still more slowly, *adagio* or, at the most *andante quasi adagio*. *Andante* in 2/4 time must be taken much faster than the tempo of the song here. As it appears, the latter cannot remain in 2/4 time, for the music is too slow for it. It appears best to set them both in ¢ time.

The first [part], in E major, must remain in 2/4 time, otherwise it would be sung too slowly.

In the past, longer note values were always taken more slowly than shorter ones; for example, crotchets slower than quavers.

The smaller note values determine the tempo; for example, semiquavers and demisemiquavers in 2/4 time make the tempo very slow.

Perhaps the contrary is also true.[60]

Beethoven's metronome marks suggest that he continued throughout his life to regard much of this view of tempo as valid, and indicate that he took great care to choose the tempo terms which, in relation to the other relevant factors, most precisely indicated the speed he conceived for his music. (This, of course,

---

[59] For further discussion of these see Ch. 10.

[60] Richard Kramer, 'Notes to Beethoven's Education', *Journal of the American Musicological* Society, 18 (1975), 75.

assumes that, in general, he did not significantly change his mind about the tempo of particular pieces between the period of their composition and the time when he gave them metronome marks.) In most cases, pieces are grouped into fairly narrow bands according to the relationship between tempo term, metre, metronome mark, and the fastest note value employed in the music. The distinctions between the three main groups, adagio, andante–allegretto, and allegro–presto, are generally quite sharp. Apparent deviations from a strictly ordered sequence within these groups (when they are not the result of an erroneous marking) are often explained by the quantity of the fastest-moving notes in the piece and the way in which they are used. For the purposes of the present discussion, the quantity of the fastest functional notes in a piece is expressed as a percentage representing the number of bars containing three or more of the fastest notes in relation to the total number of bars in the piece. This is only one way of calculating this proportion, and inevitably the results are approximate, but other methods which have been considered have been found not to make a significant difference to the end result. However, it is relevant to distinguish in orchestral music between the quantity of bars in which the fastest notes appear as figurations and those in which they are merely used as a tremolando effect, since tremolando effects are both technically feasible at faster speeds and produce less of a subjective impression of speed on the listener than figurations of notes at the same tempo. In Tables 8.2 to 8.4 below, numbers in brackets represent the percentage of bars in the movement where the fastest notes occur only as tremolando. In deciding which note value should be regarded as the fastest, occasional flourishes and purely ornamental figures, even if written out in large-size notes, are ignored. Naturally, this type of analysis cannot be usefully applied to very short sections.

Table 8.2. The Influence of Fast-Moving Notes on Tempo Indication

Opus	Tempo term	Time signature	MM	Fastest notes	Approx. % of bars with fastest notes
21/iv	Allegro molto e vivace	2/4	♩ = 88	♪	24 (16)
55/iv	Allegro molto	2/4	♩ = 76	♪	51 (8)
18/5/i	Allegro	6/8	♩. = 104	♪	18
59/2/i	Allegro	6/8	♩. = 84	♪	58

The modifying effect of this factor can be seen from a comparison of movements, such as the finales of the First Symphony and the Third Symphony or the first movements of the quartets op. 18 no. 5 and op. 59 no. 2, which have the same metre, similar tempo directions, and the same range of note values. The

Table 8.3. The Influence of Fast-Moving Notes on Tempo Indication

Opus	Tempo term	Time signature	MM	Fastest notes	Approx. % of bars with fastest notes
59/1/i	Allegro	C	♩ = 88	♫♫₃	21
59/3/i	Allegro vivace	C	♩ = 88	♪	34
68/i	Allegro ma non troppo	2/4	♩ = 66	♪	26
68/iii	In tempo d'allegro	2/4	♩ = 132	♪	60

relationship may be shown as in Table 8.2. In other words, the larger quantities of fast-moving notes in op. 55 and op. 59 no. 2 require a slower pulse rate, but in terms of subjective tempo feeling they are equivalent to pieces with faster pulse rates but fewer fast-moving notes.

A similar sort of thing can be seen from a different angle in Table 8.3, which compares the first movements of the quartets op. 59 nos. 1 and 3 and the first movement and third movement (trio section) of the Sixth Symphony op. 68. Here the same metres and metronome marks have different tempo terms, but the faster term for op. 59 no. 3 is explained by the fact that the fastest moving notes are semiquavers as opposed to quaver triplets, and the faster tempo term for the third movement of the Sixth Symphony than for the first movement seems to reflect the much greater quantity of fast-moving notes in the former.

A few cases which initially appear anomalous are elucidated by a closer look at the nature of the music; thus, the first movement of the First Symphony, an Allegro con brio ¢ with a metronome mark of ♩ = 112 and semiquavers as its fastest notes, seems as if it ought to have a faster tempo term than the Finale of the Septet op. 20, a Presto ¢ which is also marked ♩ = 112 and has triplet quavers as its fastest notes, but the virtuoso triplet figurations in the septet give a greater subjective feeling of speed than the semiquavers in the symphony, which are tremolando with an occasional four-note flourish. Sometimes the relationship between tempo term and metronome mark is also modified by other factors, especially the character of themes or a strong element of contrast (e.g. the first movements of op. 18 no. 4, op. 95, and op. 36), but in the vast majority of cases the margin of variation is relatively small, and the information conveyed by taking into account the factors described by Schulz defines the actual speed of the music quite narrowly.

The comparison shown in Table 8.4 of all Beethoven's metronomized movements in C metre containing the word 'allegro' will illustrate the degree of consistency of faster tempos in this metre (for slower tempos in most metres the

Table 8.4. Beethoven's Metronome Marks for Movements in ¢ Metre

Opus	Tempo term	MM	Fastest notes	Approx. % of bars with fastest notes
18/4/i	Allegro ma non tanto	$\half$ = 84	$\eighth$	11
125/iv	Allegro assai	$\half$ = 80	$\eighth$	17
68/iv	Allegro	$\half$ = 80	$\eighth$	70 (40)
74/i	Allegro	$\half$ = 84	$\eighth$	19
67/iv	Allegro	$\half$ = 84	$\eighth$	39 (24)
59/1/i	Allegro	$\half$ = 88	♫♫	21
59/3/i	Allegro vivace	$\half$ = 88	$\eighth$	34
95/i	Allegro con brio	$\half$ = 92	$\eighth$	52
36/i	Allegro con brio	$\half$ = 100	$\eighth$	50 (18)

paucity of examples only allows more generalized conclusions). The last two metronome markings indicate that when all the main factors are apparently equal there can be a noticeable difference in speed; but in this case it seems probable that the difference results from the fact that the quartet contains figures of separately bowed semiquavers, while in the symphony quite a number of the semiquavers are used in tremolando and all the figurations are slurred. The fastest allegro marking is, as might be expected, the first movement of the String Quartet op. 59 no. 1, which has triplet quavers rather than semiquavers as its fastest notes, and the slowest, the fourth movement of the 'Pastoral' Symphony, has the most semiquavers. The marking for the Allegro assai in the Finale of the Ninth Symphony confirms the view that for Beethoven the qualifying term 'assai' meant 'enough' rather than 'very'. [61]

The ¢ markings are fairly straightforward; greater problems of reconciling apparent differences are found in other metres. Some of these may merely reveal that Beethoven did not always light upon the combination that most accurately reflected his wishes, that he changed his mind about the speed of a movement between composing it and allotting it metronome marks, or that the metronome marks have been wrongly transmitted.[62]

[61] Advanced, for instance by Stuart Deas, 'Beethoven's "Allegro assai"', *Music & Letters*, 31 (1950), 333.
[62] For particular examination of two metronome marks in the Ninth Symphony, see Brown, 'Historical Performance', 253 ff.

The Impact of the Metronome

Before looking at what metronome marks may reveal about the attitudes of Beethoven's younger contemporaries and their tempo conventions,[63] it will be useful to consider how the success of the metronome related to early nineteenth-century concerns about tempo and to examine some of the problems inherent in the use and interpretation of metronome marks. Many early nineteenth-century musicians were particularly concerned about finding a method of indicating tempo that would be less easily misunderstood than previous ones, since their own times saw such controversy and confusion in the matter. Earlier devices or methods for indicating tempo chronometrically[64] had failed to gain currency not because of their own deficiencies, but rather, despite the occasional lament on the part of theorists that no such device was readily available, because the need was not sufficiently pressing. The acceptance and rapidly proliferating use of the metronome in the second and third decades of the century was a direct response to changing conditions. Even before the commercial success of Maelzel's metronome had become assured, some composers were attracted by the idea of regularly giving their music chronometric tempo indications by other methods. Gottfried Weber vigorously advocated the use of a pendulum in a number of articles at about the time of Maelzel's first metronome, and Spohr, among others, adopted his method of indicating tempo by this means before changing to metronome marks around 1820.

The early decades of the nineteenth century saw gradual but significant changes in composers' approaches towards specifying the tempo of their pieces. To a large extent this was because the fundamental tenets upon which the whole system was founded were breaking down, together with the pan-European aristocratic social system that had prevailed throughout much of the eighteenth century. The notion that the tempo giusto of every metre could be understood by studying all kinds of dance pieces—every dance having its definite tempo, determined by the metre and the note values employed in it[65]—could not survive the disintegration of the social order, first weakened and then finally destroyed by the French Revolution and the Napoleonic Wars, with which this aspect of musical culture had enjoyed a symbiotic relationship. Drastic social and cultural change, especially relating to the extraordinary growth in numbers and influence of the western European middle classes, saw the desuetude and gradual disappearance of the repertoire of eighteenth-

---

[63] See Ch. 10.

[64] See Rosamond E. M. Harding, *Origins of Musical Time and Expression* (London, 1938) and David Martin, 'An Early Metronome', *Early Music*, 16 (1988), 90–2.

[65] Kirnberger, *The Art of Strict Musical Composition*, 376.

century courtly dances, the yardstick by which the tempo giusto had been measured.

The older system did not break down entirely or immediately, but it seems to have become increasingly unreliable in the hands of composers who lacked a rooted and instinctive feeling for the premises on which it was based. In these circumstances, chronometric tempo measurement, which had failed to take hold in the eighteenth century despite a number of perfectly practicable proposals, was seized upon with alacrity by many musicians. It seems quite likely that the widespread adoption of the metronome, which theoretically rendered other means of specifying tempo more or less redundant, helped to accelerate the decay of the older system. Yet it would perhaps be closer to the mark to attribute the enthusiasm with which so many musicians advocated mechanical means of designating tempo at this time to the recognition that the ever-greater diversity of style and individuality of expression in late eighteenth-century and nineteenth-century music had made it increasingly difficult to perceive the relationship of a work to the sorts of conventions described by eighteenth-century theorists. Gottfried Weber's awareness of this problem is suggested by the foreword to his Requiem op. 24 of 1813, in which he provided chronometric markings in pendulum lengths; he recommended that other composers should use this method, since by that means 'the tempo intended by the composer will be immutably and unmistakably prescribed despite all changes of period, fashion, and taste'.[66] A similar awareness, expressed in typically Beethovenian style, is apparent in Beethoven's letter to Schott, promising metronome marks for the *Missa solemnis*: 'Do wait for them. In our century such indications are certainly necessary . . . We can scarcely have tempi ordinari any longer, since one must fall into line with the ideas of unfettered genius.'[67]

The fact that this remark was prompted by correspondence over the publication of the mass suggests another important impulse behind the growing use of metronome marks: the enormous expansion of publishing during Beethoven's lifetime, catering increasingly for an amateur market, carried with it the expectation that the music would come into the hands of people who had little or no knowledge of this difficult matter. That Beethoven's contemporaries were seriously concerned about a decline in the understanding of tempo conventions by professionals and amateurs alike is corroborated by the increasingly frequent complaints of early nineteenth-century writers that some music was becoming distorted almost to the point of incoherence by being performed at radically different speeds from those intended by the composer. As Andersch lamented in 1829, the consequence of composers not employing the

---

[66] (Offenbach am Main, André, [c.1816]), p. iii.
[67] Anderson, *The Letters of Beethoven*, 1325.

metronome as a matter of course was that 'the correct tempo is only too often missed and then the character of a composition is disfigured'.[68]

Early nineteenth-century comments about particular circumstances in which there were problems over tempo illuminate national and regional differences and the application of inappropriate criteria to older music, as well as misunderstandings arising from the performance of music by inexperienced performers, or those brought up in a different tradition from that of the composer. In 1809, for instance, one writer warned that 'German music must not be played in French tempos',[69] and three decades later Bernhard Romberg noted that allegro was played faster in Paris than in Vienna and faster in Vienna than in the north of Germany.[70] Another critic had observed in 1807 that some schools of performers favoured extremely fast tempos while others, especially members of the Viotti school, went to the opposite extreme; and he lamented that 'if this goes on there will be the same situation with tempo in Germany as we have with spelling—that we will no longer have any, but rather everything will be abandoned to caprice'.[71] Thus, although complaints about discrepancies in the treatment of tempo can be found in earlier periods (not everyone, for example, agreed with Quantz's ideas[72]), the frequency and nature of the references to this problem in the early nineteenth century suggest a much more intractable situation.

Concrete evidence of the way in which the widespread adoption of chronometric tempo measurement delivered the *coup de grâce* to the older system can be found in the various early nineteenth-century discussions of the metronome and its uses. Hummel's brief account is revealing of a new attitude towards indicating tempo. Like Gottfried Weber, he stressed that

To composers it offers the great advantage, that their compositions when marked according to the degrees of the metronome, will be performed in every country in exactly the same time; and the effect of their works will not now, as formerly, (notwithstanding the most carefully chosen musical terms), be lost by being played in a hurried or retarded movement.[73]

His total abandonment of the older system is indicated by his next sentence:

Long directions by means of multiple epithets are no longer necessary, since the whole system of time is divided into three principal movements, the *slow*[,] the *moderate*, and the *quick*, and therefore it will but very seldom be necessary to add more than one word, indicating the particular emotion or passion predominating throughout the piece.

Maelzel's own table of the metronome marks appropriate to slow, moderate, and quick pieces in various metres, which Hummel approvingly includes in his account, immediately implies a coarsening of the subtleties of the older system

---

[68] *Musikalisches Wörterbuch*, art. 'Allegro'.   [69] *Allgemeine musikalische Zeitung*, 10 (1809), 603.
[70] *A Complete*, 110.   [71] *Allgemeine musikalische Zeitung*, 9 (1806–7), 265.
[72] See below, Ch. 10, p. 369.   [73] *A Complete*, iii. 65.

Ex. 8.1. Hummel, *A Complete*, iii. 67

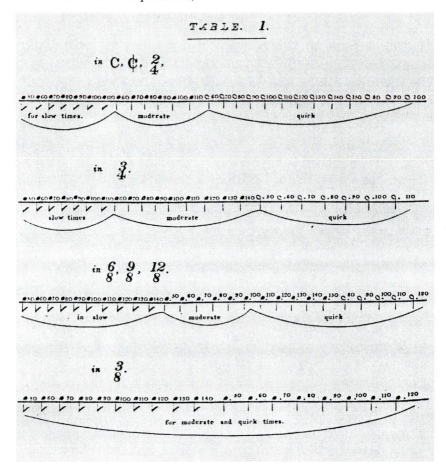

by making no apparent distinction between the time units in ¢, ¢, and 2/4 (Ex. 8.1). The graduated scale on Maelzel's original metronome listed merely numbers, but it was not long before the scale also included tempo terms, linking a particular word with a fairly narrowly circumscribed speed for the beat (Ex. 8.2), thus strengthening the idea that tempo terms were directly related to a particular pulse rate in the music.

One of the other tables reproduced by Hummel purports to show the 'inconsistency' of composers in the old system (Ex. 8.3), but in doing so it fails to compare like with like. The metres are muddled (all bars with four crotchets are indiscriminately given as ¢), and a vital element of the tempo equation— the types of notes in the piece—is omitted. Furthermore the metronome tempos, supposedly given by the composers, are in any case dubious; the three

Ex. 8.2. Metronome scale

40	Grave	42
44	Largo	46
48	Larghetto	50
52	Adagio	54
56		58
60	Andante	63
66	Andantino	69
72		76
80	Moderato	84
88		92
96	Allegretto	100
104		108
112	Allegro	116
120	Vivace	126
132		138
144	Presto	152
160		168
176	Prestissimo	184
192		200
208		

Ex. 8.3. Hummel, *A Complete*, iii. 68

68

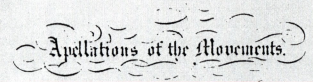

Apellations of the Movements.

Names of the Authors.	Original indication of the Movement of the Pieces.	Degrees	Measures
By Paer	Allegro Moderato	○ = 50	C
Paer	Allegro Moderato	○ = 80	C
Mehul	Allegro Moderato	○ = 72	C
Mehul	Allegro Moderato	○ = 88	C
Clementi	Allegro	○ = 54	C
Clementi	"	○ = 50	C
Cherubini	"	○ = 172	C
Cherubini	"	○ = 126	C
Cherubini	"	○ = 72	C
Mehul	"	○ = 96	C
Berton	Allegro molto	○ = 176	C
Spontini	Presto	○ = 72	C
Spontini	"	○ = 88	C
Beethoven	"	○ = 152	C
Beethoven	"	○ = 176	C
Beethoven	"	○ = 224	C
Clementi	"	○ = 96	C
Cherubini	Andantino	● = 76	2/4
Cherubini	"	● = 164	4/4
Cramer	Moderato	● = 65	3/4
Cramer	"	● = 116	3/4
Cramer	Allegro non tanto	● = 138	2/4
Cramer	Presto	● = 138	3/4
Cramer	Moderato	● = 100	3/4
Cramer	"	● = 258	6/8
Viotti	Andante	= 52	6/8
Berton	"	= 152	6/8
Nicolo	Andantino	= 52	6/8
Catel	"	= 126	6/8
Paer	Andante	= 50	6/8
Berton	"	= 100	6/8
Cramer	Più tosto Moderato	= 92	6/8
Cramer	Allegro Agitato	= 66	6/8
Paer	Lento	= 120	6/8
Paer	Andante	= 120	6/8
Paer	"	= 172	6/8
Berton	"	= 300	6/8

Time, in conformity to the Authors will and indication expressed by the Degrees of the Metronome.

Nº 3.

Graduated Scale of the Metronome.

50.	50
	52
	54
	56
	58
60.	60
	63
	66
	69
70.	72
	76
80.	80
	84
	88
90.	92
	96
100.	100
	104
	108
110.	112
	116
120.	120
	126
130.	132
	138
140.	144
150.	152
160.	160

presto illustrations in 𝄌 metre given for Beethoven do not correspond with any of his markings, and only two of them can be matched with 𝄵 prestos.

The result of the tendency illustrated by Hummel's treatment of tempo was that the tempo term came increasingly to be seen as a word that described an aural phenomenon rather than as a single modifying factor in a complex equation. A piece was designated adagio, andante, allegro, or presto because it was felt to be so. The choice of tempo term and its relation to the envisaged speed of the music seem to have become more subjective, creating very significant problems for performers unfamiliar with the composer's practice when metronome marks were not provided.[74]

Nineteenth-Century Tempo Conventions

Few composers born after 1800 seem to have shown real understanding of the older system for indicating tempo, though its influence, albeit in a diluted form, may be detected in some aspects of the practice of more conservatively trained or historically aware composers such as Dvořák and Brahms. Mendelssohn's sensitivity to the relationship between tempo term, metre, and note value has already been mentioned; this may be explained by his thorough training under Carl Friedrich Zelter. It is revealing, however, that his exact contemporary and colleague Schumann, whose early musical education was nowhere near as thorough, seems not to have possessed this sensitivity to anything like the same degree, if at all. When he revised his D minor Symphony, for example, Schumann altered the notation of the outer movements: in the first movement he kept the metre the same and halved the note values; in the Finale he changed the metre from 2/4 to 4/4 but retained the original note values. In both cases the tempo term in the first version was 'Allegro' and in the second version *Lebhaft*, indicating, in contrast to Mendelssohn's procedure in the *Sommernachtstraum* and Octet (above), a lack of responsiveness to the old relationship of tempo term, metre, and note values.

Major German theoretical studies from the 1820s onwards scarcely, if at all, allude to that relationship. Gottfried Weber, in his widely disseminated and influential *Versuch einer geordneten Theorie der Tonsetzkunst*, set the pattern for many later theoretical works. Considering the significance of metre he stressed the effect of different metres and note values on style of performance, but seems entirely to have excluded their direct relationship to tempo. Having observed that 2/1, 2/2, and 2/4 were basically 'only different ways of representing one and the same thing by signs', he continued:

It follows from this, that in a species of measure where the parts of a measure are represented by large forms of notes, such large notes, other circumstances being alike, are performed as

[74] See Ch. 10.

fast as smaller notes in those species of measure where the parts of the measure are represented by notes of a smaller form. As in 2/2 measure e.g. the half-notes represent precisely the same thing as the quarter-notes do in 2/4 measure; and the quarter notes in the former, the same as the eighth-notes in the latter; eighth-notes in the former, the same as sixteenth-notes in the latter &c;—so it appears that half-notes are executed as fast in the former, as quarter-notes are in the latter, &c. Hence it appears, finally, even a matter of indifference, which mode of writing a man chooses; every piece of music in 2/4 measure might be written not only in 2/2 measure, but also in 2/1 measure, or 2/8 measure, &c. Thus the matter stands, considered in itself and its relation to time; but it is conceded, that, the 2/2 measure should have a somewhat different mode of delivery from the 2/4 or the 2/8 measure, and that the 3/2 measure also should have a mode of delivery somewhat different from that of 3/8 measure; that is to say a piece of music is in a manner delivered more lightly and softly [delicately] in proportion as it is written in the smaller notes, or, in other words, the larger the denominator—the lower the figure of the fraction; and on the other hand, the delivery is more heavy and firm, in proportion as the species of note is greater; and thus e.g. the manner of delivering quarter-notes in allegro, is different from that of delivering sixteenth-notes in adagio though the latter are perhaps as quick in their movement as the former. In this respect, the difference in the designation of the measures furnishes the composer with an additional means of indicating, in a certain particular, the character in which he wishes to have his composition delivered; and consequently it is not unimportant to choose the most suitable designation of the measure.[75]

For determining tempo Gottfried Weber, as already mentioned, preferred to rely on chronometric tempo indications, which he included in his own compositions, advocating the use of a simple pendulum rather than a metronome.

With Liszt and, above all, Wagner a move towards simplification in the employment of metres was inevitably related to a change in the significance of note values for tempo. Liszt's *Faust-Symphonie*, with its constant time changes between **c** (4/4), 6/4, 2/4, and 3/4 ('Faust') or between 2/4, 6/8, **c**, 3/4, and ¢ ('Mephistopheles'), illustrates the imperatives in this music that caused an inevitable reassessment of the implications of metre. The ever-increasing individualism of musical gesture in a single section or movement was seen to be essentially incompatible with the 'collectivism' inherent in the old system: the intended expression of the piece could not be adequately conveyed to any extent by the choice of metre; the constantly fluctuating nuances had to be indicated by other means. Liszt's use of ¢ and **c** is particularly revealing, for the choice of one or other of these metres seems to be directly related to the convenience of the conductor. For greater clarity he even headed the sections in ¢ 'Alla breve taktieren' (i.e. beat in 2). Wagner, as in so many other respects, followed him in this approach to alla breve.[76] Richard Strauss, too, seems largely to have thought of metre in terms of conducting; in *Also sprach Zarathustra*, for instance, he followed an accelerando with the instruction 'sehr schnell (alla breve)' (very fast (alla breve)) and ten bars later 'Ziemlich langsam (in

---

[75] *Theory*, i. 88–9.   [76] See Ch. 9.

Vierteln)' (rather slow (in crotchets)).[77] Coupled with this increasingly 'practical' approach to the role of metre went a more subjective employment of tempo terms, which is examined further in Ch. 10 below.

Nevertheless, some of the other considerations that were felt to influence the speed at which a particular piece of music would be performed, besides the relationship between metre, note value, and tempo term, retained their validity and even became more pronounced in the nineteenth century. The slower tempo for church music (which, however, may have been stronger among Protestant and northern musicians than among Catholic and southern ones) is, for example, reflected in the metronome tempos (commented upon adversely by Ferdinand Ries)[78] that Spohr gave for his oratorio *Die letzten Dinge*. It seems also to be a factor in the very slow metronome marks given for Haydn's *Creation* in the Novello edition of 1858. The same appears to be true for much other nineteenth-century religious music. Mendelssohn's metronome marks for his organ sonatas op. 65 (which may perhaps be regarded as falling into the categories of both church music and 'strict' music) indicate that in this genre his tempo terms were to be interpreted as slower than they normally were in other types of work (compare for instance the common-time Allegro con brio of op. 65 no. 4 at $\downarrow$ = 100 with the Allegro vivace in his String Quartet op. 44 no. 3 at $\downarrow$ = 92, both containing semiquavers).

The possibility that a tradition of faster tempos for sacred music survived longer in southern Europe, especially in Austria and Italy, may be suggested by an article in the *Allgemeine Wiener Musik-Zeitung* in 1844,[79] where the cathedral Kapellmeister F. G. Hölzl complained about the 'modern tempo mania' which led to such music being performed, in his opinion, much faster than the composers intended. However, his remark that 'It may indeed not be an easy task once more to perform at a slower tempo a work that one has performed at the tempo of many years standing', and other such comments, indicate that these fast speeds were no recent modern craze in Vienna, but rather the speeds to which everyone had always been accustomed. He accompanied his comments with a list of metronome marks for Haydn's 'Nelson' Mass in which he supplied each movement with the metronome mark for the tempo 'to which one is accustomed' followed by that 'which I regard as appropriate', as shown in Table 8.5.

Much later in the century a distinct division between German and Italian notions in these matters is revealed by German reactions to Verdi's own performance of his Requiem in Cologne in 1877, when a critic expressed astonishment at some of the fast tempos. With respect to the 'Sanctus' and 'Libera me domine' fugues he observed: '—both tempos hardly seemed fast enough for the

---

[77] Miniature score (Leipzig, Eulenburg (EE 3506), n.d.), 94–5.
[78] Cecil Hill, *Ferdinand Ries: Briefe und Dokumente* (Bonn, 1982), 267.   [79] Vol. 4 (1844), 334.

composer. We are not accustomed to such treatment of fugues for voices. Our tempos in the choruses of Bach and Handel allow the somewhat rigid strength of German voices to unfold powerfully and fully.'[80]

Table 8.5. Hölzl's Metronome Marks for Haydn's 'Nelson' Mass

Movement, tempo term	Time signature	Usual tempo (MM)	Regulated tempo (MM)
Kyrie, Allegro moderato	𝄴 – ♩	104	92
Gloria, Allegro	𝄴 – ♩	116	104
Qui tollis, Adagio	3/4 – ♪	108	88
Quoniam, Allegro	𝄴 – ♩	116	104
Credo, Allegro con spirito	𝄵 – ♩	92	80
Et incarnatus, Largo	3/4 – ♪	96	80
Et resurrexit, Vivace	𝄴 – ♩	126	108
Sanctus, Adagio	𝄴 – ♪	104	92
Pleni, Allegro	3/4 – ♩	120	108
Agnus, Adagio	3/4 – ♪	100	80
Dona, Vivace	𝄴 – ♩	120	100

---

[80] *Kölnische Zeitung*, no. 141 (22 May), 18; cited in Marcello Conati, *Interviews and Encounters with Verdi*, trans. Richard Stokes (London, 1984), 126.

9

ALLA BREVE

❧※❧

The question of what Classical and Romantic composers meant when they used ¢, ₵, or 2 has caused and continues to cause confusion for performers. Mozart's renotation of the finale of K. 458 and Mendelssohn's two versions of the *Sommernachtstraum* overture[1] make it evident that these two composers, at any rate, did not regard ¢ as necessarily indicating a literal doubling of speed, as many theorists stated that it should. Not all theorists, however, saw the function of ¢ in the same light, and a variety of apparently contradictory explanations of its significance are found in eighteenth- and nineteenth-century theoretical writings.

c and ¢ as indications of metre were direct survivals from the old system of proportional signs. In the fourteenth and fifteenth centuries c was the sign for *tempus imperfecta cum prolatio imperfecta*, while ¢ indicated *proportio dupla* or *diminutio simplex*. Along with other proportional signs, they continued to be used, together with proportions expressed as fractions, during the sixteenth century. When, during the seventeenth century, the fractions gradually evolved into modern time signatures, some of the proportional signs were retained with modified meanings. Other signs, such as O, ⏀, and ⏁, which also continued to be used alongside the system of time signatures in the seventeenth century, are only very rarely found in the eighteenth century and then, for the most part, in theoretical works. As a rule, c and ¢ were both used to signify a metre in which each bar contained notes to the value of a semibreve (though ¢ is sometimes found where bars contain notes to the value of a breve). Already in the sixteenth century there was ambiguity about whether ¢ indicated that each note should be twice as fast as it would be if the time signature were c or whether it merely indicated that the notes should be somewhat faster than with the other; the

---

[1] See Ch. 8.

same problem bedevilled theorists and performers during succeeding centuries and has continued to challenge modern scholars and performers.

The present discussion will be confined to the use of these two signs for bars containing notes to the value of a semibreve. There are a number of ways in which these appear to be employed in the music of the Classical and Romantic periods. The most commonly encountered are:

1. the two signs seem to be synonymous;
2. ¢ is twice as fast as C;
3. ¢ is considerably faster but not twice as fast as C;
4. ¢ is somewhat faster than C.

In addition, while most authorities saw C as synonymous with 4/4 (i.e. four crotchet time, *Viervierteltakt*, etc., since the time signature 4/4 was rarely used before the nineteenth century) and ¢ with 2/2 (i.e. two-minim time), others either regarded ¢ as another kind of 4/4 or, while categorizing it as 2/2, considered it to be different from the time signatures 2/2 or 2. A selection of explanations of the significance of ¢ from the middle of the eighteenth century to the end of the nineteenth century reveals the lack of agreement.

Many writers stated as a firm rule that when ¢ was marked each note was played 'twice as fast' as when the time signature was C. Quantz commented: 'In four-four time it is important to note that if a stroke goes through the C . . . the notes receive a different value, so to speak, and must be played twice as fast as when the C has no stroke through it. This metre is called alla breve, or alla cappella.' And he was insistent that this needed to be stressed, because many people took the wrong speed through ignorance of the meaning of this time signature, which he observed had become 'more common in the Galant style of the present day than it was in the past'.[2] Despite the latter comment, Quantz was only restating a view of alla breve that had been frequently advanced by earlier theorists, including Daniel Merck and Saint-Lambert. Unfortunately, George Houle in his book *Meter in Music* 1600–1800 has recently added another layer of confusion to the question of alla breve by consistently and misleadingly translating these authors' instructions to perform it 'noch einmal so schnell' and 'une fois plus vite' as 'half as fast again'.[3]

This notional doubling of speed was described by many other writers in the second half of the eighteenth century, and a considerable number of nineteenth-century theorists continued to define it in this way. Schulz observed: 'The two-two or so-called alla breve metre, whose time units consist of two minims, is indicated by the sign ¢ at the beginning of the piece where one also takes care to put the heading alla breve. It is performed heavily but twice as fast as its note values show.'[4]

---

[2] *Versuch*, V, §13.   [3] (Bloomington, Ind., and Indianapolis, 1987).
[4] In Sulzer, *Allgemeine Theorie*, art. 'Takt'.

In the fifth edition of Löhlein's *Clavier-Schule* (1791) the editor, Witthauer, expanded on earlier editions where ¢ had been mentioned without further explanation, saying that where ¢ or ꜫ was indicated the tempo of a piece 'is usually taken twice as fast as the value of the notes seems to require'.[5] Türk modified his explanation slightly between the first and second editions of his *Klavierschule*: in the 1789 edition he had explained alla breve as every note 'once again as fast as usual', but in 1802 he changed his definition to 'approximately twice as fast as usual'.[6] In the same year as Türk's second edition H. C. Koch observed that in 4/2 and 2/2 metre 'the minim is commonly performed as fast as the crotchet in two-four metre, and for that reason both are very often called alla breve metre'.[7] The following year J. H. Knecht also instructed that in alla breve 'a minim moves as fast as a crotchet in four-four'.[8] The description of alla breve as twice as fast as 4/4 is also given by Andersch in his *Musikalisches Wörterbuch* of 1829, but here the sign for it is given as **2**, a Latin Z, or ꜫ, without any mention of ¢.[9]

It may be noted in passing that **2** was used by some eighteenth-century composers to indicate 2/2 time and by others, for example Jommelli, to indicate 2/4. In the latter part of the eighteenth century and the first half of the nineteenth century some composers, presumably influenced by earlier French practice, used **2**, ꜵ, ꜫ, and ¢ for different movements or numbers within the same work, but without any discernible difference of meaning. Examples may be found in Stamitz's six duos op. 27,[10] Spontini's *Fernand Cortez* and *Olympie*, Meyerbeer's *Les Huguenots* and *Le Prophète*; in the case of Spontini and Meyerbeer, metronome marks leave no doubt about the intended tempo, and suggest no obvious distinction between the two signs. Other anomalies in composers' uses of such time signatures can easily be found in nineteenth-century music: Spohr in the overture to *Des Heilands letzte Stunden* used **2** for music with bars containing notes to the value of a breve; Schubert used ¢¢ (Impromptu in G flat, D. 899 no. 3) and Schumann CC ('Die Löwenbraut', op. 31 no. 1) for bars of that length, while Brahms used ¢ for both 2/2 and 2/1 in *Ein deutsches Requiem*. It is not surprising that many examples of this type of essentially antiquarian notation should occur in sacred music.

Some theorists, while implying that the minim in one time was equivalent to the crotchet in the other, did not specify an exact relationship. Fröhlich in 1810 equated ¢ with 2/4, saying that it should be 'performed just like the two-four and overall has the same character, with the one difference, that here there are two minims and there there are two crotchets, thus each note in this time signature must be performed much faster than it is in the common four-four time'.[11] Schilling in the 1830s maintained that the minim 'did not receive its

[5] p. 12. [6] Ch. I, §70. [7] *Musikalisches Lexikon*, art. 'Alla breve'.
[8] *Katechismus*, 20. [9] Art. 'Alla breve'. [10] Copy in the Bodleian Library, Oxford.
[11] *Musikschule*, i. 7.

true value and is only counted like a crotchet'.[12] Some twenty years later Gollmick described alla breve, or 2/2, as 'an abbreviated 4/4 metre, with two concentrated beats'.[13] Fétis and Castil-Blaze merely took ¢ to indicate a bar of two beats.[14] Many mid- to late nineteenth-century composers seem to have taken a pragmatic and individualistic approach to this matter. As indicated in Chapter 8, Liszt and Wagner used it merely to indicate that the music should be conducted in two beats to the bar without any specific connotations of metre or tempo.

For other late eighteenth and early nineteenth-century musicians, however, especially in England, the time signature ¢ quite definitely did not signify anything like twice as fast as **C**. Holden in 1770, discussing 'common time', observed that it is notated 'when slow, by a large **C** after the cliff; when quicker, by the same **C** with a bar drawn through it'. And then, in relation to what he designated alla breve (2/1) and alla semibreve (2/2), the former of which he says is properly represented by ¢, he remarked

although, in this mood, the notes ought to be made a little shorter than in the other, yet they are not so much shortened as to bring the whole breve into the time which a semibreve requires, in the other mood; nor indeed is there any fixt rule for the comparative proportions of the time of a bar, in different moods.[15]

Other English instrumental treatises from the late eighteenth century show this to be in line with the usual interpretation of ¢ in England. These methods frequently echoed Purcell's explanation of the various signs for metres in which bars contained 'one whole note or four quarter notes': **C** as for 'very slow movement', ¢ 'a little faster' and 𝄵 'brisk and airy time'.[16] A few examples from instruction books published in London during the 1790s may stand for many: Francesco Chabran's *Compleat Instructions for the Spanish Guitar* gives the time signatures **C**, ¢, 𝄵, and 2/4, commenting: 'the first of them denotes a slow movement, the next a little faster, and the other two brisk and airy movements';[17] in J. Wragg's *The Flute Preceptor* **C**, ¢, 𝄵, and **2** are listed with an almost identical explanation;[18] the anonymous author of *Instructions for the Violin by an Eminent Master*, having discussed **C**, remarks that '¢ does not differ from the former in point of value it only shows that the time must be played a degree faster than if it had been simply marked thus **C**';[19] and in *New Instructions for*

---

[12] *Encyclopädie*, art. 'Takt'.   [13] *Handlexicon der Tonkunst*, art. 'Alla breve'.

[14] François-Joseph Fétis, *Traité élémentaire de musique* (Brussels, 1831–2) and François Henri Joseph Castil-Blaze, *Dictionnaire de musique moderne* (Paris, 1821).

[15] *Essay*, 26.

[16] Anon., *A Choice Collection of Lessons* (London 1696); repr. with attribution to Purcell in *The Third Book of the Harpsichord Master* (London, 1702).

[17] *Compleat Instructions for the Spanish Guitar* (London, [*c.*1795]), 7.

[18] (London, *c.*1795), 8: 'The first of which denotes the slowest sort of Common Time; the second a degree quicker; and the third and fourth marks denote a quick movement.'

[19] (London, [*c.*1795]), 6.

Playing the Harpsichord, Pianoforte or Organ it is merely observed that one uses 'c for slow movements and ¢ or ꝰ for brisker airs'.[20] The reference to ꝰ seems to have been pure antiquarianism at this time, for it is not encountered in late eighteenth-century music. Even ¢ seems to have become much less common in compositions written in England during the early nineteenth century than it had been in the late eighteenth century. Charles Dibdin's *Music Epitomized* of 1808 gave only c and 2/4 as species of common time, though the ninth edition, revised by John Jousse, added ¢ to the list without specifying any difference;[21] Thomas Valentine's *Dictionary*, ignoring Continental practice, noted that ¢ signified 'a species of quick common time now seldom used'.[22] Clementi's treatment of time signatures is interesting, for the 1801 first edition of his *Introduction to the Art of Playing on the Pianoforte* did not prescribe any difference between ¢ and c, but the revised eleventh edition of 1826 added the following *nota bene*: 'A composition marked thus ¢ was ANCIENTLY performed as fast again as when marked thus c, but now ¢ is performed somewhat faster than c.'[23]

The *Principes élémentaires de musique* (c.1800) suggests that in France, too, alla breve may no longer have been seen as indicating so fast a tempo as it once had. Here it was explained that the duple metre signified by **2** or ¢ 'does not differ in any respect from the quadruple metre [4/4, often written simply as **4** in French music] with regard to the number of notes which make it up; the only difference which distinguishes it is that one beats it in two because of the rapidity of movement which one formerly used to give to this kind of metre'.[24] However, this treatise also shows that the strict *proportio dupla* aspect of alla breve could sometimes still be valid, for in some of the exercises later in the volume **2** is used to specify an exact doubling of tempo from **4** or c and vice versa.[25]

Among nineteenth-century writers of a more historical bent, particularly in Germany, there was a tendency to retain the notion of alla breve meaning that the music should move twice as fast as in c, despite the practical evidence of its contrary use by many composers of the period. Gottfried Weber's account provides a good example of how a desire for clear and logical exposition of the principles of metre, combined with a knowledge of older theoretical writings, helped to perpetuate this idea. Weber's treatment of the subject shows a

---

[20] p. 5.

[21] *Music Epitomized: A School Book in which the Whole Science of Music is Completely Explained* . . . (London, 1808); 9th edn. (London, [c.1820]), 37.

[22] *Dictionary of Terms Used in Music*, 2nd edn. (London, 1824), Art. 'Alla breve'.

[23] 1st edn., p. 4 and 11th edn., p. 4. [24] Gossec et al., *Principes*, i. 40.

[25] Ibid., pt. 2. In ex. 19 the music changes from **2** (2/2) to **4** (4/4) with the verbal instruction 'here the crotchets take the speed of minims', and a similar change between c (4/4) and **2** (2/2) takes place in ex. 21. In these exercises c and **4** are apparently used interchangeably for 4/4, though it may be possible that **2** is used deliberately rather than ¢ when a real doubling of tempo is intended, despite the description of the two signatures as synonymous in the introduction.

mixture of antiquarianism with an attempt to produce order out of the chaos of centuries of inconsistent usage:

Two minims to a bar: It is represented by the sign 2/2; not unfrequently also by a large figure 2 with a perpendicular stroke through it; or also by a ¢ with a similar stroke. . . . The last two signs are frequently used also for the large alla-breve measure [i.e. 2/1]. The 2/2 measure also is sometimes called alla-breve measure, by the by it would be well always to distinguish it from the above mentioned large, proper alla-breve measure, by the additional appellation of small alla-breve measure.

Two breves to a bar: The sign for this species of measure is either 2/1, or a complete circle with a stroke through it, or a large figure 2, or which is still more distinguishing a large figure 2 intersected by a perpendicular line. . . . It is frequently represented also by the sign which is more appropriate to the two-half measure, namely ¢; or by a ¢ without a stroke; this last sign belongs rather to the four-quarter measure, which we shall treat farther on.

This species of measure, therefore, is more justly entitled to its name, alla-breve measure, than the previously introduced small alla-breve measure, inasmuch as a brevis or breve just makes out one measure in this larger species of alla-breve measure.

If we take a review of the species of measure thus far passed over, we find that all the varieties of 2/1 measure, 2/2 measure, 2/4 measure etc. are fundamentally and in principle one and the same, though presented under different forms or modes of representation, according as whole-notes, half-notes, quarter-notes, &c. are chosen for the designation of the parts of the measure; and so also the different grades of uneven measure are properly only varieties of one species, only different ways of representing one and the same thing by signs.[26]

A few pages later he observed that, other things being equal, minims would be performed as fast in 2/2 as crotchets in 2/4.[27] He then went on to show how the different metres indicated different styles of performance, but failed to examine the question of whether this had an effect on tempo, as Kirnberger, Schulz, and other eighteenth-century writers had done. Many later German writers reiterated the historically orientated but simplistic description of alla breve as doubling the speed of the notes, and this tendency seems not to have been without its effect on composers. Schumann, among others, certainly used ¢ to indicate a speed exactly or approximately twice as fast as ¢. In his opera *Genoveva*, for instance, when he changed the time signature from ¢ to ¢ at the beginning of no. 17 he instructed 'slower by about half' ('um die Hälfte langsamer'), and at the beginning of no. 19, where the time again changes from ¢ to ¢, he wrote: 'The crotchets rather slower than the previous minims'; in neither case was there a new tempo term at the change of time signature.

Clearly, the confusion over this matter ran very deep. There was no theoretical consensus, and usage differed from place to place and composer to composer. Furthermore, inconsistency or carelessness on the part of composers, copyists, and engravers compounds the difficulty of determining what these signs were intended to convey: there are many instances where composers used

---

[26] Weber, *Theory*, i. 80–1.   [27] Ibid. 88–9.

c when ₵ would seem to be more appropriate and vice versa; it is also evident that many copyists and engravers were extremely negligent in this matter, for one sign is very frequently found in manuscript copies and printed editions where the composer's autograph clearly has the other. Koch had complained about the confusion between the two signatures in the 1780s, recommending that 2 should be used instead of ₵;[28] and the continuing prevalence of this sort of discrepancy in the nineteenth century led Karl Gollmick to observe in 1857 that 'most barred cs are not alla breve but often only random decoration'.[29]

When the situation is clouded by so much disagreement it might seem an impossible task to determine with any degree of confidence what kind of distinction composers intended when they used c and ₵, but here metronome marks provide invaluable evidence. The picture that emerges supports all the theoretical approaches to some extent; different composers treated the time signatures in different ways, and while some appear to have been either careless or capricious in their use of them others seem to have been relatively, though seldom wholly, self-consistent. Despite the exceptions and inconsistencies, an understanding of the basic approach adopted by individual composers can assist in making informed decisions in particular instances.

It seems to have been the case with many Continental composers of the late eighteenth century and early nineteenth century, including Haydn, Mozart, Beethoven, Spohr, Schubert, and Mendelssohn, that, though they accepted a notional 2:1 relationship between c and ₵, this was modified in practice by the influence of the note values. Thus, the greater weight of the larger note values in ₵ held back the tempo and prevented it attaining double speed, just as in the case of the relationship between 2/4 and 2/2 (₵) illustrated by Mozart's alteration of time signature and tempo term in K. 589. However, the effect of the weight of the note values seems to have been felt more strongly at faster tempos than at slower ones, probably because the larger note values were considered to belong more naturally to slower tempos. In an adagio marked with ₵, therefore, the speed of the crotchets might be regarded as only slightly less than that of the quavers in an adagio marked with c, while in an allegro the minims of the one would tend to be quite noticeably slower than the crotchets of the other; and this would be felt even more strongly at presto.

Beethoven's metronome marks suggest that he followed these principles to a considerable extent. For very fast movements, for instance, where the heavier metre offered the greatest resistance to an increase of speed, the distinction between the two metres became somewhat blurred and Beethoven seems to have used ₵ rather inconsistently in relation to the tempo term for these types of movement. The consistency in allegro range, on the other hand, is quite

---

[28] *Versuch*, ii. 295. This use of ₵ and 2 should not be confused with French Baroque practice, where these two signs had theoretically distinct implications.

[29] *Handlexicon der Tonkunst*, art. 'Alla breve'.

striking. It is likely, however, that he did not begin to grasp this notion of alla breve until around 1800, and that he may previously have used the time signature ¢ in a more arbitrary manner. This is suggested by the metronome marks he gave for the Finale of the Septet and the first movement of the First Symphony; both movements would fit more logically into the scheme if they were in **C** metre (see Table 9.1). His comment on the time signature of the Gloria of his Mass in C also suggests a continuing uncertainty in his mind during the first few years of the century. He originally marked the movement ¢ but, as he wrote to Breitkopf & Härtel in 1812, a 'bad performance at which the tempo was too fast' induced him to change it to **C**; however, he informed them that he had changed it back to ¢, 'thus altering the tempo' (i.e. making it faster). He clearly recognized on reflection that, although not halving the original tempo, the change of time signature to **C** would imply much too slow a tempo, for he remarked 'Well, as I had not seen the Mass for a long time, this point struck me at once and I saw that unfortunately a thing like that has to be left to chance'.[30] Three of Beethoven's slow **C** movements (the Ninth Symphony op. 125/iii, the String Quartet op. 59 no. 2/ii, and the Seventh Symphony op. 92/i) seem really to have required ¢. (The same is undoubtedly true of a number of Mozart's slow movements.[31]) For very fast movements, where the fastest notes were longer than semiquavers, Beethoven usually used ¢ even if they really related more closely to the **C** scale. Table 9.1 shows the relationship of the movements in ¢ and **C** to which Beethoven gave metronome marks.

The metronome marks in Schubert's *Alfonso und Estrella*, which even if not written into the autograph by the composer almost certainly stem from him, indicate that Schubert, too, shared the concept of ¢ as indicating a speed notionally twice as fast as **C**; but his sense of the slowing effect of the weightier note values seems to have been less strong than Beethoven's. At slow to moderate tempos he appears to have regarded the minim in the one as more or less exactly equivalent to the crotchet in the other. The slowing effect of the note values seems to operate, however, in faster movements, though not entirely consistently. The note values employed and the quantity of fast notes only explain discrepancies to a limited extent (see Table 9.2).[32]

Cherubini's metronome marks in his two Requiems and his string quartets show him to have shared the view of ¢ as indicating a modified doubling of speed. As with the other composers, however, the time signatures alone (at least as given in printed editions) cannot be relied on, for the Allegro agitato first

---

[30] Anderson, *The Letters of Beethoven*, 378. Rosenblum, in her stimulating study *Performance Practices*, 308, misinterpreted the implications of this letter, apparently failing to appreciate that ¢ was the original marking and assuming that Beethoven meant to slow the tempo down by substituting ¢ for **C**.

[31] See Uri Toeplitz, 'Über die Tempi in Mozarts Instrumentalmusik', *Mozart-Jahrbuch* (1986), 171–202.

[32] Clive Brown, 'Schubert's Tempo Conventions', in Brian Newbould, ed., *Schubert Studies* (Aldershot, Ashgate, 1998), 1–15.

movement of the first quartet ($\bullet$ = 116) and the Allegro vivace Finale of the posthumous Quartet in F, though evidently alla breve, are marked **C**; the same is true of the 'Quam olim Abrahae' in the C minor Requiem which is headed 'Tempo a cappella' (see Table 9.3).

Weber's metronome marks for *Euryanthe* reveal a quite different picture. He seems to have leant towards the English notion of **¢** indicating a tempo only somewhat faster than **C**, though he used **¢** almost exclusively for fast movements where the difference could in any case be expected to be smaller. He does, however, appear to have marked some slow movements **C** where the metronome marks indicate that they stand in an alla breve relationship to other movements with the same tempo term (compare, for example, the largos nos. 17 and 23b and the overture with the largos nos. 17a and 6a in Table 9.4).

Spohr's and Mendelssohn's use of the time signature **¢** seems closer to Weber's than to Beethoven's, Schubert's, and Cherubini's. Schumann's employment of it, however, is in stark contrast with both these approaches. He does not seem to have used **¢** until about 1840, at which time he started to employ a number of less common time signatures. Its first use, in the *Thematisches Verzeichnis*, is in the String Quartets op. 41. Op. 31, *Drei Gesänge* (*c.*1840), uses 2/8 as well as **CC** (for 4/2); *Myrthen* op. 25/i (1840) uses 3/2 and 6/4. In general, as Table 9.5 shows, he seems to have regarded **¢** as indicating literally that minims should be seen in the same light as crotchets in **C**. Since Schumann lacked the practical musical apprenticeship enjoyed by many other composers of his generation, this may well have been the result of a reliance on the contemporary theoretical statements of Gottfried Weber and others that he had encountered in his reading.

Some early nineteenth century composers were very casual about the use of these time signatures. Spontini's and Rossini's employment of **¢** and **2**, mostly without any obvious purpose, has already been alluded to; but their works also include many other pieces, evidently of an alla breve type, which have a **C** time signature. Some movements in **C** that share the same or similar tempo terms have minim metronome marks, while others have crotchet metronome marks with the same or similar numbers; for instance Spontini gave both the Allegro espressivo agitato in Act I, no. 7 of *Fernand Cortez* and the Allegro agitato assai in Act III, no. 1 of *Olympie* the time signature **C**, but he fixed the metronome mark for the former at $\bullet$ = 120 and for the latter at $\bullet$ = 120.

The use of **¢** and **C** continued to be very variable in the mid- to late nineteenth century. Berlioz used **¢** in a few slow and moderate movements, but mostly confined it (and occasionally **2** or 2/2) to allegro movements which would, as his metronome marks indicate, generally have been beaten in two or sometimes one. His **C** movements are mainly composed with a crotchet pulse and have crotchet metronome marks with numbers that are close to those for the minim pulse in his **¢** movements with similar tempo terms. In quite a few cases, however, movements marked ℂ look as if they should really have been marked ¢. Berlioz does not seem to have had any clearly formulated notion of larger note values implying greater resistance to speed, even at the fastest tempos.

Wagner, like Berlioz, saw things primarily from the practical conductor's view, though more consistently. He employed ℂ mostly for slow to moderate movements and ¢ for faster ones, perhaps with the implication that ℂ should be beaten in four and ¢ in two (though there appear to be a significant number of occasions on which a metre has been wrongly transmitted or carelessly assigned). In later works his tendency was to use 4/4 and 2/2 in the same sense. There is absolutely nothing to suggest that he was influenced by the Kirnberger–Schulz view of the relationship between tempo, metre, tempo term, and note value. The list of numbers in ℂ and ¢ from operas to which Wagner gave metronome marks (Table 9.6) shows graphically how different his approach to this matter was from Beethoven's and Schubert's or even from Schumann's, and indeed from that of many of his younger contemporaries such as Brahms, Tchaikovsky, and Dvořák, who retained the notion that ¢ was twice as fast as ℂ.

Note on Tables 9.1–9.6

The term 'fastest notes' refers to the fastest functional note values employed in the movement or section (i.e. ignoring tremolando and occasional flourishes or ornamental figures of faster notes). The tables are arranged according to tempo terms, roughly in ascending order of speed, and movements or sections in each column are ranged opposite those with which they have approximately a 2 : 1 relationship. Entries enclosed in round brackets are very short sections which provide insufficient information to compare them confidently with others. Note values in brackets in the 'fastest notes' column indicate that a very small proportion of notes of this value appear in the piece. The letters that follow some of the numbers indicate the order of sections within these numbers of an opera.

Table 9.1. The Relationship of ¢ and C Metre in Beethoven's Music

The composer's metronome marks in this table are taken from the symphonies opp. 21, 36, 60, 67, 92, 93, and 125, the string quartets opp. 18 (1–6), 59 (1–3), 74, and 95, the Septet op. 20, and the cantata *Meerestille und glückliche Fahrt* op. 112. Asterisks indicate movements which appear to have an inconsistent time signature and ought more logically to belong in the other column; these movements are also given, in square brackets, at the appropriate place in the other column.

¢				C			
Opus	Tempo term	MM	Fastest notes	Opus	Tempo term	MM	Fastest notes
[125/iii	Adagio molto e cantabile	♩ = 60	♪]				
[59/2/ii	Molto Adagio	♩ = 60	♪]				
60/i	Adagio	♩ = 66	♪				
74/i	Poco Adagio	♩ = 60	♪				
[92/i	Poco sostenuto	♩ = 69	♪]				
112	Sostenuto	♩ = 84	♪				
				21/i	Adagio molto	♪ = 88	♪
				125/iii*	Adagio molto e cantabile	♩ = 60	♪
				59/2/ii*	Molto Adagio	♩ = 60	♪
				92/i*	Poco sostenuto	♩ = 69	♪
125/iv	Allegro ma non tanto	𝅗𝅥 = 120	♪				
18/3/i	Allegro	𝅗𝅥 = 120	♬♬♬ (3)				
18/4/iv	Allegro	o = 66	♪				
18/5/iv	Allegro	o = 76	♪				
95/iv	Allegro	o = 92[a]	♪				
59/1/i	Allegro	𝅗𝅥 = 88	♬♬♬ (3)				
60/i	Allegro vivace	o = 80	♪				
93/i	Allegro vivace	o = 84	♬♬♬ (3)	125/iv	Allegro assai	𝅗𝅥 = 80	♪
18/6/i	Allegro con brio	o = 80	♪	68/iv	Allegro	𝅗𝅥 = 80	♪
				18/4/i	Allegro ma non tanto	𝅗𝅥 = 84	♪
				74/i	Allegro	𝅗𝅥 = 84	♪
				67/iv	Allegro	𝅗𝅥 = 84	♪
				59/3/i	Allegro vivace	𝅗𝅥 = 88	♪
				95/i	Allegro con brio	𝅗𝅥 = 92	♪
20/i*	Allegro con brio	𝅗𝅥 = 96	♪	[20/i	Allegro con brio	𝅗𝅥 = 96	♪]
21/i*	Allegro con brio	𝅗𝅥 = 112	♪	[21/i	Allegro con brio	𝅗𝅥 = 112	♪]
36/iv	Allegro molto	𝅗𝅥 = 152	♪				
59/3/iv	Allegro molto	o = 84	♪				
20/iv	Presto	𝅗𝅥 = 112	♬♬♬ (3)				

Table 9.1. *cont.*

¢				c			
Opus	Tempo term	MM	Fastest notes	Opus	Tempo term	MM	Fastest notes
59/2/iv	Presto	𝅝 = 88	♪				
				36/i	Allegro con brio	𝅗𝅥 = 100	♪
67/iv	Presto	𝅝 = 112	♪				
125/ii	Presto	𝅝 = 116	♩				
125/iv	Prestissimo	𝅗𝅥 = 132	♪				
18/4/iv	Prestissimo	𝅝 = 84	♪				

[a] The metronome mark for this short section, which concludes the last movement, seems puzzlingly fast for Allegro ¢. It is in a proportional relationship to the preceding 6/8 Allegretto agitato, itself surprisingly fast at 𝅘 = 92. In the context of Beethoven's metronome markings as a whole, it seems distinctly possible that in both cases '92' may be a misprint for '72'.

Table 9.2. The Relationship of ¢ and c Metre in Schubert's Music

These metronome tempos are all taken from Schubert's opera *Alfonso und Estrella*.

¢				c			
No.	Tempo term	MM	Fastest notes	No.	Tempo term	MM	Fastest notes
33[a]	Andante	𝅗𝅥 = 100	♪	2	Andante molto	♪= 76	𝅘𝅥𝅯
				(3b	Andante maestoso	𝅗𝅥 = 52	𝅘𝅥𝅯)
4	Andante	𝅗𝅥 = 58	𝅘𝅥𝅯𝅘𝅥𝅯𝅘𝅥𝅯 (triplet)	35c	Andante	𝅗𝅥 = 50	𝅘𝅥𝅯
				31	Moderato	𝅗𝅥 = 96	♫ (triplet)
				3a	Andantino	𝅗𝅥 = 100	♫ (triplet)
				27a	Allegretto	𝅗𝅥 = 112	♪
				12	Andantino	𝅗𝅥 = 116	𝅘𝅥𝅯
				15	Andantino	𝅗𝅥 = 120	♫ (triplet)
				10	Tempo di marcia	𝅗𝅥 = 132	𝅘𝅥𝅯
				35d	Allegro molto moderato	𝅗𝅥 = 84	♪
10d	Allegro moderato	𝅗𝅥 = 116	♪	(6	Allegro moderato	𝅗𝅥 = 100	♪(𝅘𝅥𝅯))

¢				ℂ			
No.	Tempo term	MM	Fastest notes	No.	Tempo term	MM	Fastest notes
7a	Allegro moderato	𝅗𝅥 = 120	♪	35a	Allegro moderato	𝅗𝅥 = 120	♪ (♪)
				(34b	Allegro moderato	𝅗𝅥 = 120 (same music as 35a))	
				5	Allegro ma non troppo	𝅗𝅥 = 126	♪
31a	Allegro	𝅗𝅥 = 132	♪	28	Allegro moderato	𝅗𝅥 = 132	♪
29	Allegro assai	𝅗𝅥 = 138	♪	16	Allegro moderato	𝅗𝅥 = 138	♪
17	Allegro agitato	𝅗𝅥 = 144	♪	1	Allegro giusto	𝅗𝅥 = 144	♪
23[b]	Allegro[c]	𝅗𝅥 = 160	𝅘𝅥𝅯	8a	Allegro giusto[d]	𝅗𝅥 = 160	♪
ov.[e]	Allegro	𝅗𝅥 = 160	♪ (♪)	(8	Allegro[f]	𝅗𝅥 = 160[g]	♪)
17b	Allegro molto	𝅗𝅥 = 160	♪	9a	Allegro	𝅗𝅥 = 160	♪
				18	Allegro	𝅗𝅥 = 160	♪
				35b	Allegro	𝅗𝅥 = 160	♪
				35e	Allegro	𝅗𝅥 = 160	♪
26	Allegro molto	𝅝 = 84	♪				
				22	Allegro	𝅗𝅥 = 88	♪
				2b	Allegro	𝅗𝅥 = 92	♪
				32	Allegro agitato	𝅗𝅥 = 104[h]	♪
				17a	Allegro assai	𝅗𝅥 = 104	♪
				33	Allegro	𝅗𝅥 = 112[i]	♪(𝅘𝅥𝅮𝅘𝅥𝅮𝅘𝅥𝅮)
				20	Allegro molto vivace	𝅗𝅥 = 112	♪
				19	Allegro molto	𝅗𝅥 = 112	♪
				(10c	Allegro assai	𝅗𝅥 = 116	♪)
				22b	Allegro vivace	𝅗𝅥 = 120	♪

[a] Given as ℂ in the 1884–97 *Gesamtausgabe*.

[b] This section and the Allegro of the overture seem out of line with the other ¢ sections; they seem as if they ought to have a faster tempo term. But both are purely orchestral, and this may suggest different criteria for orchestral and vocal music, just as there seems to have been in the case of sacred and secular music.

ᶜ Originally Allegro moderato, then Allegro ma non troppo, and finally Allegro. The separately bowed semiquaver runs in the violins would only be realistic at the original tempo, and Schubert presumably omitted to alter these (by adding slurs) as his conception of the tempo increased.

ᵈ Originally Mod^to maestoso.

ᵉ See note 3.

ᶠ Originally All° mod^to.

ᵍ Incorrectly given as ♩ = 106 in the score (p. 177) in *Neue Schubert Ausgabe* and, equally incorrectly, as 100 in the 'Quellen und Lesarten' section at the end of the volume (p. 797). It should be 160. Ferdinand Schubert's copy of the opera in the Österreichische Nationalbibliothek also has 160.

ʰ The metronome mark is given in Ferdinand Schubert's copy simply as MM 104, without a note value, and the editor of the 1884–97 *Gesamtausgabe* gave it as ♩ = 104. Schubert's autograph, however, clearly has '104 ♩'.

ⁱ Given in the score of the *Neue Schubert Ausgabe* as ♩ = 112 (p. 723), though it is referred to in the 'Quellen und Lesarten' (p. 825) as 𝅗𝅥 = 112. Ferdinand Schubert's copy has 𝅗𝅥 = 112. The 1884–97 *Gesamtausgabe*, without any known authority, gave it as ¢ 𝅗𝅥 = 120. 𝅗𝅥 = 112 would be improbably slow; ♩ = 112, though slightly faster than might be expected, seems likelier to represent Schubert's intentions.

Table 9.3. The Relationship of ¢ and c Metre in Cherubini's Music

Metronome marks are taken from the Requiem no. 1 in C minor (R1), the Requiem no. 2 in D minor (R2), and the five published string quartets (Q1–Q5).

¢				c			
Piece	Tempo term	MM	Fastest notes	Piece	Tempo term	MM	Fastest notes
				R1	Largo	𝅗𝅥 = 54	♪
				R2	Lento	𝅗𝅥 = 63	♪
R1	Larghetto sost.	𝅗𝅥 = 50	♪				
R1	Larghetto	𝅗𝅥 = 56	♪				
				R1	Sostenuto	𝅗𝅥 = 60	♪
				R1	Andante	𝅗𝅥 = 66	♪
				R2	Grave ma non troppo	𝅗𝅥 = 69	♪
				R2	Andante con moto	𝅗𝅥 = 88	♪
R1	Allegro maestoso	𝅗𝅥 = 88	♪ (♪)				
				R2	Maestoso	𝅗𝅥 = 72	♪
				R2	Maestoso	𝅗𝅥 = 67! [76?]	♪
R2	Allegro (più vivo che la	𝅗𝅥 = 96					

¢				c			
Piece	Tempo term	MM	Fastest notes	Piece	Tempo term	MM	Fastest notes
R1	prima volta [i.e. Allegro mod.]) Tempo a cappella,ᵃ poco allegro	𝅗𝅥 = 120	♪				
				R2	Allegro moderato	𝅗𝅥 = 152	♪
				R2	Vivo	𝅗𝅥 = 60! [160?]	♪
Q5	Allegro vivaceᵇ	𝅗𝅥 = 108	♪	Q4	Allegro maestoso	𝅗𝅥 = 108	♪
Q1	Allegro agitatoᶜ	𝅗𝅥 = 116	♪				
Q2	Allegro vivace	𝅗𝅥 = 120	♪	Q3	Allegro comodo	𝅗𝅥 = 120	♪
Q1	Allegro assai (plus vite encore)	𝅗𝅥 = 160	♪	Q2	Allegro	𝅗𝅥 = 80	♪
				Q3	Allegro risoluto	𝅗𝅥 = 88	♫♪ (triplet)
				Q4	Allegro assai	𝅗𝅥 = 88	♪

ᵃ Time signature printed as 𝄴!
ᵇ Time signature printed as 𝄵.
ᶜ Time signature printed as 𝄵.

Table 9.4. The Relationship of ¢ and C Metre in Weber's Music

Weber's metronome marks come from *Euryanthe* and from the *Konzertstück* for piano and orchestra J. 282.

¢				C			
No.	Tempo term	MM	Fastest notes	No.	Tempo term	MM	Fastest notes
				17	Largo	♩ = 50	♪
				23b	Largo	♩ = 50	♪ (♪)
				ov.	Largo	♩ = 52	♩
				17a	Largo	♪ = 66	♪
				6a	Largo	♪ = 84	♪ (♪)
				15	Adagio non lento	♩ = 66	♪
				9a	Andantino grazioso	♩ = 54	♪
23	Maestoso energico ma non troppo	♩ = 63	♪	4	Maestoso assai	♩ = 50	♪
				14c	Maestoso assai	♩ = 66	♪ (♪)
				25	Maestoso con moto	♩ = 108	♪
				15a	Moderato	♩ = 88	♪
				1	Moderato maestoso	♩ = 92	♪
				25c	Moderato assai	♩ = 92	♪
				5b	Moderato assai	♩ = 96	♪
				7	Moderato assai	♩ = 104	♪
				8a	Moderato	♩ = 100	♪
				23d	Allegro moderato	♩ = 104	♪
				3	Allegro	♩ = 116	♪
				12a	Allegro	♩ = 120	♪
				J. 282	Tempo di marcia	♩ = 126	♪
				21a	Allegro non tanto	♩ = 132	♪
				23a	Allegro moderato	♩ = 138	♬ (3)
				11	Allegro energico	♩ = 144	♬ (3)
				8b	Allegro fiero	♩ = 144	♪
				14d	Allegro ma non troppo	♩ = 144	♪
				16	Molto passionato	♩ = 152	♪ (♪)
				22	Allegro	♩ = 152	♪
				23e	Vivace	♩ = 152	♪ (♪)
				14e	Con tutto fuoco ed energia	♩ = 160	♪ (♪)
				8	Allegro	♩ = 160	♪

¢				c			
No.	Tempo term	MM	Fastest notes	No.	Tempo term	MM	Fastest notes
				♩. 282	Allegro passionato	𝅗𝅥 = 160	♪
				10b	Allegro	𝅗𝅥 = 160	♪ (♪)
				20	Allegro con fuoco	𝅗𝅥 = 160	♪
				23c	Vivace	𝅗𝅥 = 160	♪
				4a	Allegro	𝅗𝅥 = 88	♪ (♪)
				ov.	Allegro marcato, Tempo I assai moderato	𝅗𝅥 = 88	♫♫ (3)
				15c	Allegro non tanto	𝅗𝅥 = 88	♪
				ov.	Allegro marcato, con molto fuoco	𝅗𝅥 = 92	♫♫ (3)
10	Allegro con fuoco	𝅗𝅥 = 92	♪	6	Agitato ma non troppo presto	𝅗𝅥 = 92	♪ (♪)
13	Allegro animato	𝅗𝅥 = 96	♫♫ (3)	4b	Con fuoco	𝅗𝅥 = 96	♫♫ (3)
				15b	Agitato	𝅗𝅥 = 96	♪
				25a	Agitato	𝅗𝅥 = 96	♪
14a	Allegro	𝅗𝅥 = 100	♪ (♪)	24	Con impeto	𝅗𝅥 = 100	♫♫ (3)
11a	Con strepito	𝅗𝅥 = 104	♫♫ (♪)	3a	Agitato assai	𝅗𝅥 = 104	♪
				25d	Molto passionato	𝅗𝅥 = 112	♪ (♪)
				15d	Presto	𝅗𝅥 = 116	♪
10d	Vivace feroce	𝅗𝅥 = 132	♪ (♪)				
6b	Presto	𝅗𝅥 = 128 [?138]	♪				

Table 9.5. The Relationship of ¢ and c Metre in Schumann's Music

Schumann's metronome marks are taken from the following works: *Szenen aus Goethes Faust* (*Faust*), the symphonies opp. 38, 61, 97, and 120, the Overture, Scherzo, and Finale op. 52, the overtures *Genoveva* op. 81, *Die Braut von Messina* op. 100, *Manfred* op. 115, *Fest-Ouverture* op. 123, and *Hermann und Dorothea* op. 136, the string quartets op. 41 (1–3), and the Piano Quintet op. 44.

¢				c			
Op.	Tempo term	MM	Fastest notes	Op.	Tempo term	MM	Fastest notes
				Faust	Langsam, feierlich	♪ = 112	♪
				81	Langsam	♩ = 50	♪
				120	Langsam	♩ = 52	♪
				41/1	Adagio	♩ = 54	♪
				123	Feierlich, doch nicht zu langsam	♩ = 58	♪
				41/3	Andante espress.	♩ = 60	♪
				52	Andante con moto	♩ = 60	♪
				115	Langsam	♩ = 63	♪
				41/3	Adagio molto	♩ = 66	♪
44	In modo d'una marcia Un poco largamente	♩ = 66	♪♪♪ (triplet)	38	Andante un poco maestoso	♩ = 66	♪
				128	Kräftig gemessen	♩ = 80	♪
100	Sehr lebhaft	♩ = 88	♪				
41/1	Moderato	♩ = 96	♪				
38	Allegro animato e grazioso	♩ = 100	♪				
41/3	Allegro molto vivace	♩ = 108	♪♪♪ (triplet)	123	Lebhaft	♩ = 108	♪
44	Allegro brillante	♩ = 108	♪	136	Mässig	♩ = 126	♪♪♪ (triplet)
97	Lebhaft	♩ = 120	♪				
44	Allegro ma non troppo	♩ = 126	♪	120	Lebhaft	♩ = 126	♪
81	Leidenschaftlich bewegt	♩ = 140	♪	115	In leidenschaftlichem Tempo	♩ = 144	♪
52	Allegro molto vivace	♩ = 148	♩♩♩ (triplet)				
41/1	Presto	♩ = 160	♪				
61	Allegro molto vivace	♩ = 170	♪				

Table 9.6. The Relationship of ¢ and C Metre in Wagner's Music

Metronome marks are taken from *Rienzi* (R), the *Rienzi* ballet music (RB), *Der fliegende Holländer* (H), and *Tannhäuser* (T). In *Rienzi* and *Tannhäuser* the opera is divided into a succession of numbers which run continuously throughout; *Tannhäuser* is divided into acts and scenes. Very many sections include some tremolando in the strings. This has been ignored in calculating the fastest functional note values, as have ornamental flourishes; nevertheless the fluid nature of Wagner's music makes this factor debatable in many cases. In some instances the metre is not clear, either because Wagner has not indicated a change from a previous section with four crotchets in the bar, or for another reason, but in some cases an intended change has been assumed because of the note content; these sections are marked with a dagger.

¢				C			
Work	Tempo term	MM	Fastest notes	Work	Tempo term	MM	Fastest notes
				TIII,2	Moderato	♩ = 46	triplet semiquavers
				TIII,1	Andante assai lento	♩ = 50	quaver
				H2	Sostenuto	♩ = 50	triplet semiquavers
				TIII,3	Lento	♩ = 50	quaver
				TIII,3	Lento maestoso	♩ = 50	semiquaver
				H8	Andante	♩ = 50	quaver
				TI,4	Lento	♩ = 54	quaver
				TII,4	Andante	♩ = 56	quaver
				TII,4	Adagio	♩ = 58	semiquaver
				R4c	Andante energico†	♩ = 60	semiquaver
				R1f	Moderato e maestoso	♩ = 66	semiquaver
				H2	Moderato	♩ = 66	quaver
				R6e	Un poco sostenuto†	♩ = 66	quaver
				Rov	Molto sostenuto e maestoso	♩ = 66	quaver
				R13	Lento	♩ = 66	triplet semiquavers
				H3	Lento	♩ = 66	quaver
				H6	Sostenuto	♩ = 66	quaver
				H5	Sostenuto	♩ = 69	quaver
				R9d	Maestoso	♩ = 69	quaver
				R9b	Andante	♩ = 69	semiquaver
				TIII,3	Maestoso	♩ = 69	crotchet
				R4d	Maestoso†	♩ = 72	triplet semiquavers
				TII,4	Andante†	♩ = 72	quaver
				R4b	Maestoso†	♩ = 72	semiquaver
				R1oh	Grave	♩ = 72	triplet semiquavers

Table 9.6. *cont.*

¢

Work	Tempo term	MM	Fastest notes
H3	Allegro moderato	𝅗𝅥 = 50	♪
TII,4	Moderato	𝅗𝅥 = 60	♪
TII,4	Moderato	𝅗𝅥 = 60	♪
TII,2	Moderato	𝅗𝅥 = 60	♪
TI,4	Allegro moderato	𝅗𝅥 = 60	♪♪♪ (3)

c

Work	Tempo term	MM	Fastest notes
TI,4	Andante	♩ = 76	♪♪♪ (3)
TII,3	Andante	♩ = 76	♪
R11b	Un poco lento†	♩ = 80	♪
H1	Moderato	♩ = 80	♩
H2	Allegro	♩ = 80	♬
R12b	Grave	♩ = 80	♪
H6	Moderato	♩ = 80	♪
R10f	Maestoso	♩ = 84	♪
H3	Moderato	♩ = 84	♪♪♪ (3)
R5b	Maestoso moderato	♩ = 88	♪
R6b	Moderato e un poco maestoso†	♩ = 88	♪
TII,4	Maestoso	♩ = 88	♪♪♪ (3)
R2e	Maestoso†	♩ = 80	♪♪♪ (3)
TI,3	Moderato	♩ = 84	♪
R12a	Un poco maestoso	♩ = 92	♬
R1b	Maestoso	♩ = 92	𝅘𝅥𝅰
R7a	Allegro maestoso, ma non troppo	♩ = 96	♬
R11a	Un poco sostenuto	♩ = 96	♪
R2b	Allegro non tanto	♩ = 100	♪
TII,3	Andante	♩ = 100	♪
RBe	Allegro maestoso	♩ = 108	♪
R14a	Moderato e maestoso	♩ = 108	♪♪♪ (3)
TII,4	Moderato	𝅗𝅥 = 54	♪
R10b	Allegro energico	♩ = 112	♬
H6	Allegro moderato	♩ = 112	♬
TI,2	Moderato	𝅗𝅥 = 58	♪♪♪ (3)
RBc	Maestoso	♩ = 120	♪
H3	Animato	𝅗𝅥 = 60	♪♪♪ (3)
H3	Animato	𝅗𝅥 = 60	♪♪♪ (3)
TII,4	Moderato	𝅗𝅥 = 60	♪

¢				c			
Work	Tempo term	MM	Fastest notes	Work	Tempo term	MM	Fastest notes
H3	Moderato	𝅗𝅥 = 60	♪	TII,2	Allegro moderato	𝅗𝅥 = 60	♪
				R2a	Agitato	𝅗𝅥 = 126	♪
				R6a	Moderato	𝅗𝅥 = 126	♪
				H Act II intro.	Allegro vivace	𝅗𝅥 = 63	♫₃
TI,2	Allegro	𝅗𝅥 = 69	♪	TIII,3	Allegro†	𝅗𝅥 = 69	♫₃
R15b	Molto passionato†	𝅗𝅥 = 72	♫₃				
H1	Allegro con brio	𝅗𝅥 = 72	♫₃				
TII,4	Allegro	𝅗𝅥 = 72	♫₃				
TII,3	Allegro	𝅗𝅥 = 72	♫₃				
TI,4	Allegro	𝅗𝅥 = 72	♫₃				
TI,2	Allegro	𝅗𝅥 = 72	♫₃				
H6	Allegro vivace	𝅗𝅥 = 72	♪				
H3	Vivace ma non troppo presto	𝅗𝅥 = 72	♫₃	R1e	Allegro	𝅗𝅥 = 72	♫₃
H3	Allegro agitato	𝅗𝅥 = 76	♪	H5	Allegro appassionato	𝅗𝅥 = 76	♪
TII,4	Allegro	𝅗𝅥 = 76	♪	R10a	Tempo di marcia	𝅗𝅥 = 76	♪
TI,2	Allegro	𝅗𝅥 = 76	♪	R2c	Allegro	𝅗𝅥 = 152	♫₃
TII,4	Allegro†	𝅗𝅥 = 80	♪	TIII,3	Allegro†	𝅗𝅥 = 80	♪
R10g	Allegro furioso	𝅗𝅥 = 80	♪	H3	Allegro	𝅗𝅥 = 80	♫₃
TII,4	Allegro	𝅗𝅥 = 80	♪	TIII,3	Allegro	𝅗𝅥 = 80	♪
R6d	Allegro agitato	𝅗𝅥 = 80	♪				
R3b	Allegro con moto	𝅗𝅥 = 80	♪				
TI,4	Allegro	𝅗𝅥 = 80	♪				
T ov.	Allegro	𝅗𝅥 = 80	♪				
H8	Allegro agitato	𝅗𝅥 = 80	♪				
H4	Allegro con fuoco	𝅗𝅥 = 80	♪				

Table 9.6. *cont.*

¢				c			
Work	Tempo term	MM	Fastest notes	Work	Tempo term	MM	Fastest notes
R9c	Allegro	𝅗𝅥 = 84	𝅘𝅥𝅯	R1c	Allegro	𝅗𝅥 = 84	𝅘𝅥𝅯
R ov.	Allegro energico	𝅗𝅥 = 84	𝅘𝅥𝅯𝅘𝅥𝅯𝅘𝅥𝅯 (3)				
H2	Molto passionato	𝅗𝅥 = 84	♪				
TII,4	Allegro	𝅗𝅥 = 84	𝅘𝅥𝅯				
H8	Molto agitato	𝅗𝅥 = 84	♪				
R14b	Con spirito	𝅗𝅥 = 84	♪				
H5	Allegro con fuoco	𝅗𝅥 = 84	♪				
R10c	Agitato	𝅗𝅥 = 88	♪				
TII,1	Allegro	𝅗𝅥 = 88	𝅘𝅥𝅯𝅘𝅥𝅯𝅘𝅥𝅯 (3)				
R1a	Allegro animato	𝅗𝅥 = 88	𝅘𝅥𝅯				
R11c	Allegro[†]	𝅗𝅥 = 88	𝅘𝅥𝅯𝅘𝅥𝅯𝅘𝅥𝅯 (3)				
H Act III intro.	Allegro molto	𝅗𝅥 = 88	♪				
R2d	Allegro con brio	𝅗𝅥 = 88	♪				
R8a	Molto agitato	𝅗𝅥 = 88	𝅘𝅥𝅯				
H ov.	Vivace	𝅗𝅥 = 92	𝅘𝅥𝅯𝅘𝅥𝅯𝅘𝅥𝅯 (3)				
H8	Feroce	𝅗𝅥 = 92	𝅘𝅥𝅯𝅘𝅥𝅯𝅘𝅥𝅯 (3)				
R6f	Allegro agitato	𝅗𝅥 = 92	♪				
R9e	Vivace	𝅗𝅥 = 92	♪				
R12c	Allegro molto	𝅗𝅥 = 96	𝅘𝅥𝅯				
R15a	Con impeto	𝅗𝅥 = 96	♪				
H6	Allegro molto	𝅗𝅥 = 96	♪				
TII,4	Allegro[†]	𝅗𝅥 = 100	♪				
TII,2	Allegro	𝅗𝅥 = 100	♪				
H7	Molto vivace	𝅗𝅥 = 100	♪				
H4	Prestissimo possibile	𝅗𝅥 = 100	♪				

¢				C			
Work	Tempo term	MM	Fastest notes	Work	Tempo term	MM	Fastest notes
R4a	Allegro con fuoco	♩ = 104	♫♪ (3)				
R10e	Allegro molto	♩ = 104	♪				
R9a	Molto agitato	♩ = 104	♫♪ (3)				
TI,4	Allegro	♩ = 108	♪				
R10i	Allegro molto	♩ = 116	♪				
R16	Molto passionato	♩ = 120	♪				
TI,1	Allegro molto	♩ = 132	♪♪♪ (3)				

10

Tempo Terms

❦

As the connotations of metre for tempo weakened during the seventeenth and eighteenth centuries, the Italian directions, which began increasingly often to be affixed to the beginning of a piece, became more important for determining tempo. Concomitantly with the proliferation of these terms, however, a lack of consensus about their meaning also became more apparent. Although there was no significant disagreement about the fact that 'adagio', 'andante', 'allegro', and 'presto' indicated a series of progressively faster speeds, that pieces marked 'largo', 'lento', 'grave', and 'larghetto' were all slower than those marked 'andante', or that 'adagissimo' implied a slower tempo than 'adagio' and 'prestissimo' a faster one than 'presto', there were many points of detail upon which composers' practices were at odds with one another. A particular problem with these terms was that they served a dual purpose; for composers, especially in the earlier part of the period tended to use them as much to prescribe the appropriate mood or style as to designate the tempo. As Koch observed around the turn of the century, they could be used 'merely to indicate the tempo, or merely the style of performance, or both at the same time'.[1] Thus, while there was seldom doubt about the general tempo region to which the most commonly employed terms belonged, there was often a significant lack of agreement about precisely how they stood in relation to each other, or, in the case of qualifying terms, how, if at all, these might affect the tempo indicated by the principal term. An additional matter about which there were considerable differences between regions, individuals, and generations was the absolute degree of momentum implied by the most common principal terms, particularly 'andante' and 'allegro'. There is a widely held view that 'andante' meant something more active to late eighteenth-century and early nineteenth-century musicians than it did a few decades later, and there is evidence to

---

[1] *Musikalisches Lexikon* art. 'Adagio'.

suggest that, in some places at least, early nineteenth-century composers and performers saw 'allegro' as indicating a substantially faster tempo than did those of the mid- to late nineteenth century.

Theorists, trying to make sense of a host of evident discrepancies in practice, chose a number of different courses. Some, particularly in the eighteenth century, regarded many of these terms as primarily describing expression, or signifying a particular mode of execution, rather than tempo; some grouped them in more or less broad categories; some explicitly recognized divergent usages; others simply contented themselves with prescribing a hierarchy of tempo terms without comment. A few writers attempted to fix chronometric tempos or tempo ranges for the various terms, but in most cases these provide little useful information, since by giving nothing but tempo term and metronome mark they failed to compare like with like.

The confusion and complexity that cloud this matter at every stage may be illustrated by the contrasting approaches of two British writers, William Crotch and John Jousse, in the early nineteenth century. Crotch proposed the following list of tempo terms in ascending order of speed: grave, largo, larghetto, adagio, lento, andante, allegretto, allegro, vivace, alla breve, presto, prestissimo; but he admitted that there were those who regarded adagio, lento, andante, alla breve, and vivace 'rather as terms of expression and taste, than of time'. He further observed that some considered 'adagio' to indicate a slower tempo than 'largo' and that others thought 'andantino' called for a slower one than 'andante'.[2] Jousse's *A Compendious Musical Grammar* (1825), an English translation of Bonifazio Asioli's *Principj elementari di musica*, nicely illustrates the gulf which separated English and Continental musicians in this matter. Asioli's list gave the order: largo, grave, larghetto, adagio, andantino, il tempo giusto, tempo di minuetto, andante, allegretto, allegro, presto prestissimo, but Jousse appended a footnote saying: 'The above description, which the French have adopted, is according to the Italian school; in England the following order is generally adopted: 1) Grave 2) Adagio 3) Largo 4) Larghetto 5) Andante 6) Andantino 7) Maestoso 8) Allegretto 9) Allegro 10) Vivace 11) Presto 12) Prestissimo'.[3]

In this respect, as in many others, the last decades of the eighteenth century and the first of the nineteenth were a period of transition. More conservative writers in the 1770s could still adhere primarily to the notion of these conventional Italian words as terms of expression, with a secondary connotation for tempo. Löhlein in 1774, for instance, explained them as indicating 'the ruling character [*Affekt*] of a piece', and listed them with more or less literal translations into German, which, in many cases, make no direct reference to speed. In his subsequent discussion of the meaning the performer should

---

[2] 'Remarks on the Terms at Present Used in Music, for Regulating the Time', *Monthly Magazine*, 8 (1800), 941–3.

[3] *A Compendious Musical Grammar*, 111.

derive from them, he focused largely on aspects of performance style rather than speed, considering, for instance, how the bowstroke should vary so that 'in this manner one seeks to define every degree of joy by means of the performance style [*Vortrag*]'.[4] Yet his manner of cataloguing the terms provides an unstated, albeit partial, hierarchy of speed; the first three categories imply a progressive increase of speed while the fifth, eighth, and ninth (with the exception of 'mesto') suggest a progressive decrease of speed; the relative speeds of the fourth, sixth, and seventh categories are less clearly implied. The ambiguous position of 'allegro furioso' evidently results from the difficulty of using 'allegro' as a term for fast music that was not in any way joyful. A decade after the appearance of Löhlein's treatise, Türk commented on the absurdity of the literal meaning of 'allegro furioso' as 'cheerfully angry' and suggested that 'allegro' should be regarded merely as meaning 'brisk' (*hurtig*) rather than 'merry' or 'cheerful' (*munter, lustig*).[5]

Löhlein's list reads as follows:

A moderate joy is expressed, for example, by:
    Vivace, merry, lively [*munter, lebhaft*]
    Allegro, cheerful, joyful [*lustig, freudig*]
A joy, which has more exuberance:
    Allegro assai, cheerful enough [*lustig genug*]
    Allegro di molto, very cheerful [*sehr lustig*]
    Presto, quick [*geschwind*]
An extravagant joy:
    Prestissimo, the quickest [*aufs geschwindeste*]
An angry exuberance:
    Allegro furioso, brisk and vehement [*hurtig und heftig*]
A moderated joy, that has more calmness:
    Allegro moderato, moderate [*mäßig*]
    Tempo giusto, in appropriate movement [*in angemessener Bewegung*]
    Poco allegro, somewhat cheerful [*etwas lustig*]
    Allegretto, somewhat less cheerful [*etwas weniger lustig*]
    Scherzante, funny, joking [*spaßhaft, scherzend*]
    Molto andante, at a strong walking pace [*im starken Schritte*]
Magnificence:
    Maestoso, splendid, proud [*prächtig, stolz*]
Tenderness:
    Affetuoso, with feelings [*mit Affekte*]
    Cantabile, singing [*singend*]
    Arioso, aria-like [*arienmäßig*]
Calmness;
    Andante, walking [*gehend*]
    Andantino, or poco andante, at a gentle walking pace [*im sachten Schritte*]
    Larghetto, somewhat spacious [*etwas weitläufig*]

[4] *Anweisung zum Violinspielen*, 106.   [5] *Klavierschule*, I, §70.

Sadness:
Mesto, sad [*traurig*]
Adagio, slow [*langsam*]
Largo, spacious [*weitläuftig*]
Lento, lazy, slack [*träg, saumselig*]
Grave, sluggish [*schwerfällig*]

It is not difficult to see how such lists, even where a definite hierarchy of speed was not intended, could give rise to confusion when, on the one hand, writers such as Quantz appeared to link Italian terms to precise chronometric tempos and, on the other, Kirnberger and Schulz were advocating a system in which the 'tempo' term played a crucial role in a complex equation that was intended to allow the speed of a piece to be determined as closely as possible. There can be little doubt that many late eighteenth-century musicians had a definite idea about the order of quickness or slowness indicated by particular terms and that they were by no means in agreement about it. Furthermore, as Türk observed, 'composers themselves are not entirely of the same mind with respect to indicating the tempo and the terms usually employed for that purpose; for one understands a far greater degree of speed by allegro than another'.[6]

The distinction between terms that primarily designated speed and those that denoted a type of expression or style of performance is much more apparent in Türk's treatise than in Löhlein's, but towards the end of the eighteenth century and in the nineteenth century there was a tendency to attribute definite tempo implications also to words or phrases such as 'maestoso', 'sostenuto', 'con spirito', 'vivace', or 'con brio' when these were combined with another term, or to try to assign a definite tempo region to terms that clearly described character, like 'amoroso'. This tendency is apparent in Domenico Corri's list, from the early 1780s, of 'words used to expr[e]ss the time, arranged progressively from the slowest to the most rapid movement'.[7]

The following consideration of individual tempo terms is intended to be illustrative rather than exhaustive, but it identifies some of the ambiguities that affect those most commonly used during the period under consideration. Of course, as in so many aspects of performing practice, generalized conclusions, though they may alert musicians to areas of uncertainty, are of only limited value. There is scope for several major studies of the attitudes and practices of individual composers and schools of composers towards tempo in the nineteenth century, for which the (as yet) scarcely investigated evidence of metronome marks would provide a mass of invaluable evidence. The present study attempts to draw general, and in some cases specific, conclusions from composers' metronome marks; but the correlation between a metronome

---

[6] Ibid., I, §72 n.   [7] *A Select Collection*, i. 10.

mark, a tempo term, and the speed of the music is not a simple one, hence the fallacy of theorists attempting to link terms with particular tempo ranges. The musical content within any given metre is so variable, in terms of density, texture, frequency of harmony change, and so on, that a metronome mark (linked to a particular note value) and the tempo term alone can be seriously misleading; and even when other factors are taken into account the rationale behind the choice of term and chronometric tempo is not always easy to appreciate.

Slow Tempo Terms

Grave, Adagio, Largo, Lento

Löhlein, who included these terms under the general category 'Sadness' (along with 'larghetto', though he had listed this earlier in the category of 'calmness'), made no significant reference to tempo in his description of the performance style appropriate to them. He observed:

Sadness, as a main category of feeling [*Hauptleidenschaft*], has various grades, the differences between these grades must therefore also be considered in their execution. *Larghetto, adagio* depicts more a peaceful, thoughtful and pleasant state of mind than a sad one; for that reason one must not perform it so heavily as if it were the sad *Affekt*. However, *mesto, largo, lento*, already signify a suffering *Affekt*, and must be performed with a heavy and sustained bowstroke, one note joined to the other and well supported. One must also put oneself into a sad *Affekt* if one wants to perform these melodies well, in accordance with their character. *Grave* requires even more sustaining of the bow and the tone than the previous kinds. Also with respect to the composition it must have a slow and heavy movement, consisting of long notes and strong harmonies.[8]

Reichardt, employing the general term adagio to cover the slowest tempos, similarly observed:

The different character of the pieces also requires different bowstrokes.

Thus the bowstroke in Adagio is very different from that in Allegro, and contrasts mainly in that the former remains more on the string than in Allegro.

Nothing but a rest must bring the bow entirely off the string in Adagio.

Even on the notes marked with a stroke for staccato, even before an *Abzug*, it must not entirely leave the string, but remain on it with at least an eighth of the hair.

If, however, in a completely contrasting passage, several notes in an Adagio should be very sharply staccatoed, the composer would do well if he were to signify such a passage with a particular indication, with a word, for example, *furioso* (violent) or *adirato* (angry).[9]

He added later that 'mesto' and 'grave' 'indicate in the same way that the longer bowstrokes should receive a stronger, more expressive accent, and in these cases the notes before rests, rather than being taken off short, should only come away gradually'.[10]

[8] *Anweisung zum Violinspielen*, 107.   [9] *Ueber die Pflichten*, 25.   [10] Ibid. 27.

These comments from the 1770s reflect similar remarks in Quantz's and Leopold Mozart's treatises of twenty years earlier, but there is every reason to believe that some such considerations continued to be relevant to later generations. Reichardt did not expunge or modify these passages in Löhlein's treatise when he produced a new edition of it in the 1790s.

The similar account of bowstrokes in relation to tempo terms that occurs in the Paris Conservatoire's *Méthode de violon* (1803), which is repeated more or less verbatim in Fröhlich's *Musikschule* (1810–11) and Campagnoli's *Nouvelle méthode* (1824), makes almost the same points as Reichardt. There seems though, to be a greater emphasis on broadness and legato. In Fröhlich's version it was stated that

In adagio, and in general in all cantabile places, particularly those of a deep expression, where all notes must be slowly sustained, one should use the bow from one end to the other, and perform all notes as legato as possible. Or, if they are expressly to be played staccato, one must give them their full value with the same length of bow.[11]

The growing tendency of composers to mark their requirements more clearly and their partiality for including music of an andante or adagio character in allegro movements, and so on, meant, however, that in the nineteenth century such distinctions were less clear-cut than formerly and that the term prefacing the beginning of the movement might not be appropriate throughout.

The connotations for tempo of the principal terms that were employed in slow pieces were very variable, since these words were, and remained, as Crotch had observed, essentially 'terms of expression and taste'. Also, since slow tempos were not as frequently used as moderate and fast ones, there was less opportunity for them to acquire a generally recognized order of speed. The quotations above demonstrate that different composers and theorists adopted irreconcilably different approaches. Sandra Rosenblum has identified the following writers as propounding the view that 'largo' indicated a slower tempo than 'adagio': Brossard, L. Mozart, Rousseau, Kirnberger, Lorenzoni, Türk, Galeazzi, Dussek, F. P. Ricci (J. C. Bach), Milchmeyer, Koch, Hummel, and Czerny.[12] To this list may be added Campagnoli, Crotch, Asioli, Adam, E. Miller, and Arrey von Dommer. In support of the opposite view she lists Purcell, Malcolm, Gassineau, Quantz, C. P. E. Bach (commenting on Berlin practice), J. Hoyle, Vogler, Busby, Clementi, Mason, Knecht, and Cramer. These may be supplemented by Fröhlich, Dibdin, and Jousse (on British practice). The list could be lengthened indefinitely.

---

[11] *Musikschule*, iii. 47; cf. Pierre Marie François de Sales Baillot, Pierre Rode, and Rodolphe Kreutzer, *Méthode de violon* (Paris, 1803), 130.

[12] *Performance Practices*, 313–14.

Not all musicians, however, were constant in their allegiance. Jousse, for instance, seems later to have shifted his ground some way, at least, towards the majority view, for whereas the early editions of Dibdin's *Music Epitomized* (1808) defined 'adagio' as meaning 'one degree faster [than grave] but always elegant and graceful', and 'largo' and 'lento' as 'something faster than adagio', the ninth edition, revised by Jousse, defines 'adagio' as 'one degree faster [than grave] but very expressive', and 'largo' as 'slow and in an extended style'.[13] Many authors frankly acknowledged areas of disagreement. John Holden gave the following explanation of 'largo':

Large or ample. A slow movement. There are different explanations given to this word. Some will have it, a large, and frequently, unrestricted measure, slower than Adagio; others, more conformably to its modern acceptation, define it, a slow Andante; but not so slow as Adagio; and in this sense Largo, as compared with Andante, is like an ample stride compared with an ordinary step. The diminutive Larghetto is smaller or less ample; and therefore denotes a movement something quicker.[14]

Some theorists avoided the problem by grouping terms together without explicitly ranking them within each group in order of speed. Domenico Corri regarded 'grave', 'largo assai', and 'largo sostenuto' as indicating 'very slow and with a certain gravity of expression', while he bracketed 'largo', 'lento', and 'adagio' together as meaning 'slow and with ease'.[15] Karl Gollmick, towards the middle of the nineteenth century, adopted a similarly judicious standpoint, tacitly recognizing that most of these terms often applied less to speed than to character,[16] while Mathis Lussy, whose approach illustrates the decay of the Classical tempo conventions discussed in the two previous chapters, bracketed 'largo' 'and adagio' together as indicating slow tempos within a suggested metronome range of 40–60.[17] But, as will be apparent from the following pages, many composers gave numbers outside this range for music marked with these terms.

'Grave', too, was often seen rather as a description of character rather than tempo. Holden explained it as 'A slow and solemn manner. Some authors define it as slower than Adagio; others a degree quicker than Adagio; but it ought probably, to be considered rather as a particular manner, than a mood of time.'[18] Leopold Mozart's explanation of 'grave' also emphasizes its character and prescribes a particular style of performance; he observed that it should be played 'sadly and seriously, and therefore very slowly. One must, indeed, indicate the meaning of the word *Grave* by means of long, rather heavy and solemn bowing and by means of consistent prolonging and maintaining of the various notes.'[19]

[13] 1st edn., 63; and 9th edn., 39.   [14] *Essay*, 36.
[15] *A Select Collection*, i. 10.   [16] *Kritische Terminologie.*
[17] *Traité de l'expression musicale*, 161.   [18] *Essay*, 41.   [19] *Versuch*, I, 3, §27.

A. F. C. Kollmann considered 'grave' to signify a kind of alla breve in reverse, explaining that whereas in alla breve every note should be 'as fast again as otherwise', when music is marked 'grave' one should play 'every note as slow again as otherwise';[20] and he went on to observe that 'grave' is used with 4/4 as a substitute for 4/2, which is difficult to read, and that in that case every crotchet 'should be expressed slow and heavy like a minim'.[21] Mozart's and Kollmann's descriptions should alert us once again to the very definite notions that obtained in the late eighteenth and early nineteenth centuries about the distinct performance styles appropriate to different types of pieces, which could be indicated by metre, by the note values employed, the choice of such terms as 'grave', and so on.[22] Of authors who attributed to 'grave' a definite tempo relationship to other terms, Crotch, Dibdin, Hummel, and Czerny were among those who regarded it as indicating a slower tempo than that implied by 'largo' and 'adagio'. Some of the writers who regarded 'adagio' as indicating a slower tempo than 'largo', for instance Vogler, Knecht, and Clementi, placed 'grave' between them; Hüllmandel listed them, in ascending order, 'largo', 'grave', 'adagio',[23] as, much later, did Mendel;[24] and Dommer gave the order 'largo', 'grave', 'lento', 'adagio'.[25]

The significance of 'lento' was equally unclear. Some eighteenth-century writers, such as Quantz, Löhlein, and E. Miller, seem to have regarded it as indicating a very slow tempo; many failed to include it in their lists, while others such as Crotch and Campagnoli saw it as meaning only moderately slow. A few nineteenth-century composers used it largely as a qualification to other terms (e.g. 'adagio non lento'), but it is not always quite certain whether they always considered it to mean 'slow' in the general sense or whether, unlikely as it seems, they intended to modify the main term in the direction of another term that was seen as having a definite relationship to it.[26]

The relatively small number of examples makes it difficult to determine the usages of major composers with any degree of confidence. Isidor Saslov suggests, on the basis of *Die sieben letzte Worte*, that Haydn regarded 'largo', 'lento', 'grave', and 'adagio' as signifying progressively faster tempo terms.[27] This does not seem, however, to have been the view of Haydn's contemporary Crotch, for in 1800 he gave the following tempos (in pendulum lengths, converted here to the nearest metronome mark) for movements from *Die sieben letzte Worte*: no. 4, Largo 3/4, ♪ = 120, no. 5, Adagio 𝄵, ♪ = 126, no. 6, Lento 𝄵, ♪ = 152.[28] The slower tempo for the Largo is to some extent counteracted by a greater number

---

[20] *Essay*, 72.   [21] Ibid. 74.   [22] See Ch. 16, 'Heavy and Light Performance Style'.

[23] *Principles of Music*, 8.

[24] Mendel and Reissmann, *Musikalisches Conversations-Lexikon*, art. 'Tempo'.

[25] *Musikalisches Lexicon*, art. 'Tempobezeichnungen'.

[26] See below for Berlioz's curious use of 'adagio un poco lento' and 'andante un poco lento'.

[27] 'Tempos in the String Quartets of Joseph Haydn' dissertation (Indiana University, 1969), 57–8.

[28] 'Remarks'.

of semiquavers than in the Adagio, though its opening certainly seems more expansive; the Lento, on the other hand, with some quite active semiquaver figurations, seems to have greater animation at Crotch's speed.

For Mozart the situation is similarly unclear; terms like 'Andante un poco adagio' (K. 309) do not necessarily indicate that he regarded 'adagio' as indicating a faster tempo than 'largo', since 'adagio' in this sense could merely have been used, like 'lento', with its generalized meaning of slow. However, it seems highly probable that Mozart, like his father, regarded 'largo' as having a greater implication of slowness than 'adagio', and a number of factors, such as the alteration of the second movement of K. 465 from Adagio to Andante cantabile, suggest that Mozart did not consider 'adagio' to imply a very slow tempo (since there is every reason to believe that he regarded 'andante' as indicating a fairly flowing tempo). In addition to its connotations of speed, however, 'adagio' will certainly have had implications of style which also relate to the use of 'cantabile' with 'andante'.

It seems likely that Beethoven, too, along with his younger contemporaries Hummel and Czerny, regarded a very slow tempo as appropriate for 'largo'. This is suggested by his metronome mark of $\mathbb{A}$ = 76 for the Largo in the Piano Sonata op. 106, whose fastest notes are demisemiquavers. However, he may also have considered 'adagio' as indicating a rather slower speed than Mozart; the 2/4 Adagio ma non troppo of the String Quartet op. 18 no. 6, containing demisemiquavers and a few hemidemisemiquaver triplets, has the marking $\mathbb{A}$ = 80, and the 2/4 Adagio molto e mesto of op. 59 no. 1, containing demisemiquavers and a few hemidemisemiquavers, has $\mathbb{A}$ = 88.

Metronome marks indicate continuing disagreement among nineteenth-century composers about the tempo relationships of these directions. On the strength of metronome markings in the original editions of *Le Siège de Corinthe*, *Le comte Ory*, *Moïse*, and *Guillaume Tell*, Rossini seems to have used the terms 'adagio', 'lento', and 'largo' without any clear order of slowness among them, though his use of the French term 'lent' suggests, curiously, that he regarded this as slower than the other three. His older Italian contemporary Spontini rarely used terms slower than 'andante' or 'andantino' (with various qualifiers). In the operas *Fernand Cortez*, *Olympie*, and *Nurmahal*, to which he gave metronome marks, there are no largos, lentos, or graves and only one adagio, which is in 3/4 with a metronome mark of $\flat$ = 88 and movement mainly in quavers, though with some semiquavers;[29] an Andantino passionato in the same opera,[30] which has similar note values and is also in 3/4, is only slightly faster at $\flat$ = 96, and a 3/4 Andante sostenuto in *Olympie*, admittedly with more semiquaver movement, has a slower metronome mark of $\flat$ = 76.[31]

---

[29] *Fernand Cortez*, Act I, no. 3.   [30] Act II, no. 3.   [31] Act III, no. 5.

In *Euryanthe* Weber used 'largo' much more frequently than 'adagio'; he did not use 'lento' in its own right but employed it as a qualifying term in the expressions 'adagio non lento' and 'larghetto non lento', apparently to warn against too slow a tempo. There is no clearly discernible difference in the implications for tempo of 'largo' and 'adagio' (though the sample is too small to be certain of his intentions). In Weber's case, as in so many others, it may be more appropriate to consider the terms 'largo' and 'adagio' as indicating a different character rather than a different speed. Spohr left many more metronome marks for his works, and it is fairly clear that 'largo' implied something slower and more expansive than 'adagio'. His normal term for his slowest movements, however, was 'adagio', or 'adagio molto' (he did not use 'lento'). 'Largo' appears only six times among the movements with metronome marks (and very rarely elsewhere), and of these six, four largos occur in the opera *Pietro von Abano*, and are very slow; so, too, is the opening largo section of his Fourth Symphony *Die Weihe der Töne*, which is meant to evoke the 'deep silence of nature before the birth of sound'. Spohr very rarely used 'grave' alone as a tempo term, though he used it quite often in the expression 'andante grave', which indicated a slower tempo than 'andante'.

Berlioz's metronome marks present a particularly inconclusive picture. 'Adagio', 'largo', and 'lento' seem to apply to the same tempo area without any obvious hierarchy, though, if anything, it seems that he regarded 'adagio' as indicating a somewhat slower tempo than 'largo' and 'lento'. Berlioz's use of 'lento' both as an absolute tempo term and as a qualifying term in such phrases as 'un poco lento' and 'non troppo lento' complicates the situation. Comparison of the 6/8 Lento quasi Adagio, no. 33 in *Les Troyens* ($\flat$ = 120), with the 6/8 Adagio, no. 48 in the same opera ($\flat$ = 96),[32] and the adagios in the *Symphonie fantastique* ($\flat$ = 84) and the *Reverie et caprice* ($\flat$ = 88), all of which are comparable in terms of their note values, appears to indicate that he regarded 'adagio' as indicating a slower tempo than 'lento'. The 9/8 Adagio un poco lento e dolce assai ($\flat$ = 96) of the orchestrally accompanied version of his song 'Le Spectre de la rose',[33] which in its original version with piano accompaniment[34] was given as Andante un poco lento e dolce assai with the same metronome mark, could be interpreted in a similar sense only in the unlikely circumstances that, in the former, 'un poco lento' were taken to suggest a slightly faster speed than the principal tempo term and, in the latter, a slower one! In this context it is interesting, though hardly enlightening, that Domenico Corri, who bracketed together 'Adagio' and 'Lento' as 'slow and with ease' followed these with a category of 'not so slow' terms which included 'Lento Andante' and 'Lento Adagio'.[35]

---

[32] It is wrongly given as $\flat$ = 48 in D. Kern Holoman, *Catalogue of the Works of Hector Berlioz, Hector Berlioz: New Edition of the Complete Works*, xxv (Kassel, etc., 1987). Holoman's numberings for Berlioz's works are henceforth prefixed with H.

[33] H. 83b.   [34] H. 83a.   [35] *A Select Collection*, i. 10.

The metronome marks in Wagner's earlier operas also indicate inconsistency in the use of slow tempo terms (which for Wagner and many other composers of his and subsequent generations included 'andante'). The third act of *Tannhäuser* contains the following markings: Andante assai lento 𝄴 ♩ = 50, Andante maestoso 3/4 ♩ = 50, Lento 𝄴 ♩ = 60, Moderato 𝄴 ♩ = 46, Lento 𝄴 ♩ = 50, and Lento maestoso 𝄴 ♩ = 50. In all of these the note content and character of the music gives little if any clue to the rationale behind the union of these tempo terms with the specified speed. Metronome marks in Verdi's music suggest that, like Spohr and a number of other composers, he used 'largo' for pieces in which longer note values predominated (generally crotchets and quavers and occasionally quaver triplets), while he reserved 'adagio' for pieces with more florid melodic lines, often including semiquavers; in common time both markings are most often used in the range 50–66, with occasional pieces outside that range. Dvořák's use of 'lento' is worthy of note. There can be little doubt that Dvořák regarded 'lento' as indicating a slower tempo than 'andante con moto', yet the metronome marks he gave to two movements from his string quartets to which he affixed these terms appear at first sight to indicate the opposite (Ex. 10.1). Both are in 6/8 with predominantly quaver and semiquaver movement; the Lento (op. 96) is marked ♪ = 112 and the Andante con moto (op. 51) ♪ = 100. The Lento also has many more semiquavers than the Andante con moto as well as a considerable number of bars containing demisemiquaver figures (the Andante con moto has some demisemiquavers, but fewer). Despite these factors, superficially indicating that the Lento is faster than the Andante con moto, this is not, arguably, how these two movements feel in performance. The principal melodic line of the Lento is more expansive, the fundamental harmonic movement is slower, and the movement will tend for much of the time to be felt in two beats to the bar, while the Andante con moto appears more frequently to move in six notes to the bar. Nevertheless, there does not seem to be much difference in tempo between these movements. The distinction is much more one of character; and that character distinction will be emphasized if something like the types of performance style appropriate to these tempo terms (greater weight and sostenuto for the Lento, and a lighter less sustained execution for the Andante) are applied in this instance, as Dvořák almost certainly intended they should be.

Examinations of other composers' tempo terms and metronome marks reveal a similarly baffling picture and it is scarcely surprising that many theorists were unable to offer any confident explanations of these words in terms of absolute tempo. The impression that with regard to speed alone, though not perhaps expression and execution, a neutral word meaning 'slow' would have conveyed as much information to the performer is inescapable; it is certainly the case that without their metronome marks many of these movements would be taken at significantly different speeds by musicians unacquainted with their composer's practice.

Ex. 10.1. (*a*) Dvořák, String Quartet op. 96/ii (Berlin, Simrock, 1894); (*b*) Dvořák, String Quartet op. 51/iii (Berlin, Simrock, 1879)
(*a*)

ROMANZE

Ex. 10.1. *cont.* (*b*)

II

Larghetto

'Larghetto' was almost universally understood to indicate a faster tempo than 'largo'. (An exception to this occurs in Gesualdo Lanza's *The Elements of Singing*, where for semiquavers in larghetto a pendulum length of 7 inches is suggested and for largo 6 inches, i.e. larghetto MM *c.*144 and largo MM *c.*152). But beyond that there was considerable disagreement about its relation to the other terms. For those musicians, such as Holden, Lussy, and others, who regarded 'largo' as requiring a faster tempo than 'adagio', 'larghetto' naturally formed the bridge between the slow tempos and the moderate ones. Yet the idea that 'larghetto' indicated the fastest of the slow tempos is also encountered among those who believed 'largo' to mean 'very slow'; thus, Koch described the tempo of larghetto as 'usually similar to that of andante',[36] while Fröhlich also categorized it as 'almost like andante'.[37] And about 1800 the *Principes élémentaire de musique*, which included 'largo' in the slowest of its five tempo groups, put 'larghetto' in the middle group along with 'andante' and 'allegretto'.[38] Löhlein, who similarly considered it to be the slowest of the moderate terms, regarded its performance style as tending more towards that appropriate for the slower tempos.[39] A few musicians, however, such as Campagnoli and Bernhard Romberg, who regarded 'largo' as among the slowest tempo terms, considered 'larghetto' to imply a slower pace than 'adagio',[40] and it also appears in this position on the tabulation of the metronome.

Here, too, composers' practices seem to have been variable. It has been claimed that Mozart regarded 'larghetto' as indicating a slower tempo than 'adagio',[41] but this seems unlikely in view of the discrepancies between the tempo terms in some of his later works and the entries in his autograph *Verzeichnüss*, where the Andante in K. 469 was entered as Larghetto, the Larghetto of K. 468 as Andantino, the Larghetto of K. 489 as Andante and the Larghetto of K. 593 as Adagio. This suggests that for Mozart 'larghetto' signified a tempo somewhere between those indicated by 'adagio' and 'andante', but that, in terms of speed, the differences were not very marked. It also implies, perhaps, that for Mozart, as for many other eighteenth-century composers, 'adagio' was not regarded as indicating a very slow tempo.

Beethoven's treatment of 'larghetto' also suggests that he regarded it as the bridge between 'andante' and the slower tempo terms, but seemingly closer to 'andante' than to 'adagio' (which for him may have signified a somewhat slower tempo than for Mozart). Beethoven chose the tempo terms 'larghetto' and

[36] *Musikalisches Lexikon*, art. 'Larghetto'.   [37] *Musikschule*, i. 51.
[38] Gossec et al., *Principes*, i. 43.   [39] See below, 'Andante and Andantino'.
[40] Campagnoli, *Nouvelle méthode*, v. 10; Romberg, *A Complete*, 110 (Largo MM 50, Larghetto MM 56, Adagio MM 60).
[41] Toeplitz, 'Über die Tempi', 183. This is not shared, however, by Zaslaw, 'Mozart's Tempo Conventions' and Jean-Pierre Marty, *The Tempo Indications of Mozart* (New Haven and London, 1988).

'andante con moto' respectively for the closely analogous slow movements of the Second and Fifth symphonies, both of which are in 3/8 with demisemiquavers as their fastest notes, but he later gave them the same metronome mark ($\flat$ = 92). To some extent the difference in the terms is explained by the fact that when performed at the same speed as the Larghetto of the Second Symphony, the Andante con moto of the Fifth Symphony may *seem* faster, because of its slightly greater number of demisemiquavers; but the metronome marks may also indicate that by the time Beethoven fixed them, more than a decade later, he conceived the tempo of the Larghetto of the earlier symphony as being faster than he had originally done. This is perhaps supported by the change to the tempo term 'Larghetto quasi andante' in his piano trio arrangement of the Second Symphony; however, this designation, too, confirms the position of 'larghetto' as indicating a tempo only just slower than 'andante'.

In Weber's *Euryanthe*, sections marked 'larghetto' generally contain rather more active music than those marked 'largo' and 'adagio', thus making the music seem subjectively faster. However, the metronome marks are within the same range as those for the term 'largo'. But direct comparison is impossible since all the largos are in ¢, while all but one of the larghettos (also the metronomized Larghetto ma non troppo from the *Konzertstück* J. 282) are in 3/4; the other larghetto is in 6/8. In Spohr's music 'poco adagio' and 'larghetto' share the same metronome mark range; but as in Weber's case, movements marked 'larghetto', the bulk of which (twenty-three out of thirty-one) are in triple or compound metre, tend to have a more flowing character. Spontini similarly favoured the combination of 3/4 and 'larghetto' in *Fernand Cortez, Olympie,* and *Nurmahal.* With a tempo range of ♩ = 50–4, Spontini's 3/4 larghettos in these operas have a distinctly slower pulse than his 3/4 andantes.

Berlioz, too, used 'larghetto' most often in triple or compound metres. Of fourteen larghettos in his works only three are in ¢, and they have a tempo range that makes them, in general, a little faster than his adagios, but by their metronome range and note values alone they are scarcely distinguishable from his andantes. Indeed, many of the andantes are slower than the faster larghettos. All the 3/4 larghettos have a crotchet pulse within a range from 48 for Larghetto un poco lento and 54 for Larghetto sostenuto to 76 for Larghetto espressivo; the simple Larghettos are in the range ♩ = 56–72. His 3/4 adagios are in the range ♩ = 44–58 while his 3/4 andantes, with and without qualifying terms, are in the range ♩ = 50–69.

Dvořák rarely used 'larghetto', but when he did in the *Stabat mater* op. 58 and the Symphonic Variations op. 78, he used it for movements with the unusual time signature 4/8, which he also employed with 'largo', 'adagio', and 'andante'. The two above-mentioned larghettos are not only faster than the largos and adagios, but, with the metronome marks ♪ = 104 and ♩ = 66 respectively, they are also faster than the only 4/8 andante (♪ = 92) from *Legendy* op.

59; all three movements have semiquavers as their fastest notes (op. 78 even having occasional demisemiquavers).

Andante and Andantino

Löhlein prescribed the following performance style for the group of terms from 'andante' to 'larghetto', which he considered to share the general characteristic of calmness:

Calmness is performed with a modest [*bescheiden*] and calm stroke, certainly not too powerful, but also not weak; and if places occur which depart somewhat from calmness, and approach the brilliant or indeed the pathetic, so the performance must be regulated in that direction: for just as in monotonous situations in speech the content often requires animation in the voice, so is it in music, and a piece that always flows along uninterruptedly and restfully in a monotone tires the listener and makes for boredom. This applies to the words *andante, andantino, poco andante. Larghetto* however approaches still more to peaceful rest.[42]

Reichardt observed: 'In Andante the bow must have the lightness of the Allegro bow without its sharpness and without its rapidity in leaving the string at an *Abzug*. For fast notes in Andante the above-mentioned bowstroke [Ex. 10.2] where two notes are played with a short staccato in an up-bow has a very good effect.'[43] (Reichardt had instructed that this figure was to be 'Played in the third quarter of the bow, reckoned from the heel, using no more than an eighth of the bow'.)

Ex. 10.2. Reichardt, *Ueber die Pflichten*, 17

Interestingly, the Paris Conservatoire's *Méthode de violon* and its followers failed to specify a particular style of performance for 'andante' (which was relatively infrequently used by composers associated with the Viotti school). They went straight from discussing the bowstroke appropriate to music marked 'adagio' to that required when the terms 'allegro maestoso' and 'moderato assai', were used, tempo terms which for them seem to have occupied a similar tempo area to the Classical andante.

The nature of the relationship between 'andante' and 'andantino', with respect to tempo, has been a subject of constant theoretical discussion and disagreement. Some composers and theorists regarded 'andantino' as meaning

---

[42] *Anweisung zum Violinspielen*, 107.   [43] *Ueber die Pflichten*, 26.

slower than 'andante', others as faster, and, as is the case with the slower tempo terms, some appear to have made less a distinction of speed than of character. The problem hinged on the fact that 'andante' was ranked with neither the slow nor the fast tempo terms, and so, in contrast to 'largo–larghetto' and 'allegro–allegretto', it was unclear which way the diminutive 'andantino' should modify it. Those who considered 'andante' to signify a rather spacious tempo tended to see 'andantino' as indicating a faster one, and those who regarded it as signifying a brisker tempo were inclined to take the opposite view.

The stylistic connotations of 'andante', as clear, even, distinct, and well separated, were often independent of any explicit notion of tempo until well into the middle of the eighteenth century; Quantz, for instance, observed that if instead of sustaining the dotted notes in an adagio one were to replace the dot with a rest the adagio would be 'transformed into an andante'.[44] These stylistic considerations remained an important aspect of the meaning of 'andante' throughout the eighteenth century, but from at least the middle of the century onwards it was also generally accepted that it indicated a tempo somewhere between 'adagio' and 'allegretto'. Leopold Mozart stated that its meaning, *gehend* in German (which can be translated into English as 'going' or, more specifically, 'walking'), demonstrates 'that the piece must be allowed to take its own natural course; especially if *Un poco allegretto* be added',[45] suggesting that he saw it as tending rather towards a brisk stride than a leisurely stroll. Fifty years later Knecht defined 'andante' as 'going [walking] or pace by pace (that is to say all notes should be neatly, equally and clearly well-separated from each other)' and 'andantino' as 'going [walking] somewhat'. But, recognizing that his view was not universally shared, he continued: 'Some composers are of the opinion that andantino must go somewhat faster than andante; but since the former is the diminutive of the latter, the contrary is true: andantino relates to andante like allegretto to allegro. Despite this, however, many composers take it in the first sense as going somewhat faster than andante.'[46] John Holden's slightly earlier definition shows how two musicians, even when they agreed about the meaning of the word 'andante' itself, could interpret the effect of the diminutive element quite differently. Holden explained: 'Andante, walking. A regular, distinct and moderate movement. The diminutive Andantino is somewhat quicker than Andante, as if it were to be measured by a little mincing step.'[47]

It seems probable that during the eighteenth century, in Germany and Italy at any rate, the faster interpretation of 'andante' and the slower one of 'andantino' was the more widespread. C. D. F. Schubart, for instance, referred to andante as a tempo that 'kisses the borderline of Allegro'.[48] And it has been per-

---

[44] *Versuch*, XVII, 2, §13.
[47] *Essay*, 41.

[45] Ibid., I, 3, §27.
[48] *Ideen*, 360.

[46] *Katechismus*, 39.

suasively argued that Mozart regarded 'andante' as indicating a faster tempo than 'andantino'.[49] But during the nineteenth century, as 'andante' came increasingly to be seen to signify a fairly slow tempo, the faster view of 'andantino' gradually gained ground. Carl Wilhelm Greulich still maintained in his *Kleine practische Clavierschule zum Selbstunterricht* (*c*.1831) that 'andantino' indicated a slower tempo than 'andante' but acknowledged: 'by a few composers a faster tempo than andante is indicated by andantino'.[50] However, a reviewer of Greulich's tutor, J. A. Gleichmann, commented on the above sentence: 'Not only with a few composers is this the case, however, but it is rightly rather generally used in this way', and his justification for this shows Knecht's observation about 'allegretto' and 'allegro' being turned on its head, for Gleichmann continued: 'the diminutive of andante (andantino) is analogous to that of largo (larghetto), and just as that indicates a less slow tempo, so this too indicates a less slow one'. To this remark the editor of the journal, Gottfried Weber, possibly recalling Knecht's view, merely appended the comment: '-? Allegretto -?'[51]

Karl Gollmick's comments in 1833 illustrate the growing tendency to regard 'andante' as indicating a distinctly slow tempo:

Andante belongs decidedly to the slower tempos and is only more strictly defined by the notion of walking/going. In this sense, regarded and translated as slow, the meanings of 'più andante' and 'meno andante' are no longer doubtful [i.e. 'più' is slower and 'meno' faster]. ... if one translates 'andante' as walking/going, these words obtain precisely the opposite meaning. For this reason the controversy over 'andantino' still remains undecided.[52]

He then cited Rousseau, Türk, Sommer (*Fremdwörterbuch*), and Nicolo as favouring the slower conception of 'andantino' and Wolf (*Musicalisches Lexicon*), Koch, Petri (*Handbuch*, 1823), Häuser, and Schneller as opting for the faster one.

The depth of confusion at that time is well illustrated by W. N. James's statement in 1829 that the Italians interpreted 'andantino' to mean faster than 'andante',[53] whereas only three years earlier Jousse had given the Italian view of 'andantino' as indicating a slower tempo than 'andante' and the English as indicating a faster one.[54] Searches through other authorities from the end of the eighteenth century and the beginning of the nineteenth century reveal, in addition to those authors who judiciously acknowledged the lack of consensus, a more or less balanced weight of dogmatic authority on either side of the question.[55]

---

[49] Rudolf, 'Ein Beitrag'; Nikolaus Harnoncourt, *Der musikalische Dialog* (Salzburg, 1984), 127 ff.; Zaslaw 'Mozart's Tempo Conventions'.

[50] Quoted in *Caecilia*, 14 (1832), 268.   [51] Ibid.   [52] *Kritische Terminologie*, art. 'Andante'.

[53] *The Flutist's Catechism* (London, 1829), 43.   [54] *A Compendious Musical Grammar*, 111.

[55] Andantino faster than andante: Anon., *New Instructions for Playing the Harpsichord*, 36; Castil-Blaze, *Dictionnaire*, art. 'Andante'. Andantino slower than andante: Busby *A Complete Dictionary of Music* (London, 1806), art. 'Andante', Milchmeyer, *Die wahre Art*, 52, Valentine, *Dictionary*, art. 'Andante'.

In Rossini's music, to judge by the metronome marks, 'andante' and 'andantino' seem to signify little obvious difference in speed, though in many instances sections marked 'andantino' have a very slightly slower pulse. However, as far as such a restricted sample can show, the treatment of the two terms appears closely related to the metre with which they are coupled: in **c** the pulse in andantino is equivalent to a slow andante, but there are faster-moving notes in the andantino sections; in the four operas with metronome marks mentioned above (*Le Siège de Corinthe*, *Le Comte Ory*, *Moïse*, and *Guillaume Tell*), there are five 2/4 andantes, all of which have a quaver pulse between 56 and 84, while a single andantino has a crotchet pulse of 60 but fewer fast-moving notes. In 6/8, 3/8, and 3/4 there is no obvious difference in tempo between the two terms, but it may be significant that the majority of andantinos are in these metres while a considerably greater proportion of andantes are in **c** and 2/4. Spontini certainly seems to have regarded 'andantino' as implying a tempo on the slow side of that implied by 'andante', but in *Nurmahal*, for instance, there is no obvious difference of tempo between the Andantino malinconico no. 16 ($\downarrow$ = 50), the Andantino sostenuto no. 27 ($\downarrow$ = 48), the Andante poco sostenuto no. 18 ($\downarrow$ = 50), and the Andante un poco sostenuto no. 21 ($\downarrow$ = 48), all of which are in **c** metre and have similar note values.

It seems possible that the notion of 'andantino' as indicating a gentler (i.e. somewhat more leisurely) style of performance than 'andante' remained stronger in Italy than elsewhere. Verdi may have employed it in this sense. In *Il trovatore*, for instance, there are a 3/8 Andante with the metronome mark $\flat$ = 76 (no. 3) and a 3/8 Andantino with similar note values and melodic profile marked $\flat$ = 72 (no. 14). On the other hand, in *Rigoletto* there is a 3/8 Andantino (no. 5), also with semiquavers, that is marked $\flat$ = 92. For a faster andante Verdi often used 'andante mosso'; for example, the 3/8 Andante mosso in no. 10 is marked $\flat$ = 120, thus occupying a place almost exactly half-way between his andante and allegretto (all three 3/8 allegrettos in *Il trovatore* (in nos. 4, 5, and 14) are marked $\downarrow$. = 60).

During the course of the nineteenth century, however, as a slower notion of 'andante' increasingly gained ground in Germany and France, 'andantino' was more often defined as faster. Fétis and Ignaz Moscheles considered that 'andantino' should strictly mean a slower tempo than 'andante', but that in common usage at that time it meant faster, adding, with dubious justification: 'for which we have the authority of Mozart and the practice of modern composers'.[56] In his *Handlexikon der Tonkunst* (1857) Gollmick resolved the indecision in his earlier book by coming down firmly on the side of 'andantino' meaning a faster tempo than 'andante', stating that it meant 'less andante, somewhat faster, the

---

[56] *Méthode des méthodes de piano* (Paris, [c.1840]), trans. as *Complete System of Instruction for the Piano Forte* (London, [1841]), 5.

fastest grade of the slow tempos and bordering on the allegretto'.[57] Because of its ambiguity, Beethoven rarely used the term 'andantino'. In a letter to Thomson about Scottish songs, he commented on the disagreement saying: 'Andantino sometimes approaches an Allegro and sometimes, on the other hand, is played like Adagio'.[58] But when he did use the term, as in many of the songs he arranged for Thomson, he clearly favoured the faster meaning, as his employment of such terms as 'andantino più tosto allegretto' testifies. Spohr, in line with the predominant German practice, appears to have regarded 'andantino' as indicating a somewhat more active tempo than 'andante', though both terms seem to imply roughly the same tempo area in his music. This is illustrated by comparison of three 6/8 numbers in his opera *Jessonda*, the andantinos in nos. 7 and 10 ($\downarrow$. = 58 and $\downarrow$. = 50) and the Andante no. 20 ($\downarrow$. = 52); nos. 7 and 20 have similar note values, though the music is slightly more active in no. 7, while no. 10 has considerably more semiquaver movement than the other two. Interesting light on Spohr's notion of the meaning of 'andante' and 'andantino' is shed by three holographs of the song 'Nachgefühl': the original of 1819 was marked 'Moderato', while a copy written for an album in 1834 is headed 'Andante' and another, published as a facsimile in 1839 has the direction 'Andantino'. A further peculiarity of Spohr's use of these tempo terms is that his andantinos, like his larghettos and like Rossini's andantinos, occur mainly in 6/8 with a few in 3/4, 3/8, and 9/8; none of Spohr's andantinos are in ¢, whereas his use of the term 'andante' occurs principally in ¢ and 3/4.

Berlioz, too, favoured 'andantino' for certain metres and 'andante' for others; almost all occurrences of the former are in 3/4 and 6/8, while 'andante' is frequently found in ¢. The tempo range for his andantinos is considerable and does not show any clear preference for a faster or slower conception than for movements marked 'andante'. In fact, his use of the term seems to bear out Beethoven's observation of several decades earlier. In 3/4 metre Berlioz ranges from Andantino quasi allegretto ($\downarrow$ = 108) in the romance 'Le Matin' of around 1850 (H. 125) to Andantino quasi adagio ($\downarrow$ = 50) in the Te Deum of 1848–9 (H. 118). When he revised the ballade 'La morte d'Ophélie' (H. 92a) in 1848 (H. 92b) he altered the tempo term from 'Andante con moto quasi allegretto' to 'Andantino con moto quasi allegretto' (6/8), keeping the same metronome mark of $\downarrow$. = 63. This suggests that for Berlioz, as probably for other composers at that time, the difference in the significance of 'andantino' and 'andante' was rather one of character than tempo; probably the diminutive suggested something more lightweight. This was certainly the interpretation proposed by Andersch in 1829.[59]

Schubert, who, unlike Beethoven, frequently used the tempo direction 'andantino', undoubtedly intended it to indicate a tempo considerably faster

---

[57] Art. 'Andante'.　　　[58] Letter of 19 Feb. 1813, in Anderson, *The Letters of Beethoven*, 406.
[59] *Musikalisches Wörterbuch*, art. 'Andante'.

than that indicated by 'andante'. In *Claudine von Villa Bella* no. 6 is marked 'Andantino quasi allegretto', and the same direction is given for no. 2 in *Die Freunde von Salamanka*. The second movement of the Piano Sonata op. 164 is marked 'Allegretto quasi andantino'. In the autograph of *Fierrabras*, no. 2 originally bore the heading 'Allegretto', but Schubert subsequently replaced this with 'Andantino'. These and other similar instances suggest that he regarded 'andantino' as coming between 'andante' and 'allegretto' with respect to tempo. Five numbers in *Alfonso und Estrella* have the heading 'Andantino', and for all of these there are quite strikingly brisk metronome marks, which seem well into the region of the tempo normally associated with 'allegretto'. In terms of the note values employed, the common-time Andantinos nos. 3a, 12, and 15, with the metronome marks ♩ = 100, 116, and 120 respectively, all seem faster than the common-time Allegretto no. 27a at ♩ = 112.

Composers within the Franco-German sphere of influence generally adopted the faster conception of 'andantino' during the nineteenth century, but there are many inconsistencies. Meyerbeer's notion of 'andantino' as meaning on the faster side of 'andante' may be indicated by such markings as 'Andantino quasi allegretto' in *Les Huguenots* (nos. 1c and 9); but it is difficult to see clearly from the metronome marks what Meyerbeer had in mind, since although the note content of the two numbers is comparable, they are marked ♩ = 66 and ♩ = 104 respectively. A similar movement which is headed simply 'Andantino' (no. 5) has the metronome mark ♩ = 84, and many numbers in the same opera with the headings 'poco andante', 'andante', and even 'andante sostenuto' are within the same range. Perhaps Meyerbeer's cosmopolitan musical experience (in Germany, Italy, and France) led him to use these terms inconsistently. In any case, it certainly seems that his intended tempo cannot easily be determined from the combination of metre, tempo term, and note values.

Brahms, judging from the use of such terms as 'Allegretto grazioso (quasi andantino)' for the third movement of his Second Symphony, may be supposed to have seen 'andantino' as signifying a tempo somewhat faster than 'andante'; but his heading 'Allegretto grazioso (quasi Andante)' for the final movement of the Violin Sonata op. 100 suggests that he may have made little if any tempo distinction between 'andante' and its diminutive. Dvořák used directions such as 'Allegro ma non troppo, quasi andantino' and 'Un poco allegretto e grazioso, quasi andantino' (op. 59) or 'Andante con moto, quasi allegretto' (op. 58), which imply that he saw 'andantino' along with 'andante con moto' as meaning a tempo somewhat more lively than that indicated by 'andante'. His metronome marks, however, indicate that, as in Meyerbeer's case, these terms had subjective implications, rather than a narrowly defined or clearly conceived role in determining the tempo. Many other composers (for example C. G. Reissiger in his piano trios) used these two words in a similarly ambiguous manner in relation to 'allegretto' or other terms indicating moderately fast speeds.

'Andante' as a Relative Tempo Direction

One of the more important problems for the performer, rising from the lack of consensus about whether to regard andante as tending more towards the fast or the slow tempos, is, as Gollmick observed, the meaning of terms such as 'più andante' and 'andante molto' (or 'molto andante'). If 'andante' is taken literally to mean 'walking' or 'going', such phrases ought to imply a faster tempo, while 'meno andante' and 'poco andante' should imply a slower one, and this is undoubtedly how they were used by many composers, especially in the eighteenth century. A classic example of where 'andante molto' has caused frequent confusion occurs in the finale of Act II of Mozart's *Figaro*, where Susanna unexpectedly emerges from the Countess's dressing room. Here musical sense may support the notion that the tempo should be relatively rapid, for Susanna's triplets lose their effect of pertness (suppressed laughter?) if taken too slowly. Other interpretations may be possible; David Fallows suggests that the direction 'Molto andante' is 'surely used to denote an extremely controlled and ironically measured tempo contrasting with the preceding *allegro*'.[60] But an early recognition that a rapid tempo was intended here is shown by the change of tempo direction in two editions of the opera from the early 1820s: the Schlesinger edition designated it 'Allegro [*sic*] con moto', and the Simrock edition 'Andante con moto', both giving it the metronome mark ♪ = 120.[61]

It is clear that Beethoven also kept the literal meaning of 'andante' in mind when using such expressions, for in the variation movement of op. 109 he wrote: 'Un poco meno andante ciò è un poco più adagio come il tema (Etwas langsamer als das Tema)', which translates as 'A little less Andante that is a little slower than the theme (Somewhat slower than the theme)'. His inclusion of the qualification in German, however, makes it clear that here, as in the case of 'andantino', he was well aware of the possibility of ambiguity. Schubert, however, as his fast conception of 'andantino' might suggest, seems to have taken the opposite view. The common-time Andante molto from *Alfonso und Estrella* (no. 2), with the metronome mark ♪ = 76, is notably slower than his other common-time andantes in that opera.

There remains also the possibility that some composers may not have intended the various qualifying words to have a significance for tempo. Rossini, for instance, headed a number in *Le Siège de Corinthe* with the term 'Andante assai',[62] but the given metronome mark does not show that he wanted it faster than other andantes in the same metre (2/4) to which he also

---

[60] *New Grove*, art. 'Andante', i. 397.   [61] Rudolf, 'Ein Beitrag', 209.

[62] For ambiguities in the meaning of 'assai' see Deas, 'Beethoven's "Allegro assai" '.

gave metronome marks. It seems possible that here, and perhaps with other composers too, the intensification applied more to the character of firmness and distinctness which still remained widely associated with the term in the early years of the nineteenth century (see, for instance, Knecht's description and Reichardt's comments above).

Brahms may have inclined to a somewhat brisker notion of 'andante' than some of his contemporaries, since he used the word *gehend* (walking, going) as the equivalent of 'andante' when he gave German tempo directions, though his idea of walking was probably more like strolling, as in Gollmick's 1857 definition: 'In a moderated step and calm movement',[63] than Knecht's interpretation, with its implications of a brisk walk. In Brahms's music, however, 'più andante' could sometimes mean 'faster' and sometimes 'slower', since he clearly saw it as occupying a definite central tempo area. This is shown, for example, by his employment of the sequences Adagio–Più andante in the finale of his First Symphony to indicate an increase in speed and Vivace (no. 6)—poco più andante (no. 7) in his Waltzes op. 39 to obtain a slower tempo.

Dvořák, although he does not seem to have regarded 'andante' as calling for an especially slow tempo, clearly considered 'poco andante' to mean a speed somewhat faster than that normally indicated by 'andante', indeed, apparently faster than the tempo implied by 'andante con moto'. This is suggested by comparisons of, for instance, the Andante con moto *Dumka* of the String Quartet op. 51 (2/4, ♩ = 63), which contains semiquavers, with the 2/4 Poco andante from the Humoresques op. 101 (♩ = 72), which has semiquavers, semiquaver triplets, and a few demisemiquavers, or the Poco andante in the Symphonic Variations op. 78 (♩ = 80), which has quaver triplets.

The Changing Connotations of 'Andante' for Tempo and Performance

Metronome marks provide some indication of the various attitudes of a number of nineteenth-century musicians towards the appropriate speed for 'andante'. Evidence from theorists indicates considerable differences of opinion. Lanza gave *c*.60, as does the calibration on the metronome, but in 1840 Romberg suggested 80, and a generation later Lussy proposed 72–84.[64] Of course, these pure numbers are of very limited value since they have no relationship to metres or note values (except in Romberg's case, where the 80 refers to crotchets in 4/4) and they tell us nothing about the type of music envisaged.

Composers' metronome marks, some of which have been considered above, are more interesting. Beethoven's andantes are, on the whole, very active. The

---

[63] *Handlexicon der Tonkunst*, art. 'Andante'.

[64] Lanza, *The Elements of Singing*, 19 (he gave his measurement in pendulum inches); Romberg, *A Complete*, 110; Lussy, *Musical Expression*, 232.

2/4 Andante cantabile of op. 18 no. 5 is marked ♪ = 100 and has a substantial number of demisemiquavers, making it faster, note for note, than the Allegretto in the Seventh Symphony op. 92. Comparison of the Andante con variazioni of the Septet op. 20 at ♪ = 120 (with demisemiquavers) with the Allegretto con variazioni of the String Quartet op. 74 at ♩ = 100 (with semiquavers) reveals little difference between the implications for tempo of the two terms. The 3/8 Andante scherzoso quasi allegretto of the String Quartet op. 18 no. 4 and the 3/8 Allegretto vivace e sempre scherzando of the String Quartet op. 59 no. 1 both have semiquavers as their fastest notes and received the same metronome mark (♩. = 56); the Allegretto has only a few more semiquavers than the Andante. The 3/8 Andante cantabile con moto of the First Symphony, which contains some semiquaver triplets, is scarcely slower at ♪ = 120. Beethoven's metronome mark certainly indicates that this movement should be played at a considerably faster speed than it is normally performed. The same is true of the 3/8 Andante con moto of the Fifth Symphony, which has many demisemiquavers and a metronome mark of ♪ = 92.

For Mendelssohn, 'andante' still seems to have indicated a relatively flowing tempo. The Andante con moto tranquillo (¢) in the D minor Piano Trio op. 49, with the metronome mark ♩ = 72, contains many semiquavers which, despite the broad character of the main theme, do not give it the feel of a slow movement. A similar situation obtains in the Andante maestoso (¢) no. 3 in *Die erste Walpurgisnacht* at ♩ = 80, where an expansive melodic line is accompanied by continuous semiquavers. When a rather slower metronome mark is indicated, as in the Andante of the String Quartet op. 44 no. 2 (¢, ♩ = 60), whose beginning has a more sustained character, Mendelssohn's concern that it should not be taken like an adagio is shown by his appended comment 'Dieses Stück darf nicht schleppend gespielt worden' ('this piece may not be played in a dragging manner'). But although Mendelssohn clearly did not want his andantes to be taken too slowly, there seems to be no direct evidence that he associated them with the eighteenth-century notion of a 'well separated and distinct' performance style. Yet perhaps this was still an element in his choice of the term; if this were borne in mind it might avoid the more unctuous interpretations of numbers such as 'If with all your hearts' (3/4 andante con moto, ♩ = 72) from *Elijah*.

The style of writing employed in Schumann's andantes seems, in most instances, entirely to preclude the characteristics formerly associated with the term. His andantes often feel distinctly closer to adagio, though in general those with metronome marks only have a slightly slower pulse than Mendelssohn's. The Andante con moto (¢) that opens the Overture, Scherzo, and Finale op. 52, for instance, has a metronome mark of ♩ = 60, but it moves mostly in legato quavers. It feels slower, subjectively, than the introduction to the overture to *Genoveva* (¢, ♩ = 50), which is marked *Langsam* (literally 'slow', and usually regarded as an equivalent of 'adagio')[65] and contains legato semi-quavers in comparable figurations to the quavers in op. 52. Similarly, the initial *Langsam* of the overture *Manfred* (𝄵, ♩ = 63), also with legato semiquavers, feels rather faster than the op. 52 Andante.

In Wagner's earlier operas 'andante' is fairly uncommon. Where it does occur the metronome marks range in 3/4 from ♩ = 50 to ♩ = 80 and in common time from ♩ = 50 to ♩ = 76 and even, in one case, to an anomalous ♩ = 100 (*Tannhäuser*, Act II, Scene iii). The characters and textures of these andantes differ considerably from one another, and it is difficult to see any consistent motivation for Wagner's choice of this term rather than another. Some, like Erik's Cavatina from *Der fliegende Holländer* (𝄵, ♩ = 50), are decidedly slower in effect than any of Mendelssohn's andantes. A revealing example occurs in *Tannhäuser* Act II, Scene iv, where, at Elisbeth's words 'Der Unglücksel'ge' the music is marked 𝄵 Andante ♩ = 56: the vocal line is sustained in crotchets and quavers with the occasional anacrustic semiquaver, and, apart from some tremolandos, the accompaniment is sustained in long note values with peri-odic interjections of an accelerating repeated-note figure in the bass (Ex. 10.3); after a while there is a poco ritard. to ♩ = 50, then after another six bars the tempo term changes to 'Adagio' with the metronome mark ♩ = 58 and the music becomes slightly more active, though it is essentially the same material as at the beginning of the preceding Andante (Ex. 10.4).

Ex. 10.3. Wagner, *Der fliegende Holländer*, Act II, Scene iv

[65] The equivalence of German and Italian tempo terms in the 19th c. was by no means clear, however, as the inconsistent 'translation' of German terms into Italian ones in many 19th-c. editions indicates.

Ex. 10.4. Wagner, *Der fliegende Holländer*, Act II, Scene iv

Wagner made no use of the term *gehend* after abandoning Italian directions in his later operas; any movements that might have been marked 'andante' were almost certainly designated *langsam* or *mäßig* (moderate), the latter of which, as discussed below, could also in its Italian form, moderato, mean something very slow to Wagner.

Moderate Tempo Terms

Around 1780 Corri bracketed 'allegretto', 'poco allegro', 'maestoso', and 'moderato' together as 'a small degree slower than Allegro'. This certainly represents their usage by many composers during the next century, but there were many subtle variants, and individual usages.

Moderato and Allegro Moderato

These terms were not generally regarded by eighteenth-century writers as indicating a distinct performance style, but for musicians associated with the Viotti school of string players, they were, together with 'maestoso', particularly cultivated and are often found for the opening movements of concertos. The Paris Conservatoire's *Méthode* and its plagiarists required that 'In Allegro maestoso, or Moderato assai, where the bowstroke should be faster and more decided, one must give the staccato notes as much extent as possible and use about the middle of the bow so that the strings, being put into full vibration, give a round tone. Here one should also make the down- and up-bow lively so that after each note a small gap occurs.'[66] But their view of these terms was not universally shared.

The tempo significance of 'moderato' was particularly subject to disagreement. W. N. James stated that the French regarded 'allegretto' as indicating a tempo slower than 'moderato', 'though the time is certainly faster than the latter movement'.[67] It is not clear, however, what French source he had in mind, for the *Principes élémentaires de musique* puts 'moderato' in the second slowest of its five groups of tempo terms, that is, slower even than 'larghetto' and 'andante'.[68] That interpretation of the term perhaps reflects Rousseau's use of the French word *modéré* as the equivalent of the Italian 'adagio' in his 1768 dictionary. Most authorities did not regard moderato as so slow (though Rousseau's equivalent perhaps suggests a flowing adagio); but a certain amount of confusion did arise from the fact that some composers seem to have used 'moderato' and 'allegro moderato' as two separate tempo terms, while others apparently regarded them as synonymous. Campagnoli gave the order 'allegretto', 'allegro moderato', 'allegro maestoso', 'allegro';[69] Marx gave 'allegretto', 'moderato', 'allegro';[70] Mendel gave 'andante', 'andantino', 'moderato', 'allegretto';[71] Dommer gave 'andante', 'moderato', 'maestoso', 'andantino', 'allegretto'.[72] Composers sometimes seem to have designated a slower tempo with 'moderato' and at other times used it as a qualifier to 'allegro' for movements that are well into the allegro range. Schubert's only metronomized moderato, no. 31 in *Alfonso und Estrella*, is in C metre with the marking ♩ = 96, and its fastest notes are triplet quavers; his allegro moderatos in the same metre (nos. 6, 16, 28, and 34a) are marked ♩ = 100, 138, 132, and 120 respectively. The slower marking for no. 6 may be explained by the continuous demisemiquaver tremolos in the accompaniment; the others contain semiquavers with some faster notes. However, the opera also contains one Allegro molto moderato in C metre (no. 34d) which is slower than no. 31 (♩ = 84). But the sample of Schubert's markings is too small to suggest any firm conclusions.

Metronome marks given by other composers indicate the variability of practice. Those of Rossini suggest that he may sometimes have used 'moderato' to indicate a slower pace than would have been implied by 'allegro moderato', but he was far from consistent. Weber's employment of 'moderato' and 'allegro moderato' in *Euryanthe* suggests that for him they shared the same tempo region; the Moderato assai no. 7 and the Allegro moderato no. 23d, for instance, both in C metre, have an identical metronome mark (♩ = 104) and similar note values. Spohr's metronome marks, too, reveal no obvious distinc-

---

[66] Fröhlich, *Musikschule*, iii. 47.

[67] *The Flutist's Catechism*, 42.

[68] Gossec et al., *Principes*, 43.

[69] *Nouvelle méthode*, v. 10.

[70] In Schilling, *Encyclopädie*, art. 'Tempo'.

[71] Mendel and Reissmann, *Musikalisches Conversations-Lexikon*, art. 'Tempo'.

[72] *Musikalisches Lexicon*, art. 'Tempobezeichnungen'.

tion between the two terms. Verdi's designation of successive sections in no. 9 of *Il trovatore* as 'Moderato' and 'Allegro moderato maestoso', to both of which the metronome mark ♩ = 96 was allotted, suggests that he made no distinction. Berlioz, on the other hand, seems generally to have meant a decidedly slower tempo by 'moderato', and, again contrary to James's contention about French practice, his 'allegretto' appears normally to have indicated a faster tempo than his 'moderato'.

In the case of many other composers, where sufficient data exists to hazard a conclusion, 'allegretto' and 'moderato' appear to have suggested a similar tempo range; the choice of term may have been to some extent connected with character rather than tempo. In this context it is interesting to note, once again, that a number of composers favoured particular terms for particular metres. Spohr, for instance, scarcely if ever used 'allegretto' for pieces in ¢, whereas he freely used it for pieces in 6/8; in contrast, he often used 'moderato', 'allegro moderato' or 'allegro ma non troppo' for pieces in ¢, but scarcely if ever for pieces in 6/8. Berlioz, too, showed a preference, albeit less marked, for the association of 'allegretto' with compound metres and 'moderato', 'allegro moderato', or 'allegro non troppo' with common time. Rossini scarcely ever used 'allegretto' for movements in ¢ metre, but frequently did so for those in 3/4, whereas he almost invariably employed 'allegro moderato' for music in ¢ metre.

Wagner, like Berlioz, evidently intended 'moderato', in some cases, to indicate a slower tempo than 'allegro moderato', but in others apparently regarded the two terms as synonymous. His fastest moderato at ♩ = 126 (*Rienzi*, no. 6) is actually slightly more rapid than his fastest allegro moderatos at ♩ = 120 (*Tannhäuser*, Act I, Scene iv and Act II, Scene ii), but his slowest allegro moderato (*Der fliegende Holländer*, no. 3), which is given in ¢ metre, is marked ♩ = 50. In *Der fliegende Holländer* he twice marked successive sections in the same metre 'Moderato' and 'Allegro moderato'. In one of these (no. 6) there is no doubt about the relationship, for he indicated ♩ = 80 for the Moderato and ♩ = 112 for the Allegro moderato, both in common time. In the other, from no. 3, the situation seems to be reversed, for the Moderato is marked ♩ = 60 and the Allegro moderato ♩ = 50, but the presence of sextuplet quavers and a few semiquavers in the latter, together with a decidedly more active vocal line, gives an impression of somewhat greater speed. 'Moderato', used on its own, is perhaps Wagner's most flexible marking in the operas up to *Tannhäuser*, for he gave it metronome markings in common time ranging from ♩ = 46 (his slowest ¢ marking: slower than for 'andante', 'lento', 'sostenuto', 'adagio', and 'grave') to ♩ = 126; at both ends of the scale, the music moves in crotchets. It may be reasonable to assume that he conceived a similar flexibility in terms of tempo for the German equivalent *mäßig*, which occurs very frequently in his later operas.

Maestoso

Löhlein considered that maestoso required

a firm tone, that is well sustained and well articulated. It is mostly expressed in figures where the first note is long and the second short, or, to put it more clearly: where after the first, third, fifth note, etc. there are dots. The former overtures always began with such movements. Nowadays marches, in particular, but also from time to time other musical pieces, still have these figures.[73]

And Reichardt appears to have regarded 'maestoso' as mainly appropriate to slow pieces; he observed that it indicated 'that the longer bowstrokes should receive a stronger, more expressive accent, and in these cases the notes before rests, rather than being taken off short, should only come away gradually'.[74]

The association of the term 'maestoso' with music of a majestic, processional character meant that it was pre-eminently employed in common time, though it is occasionally found in other metres. It occurs most frequently as a qualification to 'andante' and 'allegro', but, especially in the nineteenth century, is quite often found as a term on its own. Its effect on the tempo of an allegro seems always to be a moderating one; its effect on that of an andante, however, is more variable and is probably linked to some extent with a composer's feeling about the tempo area appropriate to that term. Mozart almost certainly intended andante maestoso to be slower than his normal andante.[75] Beethoven gave metronome marks to only two tempo directions that include the term 'maestoso', both in the Ninth Symphony. The 3/4 Maestoso has quite a stately pulse at ♩ = 60, but contains many demisemiquavers. The Andante maestoso in 3/2, which is marked ♩ = 72, has quavers as its fastest notes and seems similar to the 3/4 Andante moderato (♩ = 63, with semiquaver movement); but the Andante maestoso has a greater feeling of speed at that tempo, and, taking the metre into account, it seems clear that Beethoven saw this tempo marking as the faster of the two.

Some composers, probably including Beethoven, evidently felt that 'maestoso' itself occupied a particular niche in the tempo hierarchy and that the effect of its attachment to another term depended on whether the tempo indicated by the main term were slower or faster than the tempo area appropriate to 'maestoso' alone. For Spontini it apparently occupied a distinct place between 'andante' and 'allegro'. His metronome marks indicate that he regarded 'andante maestoso' as signifying a faster tempo than 'andante', while he, like other composers, regarded 'maestoso' or 'allegro maestoso', as indicating a quite distinctly slower tempo than 'allegro'. For Spohr, on the other hand,

---

[73] *Anweisung zum Violinspielen*, 106.   [74] *Ueber die Pflichten*, 25–6.

[75] Marty, *The Tempo Indications of Mozart*, 84 ff. Although Marty's arguments are largely subjective, his instinct seems very plausible in this case.

'maestoso' seems, as with Mozart, always to have had a restraining effect on the principal tempo term, and thus he undoubtedly used 'andante maestoso' to specify a slower tempo than 'andante'. The common-time sections marked 'andante maestoso' in *Jessonda* (no. 1) and in the Fourth Symphony op. 86, with the metronome marks ♩ = 56 and ♩ = 60 respectively, equate closely with sections also in common time marked 'andante grave' in the Third Symphony op. 78 and the Concertinto op. 79, to which Spohr likewise gave the metronome marks ♩ = 56 and ♩ = 60 respectively. Movements in the same metre which he marked 'andante', however, are generally in the region of ♩ = 76–92. Weber's use of 'maestoso' in *Euryanthe* is very varied, ranging from the extremes of Maestoso assai 𝄴 ♩ = 50 (no. 4), with quaver movement and a few figures consisting of a dotted quaver and a semiquaver, to Maestoso energico ma non troppo 𝄵 ♩ = 63 (no. 23) with semiquaver movement. In between come a Moderato maestoso 𝄴 at ♩ = 92 (no. 1) and a Maestoso 3/4 at ♩ = 96 (no. 1), both with semiquavers. Two other short sections, a Maestoso assai 𝄴 at ♩ = 66 and a Maestoso con moto 𝄴 at ♩ = 108, both have primarily quaver movement. Rossini, like many other composers, appears to have felt that 'allegro maestoso' and 'allegro moderato' indicated a similar speed, and perhaps differed significantly only in expression, though he may have considered the former to be a little slower, perhaps about ♩ = 120, with the central range of the latter being ♩ = 120–32 (both assuming semiquaver movement). 'Maestoso' and 'moderato' by themselves probably signified something rather slower, perhaps ♩ = 92 and 100 respectively with similar note content. Rossini's pieces in 𝄴 and 2/4 fit into the same range as those marked simply 'andante'.

Mendelssohn's metronome marks suggest that he may have seen 'maestoso' alone as occupying a similar tempo area to 'andante' (in 𝄴 with semiquaver movement ♩ = 60–80, though a Maestoso in *Antigone* has the faster metronome mark ♩ = 92) and that the effect of the term 'maestoso' in combination with 'andante' was rather one of expression than speed. The metronome marks for his Andante maestoso 𝄴 music in *Antigone* and *Die erste Walpurgisnacht* indicate, taken in conjunction with other musical factors, a similar speed to music designated 'andante', with perhaps a tendency to be slightly faster. In *Antigone*, however, the 6/8 Andante con moto maestoso (♪ = 138) does feel somewhat slower than the 6/8 Andante con moto in the same work, which is not only given a marginally higher metronome mark (♪ = 144) but also has some faster-moving notes. 'Maestoso' had a scarcely less extended meaning for Wagner than 'moderato'. His fastest use in common time (in which he chiefly employed it) in the three operas with metronome marks is ♩ = 120 (in the *Rienzi* ballet music), and his slowest ♩ = 69 (in *Rienzi*, no. 9 and in *Tannhäuser*, Act III, Scene iii). Like 'allegro moderato' and 'moderato', 'allegro maestoso' is only found in the upper part of the range, the lowest being an Allegro maestoso ma non troppo (♩ = 96) in *Rienzi*, no. 7.

Allegretto

Reichardt considered the character of allegretto to be similar to that of andante, and having described the appropriate bowstroke for andante (see above), he continued: 'It is the same in allegretto, only the bow already acquires somewhat more liveliness and from time to time some sharpness.'[76] Löhlein approached the question from the opposite angle and considered that, along with allegro moderato, tempo giusto, and poco allegro, 'it should be played with a gentler and more connected bowstroke than the completely joyful [i.e. allegro]. But it must not be sleepy, rather it must hold to the mean between cheerful and moderate.'[77]

The relationship of 'allegretto' to slower tempo terms has frequently been touched on above, and it only remains to make one or two general points here. Some composers particularly associated 'allegretto', like many other tempo terms, with particular metres, or avoided using it in some metres. Among the allegrettos to which Beethoven gave metronome marks, for instance, there are none in c or ¢; all occur in 2/4, 6/8, and 3/8. Berlioz's allegrettos are preponderantly in the latter metres, especially 6/8, though there is also a group in 3/4. Rossini too avoided c and ¢, and had a marked tendency to apply this term to movements in 3/4. Spontini, on the other hand, seems to have been quite happy to use 'allegretto' for music in common time; *Olympie* alone contains five of them. Dvořák was especially fond of writing 2/4 allegrettos.

'Allegretto' normally indicated a tempo somewhat slower than would have been signified by 'allegro', but its closeness to 'allegro' may have depended on the composer's view of that tempo term. Mozart seems not to have regarded the difference between 'allegro' and 'allegretto' as very great, for on two occasions he entered a work which he had marked 'allegretto' in the score as 'allegro' in his *Verzeichnüß*. Nevertheless, for many composers in the nineteenth century 'allegretto' does appear to have indicated a quite significantly less rapid tempo than 'allegro', but the practice of some, Berlioz for example, was very erratic; sometimes 'allegretto' was intended to specify a slower and sometimes a faster tempo than 'allegro'.[78] This ambiguity of the term for French composers may be reflected in Mathis Lussy's observation that 'some take Allegretto, the diminutive of Allegro for its augmentative, and render it by a quicker tempo instead of a slower one'.[79]

---

[76] *Ueber die Pflichten*, 26.   [77] *Anweisung zum Violinspielen*, 106.
[78] Macdonald, 'Berlioz and the Metronome'.   [79] *Musical Expression*, 224.

Fast Tempo Terms

Löhlein and Reichardt were essentially agreed about the nature of the bow-stroke in music marked with 'allegro' and closely related tempo terms. Löhlein taught that:

The joyful [i.e. allegro, vivace, presto, etc.] is performed with a cheerful, lively and articulated bowstroke, and as this passion becomes more moderate, e.g. with the words moderato, allegretto, poco allegro, one must also reduce the liveliness of the stroke and move towards calmness. In contrast, with the words allegro assai, allegro di molto, which signify greater abandon, the stroke must also be taken more fleetingly and shorter. In this manner one seeks to define every degree of joy through the performance style.[80]

Reichardt commented, after discussing the necessary style for allegretto:

Finally in allegro, however, the sharpness of the bow in detached notes and its rapidity at *Abzugs* is highly necessary.

The more extreme terms, such as, for example, *Allegro di molto, Allegro assai, Presto, Prestissimo* merely affect the tempo and alter nothing in the character of the bowstroke. For this an expression must be added which specifies the character of the piece. *Allegro e con brio, Allegro e con spirito, con fuoco, resoluto*, etc.

In the same way the terms which diminish the speed of the allegro, such as, for example, *Allegro ma non troppo, non tanto, moderato*, etc., make no difference to the character of the bowing, but merely affect the tempo. If, however, *cantabile, dolce*, or another expression which more narrowly determines the character of the piece occurs, then that has a bearing on the bow, which must go more gently and more connectedly.[81]

A rather different view of the matter is found in the early nineteenth-century string methods that were influenced by the approach of the Viotti school. Fröhlich's *Musikschule* stated:

In allegro the bowstroke must have less breadth [than in allegro maestoso or moderato assai]. One begins the notes about the end of the third quarter of the length of the bow and one plays the notes without separating them with gaps.

In presto, where the stroke must be even faster and livelier, one gives the staccato notes even less breadth. Here, too, one plays in the region of the third quarter of the bow, but one must take trouble to make the stroke as long as is necessary to put the strings into perfectly equal vibrations, so that the notes reach, as far as possible, into the distance, every note speaks properly, and one is able to give one's playing power and fire. The longer one makes the bowstrokes the better effect they will have in the right place; but one should not exaggerate, but must always take trouble to suit the stroke to the quantity of its strength.[82]

Vivace

Before examining what eighteenth- and nineteenth-century composers may have understood in terms of tempo by 'allegro', 'presto', and so on, it will be

---

[80] *Anweisung zum Violinspielen*, 105–6.   [81] *Ueber die Pflichten*, 26–7.   [82] Vol. iii. 47.

useful to consider this associated tempo word, which was used in a number of different ways. 'Vivace' is frequently encountered both as a term on its own and as a qualifier of 'allegro'. During the earlier and mid-eighteenth century it sometimes had a slower connotation than it later acquired. It was described by Leopold Mozart, along with 'spiritoso', as 'the median between quick and slow',[83] and Charles Cudworth has shown that, in eighteenth-century England at any rate, it was used by composers to indicate a relatively slow tempo.[84] Löhlein's list of terms (above) implies that he regarded it as indicating a slower tempo than 'allegro'. Koch's definition of 'vivace'—'lively, designates as much a lively tempo as a quick one, and light, flowing performance style'[85]—suggests that this signification of 'vivace' survived to some extent into the early years of the nineteenth century; elsewhere in his dictionary Koch included 'vivace' just before 'allegro' in the fourth of his five tempo categories (reckoning from slow to fast).[86] But during the late eighteenth century and the nineteenth century it seems to have been used much more, either alone or in the phrase 'allegro vivace', to indicate a tempo not only livelier but also faster than that indicated by an unqualified 'allegro'. Already around 1780 Domenico Corri regarded it, along with 'allegro con brio', as meaning 'sprightly and a degree quicker' than 'allegro';[87] Jousse, in the English usage (it was not given in Asioli's original Italian), listed it between 'allegro' and 'presto',[88] as, much later in the nineteenth century, did Mendel[89] and Dommer,[90] while A. B. Marx placed it after 'allegro', 'con brio', and 'animato'.[91]

Metronome marks indicate that Beethoven's allegro vivace is normally rather faster than his simple allegro but not as fast as his allegro con brio. When Schubert added 'vivace' to 'allegro', however, it seems to have signified a considerably faster pulse: most of the common-time allegros in *Alfonso und Estrella* are marked ♩ = 160, while the two numbers in that metre marked 'allegro vivace' (no. 22b) and 'allegro molto vivace' (no. 20) are marked ♩ = 112 and ♩ = 120 respectively. But these movements have nothing like so many semiquavers. Spohr's metronome marks suggest that he used 'vivace' alone to indicate a somewhat faster tempo than when he used the term 'allegro vivace'. For many later nineteenth-century composers it was seen, either alone or in combination with 'allegro', as indicating a faster tempo than 'allegro' on its own; but a few, for instance Dvořák, may have regarded 'vivace' alone as calling for a slower tempo than 'allegro vivace'.

[83] *Versuch*, I, 3, §27.

[84] 'The Meaning of "Vivace" in Eighteenth-Century England', *Fontes artis musicae*, 12 (1965), 194.

[85] *Musikalisches Lexikon*, art. 'Vivace'.   [86] Ibid., art. 'Zeitmaaß'.

[87] *A Select Collection*, i. 10.   [88] *A Compendious Musical Grammar*, iii.

[89] Mendel and Reissmann, *Musikalisches Conversations-Lexikon*, x. 138.

[90] *Musikalisches Lexikon*, art. 'Tempobezeichnungen'.   [91] In Schilling, *Encyclopädie*, vi. 600.

Allegro

At the beginning of the nineteenth century there was undoubtedly a tendency for some composers and performers to prefer very fast speeds. How far this tendency goes back into the eighteenth century, and which composers may have favoured it, is difficult to determine. Certainly Quantz's chronometric tempos seemed very fast to other contemporaries. Only two years after the appearance of Quantz's treatise, C. P. E. Bach, who spent many years as his colleague in Berlin, commented on the fact that in Berlin 'adagio is far slower and allegro far faster than is customary elsewhere'.[92] Türk, too, gave his opinion that the difference between adagio assai and allegro assai in Quantz's scheme was too great.[93]

Information about Mozart's preferences, as outlined earlier, is ambiguous, and it is difficult to say whether Hummel's tempos for his works, for instance, represent Mozart's own ideas or a more recent preference for faster tempos. Rochlitz's anecdote about Mozart's visit to Leipzig in 1789 (see above, p. 297) may suggest that he was capable of taking his own allegros rather quickly.

There was undoubtedly controversy in the early years of the nineteenth century, however, about excessively rapid speeds, and there were important crosscurrents in this respect. Many Viennese and Parisian musicians appear to have favoured very fast tempos. And Friedrich Guthmann complained vigorously in 1805 about the almost universal tendency to adopt very fast speeds, especially in the 'allegros of overtures' (first movements of symphonies?) and in the 'socalled minuets of symphonies'.[94] However, the French school of string players, inspired by Viotti, and their German followers (including Spohr) were noted for their very expansive allegros, at least in their concertos (as Guthmann also acknowledged), though these are very often marked 'moderato', 'allegro moderato', or 'allegro maestoso'.

Metronome marks offer the possibility of examining the basis of such claims, though the question of what 'allegro', alone or in its various combinations, meant to late eighteenth-century and nineteenth-century composers in terms of absolute tempo is difficult to determine, for many additional factors affect subjective perceptions of speed. The matter is further complicated because, while some composers frequently used simply 'allegro', or combined this with a limited number of terms that appear to have quite precise relationships, others, particularly Italian composers, employed a wide range of different expressions.

The present discussion will be confined to movements marked **c** and **¢**. It becomes clear from an examination of these that there were considerable differences in the perception of 'allegro' during the nineteenth century, but that

---

[92] *Versuch*, ii, XXXVI, §7.   [93] *Klavierschule*, I, v, §72.
[94] *Allgemeine musikalische Zeitung*, 7 (1804–5), 775.

there was a very marked predilection for extremely fast allegros among a number of composers. In the work of those composers to whom metre still seems to have been a significant factor, the fastest movement is almost invariably found in c (or dubious ϕ) movements, with semiquavers as their fastest notes, rather than in genuine ϕ movements with quavers. This is not surprising if one bears in mind the notion that larger note values did not move as fast as slower ones.

Beethoven's fastest movements of this kind are those marked 'allegro con brio'. (His movements marked 'allegro molto', 'presto', and 'prestissimo' all have the time signature ϕ, have quavers as their fastest notes, or in one case (the Septet op. 20) quaver triplets, and do not achieve as rapid an absolute tempo.) The speediest of all, in terms of the velocity of the fastest functional notes[95] (in this case semiquavers), are the Allegro con brio first movements of the First and Second symphonies at $\bm{J}$ = 112[96] and $\bm{J}$ = 100 respectively (though in the case of the First Symphony most of the semiquavers are repeated notes or short slurred scale passages). A more breathless effect may be created by the slightly slower first movement of the String Quartet op. 95 at $\bm{J}$ = 92 because of the proportion of separately bowed semiquavers and the more angular patterns in which they occur. The fastest functional notes in these movements move, therefore, at between 736–896 notes per minute (hereafter npm). Some of Schubert's fastest movements seem, on the basis of the metronome marks in *Alfonso und Estrella*, to be equally rapid, with the fastest functional notes in allegro assai and allegro molto in the dizzying range of 832–96 npm. The movements marked simply 'allegro' by both these composers are never slower than 640 npm; in Beethoven's case they reach 676 npm in the last movement of the Fifth Symphony op. 67 and the first movement of the String Quartet op. 74 and in Schubert's case 736 npm in no. 2 of *Alfonso und Estrella*, though only for a few bars. Cherubini's use of 'allegro', in the few works to which he gave metronome marks, matches Beethoven's and Schubert's; in the Second String Quartet a movement headed 'Allegro' has 640 npm, but his fastest metronome tempo of 704 npm was given to a movement in the Fourth String Quartet marked 'Allegro assai'.

Rossini's, Spontini's, Mendelssohn's, and Verdi's fastest movements attain a similar range, yet they do not quite reach the fastest speeds in Beethoven and Schubert (except in the case of some of Mendelssohn's piano figurations). Rossini's fastest movements in the operas *Le Siège de Corinthe*, *Le Comte Ory*, *Moïse*, and *Guillaume Tell*, sometimes marked 'Allegro vivace' but most just 'allegro', and with an utterly inconsistent mixture of c and ϕ, reach 836 npm; the slowest allegro vivace has 640 npm. The range for 'allegro' alone is enor-

---

[95] The expression 'functional notes' is taken here to exclude tremolando or ornamental flourishes.

[96] As explained in Ch. 9, the ϕ time signatures for this movement and the Allegro con brio of the Septet op. 20, which also has semiquavers, seem anomalous, and both movements seem really to have been intended to be in c.

mous: 504 to 836 npm. Spontini, unlike Rossini, was particularly fond of combining 'allegro' with other terms, and 'allegro' on its own appears very infrequently. His markings in the operas *Fernand Cortez*, *Olympie*, and *Nurmahal* range from Allegro nobile at 448 npm (*Nurmahal*, no. 8) through Allegro giusto at 528 npm (*Fernand Cortez*, Act III, no. 4) and Allegro agitato espressivo at 768 npm (*Olympie*, Act I, no. 4) to Allegro vivace assai at 816 npm (*Fernand Cortez*, Act I, no. 6). Mendelssohn's Allegro assai appassionato (Piano Trio op. 49 and String Quartet op. 44 no. 2), Allegro vivace (String Quartet op. 44 no. 3 and Cello Sonata op. 45), Allegro assai (Cello Sonata op. 45), Molto allegro vivace (String Quartet op. 44 no. 1), and Molto allegro con fuoco (String Quartet op. 44 no. 3) move at between 704 and 800 npm. An astonishing 1344 npm is reached in the piano figurations in the Allegro vivace of the op. 3 Piano Quartet. Verdi often expressed his liking for fast tempos. In relation to the Viennese première of *Ernani*, for instance, he wrote to Leon Herz in 1844: 'I caution [you that] I do not like slow tempos; it is better to err on the side of liveliness than to drag.'[97] And he made similar comments in connection with *Don Carlos* in 1869.[98] It is not surprising, therefore to find that his tempos are among the fastest in the later nineteenth century. Movements marked simply 'allegro' may be found in the range 480 npm (*Rigoletto*, no. 10) to 672 npm (*Il trovatore*, no. 14), while movements marked 'allegro assai mosso' (*Il trovatore*, no. 9), 'allegro assai vivo' (*Rigoletto*, no. 7, *Il trovatore*, nos. 11 and 13), and 'allegro vivo' (*Il trovatore*, no. 8) occupy the region 672 to 832 npm. Meyerbeer sometimes demanded rather quick speeds. His allegro con spirito in *Les Huguenots* varies from 576 npm (no. 6) to 736 npm (no. 12), but these are his fastest tempos. Weber specified $\downarrow$ = 132 for a Vivace feroce (¢) in *Euryanthe* (no. 10), which contained a few slurred semiquaver runs, making a rate of 1056 npm, but on the whole his tempos seem more moderate than those of Beethoven and Schubert. Nevertheless his vivace, allegro con fuoco, and allegro sometimes involve movement at between 640 and 736 npm, though his allegro movements can be as slow as 464 npm.

Composers who do not seem to have required such extremes of tempo when they marked their music 'allegro' include Clementi, Spohr, Wagner, and Dvořák. Clementi, however, did specify some fairly rapid speeds for movements with semiquavers. In the Allegro of the Piano Sonata op. 50 no. 1 the semiquavers move at 640 npm, and the Allegro ma non troppo ma con energia of op. 50 no. 2 contains semiquaver triplets moving at 576 npm and demisemiquavers at 768 npm. Spohr seldom required very fast movement; his allegro molto rarely approaches 872 npm, and his average allegro vivace is around 552. But the complicated nature of many of his figurations often makes the music

[97] G. Morazzoni, *Verdi: Lettere inedite* (Milan, 1929), 27.
[98] A. Damerini, 'Sei lettere inedite di Verdi a J. C. Farrarini', *Il pianoforte*, 7 (Aug.–Sept. 1926), letter no. 3.

seem faster. Wagner's fastest allegro tempos in *Tannhäuser* (marked ¢) reach 608 npm, and one allegro in *Rienzi* attains 676 npm, but such velocity is rare, and his allegros are often very much slower. Dvořák's allegro con brio and allegro agitato, his fastest tempos in ¢ metre, only reach 552 npm, though his allegro con brio ¢, with quaver triplets, attains 720 npm.

Other Terms Affecting Tempo

To survey all the various tempo and expression words employed during this period, many of which present no significant problems, is beyond the scope of this study, but a few fairly common terms, primarily of expression, which could also affect tempo, warrant consideration.

Amoroso

When appended to a tempo word, this sometimes implied a slowing down of the tempo. Woldemar described 'andante amoroso' as meaning 'slower than the ordinary andante'.[99] It certainly seems to have had this meaning for Spontini. The Andantino amoroso (no. 5) in *Nurmahal* belongs, together with such expressions as 'andante sostenuto' and 'andantino melancolico', among the more leisurely andantinos and andantes for which he gave metronome marks. However, Spontini often appears also to have used the word in a more purely expressive sense in such phrases as 'Andante amoroso un poco mosso' (*Nurmahal*, no. 13) and 'Allegro amoroso agitato' (*Olympie*, Act II, no. 4).

Sostenuto

'Sostenuto' was sometimes used alone as a rather imprecise tempo direction, sometimes in conjunction with another tempo term, and sometimes as a term of expression. It appears as a tempo term in a number of lists. In the *Principes élémentaires de musique* it is in the second slowest tempo category between the largo–adagio group and the andante–allegretto group. Marx, however, listed it after 'andante' and 'andantino', but before 'andante con moto'. For Beethoven it seems to have signified a tempo somewhat, but not much, faster than he might have intended by 'adagio', to judge by his metronome marks for the Sostenuto in op. 112 (♩ = 84), where movement is largely in crotchets and the Poco sostenuto in op. 92 (♩ = 69), which includes a significant number of semiquavers. Spontini employed 'sostenuto' and 'poco sostenuto' with a similar meaning in *Olympie* and *Fernand Cortez*, in a somewhat slower tempo range than Beethoven (♩ = 50–63, with movement generally in quavers), and for him it

---

[99] *Grande méthode*, 33.

seems to have been virtually synonymous with 'andante sostenuto'. Wagner used 'sostenuto' as a tempo term in its own right in *Der fliegende Holländer*, for sections which he marked with metronome marks comparable to the generally rather slow andantes (andante $\mathbf{c}$ = 50–76; sostenuto $\mathbf{c}$ = 50–69).

Brahms also used 'sostenuto' as a tempo term: an instance is the Un poco sostenuto which opens his First Symphony. This, however, led to confusion with his employment of the very similar term 'Poco sostenuto', in a quite different sense, for the last seventeen bars of the first movement. In October 1881 he wrote to his publisher, Simrock, requesting him to change 'Poco sostenuto' to 'Meno allegro' since, he observed, 'people always take the tempo of the introduction'.[100] But the change was never made, though Brahms himself pencilled it into his own copy. Elsewhere, Brahms frequently used 'sostenuto' and 'poco sostenuto' in the sense of 'meno mosso' or 'allargando', for instance in the last four bars of the third movement of his Second Symphony. At the beginning of the development section of the first movement of his G major Violin Sonata he wrote 'poco a poco più sostenuto'; the fact that in this case he required a slower tempo, not merely a different expression, is demonstrated by the direction 'poco a poco tempo 1°' just before the recapitulation. And similar instructions to return to the original tempo are found in much earlier works, for instance towards the end of the first movement of the 1854 version of the B major Piano Trio. J. A. Fuller Maitland identified this usage of 'sostenuto' with what he called the 'romantic' school, but it was certainly used in the same sense at an early stage in the nineteenth century.[101]

Spontini clearly understood 'sostenuto', when appended to other tempo terms, to mean slower, hence in *Olympie*, Act II, no. 4 he headed the section 'Andante espressivo sostenuto' with the metronome mark $\mathbf{J}$ = 56; later in the number he wrote 'Meno sostenuto' and gave the metronome mark $\mathbf{J}$ = 72. In Berlioz's music, too, the term is used, in combination with 'adagio', 'larghetto', and 'andante', to indicate slower tempos than usual. Spohr employed the tempo term 'andante sostenuto' on a couple of occasions (the male-voice part-songs op. 44 no. 1 and op. 90 no. 4), in both cases with metronome marks that equate with those he gave for movements headed 'adagio'. Mendelssohn, on the other hand, does not seem to have used it in this way, but rather as an expression marking, perhaps calling for extremely legato execution. His use of the term in the Second Symphony (*Lobgesang*) op. 52, for instance, appears not to have been intended to affect the speed. He gave the same metronome mark ($\mathbf{J}$ = 100) to the Andante and to the Andante sostenuto assai, both of which movements are in 2/4 and contain similar note values.

---

[100] *Johannes Brahms Briefwechsel*, ed. Max Kalbeck, x (Tutzing, 1974), 192.

[101] Art. 'Sostenuto', *Grove's Dictionary*, 3rd edn., ed. H. C. Colles (London, 1927).

Cantabile

'Cantabile' was employed as a tempo direction in its own right, as a modifier of tempo, and as a term of expression. Domenico Corri placed it in his third group of tempo terms along with 'larghetto', regarding it as faster than 'adagio' but slower than 'andantino'.[102] Koch, too, explained that 'cantabile', used as a tempo direction, indicated a moderately slow tempo.[103] Campagnoli, however, who regarded the term 'larghetto' as signifying a slower tempo than 'adagio', saw it as even slower, placing it between 'grave' and 'larghetto',[104] and the *Principes élémentaires de musique* put it in the slowest tempo category along with 'grave', 'largo', and 'adagio'.[105] When used in conjunction with other terms it seems, like 'sostenuto', sometimes to have indicated a modification of the tempo and at other times simply to have specified a singing style of performance. That Mozart may have considered 'andante cantabile' to indicate a slower tempo than 'andante' is implied by his modification of the tempo term of the slow movement of his String Quartet K. 465 from 'Adagio' to 'Andante cantabile'. Beethoven, in the String Quartet op. 59 no. 1, seems to have been conscious that some musicians might have regarded 'cantabile' as a modifier of tempo, but wished to indicate that he did not intend it to be so in that case, for when he gave metronome marks to his string quartets he not only marked ♪ = 88 for the Adagio molto e mesto at the beginning of the third movement, but also repeated the same metronome mark later in the movement at the section marked 'molto cantabile', presumably to ensure that the players did not take this marking to signify a new tempo. Whether Beethoven thought the players might take it slower or faster remains a moot point, though it was most likely the former.

According to some English writers, 'cantabile' could also have a more specialized meaning in the late eighteenth century and early nineteenth century. In 1771 Anselm Bayly complained in his *Practical Treatise on Singing and Playing with Just Expression and Real Elegance* that 'What are called *cantabiles* betray in general such a want of invention, and absurdity of application, that they make the hearer sick before they are half finished.'[106] Sometimes, as the anonymous author of *New Instructions for playing the Harpsichord* (*c.*1790) observed, the term 'cantabile' 'when set at the conclusion of an air signifies an extempore cadence';[107] and Dibdin, too, maintained in the first edition of his *Music Epitomized* that it indicated the 'introduction of extempore ideas gracefully'; this was changed by Jousse in the ninth edition to the simple definition 'in a singing style', perhaps indicating that the earlier definition was by that time regarded as obsolete.[108]

---

[102] *A Select Collection*, i. 10.   [103] *Musikalisches Lexikon*, art. 'Cantabile'.
[104] *Nouvelle méthode*, v. 10.   [105] Gossec et al., *Principes*, 43.   [106] (London, 1771), 65.
[107] p. 36.   [108] 1st edn., 67; 9th edn., 41.

II

TEMPO MODIFICATION

❧

A degree of deviation from absolutely mechanical adherence to a constant beat is inevitable in a musically effective performance of any reasonably extended piece, even if the performer's primary intention is to adhere strictly to the initial tempo.[1] Departures from an unyielding observation of the beat, when they do not merely arise from lack of skill or negligence, will be the natural outcome of a musician's deliberate or subconscious response to the expressive content of the music. Throughout the Classical and Romantic periods there was a general recognition (as there had also been in the Baroque) that, as long as certain aesthetic borderlines were not crossed, holding back some notes and hurrying others was not merely permissible but was an indispensable adjunct of sensitive performance. As C. P. E. Bach commented: 'whoever either does not use these things at all, or uses them at the wrong time, has a bad performance style.'[2]

The important question was where, how, and to what extent such flexibility should be introduced. This was often a highly controversial matter. At the one extreme were those musicians who believed that this expressive resource should be used sparingly and with extreme subtlety, while at the other were those who introduced frequent and obvious tempo modifications. There is abundant evidence that examples of both these extremes could have been heard in professional performances throughout the period. But the balance between them did not remain constant; at different times and in different places influential opinion and practice varied significantly. During the eighteenth century and the early part of the nineteenth century the opinion of the majority of eminent authorities was in favour of a restrained, even extremely restrained employment of tempo flexibility where it was not marked by the composer (except in

[1] The word 'tempo' is used here with the dual sense of the German word *Bewegung* so that the phrase 'tempo modification' encompasses both localized departures from mathematical observance of the note values in one or all parts and more extended alterations to the speed of the beat.
[2] *Versuch*, i, III, §3.

certain specific types of piece such as fantasias or recitative); and, where it was felt to be appropriate, particular emphasis was often laid on the use of specialized techniques of tempo rubato, which did not disturb the underlying unity of tempo. Exceptions to this general rule seem largely to have been confined to a few individuals and schools of solo instrumentalists and singers. In the course of the nineteenth century a more pronounced degree of tempo modification, in a wider range of musical genres, was sanctioned by influential sections of the musical élite, although some of the older established techniques of tempo rubato seem to have been less widely cultivated as the century drew to its close. During this period the employment of more conspicuous tempo modification, which affected the steadiness of the beat, spread increasingly from solo and small ensemble performance to orchestral performance, largely as a result of the advocacy of 'interpretative' conducting by Wagner and his disciples. The influence of this approach, persuasively advanced by Wagner in his polemical writings, was closely tied to the growing prestige of the so-called New German School in the middle of the century, and in due course made itself felt in France, Italy, and elsewhere.

Despite the evidence for significant modification of the beat by particular musicians during the eighteenth century, there is little to suggest that musicians of that period explicitly challenged the notion that the beat should remain fundamentally steady unless the composer decreed otherwise. In the nineteenth century, on the other hand, the promotion of such ideas, and their practice as a matter of conviction by leading musicians of the day, provoked strong reactions from those who remained true to the older aesthetic, espoused most notably perhaps by Mendelssohn and his followers. The strength of feeling may partly be explained by an apparent discrepancy between theory and practice among the champions of freedom of tempo. Although most of those who supported this approach in theoretical or polemical writings, including Wagner, were insistent that whatever type of tempo modification might be under consideration it must be employed with discretion, it is evident from frequent complaints that one person's discretion was another's excess.

Types of Tempo Modification

There are a number of distinctly different ways in which, where no modification of tempo has been indicated by the composer, the steadiness of the beat can be manipulated by the performer for expressive purposes. These fall into two basic categories: one involves genuine disruption of the tempo; the other, which is intimately related to improvisation and embellishment, although it causes a redistribution of note values and accents in an individual strand of the music, leaves the regularity of the beat fundamentally undisturbed. C. P. E.

Bach described and recommended both types of rubato (without, however, using the word) to keyboard players, though he considered each of them to be appropriate to different circumstances, observing:

One can often intentionally commit the most beautiful offences against the beat, but with the distinction that, if one is playing alone or with a few intelligent people, it is permissible to make an impact on the tempo as a whole, for the accompanying players will be far more likely to become alert than to let themselves be led astray, and will enter into our intentions; but if one is playing with a larger accompanying body, and if indeed the latter consists of a mixture of people of unequal accomplishment, it is only within one's own part alone that one can undertake a variation that goes against the regular distribution of the beat, for the overall pace of the beat must be precisely maintained.[3]

The term 'rubato' has been used to describe both these types of tempo modification at least since the end of the eighteenth century, although it was predominantly employed at that time to designate techniques in the latter category. During the nineteenth century the expression 'rubato' was increasingly invoked to describe the former type, but general acceptance of that meaning was slow to develop. An early example of a definition of 'tempo rubato' that could possibly imply this kind of tempo modification is found in Busby's 1801 *Complete Dictionary of Music*, where it is explained as 'An expression applied to a time alternately accelerated and retarded for the purpose of enforcing the expression';[4] but this is ambiguous and could equally refer to fluctuation within a steady beat. However, Türk had acknowledged in a gloss on the index entry for 'Tempo rubato' in his *Klavierschule* that some considered the use of accelerando and ritardando to be covered by this expression. Yet the majority of dictionaries and treatises continued to use the term in its traditional sense right through the nineteenth century; thus, 'rubato' and 'tempo rubato' were defined by Hamilton in the 1830s as borrowing from one part of the bar to give back elsewhere 'so that the time of each bar is not altered in the aggregate', and this definition was still reproduced in the 1882 edition.[5]

The history of tempo modification during the period 1750–1900 reveals many different approaches and aesthetic attitudes, and changing notions of where one or the other type might be most appropriate. The principal techniques and practices may be categorized as follows:

1. Modification of the basic pulse of the music either momentarily or for a more extended period can occur in different ways and for dramatic, expressive or structural purposes.

    (a) This can occur on the small scale as the lengthening, without restitution, of a single beat or rest.

---

[3] *Versuch*, i, III, §8.   [4] Art. 'Tempo rubato'.
[5] *Dictionary*, 4th edn., and *Hamilton's Dictionary of Musical terms. New Edition . . . Enlarged* (London, [1882]), art. 'Tempo rubato'.

(b) There can be a gradual slowing down or speeding up of the pulse over several beats or bars.

(c) It can involve the adoption of a slower or faster basic tempo for a whole phrase or section, either abruptly or preceded by a ritardando or an accelerando. In such cases the change of speed can either be slight, and scarcely perceptible to the casual listener, or can result in the establishment of an unmistakably different tempo.

2. The classic tempo rubato occurs when the accompaniment (or in the case of a keyboard instrument usually the left hand) remains steady, while the melodic line is modified for a more or less extended passage.

(a) A single note or occasionally a rest may be lengthened where it has a particular expressive or structural function, and the time that is lost will be regained by hurrying the immediately following beats.

(b) Sometimes the relationship of the melodic line to the bass will be modified throughout a phrase, an extended passage, or even a whole movement. This technique was widely used, particularly in the eighteenth century, to create a special effect or to vary a passage on repetition. It required particular skill and understanding of the rules of composition on the part of the performer not to produce intolerable harmonic clashes with the bass, though it is clear that the retardation and anticipation of essential harmony notes, even when the technique was employed by experts, will sometimes have caused effects that would not normally have been written down.

(c) In addition to or instead of redistribution of the note values, embellishments in the form of fiorituras might be added to the melodic line in such a way that it appears to be rhythmically independent of the accompaniment. The employment of this technique can be traced from C. P. E. Bach and Franz Benda to Dussek, Chopin, and beyond, though with the passage of time, as with many of the above-mentioned tempo rubato devices, the technique became a resource for the composer rather than for the performer.

Modification of the Basic Pulse

Many eighteenth-century musicians besides C. P. E. Bach discussed the types of tempo modification that involved a real disturbance of the basic pulse, and a few more pedagogically minded or meticulous ones attempted to indicate it graphically. Georg Friedrich Wolf used signs for various kinds of ritardando in his keyboard method of 1783,[6] and Türk introduced several symbols for tempo modification into his *Sechs leichte Klaviersonaten* published the same year.

---

[6] *Unterricht,* 85 ff.

Türk's consideration of tempo modification, which is perhaps the most detailed of late eighteenth-century treatments of the subject, provides valuable information about where such things should be applied. He suggested that accelerando could be effective:

1. for the most powerful places 'in pieces which have a character of vehemence, anger, rage, fury and the like';
2. for single motifs 'which are repeated more powerfully (usually higher)';
3. occasionally 'when gentle feelings are interrupted by a lively passage'; or
4. for a passage that should 'unexpectedly arouse a violent emotion'.

He considered that 'tardando' could produce a telling effect

1. in 'exceptionally tender, languishing, sad passages in which the feeling is, so to speak, concentrated on a single point';
2. before certain fermatas 'as if the strength is gradually exhausted';
3. when places 'towards the end of a piece (or section) are marked with *diminuendo*, *diluendo*, *smorzando*, and the like';
4. for lead-in figures, not only when they are written in small notes or explicate 'senza tempo', but also 'when the composer has kept to the normal method of writing a)' (Ex. 11.1); or
5. for 'a delicate idea [*matter Gedanke*] on its repetition b)' as in Ex. 11.2.

He also proposed that an abrupt change of speed could sometimes be appropriate. For instance, a somewhat slower tempo could be adopted

1. for a 'tender, moving passage between two lively, fiery ideas' (his *Sechs leichte Klaviersonaten* provide examples of this kind marked with Türk's special sign ⌐⌐ (Ex. 11.3));

Ex. 11.1. Türk, *Klavierschule*, VI, §69

(*a*)

(*b*)

Ex. 11.2. Türk, *Klavierschule*, VI, §69

Ex. 11.3. Türk, *Sechs leichte Klaviersonaten*, pt. I, 10

2. in general in passages in a slow tempo (this suggestion seems rather vague, but another example from Türk's *Sechs leichte Klaviersonaten* probably indicates the type of passage he had in mind (Ex. 11.4)).

Like Bach, Türk recommended that such things should only be attempted when playing alone 'or with very alert accompanists',[7] and, referring to 'tardando', he stressed that the marked passages should be taken 'imperceptibly a little slower than is required by the tempo', noting that 'many players also observe these signs very carefully, only they make mistakes by not following the instruction. Thus they go from an allegro almost into an adagio, which has a very bad effect'.[8] Türk was clearly in agreement with the general view that although this type of tempo modification was a legitimate, indeed necessary aspect of cultivated performance, it was something to be used occasionally and very judiciously with respect to the degree of modification, except in such things as fantasias, preludes, and caprices, where the notation itself often indicates a requirement for considerable freedom of pulse. However, Türk's

[7] *Klavierschule*, VI, §§65–9.   [8] Ibid. §48.

Ex. 11.4. Türk, *Sechs leichte Klaviersonaten*, pt. I, 22

remarks also imply that, in practice, more extreme modifications of the tempo than would have been approved of by the majority of accomplished musicians were often to be heard. Such things were by no means confined to performances by less experienced or amateur musicians; they were also associated with soloists of distinction and reputation. After a visit to Salzburg by the violinist Janitsch and the cellist J. Reicha, for instance, Leopold Mozart, who had warned against the wilful treatment of tempo in his *Violinschule*,[9] described their playing in a letter to his son, praising many aspects of their performance; but he remarked: 'Both, however, have Becke's fault of dragging the time, holding back the whole orchestra by a wink and by their movement, and then returning to the original tempo.'[10] Since Janitsch and Reicha were both musicians at the Oettingen-Wallerstein court, this suggests the possibility of localized practices, but it seems likely that such habits were and remained widespread.

　Discussion of tempo modification involving alteration of the pulse of the music assumed some prominence in music journals and instruction books in the first few decades of the nineteenth century, suggesting that the appropriateness, or otherwise, of this expressive resource was very much a live issue at that time. The writers were all, more or less, concerned to caution restraint. In the *Allgemeine musikalische Zeitung* of 1804 Friedrich Guthmann considered 'the localized hurrying and hesitating which the player allows himself out of feeling or principle without the composer having clearly indicated it', observing: 'the beat is the means by which we are so much the more freely and better able to express our feelings. It should not, however, inhibit us.' Developing the idea that the performer should be impelled by the emotion of the music, he continued: 'is it to be wondered at if, without himself being aware of it, he gradually hurries or drags? Would it be right, would it make the proper effect if he did not do it . . . (Naturally I am only talking about solo playing and singing.)' But unlike Türk he stopped short of giving detailed information about the sorts of circumstances in which tempo modification might take place, merely

---

[9] See esp. ch. XII, §20.　　[10] Anderson, *The Letters of Mozart*, 455.

remarking that the sensitive musician 'will also, if he only to some extent understands his feelings and knows how to control them, rightly perceive, in the majority of cases, the places where he may deviate from the prescribed tempo—how much and for how long'. He was at pains to point out, however, that a distinction needed to be made between this type of artistically effective flexibility and mere unrhythmicality, asserting: 'Taken as a whole the tempo must always remain constant, even if it constantly deviates in individual places. Where a theme is presented from different angles, one can later on also easily modify the tempo a little according to circumstances without its being specifically suggested.'[11]

Shortly afterwards, G. W. Fink also addressed the issue in the same journal. In a series of articles on dynamic and articulation markings he touched upon the subject of holding back or hurrying the tempo on short phrases, single bars, or individual beats. He observed:

It would be extremely pedantic if anyone were to venture to rob the player of this freedom, which, applied with taste, is able to invest the simplest ideas with a splendid, exalted spirit (as the sensitive singer, Mlle Jagemann, as Sextus in Titus [*La clemenza di Tito*], does at the often repeated words 'That is more than the pains of death'). I treasure and love this manner of performance, just as I and anyone else who is receptive to beauty must treasure and love it. But the finer and tenderer something is, the more it can be spoiled.[12]

And he went on to warn against the over-frequent use of the device which he believed would seriously weaken its effect.

In fact, even allowing for the exaggeration to which writers, trying to make a point, are prone, many sources indicate that around 1800 the habit of soloists indulging in exaggerated changes of tempo within a movement had become endemic to the point where it was beginning to be accepted as normal, at least by a considerable portion of the concert-going public. In 1799 the *Allgemeine musikalische Zeitung*, in its report on a concert given by the horn-playing Brün brothers, felt it worthy of mention as something remarkable that they kept regular time during their concerto performance, noting: 'So, for example, they never beat time—it was also not necessary, for they themselves held the tempo very exactly; therefore they were also so well accompanied, as certainly no ever-so-efficient time beater has been or will be accompanied here.'[13]

More direct evidence is provided by Heinrich Christoph Koch's complaint in his 1802 *Lexikon* that 'people are becoming more and more accustomed to excuse the unrhythmical performance of solo singers and concert players as an insignificant trifle, and make it increasingly into an unconditional duty for the orchestral player to yield to the concert player who now hurries, now holds back the beat'.[14] And at about the same time, referring specifically to pianists,

---

[11] 'Ueber Abweichung vom Takte', *Allgemeine musikalische Zeitung*, 7 (1804–5), 347–9.
[12] Ibid. 11 (1808–9), 230. [13] Vol. 1 (1798–9), 622.
[14] *Musikalisches Lexikon*, art. 'Concert'.

Louis Adam observed: 'Some have made it fashionable not to play in time, and perform every type of music like a fantasia, prelude, or caprice. They believe thus to give more expression to a piece and they change it in such a manner as to make it unrecognizable.'[15] Johann Friedrich Reichardt, too, complained in the pages of the *Berlinische musikalische Zeitung* about wayward timekeeping. This was one of his criticisms of the 21-year-old Spohr's performances in Berlin in 1805.[16] The consequence of Reichardt's criticism in this instance is particularly interesting. Spohr recalled:

I was obliged to confess that[,] yielding to my depth of feeling, I had kept back in the Cantabile, perhaps, too much, and in the Passages and more impassioned parts[,] carried away by my youthful fire, I had precipitated them too much. I therefore determined to correct such blemishes in my execution without diminishing its force of expression, and by unremitting attention I succeeded.[17]

As accounts of his playing together with the instructions he gave in his *Violinschule* show, he became a powerful opponent of exaggerated modification of tempo. Other soloists, however, continued their errant ways, apparently in considerable numbers. In 1807, the reviewer of some fugal quartets by Gassmann and Monn, commenting that fugues above all require a very strict observance of the beat, digressed to remark:

Now, however, it is known that the majority of those musicians who particularly dedicate themselves to the performance of solo parts have for a long time dealt very wilfully with the tempo, and that they are ever more inclined to shake off the yoke of the beat. However, it is absolutely inappropriate in the performance of fugue to justify the wavering back and forth of the tempo, which is offensive to every uncorrupted feeling and cultured ear, with the indeed customary but very unsustainable gloss that a perfected expression is thereby obtained.[18]

To this statement the editor, Friedrich Rochlitz, appended a comment in which, having averred that in his opinion the now widespread habit had arisen simply from careless self-indulgence during private practice, he stated:

The pretence that the expression might gain from holding back or pushing forward the tempo, is, except in very rare cases, nothing more than a pretence, intended only to throw sand in the eyes of the listeners and make it necessary for the accompanists to give way, so that, if all the parts do not give way at one and the same moment, which in many cases is not possible, one can blame the error against the beat, which is one's own fault, on the accompaniment. Unfortunately fashion still continues to allow this to the singer or solo player; unfortunately the result of this is that the performance of orchestral parts becomes ever more discredited, and the consequence of this usual procedure is that the orchestral players are often insulted in public music-making to the point of an offence against their sense of honour. Are authorities against this misuse required? Well then: Mozart played to

---

[15] *Méthode*, 160.   [16] Vol. 1 (1805), 95.
[17] *Louis Spohr's Autobiography* (London, 1865), 80–1.
[18] *Allgemeine musikalische Zeitung*, 10 (1807–8), 438–9.

a nicety in time, Ph. Em. Bach did it likewise, and Clementi, Romberg, and Rode still do it! . . . Although there may occasionally be a few places in a solo part which, through a somewhat increased or decreased rapidity of movement, are not merely apparently but also actually able to gain in respect of the expression: at least in these the case cannot by far be so frequent, or by far so bad, as when such a so-called piquant solo player deviates from the beat; and a sudden holding back and pulling out, a sudden alteration of the tempo, perhaps to the extent of a third, if not a half of the measure, as one now not infrequently hears, definitely can and may absolutely never and nowhere be tolerated.[19]

There can be little doubt that despite the constant warnings from respected authorities about the dangers of excessive tempo modification, and the examples of many leading performers such as Hummel and Spohr, an ever-increasing number of solo players and singers went far beyond what these musicians would have regarded as tasteful. By the 1830s there are signs that, as Koch had feared a generation earlier, this sort of thing had become so general that it was perceived by the public as the norm. In 1833 J. Feski observed:

Ritardando and accelerando alternate all the time. This manner has already become so fixed in the minds of the musical public that they firmly believe a diminuendo must be slowed down and a crescendo speeded up; a tender phrase (e.g. in an allegro) will be performed more slowly, a powerful one faster. At times this kind of treatment may well be applicable; but how to determine where requires very deep insight into the composition and very correct feeling. Furthermore, the compositions of the older composers tolerate this type of treatment extremely rarely, and the newer ones are well enough endowed with markings of this kind! In these, on the other hand, one misses the exalted calm, in which the older composers distinguished themselves.[20]

A few years later, Czerny, employing the term 'tempo rubato' in the looser sense that was by that time accepted in common parlance, complained: '*tempo rubato*, (that is the arbitrary retardation or quickening of the degree of movement) is now often employed even to caricature', and he noted that in playing the first movement of a Hummel concerto many soloists alternate allegro for the first subject with andante for the second and presto for the concluding section, 'whilst Hummel himself performed his compositions in such strict time, that we might nearly always have let the metronome beat time to his playing'.[21] Similar remarks were made about Mendelssohn's playing. As Sir George Grove explained:

Strict time was one of his hobbies. He alludes to it, with an eye to the sins of Hiller and Chopin, in a letter of May 23, 1834, and somewhere else speaks of 'nice strict *tempo*' as something particularly pleasant. After introducing some *rallentandos* in conducting the introduction to Beethoven's second symphony, he excused himself by saying that 'one could not always be good,'* and that he had felt the inclination too strongly to resist it. In playing, however, he never himself interpolated a *ritardando* or suffered it in anyone else.** It

---

[19] *Allgemeine musikalische Zeitung*, 10 (1807–8), 439.   [20] *Caecilia*, 15 (1833), 270.
[21] *Piano Forte School: Second Supplement*, 29.

specially enraged him when done at the end of a song or other piece. 'Es steht nicht da!' ['It is not there'] he would say; 'if it were intended it would be written in—they think it expression, but it is sheer affectation.'***[22]

* Kellow Pye.
** Hans von Bülow.
*** Mrs Moscheles and W. S. Rockstro.

Despite such accounts and Rochlitz's references to C. P. E. Bach, Mozart, Rode, and Clementi playing strictly in time, it is undoubtedly mistaken to believe that it would really have been possible to let the metronome beat time to their playing. Czerny's assertion is contradicted by Hummel himself, who clearly supported the idea of tempo flexibility as a concomitant of sensitive performance, observing: 'Many persons still erroneously imagine, that, in applying the metronome, they are bound to follow its equal and undeviating motion throughout the whole piece, without allowing themselves any latitude in the performance for the display of taste or feeling.'[23] Yet numerous accounts of his playing leave no doubt that his own use of the resource was exceedingly subtle and unobtrusive. The same could surely have been said of Mendelssohn, Spohr, and all those musicians, such as Joseph Joachim and Johannes Brahms, who, throughout the century, represented the 'classical' approach to flexibility of tempo.

Before considering the growing influence of the opposite approach, in theory as well as practice, it will be helpful to consider the circumstances in which some early nineteenth-century musicians regarded discreet tempo modification as appropriate and effective. Though nineteenth-century writers constantly mentioned the importance of knowing where, how, and to what extent tempo modification should be introduced, most recognized that such things could only be dictated by the sensitivity of a cultivated musician, and few attempted to give detailed instructions. Among those who did offer more specific advice was Crelle (1823). Having stated that 'An exact and strictly measured tempo is an essential aspect of music', he went on to identify a number of situations in which a degree of speeding up and slowing down might be appropriate. He linked this to some extent with articulation and accent markings. After describing the three principal categories of strokes, dots, and dots under slurs, and explaining the extent to which these affected the length of the note (in the same terms as Adam), he observed: 'Apart from this, however, these signs also have significance for the tempo of performance. The staccato [i.e. '] hurries rather than drags. In the case of notes with dots, however, this is rather reversed and even more so if the dots are under slurs.' He further observed that all 'strengthened' notes do not hurry and, discussing phrasing, advised: 'as a rule, the beginning of a musical unit commences powerfully and importantly,

---

[22] *Dictionary*, art. 'Mendelssohn', ii. 299.   [23] *A Complete*, iii. 65.

the middle carries on in a measured and regular manner and the end increases in speed and decreases in power'.[24]

Crelle's recommendations for expressive performance have much in common with those provided by Kalkbrenner, but rather than giving a general instruction that the ends of phrases should hurry, Kalkbrenner prescribed that 'all terminations of cantabile phrases should be retarded', and he added that 'when a frequent change of harmony occurs, or modulations succeed each other rapidly the movement must be retarded'. This agrees essentially with Crelle's comment that strengthened notes do not hurry, for Kalkbrenner also restated the traditional view that 'all notes foreign to the key, and those which bear accidentals, should be well marked'.[25] Czerny, with characteristic thoroughness, gave a much fuller list of circumstances that invite a modification of the tempo, though his analysis is less exhaustive than Türk's. He stated that a ritardando or rallentando is used:

1. on the return of the principal subject;
2. when we separate a phrase from the melody;
3. on long notes strongly accented;
4. in the transition to a different time;
5. after a pause;
6. on the diminuendo of a quick lively passage;
7. where the ornamental notes cannot be played 'a tempo giusto';
8. in a well-marked crescendo serving as introduction or wind-up to an important passage;
9. in passages where the composer or performer gives free play to his fancy;
10. when the composer marks the passage 'espressivo';
11. at the end of a trill or cadence.

He also observed that an accelerando is required in an ascending phrase, and implies passion and agitation. In addition he noted that the words 'calando', 'smorzando', and so on are also used for ritardando.[26]

At about the same time as Czerny's piano method appeared in print, Anton Schindler published very different views on the subject of tempo. Schindler, whose desire to be seen as the only true disciple of Beethoven made him intensely jealous of those whose claims to know and understand Beethoven were better than his own, criticized Czerny's notion of tempo indirectly. He attacked not only Czerny's recommendations for absolute tempos (i.e. his metronome marks for the sonatas[27]) but also his attitude towards flexibility of tempo.[28] In his discussion of the proper performance style for Beethoven's

---

[24] *Einiges*, 61.   [25] *Méthode*, 12.   [26] *Pianoforte School,* iii. 21.
[27] *Biographie von Ludwig van Beethoven*, 216.
[28] For a thoughtful discussion of the conflicting approaches of Czerny and Schindler, see Rosenblum, *Performance Practices*, 387 ff.

music, Schindler was perhaps the most insistent advocate of substantial tempo modification in the first half of the nineteenth century.

The reliability of his claims about Beethoven's intentions and his own quality as a musician have been seriously and convincingly brought into question.[29] He claimed (and provided 'evidence' for his claims by forging entries in Beethoven's conversation books) that Beethoven had adopted a new 'manner of performance in the first years of the Third Period of his life, and that it totally departed from his earlier, less nuanced one'.[30] He promulgated the notion of 'two principles' for contrasting 'subjects' within a movement, which affected the performance style (including tempo) of the passages concerned. Schindler summed these up, in the case of the first movement of the Piano Sonata op. 14 no. 2 for instance, as an interaction between a 'pleading' (*bittende*) one and a 'resisting' (*widerstrebende*) one. Despite their unreliability as evidence of Beethoven's own practice or intentions, Schindler's comments undoubtedly reflect an aspect of musical performance in his lifetime that was rapidly gaining ground among prestigious and influential musicians. Far greater musicians than he, such as Franz Liszt, were powerful practical advocates of such an approach; but there can be little doubt that Schindler's testimony that this approach had been sanctioned by Beethoven, suspect though it might be, may well have facilitated a more widespread acceptance of its orthodoxy. Furthermore, it does not seem beyond the bounds of possibility that Richard Wagner's ideas about tempo modification were directly influenced by what Schindler had to say about Beethoven, particularly with respect to his orchestral music (which is considered further below).

The growing influence of the ideas promulgated by Schindler can be seen, a generation later than Czerny and Schindler, in the writings of the Swiss musician Mathis Lussy (who worked principally in Paris). Lussy referred directly to Czerny's instructions, objecting that they were both vague and misleading, and his discussion of tempo modification seems to reflect the shift of emphasis towards a more obtrusive use of this resource. His comments explicitly identify rhythmic flexibility and tempo modification with expressive performance. However, they also indicate that there were still musicians who chose to use this resource very sparingly. He observed that two schools existed, the tone of his comments leaving no doubt as to his own allegiance:

One demands a uniform rate of time, without *accelerando* or *ritardando*; the other, on the contrary, is accustomed to quicken and slacken with every rhythm, every change. The first

---

[29] See e.g. Dagmar Beck and Grita Herre, 'Einige Zweifel an der Überlieferung der Konversationshefte', in Harry Goldschmidt, Karl-Heinz Köhler, and Konrad Niemann, eds., *Bericht über den Internationalen Beethoven-Kongress . . . 1977 in Berlin* (Leipzig, 1978), 257–74, and also Peter Stadlen, 'Schindler's Beethoven Forgeries', *Musical Times*, 118 (1977), 551, and id., 'Schindler and the Conversation Books', *Soundings*, 7 (1978), 2–18.

[30] *Biographie von Ludwig van Beethoven*, 228.

regards regular and mechanical precision as the height of perfection; the second will alter the time at every phrase, and will not feel anything objectionable in the constant irregularity. Now we have observed that the warmest partisans of the uniform and regular rate of time are precisely those who have no feeling for expression.

He went on to admit, however, that not every piece required or tolerated the same degree of tempo modification:

In Prestos, Allegros, Galops Valses etc. it seems natural to keep up a uniform rate, only slackening with the loss of power and impetus, or when there is an evident change of structure. And in slow impressive pieces, such as Nocturnes, Rondos, Reveries, Andantes, Adagios, Romances etc. it seems equally natural to modify the time. In such pieces there should be *accelerandos* and *ritardandos* according to every change of feeling, and whenever the expressive structure of the phrases, or their motion up or down seems to require them.[31]

It is clear from these accounts that there was a well-recognized distinction between the slight flexibility that was always intended to be present in a sensitive performance, and more major disturbances of the rhythmic flow, such as pronounced rallentandos at the ends of sections and perceptible alternation of slower and faster tempos within a single movement. As Lussy's comments indicate, there was also seen to be a difference between various genres of music. Perhaps more importantly, the development of a repertoire that contained an increasing proportion of established masterpieces from different periods and traditions, and (particularly after the establishment of the railways from the 1840s) the increasing internationalization of musical culture, fostered the growth of stylistic awareness and the recognition that different kinds of music required different approaches. Thus, with respect to tempo modification, García observed that 'The compositions of Mozart, Cimarosa, Rossini &c., demand great exactitude in their rhythmic movements,' but he also remarked: 'Donizetti's music—and above all Bellini's contains a great number of passages, which without indications either of rallentando or accelerando, require both to be employed.'[32]

The discussion so far has been concerned largely with solo playing and singing. It seems to have been understood, however, that the same principles applied to a considerable extent to playing in small ensembles, especially in passages where an individual instrument was to the fore. Spohr, for instance, cautioned the second violinist in a quartet to be careful to follow 'the slight changes of time which the first violinist may possibly introduce'.[33] And accounts of performances by the Schuppanzigh Quartet suggest that they employed some degree of tempo modification as an expressive resource.[34]

---

[31] *Musical Expression*, 163.   [32] *New Treatise*, 50.   [33] *Violin School*, 233.
[34] Schindler, *Biographie von Ludwig van Beethoven*, 242. (Although Schuppanzigh himself had died in 1830 it seems unlikely that this statement can have been entirely groundless, since other members of the quartet were still alive and there would still have been many in 1840 who would have remembered their performances.)

Naturally, the individual string player in an orchestra could not modify the time at will. Many eighteenth-century and early nineteenth-century writers specifically made the obvious point that such things were completely out of the question in orchestral music, though in accompanying a concerto it might become necessary. Reichardt instructed that 'it is the orchestral player's duty to keep in the most exact manner to the tempo once it has been set by the leader'.[35]

Some degree of tempo modification in orchestral performance, if adequate rehearsal time were available and the direction efficient, would certainly not have been unacceptable in principle; but on the whole, it seems that in performances of purely orchestral music during the late eighteenth century and early nineteenth century little use of unwritten rallentando or accelerando was envisaged, since the necessary conditions were rarely present. In the first place, the repertoire of most eighteenth-century and early nineteenth-century orchestras consisted of new or unfamiliar music, which they generally had to perform after minimum rehearsal. Thus Reichardt stressed the necessity for the orchestral violinist to be a good sight-reader, and for the same reason Anton Reicha recommended that in orchestral pieces the composer should not write anything higher than f''' for the violins.[36] Furthermore, the absence of a conductor in purely orchestral music and the customary divided direction in the theatre (the maestro al cembalo or Kapellmeister being concerned with the singers and the first violinist with the orchestra) militated against controlled manipulation of the beat for interpretative purposes. This situation persisted well into the nineteenth century in many places; direction by an independent time-beater in purely orchestral music at the Gewandhaus concerts in Leipzig, for instance, did not become usual until Mendelssohn's advent in 1834. The most that is likely to have been expected in these circumstances is a degree of discreet tempo rubato, in the strict sense discussed below, where individual wind instruments had genuine solo passages. (There is some suggestion that Beethoven encouraged this in performances of his orchestral music.)

Nevertheless, in accompanying a singer or instrumental soloist, even without a conductor, there must often have been occasion to modify the tempo. That this frequently caused serious ensemble problems is suggested by many comments (for instance Rochlitz's, above), but there is evidence that in rare circumstances, with a highly trained orchestra, it could be very successful. A visitor to Vienna in 1790 observed of the opera orchestra at the Hoftheater: 'Such order rules here, such a rare unanimity of ensemble, depending not merely on the beat, and such an equal and unanimous feeling in the subtleties of expression, that no orchestra in Europe, even though it might surpass it in detail,

---

[35] *Ueber die Pflichten*, 78.

[36] *Cours de composition musicale*, trans. and ed. Carl Czerny as *Vollständiges Lehrbuch der musikalischen Composition* (with parallel Fr. and Ger. text) (Vienna, 1834), i. 3, 303.

surpasses it as a whole.'[37] After discussing the relative merits and demerits of the orchestras in London, Paris, Naples, and Munich, he described the marvellous flexibility of the orchestra in a performance of Salieri's *Axur*, during which he observed:

a manner and method of expressing the dying fall of passion which were till then unknown to me. As the storm of passion gradually sank to exhaustion and the most violent agitation gave way to milder feelings, so the orchestra allowed the beat to relax in the most perfect accord with the singers and the melodies to ebb away more and more slowly, as the mood was intended to become more and more gentle. When the passion grew again, so the pulse became more impetuous and emphatic, and they also accelerated the flow of the melody with rare unanimity of ensemble. [38]

The rarity of this type of performance is evident from the fact that this experienced and musically aware traveller considered it to be exceptional; but, theoretically at least, a good eighteenth-century orchestra must have been expected to follow a soloist's deviations from strict tempo, if only to avoid an embarrassing breakdown in the performance.

It seems possible that an expectation of controlled tempo flexibility in orchestral playing, not only to follow a soloist, may have been growing during the early nineteenth century. Weber was concerned that his metronome marks for *Euryanthe* should not induce the conductor to keep rigidly to an unvarying beat. In his accompanying instructions he was explicit about his requirement for real modification of the tempo:

The beat (the tempo) should not be a tyrannical and inhibiting one, or a driving mill-hammer, it must rather be to the piece of music what the pulse beat is to the life of mankind. There is no slow tempo in which passages might not occur that encourage a quicker pace in order to combat the feeling of dragging.—There is no presto which does not also in contrast require calm performance in some passages, in order not to take away the means of expression through excessive hurrying.[39]

And a couple of years later Lichtenthal observed in the article on the metronome in his *Dizionario*: 'If the beat is always kept with an extreme exactness, a perfect ensemble is necessarily achieved. But such a symmetrical and square performance lacks magic. One should deck the yoke that is imposed on the beat with flowers, and from time to time free oneself from it with felicitous licence.'[40] A few years later Spohr, discussing the duty of the orchestral violinist, remarked:

The timing of the several members of the bar according to their duration, must, in orchestral playing be strict in the extreme, or unity could not possibly exist among the performers. Consequently, the *tempo rubato*, (that is tarrying upon one or more notes,) which in solo playing is frequently productive of great effect, cannot here be permitted.

[37] Anon., *Reise nach Wien* (Hof, 1795), 253.   [38] Ibid. 256.
[39] Quoted in Jähns, *Carl Maria von Weber*, 374.   [40] Art. 'Metronomo'.

However, he certainly did not exclude the possibility of a certain amount of tempo modification by the director of the orchestra, for he also noted:

With respect to the time or degree of movement, the orchestral player must be guided entirely by the conductor, whether he leads or simply wields the baton. It is also his duty frequently to cast a glance at him, in order that he may not only remain true to the time, but also immediately fall in with any retardation or acceleration of it.

Regarding the orchestral accompaniment of a soloist, he instructed: 'The accompanist must be careful not to hurry or retard the solo player, though he must instantly follow the latter whenever he slightly deviates from the time.'[41]

Since Spohr was among those who favoured a very restrained approach to tempo modification in general, and since he was in any case among the earliest effective baton conductors, there will have been no significant discrepancy between what he sought to achieve as a soloist and as a conductor, though naturally the minute subtleties of expression that he aimed for in the one could not be attained in the other. In the case of a musician like Liszt, however, whose solo performances involved much greater and more pervasive manipulation of the tempo, the conventional orchestral performance in the first half of the nineteenth century, which allowed little flexibility, must have seemed far from satisfactory. It is surely this kind of thing that lies behind his statements in the preface to his symphonic poems about freeing performance from the 'mechanical, fragmented up and down playing, tied to the bar-line'.[42] The difference between his approach and Spohr's is nicely suggested by their very different styles of conducting, which must have made a striking contrast when they were joint conductors of the great Beethoven Festival at Bonn in 1845. Spohr was noted for his extremely calm and dignified presence on the rostrum but Sir George Smart, in his diary of the festival, referred to Liszt as conducting 'with much twisting of the person'.[43]

The gradual development of conducting technique during the early nineteenth century did not immediately encourage conductors to manage their orchestras as the more wilful soloists managed their instruments. Many musicians continued to believe that the ideal in orchestral performance was steady maintenance of the tempo throughout a movement with only, perhaps, the subtlest of nuances at important points. A writer, probably Schumann, in the *Neue Zeitschrift für Musik* of 1836 recommended that a conductor should only beat at the beginning of a movement or at tempo changes, though he conceded that it might be helpful to beat regularly in very slow tempos.[44] This seems to have been close to the practice adopted by Mendelssohn, and under the general conditions of rehearsal and performance at that time it certainly ruled out any frequent or substantial modification of tempo. Mendelssohn was particularly

---

[41] *Violin School*, 234.   [42] *Liszts Symphonische Dichtungen.*
[43] Smart Papers, British Library, London, Dept. of Manuscripts, vi, 16.   [44] Vol. 4 (1836), 129.

noted for his regularity of tempo (any deviation from which, as the quotation cited earlier indicates, he regarded as a scarcely excusable indulgence).

In 1840 Schindler conceded that 'it goes without saying that in orchestral music in general it is not permissible [he seems really to mean 'practicable'] to change the tempo so often as in chamber music',[45] but he went on to suggest that a much greater degree of tempo modification was appropriate in the performance of Beethoven's symphonies than had hitherto been the case. He argued that the tradition of 'in tempo' performance, which he could not deny to have been prevalent in Beethoven's Vienna, was simply a consequence of circumstances; that, if Beethoven could have had his own orchestra for unlimited rehearsal, he would certainly have wanted the symphonies performed in a more flexible manner.[46] Schindler's specific suggestions, purportedly coming from Beethoven himself, are interesting because they prefigure the kind of treatment that Wagner and his disciples were later to give to the symphonies, in the belief that this was what the composer had really wanted. In the 'Eroica', for instance, Schindler claimed that the passage beginning at bar 83 of the first movement should be played somewhat more slowly until the following *pp* (Ex. 11.5), where 'by means of a gently held accelerando it hurries into the original tempo of the movement, which is finally attained with the phrase in B flat major *f*'.[47] Most notably, he attributed to Beethoven the expression 'thus fate knocks at the door' as an explanation of the opening gesture of the Fifth Symphony, and claimed that at each of its appearances it should be much slower than the rest: '♩ = 126, approximately an Andante con moto'.[48] His most elaborate example of tempo modification in the symphonies, however, is the Larghetto of the Second Symphony; this gives a clear idea of the extent to which Schindler believed such flexibility of tempo was apposite (Ex. 11.6).

Ex. 11.5. Beethoven, 'Eroica' Symphony op. 55/i, in Schindler, *Biographie von Ludwig van Beethoven*, 239

[45] *Biographie von Ludwig van Beethoven*, 235.   [46] Ibid. 242–3.   [47] Ibid. 239.
[48] Ibid. 241.

Ex. 11.6. Beethoven, Second Symphony op. 36/ii, in Schindler, *Biographie von Ludwig van Beethoven*, 237

Wagner, too, looking back on his youth, observed in 1869 that 'modification of tempo' was 'not merely entirely unknown to our conductors but, precisely because of that ignorance, treated with foolishly dismissive contempt'.[49] He later remarked that it was not surprising that Beethoven's 'Eroica' Symphony made a poor impression when played in strict time by the pupils at the Prague

---

[49] 'Ueber das Dirigieren', *Gesammelte Schriften*, viii. 287.

Conservatoire under Dionys Weber; observing that at that time 'it was nowhere played any differently',[50] he argued that it was only when the symphony was played on the piano with the proper flexibility of tempo that people began to appreciate the true import of the music. Wagner regarded each section of a movement as having its own appropriate tempo, and believed that the fundamental adagio element in lyrical melody should be emphasized. He claimed that he only expected this to take place in a discreet manner, but accounts of performances conducted by him suggest that, in fact, his modifications of tempo were quite extreme. During his conductorship of the Philharmonic Society in London in 1855 one of the most frequent complaints against him concerned his distortion of tempo. Henry Chorley described Wagner's conducting of a Beethoven symphony as 'full of . . . ill measured rallentandos',[51] while Henry Smart objected to his tempos in every respect, saying:

Firstly he takes all quick movements faster than anybody else; secondly he takes all slow movements slower than anybody else; thirdly he prefaces the entry of an important point, or the return of a theme—especially in a slow movement—by an exaggerated ritardando; and fourthly, he reduces the speed of an allegro—say in an overture or the first movement—fully one-third, immediately on the entrance of its cantabile phrases.[52]

In Wagner's own later works frequent changes and modifications of tempo are specified in the score, though there is no reason to think that these are the only places where flexibility is permissible or desirable. Porges records, for instance, that in *Siegfried*, Act I, Scene i, Wagner asked for a rallentando, not marked in the score, to round off the scene.[53] With regard to tempo Wagner trusted the instincts of the conductor who was in tune with his general principles and with the dramatic meaning of his music. He abandoned the practice of including metronome marks after *Tannhäuser*, largely because he believed that things would be in a sorry state 'if conductor and singers are to be dependent on metronome marks alone' and that 'They will hit upon the right tempo only when they begin to feel a lively sympathy with the dramatic and musical situations and when that understanding allows them to find the tempo as though it were something self-evident, something that did not require any further searching on their part.'[54] He himself was capable of taking the same music at considerably different tempos in response to the dramatic mood of the moment.

The fundamental difference here was that this practice, which had previously been confined to solo performances, small ensembles, and orchestral performances involving a soloist, was on the way to becoming established, through the medium of the virtuoso conductor, as a legitimate and admired

---

[50] 'Ueber das Dirigieren', *Gesammelte Schriften*, viii. 296.   [51] *Athenaeum*, 28 (1855), 329.

[52] *Sunday Times* (17 June 1855), 3.   [53] *Die Bühnenproben*, 82 n. 21.

[54] 'Ueber die Aufführung des Tannhäuser', *Gesammelte Schriften*, v. 144.

aspect of purely orchestral performance. Wagner's tremendous prestige and the influence of his writings in the second half of the century, together with the adulation accorded to his aesthetic ally Liszt, legitimized and encouraged, indeed glamorized, an approach to tempo modification that had previously been resisted by most musical authorities. A particularly clear and informative account of the change that took place in the second half of the nineteenth century is contained in Heinrich Ehrlich's record of a discussion with the 84-year-old Verdi in 1897. In reply to Verdi's enquiries about the 'new school of German conductors', Ehrlich replied that they

are orchestral virtuosi, highly gifted, with a thorough musical education; the instrument they play is the orchestra and they have developed its technique to an extent hitherto unknown and impose their individual interpretations on a great variety of works. They are the precise opposite of the conductors of former generations, whose overriding concern was to play everything accurately and scrupulously in time. This endeavour led with rare exceptions to mechanical routine. Operas and symphonies were sung and performed correctly; the most popular singers were allowed to take liberties with the tempi, but the conductor resisted their temptations. Today the opposite applies. The young conductors, who all follow Richard Wagner's example and teachings, do not hesitate to change the tempo of an aria or any piece of music, according to how they see fit . . . They make the most intensive and detailed study of operas and orchestral works, and are able to throw into bold relief, in the most masterly fashion, beautiful and interesting moments that until then have gone unnoticed, and thus obtain remarkable effects . . . yet during their performances of orchestral works the audience will often attend more to the orchestra's virtuosity and the conductor's individuality than the sequence of ideas in the work itself.[55]

Verdi concurred, and remarked that after hearing a virtuoso performance of Beethoven's First Symphony in Paris he had similarly felt that

everything sounded so beautiful, that sometimes you only seemed to hear the sound and not the composition itself—and it occurred to me that the essence of the work of art was more obscured than emphasised. Moreover, what you were just telling me about German conductors and their arbitrary treatment of tempi—that is beginning to spread rapidly in Italy too; it is almost comic to observe how many of our young conductors endeavour to change the tempo every ten bars or introduce completely new nuances into every insignificant aria or concert piece.[56]

The consequences of the new orthodoxy can be heard in early recordings, for instance Nikisch's interpretation in 1913 of Beethoven's Fifth Symphony with the Berlin Philharmonic Orchestra, and in many performances by Fürtwängler, Mengelberg, and others recorded during the first half of the twentieth century.

---

[55] Ehrlich, 'Beim 84jährigen Verdi', *Deutsche Revue* (Stuttgart), 22/2 (1897), 325 ff., quoted in Conati, *Interviews and Encounters with Verdi*, 294–5.
[56] Ibid.

Modification over a Steady Beat

During the nineteenth century, the gradual acceptance of tempo modification that necessitated an alteration of the basic pulse led to decreasing emphasis on the types of tempo rubato that were obtained without disturbance of the beat. Many eighteenth-century and early nineteenth-century accounts, however, show the extent to which, until at least the 1830s, tempo rubato in its various forms was still widely regarded as the principal legitimate method of bending the tempo. Some writers, even in the early nineteenth century, seem not to have recognized any other kind of tempo modification as permissible. Tempo rubato could apply to a single note or small group of notes that were slightly longer or shorter than their written length, and in this sense, as an almost imperceptible flexibility, it was present for much of the time in the performance of a sensitive musician. But tempo rubato seems often to have been understood to mean a more radical reorganization of the note values, a redistribution of accentuation, or even the addition of rhythmically free embellishment, any of which could be introduced in particular passages as a special effect. Tempo rubato, under the name 'rubamento di tempo', was explained by Pier Francesco Tosi's translator, J. E. Galliard, in 1742 as 'when the Bass goes an exactly regular Pace, the other Part retards or anticipates in a singular Manner, for the Sake of Expression, but after a Time return to its Exactness, to be guided by the Bass'.[57] Many other eighteenth-century writers, including Leopold Mozart, elaborated on this manner of 'postponing or anticipating the notes' against a steady accompaniment. Leopold Mozart, apparently referring primarily to note redistribution, remarked that an effective tempo rubato was 'more easily demonstrated than described'.[58]

J. A. P. Schulz's discussion of the subject in the 1770s provides a good example of the view, widespread in the late eighteenth century, that this was the most artistic manner of obtaining flexibility of tempo in performance, though it also confirms that real alteration of the pulse was often encountered. Schulz observed:

Singers and players often introduce a holding-back or a pressing-forward [*Verzögerungen oder Voreilungen*] which the composer has not marked, and they are certainly often of very good effect. But whoever does this must have an adequate knowledge of harmony, so that he does not go against the rules of strict composition. In addition one must be aware whether the other accompanying parts allow such alterations in the movement. If the violins or flutes accompany the principal part in unison, it can neither delay nor hurry, since it would only make seconds with the other parts.

---

[57] Tosi, *Opinioni de' cantori antici e moderni, o sieno Osservazioni sopra il canto figurato* (Bologna, 1723), trans. and ed. Galliard as *Observations on the Florid Song; or, Sentiments on the Ancient and Modern Singers* (London, 1742), 156 n. 41.

[58] *Versuch*, XII, §20.

One should not confuse the so-called dragging and hurrying [*Schleppen und Eilen*], which results from a real lack of feeling for the true tempo, with the appropriate and expressive holding-back and pressing-forward; for these are real and serious errors, which ruin the whole harmony of a piece.[59]

Some musical authorities continued to take a very hard line on the matter into the nineteenth century, requiring an extremely restrained approach. In 1804 Louis Adam, for instance, wrote:

One of the first qualities that is required in musical performance is to observe the beat; without this there would be nothing but indecision, vagueness, and confusion. It is necessary, therefore, that the pupil habituates himself to play exactly in time and endeavours to keep the same tempo from beginning to end of a piece. It is not permissible to alter the beat unless the composer has indicated it or the expression demands it; still it is necessary to be very sparing of this resource. . . . Doubtless expression requires that one holds back or hurries certain notes in the melody, but these rallentandos should not be continual throughout a piece, but only in those places where the expression of a languid melody or the passion of an agitated melody requires a rallentando or a more animated tempo. In this case it is the melody which must be changed and the bass should strictly mark the beat.[60]

Thus Adam qualified his limited acceptance of tempo modification where 'the expression demands it', but where the composer had not specified it; he required it to take place within the framework of a stable tempo, that is, as tempo rubato in the strictest sense of the term.

A somewhat more relaxed attitude, which nevertheless indicates that the basic pulse was expected to remain more or less constant, can be found in a Viennese reissue, much altered and expanded, of Leopold Mozart's *Violinschule*, published in Vienna in 1805. The writer commented:

An appropriate hurrying and holding-back is a helpful adjunct of expression, if it is applied with taste and in the right place. In order to strengthen the effect of his playing it may be permissible that the solo player perform the lyrical passages in his piece somewhat slower, but seeks to give the passagework more life and strength through a slight hurrying of the tempo. We are only talking, however, about a small, imperceptible alteration of the tempo. What is even more permissible, however, for the sake of expression and is often of very beautiful effect, is a slight alteration of the individual beats without displacing the bar as a whole. The player may dwell somewhat longer than written on the most important, emphatic notes; the thus modified time is regained by hurrying on the following notes. It is understood that also this expressive hesitating and hurrying must be introduced rarely and with taste. It is no more permissible for it really to displace the beat than it is for it to confuse the [musical] ideas. Finally, it should not occur too often, so that it does not degenerate into an affectation and lose its effect.[61]

---

[59] In Sulzer, *Allgemeine Theorie*, 2nd edn. iv. 685.   [60] *Méthode*, 160.
[61] Anon., *Violinschule oder Anweisung die Violine zu spielen von Leopold Mozart. Neue umgearbeitete und vermehrte Ausgabe* (Vienna, [*c*.1805]), 75.

Türk had stressed the necessity of employing this kind of expressive lingering as an adjunct of fine performance, cautioning: 'It is understood that the following note loses as much of its value as the accented note receives from it.'[62] His explanation of the circumstances in which its introduction might be appropriate is similar to his discussion of expressive accent. The correspondence between Türk's rules for the employment of expressive lingering and those usually given for the application of accent indicate their relationship, which has already been discussed in Chapter 2.

Ex. 11.7. Rode, Third Caprice, in Joachim and Moser, *Violinschule*, iii. 7

A generation later, Spohr in his *Violinschule* described this type of expressive lingering in his explanation of how Rode's Seventh Concerto should be performed (see Ex. 12.10). A similar procedure is evidently intended to be applied, probably together with vibrato, in many of Rode's own caprices in instances where he marks notes with the sign <>; the passage from Rode's Third Caprice shown in Ex. 11.7, was analysed and described thus in the Joachim and Moser *Violinschule*:

Here the vibrato necessitates not only a slight lingering on the notes marked <>, but the bow should also support the vibration by a soft pressure on the string. The time lost on the vibrated note must be regained from the notes that follow, so that the proceeding takes place without in any way interrupting the rhythmic flow of the passage.[63]

Joachim's own recorded performances show that, along with more obtrusive modifications of tempo, he continued to employ this type of tempo rubato. Indeed, even in the later nineteenth century many writers who discussed expressive lingering, both on notes and rests, emphasized the necessity of regaining the lost time. But in practice there were undoubtedly many instances where a real disturbance of the beat would have occurred, and this seems increasingly to have been envisaged during the course of the nineteenth century.

Tempo rubato could, however, involve a more radical redistribution of the note values during an extended passage. In its most straightforward form this might amount to little more than simple syncopation, and it is shown thus by, among others, Marpurg, Agricola, Hiller, Lasser, Koch, and Türk. Koch and Türk elaborated the idea of tempo rubato as being more or less confined to a

---

[62] *Klavierschule*, VI, §18.   [63] Pt. iii. 7.

kind of regular cross-rhythm or displacement of the metrical accent, and as such it came to be regarded primarily as a resource for the composer. Indeed, Koch declared in 1808 that the improvisatory tempo rubato was as good as obsolete, and that where it was still used it was much more unobtrusively employed than formerly. He suggested that this development was no bad thing:

partly because modern composers work out in full the adagio movements of their concertos, not at all representing them only as skeletons like the old composers who left their elaboration to the solo player; partly and especially also because the quest for imitation easily oversteps the bounds beyond which this type of performance sinks into ridiculousness and nonsense.[64]

In fact, however, many performers of Koch's generation and younger continued to advocate and employ tempo rubato, though always with the proviso that it should be tastefully and sparingly introduced. Two years after the publication of Koch's article the veteran singer Domenico Corri issued *The Singer's Preceptor* in which he observed that tempo rubato

is a detraction of part of a time from one note, and restoring it by increasing the length of another, or vice versa; so that whilst a singer is, in some measure, singing ad libitum, the orchestra, which accompanies him keeps the time firmly and regularly. Composers seem to have arranged their works in such a manner as to admit of this liberty, without offending the laws of harmony: one caution, however, becomes highly necessary; namely that this grace, or licence, is to be used with moderation and discretion, in order to avoid confusion; for too frequent a use of Tempo Rubato, may produce *Tempo indiavolato*.[65]

Spohr, in his 1832 *Violinschule*, did not give any specific examples of tempo rubato except the lingering on a single note, mentioned above, but various comments suggest that he might have envisaged a more elaborate employment of it; he warned the orchestral player, for instance, that when accompanying a soloist he 'must instantly follow the latter whenever he slightly deviates from the time. This, however, does not apply to the *tempo rubato* of the soloist, during which, the accompaniment must continue its steady, measured course.'[66]

Shortly afterwards Baillot described Viotti's tempo rubato (which he called *temps dérobé*) and attempted to notate two examples of his use of it, warning, however, that 'Up to a certain point this device can be notated, but like all impassioned accents it will lose much of its effect if it is performed literally'.[67] Baillot's examples show less a redistribution of notes, than a redistribution of accent and articulation (Ex. 11.8).[68]

A few examples in which great composers wrote out an elaborate tempo rubato of this kind nicely illustrate the effect of more flexible and radical note

[64] *Allgemeine musikalische Zeitung*, 10 (1808), 519.   [65] p. 6.
[66] *Violin School*, 234.   [67] *L'Art du violon*, 136–7.
[68] These examples are reproduced in full in Stowell, *Violin Technique*, 274–5.

Ex. 11.8. (*a*) Viotti, Violin Concerto no. 19, in Baillot, *L'Art du violon*, 137–8; (*b*) Viotti, Violin Concerto no. 18, in Baillot, *L'Art du violon*, 8

(*a*)

Maestoso ♩ = 104

p

as written

General indication of the manner of playing

f

(*b*)

Presto ♩ = 116

redistribution. The second movement of Haydn's String Quartet op. 54 no. 2 provides a particularly extended and subtle example, showing how a practised exponent of the art might have applied a combination of rhythmic redistribution and melodic embellishment to the whole of an adagio (Ex. 11.9). Mozart's piano music contains several revealing examples of the type of rubato he might have introduced into his own performances to vary the repetitions of a melody in accordance with the principle referred to in an often-cited passage from his letter of 1777 where he reported, 'What these people cannot grasp is that in tempo rubato, in an adagio, the left hand should go on playing in strict time. With them the left hand always follows suit.'[69] The difference between the autograph and the Artaria edition of the Piano Sonata K. 332 is particularly revealing, for in preparing the work for publication, Mozart seems to have decided to include a stylized version of the kind of ornamentation and rubato that, in his own performance, he might have introduced on repetitions of the theme (Ex. 11.10). And the A minor Rondo K. 511 contains variants that are likely to reflect his practice (Ex 11.11).[70] The Cavatina from Beethoven's String Quartet op. 130 contains a shorter

---

[69] Anderson, *The Letters of Mozart*, 340.   [70] Rosenblum, *Performance Practices*, 379–80.

Ex. 11.9. Haydn, String Quartet op. 54/2/ii

Ex. 11.9. *cont.*

Ex. 11.9. *cont.*

Ex. 11.10. Mozart, Piano Sonata K. 332/ii: (*a*) autograph; (*b*) first edition

(*a*)

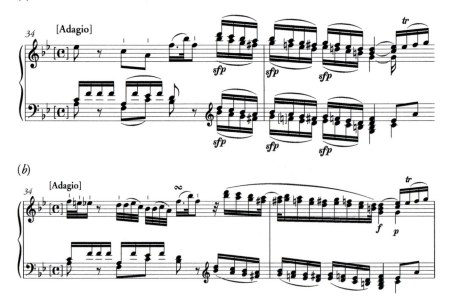

(*b*)

Ex. 11.11. Mozart, Rondo K. 511

(*a*)

(*b*)

passage illustrating how he might perhaps have envisaged the use of the technique at moments of particular expressiveness (Ex. 11.12).

On occasion, nineteenth-century composers incorporated the stylized, syncopated tempo rubato into their music. Good examples are to be found in Liszt's *Canzona napolitana,* in which for the first sixteen bars the right hand is a semiquaver behind the left (Ex. 11.13), and the fourth piece from Schumann's *Noveletten* op. 21, where a theme is varied in this way on its repetition (Ex. 11.14). Yet, despite the neat and convenient notation of tempo rubato by many writers as simple syncopation or displaced accent, it seems clear that rhythmic displacement as practised by many of the best players and singers was, as Baillot's caveat suggests, considerably more complex. Perhaps the most subtle attempts to notate tempo rubato are to be found in the works of Chopin, who was noted for his mastery of the type of keyboard tempo rubato, practised by Mozart, in which the left hand remained firmly in time while the right hand anticipated or retarded the notes of the melody. Chopin employed intricate, carefully elaborated notation to convey the free and improvisatory impression that his performances conveyed; indeed he was criticized in a Parisian review of his Nocturnes op. 15 in 1834 for his 'affectation' in writing his music 'almost as it should be played'; the reviewer went on to remark that, in any case, it was not possible to notate adequately 'this swaying, languid, groping style, this style which no known arrangement of note values can well express'.[71] Since Chopin

---

[71] *Le Pianiste,* 1/5 (Mar. 1834), 78, cited in Richard Hudson, *Stolen Time: A History of Tempo Rubato* (Oxford, 1994), 190.

Ex. 11.12. Beethoven, String Quartet op. 130/v

Ex. 11.13. Liszt, *Canzona napolitana*

Ex. 11.14. Schumann, *Noveletten* op. 21/4

Ex. 11.14. *cont.*

expected ornaments, as a matter of course, to be executed on the beat, he often used small notes, additional to the time of the bar, to indicate displacement of the melody from the bass, as in the Nocturne op. 15 no. 2 (Ex. 11.15).

Among nineteenth-century performers who appear to have continued the practice of this art in a more elaborate form were the violinist Paganini and the singer Manuel García (1775–1832, Rossini's first Almaviva in *Il barbiere di*

Ex. 11.15. Chopin Nocturne op. 15 no 2: (*a*) bar 1; (*b*) bar 9

(*a*)

(*b*)

Siviglia). García's son (also Manuel) cited an example of his father's style of employing tempo rubato, which is particularly instructive, since he attempted to notate it much more literally than was usual. García's account as a whole is worthy of consideration, for it gives a clearer idea of how, in Italian opera especially, tempo rubato remained a significant means of expression well into the nineteenth century. Having prefaced his remarks by the statement that 'Every change introduced into the value of the notes, should, without altering the movement of the time, be procured from adopting the *tempo rubato*', he continued:

By *tempo rubato* is meant the momentary increase of values, which is given to one or several sounds, to the detriment of the rest, while the total length of the bar remains unaltered.

Ex. 11.16. García, *New Treatise*, 51

(*a*)

Ex. 11.16. *cont.*

(*b*)

(*c*)

This distribution of notes into long and short, breaks the monotony of regular movements, and gives greater vehemence to bursts of passion. Example—[Ex. 11.16(*a*)]

To make *tempo rubato* perceptible in singing, the accents and time of an accompaniment should be strictly maintained: upon this monotonous ground, all alterations introduced by the singer will stand out in relief, and change the character of certain phrases. Accelerando and rallentando movements require the voice and accompaniment to proceed in concert; whereas *tempo rubato* allows liberty to the voice only. A serious error is therefore committed, when a singer, in order to give spirit to the final cadences of a piece, uses a rallentando

(*d*)

at the last bar but one, instead of the *tempo rubato*; as while aiming at spirit and enthusiasm, he only becomes awkward and dull. This prolongation is usually conceded to appoggiaturas, to notes placed on long syllables, and those which are naturally salient in the harmony. In all such cases, the time lost must be regained by accelerating other notes. This is a good method for giving colour and variety to melodies. Example:—[Ex. 11.16(*b*)]

Two artists of a very different class—García (the author's father) and Paganini—excelled in the use of *tempo rubato*. While the time was regularly maintained by an orchestra, they would abandon themselves to their inspiration, till the instant a chord changed, or else to the very end of the phrase. An excellent perception of rhythm, and great self-possession on the part of the musician, however, are requisite for the adoption of this method, which should be resorted to only in passages where the harmony is stable, or only slightly varied— in any other case, it would appear singularly difficult, and give immense trouble to an executant. The annexed example illustrates our meaning [footnote: This passage presents an approximate example of the use which the author's late father made of the *tempo rubato*]:- [Ex. 11.16(*c*)]

The *tempo rubato*, again, is useful in preparing a shake, by permitting this preparation to take place on the preceding notes; thus:—[Ex. 11.16(*d*)] The *tempo rubato*, if used affectedly, or without discretion, destroys all balance, and so tortures the melody.[72]

Tempo Rubato as Arhythmical Embellishment

A somewhat different type of tempo rubato goes back at least to C. P. E. Bach, who used this term to describe an irregular number of notes performed independently above a regular bass; Ex. 11.17, from his *Sechs Sonaten . . . mit veränderten Reprisen*, illustrates the sort of situation to which he refers. Illustrations of similar procedures can be found in the embellishments that Bach's Berlin colleague Franz Benda introduced into his own violin sonatas. Though this

[72] *New Treatise,* 50–1.

Ex. 11.17.   C. P. E. Bach, *Sechs Sonaten . . . mit veränderten Reprisen* Wq. 50/4/i

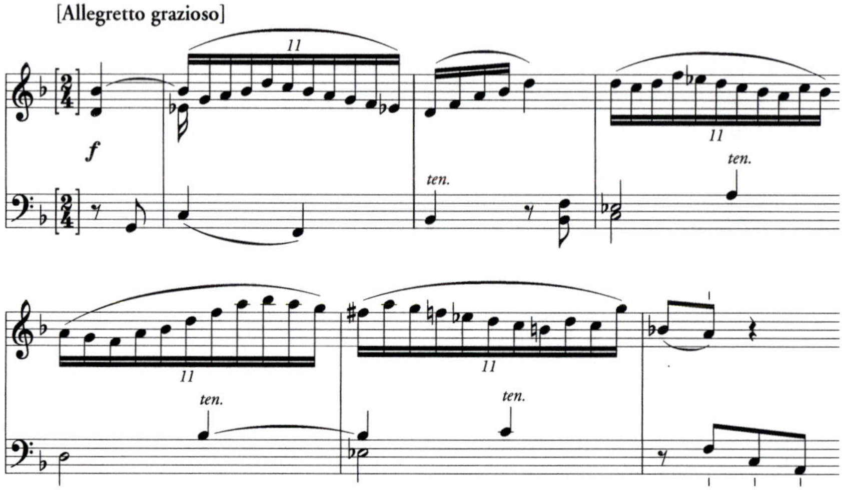

[Allegretto grazioso]

sort of thing was sometimes written out, it seems more often to have been introduced in the form of improvised ornamentation. Examples similar to Bach's and Benda's are also preserved as additions to the original text of Viotti's slow movements, which he is known to have embellished lavishly in this manner; some are found as pencilled additions by the composer himself, others are suggested by elaborations of the melodic line in editions by his pupils and followers (Ex. 11.18).[73] In the piano music of Dussek, Field, Hummel, Chopin, and others such things may well have occurred as improvised additions in performances by the composers themselves, but they are also frequently indicated in the notation. The well-known description of Chopin's tempo rubato— 'Fancy a tree with its branches swayed by the wind; the stem represents the steady time, the moving leaves are the melodic inflections. This is what is meant by *Tempo* and *Tempo rubato*'[74]—seems neatly to describe the effect appropriate to many passages in Chopin's works (Ex. 11.19).

The two principal types of tempo rubato, the one consisting of a redistribution of note values and the other involving the performance of fiorituras that were rhythmically independent of a regularly moving bass, represent, in some

---

[73] Other published examples may be found in Baillot's *L'Art du violon*, 159 (also in Stowell, *Violin Technique*, 351) and in Ferdinand David, ed., *Concert-Studien für die Violine. Eine Sammlung von Violin-Solo-Compositionen berühmter älterer Meister, zum Gebrauch beim Conservatorium der Musik in Leipzig* (Leipzig, Bartholf Senf, n.d.), i.

[74] Edward Dannreuther, *Musical Ornamentation* (London, 1893–5), ii, 161. Richard Hudson, in his wide-ranging and informative study *Stolen Time*, 191 ff., gives other versions of this statement from Chopin's contemporaries together with descriptions of his treatment of tempo rubato.

Ex. 11.18. Viotti, Violin Concerto no. 27/ii, in Chappell White, ed., *Recent Researches in the Music of the Pre-Classical, Classical, and Early Romantic Eras,* v (Madison, Wis., 1976)

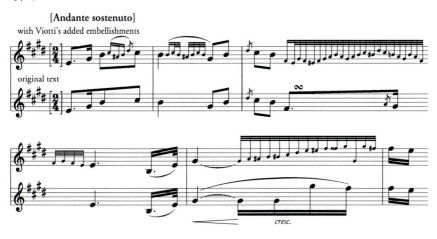

Ex. 11.19. Chopin, Impromptu op. 36/2

sense, two quite distinct techniques. In the hands of the most accomplished artists, however, the distinction became blurred, since, as can be seen from García's examples, redistribution of notes and accents and addition of ornamentation seem often to have been used in combination. Henri Herz, apparently oblivious of the use of tempo rubato by his contemporary Chopin, provides some interesting insights into Dussek's employment of the technique, but certainly implies that the technique was encountered much less frequently towards the middle of the nineteenth century than formerly:

A too exact and uniform tempo at times produces monotony. A phrase of melody may require to be slower than the brilliant passage which follows it; sometimes even the double character of the accompaniment and the melody requires a different rhythmic effect from each hand. Thus while the right hand seems to lose itself in frivolous variations, the left, accenting the off-beats in the bass, follows it in heavy steps and with syncopated notes. This case, like all those where the expression is complex, requires not only hands which are perfectly independent from one another, but also, if I may say so, a different soul in each of them. It is thus that Dussek spread a hazy and melancholy atmosphere over certain passages, by letting the right hand sing in a vague and careless manner, while the left performed arpeggios strictly in time. I do not know why this manner of phrasing, formerly so widespread, has now fallen into oblivion.[75]

[75] *Méthode,* 33.

I2

EMBELLISHMENT, ORNAMENTATION, AND IMPROVISATION

✎

Throughout the period 1750–1900 musical notation in European art music was generally viewed as something much more flexible with respect to pitch, rhythm, and embellishment than it has been for much of the twentieth century. But as the tendency for composers to specify their requirements with ever greater precision grew progressively during that period, performers became inclined to observe the letter of the notation ever more punctiliously. Between the middle of the eighteenth century and the middle of the twentieth century the scope for performers to modify and elaborate on the strict meaning of the notation became increasingly restricted, and the orthodoxy of the second half of the twentieth century (based largely on misconceptions of eighteenth- and nineteenth-century practice), upon which scholarship has only recently begun to make a modest impact, is to regard Classical and Romantic composers' notation as literal and definitive, and to adhere to it as closely as possible in performance. For the vast majority of modern performers, the addition of a few cadential trills and prosodic appoggiaturas, together with minor modifications of phrasing and dynamics, is the most extreme alteration to the received text that they feel to be justified in the performance of late eighteenth-century and nineteenth-century music (apart from the employment of a patently unhistorical continuous vibrato, now almost ubiquitous on many instruments and in singing, which appears to be regarded as an essential element of the sound and therefore not dependent on the notation).

In fact, during the first half of the period the embellishment and elaboration of all kinds of music by performers was endemic and, in many respects, fundamental to the aesthetic experience of composer, performer, and listener alike. The alteration of attitudes during the course of the nineteenth century was slower than might be imagined. Change was most gradual in vocal music, especially opera, and most rapid in German chamber music, yet by the end of the century it seems probable that in all these areas performers' practices, and their perceptions of what the notation implied, were still considerably closer to those of the late eighteenth century than late twentieth-century performers' practices and perceptions are to theirs.

The present-day musician who wishes to understand the ways in which, with respect to embellishment, eighteenth- and nineteenth-century performers might have responded to the notation of their day, or the sorts of expectations that composers might have had about the interpretation of their notation, needs to be conscious of a number of important distinctions. At one extreme was the addition of more or less elaborate fioriituras to the given musical text, substantially modifying the melodic line or introducing new material at cadences: at the other was the application of various less obtrusive embellishments, ranging from vibrato, portamento, and subtle modifications of rhythm to the interpolation of arpeggiation, trills, turns, and appoggiaturas. The former type of embellishment was considered appropriate and necessary in specific circumstances and genres of music, especially in vocal or instrumental display pieces: the latter (though its precise nature was subject to changes of taste and fashion) was regarded as an essential aspect of musicianly performance in all circumstances, without which the music would be lacking in communicative power. The distinction that Spohr made so clearly in 1832 between a 'correct' style and a 'fine' style[1] was the distinction between music rendered in a literally correct manner and music in which the performer subjected the text to a host of small modifications for the sake of expression. There were also a number of specific situations in which the performer was expected to see beyond the literal meaning of the composer's text. Sometimes, by generally understood convention, the given notes were recognized as standing for different ones, or a particular type of execution was implied by the musical context. Conventions of this sort applied especially to appoggiaturas and in recitative, but were also operative in respect of variable dots, the arpeggiation of chords in keyboard playing, the application of slurs and dynamics, and a whole series of consequences arising from metre and musical genres, which were discussed by German writers under the heading of 'heavy and light performance style' ('schwerer und leichter Vortrag').[2] The area in which these latter considerations applied, however, shrank gradually in the course of the period as notation became more prescriptive.

During the second half of the eighteenth century and the first decade or so of the nineteenth century all these kinds of embellishment were a prominent feature of musical life wherever solo performance was involved, but the type of performance in which a large element of fairly elaborate improvised ornament

[1] *Violin School,* 181.   [2] See Ch. 16 below.

was envisaged played a much greater part than it was later to do. In the last decades of the eighteenth century there was still a widespread view that it was the composer's duty to provide solo performers with an outline on which they could elaborate in a manner that displayed their own abilities to best advantage; and even where ornament signs or notated ornaments were included by the composer it was commonly taken for granted that performers were fully at liberty to substitute others that might suit them better. This attitude was clearly enunciated by many writers of the period. Anselm Bayly, for instance, observed in his *Practical Treatise on Singing and Playing with Just Expression and Real Elegance* in 1771:

Many composers insert appoggiaturas and graces, which indeed may assist the learner, but not a performer well educated and of a good taste, who may omit them as he shall judge proper, vary them, or introduce others from his own fancy and imagination. . . . The business of a composer is to give the air and expression in plain notes, who goes out of his province when he writes graces, which serve for the most part only to stop and confine the invention and imagination of a singer. The only excuse a composer can plead for this practice, is the want of qualifications in the generality of singers.[3]

Domenico Corri, approaching the matter from the opposite direction, made much the same point when he stated in the early 1780s that 'either an air, or recitative, sung exactly as it is commonly noted, would be a very inexpressive, nay, a very uncouth performance; for not only the respective duration of the notes is scarcely hinted at, but one note is frequently marked instead of another'.[4] However, as Corri's editions and his other writings suggest, he was concerned rather with the discreet embellishment of the melodic line demanded by 'good taste', and proper understanding of composers' notational conventions, than with the addition of elaborate fiorituras.

For many connoisseurs of that period the individuality of a performer's embellishment of the given notation was a vital part of the musical experience. Burney commented in 1778 on 'La Bernasconi' that she 'has no great voice, but she has a very elegant style of singing, and many embellishments and refinements that are wholly new here'.[5] And three years later he remarked approvingly of Teresa Maddalene Allegranti: 'Indeed she seems to me original—her graces and embellishments do not appear to have been copied from any other singer, or to have been mechanically taught by a master.'[6] These comments confirm that in Burney's opinion the ability to invent new modes of embellishing familiar music was an essential attribute of a successful solo singer. The continuation of similar attitudes well into the nineteenth century is suggested by the cellist J. J. F. Dotzauer, who observed in the 1820s: 'There are a mass of

[3] pp. 47–8. [4] *A Select Collection*, i. 2.

[5] Alvaro Ribeiro SJ ed., *The Letters of Dr Charles Burney* (Oxford, 1991), i. 264–5.

[6] Ibid. i. 334

ornaments which fashion and the humours of virtuosos have increased to such a number that suitable names have not even been found for them.'[7]

By the early years of the nineteenth century the excess and misuse that inevitably arose from ignorance and incapacity on the part of less gifted solo singers and instrumentalists led to increasingly frequent criticism. Domenico Corri, whose own notions of the appropriate embellishment of vocal music are clearly illustrated by his publications of the 1780s and 1790s (see below), complained in 1810 about 'the abuse of ornament', considering it to be 'of recent date'. He observed:

within my memory, those famous singers Farinelli, Cafarello, Geziello, Pacchiarotti, Millico, Aprile, David, Raff and others of the first eminence, sung compositions with little ornament, exerting their talents, on the parts appointed to them; nor were they permitted to introduce, at random, any graces, ornaments etc., as caprice directed, but in such places only as the composer had allotted.[8]

He added that the talent of these singers was principally shown by their *portamento di voce*, though his own publications suggest that, from our perspective, they appear to have modified the musical text to a considerable degree.

The extremely intricate embellishment that was typical of some of the leading performers of the early nineteenth century is exemplified in numerous printed and manuscript sources.[9] As an illustration of the sort of treatment expected in a particular genre of aria, Anton Reicha gave examples by Cimarosa, Giordanello, and Lamparelli with extensive added embellishment. He was not, however, entirely happy about the predominance of the practice, commenting:

Singers, at the period of this decadence, only want songs to embroider [*airs à broder*]: and one might say that for almost forty years [i.e. *c*.1770–1810] we have lived in the period of musical embellishment, of which the three arias which we have cited may henceforth provide an idea, and serve as a tradition for the history of this art; for it may be presumed that this manner of singing, as a result of the abuse to which it leads, will pass out of fashion, or at least be restrained within reasonable bounds . . . one might see [these airs] as a special genre and distinguish them from others by calling them *air à broder*.

But he went on to ask, rhetorically, whether the composer could not write in all the required decoration. For instrumental music his answer was 'yes'; for vocal music 'no', since he clung to the view, enunciated by Bayly, that the singer

---

[7] *Méthode de violoncelle*, 40.   [8] *The Singer's Preceptor*, 3.

[9] Johann Adam Hiller, *Sechs italienische Arien verschiedener Componisten* (Leipzig, 1780); Douglas Lee, 'Some Embellished Versions of Sonatas by Franz Benda', *Musical Quarterly*, 62 (1976), 58–71; Corri, *A Select Collection*; Mozart's ornamented arias: Austin Caswell, 'Mme Cinti-Damoreau and the Embellishment of Italian Opera in Paris 1820–45', *Journal of the American Musicological Society*, 28 (1975), 459–2; Baillot, *L'Art du violon*; Chappell White, ed., Viotti's Violin Concerto no. 27 (Recent Researches in Classical Music, 5; Madison, Wis., 1976) (containing Viotti's additions to the autograph).

would be bound to do it better. Only in bravura arias did he consider it proper for the composer to specify all the embellishment.[10]

There is much evidence of changing attitudes during the second decade of the nineteenth century. An anecdote about Manuel García senior provides a glimpse of the developments that were taking place, even in Italy, where the tradition in which composers provided merely the skeleton of an aria was giving way to one in which they assumed greater responsibilities for the detail of the music. Manuel García junior recalled an incident in about 1815 when, at the first rehearsal of a new opera by a composer of the older Italian school, his father was given his part to read at sight:

When his first aria had been reached he sang it off with perfect phrasing and feeling, but exactly note for note as written. After he had finished the composer said 'Thank you signor, very nice, but not at all what I wanted.' He asked for an explanation, and was informed that the melody was merely a skeleton which the singer should clothe with whatever his imagination and artistic instinct prompted . . . The elder García was skilful at improvising . . . he made a number of alterations and additions, introducing runs, trills, roulades and cadenzas . . . The old composer shook him warmly by the hand. 'Bravo! magnificent! That was my music as I wished it to be given.'[11]

About the same time, Rossini had begun to notate embellishments more fully in his own scores, and he was clearly unhappy to trust his music entirely to the chance of finding a singer with sufficient skill, taste, and understanding to achieve the effects he desired; but there is no reason to believe that either Rossini or the singers with whom he worked would have regarded his embellishments as binding or exclusive. As indicated by the treatment of some of his arias by late nineteenth-century singers, whose performances are preserved on early recordings, the tradition of elaborate and individual interpolated embellishment in this repertoire was far from defunct, even in the generation after Rossini's death. The cavatina 'Una voce poco fa' from *Il barbiere di Siviglia* (1816) is typical of the type of early nineteenth-century display aria that lent itself admirably to the inventive embellishment cherished by nineteenth-century singers and audiences alike. In the performance of such long-established repertoire pieces, an element of tradition undoubtedly crept in, so that one might expect to find correspondences between the interpretations of different artists; but the desire for individuality was just as important, if not more so, even to the extent that many nineteenth-century singers were renowned for their fertility of invention in elaborating the same aria differently on different occasions.[12] Recordings of Rossini's 'Una voce poco fa' by three great sopranos born during the second half of the nineteenth century reveal consistency in the choice of places that invited elaboration and in some

---

[10] *Cours de composition /Vollständiges Lehrbuch*, ii. 498–9.

[11] Malcolm Sterling Mackinlay, *García the Centenarian and his Times* (Edinburgh, 1908), 34.

[12] See Caswell, 'Mme Cinti-Damoreau'.

traditionally sanctioned changes, but they also show how other passages were regarded as an opportunity for the singer to introduce the types of ornamentation that displayed the individuality of their voices and technique to the best advantage.[13] The modern approach to this repertoire is very different, and it is rare to hear more than one or two very minor conventional modifications and departures from Rossini's notated text.

Rossini's own attitude towards the embellishment of his music remains enigmatic; after Adelina Patti had given a particularly florid rendition of 'Una voce poco fa' at one of his Saturday soirées he politely remarked: 'Very nice, my dear, and who wrote the piece you have just performed?'[14] Perhaps Patti's rendition seemed musically inappropriate to him, or perhaps he objected to the aria (which he had written for alto) being sung by a soprano. Yet Rossini would certainly have expected a degree of vocal display, if only at the allotted places for cadenzas. Whether ornamentation of the kind that is preserved on early recordings was enjoyed, merely tolerated, or even detested by the composer, however, does not alter the fact that it was a pervasive aspect of nineteenth-century musical life.

The tendency for nineteenth-century composers to provide examples of appropriate embellishment, if not obligatory fioriituras, was probably prompted less by concern about performers altering and adding to the musical text than by incorrect or inappropriate ornamentation on the part of inexperienced or unmusical performers. There is considerable evidence that, even in Verdi's generation, opera composers did not necessarily expect the singer to execute written-out cadenza-like passages literally; they provided them rather as a guide to length and correct positioning,[15] whereas earlier composers had tended to leave such decisions almost entirely to the singer. Thus, although writers and musicians, throughout the Classical period, had inveighed against excessive embellishment and its application incorrectly or in the wrong places, such comments should not be taken to mean that these writers advocated no or even very little embellishment. As Reicha remarked:

One should not confound a thing with the abuse that is made of it; for there is always a great difference between the two. It is necessary also to distinguish between a singer of talent who embellishes a melody with a flexible and pleasant voice, and with exceptional tact and exquisite taste, with those bad mimics and pitiful caricatures who make something worse of it. And if the former has, in addition, enough spirit to place his embellishments in just the right manner, one should not confuse him with the latter who use them profligately.[16]

---

[13] Compare e.g. recordings of the aria by Marcella Sembrich (1858–1935), Luisa Tetrazzini (1871–1940), and Amelita Galli-Curci (1882–1963).

[14] Cited by Richard Osborne in '*Barbiere di Siviglia, Il* (ii)', *The New Grove Dictionary of Opera*, ed. Stanley Sadie (London, 1992), i. 311.

[15] David Lawton, 'Ornamenting Verdi Arias: The Continuity of a Tradition' (forthcoming).

[16] *Cours de composition/Vollständiges Lehrbuch*, ii. 491.

Complaints about embellishment from this period seem often to have been misinterpreted. Frederick Neumann, for instance, in support of his contention that no embellishment should be introduced in Mozart's later operas, cites early nineteenth-century objections in the *Allgemeine musikalische Zeitung* to the decoration of arias in *Figaro* and *Die Zauberflöte* by the bass I. L. Fischer (who had been the first Osmin in *Die Entführung*). These reports suggest, however, not so much that Fischer was taken to task because he added fio;rituras and ornaments, but because he added them unskilfully. In 1802 a reviewer complained about his ornamentation of 'In diesen heil'gen Hallen' (*Die Zauberflöte*), where the harmony was complex and where Mozart had in any case written many notes; yet three years earlier, criticizing the same piece, the journal had merely asked that he employ 'somewhat fewer embellishments'. The fact that Fischer's use of embellishment, despite his distinguished career, was by no means exemplary is illustrated by a report from Hamburg of his elaboration of a fermata in Haydn's *Die Schöpfung*; having criticized a French singer's harmonically false embellishment in the same work, the reviewer observed: 'The lack of basic knowledge and the concomitant French levity can to some extent be credited; but how astonished I was when I heard the German singer who has been famous for more than thirty years do the following [Ex. 12.1] and introduce several similar embellishments and decorations.'[17]

Ex. 12.1. *Allgemeine musikalische Zeitung*, 4 (1801–2), 14

Other complaints about embellishment from the same journal are revealing both of attitudes and of the types of interpolation that were common. In a report from Hamburg in 1799 a reviewer commented of Madam Righini that

her singing was clean and correct throughout; also she rarely made superfluous ornaments and embellishments [*Manieren und Verzierungen*], and when one heard these, they nevertheless fitted with the harmony and the accompaniment. How much good that did me, and how I rejoiced over it!—For the following examples may prove how right are my frequent complaints about the widespread mania for making bad and often harmonically quite incorrect embellishments and alterations which not only are tolerated by music directors, but even, to judge by the loud applause of the public, are taken for the *non plus ultra* of art.

He then gave several examples from Mozart operas. Herr Rau, as Tamino in *Die Zauberflöte*, sang embellishments as in Ex. 12.2. The reviewer added sarcastically that in the aria 'In diesen heil'gen Hallen' Herr Krug as Sarastro 'every

[17] *Allgemeine musikalische Zeitung*, 4 (1801/2), 14–15.

Ex. 12.2. *Allgemeine musikalische Zeitung*, 1 (1798–9), 604

Ex. 12.3. *Allgemeine musikalische Zeitung*, 1 (1798–9), 604

time sang the following excellent appoggiatura' (Ex. 12.3). He continued: 'All this cannot in any way be compared with the embellishment of a fermata in the last duet of Mozart's opera *Così fan tutte* by which Mad. Lange was able to gain equally universal and loud applause. This went as follows:' (Ex. 12.4).[18]

Ex. 12.4. *Allgemeine musikalische Zeitung*, 1 (1798–9), 604

The kind of embellishment that was considered appropriate may be illustrated by a multitude of examples from the period. Instances by composers themselves are particularly enlightening and provide useful models for modern performers. Mozart's embellishments for arias by himself and J. C. Bach, evidently intended to assist an inexperienced singer, are readily available,[19] though whether embellishment should ever be applied in quite the same way to his later operas is a legitimate question. Interesting examples in Salieri's

---

[18] *Allgemeine musikalische Zeitung*, 1 (1799), 604 f.

[19] See e.g. *New Grove*, ix. 46, art. 'Imrpovisation', §1, 3. An example of embellishment indicated by Haydn, in *Il ritorno di Tobia*, is also given there on p. 45.

Ex. 12.5. Salieri, *Venti otto divertimenti vocali*, no. 2

music are contained in a copy of his *Venti otto divertimenti vocali* in the British Library,[20] where the composer himself has pencilled in simple embellishments to the vocal line. In no. 2, for instance, he changed the printed text from Ex. 12.5(*a*) to Ex. 12.5(*b*). Much later, Meyerbeer's acquiescence in the modification of display passages in his vocal music is implied by his own practice of providing different versions. This is nicely illustrated by comparison of a transposed version of the Page's aria from *Les Huguenots* with the original (Ex. 12.6).

There seems little doubt that, as implied by Reicha's treatise, during the early decades of the nineteenth century there was a growing reaction against the kind of butchery practised by Fischer and others. This was combined with the composers' assumption of greater control, especially in German music, something evident, for instance, in Weber's well-known insistence that his singers abstain from embellishing their parts. By the 1830s and 1840s a widespread prejudice was developing against the addition of ornaments where the composer had not indicated them, particularly in music that was increasingly coming to be seen as 'Classical'. But in 1844 the English critic Henry Fothergill Chorley advocated a broader view:

That the Vienna tradition of singing Mozart's operas does not bind the vocalist to a bald and literal enunciation of the text and nothing but the text, we have had proofs in the singing of Madam van Hasselt-Barth, Madam Jenny Lutzer, and, most recently, Mdlle. Zerr—all vocalists formed in Mozart's own town, and who may naturally be supposed to possess some idea of the manner of executing his operas, sanctioned and provided for by himself. But this newly fashioned edict, in command of an utterly and servile plainness, which, if carried out, would utterly destroy all the singer's individuality in art, seems to me to receive contradiction from the music of Mozart itself—even if we had not tradition to confirm us—even if we did not know that Mozart wrote for singers, who were nothing

---

[20] Pub. (Vienna, [c.1803]); Shelfmark K.7.c.26.

Ex. 12.6. Meyerbeer, *Les Huguenots*, no. 6b, transposed German version from MS in the Meyerbeer Archiv, Staatliches Institut für Musikforschung Preussische Kulturbesitz, Berlin; original French version from printed full score (Paris, Schlesinger, 1836)

without their changes and their closes. That to apply ornament unsparingly would be an insolence—that to employ it out of place and out of style is a musical offence, to be repudiated by all musical people—are facts which by no means imply that to apply and employ it *at all* are cardinal sins. It is the promulgation of such a canon by modern Pedantry, which has caused one-half of the transgressions found so nauseous by severe folks and purists who are never so complacent as when they can 'make *those* singers keep in their right places.' Without some discretionary taste, delicately and scientifically exercised by the *Susanna*, the *Zerlina*, the *Fiordiligi*, and the *Pamina*, of Mozart's operas, I am satisfied that no performance of his music is classical—otherwise in conformity with his intentions.[21]

However, referring to ornamentation in the music of Gluck and Beethoven, he added, with dubious historical justification, especially with respect to the former, that 'the addition of even an appoggiatura would be intolerable'. That Beethoven was generally opposed to *ad libitum* additions in his music is beyond dispute; but there were certainly occasions on which he might add ornaments himself, though Ferdinand Ries recalled that he did this 'very rarely',[22] or extravagantly embellish a fermata, as occurred in a performance of the Quintet for piano and wind op. 16, or even applaud a performer's initiative in similar circumstances, as happened during a performance of the 'Kreutzer' Sonata by Bridgetower.[23]

Of course, everything hung on what was tasteful embellishment and where it might be appropriate, but it is beyond question that the propriety of introducing a degree of embellishment, even, say, in some of Mozart's string quartets, was accepted by leading musicians of the day. The fact that Friedrich Rochlitz, for instance, considered a certain amount of embellishment permissible in the late Mozart quartets is indicated, in a rather roundabout way, during his discussion of the six quartets dedicated to Haydn, in which he observed: 'His later quartets are more galant and concertante: in the former, however, every note is thought out; they must therefore be executed precisely as they stand, and no figure may be altered.'[24]

Most of the chamber music from Mozart onwards that still remains in the repertoire belongs to the kind in which 'every note is thought out' and which tolerates virtually no ornamental additions of the type under consideration here, but the dividing line between this kind of music and works in which some latitude for the performer was still envisaged is difficult to determine. Mendelssohn's music, for instance, belongs quite definitely to the mainstream German tradition, and what is known of the composer's strict views about unwritten rallentando and accelerando and other performance matters suggests that he would have set himself firmly against any alteration of his melodic line or addition of ornament. In most cases it is probably inappropriate to consider ornamenting his music, yet Mendelssohn is reported by Henry Chorley, who knew him quite well, to have permitted Staudigl to modify his part in

[21] *Modern German Music* (London, [1854]), ii. 376–7.

[22] See Franz Gerhardt Wegeler and Ferdinand Ries, *Biographische Notizen über Ludwig van Beethoven* (Koblenz, 1838).

[23] F. G. Edwards, 'George P. Bridgetower and the "Kreutzer" sonata', *Musical Times*, 49 (1908), 302.

[24] *Allgemeine musikalische Zeitung*, 1 (1798–9), 52.

Elijah and to have smiled at the effect of an added trill in his 'Frühlingslied'. He observed:

> Mendelssohn . . . wrote so as to allow no space or exercise of fancy for the vocal embroiderer; and thus, to alter or add to his music, would be to injure it, by showing an arrogant disloyalty to the master's wishes and meanings. Nevertheless, I well recollect the quiet smile of pleasure with which even Mendelssohn used to receive a shake exquisitely placed in the second verse of his delicious 'Frühlingslied' (Op. 47); and it must not be forgotten, by all who desire to see the question fairly argued out, and illustrated by facts, not dogmas, that the first singer of *Elijah* in Mendelssohn's *Oratorio*—Herr Staudigl—was sanctioned, in one of the finest pieces of dramatic *recitative* which the work contains, to heighten the effect, by substituting one note for another—the upper G flat, I mean, in place of D flat—in the scene with Baal's priests, on the last repetition of the words 'Call him louder.'[25]

In instrumental music in the middle of the century, there were still genres of contemporary music that required considerable embellishment, and few which wholly excluded it, as Charles de Bériot's treatment of the subject in his *Méthode* demonstrates. Discussing fioriituras, he remarked that

> the melody which is best adapted to the type of embellishments we are discussing here is that which aims to please by its amiable, flowery, and graceful style, and of which the accompaniment is light and simple in harmony. But all melody that contains a very pronounced sentiment, whether profound, solemn, or serious, and of which the accompaniment produces complicated harmony, excludes, in part, all kinds of ornament.
>
> Hence it comes about that German music, more bound by harmony than Italian music, lends itself less to embellishment. In proportion as this harmonic complexity has won over all the modern schools, ornamentation has become rarer, while the old melody, more simply accompanied, lends itself more advantageously to it.
>
> These changes are due more to progress than to fashion. It is for the performer to accept these diversities of expression, and to adapt his playing with discrimination, only embellishing music of which the character is suitable: that is a matter of taste.[26]

It is clear that in mid- to late nineteenth-century music, major elaboration which substantially changed the shape of the melodic line, or the interpolation of fioriituras, was confined to specific genres of music and particular circumstances, such as cadenzas in concertos (though Brahms was conservative in leaving this to the performer in his Violin Concerto). There was, nevertheless, an expectation throughout the century that performers would modify the written notation in a multitude of less obtrusive ways, which, although they involved departures from or additions to the strict meaning of the notation, were probably not seen as significant alterations to the composer's text any more than a modern performer regards continuous vibrato as an embellishment. These kinds of embellishment were seldom included in the elaborations of arias or instrumental pieces that were provided by composers or theorists as a guide to the inexperienced performer, but they are present in a few sources, considered below, that specifically concerned themselves with the characteristics of a 'fine style'. It is questionable whether even the most informed and imaginative modern musicians have more than a generalized and theoretical notion of the many small ways in which performers of late eighteenth- and early nineteenth-century music might have deviated from the preserved notation in pursuit of a 'fine style'. The weight of documentary evidence certainly suggests that musicians of the Classical era would have approached the repertoire of their own day with a freedom far greater than that attempted by the most adventurous present-day period performers. Indeed, Corri's opinion that a piece of music performed exactly as it is written would be a poor if not a 'very uncouth performance' seems to have been widely shared by solo singers, and also by solo instrumentalists, for more than a century afterwards. Leaving aside more elaborate embellishment, it may be useful to consider in general the other kinds of discreet embellishment that were seen as essential to 'fine' performance at various stages during the period. By making a careful comparison of the instructions given by Corri, and other writers of the late eighteenth century and early nineteenth century, with the performances by singers and instrumentalists trained during the middle of the nineteenth century that are preserved on early recordings, we find some vital clues to interpreting the necessarily ambiguous verbal and graphic attempts to explain the ways in which 'fine' interpreters of the late eighteenth century and early nineteenth century were expected to manifest taste and understanding in their realization of the notated text.

It seems likely that many of the so-called graces that Corri described and illustrated were still employed, though probably to a lesser extent and perhaps not in quite the same manner, by singers who were born in the generation after his death. Vocal effects, quite different from anything a twentieth-century singer would produce, can be heard, for instance, in recordings by one of the oldest of the great singers on record, Adelina Patti (1843–1919), and many of them appear to correspond with Corri's graces. Such effects are considerably less evident in performances by opera singers of the next generation; they are much more prominent, however, in performances by one younger singer whose recordings, though they certainly do not belong in the first rank artistically, are in another respect unique: the castrato Alessandro Moreschi (1858–1922). Moreschi's recordings give a vivid impression of what, in aural terms, Corri's notational conventions may have been intended to convey. Although the vocal sounds produced by Moreschi and Patti[27] may not be what we would naturally conceptualize from Corri's notation of the graces or his descriptions of their execution, there can be little doubt that they are very closely related to, if not directly derived from, the types of ornament that he

[27] These singers may be heard on CD. Patti's recordings are available on *The Era of Adelina Patti* from Nimbus Records (NI 7840/41), and Moreschi's have been issued on Opal 9823.

described, many of which seem intended to indicate various portamento techniques.[28] If a couple of these recordings are transcribed using the notational conventions employed by Corri (which seems a very reasonable way of notating the effects that can be heard there), the results look remarkably similar to examples in Corri's *Select Collection*, for instance in his version of J. C. Bach's aria 'Nel partir bell' idol mio' from his 1778 opera *La clemenza di Scipione* (Ex. 12.7). In this example the grace-notes are given exactly as in Corri's edition, some with two and some with three tails. It is questionable whether a distinction was intended in most cases, for in his instructions (where the grace-note has two tails) he gave the general instruction that they should be 'so rapid that, while the effect is felt, the ear shall yet be unable to determine the character of the sounds or to distinguish them from the predominant note' (for the full quotation see Ch. 13 and n. 60). Corri's specific instruction for the 'Grace of more intervals' (e.g. in b. 1), which in his later *Singer's Preceptor* he called the 'leaping grace', was that it 'is to be taken softly, and to leap into the note rapidly'. The grace 'close after the note' (e.g. at the ends of bb. 70 and 93), called the 'anticipation grace' in the *Singer's Preceptor*, was 'to show that the time necessary for its execution is to be deducted from the last part of that note', and he advised that 'in executing it, it is necessary to swell the note into the Grace, and the Grace must melt itself again into the note following'.[29] For the 'Turn Grace' (e.g. in b. 2), he instructed that it should be 'taken strong, and melted into the note'. His two signs for breathing meant either a pause 'about as long as that made by a Comma in reading' (as in b. 2) or a pause that is to be made 'as imperceptile as possible' (as in b. 12). The sign above the fourth note of b. 4 is an accent.[30]

It may not be too far-fetched to suggest that the pervasiveness of comparable ornaments in Moreschi's performances resulted from the preservation of older practices among the increasingly isolated traditions of the castrati in the nineteenth century. Many of the arias in Corri's collection were originally intended for castrati, and their unfortunate successors, as members of an increasingly marginalized tradition, may well have clung to the style and methods employed during the period of its final ascendancy in the eighteenth century, while changing tastes and fashions conduced to much more rapid stylistic development in the world of nineteenth-century opera. Allowing for deficiencies in Moreschi's technique and in the recording conditions, a transcription of his 1904 performance of the 'Crucifixus' from Rossini's *Petite messe solennelle* might appear as in Ex. 12.8. It is not always possible to represent Moreschi's vocal effects in conventional notation. The present transcription uses Corri's notation where it seems probable that similar embellishments were intended,

[28] Discussed as such in Ch. 15.
[29] For further discussion of these types of vocal portamento see Ch. 15.
[30] *A Select Collection*, i. 8.

Ex. 12.7. J. C. Bach, 'Nel partir bell' idol mio', original edition (lower stave) and D. Corri's version from *A Select Collection*, i. 90–4

Ex. 12.7. *cont.*

Ex. 12.7. *cont.*

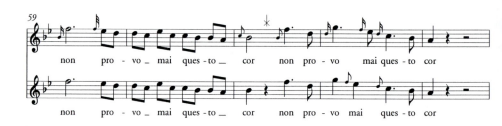

Ex. 12.8. Rossini, *Petite messe solennelle*, Crucifixus, original text (lower stave) and transcription from 1904 recording by the castrato Alessandro Moreschi

though the starting pitches of the 'leaping grace' ornaments are not always distinct. Rhythmic differences from the standard text have been transcribed as accurately as is practicable with regular, conventional notation. Variations in tempo have not been indicated, though this recording and those transcribed in Ex. 12.9 and Ex. 12.12 exhibit considerable flexibility.

The recording of Mozart's 'Voi che sapete' (*Le nozze di Figaro*) that Patti made in 1905 (Ex. 12.9), which has also been transcribed using Corri's notation, shows a number of the same traits, though not all her portamentos correspond with the apparent implications of Corri's notation. It is interesting to note that many of the same characteristics are also found in Patti's performance of a piece much closer to her own time, 'Ah non credea' from the beginning of the finale of Bellini's *La Sonnambula* (1831), a transcription of which also looks remarkably similar to Corri's texts.[31] Particularly striking is Patti's frequent use of the type of portamento indicated by Corri in bars 1, 11, etc. of Ex. 12.7, in view of Manuel García's description of this type as an old-fashioned ornament.[32] But equally notable are the many other small deviations from the strict letter of Bellini's notation, especially with respect to rhythm, including the assimilation of both dotted figures and pairs of equal notes to the triplet rhythms of the accompaniment.[33]

It is evident from comparison of these transcriptions of Moreschi's and Patti's recordings with Ex. 12.7 that, apart from their similarity in respect of the graces, many of the slight and not so slight changes of rhythm and pitch in the recorded performances, which may at first seem merely capricious, are also paralleled in Corri. Vibrato and portamento are considered in detail below, but it may be appropriate to draw attention here to the frequent employment of the latter (corresponding, again, with what is implied in Corri and other late eighteenth-century sources) and the discreet and varied use of the former, which on the earliest recordings is perceived more often as a fluctuation of intensity than as one of pitch.

Though vocal music, and opera in particular, may have exhibited the most extreme manifestations of artistic freedom in the late eighteenth century and nineteenth century, a similar approach was by no means excluded from the performance of solo instrumental music. Violin music, which allowed the closest approach to the eighteenth- and nineteenth-century instrumentalist's ideal of emulating the human voice, provides some illuminating examples. Comparison of the original text of Rode's Seventh Violin Concerto with Spohr's version, included in the final section of his 1832 *Violinschule*, reveals many deviations, the reasons for which are partly explained in the accompanying

---

[31] For a full transcription of this recording see Clive Brown, 'Nineteenth-Century Notation: Appearance and Meaning' in *Musical Theatre in Nineteenth-Century Europe, Venice 1997* (forthcoming).

[32] See below, Ch. 15, especially pp. 567 ff.

[33] See below, Ch. 16, 'The Variable Dot', esp. pp. 618 ff. and Ex. 16.36.

Ex. 12.9. Mozart, *Le nozze di Figaro*, 'Voi che sapete', original text (lower stave) and transcription of recording by Adelina Patti

Ex. 12.9. *cont.*

commentary and partly passed over in silence. Since Spohr had heard the concerto performed by its composer in 1804 and had, by his own admission, striven to perform it as much like Rode as he was able, it is tempting to believe that Spohr's text furnishes a hint as to the manner in which Rode himself might have played it at that time; but it is probably more representative of Spohr's own manner, and, in any case, Rode himself almost certainly varied his performance considerably with the passage of time. In fact, another version of the concerto, edited by Spohr's pupil Ferdinand David, includes the note: 'The markings and ornaments are precisely those which the composer was wont to employ in performance of this concerto, and the editor thanks his late friend Eduard Rietz, one of Rode's most prominent pupils, for the information.'[34] David's version is quite different from Spohr's with respect both to notes and to bowing, though much of the fingering is similar; in so far as it approaches what Rode might have played, it presumably represents the version of his later years, when Rietz studied with him. Spohr's and David's versions of the first movement of the concerto are compared with the text of the original edition in Ex. 12.10. Spohr marked four types of vibrato with different forms of wavy line, indicating fast (b.3), slow (not included in Ex. 12.10), accelerating (b.5), and decelerating (b.37). The following aspects of performance are indicated by notational changes or added instructions in Spohr's and David's texts:

1. Rhythmic modification/agogic accent/tempo rubato. Spohr: bars 16–19, 25, 28, and 30 (Spohr's commentary (p. 185) reads: 'The second half of the 28th and 30th bar must be so played as slightly to augment the duration of the first notes beyond their exact value, compensating for the time thus lost, by a quicker performance of the following notes. (This style of playing is called *tempo rubato*). But this acceleration of the time must be gradual, and correspond with the decrease of power'), 31–4, 58, and 60 (Spohr's commentary (p. 187) reads: 'In the 58th and 60th bar, the ninth note (G natural) should be dwelt upon a little, and the lost time regained by increasing the rapidity of the following notes'), 66, 71, 81, and 83 (Spohr's commentary (p. 189) reads: 'The last two quavers of the 81st and 83rd bar are to be slightly prolonged, yet so as not to occasion any marked difference in the time'). David: bars 4, 12, 16, 17, 31, 33, 80–2, 83–5.

2. Accent. Spohr: bars 10, 11, 15, 22, 26, 42, 44, 51, 66, 67, 69, 77. David: bars 14, 22, 42, 44, 60, 80–5, 90, 91.

3. Articulation. Spohr: bars 5, 13, 31–4, 80, 82. David: bars 5, 13, 85.

4. Embellishment (added notes). Spohr: bars 40 and 48 ('leaping grace'), 69, 77, 92. David: bars 3, 7, 25, 50, 69, 74, 75.

5. Realization of Rode's small notes as appoggiaturas or grace-notes (where different from Rode's notation or from each other). Appoggiaturas: Spohr: bars

---

[34] *Concert-Studien für die Violine*, no. 7.

8, 11, 21, 42, 77, 79, 85; David: bars 6, 11, 14, 21, 42, 77, 85. Grace-notes: Spohr: bars 6, 14, 52, 54; David: bars 8, 52, 54, 79.

6. Vibrato (not specifically marked by David). Spohr: bars 3, 5 (accelerating), 11, 13, 21, 22, 24, 26, 37 (decelerating), 43, 44, 52, 58, 60. David: bar 44? (<>).

7. Portamento, implied by fingering or specified by Spohr's commentary. Spohr: bars 5, 132, 36, 40, 48, 68, 69, 76, 77, 79, 90. David: bars 5, 13, 36, 68, 69, 76, 77, 79. (The portamentos in 68, 69, 76, and 77 occur between different notes in Spohr's and David's versions).

Ex. 12.10. Rode, Violin Concerto no. 7 in A minor, i, first solo section, original text (bottom stave) compared with versions by F. David and Spohr

Ex. 12.10. *cont.*

Ex. 12.10. *cont.*

Ex. 12.10. *cont.*

Ex. 12.10. *cont.*

Interestingly, a review of a performance of the concerto by a Russian violin-ist, Raczynski, in 1818, which referred to his 'tasteless additions' and cited the opening of the first movement as an example,[35] indicates that some of the embellishment preserved in David's edition may to some extent have become 'traditional' at an early stage (Ex. 12.11). (The tied notation and accents in the first, second, and fifth bars, however, are meant to illustrate Raczinski's 'poor management of the bow', also referred to in the review.)

Ex. 12.11. *Allgemeine musikalische Zeitung*, 20 (1818), 317

Aural evidence of the discrepancy between text and performance, which confirms the testimony of Spohr's and David's editions of Rode's concerto, both in terms of personalities and musical similarities, can be heard in a record-ing of Joseph Joachim playing one of his own pieces. Joachim, widely seen as the 'High Priest' of Classical violin playing in the second half of the nineteenth century, studied principally with Rode's pupil Joseph Boehm, knew Spohr, and

[35] *Allgemeine musikalische Zeitung*, 20 (1818), 317.

was associated with David. His five recordings, made in 1903, when he was 72, include two pieces of solo Bach, which are free and individual in their interpretation of the written text, two performances of his own arrangements of Brahms's Hungarian dances, which also reveal considerable flexibility in the realization of the notation, and a performance of his own Romance in C major. Of all these pieces, the Romance is the closest to the mainstream nineteenth-century Classical tradition and the one from which we are most likely to gain some idea of the manner in which he might have treated the musical texts of his friends Brahms, Mendelssohn, and Schumann. The many small deviations from the literal text and the occurrence of vibrato and portamento reveal remarkable similarities to the kinds of amplifications of Rode's text by Spohr and David and, in the broadest sense, to many of the features that are apparent in the vocal music discussed above.

Joachim's performances provide particularly revealing evidence of what a great musician of the nineteenth century felt to be essential in a composition and what he regarded as incidental. For Joachim the concept of 'rubato' clearly extended to allowing the executant extensive licence to alter rhythms within the framework of correct harmony and essential melodic contours. In terms of embellishment, too, he permitted himself considerable freedom. Comparison of a transcription of Joachim's performance of his C major Romance with the published text reveals many disparities; some of these may be genuine 'second thoughts' on the part of the composer, but most seem typical of the artistic freedom that was regarded as integral to a fine style (Ex. 12. 12). Similar principles have been followed in this transcription to those employed in Exx. 12.8 and 12.9, insofar as they are applicable to instrumental performance. However, clearly perceptible vibrato has been marked using Spohr's signs; in very many cases where vibrato is not marked the notes appear to be played with a completely still left hand. Prominent portamento has been indicated here by slanting lines above the stave. Rhythmic deviations are notated to the nearest standard pattern, although many subtle rhythmic nuances in Joachim's performance defy notation.

Many similar things would undoubtedly also have been heard in solo performance on wind instruments. Keyboard music provided less scope for imitating the voice, since it entirely excluded vibrato and portamento (in the sense of an audible slide, though not as extreme legato) and many varieties of dynamic nuance on a single note; yet some keyboard players were noted for the vocality of their playing (for instance, Thalberg[36] and Chopin), which became increasingly possible as the sustaining power of the instrument was improved. But some freedoms, such as tempo rubato in the strict sense, or modifications of notated rhythms, were just as prominently employed as in other solo instrumental and

---

[36] His publication *L'Art du chant appliqué au piano* (The Art of Singing Applied to the Piano) aimed to aid the cultivation of this quality.

Ex. 12.12. Joachim, Romance in C major, original text (lower stave) and transcription of Joachim's 1903 recording

* The grace-notes very rapid and more or less on the beat.

Ex. 12.12. *cont.*

Ex. 12.12. *cont.*

etc. (15 more bars)

vocal performance; and some idiomatic keyboard techniques, such as arpeg-giando, were widely applied where they were not indicated in the notation.[37]

More detailed consideration of some of the major types of 'discreet' embellishment is included in the following chapters. In addition, these chapters examine significant issues surrounding the most important classes of ornaments, as well as a few other related aspects of performing practice.

[37] See Ch. 16, 'Arpeggiation'.

13

Appoggiaturas, Trills, Turns, and Related Ornaments

꿍᷐꿍

In the matter of ornament notation, the musical archaeologist is working in extensively excavated ground. The finds are abundant, but their identification and ordering are by no means straightforward; much of the information derived from them is confusing and controversial. Considerable scholarly attention has been focused on ornament signs in the music of the period and on theorists' accounts of the realization of ornaments; but these durable survivals, like the artefacts from an excavation, represent only a relatively small proportion of what once existed. The ephemeral nature of the aural experience has only left us with traces of evidence that are not easy to interpret. In the first half of the period, especially, a mass of ornamentation was associated with the performance of all sorts of contemporary music, and only a small proportion of it was indicated in the music by means of ornament signs; yet its absence from the musical text does not by any means imply its absence from a good performance. As C. P. E. Bach observed: 'pieces in which all ornaments are indicated need give no trouble; on the other hand, pieces in which little or nothing is marked must be supplied with ornaments in the usual way.'[1]

To ornament the music of the period convincingly it is important to understand not only the types of ornament that are stylistically appropriate, but also the perceived function of ornaments at that time; this is nicely summed up by Schulz, who observed that

They give the notes on which they are brought in more accent, or more charm, set them apart from the others and, in general, introduce variety and to some extent light and shade into the melody. They are not to be seen merely as something artificial, for feeling itself often generates them, since even in common speech abundance of feeling very often brings

[1] *Versuch*, i. II, 1, §11.

forth a change of tone and a lingering on accented syllables which is similar to ornaments in the melody.[2]

In the second half of the period the situation was rather different, and a greater proportion of concrete evidence survives for later nineteenth-century practice; yet even here the relationship between what was written and what was expected to be performed often remains equivocal.

In the late eighteenth century and early nineteenth century, ornaments were frequently marked in a very casual manner. Different notations were employed in close proximity for what appears to be envisaged as the same ornament, or the same sign was used with obviously different meanings. During the course of the period almost all ornaments apart from trills and mordents came to be either notated in normal note values or indicated in small notes that are not counted in the value of the bar. Sometimes even trills were written out fully: Beethoven and other pianist composers had notated continuous trill-like figures in certain contexts, where they were an integral part of the texture, and ordinary decorative trills were occasionally written out in the later nineteenth century (Ex. 13.1). In his String Quartet op. 106 Dvořák evidently felt it necessary to spell out the trill at the opening of the first movement because he wished it to be without a turn, but having made his intentions clear he used the conventional *tr* at the recapitulation (Ex. 13.2). Many composers continued to employ turn signs, but this figure, too, was written out with increasing frequency in the second half of the nineteenth century. The progression is nicely illustrated by Wagner who went from using a sign for connecting turns (in the operas up to *Tannhäuser*) to either writing his turns in small notes or incorporating them into the text (for instance in *Tristan und Isolde*) to consistently notating them in full size notes in the last operas. Brahms used the turn sign in his Sextet in G (though he wrote the ornament out in full at one point in the first movement), and it occurs from time to time in his later music.[3] Some composers in the late nineteenth century, such as Dvořák, continued to use turn signs occasionally,[4] but many others did not employ them at all.

Appoggiaturas and Grace-Notes

The employment of small notes, extra to the value of the bar, was a feature of musical notation throughout the period; but the types of small notes used, and their meanings, changed with time. Until the early decades of the nineteenth century small notes, occurring singly, were widely employed to mean a number of very different things. There was, and is, no universally or even generally agreed terminology for specifying their various functions. The Italian term

---

[2] In Sulzer, *Allgemeine Theorie*, iii. 360.   [3] e.g. in the first movement of the C major Piano Trio.

[4] A late example occurs in the second movement of the String Quartet op. 106.

Ex. 13.1. (*a*) Liszt, Hungarian Rhapsody no. 19 (1885), autograph, p. 7; (*b*) Liszt, *Eine Faust-Symphonie*, i, 'Faust'; (*c*) Tchaikovsky, Fifth Symphony op. 64; (*d*) Tchaikovsky, Sixth Symphony op. 74/iii

(*a*)

(*b*)

Ex. 13.1. *cont.*

(*c*)

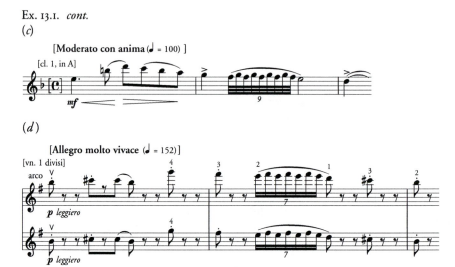

(*d*)

Ex. 13.2. Dvořák, String Quartet op. 106/i

(*a*)

(*b*)

'appoggiatura' was often applied to any of these single small notes, though it was also used in more specialized, often contradictory senses by particular writers. In Germany small notes associated with the note they precede were commonly known as *Vorschläge* (singular *Vorschlag*), and those associated with the note they follow *Nachschläge* (singular *Nachschlag*); in England they were usually referred to by the general term 'graces', with a profuse array of qualifying words; while in France a range of expressions, including *accent, appuy, coulé*, and *port de voix* were employed to describe their various functions.[5] The Italian word 'acciaccatura' was sometimes applied to the very short appoggiatura instead of to the more specific keyboard ornament where two notes are sounded simultaneously; already at the beginning of the nineteenth century the distinction seems to have become somewhat blurred, for Koch, describing the difference between the acciaccatura and the short *Vorschlag*, commented:

---

[5] For further information on nomenclature see *New Grove*, xiii, art. 'Ornaments', esp. pp. 828 ff.

'The distinction between the two consists merely in the fact that in the case of the acciaccatura the little note is performed more simultaneously [*sic: mehr gleichzeitig*] with the main note than in the case of the short *Vorschlag*.'[6]

In the ensuing discussion of single-note ornaments that are a second above or below the following note, the term 'appoggiatura' will be used for one that should take a significant part of the value of the note it precedes; the term 'anticipatory note' will be used for one taking a significant part of the value of the note that precedes it, and the term 'grace-note' will be used to describe a very short ornament that barely removes anything from the value of the notes between which it stands, and which is so fleetingly heard that the ear may not register whether it comes with or slightly before the beat;[7] the term's employment here carries no necessary implication of pre-beat performance as it does when used by some twentieth-century writers.[8] These basic categories cannot be regarded as entirely exclusive, for borderlines are often blurred in performance, especially over the question of when an ornamental note is so short that it may be perceived as a grace-note rather than an appoggiatura or anticipatory note.

Many eighteenth-century and early nineteenth-century theorists attempted to clarify distinctions between different types of single-note ornaments, to suggest ways of linking their appearance with their function, and to adduce rules for determining what they were intended to convey in any specific set of circumstances; but the haste and negligence of composers and copyists, and the lack of any universally accepted or recognized notational principles for these ornaments, seem to have made the interpretation of them quite as troublesome to many less experienced musicians at that time as it has to their successors. (Accomplished performers would, as implied by what was discussed earlier about the executant's attitude to notation, generally have been content to follow their instincts.) Eighteenth-century theorists, primarily with the musical novice in mind, periodically urged composers to minimize ambiguity by writing appoggiaturas with their intended value or even as full-size notes.[9] During the late eighteenth century these recommendations, and the acceptance of them by composers, gradually become more frequent.[10] Changing attitudes, and the concerns that lay behind them, are illustrated by a passage

---

[6] *Musikalisches Lexikon*, 56.

[7] This use of 'grace-note' conforms with the definition in the *Oxford English Dictionary* (Oxford, 1933) of 'additional notes introduced into vocal or instrumental music, not essential to the harmony or melody' (vi. 326).

[8] Frederick Neumann, *Ornamentation and Improvisation in Mozart* (Princeton, 1986); Rosenblum, *Performance Practices*.

[9] Türk, *Klavierschule*, III, §4 and n., recommended that composers write appoggiaturas in full-size notes, leaving the small notes for grace-notes.

[10] Quantz, who, unlike C. P. E. Bach, did not advocate the practice of showing a precise value for appoggiaturas, still used a quaver indiscriminately for almost all of them in his *Versuch*, but according to Edward R. Reilly (Quantz, *On Playing the Flute*, 91) his *Sei duetti* op. 2 of 1759 began to show a change of attitude.

that appears for the first time in the fifth edition of Löhlein's *Clavier-Schule*; having urged composers to indicate the length of appoggiaturas, the editor, Witthauer concluded: 'How many pieces would then, at least with respect to the appoggiaturas, be less badly performed, and how much trouble would be spared to the beginner!'[11] By the early decades of the nineteenth century the practice of indicating appoggiaturas in normal notes was increasingly being adopted, and the use of single-note ornaments became progressively more restricted, so that by the 1830s composers very rarely employed them except as grace-notes. Carl Czerny's commentary on a section dealing with ornamentation in his translation of Reicha's *Cours de composition* is among the latest admonitions on this subject, and his concern seems primarily to be focused on the confusion that was engendered by these signs in the performance of older music. He observed that it is much better if the composer 'writes all embellishments, long appoggiaturas, appoggiaturas etc. everywhere in a definite manner, where there obtains the slightest doubt over their execution', adding, 'Many, often very unpleasant-sounding, mistakes by the performer (particularly in piano music) are thereby avoided. The former customary manner of writing the ornament sign for mordents, turns, pralltrills, etc. is all too obviously imprecise, frequently quite unknown to many players, and often abandons the most beautiful ornaments to tasteless caprice.'[12] But as earlier comments indicate, uncertainty about the significance of such ornaments was scarcely less widespread during the period in which this notational practice was current.

Until the habit of notating appoggiaturas with small notes was abandoned, the problem of how to recognize when they were meant to indicate grace-notes rather than appoggiaturas or anticipatory notes was particularly vexatious. Nevertheless, there was broad agreement about many of the circumstances in which small notes were unlikely to indicate anything other than grace-notes. Perhaps the most comprehensive examination of contexts for grace-note interpretation is Türk's, which seems to have provided the basis for similar accounts by Witthauer, J. F. Schubert, A. E. Müller, F. J. Fröhlich, and others. Türk considered that this type of performance would almost certainly be appropriate to small notes:

1) Which stand before a note . . . that is repeated several times: [Ex. 13.3(*a*)]
2) Before a note (particularly a short one) after which several of like duration follow one another: [Ex. 13.3(*b*)]
3) Before notes which should be performed short (staccato): [Ex. 13.3(*c*)]
4) Before leaping intervals: [Ex. 13.3(*d*)]
5) At the beginning of a movement, or an individual idea and, similarly, after a rest: [Ex. 13.3(*e*)] . . .

---

[11] p. 25.   [12] Reicha, *Cours de composition/Vollständiges Lehrbuch*, i. 537.

Ex. 13.3. Türk, *Klavierschule*, III, §21

6) Before syncopations . . . : [Ex. 13.3(f)]
(Often the appoggiaturas before notes after which syncopations follow, as at a), fall under this rule.)
7) If a similar pattern is previously required: [Ex. 13.3(g)]
8) Before dotted notes in rather fast tempo a), particularly between leaps b): [Ex. 13.3(h)]
9) Before breaks between phrases [*Einschnitten*] a),* particularly when monotony . . . might result from a rather slow appoggiatura in this case, as at b): [Ex. 13.3(j)]
10) If the melody rises a step, and then goes back to the previous note:* [Ex. 13.3(k)]

* [Türk's footnote] There are frequent exceptions to these two rules, e.g. in slow tempo, or when an ornament (over the main note) follows after the appoggiatura

Further situations in which he considered a grace-note to be likely, but not certain were

11) Before several slurred rising or falling seconds [Ex. 13.4(a)] . . .
12) Before falling thirds [Ex. 13.4(b)] . . .
13) Before two-note figures [Ex. 13.4(c)] . . .
14) Before triplets and other three-note figures [Ex. 13.4(d)] . . .
15) Before a note after which two of half its length follow: [Ex. 13.4(e)] . . . (for Türk's qualifications about such notes see below)
16) If the pitches indicated by the small notes are not diatonically related to the following main note: [Ex. 13.4(f)] . . .
17) If the independently entering appoggiaturas are separated from the main note by more than a second or make a leap to it: [Ex. 13.4(g)] . . . [13]

Türk confessed that in all these circumstances some theorists and some composers held a different opinion. In such doubtful cases, many theorists took refuge in appeals to experienced performers to take counsel of their taste and to be aware of the character of the whole piece and of the individual sections, or, in the case of singers, to take account above all of the text.

During the early nineteenth century, as the practice of writing out appoggiaturas in normal notes became commoner, these sorts of comprehensive lists were no longer felt to be so necessary, at least for the performance of the contemporary music that formed the bulk of the repertoire. It is symptomatic of this change of practice and attitude that in Philip Corri's *L'anima di musica* (1810) the main focus of discussion was the 'short appoggiatura' (grace-note) and its execution. Corri, reversing the procedure of Türk and his followers, gave several examples of how to perform the short variety and then observed: 'Note: the Appoggiatura is always to be played short, as above, except in the following instances.'[14] He then considered a few situations in which the long species might be encountered (Ex. 13.5).

One of the latest repetitions of the gist of Türk's instructions, which was clearly intended, at least in part, as a guide to performing contemporary music, occurs in the 1830s in Schilling's *Encyclopädie*. The author of the article felt

Ex. 13.4. Türk, *Klavierschule*, III, §23

(a)

(b)

(c)

(d)   (e)

(f)

(g)

Ex. 13.5. P. A. Corri, *L'anima di musica*, 14

that, despite the widespread adoption of the notation of grace-notes by means of a small stroke through the tail of the note, there was still occasional ambiguity. By that stage, though, the main purpose of the list was to assist performers in interpreting the older music that constituted an ever increasing proportion of the contemporary repertoire. By the end of the nineteenth century, treatises such as Dannreuther's *Musical Ornamentation* approached the subject from a much more obviously historical viewpoint.

The Appoggiatura

Should the performer have resolved that a small note was intended to signify an appoggiatura rather than a grace-note, there remained the problem of deciding what its duration should be. The matter was obfuscated, both during the period of their general use and later, by the existence of two widely disseminated but sometimes incompatible guidelines for determining their length.

On the one hand was a series of not entirely consistent prescriptions for deciding what proportion of the value of the main note should be given to the appoggiatura in any given circumstances: on the other was the idea that the notational value of the small note would show the approximate value that the composer intended it to receive.

The theory, promulgated by Tartini, Quantz, Leopold Mozart, C. P. E. Bach, and others in the mid-eighteenth century, that an appoggiatura should normally take half of a binary main note and two-thirds of a ternary main note, was widely repeated by eighteenth- and nineteenth-century authors. Some musicians (including Francesco Galeazzi[15] and Romberg [16]), however, taught that before a ternary note the appoggiatura should only take a third of its value; others (for instance, Clementi[17]) allowed it to take either one-third or two-thirds of a dotted note according to context. A further principle, for what is sometimes called an 'overlong' appoggiatura, was expounded by C. P. E. Bach, Leopold Mozart, and Quantz and followed by many other German theorists in the eighteenth century: this proposed that where a small-note appoggiatura stood before a tied note or one followed by a rest, it took the whole value of the note before which it stood (Ex. 13.6). It was admitted, however, that the resolution onto a rest might not always be permitted by the harmony. Other rules may be found in the works of individual theorists. A late authority, Baillot, for instance instructed that, in realizing the *appoggiature préparée*, where a small-note appoggiatura was preceded by a normal note at the same pitch, the appoggiatura should be half the length of the preparatory note, and he gave the opening of Mozart's D major String Quartet K. 575 (but with all three small notes incorrectly shown as crotchets[18]) as an example of where this rule would operate (Ex. 13.7).[19] Yet whatever general rules were expounded, these musicians would almost certainly have agreed with C. P. E. Bach that the theoretical length of appoggiaturas must sometimes be modified for the sake of expression or to avoid corrupting the purity of the voice-leading.[20]

A convention similar to the 'overlong' appoggiatura, apparently unremarked by theorists of the day, seems also to have been widely observed by late

Ex. 13.6.

[15] *Elementi teorico-pratici di musica, con un saggio sopra l'arte di suonare il violino annalizzata, ed a dimostrabili principi ridotta*, 2 vols. (Rome, 1791–6), i, pt. 2, art. 15.

[16] *A Complete*, 43.   [17] *Introduction*, 10.

[18] Mozart's original has a quaver (originally a crotchet) in the third bar and semiquavers in the fourth bar.

[19] *L'Art du violon*, 74.   [20] *Versuch*, i. II, 2, §17.

Ex. 13.7. Mozart, String Quartet K. 575/i, in Baillot, *L'Art du violon*, 74

eighteenth- and early nineteenth-century composers: this was that when a small-note appoggiatura occurred, at the interval of a second above or below, before a pair of notes of the same length and the same pitch, the appoggiatura was to be conceived as taking the whole value of the initial note, not merely a proportion of it (Ex. 13.8). This convention was certainly employed by Haydn.

Ex. 13.8.

In a letter of 1768 he explicitly stated that the notation shown in Ex. 13.9(*a*) should be rendered as in Ex. 13.9(*b*) not as in Ex. 13.9(*c*).[21] It is probable that this was also intended by J. C. Bach; certainly Domenico Corri considered it to have this meaning in his music, and realized it thus in his version of Bach's 'Nel partir bell' idol mio' (see Ex. 12.7, bars 18, 31, 33, 76, 78, etc.). Later examples of the use of appoggiaturas in this manner can be found in Schubert. Where two syllables of this kind occur in Schubert's vocal music, he generally indicated the desired appoggiatura with a small note before the first of the pair, but wrote the small note with only half the intended value of the appoggiatura. Clear illustrations of this practice may be taken from his late opera *Fierrabras* (Ex. 13.10). The intended realization is made clear by the many occasions on which the orchestral parts have the same figure fully written out (Ex. 13.11). If Schubert required the figuration that his appoggiaturas seem to indicate, he wrote it in full (Ex. 13.12). Where appoggiaturas occur before single syllables (or in instrumental parts before single notes), however, he generally gave them the value

Ex. 13.9. Haydn, 'Applausus' letter (1769), cited in Landon, *Haydn at Eszterháza*, 147

---

[21] H. C. Robbins Landon, *Haydn at Eszterháza 1766–1790* (London, 1978), 147.

Ex. 13.10. Schubert, *Fierrabras*, no. 4

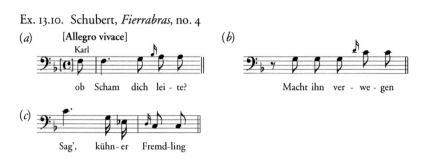

Ex. 13.11. Schubert, *Fierrabras*, no. 10

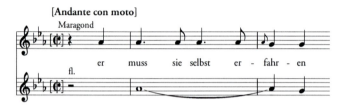

Ex. 13.12. Schubert, *Fierrabras*, no. 10

Ex. 13.13. Schubert, *Fierrabras*, no. 10

with which he intended them to be performed (Ex. 13.13); but since he did not use minim small notes this is not the case before notes longer than a minim (Ex. 13.14). Ernest Walker believed that this notational habit of Schubert was peculiar to him and not mentioned in theoretical writings.[22] However, the practice was evidently widespread, and late examples may also be found in Weber. At least one late nineteenth-century writer, Franklin Taylor, recognized and described the convention in the nineteenth century.[23]

[22] 'The Appoggiatura', *Music & Letters*, 5 (1924), 121–44.
[23] Grove, 'Appoggiatura', in *Dictionary*, i. 78.

Ex. 13.14. Schubert, *Fierrabras*, no. 17

The problem with the rules advanced by theorists was not only that they disagreed among themselves, but also that, where persuasive evidence exists to show how appoggiaturas were intended to be realized in specific instances, even the rules about which most of the theorists were in agreement seem to have had a rather tenuous relationship with many composers' and performers' practices. This is particularly the case with appoggiaturas before notes of longer duration than crotchets.

The practice of giving the small-note appoggiatura the approximate value intended for its realization offered a potentially much more reliable means of avoiding confusion. C. P. E. Bach observed in 1753: 'people have recently begun to indicate such *Vorschläge* according to their true value'.[24] Although this was true of a few composers, the practice was certainly not widespread at that stage; and even where composers did begin to use different lengths of small notes for their appoggiaturas, it would be rash to assume that these always represented the desired length, or that they might not admit of equally acceptable alternative solutions, with respect to either length or embellishment. Nevertheless, during the second half of the eighteenth century, an increasing number of composers did begin to use differentiated note values for small notes and to write many of their longer appoggiaturas in normal notation, in order to convey to the performer their preferred approximate duration for the dissonance (it was approximate because by convention the appoggiatura required a degree of metrical freedom in its execution).

A progression from undifferentiated to varied small-note appoggiaturas can be traced in the music of major composers of the Classical period. Gluck used small quavers for appoggiaturas of all lengths and types in his earlier operas (in *Semiramide riconosciuta* (1748), for instance), and the actual performing

---

[24] *Versuch*, i. II, 2, §5.

Ex. 13.15. Gluck, *Semiramide riconosciuta*: (*a*) Act II, Scene vi; (*b*) Act I, Scene iv. Österreichische Nationalbibliothek, Vienna, Cod. mus. 17.793

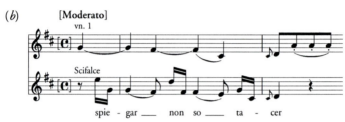

lengths of these small notes are governed by no discernible rules; sometimes they evidently obey the rule to take half the note (Ex. 13.15(*a*)), but they seem never to follow the 'two-thirds or longer' rule and appear most frequently to be intended to be short (Ex. 13.15(*b*)). The only guiding principle for interpreting these notes appears to have been confidence in the musical instinct—*le bon goût*—of the performer. In his later operas, especially those written for Paris, Gluck differentiated the values of small notes. Haydn began increasingly to notate small notes in a more differentiated manner from about 1762.[25] In works after this date the value of the small note is likely to be a useful indicator of how it should be realized; but there remained habitual oddities, such as his use of a semiquaver small note in the pattern shown in Ex. 13.16, where something shorter is clearly meant (either a demisemiquaver or a grace-note). Mozart had already begun to use small notes of different values in very early works. At first he employed minim, crotchet, quaver, semiquaver, and occasionally demisemiquaver small notes, but after about 1780 he stopped using minim small notes, and wrote out his longer appoggiaturas as full-size notes.

Ex. 13.16

[25] See Laslo Somfai, 'How to Read and Understand Haydn's Notation in its Chronologically Changing Concepts', in Eva Badura-Skoda, ed., *Joseph Haydn: Bericht über den internationalen Joseph Haydn Kongress, Wien . . . 1982* (Munich, 1986), 25.

Neither Haydn nor Mozart seems to have used dotted small notes (which are extremely rare anywhere in eighteenth-century music). In the majority of cases where appoggiatura treatment is called for in Mozart's music, the length of the small note is likely to be a useful guide to its duration, though it should not necessarily be regarded as enjoining a rhythmically exact execution or precluding some form of nuanced or embellished performance. In view of his obvious care in specifying different values for small notes, however, it is difficult to see the logic of suggestions such as those in some of the *Neue Mozart Ausgabe* volumes, for instance in the Violin Sonata in E minor K. 304, where a different notational value for the resolution is suggested (Ex. 13.17). Many minor composers in the late eighteenth century, such as J. F. Reichardt and G. J. Vogler, similarly adopted the practice of differentiating the values of their appoggiaturas; but others, probably the majority, were much more casual; and there is every reason to suspect that Italian composers, especially, were extremely indifferent in this matter.

Ex. 13.17. Mozart, Violin Sonata K. 304/i, piano part (*Neue Mozart Ausgabe*)

It is clear from a mass of manuscript and printed music by minor figures, as well as from reiterated complaints about the difficulties presented to less experienced players by this notation, that considerable scope for misunderstanding remained throughout the eighteenth century. This was true not only in compositions, but also in instruction books, where a more consistent approach might have been expected. Löhlein's widely disseminated *Clavier-Schule* and *Anweisung zum Violinspielen,* for instance, contain many ambiguous small notes in the musical exercises; hence Witthauer's comments (above) in the fifth edition of the *Clavier-Schule* in 1791 and J. F. Reichardt's similar remarks in the fourth edition of the *Anweisung zum Violinspielen* in 1797. Reichardt observed of one of Löhlein's examples, where quaver small notes were employed: 'this manner of writing is not the most correct one; for most people will, in accordance with the convention, execute the quaver appoggiatura as a quaver. A short appoggiatura of this kind [he evidently means a grace-note] should reasonably be designated by a semi- or demisemiquaver.'[26] But he, too, left the notation unaltered.

[26] p. 44.

Despite the ambiguities resulting from the custom of using small notes for appoggiaturas, there were undoubtedly factors, apart from force of habit, that favoured its survival into the nineteenth century. In an age when the addition of improvised ornaments was endemic, the notation of the appoggiatura as a small note would, as Leopold Mozart observed, warn the player or singer against distorting the harmony by the addition of inappropriate embellishments to notes that were already ornamental.[27] More importantly, writing an appoggiatura in this manner encouraged the executant to give it a particular style of performance and a certain degree of rhythmic freedom, which might have been inhibited if it were indicated in precise note values. Many comments from the period suggest that this was the case. John Holden remarked: 'The appoggiatura should always be tied to one of the principal notes; and, though we are not strictly obliged to give it just the time which its figure would require, yet whatever length of time is bestowed on it, must be, as it were, borrowed from the principal note with which it is tied.'[28] Forty years later Anton Reicha gave an example of appoggiaturas and their possible realization (Ex. 13.18), observing: 'one may perform them with a greater or lesser value according to the character of the piece';[29] he later remarked that composers write appoggiaturas as normal notes if they definitely want them a certain length, 'neither more nor less'.[30] And Domenico Corri's *The Singer's Preceptor*, published at about the same time as Reicha's treatise, contains the comment: 'The length of time given to Graces, tho' in general marked, yet never can be given so accurately as to direct the true expression of the words, which must be therefore regulated by the judgement, taste and feeling of the Singer.'[31] There is every reason to believe that, as C. P. E. Bach's comment about modifying the length of appoggiaturas for the sake of expression implies, a similar attitude was taken in instrumental performance. Michel Woldemar, in his revision of Leopold Mozart's *Violinschule* (which, in fact has only a tenuous relationship with the original), gave several examples of how to perform appoggiaturas, remarking: 'One sees here that the little note requires half the note that it precedes; it may

Ex. 13.18. Reicha, *Cours de composition/Vollständiges Lehrbuch*, i. 100

---

[27] *Versuch*, IX, §3.   [28] *Essay*, 39.   [29] *Cours de composition/Vollständiges Lehrbuch*, i. 100.
[30] Ibid. 536–7.]   [31] p. 32.

Ex. 13.19. (*a*) Woldemar, *Méthode de violon par L. Mozart*, 30; (*b*) L. Mozart, *Versuch*, IX, §3

(*a*)

(*b*)

however be worth less, but never more'.[32] He included two examples from the original edition, but realized them differently from Mozart (Ex. 13.19).

It seems likely, in fact, that appoggiaturas were very often executed shorter than is suggested by many ornament tables and theoretical guidelines, though without being performed as short as grace-notes. A passage from an *opera buffa* by Gassmann, *L'opera seria*, in which a Kapellmeister instructs the orchestra how to play his music, is instructive: the orchestra parts have Ex. 13.20(*a*)), and the singer's demonstration is notated as in Ex. 13.20(*b*)). Much later, in music by Beethoven's Viennese rival Anton Eberl, there is similar evidence of a shorter realization than might be expected in the different notation employed for a unison passage between violin and piano in the Rondo of his Violin Sonata op. 49 (Ex. 13.21), though this may perhaps be taken as notation for a grace-note rather than an appoggiatura. In contrast, an appoggiatura in the violin part of the Rondo of his Violin Sonata op. 50 is given a longer realization in the piano part than its apparent value, but a shorter one than might be expected from the 'two-thirds of a dotted note' rule (Ex. 13.22).

Ex. 13.20. Gassmann, *L'opera seria*, Act II, Scene vi, MS score in Österreichische Nationalbibliothek, Vienna, ms. no. 177775; pub. in fac. in the series *Italian Opera 1640–1770* (New York and London, Garland 1982)

---

[32] *Méthode de violon par L. Mozart*, 30.

Ex. 13.21. Eberl, Violin Sonata op. 49/iii

Ex. 13.22. Eberl, Violin Sonata op. 50/iii

When a singer or solo instrument and an accompaniment part were in unison, it was not uncommon for composers to include small-note appoggiaturas in the solo part and to write the ornament in full-size notes in the accompaniment, as in the examples from Eberl and the passages from Schubert's *Fierrabras* cited above. Such instances provide useful indications of the duration envisaged for the appoggiatura. But this cannot be relied on in all cases, especially with semiquaver small notes, where, as in the example from Eberl's Sonata op. 49, the choice between a grace-note and a literal semiquaver is often unclear.

While unison passages shed light on the length of appoggiaturas, they do not necessarily prove that a performance in which the soloist delivers the appoggiatura in complete synchronization with the orchestra was what the composer wanted or what accomplished singers of the day would actually have given. Corri's *Select Collection*, which, as far as the notation of the period allowed, purports to give the ornaments precisely as they might have been rendered, provides examples of the sort of thing that could have occurred (Ex. 13.23). Corri's collection also includes interesting examples of less predictable realizations of appoggiaturas in some instances, which indicate that the use of a single small note might well have been understood to allow a variety of more elaborate types of performance (see Ex. 12.7, bb. 33, 47, etc.).[33] The pervasiveness of this

Ex. 13.23. D. Corri, *A Select Collection*, i. 6

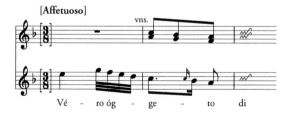

Vé - ro óg - ge - to di

---

[33] See also Ex.c 13.72 for examples of the appoggiatura combined with an extempore turn.

Ex. 13.24. (*a*) Notated appoggiatura; (*b*)–(*c*) realizations in Baillot, *L'Art du violon*, 74–5

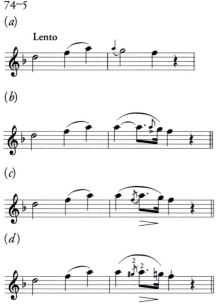

kind of ornamental treatment in different times and schools is suggested by Pierre Baillot's discussion, half a century later, of very similar methods of varying an appoggiatura (Ex. 13.24(*a*) might be realized as in Ex. 13.24(*b*)–(*d*)).

One aspect of the execution of appoggiaturas on which there was general agreement was that they should be smoothly connected to their main notes[34] and that the appoggiatura received the greater stress, the main note being phrased off and sometimes shortened. Some writers of string, wind, and singing methods, however, suggested that this should normally be a very different kind of emphasis from the simple accent that would be given to the same figure written in normal notes. According to some authors,[35] where time allowed, as Johann Georg Tromlitz explained, the player should 'sound the appoggiatura softly, allow it to grow in strength, and slur it to the following note very softly, allowing it to decrescendo at the same time'.[36] This treatment of the appoggiatura is explicitly shown in many of the exercises in Campagnoli's *Nouvelle méthode*, where the notation (illustrating a rare

---

[34] e.g. Türk, *Klavierschule*, III, 2, §19; Joseph Gehot, *A Treatise on the Theory and Practice of Music together with the Scales of Every Musical Instrument* (London, 1784), 3; Löhlein, *Klavierschule*, 5th edn., 25; Romberg, *A Complete*, 43.

[35] Giuseppe Tartini, *Traité des agréments de la musique*, ed. E. R. Jacobi (Celle and New York, 1961), 66; Quantz, *Versuch*, VIII, §4; Jean Baptiste Cartier, *L'Art du violon ou collection choisie dans les sonates des écoles italienne, françoise et allemande précédée d'un abrégée des principes pour cet instrument* (Paris, [1798]), 4.

[36] *Ausführlicher und gründlicher Unterricht die Flöte zu spielen* (Leipzig, 1791), 242.

Ex. 13.25. Campagnoli, *Nouvelle méthode*: (*a*) p. 38; (*b*) p. 39; (*c*) p. 43

employment of dotted appoggiaturas) sometimes also indicates a longer appoggiatura than might be expected (Ex. 13.25).

Koch's consideration of the performance of appoggiaturas and the reason for writing them with small notes neatly synthesizes the views of many of his contemporaries. He observed that many dissonances are

> distributed properly in the bar and indicated in normal notes. The reason why this does not likewise happen with the appoggiatura has its origin in the particular and exceptional manner in which the appoggiatura is performed. That is to say, it is agreed that in delaying a melodic main note by means of the appoggiatura, one should markedly bring out the appoggiatura itself with a particular accent, or sound it with a certain rapid swelling of the strength of the note: and then slur the following melodic main note to it softly or with decreased strength.[37]

With the demise of the small-note appoggiatura and the growing precision of composers' notation, any such special treatment as was specified by eighteenth-century writers was more likely to be indicated by dynamic marking; and the persistence of this style of performance for written-out appoggiaturas in the nineteenth century is attested, for instance, by dynamic markings on appoggiaturas in the Largo of Mendelssohn's String Quartet op. 12, and in many Lieder by his teacher Zelter, that are the same as those used by Campagnoli. Later in the nineteenth century, Charles de Bériot seems to have been describing a similar procedure when he instructed: 'In order to render the appoggiatura well we must press softly with the bow on the long note, making it vibrate with the finger when the expression admits and letting the sound expire

---

[37] *Musikalisches Lexikon*, art. 'Vorschlag'. (See Ch.6 above for Koch's and other writers' further views on the performance of the *Abzug* in such instances.)

on the final note (which represents the mute E [in the French language]) with as much purity as elegance.'[38]

For keyboard players, this kind of nuanced performance was obviously not possible; and in their discussion of appoggiaturas most writers of keyboard methods mentioned simply that the small note requires greater emphasis than the main note.[39] But it is evident from occasional examples that, at least in the nineteenth century, there might be circumstances in which this rule of emphasizing the appoggiatura did not operate. In an editorial note to his translation of Reicha's *Cours de composition*, Carl Czerny gave an example of ornaments and their resolutions in which he showed the main note with the accent (Ex. 13.26).[40] Naturally individual cases were likely to be conditioned by their particular contexts, and where, as in the vast majority of cases, the small-note appoggiatura is dissonant, the usual convention of stressing dissonances would be likely to apply; Czerny did not indicate the harmony in his example, but, whatever the harmony, it appears that in this instance he felt that the principle of displacement of accent by a syncopation overrode that of accenting an appoggiatura.

Ex. 13.26. Reicha, *Cours de composition/Vollständiges Lehrbuch*, i. 537

It was probably the association of dissonance with a stronger accent than usual that led Philip Corri to state in his piano method that though figures like Ex. 13.27 were to be performed as four equal notes, the first of the group received more accent if it was written in this manner rather than with full-size notes.[41] Like so many rules in instruction books, this offered only rough guidance to the inexperienced player, for while in many cases the small note was dissonant, this was not always so. Corri's treatment of these figures may indicate a change of attitude around the beginning of the nineteenth century, as

Ex. 13.27. P. A. Corri, *L'anima di musica*, 14

[38] *Méthode*, 204.   [39] e.g. Türk, *Klavierschule*, III, §19; Löhlein, *Clavier-Schule*, 5th edn., 25.
[40] *Cours de composition/Vollständiges Lehrbuch*, i. 537.   [41] *L'anima di musica*, 14.

comparison with Türk's discussion of the matter implies. Türk explained that (according to generally accepted theory) the appoggiatura in figures such as Ex. 13.28(*a*) required a short (i.e. grace-note) performance; but he felt that in many cases this was frequently unsatisfactory, remarking:

With these and similar figures almost all music teachers require, indeed, that the appoggiaturas should be short, as at b) [Ex. 13.28(*b*)]; and in various cases, if, for example, single figures of this kind occur, as at c) [Ex. 13.28(*c*)] below, or when several similar figures follow immediately one after another, as at d) [Ex. 13.28(*d*)] etc., this realization may be good and necessary on harmonic grounds. Yet still I cannot convince myself that this rule should apply so generally and in every instance. If one makes the appoggiatura short in example e) [Ex. 13.28(*e*)], after the preceding and following four-note figures, the flow of the melody seems to me to become, at the same time, limping.

Also, I have heard only few tasteful, practical musicians realize passages like f) [Ex. 13.28(*f*)] as at g) [Ex. 13.28(*g*)], but many more as at h) [Ex. 13.28(*h*)].

Although the realization at g) may be commoner than that at h), I desire that the latter should be used in my works, except where in individual cases other rules are against it.[42]

Türk's preferred realization of such figures, with equal notes and an accent, appears to reflect an approach that was gaining ground in the eighteenth century and which by the time of Philip Corri's treatise of 1810 had become the standard method. (By that date, too, the use of a small note in notating these figures was becoming increasingly uncommon.) Interestingly, Philip Corri's approach was somewhat at odds with his father's more varied treatment of figures of this kind in vocal music. In the aria from J. C. Bach's *La clemenza di Scipione* cited earlier, for instance, Corri rendered the notation in two different manners (see Ex. 12.7, bb. 22 and 29).

There were also circumstances in which some musicians, principally singers, seem to have regarded it as stylish to reverse the usual dynamic pattern for appoggiaturas; this was when they were taken from the semitone below. In 1810 Domenico Corri explained that in such cases, one should 'Take the Grace softly and force it into the Note'.[43] Some thirty years earlier he had given similar instructions in the preface to *A Select Collection*. Corri's extensive annotations to the pieces in that collection provide some interesting practical illustrations of where this technique might be applied (Ex. 13.29), and all of them indicate that despite the reversed dynamic, the second note was still shortened. Gesualdo Lanza was also quite explicit about performing the rising appoggiatura in this manner. He observed of long appoggiaturas in general that they 'should be sung much stronger than the note which follows them', but his examples show the realization of a rising appoggiatura with a crescendo to the note of resolution and a shortening of that note (Ex. 13.30).[44] Somewhat later he observed: 'The under appoggiatura generally rises and the upper diminishes

[42] *Klavierschule*, III, §23.   [43] *The Singer's Preceptor*, 32.   [44] *The Elements of Singing*, i. 68.

Ex. 13.28. Türk, *Klavierschule*, III, 3, §23

(*a*)

(*b*)

(*c*)

(*d*)

(*e*)

(*f*)   (*g*)

(*h*)

in strength.'[45] However, many other musicians evidently performed rising appoggiaturas, whether written in normal notation or indicated by small notes, in a similar manner to falling ones. Leopold Mozart, for example, instructed that they must still be performed stronger than the main note.[46]

Another practice, peculiar to many early nineteenth-century French violinists, seems to have been the habit of ending phrases, even apparently after a falling appoggiatura, with an accent and vibrato. This mannerism, however, was regarded as ugly by some German musicians. A writer in the *Wiener*

[45] Ibid. 82.   [46] *Versuch*, IX, §20.

Ex. 13.29. D. Corri, *A Select Collection*, i. 5

Vé - ro óg - get - to di ___ pié - ta ___

Ex. 13.30. Lanza, *The Elements of Singing*, i. 68

is realized as

allgemeine musikalische Zeitung in 1813, noting this habit in Rode's playing, remarked: 'Whether Herr Rode's mannerism, or rather that of the new French school, of accentuating the last note of a passage with a powerful vibrato [Tremolando] is an essential aspect of a brilliant performance style, would still have to be proved in accordance with the principles of the aesthetics of music.'[47] Seven years later Spohr, referring to Lafont's playing, also deprecated 'the bringing out of the last note of a phrase by means of reinforced pressure and rapid, accented up-bow, even when a note comes on a weak beat', which, he reported, was common to all French violinists. And he added: 'It is incomprehensible to me how this unnatural accentuation, which sounds just as if a speaker were to stress the weak final syllables particularly strongly, could have come about.'[48] A generation later Charles de Bériot described this procedure as appropriate when one or more ornamental notes occur between the appoggiatura and its resolution, though he did not call for an accent on the final note.[49]

The Grace-Note

The matter of whether grace-notes should precede or coincide with the beat was already controversial in the eighteenth century and has remained so until the present day. The belligerent positions adopted by modern scholars, combined with the disagreements of eighteenth- and nineteenth-century writers, have fuelled a heated debate that has sometimes tended to confuse rather than clarify the issue.

There is abundant evidence that either conception of the rhythmic placement of grace-notes would have found partisans at any stage during the period. Some musicians would have taken a dogmatic stand on one side of the argument, while many would have been more flexible, favouring one or the other

[47] Vol. 1 (1813), 48. [48] *Allgemeine musikalische Zeitung*, 23 (1821), 191.
[49] *Méthode*, 205.

interpretation according to context. Even among those who admitted both possibilities there would doubtless have been disagreement in specific instances; but this simply illustrates the diversity and mutability of musical taste. In very many cases, though, the problem is essentially an illusory one, for grace-notes will often be performed so rapidly that their precise relationship to the beat, which may itself be somewhat flexible, is virtually incapable of being distinguished either by the listener or, frequently, by the performer.

General rules for the appropriate style of grace-note performance in any given period are impossible to formulate. During the Classical period, however, it is evident that the vast majority of writers who addressed the problem favoured an on-beat conception (i.e. beginning the grace-note simultaneously with the bass note) in most, if not all, circumstances. Some writers described a type of single-note ornament, principally in the context of *tierces coulées*, which could be regarded either as an anticipatory note or pre-beat grace-note, and internal evidence suggests that composers sometimes used small notes with this meaning in other contexts (see below); but Milchmeyer's *Die wahre Art das Pianoforte zu spielen* (1797), which was very severely criticized for its treatment of ornaments in a review in the *Allgemeine musikalische Zeitung*, was among the few late eighteenth-century sources unequivocally to recommend a pre-beat conception of grace-notes as the norm. There appears to have been greater diversity of opinion in the nineteenth century, especially with regard to the placement of ornaments of more than one note; yet many musicians of standing seem still to have regarded it as good practice to consider single grace-notes as occurring on the beat in most cases, and many of them recommended the same treatment for ornaments of several notes. Throughout the century German writers continued to advance the traditional view.[50] Performers and composers were probably more pragmatic, though the majority, especially in the German sphere of influence, apparently continued predominantly to envisage single grace-notes as coinciding with the beat. This is clearly demonstrated by late nineteenth-century annotated editions of earlier music that include realizations of the ornaments. Examples may be found in the editions of Sigmund Lebert and Immanuel von Faisst for instance in Ex. 13.31 (but note the accent on the main note),[51] or those of Hugo Riemann (though unlike the majority of his contemporaries, Riemann appears in general to have favoured an accented performance of the grace-note; see Ex. 13.32). The treatise *Musical Ornamentation* by Edward Dannreuther, a practising concert pianist and a friend of Wagner, Tchaikovsky, and other prominent musicians of the period, which pursues its historical survey right up to the practices of Dannreuther's own day, also confirms the continuing strength of an on-beat, generally unaccented, conception of grace-notes among his contemporaries. In individual

[50] Schilling, Dommer, Paul, Mendel.
[51] e.g. Beethoven, Sonata op. 2 no. 3 (Hamburg, Schuberth, 1891).

Ex. 13.31. Beethoven, Sonata op. 2/3, ed. S. Lebert and I. von Faisst

Ex. 13.32. Schubert, *Moment musical* in A flat op. 94/2, ed. H. Riemann
(*a*)

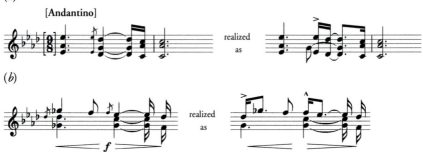

(*b*)

instances, however, there always remained the possibility of disagreement. Dannreuther, for instance, considered that the short appoggiatura in bar 3 of Schubert's A flat *Moment musical* op. 94, which Riemann would have executed on the beat, 'is meant for a *Nachschlag*'[52] and illustrated it as in Ex. 13.33.

Ex. 13.33. Schubert, *Moment musical* in A flat op. 94/2, in Dannreuther, *Musical Ornamentation*, ii. 131

Some nineteenth-century musicians, however, especially those under French influence, were much more inclined to regard grace-notes as quite definitely preceding the beat. Fétis and Moscheles, in their treatise on piano playing, were specific about a change in practice during the nineteenth century: 'Acciaccaturas, slides and groups of two or three notes are placed immediately before the principal note. In the old school it was understood that they should share in the time of the principal note, but they are now to be played quickly and lightly before the time of the large note';[53] their examples are shown in Ex. 13.34. The contemporary Belgian violinist Charles de Bériot specified that small notes should precede the beat when they occurred 'at the beginning of a piece or a phrase' (Ex. 13.35), which 'only serve as a preparation, to give more

[52] *Musical Ornamentation*, ii. 131.   [53] *Complete System*, 6.

Ex. 13.34. Fétis and Moscheles, *Complete System*, 6

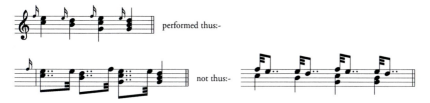

performed thus:-

not thus:-

Ex. 13.35. Bériot, *Méthode*, 204

force to the note which marks the strong time of the measure';[54] but he remained silent about grace-notes in other contexts.

Practices in this matter seem not only to have been affected by national preferences, but may also, to some extent, have been specific to particular instruments, especially in the later nineteenth century. The German violinist Andreas Moser, writing at the beginning of the twentieth century, supported a pre-beat conception in many situations, arguing that the approach was largely determined by the nature of different instruments. He observed that even at that time 'there were the most contradictory opinions among practical musicians';[55] he noted that keyboard players still tended to favour placing grace-notes firmly on the beat while the majority of singers and string players anticipated them, and he suggested that this had been the case continuously since the middle of the eighteenth century. There is little firm historical evidence to support Moser's claim for practices before his own day, but it probably reflects the views of Joseph Joachim, whose practical experience and association with the leading musicians of the day in Vienna and Leipzig stretched back to the 1840s. Joachim's own performance of grace-notes in his 1903 recording of his Romance in C was very rapid, and it is difficult to tell whether they fall on or before the beat.

Some of the argument that has led, perhaps, to an over-reaction against the on-beat conception of the grace-note is worthy of closer examination. Frederick Neumann, in his extensive studies of ornamentation,[56] advanced the opinion that an accent or staccato on the main note before which a grace-note stands precludes the performance of that grace-note on the beat; he felt that the

[54] *Méthode*, 204.　　　　　　　　　　　　　　[55] Joachim and Moser, *Violinschule*, iii. 28.
[56] *Ornamentation in Baroque and Post-Baroque Music* (Princeton, 1978) and *Ornamentation and Improvisation in Mozart*.

Ex. 13.36.

rhythmic displacement of the accent, which would arise from following the instructions laid down by Leopold Mozart, Koch, Türk, and others for a softer rendering of the grace-note than the main note, would weaken the accent or staccato and thus the rhythmic structure. He also, in contrast to Lebert and Faisst (see above, Ex. 13.31), regarded a 'Lombard' rhythm with the dynamic soft–loud (Ex. 13.36) as scarcely feasible, especially in fast music. With respect to the theoretical prescriptions for regarding the long note as bearing the accent in such figures, he argued:

Apart from the sense of affectation emanating from a routinely applied reverse dynamic pattern, it is for a simple reason highly improbable that anybody, including the authors themselves, followed this prescription with any degree of consistency. Such reverse dynamics are feasible only in a slow tempo, before single, long principal notes. The faster the tempo, the less feasible they become. We never find Mozart, nor presumably any other classical master, combining his frequently spelled-out 'Lombard' rhythm [Ex. 13.37(*a*)] with reverse dynamics [Ex. 13.37(*b*)], not even in slow tempos. The very point of the Lombard rhythm is the snap effect produced by the accentuation of the short note.[57]

Ex. 13.37. Neumann, *Ornamentation and Improvisation*, 9

His argument is only valid, however, if the 'Lombard' rhythm is performed strictly as notated in a fairly steady tempo and with a very powerful attack on the first note followed by an abrupt piano, for the slighter the dynamic contrast between the two notes, or the more the initial note of the figure is shortened, the more prominently the second note will appear to bear the accent. A number of theorists of the period who specifically discussed the accentuation of 'Lombard' rhythms considered that they would normally have the stress on the dotted note.[58] Discussion of 'Lombard' rhythms in Neumann's terms is scarcely relevant, since, with a very rapidly delivered grace-note, not only is it virtually impossible to give the small note more accent than the following one, but also the ear no longer perceives a distinct 'Lombard' rhythm even if the grace-note coincides exactly with the bass.

Some of the confusion seems to arise from the very reliance on ornament tables, of which Neumann was rightly so suspicious. The sections on 'Graces' in Domenico Corri's *A Select Collection* (*c*.1782) and *The Singer's Preceptor*

---

[57] *Ornamentation and Improvisation*, 9.   [58] See above, Ch. 2, 'Slurred Groups'.

(1810) provide good examples of the caution that is necessary. In the latter he illustrated his discussion of the 'Leaping Grace' with what is apparently a conventional 'Lombard' rhythm (Ex. 13. 38):[59] in the former he instructed that this grace was 'to be taken softly and to leap into the note rapidly'. Corri's fuller verbal description in the earlier publication clearly indicates that the rhythmic pattern of the example in the later work was not to be taken literally:

> They are not to be considered as forming any part of the air; but are only intended to give to certain notes a particular emphasis or expression. The execution of them, therefore, ought to be so rapid, that, while the effect is felt, the ear shall yet be unable to determine the character of the sounds or to distinguish them from the predominant note[;] by no effort whatever indeed can they be rendered totally imperceptible, or if they could they would not then exist. But the more imperceptible they are, the more happy is the execution, the more perfect the union, and the more delicate the effect, whereas, by an execution that renders them distinctly perceptible, they would lose their nature and instead of the adventitious graces now under consideration, become part of the melody itself.[60]

Ex. 13.38. D. Corri, *The Singer's Preceptor*, 32

All the graces to which Corri applied this description were unequivocally conceived as taking place on the beat; he described anticipating and connecting graces quite separately. The continuity of an on-beat style of performance for grace-notes of this kind in Corri's own family is attested to by Philip Corri's *L'anima di musica*, where, discussing an example of a grace-note (for which he uses the term 'appoggiatura'), he commented: 'The general fault is playing the Appoggiatura before the bass'.[61] This, of course, like similar remarks by other writers, makes it clear that many people at the time did play these notes distinctly before the beat.

Whatever support individual preference for a pre-beat conception of grace-notes may receive from this kind of negative evidence, the fact remains that in the late eighteenth century and early nineteenth century most of the leading musicians of the day who expressed themselves on the subject were strongly opposed to it. One of the few alterations, for instance, that J. F. Reichardt made to the text of Löhlein's *Anweisung zum Violinspielen*, the fourth edition of which he edited in 1797, concerns this matter. Earlier editions contained the passage and realization as shown in Ex. 13.39(*a*), but Reichardt changed the realization to Ex. 13.39(*b*). The evident objection of Reichardt and many other musicians and teachers in the eighteenth and nineteenth centuries to the concept of pre-beat performance of small notes, even in such instances of *tierces*

---

[59] p. 32.   [60] *A Select Collection*, 8.   [61] p. 13.

Ex. 13.39. Löhlein, *Anweisung zum Violinspeilen:* (*a*) 1st edn., 44; (*b*) 4th edn., ed. J. F. Reichardt

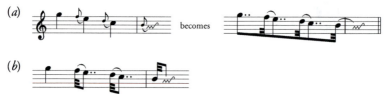

coulées, may well have reflected their concern to ensure that grace-notes created the effect so clearly described by Domenico Corri and were not given greater length than they required.

There is a good deal of musical common sense in this approach, for when grace-notes are conceived as preceding the beat there is a real danger that they will be performed somewhat longer and more lazily, thus giving the effect of anticipatory notes, than if they are thought of as coinciding with it. On the other hand, the laboured rendition that grace-notes sometimes receive from modern performers who are anxious to leave no doubt that they are performing them on the beat (often attempting, futilely, to give them a greater accent than the main note) seems equally contrary to the nature of these notes. Neumann's arguments notwithstanding, it seems clear that in the case of the short appoggiatura there was no requirement that it should really be louder than its main note. A sharper attack on the grace-note, as recommended by C. P. E. Bach, or a more caressing one, as suggested by Leopold Mozart, has little to do with the player's or listener's perception of metric or expressive accent. This misconception of the grace-note has undoubtedly been encouraged by the idea that they are performed with a deliberate rhythm in the manner that many musical examples, such as those of Corri, seem to imply. This once again results to a great extent from the modern, literal approach to musical notation, which, especially with regard to minor modifications of the given rhythm, would have been quite alien to an eighteenth-century musician. At that time Ex. 13.40(*a*) could, in some circumstances, just as well mean Ex. 13.40(*b*), (*c*) or even (*d*) according to context, and, taken in conjunction with verbal descriptions, the sense in which these graphic illustrations are to be understood becomes quite clear. Grace notes should, as Schilling's *Encyclopädie* commented in the 1830s, 'always be rendered as short as possible, for which reason, doubtless, they are also called pinched appoggiaturas'; in addition it confirmed the view that they should as far as possible be accentless, commenting that they

Ex. 13.40.

(*a*) ♪♩. (*b*) ♪♩ (*c*) ♪♩.. (*d*) ♪♩...

'should be performed as lightly as is possible without losing their clarity'; but no doubt was entertained about their placement on the beat, for it continued: 'All appoggiaturas, without exception, fall in the time of their main note.'[62]

The concept of an extremely light and rapid performance of grace-notes is, in fact, implicit in the vast majority of instructions for their execution throughout the Classical and Romantic periods. Reichardt referred to 'very short appoggiaturas' which are performed so that the main notes 'do not seem to lose any of their value'.[63] Koch similarly observed that such notes are 'slurred so fast to the main note that the latter seems to lose nothing of its value'.[64] Both these writers specified performance on the beat. Baillot, apparently envisaging prebeat performance, characterized the grace-note (which he called the *appoggiature rhythmique*) as being played 'briskly and almost on the main note', adding 'in animated movements one naturally makes it faster than in slow movements: however, it always retains a certain speed which distinguishes it from melodic small notes'.[65] Spohr, writing two years earlier and requiring on-beat performance, instructed in the typical German way that it 'deprives the note before which it stands of scarcely any of its value. With this note it is quickly and lightly connected in one bow.'[66] Moser, too, emphasized the light, fleeting nature of this ornament, saying that since it has 'an extremely short, often immeasurable duration, it cannot have any good claim to special accentuation'.[67]

The impression gained from these and numerous other eighteenth- and nineteenth-century descriptions is that, regardless of whether the writers thought they were performing grace-notes on or before the beat, they were very closely in agreement about their effect. This being so, a good criterion for the stylish performance of single grace-notes in most instances might be that the listener should not be conscious of whether the note occurs on the beat or anticipates it slightly. In the long run, it seems far more important that grace-notes fulfil their intended musical function than that, in a mathematically exact sense, they actually occur on the beat. As implied earlier, the minute deviations of rhythm and tempo that are a quintessential element of sensitive performance will, in any case, frequently make it impossible to detect the precise placement of an effectively executed grace-note.

Arguments for real anticipation of the grace-note, on the grounds that the principal notes of a chord should be sounded together on the beat, also reflect a misconception of eighteenth- and nineteenth-century attitudes; in a period which favoured three- and four-part chords in orchestral string writing (usually executed divisi today, but certainly intended at the time to be 'broken') and when frequent unnotated arpeggiando effects were recommended and employed by keyboard players, it seems highly improbable that the very

---

[62] Art. 'Vorschlag'. [63] *Ueber die Pflichten*, 41. [64] *Musikalisches Lexikon*, art. 'Vorschlag'.
[65] *L'Art du violon*, 75. [66] *Violin School*, 159. [67] Joachim and Moser, *Violinschule*, iii. 29.

slightly staggered accentuation that might result from the introduction of a grace-note with the beat would have been regarded as disturbing. Concern for absolute regimentation in such matters (largely a product of recording) has been the norm only since the middle of the twentieth century.

There is little firm information about the attitudes of the major composers of the Classical period towards the performance of grace-notes: however, three musical clocks, two dated (1792 and 1793) and one undated (*c.*1796), provide a particularly valuable source for illustrating how contemporary musicians intimately associated with Haydn realized his ornaments. The barrels of the clocks were apparently pinned either by Joseph Niemecz, who was both librarian and cellist at Eszterháza and, probably, Haydn's composition pupil, or by his assistant Joseph Gurck. They realized the ornaments on these mechanical instruments in a variety of ways, and comparison with the surviving autographs, and copies by Haydn's amanuensis Johann Elßler, shows conclusively that whoever pinned the barrels did not recognize any one immutable method of executing particular ornament signs or small notes. The editors of these *Flötenuhrstücke* in volume XXI of *Joseph Haydn Werke* have this to say about the performance of the grace-notes:

Unfortunately it is not possible to determine, either through listening or through measuring the impressions from the cylinders, whether the organ-builder took the value of a grace-note from the following or preceding note or whether, perhaps, he placed it in between [*sic*!]. Performance on the beat, however, seems to predominate.[68]

What is abundantly clear about these grace-notes is that they are, in agreement with the instructions of Reichardt, Koch, Corri, Baillot, Spohr, Schilling, Moser, and many others, rendered very fleetingly.

Most of the time, nineteenth-century composers, like their eighteenth-century predecessors, were content to rely on the performer's taste and skill in the execution of grace-notes. In a significant number of instances, though, the more painstaking among them were concerned to indicate special requirements. Some pianist composers, including Chopin, Schumann, and Alkan, periodically specified the performance of grace-notes before the beat by the positioning of the small note (Ex. 13.41). Schumann also employed this form of notation in his string writing (Ex. 13.42). Berwald, a string player, carefully marked accents on some of the grace-notes (apparently to be played on the beat) in the Finale of his Quartet in A minor (1849), whereas elsewhere in the same movement he put accents on the main notes (Ex. 13.43).

Some late eighteenth- and early nineteenth-century composers occasionally used single small notes that did not fit into the conventional categories of grace-notes, anticipatory notes, or appoggiaturas. Such small notes, which often stand for short notes of precise value, were a form of shorthand, generally

[68] p. 66.

Ex. 13.41. (*a*) Schumann, Noveletten op. 21/3; (*b*) Alkan, *Douze Études*, no. 10

(*a*)

(*b*)

employed to avoid notational complications that not only would have been troublesome to write but also might have appeared confusing to the performer. These 'pseudo-grace-notes' may involve performance either on or before the beat. Haydn's string quartets op. 76 no. 1 and op. 76 no. 4 and Mozart's Duo for violin and viola K. 423, for instance, contain examples of small notes standing for normal notes on the beat (Ex. 13.44). An example of similar notation indicating a note before the beat occurs in Beethoven's Violin Sonata op. 12 no. 1; comparison with the corresponding passage in the recapitulation clarifies its

Ex. 13.42. Schumann, String Quartet op. 41/1/iv (violin 1)

Ex. 13.43. Berwald, String Quartet in A minor, iv

(*a*)

(*b*)

Ex. 13.44. (*a*) Haydn, String Quartet op.76/2/i; (*b*) Haydn, String Quartet op. 76/4/i;
(*c*) Mozart, Duo K. 423/ii

(*a*)

(*b*)

(*c*)

meaning (Ex. 13.45). In later works, too, Beethoven occasionally used this kind
of shorthand where a precise rhythmic placement of the note would make the
music look unduly complicated and distort the clarity of the phrasing (Ex.
13.46). Like so much else in the music of the Classical period, instances of this
kind are recognizable not so much by the notational symbols employed as by
their musical context.

Anticipatory Notes

Despite the strictures of most German theorists, there were some single small-
note ornaments which, like the two-, three-, or occasionally four-note

Ex. 13.45. Beethoven, Violin Sonata op. 12/1/i

(*a*)

(*b*)

Nachschlag (most commonly occurring after a trill), were definitely conceived as belonging to the time of the note they follow. Among them were *tierces coulées*, which were difficult to distinguish by their context from appoggiaturas or grace-notes and presumably, as the example from Reichardt's edition of Löhlein's *Anweisung zum Violinspielen* (Ex. 13.39) implies, frequently taken in different senses by different musicians. The same kind of appoggiatura or grace-note was considered by Türk, who illustrated both ways of realizing it, but he observed that in German compositions he would not recommend the realization in which the small note took its value from the previous note 'because one cannot presume that the composer had been thinking of the

Ex. 13.46. Beethoven, Rondo op. 51/1

French style or the so-called *Lombard taste*.[69] Other ornaments that presupposed anticipation were connected with particular types of portamento (*cercar della nota, port de voix*) and are considered under that heading in Chapter 15.

Trills, Turns, and Related Ornaments

Trills and turns are closely related ornaments, involving, for the most part, a number of auxiliary notes decorating the main harmony note with notes a second above and below. Some ornaments that share many of the characteristics of trills and turns may involve notes that are further than a second from the main note; and a variety of inconsistent names and signs may be found in those eighteenth- and nineteenth-century writings that attempt to categorize the numerous forms these ornaments could take. The variants described by theorists provide a useful digest of the sorts of patterns employed by musicians of the period, but any attempt to link these formulas with the practice of individual composers and their ornament signs must be made with the greatest circumspection. It is important, once again, to remember that even where the composer has notated an ornament with small notes, or in those relatively rare instances where we can confidently associate a composer's ornament sign with a particular pattern of notes, there may, depending on the musical circumstances, be more room for flexibility and initiative on the performer's part than is commonly believed. Composers would certainly have considered some realizations of their ornament notation inappropriate, but this does not mean, especially in the late eighteenth century and early nineteenth century, that they would have considered a single realization, in a given instance, to be the only possibility with regard to either rhythm or the pattern of notes employed. As in other aspects of notation, later nineteenth-century composers were often more prescriptive, and where a precise rendition of an ornament was considered integral to their musical intentions they tended to write the ornament out in full, at least on its first appearance.

It will be useful first to consider these types of ornament independently of the notations employed to indicate them in the music of the period, and to look in a general way at the sorts of contexts and situations in which eighteenth- and nineteenth-century musicians believed them to be appropriate. A comprehensive survey of the relationships between signs and particular patterns of notes is beyond the scope of this chapter, but a few of the most commonly encountered problems will be illuminated by examples and extracts from music and writings of the period.

In its simplest form a turn consists of four notes: the normal turn (Ex. 13.47(*a*)) and the inverted turn (Ex. 13.47(*b*)). It may also have five notes (Ex.

---

[69] *Klavierschule*, III, §23.

Ex. 13.47.

(a)    (b)

13.48). If further repetitions of the main note and its upper auxiliary are added, these turns will be heard as trills. Trills, turns, and associated embellishments tend to act as accenting ornaments when they occur at the beginning of a strong beat, and as connecting ornaments when they occupy a weak beat. On long notes, of course, the repetitions of the main note and its upper auxiliary, which differentiate the trill from the turn, are necessary to fill out the note; on short notes the rapidity of the music or the expression aimed at by the performer will determine whether a simple turn (which can be seen as synonymous with a short trill) or a more extended trill is employed.

Ex. 13.48.

(a)    (b)

Trill Beginnings

Much attention has been focused on the manner in which trills were expected to be performed in the second half of the eighteenth century and early years of the nineteenth century. Discussion has concentrated, in particular, on the extent to which the apparently rigid prescription of some influential theorists (Marpurg, C. P. E. Bach, etc.) and their followers, that the trill should (almost) invariably begin with the upper auxiliary, and especially that the upper note should fall on the stronger part of the beat, was accepted by performers and composers of the period. There can be little doubt that these musicians mostly, if not always, required an upper-note, on-beat beginning to trills in their own music, but the situation with regard to the music of major composers of the period is by no means clear-cut. The issue was already a matter for discussion during the eighteenth century, and the concurrent employment of both types is amply demonstrated in documentary and musical sources.[70] Koch, for example, wrote: 'The majority hold, with C. P. E. Bach, that the beginning of the trill must be made with the upper auxiliary; . . . others, however, that one should always begin it with the main note.'[71] And in a footnote he referred to Tromlitz as a supporter of the latter view in his *Ausführlicher und gründicher Unterricht die Flöte zu spielen*. J. F. Reichardt strongly advocated the upper-note

---

[70] See Neumann, *Ornamentation in Baroque and Post-Baroque Music*.
[71] *Musikalisches Lexikon*, art. 'Triller'.

start, but his comment that it should begin with the upper note, 'not as many mistakenly believe with the note itself',[72] also reveals the diversity of eighteenth-century practice.

Those who advocated an upper-note start as the rule during the second half of the eighteenth century were undoubtedly, as Koch remarked, in the majority; but Koch expressed no preference and observed that it was scarcely a matter of much importance whether the trill began one way or the other, since there was no audible difference after the initial note had been sounded. Despite Marpurg's often-quoted remark about the trill being a series of reiterated appoggiaturas, it seems highly unlikely that this view, emphasizing the dissonance of the auxiliary throughout the length of the trill (which, in any case, would only have been obvious in a rather slow trill), was significant in the late eighteenth century. The trill was overwhelmingly seen as an embellishment in which the harmonic and melodic primacy of the main note remained distinct. Domenico Corri acknowledged two principal manners of performing a trill in singing, remarking that some recommended a 'close rapid shake, giving a brilliancy and shortness to the upper Note', while others, including himself (following his master Porpora), required it with 'equality of notes, distinctly marked and moderately quick. Also that the Note which bears the Shake ought to be the most predominant, and if the auxiliary Note is too closely blended the principal cannot be sufficiently distinguished.'[73] In his publications Corri appears to indicate some cadential trills beginning with the main note, others with the upper note. However, Philip Corri, in *L'anima di musica*, published in the same year as his father's *Singer's Preceptor*, instructed, 'The turn and sometimes the first note of the shake is written (tho' it is understood without it)', observing that the figures in Ex. 13.49(*a*) 'would be played alike', and added 'Sometimes the shake begins with an inverted turn [Ex. 13.49(*b*)] Hence the shake must begin either above or below, and end on the principal note, but never begin on the principal note.'[74] On the other hand, Domenico Corri's younger son Haydn Corri gave examples of trills beginning on the main note; but, eschewing dogmatism, he added the following *nota bene*:

Ex. 13.49. P. A. Corri, *L'anima di musica*, 18–19

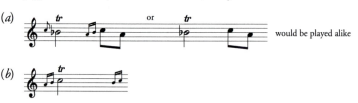

---

[72] *Ueber die Pflichten*, 46.   [73] *The Singer's Preceptor*, 30.   [74] pp. 18–19.

When a perfect shake is obtained there are many very elegant additions, as the preparing note and the closing ornament, but this I leave to the taste of the Master, as there are too many for imitation in a work founded upon brevity. Also it would appear presumptuous, were I to dictate which was most graceful as that is all matter of opinion.[75]

Scholarship has produced an impressive body of evidence and argument to support the view that there was far greater diversity of practice than the most frequently cited sources might suggest, and that the supposed hegemony of the 'appoggiatura trill' in the late eighteenth century is a fiction. Further examples (if such are needed) of late eighteenth-century sources which demonstrate theoretical support for main-note starts, and are not cited by Neumann or others, can be found in English instruction books. The anonymous *Instructions for the Violin by an Eminent Master* shows the trill beginning on the main note.[76] J. Mc Kerrell's *A Familiar Introduction to the First Principles of Music* gives further examples of trills starting on the note[77] (Ex. 13.50). During the nineteenth century an increasing number of musicians, including composers of importance such as Hummel and Spohr, stated that trills would normally begin with the main note and that composers who required an alternative beginning should indicate this. But there is no good reason to imagine that experienced musicians would have felt themselves inhibited from varying their trill beginnings (or endings), nor that composers would have wished to interdict a reasonable degree of licence in the matter.

Whatever may have been the views and practices of individual composers, it seems certain that the majority of performers employed trills beginning from the note above, the main note, or the note below, as it suited their musical purpose. Despite the apparently prescriptive teaching of some theorists, there are abundant indications in others of an acceptance that the execution of trills, like other ornaments, would be left to the taste of the performer, especially since few composers took the trouble to spell out their requirements clearly. In 1770 John Holden, for instance, whose musical examples show trills beginning on the main note, some with and some without a concluding turn, remarked:

Ex. 13.50. Mc Kerrell, *A Familiar Introduction*, 3

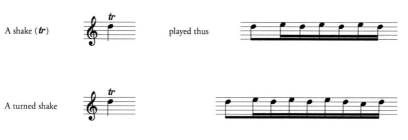

[75] *The Delivery of Vocal Music* (London, 1823), 5.   [76] p. 17.   [77] (London, [*c.*1800]), 3.

'Sometimes the shake is not begun until one half of the note be sung plain. These and other such varieties are generally left to the performer's choice, being all indiscriminately marked in the same manner . . .'[78] (Ex. 13.51). Much the same attitude is apparent in Baillot's treatment of the matter some sixty years later when he offered the performer a choice of four possibilities for the execution of trill beginnings (Ex. 13.52). Like Holden and Haydn Corri he considered the executant's choice to be determined by taste, though he observed that beginning with the upper auxiliary was the norm.[79]

Ex. 13.51. Holden, *Essay*, 39

Ex. 13.52. Baillot, *L'Art du violon*, 78

Concrete evidence of practices closely associated with a major composer of the Classical period can again be found in the performances of Haydn's *Flötenuhrstücke* preserved on musical clocks; this may lend support to Moser's statement about Viennese customs (below), while at the same time indicating a lack of rigidity in approach. The majority of the trills begin with the main note. Specially instructive are a number of pieces which appear on more than one clock; here there is frequent disagreement about the realization of trills and other ornaments. In these duplicated pieces, the undated clock almost exclusively begins trills on the main note (exceptions occur only in Hob. XIX:13 and, once, in Hob. XIX:16). Much of the time the other clock is in agreement, but

---

[78] *Essay*, 39.   [79] *L'Art du violon*, 78.

on a significant number of occasions it has an upper-note start where the undated clock begins on the note. None of these upper-note starts appears to precede the beat. In other instances one clock may have a turn at the end of the trill while the other carries on to the end with repetitions of the main note and its upper auxiliary. Another interesting point is that where a passage recurs within a piece a clock may execute a trill differently on the two occasions (in Hob. XIX:18 the trill in bar 1 begins with the upper note but in the repetition of the passage at bar 33 it starts with the main note; in Hob. XIX:18 the trill in bar 26 is longer than that in bar 2). None of these variant versions derive support from the notation of the surviving autographs or copies, and few consistencies of practice seem to emerge. Both the undated clock and the 1793 clock agree in adopting an upper auxiliary start in an ascending chains of trills (Hob. XIX:13, bars 21–2), but even here they differ on whether the trills should conclude with a turn. Frederick Neumann argued that since the 1792 and 1793 clocks were made while Haydn was away from Austria and the undated clock was probably made after his return in 1796, the versions on this clock, which has a greater preponderance of main-note starts to trills (as well as pre-beat ornamentation), probably indicate Haydn's preferred treatment.[80] Another tenable explanation would be that the third clock was pinned by Niemicz's assistant, Gurck, and therefore indicates a difference in practice between these two musicians.[81] Far more important is the evidence for diversity. Niemicz's evident musical abilities and the closeness of his association with Haydn lend strong support to the assumption that the composer's own attitudes in this matter were not inflexible.

Despite all the evidence for diversity of practice, the question of stylistic propriety in the execution of trill beginnings occupied the minds of some late nineteenth-century musicians of a theoretical bent. The violinist Andreas Moser, having quoted C. P. E. Bach's comment that since all trills begin with the upper auxiliary note it is unnecessary to indicate it unless an appoggiatura is intended, observed: 'Apparently this remark is occasioned by the special approach of the Mannheim School, where the practice obtained only to begin the trill with the upper auxiliary if this were specifically required by a gracenote.' He identified the strongest support for the upper-note trill as being in north Germany, though C. P. E. Bach's authority gave the doctrine wider currency and remarked: 'the powerful influences which stemmed from the Viennese masters of instrumental music seem finally to have broken its hegemony.'[82] The basis for Moser's assertions about Mannheim and Vienna are unclear, but it seems likely that they stem directly from opinions relayed by

---

[80] 'More on Haydn's Ornaments and the Evidence of Musical Clocks', in *New Essays on Performance Practice* (Ann Arbor, 1989), 105–19.

[81] See *Joseph Haydn Werke*, XXI, p. ix.   [82] Joachim and Moser, *Violinschule*, iii. 20.

Joachim, who would have acquired them from his early studies in Vienna with Joseph Boehm (b. 1795) and Georg Hellmesberger (b. 1800).

Another nineteenth-century musician, the pianist Franklin Taylor, noted in the first edition of *Grove's Dictionary* that the trill beginning on the main note was the 'manner most shakes in modern music are executed', but went on to suggest that composers' methods of notating a trill that was required to begin from below will reveal whether they intended a normal trill to start with the upper auxiliary or the main note (Ex. 13.53). He observed:

From a composer's habit of writing the lower prefix with one, two or three notes, his intentions respecting the beginning of the ordinary shake *without* prefix, as to whether it should begin with the principal or subsidiary note, may generally be inferred. For since it would be incorrect to render Ex. 23 or 24 [see Ex. 13.53] in the manner shown in Ex. 27 [Ex. 13.54(*a*)], which involves the repetition of a note, and a consequent break of legato—it follows that a composer who chooses the form Ex. 23 to express the prefix intends the shake to begin with the upper note, while the use of Ex. 24 shows that a shake beginning with the principal note is generally intended.

That the form Ex. 22 [see Ex. 13.53] always implies the shake beginning with the principal note is not so clear (although there is no doubt that it usually does so) for a prefix is possible which leaps from the lower to the upper subsidiary note. This exceptional form is frequently employed by Mozart, and is marked as in Ex. 28 [Ex. 13.54(*b*)] . . . Among later composers Chopin and Weber almost invariably wrote the prefix with two notes (Ex. 23); Beethoven uses two notes in his earlier works (see op. 2 no. 2, Largo bar 10), but afterwards generally one (see op. 57).[83]

More recent authors, writing primarily about Mozart, have suggested various general musical criteria for deciding on the appropriate treatment of trills, which may just as well be applied to the music of later composers, and, in the

Ex. 13.53. Taylor, 'Shake', in Grove, *Dictionary*

Ex. 13.54. Taylor, 'Shake', in Grove, *Dictionary*
(*a*)

(*b*)

---

[83] 'Shake', in vol. iii. 483.

absence of firm information about a composer's intentions in general or in particular instances, they may be helpful to the uncertain performer. Eva and Paul Badura-Skoda recommended a main-note start when:

1. in legato the trill is preceded by the next note above;
2. the trill is preceded by three rising or falling notes like a 'slide';
3. the trill is on a dissonant note;
4. the trill is in the bass;
5. the trill comes at the end of a rising scale;
6. the trill is preceded by the same note as a sharply attacked anacrusis;
7. the trill is part of a chain of trills;[84]
8. the trill is in the formula [Ex. 13.55];
9. in other special cases.[85]

Ex. 13.55.

Frederick Neumann proposed a simpler rule of thumb, which he saw as 'rooted in musical logic'. He suggested that

1) a trill starting with the upper note on the beat has the effect of a short appoggiatura; 2) a trill starting with a lengthened upper note has the effect of a long appoggiatura; 3) a trill starting with the upper note before the beat has the effect of a grace-note [in his terminology, a note sounded before the beat]. We find guidance by leaving out the trill and judging whether one of these ornaments would be a desirable addition to the bare melody; if so, the corresponding trill type is likely to be the proper or at least an acceptable choice. Where none of these ornaments seems to fit, the main-note trill is indicated.[86]

These are all perfectly good and sensible recommendations, and can to some extent be supported by theoretical writings; but it may be legitimate to maintain a degree of scepticism about assuming too readily that what seems musical and tasteful to us in these matters would necessarily have done so to musicians of previous generations.

Trill Endings

There were as many views about the endings of trills as about their beginnings, and here, too, it seems unlikely that experienced executants would have been greatly inhibited by the composer's notation in varying the endings as they saw

---

[84] But see the evidence of the Haydn clock (above) with respect to a rising chain of trills where each begins with the upper note.

[85] *Mozart-Interpretation* (Vienna and Stuttgart, 1957), trans. Leo Black as *Interpreting Mozart on the Keyboard* (London, 1962), 111–16.

[86] *Ornamentation and Improvisation*, 114.

fit, nor that composers, at least until the second half of the nineteenth century, would always have taken exception to this practice. A number of different endings are commonly encountered. In the eighteenth century it seems likely that the trill would often conclude with an anticipation of the next note, as illustrated in the second example from Holden (Ex. 13.51 above), or as notated in Anton Bemetzrieder's *New Lessons* (Ex. 13.56).[87] Many musicians seem to have

Ex. 13.56. Bemetzrieder, *New Lessons*, 14

favoured the familiar turned ending as a rule: Reichardt, for instance, remarked: 'The trill often has a turn [*Nachschlag*], which in orchestral parts is normally written out [Ex. 13.57], but sometimes omitted. In this case one

Ex. 13.57. Reichardt, *Ueber die Pflichten*, 46

should see that at least every trill on a long note has a turn.'[88] The instruction to end trills with a turn as a matter of course is often encountered in instruction books; some authors, such as the 'eminent master' whose *Instructions for the Violin* was published in London in about 1795, were quite definite that 'a shake should never be finished without [a turn]'.[89] In the nineteenth century, Joachim also firmly believed that in the vast majority of cases trills should have a turn of some kind, whether it was indicated or not; thus he, and probably most violinists of the early nineteenth century, would have concluded the trill at the beginning of Beethoven's Violin Sonata op. 96 with a turn, which was most likely what the composer wanted, although he did not indicate one. It was in descending figures that a turn seems most often to have been omitted; the omission of the turn was explicitly required by Philip Corri, for instance, in figures such as Ex. 13.58(*a*), though he remarked that turns should be included in similar ascending figures (Ex. 13.58(*b*)). He too commented that trills, as a rule, conclude with a turn, whether or not one was notated. On the other hand, where a chain of ascending trills in solo violin playing was concerned, Spohr and Baillot instructed, contrary to the keyboard practice of C. P. E. Bach, that no turn should be included.

[87] *New Lessons for the Harpsichord* (London, 1783), 14.   [88] *Ueber die Pflichten*, 46.
[89] Anon., *Instructions for the Violin by an Eminent Master*, 17.

Ex. 13.58. P. A. Corri, *L'anima di musica*, 19

A nice, but by no means unusual, example of notational inexactitude in the matter of trill endings and beginnings can be found in the printed orchestral parts of Anton Flad's Oboe Concertino in C (*c*.1800); in the opening tutti the solo oboe and the first violin are in unison throughout but the trills are notated quite differently (Ex. 13.59). Despite three different ways of showing the trills, it seems likely that a trill beginning with the upper note and ending with a turn was envisaged in each case.

Ex. 13.59. A. Flad, Concertino in C, i

More elaborate trill endings were commonly interpolated by solo players until the middle years of the nineteenth century. In 1811 John Jousse gave examples of highly decorative endings, which, he remarked, 'are become very fashionable' (Ex. 13.60).[90] Baillot's examples of terminations for trills indicate the most usual variants of the normal turned ending (Ex. 13.61); but he also included forty-eight more elaborate endings in his instructions for the embellishment of fermatas (Ex. 13.62).

Ex. 13.60. Jousse, *Theory and Practice of the Violin*, 47

---

[90] *Theory and Practice of the Violin*, 47.

Ex. 13.61. Baillot, *L'Art du violon*, 78

Ex. 13.62. Baillot, *L'Art du violon*, 171–2

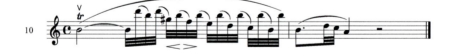

In general, however, it seems likely that in ensemble playing, and in the majority of normal circumstances, trills would most commonly have concluded with the familiar two-note pattern. When composers in the later part of the nineteenth century quite definitely did not want this they would certainly have had to indicate it, as Dvořák did at the beginning of his String Quartet op. 106 (see Ex. 13.2).

Turns

The expressive effect of the turn depends on its position in relation to the note it ornaments, on its rhythmic configuration, and on the speed at which it is executed. The relationship between the turn that embellishes the beginning of a beat and the trill has always been close. C. P. E. Bach considered that the two ornaments were interchangeable in many instances and felt that the principal difference was that, since his turns were normally more rapid at the beginning than at the end, 'there is always a small space between them and the following note'. His examples of turns show that only at a very fast tempo might the notes of the turn be even (Ex 13.63). For Bach the turn (*Doppelschlag*) was principally

Ex. 13.63. C. P. E. Bach, *Versuch*, table v, fig. L

an accenting ornament.[91] Leopold Mozart used the term 'mordent' for a similar pattern of notes (and the inverted form), but his explanation of its performance, influenced by Italian practice, was different from Bach's, for he considered that 'The stress of the tone falls on the note itself, while the mordent, on the contrary, is slurred quite softly and very quickly on to the principal note' (Ex. 13.64). He was particularly emphatic about the speed of the ornament. For Mozart this was essentially an improvised ornament, to be applied where a note was to be given particular liveliness.[92] Domenico Corri, from the singer's point of view, gave a somewhat different explanation of their execution, instructing that 'The Ascending Turn, begins softly, and encreases [*sic*] its strength as it rises, then gently again sinks into the note' (Ex. 13.65(a)), while 'The Descending Turn, begins strong, and decreases its strength as it falls, then rises into the note strong again' (Ex. 13.65(*b*)).[93] Corri, Niccolo Pasquali, Justin Heinrich Knecht, and other writers also, however, illustrated

---

[91] *Versuch*, i. II, 4, §§1 ff.   [92] *Versuch*, XI, §§10 ff.   [93] *A Select Collection*, i. 8.

Ex. 13.64. L. Mozart, *Versuch*, XI, §13

Ex. 13.65. D. Corri, *A Select Collection*, i. 8

these kinds of turn with a longer first note, suggesting, perhaps, a degree of agogic accent (Ex. 13.66).[94] Yet another explanation of the execution of this kind of turn (*grupetto*) was given in the nineteenth century by Manuel García, who instructed that it should 'begin with a bold sforzando on the first of the three notes composing it. The stress given to this note should carry off the two others that follow.'[95] (García considered this form of turn the most common ornament after the appoggiatura and evidently regarded what he called *mezzi-grupetti* and double appoggiaturas as ornaments closely related in their musical function; see Ex. 13.67).

Ex. 13.66

Ex. 13.67. García, *New Treatise*, 33

Most authors stated that these kinds of turn should be performed quickly; but a variety of speeds, depending on context, might certainly have been employed by musicians throughout the period. An example from the eighteenth century illustrates how, even with the same notation, two turns might be differently executed in close proximity; Löhlein gave the realization shown in Ex. 13.68, indicating varied treatment of the two on-beat turns. In the nineteenth century, just as there was a greater tendency for trills to begin with the

[94] Corri, *The Singer's Preceptor*; Pasquali, *The Art of Fingering the Harpsichord* (Edinburgh, [c.1760]); Knecht, *Kleine theoretische Klavierschule für die ersten Anfänger* (Munich, [1799]).

[95] *New Treatise*, 33.

Ex. 13.68. Löhlein, *Anweisung zum Violinspielen*, 48

principal note, there is evidence that in some circumstances performers may have been inclined to start these kinds of turns with the main note. Baillot, for example, suggested realizing the turn sign in the Allegro of Mozart's Violin Sonata K. 379 as in Ex. 13.69, though it seems more likely that Mozart intended something like his father's mordent or García's explosive turn or *grupetto*, beginning from the note above. Baillot's instinct to begin such figures with the main note was evidently shared by his younger colleague Charles de Bériot, who illustrated the resolution of a turn sign, in almost identical circumstances, in a very similar manner (Ex. 13.70).

Ex. 13.69. Baillot, *L'Art du violon*, 84

Ex. 13.70. Bériot, *Méthode*, 205

For the most part such turns, along with other short ornaments, would have been added at will in the performance of eighteenth-century and early nineteenth-century music, and remained appropriate as improvised embellishment in some later nineteenth-century repertoires, especially Italian vocal music. With respect to their positioning on or before the beat, many of the same factors apply as in the case of the grace-note; the majority of authorities favoured on-beat performance, but some advocated performance before the beat.

The form of turn for which Leopold Mozart used the conventional German term *Doppelschlag* was clearly considered by him as a connecting ornament, whose principal use was as an extempore embellishment to an appoggiatura,[96] and the same usage was still recommended in the nineteenth century by Campagnoli[97] (Ex. 13.71(*a*), Ex. 13.25(*c*)). In the revised 1787 edition of his *Versuch* Mozart also illustrated it as a simple connection between two notes (Ex. 13.71(*b*)).[98] Both these patterns were standard eighteenth-century usages, varying slightly from author to author in their exact rhythmic configuration and placement (see, for instance, Ex. 13.68). In the eighteenth century it seems to

Ex. 13.71. L. Mozart, *Versuch*: (*a*) first edition (1756), XI, §10; (*b*) third edition (1787), IX, §28

(*a*)

(*b*)

---

[96] *Versuch*, IX, §27.   [97] *Nouvelle méthode*, 43.   [98] Ch. IX, §28.

have been generally accepted that the connecting turn would be performed rapidly, and this remained true for many nineteenth-century musicians, for instance Spohr, who instructed that 'the turn is always played quickly, whether in slow or quick degree of movement'.[99] And García took a similar view of all turns (*grupetti*), whether accented, connecting, or anticipatory. He illustrated and explained the three types:

In the first case, the note must be struck by the turn; example:- [Ex. 13.72(*a*)]

In the second case, the note should be fixed, and the turn placed in the middle of its duration; example:- [Ex. 13.72(*b*)]

In the third case, the value of the note must be accomplished by the turn; example:- [Ex. 13.72(*c*)]

The essential character of the turn being rapidity and animation, its duration should be that of a semiquaver, at No. 100 of Maelzel's metronome.[100]

Ex. 13.72. García, *New Treatise*, 33

(*a*)

Las mu - cha - chas ___ de l'Ha - va -

(*b*) ROSSINI–*Semiramide*

Bel - la im - ma - go

(*c*) CIMAROSA–*Il Matrimonio segreto*

Pria che spun -ti in cie - l l'au -ro - ra.

There was, however, a growing tendency towards the middle of the nineteenth century to perform some turns in a more leisurely manner. A. B. Marx thought that the turn should be 'performed in moderately fast or even fast tempo'.[101] And a generation later Dannreuther recorded:

The turn in Bellini's cantilena, both andantino and largo, was sung in a very broad way, so the notes formed part of the principal phrase, just as it is now to be found written out and incorporated in Wagner's *Tristan*. The ornamental notes, resembling a turn at the end of a long breath, were always given piano, diminuendo, leggiero as in Chopin. [Ex. 13.73][102]

[99] *Violin School*, 157.
[101] In Schilling, *Encyclopädie*, ii. 461 (art. 'Doppelschlag').
[100] *New Treatise*, 33.
[102] *Musical Ornamentation*, ii. 141.

Ex. 13.73. Bellini, *I Puritani*, in Dannreuther, *Musical Ornamentation*, ii. 141

In Joachim's C major Romance, the composer performed the turns in bars 7 and 98 of Ex. 12.12 as five equal notes commencing at the beginning of the bar, rather than starting half-way through the first note as suggested by most nineteenth-century theorists.

The Notation of Turns and Trills

Most of the instructions about ornaments in theoretical writings were less an objective record of contemporary notational practice than an essentially vain attempt to produce order out of the chaos of conflicting signs and practices. In reality composers were remarkably casual about how they indicated ornaments, and where evidence exists to show what particular composers meant by particular signs, this frequently appears to be different from the realizations proposed in standard theoretical writings. Even when composers complained about engravers failing accurately to transcribe the signs they had written (as Haydn did to Artaria), it is clear from numerous instances in their own autographs that they were often not at all consistent in their employment of them. Bernhard Romberg confessed in his *Méthode de violoncelle* to a laxity in the use of signs for standard and inverted turns which was probably typical of many composers' attitudes to the notation of ornaments; having explained the meaning of the two signs conventionally used for normal and inverted turns, Romberg commented: 'There are however some Composers (among whom I include myself) who write in such haste that they do not take the trouble to mark this grace in such a way as to show whether they intend it to be made from above or below.'[103] Spohr, in his *Violinschule*, followed Hummel's piano method in giving ∞ for a normal turn and ∾ for an inverted turn,[104] in contrast to most writers, who employed these signs in the opposite sense. But in his autographs Spohr does not seem to have adopted his own recommendations. In the works of his Vienna period (1812–15) he invariably notated turns, like Pleyel, as ᠲ;[105] and in the year of Hummel's treatise he was still using the same notation,[106] though in all cases the first editions printed the normal turn sign

---

[103] *A Complete*, 86.   [104] *Violinschule*, 156 ff.

[105] See e.g. the autographs of op. 29 no. 2 and op. 30 shown in facsimile *The Selected Works of Louis Spohr*, ed. Clive Brown, ix/2 (New York, Garland, 1988).

[106] See the autograph of op. 82 no. 2 in ibid.

(∾). In a copy of his song 'Nachgefühl' written in an album in 1834, just after the publication of the *Violinschule*, Spohr indicated what was evidently meant to be a direct turn with the sign he had recommended in his treatise, but when he prepared another copy of this song for publication as a facsimile in the *Allgemeine musikalische Zeitung* in 1839, he employed the conventional direct turn sign (Ex. 13.74).

An interesting, more general case-study is provided by late eighteenth- and early nineteenth-century employment of the signs and formulas shown in Ex. 13.75. These often seem to have been used synonymously, sometimes in close proximity in the same piece of music, with the meaning shown in Ex. 13.76. Haydn, for instance, employed the forms found in Ex. 13.77. Haydn was certainly not alone in this; his pupil Pleyel used them in a similar manner and with similar meanings. Comparison of different notations in Pleyel's own edition of his twelve string quartets (in four books of three quartets) dedicated to the King of Prussia of 1787 is instructive.[107] In many places in these quartets *tr* seems to be used as a shorthand for Ex. 13.75(*a*), as in the first movement of the third quartet in book 1 (Ex. 13.78(*a*), or the second movement of the third quartet in book 2 (Ex. 13.78(*b*)). The first movement of the third quartet in book 3 provides a very good example of how cautious one should be about making assumptions of pre-beat performance for such ornaments, even before staccato notes; for while the first violin has three small notes, the second violin, in thirds with it, simply has *tr* (Ex. 13.79). The synonymity of these notations and the turn sign is suggested by passages in the third movement of the second quartet in book 2: the first violin has a turn sign on the initial appearance of the figure (Ex. 13.80), then a trill in its subsequent appearance. Where viola and cello play the figure in thirds later in the movement, the viola has a turn (this time without the vertical line) while the cello has *tr*. In addition, the first movement of the second quartet in book 3 shows an apparent equivalence between the notations in Ex. 13.81.

Further examples of this kind of inconsistent notation for ornaments may be drawn from numerous printed editions and manuscript sources of the period; some of them may reflect an intention to vary ornamentation at the return of an earlier passage, but most do not seem likely to have any such implication. In many instances these alternative methods of notation offer useful clues to the kinds of thing the composer may have imagined. Comparison of Mozart's draft of the first movement of his Violin Sonata K. 306 with the final version (1778) appears to show different methods of notating the same ornaments. In bar 18 both versions have the notation shown in Ex. 13.82(*a*); in bars 40 ff. the same figure occurs in the finished manuscript while the draft has a simplified notation, probably meaning the same thing (Ex. 13.82(*b*)–(*c*)). In the draft, a

[107] *Douze Nouveaux Quatuors dédiés A sa Majesté Le Roi De Prusse* (Paris, Pleyel, n.d.).

Ex. 13.74. Spohr, 'Nachgefühl' WoO. 91, autographs

(*a*)

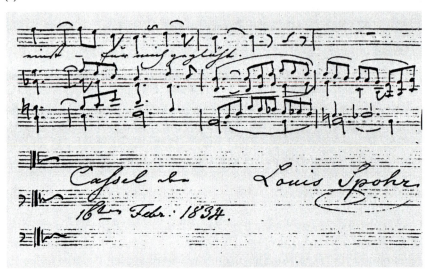

(*b*)

Ex. 13.75

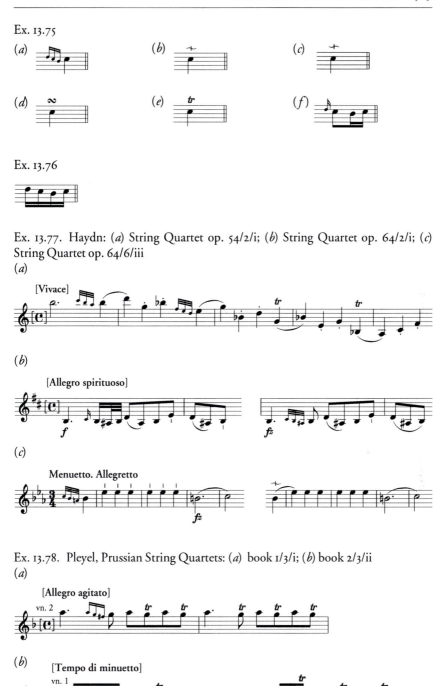

Ex. 13.76

Ex. 13.77. Haydn: (*a*) String Quartet op. 54/2/i; (*b*) String Quartet op. 64/2/i; (*c*) String Quartet op. 64/6/iii
(*a*)

(*b*)

(*c*)

Ex. 13.78. Pleyel, Prussian String Quartets: (*a*) book 1/3/i; (*b*) book 2/3/ii
(*a*)

(*b*)

Ex. 13.79. Pleyel, Prussian String Quartets, book 3/3/i

Ex. 13.80. Pleyel, Prussian String Quartets, book 2/2/iii

Ex. 13.81. Pleyel, Prussian String Quartets, book 3/2/i

connecting turn is shown at bars 36 f. as in Ex. 13.82(*d*), while in the final version it is fully written out as in Ex. 13.82(*e*). In Clementi's Piano Sonata op. 40 no. 1, as in many examples from Haydn, a turn is written the first time as three small notes, and the second time as ∞ (Ex. 13.83). Wenzel Müller, in *Das Sonnenfest der Braminen*, employed a somewhat differently notated version of this ornament and abbreviated it later as *tr* (Ex. 13.84). Süssmayr's opera *Der Spiegel von Arkadien* presents another example of the interchangeability of the accenting turn or mordent, written this time as three notes, and the short trill beginning from above (Ex. 13.85). As an abbreviation for the same figure, Salieri used ✢ rather than *tr* in his Singspiel *Der Rauchfangkehrer*; in this case the synonymity of the two signs is confirmed by a passage in which the flute is written

Ex. 13.82. Mozart, Violin Sonata K. 306/i

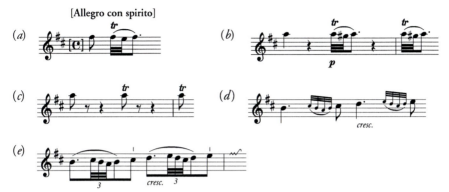

Ex. 13.83. Clementi, Piano Sonata op. 40/1/i, printed edn. (London, Clementi, [1802])

Ex. 13.84. Müller, *Das Sonnenfest der Braminen*, no. 11

Ex. 13.85. Süssmayr, *Der Spiegel von Arcadien*, no. 5

one way and the oboe the other (Ex. 13.86(*a*)). In the same number of the opera Salieri employed the sign ✛ together with notation clearly indicating a turn of four equal notes (Ex. 13.86(*b*)). This convention was not apparently confined to Viennese composers, for Weber employed it in *Der Freischütz* (Ex. 13.87), though perhaps he derived it from his brief period of study with Michael Haydn.

It is worth noting that theorists gave a number of quite incompatible explanations of the sign ✛ or ✛ (often impossible to distinguish from ∾ in

Ex. 13.86. Salieri, *Der Rauchfangkehrer.* (*a*) Act I, no. 6; (*b*) Act II, no. 5

(*a*)   [con moto]

(*b*)   [Allegro]

Ex. 13.87. Weber, *Der Freischütz*, no. 2, autograph (poco più moderato (following Allegro), 6/8)

manuscript sources). Cartier, in *L'Art du violon*, considered ᚠ it to mean a trill with a turn, whereas *tr* was a simple trill without turn;[108] and Philip Corri saw the line through the middle as a sign that the ornament should be a 'close turn' (i.e. with an accidental before the first or third notes).[109] Also with respect to accidentals in turns, Reichardt rather confusingly suggested Ex. 13.88(*a*) as a notation for Ex. 13.88(*b*) and Ex. 13.88(*c*) for Ex. 13.88(*d*). Idiosyncratic notation of this sort may lie behind the ambiguity of the accidentals in some Beethoven turns, for example in the *Chorfantasie* op. 80, where a turn sign in bar 33 with a sharp followed by a natural sign above it almost certainly indicates a turn with a sharpened under-note;[110] or in the 'Kreutzer' Sonata, where the turn added to the violin's G♯ in the *Stichvorlage* at bar 95 of the first movement (it is missing in the autograph) has a pair of sharp signs beneath it (evidently signifying an F𝄪, notwithstanding the opinion of the new Beethoven *Gesamtausgabe*, where it is given as F♯), while at the equivalent place in the recapitulation the sign after the violin's C♯ is written with a sharp above it, signifying a B♯.

Ex. 13.88. Reichardt, *Ueber die Pflichten*, 57

(*a*)   (*b*)   (*c*)   (*d*)

Mendelssohn's notation in a number of early works provides some interesting comparisons between trill signs and turns. In the Scherzo of the Octet for Strings op. 20 he first wrote the ornament at bar 95, as in Ex. 13.89(*a*), but subsequently changed it to Ex. 13.89(*b*). (In all subsequent occurrences of the figure Mendelssohn wrote out the turn after the trill.) In his own piano duet arrangement of the Octet this bar occurs as in Ex. 13.89(*c*), and the notes marked *tr* in this passage in the autograph are all written out as similar four-note turns. Where the string version has Ex. 13.89(*d*), the piano duet has an inverted turn, or three-note trill, beginning on the main note. Where he used a similar notation to the latter in the almost contemporaneous opera *Die Hochzeit des Camacho*, however, he gave it as a short trill from above or a turn in his vocal score arrangement (Ex. 13.90). At bar 202 of the Finale of his op. 6 Piano Sonata he wrote a trill in the autograph (Ex. 13.91(*a*)), but at this point in the first edition, and elsewhere where a similar figure occurs in the autograph, it is written as four semiquavers (Ex. 13.91(*b*)).

Apart from the evidence of inconsistent notation, such examples lend support to the idea that those composers regarded these kinds of accenting ornaments as coinciding with the beat rather than preceding it, and that they

---

[108] p. 4.   [109] Corri, *L'anima di musica*, 16.
[110] Ed. Clive Brown (Wiesbaden, Breitkopf & Härtel, 1993), 4 and 64–5.

Ex. 13.89. Mendelssohn, Octet op. 20/iii

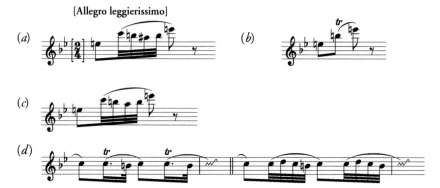

Ex. 13.90. Mendelssohn, *Die Hochzeit des Camacho*, no. 14: (*a*) autograph; (*b*) vocal score

Ex. 13.91. Mendelssohn, Piano Sonata op. 6/iv: (*a*) autograph; (*b*) first edition

retained a fairly strong notion of an upper-note start to trills. However, it would be contrary to the spirit of eighteenth- and nineteenth-century performance to conclude from this that a metrically regimented or uniform execution of ornaments in these or similar circumstances was envisaged; the rhythmic placement, in particular, may be subject to many subtle variations depending on context and the effect desired by the performer. There is no reason to suppose, for instance that the turn signs and trill signs in the piano part of Beethoven's *Chorfantasie* op. 80 (Ex. 13.92(*a*)) should not be capable of a number of different realizations. In bar 63 any of the forms shown in Ex. 13.92(*b*)–(*f*) seem plausible. In relation to the last of these examples, it is interesting to note that Karl Klindworth suggested a similar approach to the inverted turn in Mendelssohn's *Lieder ohne Worte* no. 2 (Ex. 13.93).

Ex. 13.92. Beethoven, *Chorfantasie* op. 80

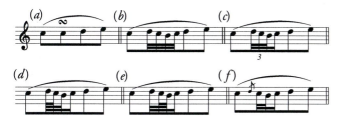

Ex. 13.93. Mendelssohn, *Lieder ohne Worte* op. 19/ii, ed. Klindworth

Direct and Inverted Turns

At the end of the nineteenth century Edward Dannreuther, discussing the notation of turns, emphatically asserted that 'with Hummel, as with all contemporary instrumentalists and vocalists, ∞, when connecting one note with another, meant a turn from above, and nothing else'.[111] The remark by Bernhard Romberg quoted above shows that this was not true of at least one important figure among Hummel's contemporaries, as do the inconsistencies in Spohr's notation of turns. Other information from the mid-nineteenth century indicates that Romberg's apparent willingness to leave the choice to the performer was by no means eccentric. Adolf Bernhard Marx, a leading theoretical authority of his generation, considered that 'The turn from below is mostly explicitly written out with notes; but one can also introduce it at the sign ∞, if a gentler, more pensive expression is aimed at; and in this case it will be executed more slowly.' He also felt, like Romberg, that the turn from below was generally more appropriate where the melody falls, and, referring to both forms of turn, continued:

It is left to the taste of the performer to introduce this often very graceful ornament, which at the same time wreathes and seeks the main note, even where it is not marked. But one should be sparing and thoughtful about it, since a mass of such small figures easily becomes fussy and obscures and disturbs the deeper meaning and character of the melody.[112]

Among major composers of the second half of the nineteenth century in whose music the turn (either written out or indicated by a sign) played an important part was Wagner. His practice in this matter, and the manner in

---

[111] *Musical Ornamentation*, ii. 174.   [112] In Schilling, *Encyclopädie*, art. 'Doppelschlag'.

which his instructions were interpreted by leading contemporaries, nicely illustrate the flexibility which persisted even in that period of ever-increasing prescriptiveness in notation. In his operas up to *Lohengrin* Wagner used a variety of conventional ornament signs; in the later operas, with very few exceptions other than trills (which according to Dannreuther were normally meant to start on the main note[113]), he dispensed with signs, and either indicated his ornaments with small notes or incorporated them into the musical text in normal-size notes. In the overture to Raupach's *König Enzio* of 1832 Wagner employed the turn sign ∿. In *Rienzi, Der fliegende Holländer*, and *Tannhäuser* he regularly used the sign ⌘ for turns. He does not seem to have employed a different sign to indicate an inverted turn, but in his later works, where the turns are written out, some begin from above and others from below. The *Vorspiel* to *Götterdämmerung*, for instance, has inverted turns and direct turns closely juxtaposed. A written-out inverted turn also occurs in the 1855 version of his *Faust* overture; this example is particularly interesting, since in the 1844 version of the overture the turns are indicated by Wagner's usual turn sign. Whether Wagner originally envisaged an inverted turn in the *Faust* overture is open to question.

How Wagner wished the turn signs in earlier operas to be interpreted was by no means clear even during his own lifetime. In Liszt's piano versions of the Prayer from *Rienzi* and the March from *Tannhäuser* (Act II, Scene iv), the turn signs are realized as direct turns. Hans von Bülow, however, apparently without any authority from the composer, insisted for a while on his Meiningen orchestra performing many of the turns in *Rienzi* and others of Wagner's earlier operas as inverted turns. This was the subject of considerable controversy in the late nineteenth century, but though Bülow later changed his mind, other conductors adopted the habit. Dannreuther reported that at Munich in the 1890s, for instance, the inverted turn was routinely used in *Rienzi*;[114] this practice was perpetuated by Karl Klindworth's vocal score, in which the signs are realized as inverted turns. Wagner himself seems to have added to the confusion over the meaning of his turn signs, for when present at rehearsals of *Tannhäuser* in Vienna in 1875, he asked the conductor, Hans Richter, to take the turns (marked by the sign for a normal turn) that follow the words 'So stehet auf!' in Act II, Scene ii as inverted turns. In the revised vocal score of *Tannhäuser* (1876), prepared by Joseph Rubinstein under Wagner's direct supervision, however, these turns were written out as normal turns, and they also appear thus in Klindworth's vocal score.

---

[113] *Musical Ornamentation*, ii. 172.   [114] Ibid. 174.

14

VIBRATO

☙❧

The term 'vibrato' has acquired its present universally understood meaning of a more or less rapid oscillation of pitch relatively recently, though it has had implications of this meaning since at least the first half of the nineteenth century. It may therefore be helpful to clear up some terminological confusion before considering more closely the use of vibrato and related techniques during the late eighteenth century and nineteenth century.[1] Throughout that period many different terms were used to describe the various kinds of wavering that are now generally subsumed in the word 'vibrato', and some of these terms were, in their turn, often used to characterize a number of different things. Thus *tremolo* could mean vibrato, rapid repetition of notes on the same pitch, or rapid alternation of notes at different pitches (i.e. on the piano). In Germany until the middle of the nineteenth century *Tremolo* and *Bebung* were the terms most commonly used to signify vibrato (in 1756 Leopold Mozart had used *Tremulant* and *Tremoleto*; Löhlein in 1774 employed the term *ondeggiamento* as well as *Bebung*, and in 1832 Spohr used *Tremolo*). In England, too, *tremolo* was frequently used for vibrato (older terms such as 'close shake', 'dumb shake', and 'sweetnings' gradually dropped out of usage in the nineteenth century). Pierre Baillot in *L'Art du violon* (1834) used *ondulation*; Charles de Bériot's *Méthode de violon* (1858) called it *sons vibrés* (translated literally in the original English version as 'vibrated sounds'), while Hermann Schröder's *Die Kunst des Violinspiels* (1887), under the main heading *Bebung*, gave the alternative terms *Tremolando, Vibrato, Balancement*.[2] But most of these terms could

---

[1] The word 'vibrato' is printed here in roman type whenever it is employed in its modern sense or as a general term for pulsating or undulating effects; it is given in italic type when it appears in the context of other specific usages. Italic type is also employed where words such as 'tremolo' are used in connection with techniques that are not normally associated with these words in modern English usage.

[2] Baillot, *L'Art du violon*, 138; Bériot, *Méthode*, 242; Schröder, *Die Kunst des Violinspiels*, 26.

also have been applied to techniques that would not be called vibrato in modern terminology

In fact, the Italian word *vibrato*, though it is already encountered as a performance direction during the eighteenth century, appears scarcely, if at all, to have been used with its present meaning until well into the nineteenth century, and even at the end of the century its meaning was not fixed; the contexts in which it is found in earlier periods show clearly that it was not meant to convey the same as now. The term was used on a number of occasions by G. J. Vogler in passages of relatively rapid staccato notes (Ex. 14.1). *Vibrato, vibrate,* and even *vibratissimo* occur frequently, too, in the scores of early nineteenth-century Italian operas. Most of the circumstances in which these appear, in works by Rossini and Meyerbeer for instance, suggest rather that the term implies a particular style of delivery than a vibrato in the modern sense.

In 1826 Lichtenthal defined *vibrato* simply as 'strongly marked' (*marcato fortamente*);[3] for a technique more closely related to modern vibrato he used

Ex. 14.1. Vogler, Symphony in G, Allegro, autograph, Bayerische Staatsbibliothek, Munich, mus. ms. 4309; pub. in fac. in the series *The Symphony 1720–1840* (New York and London, Garland 1983)

---

[3] *Dizionario*, art. 'Vibrato'.

the term *vibrazione di voce* (vibration of the voice).[4] At about the same time Busby's *Dictionary* explained *vibrato* as 'A term used in Italian opera, to signify that at the note or passage, to which it refers, the voice is to be thrown out, in a bold heroic style'.[5] A few years earlier the *Wiener allgemeine musikalische Zeitung* had somewhat cryptically characterized *vibrato* as indicating that 'Here, the notes will not be pulled out at the roots but only tickled at their tips',[6] an explanation which also suggests that the primary meaning is accent, but indicates, perhaps, a less forceful treatment than Busby and Lichtenthal. This Viennese definition implies a treatment that would seem to fit Vogler's use of the term, with its piano dynamic and light texture.

Other definitions carry more connotation of the modern meaning of 'vibrato' while still implying an element of accentuation. J. A. Hamilton gave the definition of *vibrato* or *vibrante*: 'With a strong, vibrating quality of tone';[7] and this was echoed a generation later by John S. Adams, who defined it as 'with much vibration of tone'.[8] These explanations recall Leopold Mozart's analogy between vibrato and the effect of striking a slack string or bell.[9]

The connection between accent and vibrato was widely felt to be a close one. As early as the mid-eighteenth century, William Tans'ur had rather oddly defined 'Accent' as 'a sort of wavering or shaking of the *Voice* or *Instrument* on certain *Notes*, with a stronger or weaker Tone than the rest, to express the *Passion* thereof; which renders *Music* (especially *Vocal*) so very agreeable to the Ear, it being chiefly intended to move and affect'.[10] A century later, in M. E. von Glehn's translation of Lussy's treatise on musical expression, it was noted: 'The longer a note, especially if it is the first of the bar, the more it must be accented. It is on these notes that singers and violinists produce the effect called *vibrato*' (Lussy's original does not include the second sentence);[11] and later, the translator again introduced the word '*vibrato*' where Lussy had not used it, remarking: 'If a long note follows by exception several short ones, it acquires great force, and will produce a crescendo, a *vibrato*' (Ex. 14.2).[12] Here the association between function and terminology is more explicit, for Lussy's example includes the sign <>, widely used in the nineteenth century where a vibrato of pitch on string instruments was envisaged.[13] Spohr, among other authorities, identified violin vibrato as particularly appropriate 'in strongly accenting notes marked with *fz* or >'.[14]

Other nineteenth-century writers recognized that the word was acquiring two quite distinct meanings; Gollmick (1857) gave the following definition of

[4] Ibid., art. 'Messa di voce'.   [5] Art. 'Vibrato'.   [6] Vol. 1 (1813), 435.
[7] *Dictionary*, art. 'Vibrato'.   [8] *5000 Musical Terms* (Boston, 1851), 106.
[9] *Versuch*, XI, §1.   [10] *A Musical Grammar and Dictionary* (London, [c.1770]), 25.
[11] *Musical Expression*, 33; *Traité de l'expression musicale*, 6th edn., 25.
[12] *Musical Expression*, 129–30; *Traité de l'expression musicale*, 6th edn., 95.
[13] See below; also Brown, 'Bowing Styles'.   [14] *Violin School*, 163.

Ex. 14.2. Lussy, *Musical Expression*, 130

Quand ton des - tin   au mien al - lait   s'u - nir!   Ange   a - do - ré

vibrato: 'vibrated 1) similar to the Tremolo 2) to push out a note powerfully, in that case synonymous with sfz and ∧'.[15] (In his earlier *Kritische Terminologie* (1833) he had merely given *vibrato* together with *tremolo* and *tremolando* as meaning 'trembling, shaking'.) The complications of the terminology can clearly be seen in Gottfried Weber's more detailed examination of meanings applied to the words *vibrato* and *tremolo* in 1822. For *vibrato* he gave: 'This word (literally translated: hurled or vibrated) is sometimes used to signify the powerful pushing out of a note and to that extent means the same as *Forzando* or *Sforzato*;—sometimes, however, also to signify the whirring and at the same time oscillating execution of fast notes [Ex. 14.3] and the like.'[16] For *tremolo* he gave the German equivalent *Bebung* and explained:

[it] is used for 1) the pulsating and at the same time wave-like recurring waxing and waning of the strength of a held note, with which also, sometimes, a change in the type of sound or tone colour, and also even an imperceptible rising and falling of pitch, is united . . . 2) . . . a roll [i.e. rapid note repetition on timpani on strings or piano] 3) *vibrato*.[17]

Ex. 14.3. G. Weber, *Allgemeine Musiklehrer*, p. cxci

A curious divergence of terminology developed between singing and instrumental playing during the course of the nineteenth century. In string playing the words 'vibrato' and 'tremolo' gradually came to be used with their modern meanings. By the end of the century this usage was firmly established; both the German and English versions of the Joachim and Moser *Violinschule* employ the word 'vibrato' for undulation of pitch, and Siegfried Eberhardt's treatise of 1910,[18] which examined vibrato as an adjunct of tone production in violin playing, is entitled *Violin Vibrato* in its 1911 English translation. In vocal music, however, usage of the words *vibrato* and *tremolo* during the later part of the nineteenth century was different. Franklin Taylor commented on the discrepancy in 1880 before defining vocal *vibrato* as 'an alternate partial extinction and

---

[15] *Handlexicon der Tonkunst*, 96.

[16] *Allgemeine Musiklehrer zum Selbstunterricht für Lehre und Lernende* (Darmstadt, 1822), p. cxci.

[17] Ibid.

[18] *Der beseelte Violin-Ton* (Dresden, 1910), trans. as *Violin Vibrato: Its Mastery and Artistic Uses* (New York, 1911).

reinforcement of the note'.[19] Taylor then went on to explain *tremolo* in singing as: 'an undulation of the notes, that is to say, more or less quickly reiterated departure from true intonation'.[20]

Changing Attitudes towards Vibrato

During the period from 1750 to about 1900 the various types of vibrato then in use were regarded almost exclusively as ornamental. Approaches to their execution and artistic function varied from school to school, individual to individual, and instrument to instrument, yet there seems to have been a broad consensus among the great majority of musical authorities that the basic sound should be a steady one and that vibrato, along with other ornamental techniques, should occur as an incidental colouring or embellishment on particular notes. The modern concept of continuous vibrato as a fundamental element of tone production began to evolve, under Franco-Belgian influence, only towards the end of the nineteenth century; but it was not until the early decades of the twentieth century that this new aesthetic began to be firmly established and widely accepted. Eberhardt's *Der beseelte Violin-Ton* was the first treatise to deal at length with the mechanism of vibrato on string instruments, clearly identifying left-hand vibrato rather than the bow with the production of a fine and individual tone quality. Indeed, Eberhardt commented:

Beauty of tone has always been considered a special gift; and to acquire it we have contented ourselves with experiments upon the right arm, and have sought for secrets where no secrets exist.

In regard to the vibrato, I can claim that:-

Artistic finish in playing is impossible without a correctly made vibrato. The bow occupies a dependent relationship—is dependent on the left hand. The left hand is entirely dependent on the oscillation.[21]

Universal acceptance of continuous vibrato in singing and on other instruments followed even later. At least until the 1930s there were still many influential performers and teachers who remained unreconciled to this new attitude towards vibrato, continuing to believe that its too-frequent use impaired rather than improved tone quality, that it deprived performance of an important level of expressiveness, and that it was inimical to purity of intonation and ensemble.

A number of discussions of vibrato by musicians whose careers flourished during the first half of the twentieth century provide a revealing picture of the radical changes that came about at that time. Sir Henry Wood in his book *The Gentle Art of Singing* (1927) gave an interesting account of the increase of

---

[19] 'Tremolo' in Grove, *Dictionary*, iv. 166.   [20] Ibid. 167.   [21] *Violin Vibrato*, 23.

vibrato in singing (for which, like Taylor, he used the word 'tremolo') that had taken place in his lifetime.[22] His own reservations about these developments are evident from his comments:

There has been a good deal written and said lately about the vocal tremolo which is out of place, but it is no new fault. I think I have explained fairly clearly why it exists, and how it can be cured. If it is not taken in hand at the very first singing lesson, it grows rapidly into a habit, and becomes so firmly established that it is most difficult to eradicate and is always liable to crop up from time to time. A tremolo often reaches the audience as out-of-tuneness, and any teacher who has tried to teach the octave duet for soprano and mezzo soprano, Agnus Dei in Verdi's *Requiem*, to singers of whom one has a decided tremolo and the other a true even, still tone, will understand why. It is impossible to get the octaves to sound in tune. The voice with the tremolo never blends in with the still tones of the other. The sharpness and flatness of the tremolo become clear.[23]

From the point of view of the string player, Leopold Auer, a pupil of Joachim and a highly respected teacher, inveighed in vain against the use of continuous vibrato; his strong language in *Violin Playing as I Teach it* (1921) reflects the hopelessness of his attempt to stem the tide. He considered that both singers and string players had, through the abuse of vibrato, 'called into being a plague of the most inartistic nature, one to which ninety out of every hundred vocal and instrumental soloists fall victim', and went on to criticize players who resort to vibrato 'in an ostrich-like endeavour to conceal bad tone production and intonation', observing:

Those who are convinced that an eternal *vibrato* is the secret of soulful playing, of piquancy in performance—are pitifully misguided in their belief. . . . But their own appreciation of musical values ought to tell them how false is the notion that vibration, whether in good or bad taste, adds spice and flavour to their playing . . . Their musical taste (or what does service for them in place of it) does not tell them that they can reduce a programme of the most dissimilar pieces to the same dead level of monotony by peppering them all with the tabasco of a continuous *vibrato*. No, the *vibrato* is an effect, an embellishment; it can lend a touch of divine pathos to the climax of a phrase or the course of a passage, but only if the player has cultivated a delicate sense of proportion in the use of it.

After a further diatribe, in which he sarcastically postulated that continuous vibrato is an 'actual *physical* defect' resulting from a 'group of sick or ailing nerves', he concluded:

In any case remember that only the most sparing use of the *vibrato* is desirable; the too generous employment of the device defeats the purpose for which you use it. The excessive *vibrato* is a habit for which I have no tolerance, and I always fight against it when I observe it in my pupils—though often, I must admit, without success. As a rule I forbid my students using the *vibrato* at all on notes which are not sustained, and I earnestly advise them not to abuse it even in the case of sustained notes which succeed each other in a phrase.[24]

[22] (Oxford, 1927), iv. 87.   [23] Ibid. 55.
[24] *Violin Playing as I Teach it* (London, 1921), 22–4.

It is noteworthy that Auer's most distinguished students, who included Jascha Heifetz, Mischa Elman, and Efrem Zimbalist, where all enthusiastic exponents of continuous vibrato.

Acceptance of the new aesthetic, however, was more rapid in some areas than in others. As late as 1934 Ronald Foster, writing about singing, observed that vibrato was liked by Latin races but not by Anglo-Saxon ones.[25] A few wind instrument players quickly followed the lead of singers and violinists in adopting a continuous vibrato: flautists, oboists, and bassoonists seem to have considered that the tone of their instruments was improved by vibrato while clarinettists and brass players in serious music generally did not, though vibrato was used on these instruments in some schools of playing and in popular music.

The history of vibrato in the twentieth century is documented not only by written accounts, but also in recorded sound. Comparison of the two is instructive, for it illustrates that words do not always prepare us for what we hear; different speeds, degrees of pitch variation, and fluctuations of intensity in continuous vibrato have strongly characterized musicians of various schools and successive generations in a manner that would be difficult if not impossible to extrapolate from the written record. So in the study of earlier periods, when the aural resource is not available, it is necessary to accept that however much information is assembled and whatever patterns of change are identified, we are still far from knowing what kinds of sounds would have been considered tasteful and beautiful by our forebears. Yet much can be learned from careful scrutiny of the eighteenth- and nineteenth-century accounts and, at the very least, it is possible to appreciate the extent to which musicians of past generations did not share the predilections of their late twentieth-century successors.

To a considerable extent, the history of vibrato during the earlier part of the period under consideration here is closely connected with the far-reaching changes of attitude to ornamentation, and style of performance in general, that occurred in the second half of the eighteenth century. A passion for elaborate ornamentation in many kinds of music seems to have grown exponentially in the middle of the eighteenth century, and it almost certainly brought with it a tendency for performers to use 'vibrato' techniques quite frequently. (The word 'vibrato' is used here advisedly, since it would be rash to assume that the various kinds of wavering effects employed by eighteenth- and early nineteenth-century musicians would have equated with what present-day musicians regard as vibrato.) It may be suspected that there were many mid-eighteenth-century performers who would have found a pure, unembellished note (especially if of any considerable length) inexpressive or even distasteful, and would have employed a vibrato where other ornaments were inappropriate or impossible.

[25] *Vocal Success* (London, 1934), 53.

Studies of wind instrument tablatures from the late seventeenth century, and tutors from the early eighteenth century, suggest that many players may have left few notes of any length without some kind of ornament.[26] Eighteenth-century advice to use vibrato where no other ornament is appropriate should probably be seen in this context. Francesco Geminiani's much-quoted comment that the violinist should introduce the close shake or *tremolo* 'as often as possible', even on shorter notes, since when made on short notes 'it only contributes to make their Sound more agreeable'[27] is, however, the only known endorsement by a significant musician of the mid-eighteenth century of frequent vibrato specifically as a means of enhancing tone. Interestingly, Geminiani considered that, whereas in violin playing the *tremolo* could 'be made on any Note whatsoever', in flute playing it 'must only be made on long Notes'.[28] The reason for this was undoubtedly that the type of flute vibrato to which he referred (produced by stopping or almost stopping an open hole in the manner of a trill) could scarcely be used, from a technical point of view, except on longer notes. It was left to the French flautist Charles Delusse, who in his tutor of about 1761 repeated most of the passage on the tremolo from Geminiani's violin treatise in an almost verbatim translation, to devise a means of imitating Geminiani's ornament on the flute. He considered that his *tremblement flexible*, produced by rolling the instrument between finger and thumb while playing the note in the normal way, 'contributes to render the melody more pleasant and tender. One ought to use it as often as possible; it is for this reason that it is never marked in music, taste alone inspires it.'[29] The final statement indicates, though, that Delusse still considered the vibrato an ornament, not a continuous colouring to the sound. In any case, Geminiani's (and Delusse's) opinion has no parallel in other instrumental or vocal methods during the succeeding century and a half. In fact, it seems clear that their attitude, which implies a reluctance to leave any note without embellishment, represented the final phase of an aesthetic that was already beginning to give way to one in which a broader, nuanced style of performance with fewer extempore ornaments was favoured. Significantly, as Roger Hickman has shown,[30] Geminiani's recommendations for the frequent employment of vibrato were even suppressed in later eighteenth-century editions of his treatise.

The process of transition from the predominance of one aesthetic to that of another was by no means simple and straightforward. Copious evidence makes it clear that many performers continued to employ vibrato, in its various forms,

[26] See Bruce Dickey, 'Untersuchung zur historischen Auffassung des Vibratos auf Blasinstrumenten', *Basler Jahrbuch für historische Musikpraxis*, 2 (1978), 88 ff.

[27] *The Art of Playing on the Violin* (London, 1751), 8.

[28] *Rules for Playing in a True Taste* (London, 1748), preface.

[29] *L'Art de la flûte traversière* (Paris, [c.1761]), 9.

[30] 'The Censored Publications of *The Art of Playing on the Violin* or Geminiani Unshaken', *Early Music*, 11 (1983), 71–6.

along with other types of ornament fairly lavishly in the second half of the eighteenth century. Indeed, there is the implication that vibrato, once acquired, tended to become a habit that was unconsciously indulged, and in that sense many players of the period may have possessed something approaching a continuous vibrato (though it is scarcely likely to have sounded anything like a modern continuous vibrato). This is suggested by Leopold Mozart's well-known condemnation of those who 'tremble consistently on each note as if they had the palsy',[31] which is echoed in other eighteenth-century treatises. Löhlein, for instance, observed sarcastically:

one must not be too liberal in its use: for if, as many do, one introduces it too frequently, the hearer will feel a sympathetic anxiety, for he believes that this constant trembling comes from an attack of cold fever, which has just seized the player. . . . Many have the praiseworthy habit of trembling on the open strings. This is worse than bad and belongs in the beer cellar.[32]

The mass of evidence does not support Donington's contention that some kind of fairly continuous vibrato, in the modern sense, has been a common aspect of string playing at least since Geminiani. His assumption that Geminiani's description 'corresponds to modern usage'[33] is highly questionable, and his statement that '[Leopold] Mozart preferred a more selective but still fairly continuous vibrato'[34] has absolutely no foundation in anything written by or about Leopold Mozart. Written evidence from the late eighteenth century and, indeed, from most of the nineteenth century implies that many musicians used more vibrato, sometimes much more, than was approved of by the most authoritative writers of the day. But this over-use of such techniques does not appear ever to have corresponded with a modern notion of continuous vibrato as an essential element of tone production (despite Donington's assertions); it is much more likely that, as suggested above, it was linked with abundant use of ornamentation as a whole.

The link between vibrato techniques and other forms of ornamentation in the early to mid-eighteenth century is of great importance, for the reaction against the one was undoubtedly part of a fairly powerful reaction, evident in many late eighteenth- and early nineteenth-century writings, against the overuse of the other. The reaction against vibrato, therefore, was not against a technique that was used to colour the tone continuously (something that was certainly unknown in those terms), but may rather be seen as part of a growing rejection of excessive ornamentation and a move towards an aesthetic in which simplicity of utterance was prized above artifice; thus Woldemar commented around the turn of the century:

[31] *Versuch*, XI, §3.   [32] *Anweisung zum Violinspielen*, 51.
[33] 'Vibrato', in *New Grove*, xix. 697.
[34] *Early Music*, 16 (1988), 571, in his review of Greta Moens-Haenen's impressive study *Das Vibrato in der Musik des Barock* (Graz, 1988).

whether the adagio is played simple or decorated it is always necessary that it expresses tenderness: see the most beautiful adagio of Tartini [he gave an example]; whoever would study the manner of ornamentation of that great master may consult his great pamphlet, but one ought to ornament adagios very little, developing a predilection on the contrary for nuancing the notes [*filer les sons*].[35]

Thus, with the example of Viotti before them, many musicians and connoisseurs in the late eighteenth century and early nineteenth century saw expressiveness and emotional truth as higher virtues than the display of dexterity and ingenuity. Such a view was entirely in tune with the spirit of an age which was influenced by Rousseau to prize directness and naturalness over elaboration and artificiality. It is noteworthy that the strongest reactions against vibrato techniques, such as Robert Bremner's, imply a general rejection of what English writers referred to as 'graces of the finger', while the texts that support their moderate and proper use often seem explicitly or implicitly to link them with the expression of natural emotion.

For Bremner a prime consideration in his rather extreme condemnation of vibrato (along with other forms of extempore ornamentation) seems to have been that it destroyed the purity of harmony; he commented: 'To bear a part in concert [i.e. in ensemble] with propriety, the fingers must be considered only as meer stops to put the notes in tune; or, which is the same thing, every tone should be as void of ornament as if produced by an open string.'[36] When he extended his objection to the use of any vibrato at all also to solo playing he went further than many of his contemporaries. Cramer's *Magazin der Musik* in 1783, commenting on Bremner's 'very thoughtful article, the consideration of which would be very salutary in Germany too', agreed with his objections to the use of vibrato in concerted music, but considered that in solo music 'the instrumentalist not only *may* make use of it, but *must*. That, like all niceties and ornaments, however, it must occur not too frequently, but with discretion and reflexion, I have no desire to argue with our author.'[37]

The majority of the more substantial German and French tutors for voice and violin, including those by Leopold Mozart, Löhlein, Hiller, and others, discussed vibrato and, while warning against abuse of the ornament, gave serious consideration to the manner of its execution and the situations in which it was appropriate. But there were others besides Bremner who adopted a more hostile approach to the whole gamut of vibrato techniques, and there is some evidence that reaction against them may have become stronger as the century

---

[35] *Méthode de violon par L. Mozart*, 78–9.

[36] 'Some Thoughts on the Performance of Concert Music', pub. as preface to J. G. C. Schetky, *Six Quartettos for Two Violins, a Tenor, and Violoncello op. VI. To which are prefixed some thoughts on the performance of concert-music by the publisher* (London, R. Bremner, [1777]); repr. in Neil Zaslaw, 'The Compleat Orchestral Musician', *Early Music*, 7 (1979), 46.

[37] Trans. by Neil Zaslaw in 'The Orchestral Musician Compleated', *Early Music*, 8 (1980), 71.

wore on. In the 1790s the Italian violinist Galeazzi, having remarked that vibrato 'consists in pressing the finger well on the string to perform a long note, and then, marking with the hand a certain paralytic and trembling motion, performing so that the finger bends now to this side and now to that', went on to observe that the result was 'a vacillating pitch and a certain continual trembling not unpleasing to those people [who do it]; but these are most genuine discords which can please only those who are accustomed to them and which should be entirely banned from music by anyone equipped with good taste'.[38] In England at about the same time John Gunn, in *The Art of Playing the German Flute*, showed a similar attitude; and his account strengthens the view that the reaction against vibrato was connected with changing attitudes towards ornamentation. He observed:

The Modern refinements in the performance of music, however multifarious and complicated they may be thought, have certainly not increased the number of what may be called *graces*, but on the contrary, have considerably reduced their number, and greatly simplified them. The performers of the *old school* had much more of what may be called *graces of the finger*, than the modern, which cultivates more the expression and powers of the bow, and the management of *tone*. There was formerly in use a numerous list of graces, some with and others without characters to represent them, and for the most part discontinued.

Among these was the dumb shake [i.e. close shake], on stringed instruments, corresponding to what the French call *flattement* on the flute, and in our language, I think, called Sweetenings, . . . producing a trembling palsied expression, inconsistent with just intonation, and not unlike that extravagant trembling of the voice which the French call *chevrotter*, to make a goat-like noise; for which the singers of the Opera at Paris have so often been ridiculed.[39]

A particularly strong reaction against vibrato around the end of the eighteenth century and the beginning of the nineteenth century in England may be suggested by John Jousse's violin methods. His *Modern Violin Preceptor* (*c*.1805) merely described the mechanism of vibrato (there called close shake) in a single sentence, without comment on its use. His later *Theory and Practice of the Violin* (1811) has the following curious heading: 'Of the Tremolo or Close Shake. (it is become obsolete)'; and Jousse went on to observe:

The Tremolo (improperly called by Geminiani and others the Close Shake) is that quivering Sound made by moving the left hand backwards and forwards, keeping at the same time the finger on the String, and pressing the Bow harder and closer to the bridge; this obsolete grace has a resemblance to that quivering sound given by two of the unisons of an organ a little out of tune; or to the voice of a person affected by a Palsy a song from whom would be one continued Tremolo from beginning to end.

Though for the sake of variety, the Tremolo might at times be introduced on a long note in a single melody; yet if it be introduced in a piece of harmony, in which the beauty and energy of the performance depends on the united effect of all the parts being exactly in tune with each other, it becomes hurtful and disgusting.[40]

---

[38] *Elementi*, i. 171.   [39] (London, [1793]), 18.   [40] *Theory and Practice of the Violin*, 48.

Such views, though perhaps extreme, do not seem to have been confined to England and to a few provincial musicians such as Galeazzi. A number of comments by distinguished and cosmopolitan German musicians, which appear to refer to the period between 1780 and 1820, suggest that a distinct change occurred throughout Europe at about that time. The internationally acclaimed cellist Bernhard Romberg referred retrospectively to an earlier period (probably the 1780s and 1790s, when his career began) as one in which cellists employed left-hand vibrato very frequently, but identified himself with a younger generation that rejected that approach. He observed: 'Formerly the close shake was in such repute that it was applied indiscriminately to every note of whatever duration. This produced a most disagreeable and whining effect, and we cannot be too thankful that an improved taste has at length exploded the abuse of this embellishment.'[41] Another cellist, J. J. F. Dotzauer, also implied that vibrato techniques were regarded as old-fashioned in the early nineteenth century. He devoted just two sentences to them in his *Violoncell-Schule*:

To shake or tremble with the finger on a long note is indeed an old ornament [*Manier*], nevertheless, introduced infrequently and in the right places,—which is a matter of good taste—, it ought not to be wholly rejected. This ornament even has precedence before that vibrato [*Tremolo*] which comes from the bow, particularly when the latter is a result of nervousness.[42]

It may also be indicative of the changing taste in such matters that the only feature in the playing of the almost legendary Viotti that came in for criticism when he gave one of his rare public performances in Europe in the late 1790s was his 'somewhat strong *tremulando*',[43] though the reaction may have been stimulated as much by the speed of the vibrato as by its frequency.

The situation in the second half of the eighteenth century and the early years of the nineteenth century seems, therefore, to have been that, when writers mentioned vibrato at all, they almost always accompanied their discussion of it with the recommendation that it be used with great discretion. At the same time many players appear to have employed more vibrato than was felt appropriate by those musicians who set themselves up as authorities. Bremner, the most extreme opponent of Geminiani's position, seems to have objected to any use of vibrato in either solo or ensemble playing. Others regarded it as an appropriate, indeed necessary, embellishment of solo playing when used in moderation.

The view that vibrato was detrimental in ensemble playing seems to have been generally acknowledged. Reichardt's treatise *Ueber die Pflichten des Ripien-Violinisten*, which dealt solely with orchestral playing and purported to inform orchestral players of the skills necessary to their profession, did not

---

[41] *A Complete*, 87.   [42] p. 28.   [43] *Allgemeine musikalische Zeitung*, 1 (1798–9), 762.

mention vibrato at all. Löhlein, whose *Anweisung zum Violinspielen* was also aimed primarily at the orchestral player, having warned fiercely against using it too often, did mention a few circumstances in which it could be introduced in his practice pieces. The statement, later in the book, that he had paved the way just up to the borderline between orchestral and solo playing suggests, perhaps, that he may have envisaged its occasional use in the orchestra if it was confined to such places.[44] (The possible employment of orchestral vibrato as a particular effect in the music of Gluck and some of his contemporaries is considered below, but it may be remarked at this point that, notwithstanding the arguments of Erich Schenk,[45] it seems improbable that a left-hand vibrato was envisaged.)

In the nineteenth century, contrary to current notions of what is appropriate to the performance of so-called Romantic music, it seems very likely that vibrato occurred somewhat less frequently in vocal and instrumental performance than in the middle of the previous century; or rather, perhaps, that it was introduced more for its expressive qualities than as one among a host of ornaments with which an individual note could be enlivened. (This is not to deny that early to mid-eighteenth-century musicians sometimes linked vibrato and other ornaments with affective performance; but it seems chiefly to have been the view articulated by Leopold Mozart, that vibrato 'must be employed only in such places where Nature herself would produce it',[46] that pointed the way to later attitudes, rather than Geminiani's more stylized notion that it could represent affliction, fear, dignity, majesty, etc.)

Despite the comment about Viotti's vibrato in 1798 and the relative frequency of his use of it suggested by the examples in Baillot's 1834 treatise,[47] his pupil Rode and disciples Kreutzer and Baillot almost certainly employed the device quite sparingly. Michel Woldemar, whose admiration for Viotti is obvious alongside his veneration of Lolli and Mestrino, interestingly omitted all mention of vibrato from his 1801 version of Leopold Mozart's violin school, despite the extensive consideration of it in the original, and it is also absent from his slightly earlier *Grande méthode*. The Conservatoire *Méthode* of 1803, overseen by Rode, Kreutzer, and Baillot, deals with tone, style, and embellishment in considerable detail, but makes no mention of left-hand vibrato, though it describes a vibrato (*ondulation*) produced by the bow alone.[48] In his 1834 treatise Baillot demanded the greatest discretion in the use of left-hand vibrato. He noted that it

---

[44] See Clive Brown, 'String Playing Practices in the Classical Orchestra', *Basler Jahrbuch für historische Musikpraxis*, 17 (1993), 44–5.

[45] 'Zur Aufführungspraxis des Tremolo bei Gluck', in Joseph Schmidt-Görg, ed., *Anthony von Hoboken: Festschrift zum 75. Geburtstag* (Mainz, 1962), 137–45.

[46] *Versuch*, V, §4.

[47] *L'Art du violon*, 138–9 (for copies of these examples see Stowell, *Violin Technique*, 209–10).

[48] Baillot et al., *Méthode de violon*, 137.

gives the sound of the instrument a close analogy with the human voice when it is strongly touched with emotion. This type of expression is very powerful, but if frequently used it would have only the dangerous disadvantage of making the melody unnatural and depriving the style of that precious naïvety which is the greatest charm of art and recalls it to its primitive simplicity.

And he concluded his survey of the ways in which it could be produced and the circumstances in which it was appropriate by requiring the player to 'avoid making a habit of vibration of the hand, which must be employed only when the expression renders it necessary and, furthermore, conforming with all that has been indicated in order to prevent its abuse.'[49]

Many French violin methods during the first half of the nineteenth century, including some quite substantial ones, seem to have considered vibrato worthy of little or no attention; François Habeneck's *Méthode* of about 1840, for instance, ignored it entirely, as did Alard's *École de violon* of 1844, despite its subtitle *Méthode complète et progressive*.

Baillot's account of the function of vibrato is broadly in line with that of leading German musicians during the third and fourth decades of the nineteenth century. Carl Maria Weber's friend Adolf Bernard Fürstenau, like Baillot, compared the flautist's use of vibrato with that of the singer. He instructed that it should only be used to express

true, self-experienced deeper feeling and then too, even in a piece where passages of passionate gesture frequently occur, far from everywhere, but only there where that gesture expresses itself most strongly, and in immediately repeated passages of the same kind it should for instance only be used the first or second time, since it is all too easy for the heaping-up of this embellishment to seem like a sickly mannerism, the continuous use of it even becoming a piteous whining, which is naturally of an extremely repulsive effect; thus the vibrato [*Bebung*], if it is to be wholly certain of its aesthetic success, must finally be confined every time to a single note, and, indeed, to the one on which the culmination point of the passionate feeling occurs, and even here, yet again, confined to a three- or four-fold quivering motion—notwithstanding that a longer continuation of the latter is very difficult to perform well—, where, according to the circumstances, an accompanying *crescendo* or *sforzato* significantly increases the effect.[50]

Numerous other flute methods into the second half of the century reiterated, in more or less strong language, Fürstenau's instructions to introduce vibrato (both that produced by the breath and the finger vibrato) very sparingly.[51]

---

[49] *L'Art du violon*, 138–9. For a translation of Baillot's account see Stowell, *Violin Technique*, 208–10.

[50] *Flöten-Schule* (Leipzig, [1826]), 79.

[51] Charles Nicholson, *Complete Preceptor for the German Flute* (London, [c.1816]); id., *A School for the Flute* (New York, 1836); Charles Weiss, *A New Methodical Instruction Book for the Flute* (London, [c.1821]); James Alexander, *Complete Preceptor for the Flute* (London, [c.1821]); Thomas Lindsay, *The Elements of Flute Playing* (London, [1828]); John Clinton, *A School or Practical Instruction Book for the Boehm Flute* (London, [c.1850]).

In Germany, Spohr, who freely acknowledged the powerful influence of the Viotti school on the early formation of his style, also drew a parallel with singing and warned against too-frequent vibrato, though in less colourful language than Fürstenau, instructing in his 1832 *Violinschule* that the player 'should guard against using it too often, and in improper places. In cases corresponding to those in which . . . this trembling is observed in the singer, the violinist may also avail himself of it.'[52]

Spohr's authority remained strong in the German school of violin playing for more than seventy years, and in the Joachim and Moser *Violinschule* (1905) Spohr's account was cited at length, taking up more than half of the short section on vibrato; the rest consisted of a few additional technical hints on its execution and a further caveat: 'the pupil cannot be sufficiently warned against its habitual use, especially in the wrong place. A violinist whose taste is refined and healthy will always recognize the steady tone as the ruling one, and will use vibrato only where the expression seems to demand it.'[53] And in part 3 of the *Violinschule*, Joachim's colleague Andreas Moser stressed the necessity for extreme restraint in the use of vibrato; giving the opening bars of Joachim's Romance op. 2 as an example, with words added to clarify the accentuation and character (Ex. 14.4), he observed: 'If therefore the player wishes to make use of the vibrato in the first bars of the Romance (which, however, he certainly need not do), then it must occur only, like a delicate breath, on the notes under which the syllables "früh" and "wie" are placed.'[54]

Ex. 14.4. Joachim and Moser, *Violinschule*, iii. 7

In the French (Franco-Belgian) school, too, the position adopted by Baillot was maintained into the sixth decade of the century. Charles de Bériot's admonitions against the overuse of vibrato in his 1858 *Méthode* were even stronger than Baillot's (perhaps because its incidence was on the increase):

Vibrato (*son vibré*) is an accomplishment with the artist who knows how to use it with effect, and to abstain from it when that is necessary: but it becomes a fault when too frequently employed. This habit, *involuntarily acquired*, degenerates into a bad shake or nervous trembling which cannot afterwards be overcome and which produces a fatiguing monotony. The voice of the singer, like the fine quality of tone in the violinist, is impaired

---

[52] *Violin School,* 163.   [53] Pt. ii. 96a.

[54] p. 7. Alfred Moffat's 1905 translation inaccurately has 'should certainly not do' for the last four words in parenthesis.

by this great fault. The evil is the more dangerous from the fact that it is increased by the natural emotion which takes possession of the performer when he appears in public. In artistic execution there is true emotion only when the artist gives himself up to it: but when he cannot direct it it always exceeds the limit of truth. Whether he be singer or violinist, with the artist who is governed by this desire to produce an effect, vibrato is nothing but a convulsive movement which destroys strict intonation, and thus becomes a ridiculous exaggeration. We must, then, employ vibrato only when the dramatic action compels it: but the artist should not become fond of having this dangerous quality, which he must only use with the greatest moderation.[55]

Much the same picture emerges from a survey of other instrumental and vocal treatises, dictionary articles, and so on in the nineteenth century. A number of woodwind methods, particularly those for the flute, contain sections on various kinds of vibrato obtained by means of the fingers or the emission of the breath, and a few singing methods deal with the matter in some detail, but many continued to regard it as of little or no importance, and in all those that did address vibrato in any detail it was treated as an ornament to be introduced for special effect.

It is interesting to compare Bériot's comments with those of his brother-in-law, the singer Manuel García.[56] In his influential treatise, García included discussion of the *tremolo* under the heading 'Emotion of the voice', observing:

The *tremolo* is employed to depict sentiments, which, in real life, are of a poignant character,—such as anguish at seeing the imminent danger of any one dear to us; or tears extorted by certain acts of anger, revenge, &c. Under these circumstances, even, its use should be adopted with great taste, and in moderation; for its expression or duration, if exaggerated, becomes fatiguing and ungraceful. Except in these especial cases just mentioned, care must be taken not in any degree to diminish the firmness of the voice; as a frequent use of the *tremolo* tends to make it prematurely tremulous. An artist who has contracted this intolerable habit, becomes thereby incapable of phrasing any kind of sustained song whatsoever. Many fine voices have been thus lost to the art.[57]

The vibrato that García considered here is surely to be equated with the 'natural' quivering of the human voice described by Mozart in his often quoted letter of 1778 and the type of left-hand vibrato described by Bériot, Spohr, Baillot, and others; and, in view of the terminology discussed by Franklin Taylor, the use of the word *tremolo* indicates that an undulation of pitch was envisaged in this instance. That there were other techniques in singing which would have been classed rather as *vibrato* than *tremolo* is evident from other passages in García's treatise, and that these also had parallels in instrumental music is substantiated from many sources. All these types of vibrato were clearly considered not as elements of tone production, but as expressive ornaments, the overuse of

[55] p. 242.
[56] Bériot was briefly married to García's sister, the celebrated soprano Marie Malibran (1808–36), just before her death.
[57] *New Treatise*, 66.

which revealed lack of technique or poor taste. There were also those, even in the second half of the nineteenth century and early twentieth century, who could maintain that vibrato was either inessential or entirely to be avoided in some contexts. It was said that Joachim 'in describing the playing of [the violinist Bernhard] Molique (d. 1869) used to assert that it was without any vibrato whatsoever. Nevertheless, he considered him "a most distinguished musician."'[58] In 1863 Moritz Hauptmann objected to any vibrato in wind playing, claiming that 'a vibrated wind note was as impossible as a vibrated harmonic',[59] though this view was directly challenged two years later by Arrey von Dommer, who asserted that vibrato was good and effective on the flute and oboe.[60] A growing tendency to use it in wind playing seems to be implied by Carl Reinecke's instruction, at the beginning of the Intermezzo of his 'Undine' Flute Sonata op. 167, that it should be played 'without any vibrato at all' (*ohne jegliche Bebung im Ton*).

At about the time when controversy over the advent of a genuine continuous vibrato in violin playing was raging fiercely, it was still possible for some writers to claim that a complete absence of vibrato was perfectly appropriate for some repertoires. J. Winram's book *Violin Playing and Violin Adjustment* (1908) observed of vibrato (for which he still used the old English term 'close shake'):

it should be judiciously used at all times, as it is quite possible to have too much of a good thing. Beethoven's music will sound lovely with very little close shake, or if preferred with none at all; whereas Wagner's will gain rather than lose by its introduction. The character of the music must be taken into consideration, and good taste will surely be sufficient guide.[61]

There is no doubt that during the second half of the nineteenth century a growing number of singers and instrumentalists employed vibrato more frequently and more prominently than most authorities considered proper, perhaps even to the extent that, in some cases, it became a constant feature of their performance; and it seems likely that this trend strengthened markedly during the last decades of the century. Sir Henry Wood remarked in 1927 on the progressive increase of vibrato in his lifetime,[62] but Franklin Taylor, writing in 1880, confirmed that this began even before Wood's birth (1869), for he recorded that *tremolo* (i.e. vibrato of pitch) 'assumed the character of vocal vice about 40 years ago, and is supposed to have had its origin in the *vibrato* of Rubini, first assuming formidable proportions in France, and then quickly spreading throughout the musical world'.[63] And he added: 'In some cases this has been cultivated (evidently) to such an extent as to be utterly ludicrous. Ferri, a baritone, who flourished about 35 years ago, gave four or five beats in the second, of a good quarter tone, and this incessantly.'[64]

[58] Samuel B. Grimson and Cecil Forsyth, *Modern Violin-Playing* (New York, 1920), 34.
[59] In *Jahrbuch für musikalischen Wissenschaft*, 1 (1863), 22.   [60] *Musikalisches Lexikon*, art. 'Bebung'.
[61] (Edinburgh and London, 1908), 34.   [62] *The Gentle Art of Singing*, iv. 87.
[63] 'Tremolo', in Grove, *Dictionary*, iv. 166.   [64] Ibid. 167.

At about the same time as Taylor's article the anonymous author of *Hints to Violin Players* confirmed that many singers and violinists had been introducing very frequent, or more or less continuous, vibrato (which he called the close shake or *tremola* (*sic*)) for some time, but like Taylor he linked this habit with fundamental deficiencies of taste or schooling:

The close shake is an imitation of that tremulous wave which often comes unbidden into the human voice during the performance of a strained note. Some singers, through ignorance or a pernicious training, introduce this wave so often that they eventually lose all control of the voice, and cannot sing a note without the detestable and irritating quiver rattling through it. Many good tenor and treble singers remain in the second or third class, who might easily advance into the first, but for this wretched and damning *tremola*. A singer thus afflicted, or a harmonium with the *tremola* stop out, are the two things which any one with a sensitive ear wishes to be leagues away from. On the violin this *tremola* or close shake is not nearly so intolerable, yet even there it is often sadly overdone, and many violinists, like the singers above noted, seem to lose all control of their left hand, and cannot play a long note without the persistent trembling. My earnest injunction, therefore, to the student before trying to throw a little light on the study, is, master the close shake, but do not let the close shake master you.[65]

He went on to describe 'those benighted beings trained to sing in the "Italian style"' as particularly incapable of producing 'a plain, pure note'.[66] His own view of the importance of vibrato in violin playing is well summed up in his comment elsewhere that

The power to swell and diminish the tone by graduating the pressure of the first finger on the stick of the bow . . . is a much more valuable and legitimate aid to art than the close shake, and one which *can never be abused*. . . . The student will get more real benefit from half-an-hour's practice at that, than from twenty devoted to the close shake.[67]

In string playing the division, increasingly apparent around the turn of the century, seems to have been principally between those trained in the German and those trained in the Franco-Belgian school. Joseph Joachim and his most faithful pupils represented the last phase of the older aesthetic while Fritz Kreisler (1875–1963), who spent several formative years at the Paris Conservatoire, was a leading exponent of the new. Kreisler gave the following account of the origins of the newer attitude, which saw vibrato not as an embellishment but as an essential element of tone production: 'Wieniawsky [1835–80] intensified the vibrato and brought it to heights never before achieved, so that it became known as the "French vibrato". Vieuxtemps [1820–81] also took it up, and after him Eugene Ysaÿe [1853–1931] , who became its greatest exponent, and I. Joseph Joachim [1831–1907], for instance, disdained it.'[68]

---

[65] (Edinburgh, [*c.*1880]), 61.   [66] Ibid. 64   [67] *The Violin: How to Master it*, 80.
[68] Quoted in Louis Paul Lockner, *Fritz Kreisler* (London, 1951), 19.

Kreisler's own account is broadly confirmed by the observations of Carl Flesch (1873–1944), who wrote:

We must not forget that even in 1880 the great violinists did not yet make use of a proper vibrato but employed a kind of *Bebung*, i.e. a finger vibrato in which the pitch was subject to only quite imperceptible oscillations. To vibrate on relatively inexpressive notes, not to speak of runs, was regarded as unseemly and inartistic. Basically quicker passages had to be distinguished by a certain dryness from longer and more expressive notes. Ysaÿe was the first to make use of a broader vibrato and already attempted to give life to passing notes, while Kreisler drew the extreme consequences from the revelation of vibrato activity; he not only resorted to a still broader vibrato, but even tried to ennoble faster passages by means of a vibrato which, admittedly, was more latent than manifest.[69]

Further confirmation may be derived from early recordings. Kreisler's 1905 Berlin recordings show a constant and fairly intense vibrato. Ysaÿe's tone in his 1912 New York recordings is coloured by a more or less constant though generally narrow vibrato, less pronounced than Kreisler's. The 1904 recordings of Pablo de Sarasate (1844–1908), another product of the Paris Conservatoire, reveal a discreet vibrato on most longer notes, noticeably slower than Kreisler's or Ysaÿe's, but many notes have little or none. A very similar slow and frequent vibrato can be heard in the 1909 recordings by Hugo Heermann (1844–1935), who also studied at the Paris Conservatoire. It is a different matter with Joachim; his five recordings of 1903 contain many prominent, long notes that appear to be played with absolutely no left-hand vibrato, some that have a mere hint of vibrato and others on which vibrato of varying intensity is quite distinct. Leopold Auer (1845–1930), a pupil of Joachim and one of the last important advocates of the old aesthetic, made a couple of recordings in 1920 which show him to have used slightly but not much more vibrato than Joachim.[70]

The vibrato used by singers on early recordings shows similar variation to that of violinists. Some singers produce a significant number of relatively long notes with little or no vibrato, while the voices of others have a fairly continuous vibrato. However, as with the violinists on these recordings, vibrato, where it is used, is almost always very narrow and controlled, and indeed in many cases it seems to be more a vibrato of intensity than one of pitch.

Types of Vibrato and their Application

As suggested above, vibrato is rather a class of ornaments than a single technique, and there were many different kinds of vibrato which have no close parallel in modern performance. Even types that appear from descriptions of the means used to produce them to be similar to modern vibrato would probably

[69] *Mémoires* (London, 1957), 120.
[70] All these violinists can be heard on the CD 'Great Violinists', vol. i (Symposium 1071).

have sounded quite different from the effect that the present-day performer, who has a clear aural concept of what a vibrato should be, would instinctively produce by application of the same method.

It may be useful first to focus on string vibrato, since the quantity and detail of the information available about the techniques employed to execute it makes it more feasible to form an idea of the effects that might have been produced than is the case with the more subjective descriptions of the techniques involved in vocal vibrato. Vibrato on wind instruments in the nineteenth century still requires some fundamental research, but a number of conclusions can be drawn about the predominant types employed and their relationship to vibrato in string and vocal music.

There were several types of vibrato available to a string player in the second half of the nineteenth century, some of them not at all what would now be classed as vibrato. Luis Alonso, in his violin method *Le Virtuose moderne* (*c*.1880), described five types with more than a hint of disapproval of most of them:

The vibrato is a major thing for a virtuoso. There are several vibratos: finger vibrato, wrist vibrato (or rather a sort of regular rocking of the hand), nervy vibrato [*vibrato nerveux*] (which comes from the left arm), vibrato by attraction or sympathy, and bow vibrato. The first is made by stopping the string with a finger while at the same time making the imitation of a trill with a higher finger but without this latter finger touching the string; this primitive vibrato is no longer used, only Italian players still do it. The wrist vibrato is normally too slow. It produces a kind of quavering resembling that of street singers. It should be avoided, for it quickly tires the audience.—The arm vibrato is insufferable, it is a nervy, stiff vibrato, it is comparable to a counterfeit chromatic trill, in a large hall it would difficult to pick out the note on which one vibrates, it tires your hearing, and when the violinist plays in high positions and especially double stops, it is with pleasure that one sees the end of the piece approaching. The vibrato by sympathy or attraction [*par sympathie ou attraction*] is soft, pearl-like, superb, but one may only use it where one finds a note doubled by an open string or on a harmonic note which makes the octave.[Ex. 14.5] The bow vibrato is very elegant and is little used, for one hardly hears it, but it produces its visual effect, its elegance; it is a kind of serpentine slur [*une espèce de coulé, serpenté*].[71]

Curiously, the two kinds that elicited Alonso's enthusiasm are those least likely to be classed as vibrato nowadays, though both seem to have been practised for much of the period under consideration.

Alonso's fourth kind of vibrato was described at some length (greater length than left-hand vibrato) by Hermann Schröder in his *Die Kunst des Violinspiels* of 1887. Having discussed left-hand vibrato, he observed of this 'vibrato by sympathy or attraction', which was produced by bowing on one string while rhythmically touching another with a finger of the left hand at an appropriate pitch:

[71] (Paris, [*c*.1880]), p. IV.

Ex. 14.5. Alonso, *Le virtuose moderne*

This preferable most clearly appealing vibrato [*Bebung*] is known to most violinists under the name *vibrato* or *vibration*. In practice this phenomenon is still not made use of because it often speaks too weakly and unreliably, yet on every good violin places similar to the following example ought not to fail in their highly individual effect. [Ex. 14.6][72]

Ex. 14.6. Schröder, *Die Kunst des Violinspiels*, 27

It was also mentioned, much earlier in the century by, among others, the cellist Dotzauer, who called it the *Pochen* and referred to it as a technique for embellishing those long notes on which it was possible to produce it.[73] There are many major string methods, however, that fail to make any allusion to it, and in view of its limitations, its use is likely, as Schröder's account suggests, to have been relatively infrequent.

Alonso's fifth type of vibrato, the bow vibrato, though discreet in its result, was much more frequently described and was probably part of the technique of

[72] p. 27.   [73] *Méthode de violoncelle*, 47 and 52–3, and *Violoncell-Schule*, 27.

most solo players.[74] Like so many string-playing effects it had clear parallels with singing—in this case with the confusingly named singer's *vibrato* (see above, p. 520 f.). It is also closely related to portato, being the most extremely legato form of that technique. Dotzauer apparently considered bow vibrato to be virtually interchangeable with left-hand vibrato (this is further evidence of how very little pitch variation there was expected to be in the latter), observing: 'Many solo players are accustomed to perform sustained notes with *Bebung* (i.e. Tremolo) [Dotzauer's terms], that is, the finger rocks back and forth [the French version adds 'with little velocity']; and many seek to produce the same effect by means of the bow, which might be roughly notated: [Ex. 14.7].' At this point the French version continued with another comment missing from the German: 'It is composed of many nuanced sounds [*sons filés*], of which one makes the *forte* apparent at the beginning of each beat or half-beat.'[75]

Ex. 14.7. Dotzauer, *Méthode de violoncelle*, 47

In the Paris Conservatoire *Méthode* of 1803, which made no mention of left-hand vibrato at all, this kind of bow vibrato was included in the context of dynamic nuances on sustained notes, especially as a means of intensifying a *messa di voce*. The authors advised: 'The swelling and diminishing of a single note may be played [*on peut filer les sons*] in another manner by giving the bow a kind of undulating motion. It is sometimes used in long holding notes and pauses, but this method should be introduced but seldom. Composers generally indicate it by this sign ∿' (Ex. 14.8).[76]

Mention of an 'undulating motion' seems clearly to link this description closely with the 'serpentine slur' of Alonso, but the distinction between this kind of bow vibrato and portato is not always clear. When, for instance, the notation of dots under a slur is encountered the temptation might be to make a distinct separation of the sound, though this may, in many cases, not be what

---

[74] Whether an account given in 1799 of Christoph Schetky's playing refers to this technique is difficult to determine, but it contains one of the earliest references specifically to *vibrato* in relation to bowing. Having described his distinctive manner of holding the bow, the writer continued: 'With this bowhold Schetky made staccato upwards and downwards, but in Adagio he drew the tone out of his instrument as one presses the sweet oil from the ripe olive, and in allegro there was such dexterity in going over the strings that one would have needed ten eyes to notice his viprato [*sic*], although one only needed one ear for it' (*Allgemeine musikalische Zeitung*, 2 (1799–1800), 34).

[75] *Méthode de violoncelle*, 47.

[76] Baillot et al., *Méthode de violon*, 137; translation from *R. Cocks and Co's improved and enlarged Edition. Of the Celebrated Method for the Violin by Rode, Kreutzer and Baillot*, trans. J. A. Hamilton (London, Cocks, [1828]), 16.

Ex. 14.8. Baillot et al., *Méthode*, 137

was intended. In the case of the above passage from the Conservatoire's *Méthode de violon*, the wavy line was given as dots in Boosey's English translation and as a wavy line in J. A Hamilton's translation.[77] In Bailleux's *Méthode raisonné* of 1779 the description of what he calls *balancement*, equating it with the Italian *tremolo*[78] and marking it with dots under a slur, as imitating the 'tremulous effect of the organ',[79] certainly suggests that it is less detached than what might conventionally be understood by portato. There seems likely to have been no sharp distinction between Bailleux's *balancement* and the effect that Joseph Riepel, in 1757, indicated by a wavy line under a slur.[80] In this context it must always be borne in mind that not only was the *Bebung* on the clavichord normally marked by dots under a slur, but that left-hand vibrato was frequently indicated in the same manner.[81] Nevertheless, in all these cases there is often an implication of a regular, perceptible pulsation in the sound.

In singing, this type of pulsation was undoubtedly cultivated in some quarters. Certainly, what W. A. Mozart described and objected to in Meissner's singing in Munich in 1778 ('turning a note that should be sustained into distinct crotchets, or even quavers',[82] which he contrasted with the natural quivering of the voice at moments of emotion) seems likely to have been a stylized embellishment of this type. Mozart's account seems to tally closely with the description of the *Bebung* in a treatise published twenty years later in Munich, Lasser's *Vollständige Anleitung zur Singkunst*. Lasser considered a *Bebung* to be produced 'if, on a semibreve, during the sustaining of the same, one allows four crotchets or eight quavers to be clearly heard by means of a slight pressure' (Ex. 14.9).[83]

Whether such effects in singing were produced by the chest, as suggested by Agricola in 1757,[84] or by the throat, as instructed by others, is unclear; a number of different means of producing these types of effect were probably employed. Johann Adam Hiller observed in 1780 that the *Bebung*

consists in not holding a long tone steadily, but allowing it to weaken and strengthen somewhat, without its thereby becoming higher or lower. On string instruments it is most easily

---

[77] *Rode, Baillot, & Kreutzer's Method of Instruction for the Violin*, edited by Baillot . . . (London, Boosey, [*c*.1880]), 15; *R. Cocks and Co's improved and enlarged Edition*, 17.

[78] For the 17th-c. antecedents of this practice see Stewart Carter, 'The String Tremolo in the 17th Century', *Early Music*, 19 (1991), 43–58.

[79] *Méthode raisonné à apprendre le violon* (Paris, 1779), 11.   [80] *Gründliche Erklärung*, 16.

[81] See e.g. Ex. 14.13.   [82] See Anderson, *The Letters of Mozart*, 552.

[83] p. 158.   [84] *Anleitung zur Singkunst*, 135.

Ex. 14.9. Lasser, *Vollständige Anleitung*, 158

done by a back-and-forth rocking of the fingers that stop the strings. For the singer it is more difficult if he wants to produce it purely with the *throat*; some make it easier for themselves by the motion of the jaw. Carestini did it often, and always with good success.[85]

It may be noted in passing that Hiller's equation of a pulsation without variation of pitch with left-hand vibrato on string instruments rather than bow vibrato, implies that this was the most common type of string vibrato and again indicates that it was expected to be very narrow.

The continuation of such vibrato techniques in nineteenth-century singing is attested by diverse sources, though it may have been less commonly employed then than at an earlier period. Franklin Taylor observed that the 'alternate partial extinction and reinforcement of the note', which he called *vibrato,*

seems to have been a legitimate figure, used rhythmically, of the fioritura of the Farinelli and Caffarelli period, and it was introduced in modern times with wonderful effect by Jenny Lind in 'La figlia del reggimento'. In the midst of a flood of vocalization these groups of notes occurred [Ex. 14.10(*a*)] executed with the same brilliancy and precision as they would be on the pianoforte thus—[Ex. 14.10(*b*)].[86]

Ex. 14.10. Taylor, 'Tremolo', in Grove, *Dictionary*

(*a*)

(*b*)

The influential treatise on singing by Manuel García, Jenny Lind's teacher, contains particularly detailed descriptions of similar techniques as they would have been used by singers of the Swedish Nightingale's generation, and it is evident from his account that there were many subtle variations in the ways in which different singers might have employed them. The first type described by García is designated 'Swelled Sounds with Inflexions or Echoed Notes (Flautati)', and he explained that they

[85] *Anweisung zum musikalisch-zierlichen Gesang* (Leipzig, 1780), 75–6.
[86] 'Tremolo', in Grove, *Dictionary*, iv. 166.

consist in an uniformly continued series of small swelled sounds, multiplied to as great an extent as the breath will allow.* These inflexions may be arranged in different ways; that is they may be of equal duration and power; may follow an increasing or decreasing progression; and so on. Great singers usually employ them according to the following method:— they first hold out a sustained sound with a third of the breath, which sound is followed by another of less power and duration; after which follows a long succession of echoes, becoming weaker as they approach the end—the last, indeed, can scarcely be heard. The throat must contract and dilate with elasticity at each inflexion.**

    * Some authors call this *making the voice vibrate* (Italian, *vibrar di voce*), and indicate this effect by syncopated notes:—[Ex. 14.11]

    ** Echoed notes must be executed from weak to strong [Ex. 14.12].[87]

Ex. 14.11. García, *New Treatise*, 31

Ex. 14.12. García, *New Treatise*, 31

The second type, which he referred to simply as 'Repeated Notes', seems from his description closer to a pitch vibrato, though García dealt with *tremolo* as such at a later point in his treatise and in a rather different manner, treating it less as a decorative embellishment than as a natural expression of emotion when 'agitation is produced by grief so intensely deep as wholly to overpower the soul'.[88] The distinction between the technique described here and *tremolo* is made clear by García's insistence that the 'repeated notes' should not be a 'mere trembling of the voice', but a regular and controlled pulsation. He explained:

Notes repeated while remaining on the same vowel, constitute a variety of sustained sounds; but, in this case, the voice performs without interruption a series of percussions, in order to subdivide the note which at first would have been a sustained one. Each percussion is effected by the larynx rising or falling, as in the act of executing the shake [trill]. These movements are slight and rapid; moreover, the note should be pinched by a sort of appoggiatura of less than a quarter of a tone below, for each repetition. These articulations must neither be aspirated, nor a mere trembling of the voice. The percussions not being perceptible and pleasing unless produced by light voices, are only suitable to women; and to produce a fine effect, they should never exceed four semiquavers for each beat of No. 100 on Maelzel's Metronome; their succession also should always be smooth and delicate.[89]

A direct equivalent for wind instruments of the pulsation without pitch variation that was widely used in singing and string playing is much less frequently

    [87] *New Treatise*, 31.   [88] Ibid. 65.   [89] Ibid. 31–2.

mentioned. For the flute, Quantz referred to a method of performing repeated notes that were notated solely with a slur by means of 'exhalation, with chest action'[90] exactly the same terms as those used by Agricola for singing (the French translation adds 'without employing the tongue'). The technique was also described by Delusse as coming from the lungs, using the syllable 'Hu', though he notated it with dots under a slur. The only form of vibrato (*Bebung*) for the flute that A. E. Müller discussed in the early nineteenth century was evidently the same effect. He observed:

> The vibrato will be specified by the Italian word: Tremolo (trem.) or by more or fewer dots over a note, according to whether this ornament [*Manier*] should be performed faster or slower: e.g. [Ex. 14.13(*a*) and (*b*)]. On the flute this embellishment [*Verzierung*] can only be produced by a moderate increase and decrease of wind pressure, which would have to be specified thus in the notation; e.g. [Ex. 14.13(*c*)]. By means of a small movement of the chin the performance of this ornament becomes easy.[91]

Ex. 14.13. Müller, *Elementarbuch für Flötenspieler*, 31

His account, particularly the third music example, links its effect closely with the string player's bow vibrato as described and notated, for instance, by Dotzauer, while his final comment recalls Hiller's remarks about Carestini. His discussion solely of this type of vibrato suggests comparison with the *Méthode* of Rode, Kreutzer, and Baillot. A similar type of vibrato produced by the chest, without pitch variation, was also employed on brass instruments, perhaps more frequently, since these instruments were incapable of producing a finger vibrato. Its use by trumpeters is dealt with in Johann Ernst Altenburg's 1795 treatise, where his description of its execution (he marked it like the clavichord *Bebung* (Ex. 14.14)), as 'a sustained strengthening and weakening of a particular note'[92] again seems to put it in the same category as the devices described by Müller, Dotzauer, and others. Such devices in wind playing had antecedents going back at least two centuries.[93]

By far the most common type of vibrato technique described for use on wind instruments during the second half of the eighteenth century and the first half of the nineteenth century (though perhaps not the most commonly employed) was that produced by making a trill-like motion on or over an open hole. Quantz was among many who mentioned the former type in the context

---

[90] *Versuch*, VI, 1, §11. The German phrase in both Agricola (*Anleitung zur Singkunst*, 135) and Quantz is *mit der Brust gestoßen*.

[91] *Elementarbuch für Flötenspieler* (Leipzig, [1815]), 31.

[92] *Versuch einer Anleitung zur heroisch-musikalischen Trompeter- und Paukenkunst* (Halle, 1795), 118.

[93] See Dickey, 'Untersuchung zur historischen Auffassung', 88 ff.

Ex. 14.14. Altenburg, *Versuch*, 118

of the *messa di voce*, calling it *Bebung* and in the French version *flattement* and saying that it should be made 'on the nearest open hole';[94] and John Gunn, along with other English writers, described the latter, which he designated with both the English term 'sweetening' and the French *flattement*, instructing that it is 'made by approaching the finger to the first or second open hole, below the proper note that is sounded and moving it up and down over the hole, approaching it very near each time, but never entirely upon it; thus occasioning an alternate flattening and sharpening of the note'.[95]

Late eighteenth-century instructions for the use of this type of vibrato on wind instruments broadly parallel those for the violin except that whereas the violin vibrato could easily be made on any note, the possibilities for wind players were somewhat more restricted. Many writers, like Quantz, mention the finger vibrato principally in connection with the *messa di voce*; some also mention the pause note before a cadenza or suggest that it might be used on any long note, and as in violin methods, the player is often warned not to use the embellishment too often. Tromlitz's account may fairly sum up the standard opinion at the end of the century:

The vibrato [*Bebung*] is a wave-like, quivering movement that is introduced on a long held note, which can be slow or fast, uniform, increasing or decreasing . . . It is not advisable to use this embellishment often. It can be used on held notes, pauses, and on the note before a cadenza . . . I once again remind you only to use this embellishment rarely, thus it will not fail in its good effect, for if it appears too often it will on the contrary rouse a certain disgust.[96]

Tromlitz had warned flautists against using a breath vibrato, remarking: 'One does not do it on the flute, it does not make a good effect, it wails, and whoever does it spoils the chest and ruins his whole playing, for he loses firmness and is consequently unable to hold a firm and pure note; he makes everything come from his chest in a trembling manner.'[97] But descriptions of breath vibrato and its artistic use are increasingly encountered in nineteenth-century

[94] *Versuch*, XIV, §10.
[95] *The Art of Playing the German Flute*, 18.
[96] *Unterricht*, 239–40. See also Andreas Daschauer, *Kleines Handbuch der Musiklehre* (Kempton, 1801), 98.
[97] *Unterricht*, 239.

flute methods. It is difficult, however, to determine to what extent this breath vibrato is a true vibrato of pitch and to what extent it is merely a refinement (or refined description) of the well-established note repetition vibrato. Nicholson's description in his 1836 *School*, for instance, with its clear representation of the manner in which the 'Vibration' should become increasingly rapid (Ex. 14.15),[98] suggests something rather closer to the singer's *vibrato* than to the *tremolo*. He and other writers of wind methods consider that the type of long-drawn-out vibrato illustrated here might be performed by means of a kind of imitation of panting, as in extreme exhaustion.

Ex. 14.15. Nicholson, *School for the Flute*, 71

The finger vibrato remained a standard part of the flautist's technical equipment for at least the first half of the nineteenth century. Fürstenau, who called it *Klopfen* to distinguish it from the breath vibrato, devoted as much space to it as to the latter, as did the writers of most major flute methods at that time; some, indeed, even in the middle of the century, seem to have regarded this type of vibrato as preferable. Thus John Clinton around 1850 focused on finger vibrato, observing that 'When judiciously employed it considerably heightens the effect'. He explained its effect in the same way that Nicholson described breath vibrato, writing: 'The beats (which are made with the finger in a similar manner to the movement in the shake) may be commenced slowly, but with firmness (or even, force) then gradually increased in rapidity, and the force (or strength) of the beats, gradually lessened.' He then gave a detailed chart of how this 'Vibration' could be obtained, marking the position of the trilling finger ⁓ (Ex. 14.16), and concluded: 'For the first four notes, the Vibration (if required) can only be produced by a tremulous action of the flute, at the Embouchure, which however cannot be recommended for the lowest notes; it however may be applied to the middle and upper notes with good effect, if skilfully managed.'[99] (The 'tremulous action of the flute' had also been recommended by Nicholson, but as a means of continuing the breast vibrato when the accelerating note repetitions became too fast for the chest.) Evidence for the production of vibrato on other wind instruments may also be found, and there can be no doubt, from occasional references throughout the period, that equivalent effects were widely imitated on all instruments that were capable of producing them.

---

[98] *School for the Flute*, 71.   [99] *A School or Practical Instruction Book*, 72.

Ex. 14.16. Clinton, *A School or Practical Instruction Book,* 72

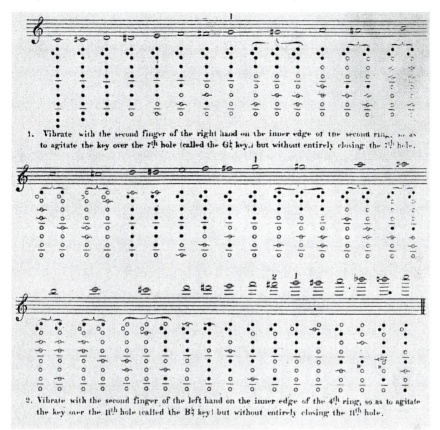

1. Vibrate with the second finger of the right hand on the inner edge of the second ring, so as to agitate the key over the 7th hole (called the G♯ key.) but without entirely closing the 7th hole.

2. Vibrate with the second finger of the left hand on the inner edge of the 4th ring, so as to agitate the key over the 11th hole (called the B♮ key) but without entirely closing the 11th hole.

Speed and Intensity of Vibrato

Ideas about how fast the pulsations of a vibrato were expected to be clearly varied from time to time, instrument to instrument, and performer to performer. Evidence as firm as García's is exceptional; nevertheless, some tentative conclusions about broad trends may be elicited from references to the technique in contemporary instruction books or descriptions. It seems probable that in the eighteenth century most performers employed a fairly slow vibrato as a rule and that in the nineteenth century a faster one was generally preferred. There were, of course, always faster and slower vibrato effects, depending on the context, but a fair amount of evidence points towards a faster norm in the period after 1800.

Indications of a change of taste in this direction around 1800 may perhaps be found in warnings, such as Baillot's in 1834, to 'avoid giving the vibrato a slackness that would make the playing old-fashioned'.[100] More concrete are the numerous eighteenth-century sources that specify the number of oscillations to be made on the note, either in the context of general instruction or in particular musical instances. Leopold Mozart's account, giving the illustration in Ex. 14.17 for three different manners of producing a left-hand vibrato,

Ex. 14.17. L. Mozart, *Versuch*, XI, §4

uuuu
The slow   o

uUuuuu
The increasing   o

uuuuuuuu
The rapid   o

observes: 'The larger strokes can represent quavers, the smaller semiquavers, and as many strokes as there be, so often must the hand be moved,'[101] though he does not specify a tempo for his semibreves. His other music examples, however, strongly suggest a rather slow tempo (Ex. 14.18), as does his insistence on the regular distribution of metrical stress in the vibrato. Interestingly, his description of this technique on the violin seems intended to produce an effect very like the one that his son condemned in the singing of Meissner twenty years later. This may indicate that, in practice, Leopold Mozart's violin vibrato was freer than his account suggests. But it may also indicate a rather different attitude on the part of the young Mozart; after all, he described the use of vibrato on instruments as an imitation of the natural quivering that comes into the human voice (maybe he implied that this occurred in connection with strong feeling, though he did not explicitly say so) rather than comparing vibrato in singing and playing to the dispassionate phenomenon of striking a bell or a slack string.

Like Leopold Mozart, many eighteenth-century writers, especially of the older generation, linked the number of dots or undulations in the graphic signs

[100] *L'Art du violon*, 139.   [101] *Versuch*, XI, §4.

Ex. 14.18. L. Mozart, *Versuch*, XI, §5 (Mozart's instruction: 'In the two examples in No. 1 the strong part of the movement falls ever on the note marked by the numeral 2 for it is the first note of the whole or half-crotchet. In example No. 2, on the contrary, the stress falls, for the same reason, on the note marked with the numeral 1.')

N.1

Thus must one express the tremolo

N.2

Thus does one make the movement

used occasionally to designate vibrato with the number of pulsations required. Marpurg's instructions for *Bebung* on the clavichord, 'One takes care always to set as many dots over the note as movements of the finger should be made', were echoed in many German string, voice, and wind methods. Among the sources encountered by the present author, the latest one to repeat this, more or less literally, is Knecht's *Musikalischer Katechismus* of 1803, which explains *Bebung* as 'A slow trembling motion on one and the same note which is produced by the breath in singing and wind playing, by means of the tip of the finger on strings. One indicates the same by as many dots or *Düpschen*, which are set over a long note, as movements should be made' (Ex. 14.19).[102]

Ex. 14.19. Knecht, *Katechismus*, 53

written   **ö**   performed

In practice this sign for vibrato is quite rarely encountered, but in cases where it was used the number of dots, even if they were only meant roughly to indicate the frequency of pulsations, suggests a very measured movement. Löhlein, for instance, indicated a vibrato in one of the practice pieces in his *Anweisung* as in Ex. 14.20. (His commentary makes it clear that this is a *Bebung*

[102] p. 46.

Ex. 14.20. Löhlein, *Anweisung zum Violinspielen*, 68

with the left hand.) Heinrich Christoph Koch, a musician of great experience, was in any case apparently in no doubt that composers who did employ the sign intended it in the manner described by so many theorists, for, having remarked that the introduction of the *Bebung* was usually left to the performer, he added: 'various composers, however, are accustomed to mark it with dots over the note, and indeed with as many dots as movements should be made with the finger.'[103]

Many nineteenth-century accounts imply a faster basic vibrato. In the updated version of Leopold Mozart's violin school published by Cappi in about 1806 and reprinted by Peters in 1817, the replacement of Mozart's section on vibrato begins with the explanation that vibrato (*Bebung*) is 'a quick movement of the fingers pressed on the string',[104] and another difference is that it required players to be able to decrease as well as increase the speed of the embellishment. Baillot's illustration of the effect of the vibrato (Ex. 14.21), too, suggests something very much quicker than Leopold Mozart's, despite his verbal description of it as a 'more or less moderate movement'. In fact his illustration of vibrato as performed by Viotti indicates the vibrato as demisemiquavers at a tempo of ♩ = 104, though he stressed that the vibrato should not be precisely measurable.[105] But Baillot's account, like most other important ones in the nineteenth century,[106] also stressed that the player should be able to vary the speed of the vibrato according to the musical context.

Ex. 14.21. Baillot, *L'Art du violon*, 138

In many details different performers would have approached the matter differently, just as they would have done the performance of trills and other ornaments, and it is salutary for the student of performing practice to consider, for instance, three treatments of the relationship between the changing speed of vibrato and dynamic nuance. Leopold Mozart, giving the example of the note

---

[103] *Musikalisches Lexikon*, art. 'Bebung'.
[104] *Violinschule oder Anweisung die Violine zu Spielen von Leopold Mozart*, 59.
[105] *L'Art du violon*, 138.   [106] e.g. those of Spohr, Bériot, and Schröder.

Ex. 14.22. L. Mozart, *Versuch*, XI, §7

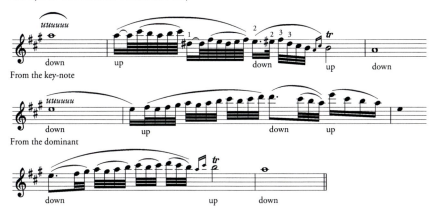

before a cadenza, which he marked with an accelerating vibrato (Ex. 14.22), instructed: 'the stroke must begin softly and gather strength towards the middle, in such fashion that the greatest strength falls at the beginning of the more rapid movement; and at last the stroke must finish softly again.'[107] He did not indicate nor specify a decrease in the speed of the vibrato, though this is implied by his earlier treatment of vibrato in connection with the *messa di voce*.[108] If the latter is what Mozart meant, his account tallies fairly closely with that of Spohr, who prescribed accelerating vibrato for crescendo and decelerating vibrato for diminuendo.[109] Charles Nicholson, on the other hand, together with many other nineteenth-century flautists, seems to have taken a very different view. They associated an accelerating vibrato with a diminuendo rather than a crescendo, though, curiously perhaps, Nicholson explained this effect as deriving from the same phenomenon that Mozart claimed to be imitating with his violin vibrato. In his *Preceptive Lessons for the Flute* of 1821 Nicholson observed: 'Vibration on the flute ought to resemble that of a Bell or Glass, the beats or pulsations of which are never rapid at first, but are governed by the strength of the Tone; for example, if your tone is full and strong, the beat should be slow, but gradually increased in proportion as you diminish the Tone—thus' (Ex. 14.23).[110] The vibrato in this case was made with the breath,

Ex. 14.23. Nicholson, *Preceptive Lessons*, 5

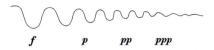

f p pp ppp

[107] *Versuch*, XI, §7.   [108] Ibid. V, §5.   [109] *Violin School*, 176.
[110] (London, 1821), p. 5.

and in his later flute method of 1836 Nicholson gave a similar description, but added that 'When the Vibration becomes too rapid to continue the effect with the breath, a tremulous motion must be given to the Flute with the right hand, the lips being perfectly relaxed, and the tone subdued to a mere whisper.'[111]

A final point about the execution of vibrato on which there seems to have been very diverse opinions was whether the pulsation should occupy the whole length of the note to which the vibrato was applied. Some authors, since they gave no instructions to the contrary, imply that this should be the case, and indeed in the case of the vibrato that is closely related to portato, where little or no pitch variation is envisaged, this would seem to be the expected procedure. In the case of pitch vibrato, however, there was considerable concern that it should not detract from accuracy of intonation, and several authoritative musicians recommended that a portion of the vibrated note should be pure. Baillot required that the beginning and end of the note should, as a rule, be free of vibrato.[112] The cellist Bernhard Romberg taught that 'it should be made only at the beginning of the note, and ought not to be continued throughout its whole duration'.[113]

There were a couple of major issues on which all nineteenth-century writers for instruments or voice who dealt with the matter seem to have been in full agreement. They considered that a vibrato should never involve more than a very small deviation from pure intonation, many using phrases like 'the deviation from true pitch should be scarcely perceptible to the ear'.[114] And they maintained that the effectiveness of all types of vibrato techniques depended on their not being used too frequently or in inappropriate places.

The Notation of Vibrato

Although the introduction of vibrato was almost always left to the discretion of the performer, a number of means, many of which have already been alluded to, were occasionally employed to indicate vibrato explicitly or implicitly. By far the most familiar signs are dots under a slur or a wavy line but both of these could have other meanings. The notations with dots and slur, and wavy lines are quite common in eighteenth-century orchestral scores, though seldom marked in solo music, except, as Petri remarked in connection with the *Bebung* (marked with dots under a slur), 'occasionally for the sake of beginners who do not yet know where they should introduce ornaments'.[115] In the nineteenth century the notation with dots and a slur became increasingly rare as a notation for vibrato, whereas the use of the wavy line became more strongly connected with vibrato and other kinds of *tremolo*. But the wavy line as an instruction to

---

[111] *A School for the Flute*, 71.   [112] *L'Art du violon*, 138.   [113] *A Complete*, 87.

[114] Spohr, *Violin School*, 175.   [115] *Anleitung*, 63.

use left-hand vibrato is rarely found outside textbooks. Spohr included it in a few of his later publications (Ex. 14.24), in all of which the relative infrequency of its occurrence is noteworthy. Wagner used it in *Siegfried* (Ex. 14.25) together with the instruction 'with trembling voice', and in *Die Meistersinger*. And Joachim employed it in some of his arrangements of Brahms's Hungarian dances.

Ex. 14.24. Spohr, Lieder op. 154/ii

Ex. 14.25. Wagner, *Siegfried*, Act I, Scene iii

Various other notations that have connotations of vibrato are occasionally encountered. Hamilton described >>>> or ~~~~ as indicating 'the vibration or close shake'.[116] Here the former notation seems likely to have been associated with the series of small accents which are apparent in a vibrato of intensity, while from the wavy line it might, perhaps, be reasonable to infer a graphic representation of pitch vibrato. Examples of similar notation can be found in Meyerbeer's scores, but as with numerous notational matters at this period, there are inconsistencies. The notation shown in Ex. 14.26(*a*) occurs in an early Italian copyist's score of *Il crociato in Egitto*, while in the printed vocal score of the same work (overseen by the composer) this is given as Ex. 14.26(*b*).[117] In *Les Huguenots* ≶≶≶≶ again seems to be used to indicate a vibrato (see Ex. 14.29 below).

Ex. 14.26. Meyerbeer, *Il crociato in Egitto*: (*a*) MS full score, no. 9; (*b*) printed vocal score (Paris, Pacini, [*c*.1826]), no. 8

(*a*)   𝄽 𝄽 ♩ ♩ ♩ ♩

(*b*)

---

[116] *Dictionary*, 88.
[117] MS score copy in the archives of Teatro La Fenice, Venice; pub. in fac. in the series *Early Romantic Opera* (New York and London, Garland, 1979), 459; vocal score (Paris, Pacini, [*c*.1826]), 107 (copy in Bodleian Library, Oxford).

Ex. 14.27. Baillot, *L'Art du violon,* 138

In nineteenth-century string music particularly the sign <>, evidently related to the traditional *messa di voce* which was normally associated with vibrato, came increasingly to imply a vibrato when placed over a single note. It is present in Baillot's *L'Art du violon,* together with the wavy line, in his example from Viotti's Concerto no. 19 (Ex. 14.27). Campagnoli, too, specifically linked it with vibrato in his *Nouvelle méthode.* It is also equated explicitly with vibrato in the Joachim and Moser *Violinschule,* where Moser explained: 'The vibrato, however, is not only employed for the beautifying of notes of longer duration in slow movements, but also in the fleeting course of passages that are to be rapidly played. Rode has made a speciality of this, and has indicated its use by the mark <> in many of his compositions, even on demisemiquavers and hemidemisemiquavers.' He followed this with an example of its use on selected semiquavers in Rode's Third Caprice.[118] The link from Joachim back to Rode via Boehm is a sufficiently direct one to instil confidence in the reliability of this interpretation of the sign. The sign is frequent throughout Rode's caprices and elsewhere in his music, for instance in the Violin Concerto no. 13; it is not widely found in other early nineteenth-century composers' music, but it occurs relatively often in the music of Zelter, his pupil Mendelssohn (whose close friend and violin teacher, Eduard Rietz, was a pupil of Rode), Schumann, and Brahms. In the music of all these composers, it seems probable that, whatever else it might be intended to convey, the sign generally implied a vibrato. There are certainly instances where, as in Rode's use of it on very short notes, it could hardly, for technical reasons, mean anything but vibrato combined with a gentle accent (possibly with an agogic element[119]). The use of the sign in Ex. 14.28 almost certainly invites vibrato as part of the accentuation.

Vibrato in Orchestral and Ensemble Music

Most vibrato techniques were essentially for soloists. It may be legitimate to presume, however, that this did not necessarily preclude their use in orchestral or ensemble music by instruments that momentarily took on a clearly soloistic role. Thus in performing string quartets Spohr insisted that only when the player 'has a decided solo part, and the other instruments merely an accompa-

---

[118] Vol. iii. 7. See above Ch. 11 and Ex. 11.7 for music example and quotation.
[119] See above, Ch. 3.

Ex. 14.28. (*a*) Mendelssohn, String Quartet op. 13/iv; (*b*) Schumann, Violin Sonata
op. 105/i; (*c*) Brahms, Violin Concerto op. 77/iii

niment, can he be allowed to embellish in the ordinary manner of solo
pieces'.[120] (He had earlier explained that the appropriate addition of vibrato
was an element of solo embellishment.) And in orchestral playing he instructed
the string player to abstain from 'everything appertaining to the embellishment
of solo playing which, if transferred to the orchestra, would destroy all unity of
performance'.[121] Nevertheless, some wind players can be expected to have
applied the same principles to the performance of solo passages in the orchestra as they would have done in purely solo music, and string solos in orchestral
pieces would have invited a similar treatment. Examples of this can be found in
Meyerbeer's scores, in which his detailed performance instructions are often
exceptionally revealing; in the viola solo in no. 2 of *Les Huguenots*, for instance,
he provided what is evidently an indication for bow vibrato (Ex. 14.29).

There is every reason to think therefore that, unless a composer specifically
requested it, orchestral string sections and wind instruments in tutti passages

Ex. 14.29. Meyerbeer, *Les Huguenots*, no. 2

---

[120] *Violin School*, 233.   [121] Ibid. 234.

would have been expected not to use any vibrato. Very occasionally, though, a composer might require an orchestral string section to produce what appears to be a left-hand vibrato. One such instance occurs in Carl Loewe's oratorio *Die Festzeiten* (Ex. 14.30); others can occasionally be found in Wagner's operas (Ex. 14.31); and at the end of the first decade of the twentieth century, when orchestral string sections still used little or no vibrato (as can be heard on pre-First World War recordings[122]), Elgar specifically asked for vibrato at the climax of the Larghetto of his Second Symphony (Ex. 14.32). But a certain degree of caution is needed in interpreting the instruction *vibrato* that is quite frequently encountered in late eighteenth-century and early nineteenth-century scores, for, as mentioned earlier, this often appears to have more to do with accent and

Ex. 14.30. Loewe, *Die Festzeiten* op. 66, fac. edn. of autograph (Mainz, Schott, 1842), 27

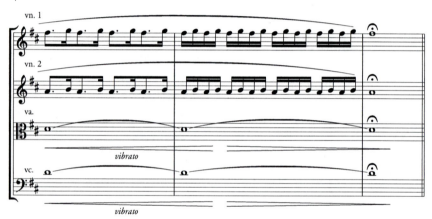

Ex. 14.31. Wagner: (*a*) *Siegfried*, Act III, Scene iii; (*b*) *Parsifal*, following rehearsal number 191

(*a*)

(*b*)

[122] e.g. Nikisch's recordings with the Berlin Philharmonic and, even more, with the London Symphony Orchestra in 1913, or Elgar's 1916 recording of an orchestral version of *Salut d'amour*.

Ex. 14.32. Elgar, Second Symphony op. 63/ii

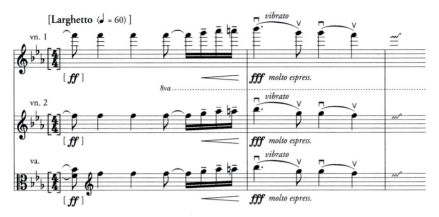

projection than with vibrato techniques in the commonly understood sense of the term.

One type of vibrato technique that does, however, seem quite often to have been asked for in orchestral contexts is the pulsating bow (or, more rarely, breath) vibrato which is related to portato. This may well be the intended execution in many cases where the notation of dots under slurs or wavy lines occurs in eighteenth-century and early nineteenth-century orchestral scores. The context sometimes makes it fairly clear that a normal measured portato was intended. On occasion it is impossible to be certain whether left-hand (or finger) vibrato was envisaged, but in the majority of cases this seems much less likely. Particularly in passages of accompanied recitative, or similar contexts, it may be necessary to consider whether uniform pulsations were intended or whether the effect was to be freely rendered by each individual player. In many cases uniform pulsations seem no more likely than in instances of tremolo indicated nominally with demisemiquavers, and in some they seem unlikely on technical grounds. In the Wolf's Glen scene in Weber's *Der Freischütz*, at an allegro tempo that has already been marked *stringendo*, the effect required in the fifth and tenth bars of Ex. 14.33 is (despite the sextuplet indication) very possibly an unmeasured bow vibrato, which would also fit the dramatic circumstances. Such an interpretation for this passage and for many passages in Gluck's and Spontini's operas may be supported by Berlioz's remarks in his *Traité*, after discussing the normal tremolo with rapidly repeated notes, that

there is another kind of tremolo, never employed nowadays, but of which Gluck has made admirable use in his recitatives. It may be entitled the *undulating tremolo* and consists of a not very rapid utterance of tied notes on the same pitch, while the bow never leaves the string.

Ex. 14.33. Weber, *Der Freischütz*, no. 10

In these non-measured accompaniments, the performers cannot precisely hit the same number of notes in each bar,—some playing more, others fewer; and from these differences results a sort of fluctuation or indecision in the orchestra, perfectly adapted to express the uneasiness and anxiety of certain scenes. Gluck wrote thus: [Ex. 14.34].[123]

Ex. 14.34. Berlioz, *Traité*, 19

Later nineteenth-century treatises on the orchestra appear not to have concerned themselves with special vibrato effects or selective vibrato in the string section, made either with the bow or with the left hand. François-Auguste Gevaert's monumental *Nouveau traité d'instrumentation*,[124] for instance, is silent on the subject, and instrumental tutors, without exception, continued to treat these techniques as something for the soloist. Nevertheless, it seems likely that, particularly where the influence of the Franco-Belgian school of string players was strong, a certain amount of vibrato on the part of individual players, in circumstances where they would have used it as soloists, might have been observed in orchestral string sections during the last decades of the century. Where the influence of the German school was strongest, however, it seems less probable that this would have been the case. These tendencies will have been

[123] p. 19.   [124] (Paris and Brussels, 1885).

particularly strong in the major orchestras, which were increasingly composed of players who had been trained predominantly as soloists rather than orchestral players in the rapidly proliferating music schools and conservatoires of Europe.

15

PORTAMENTO

❦

The term 'portamento' or *portamento di voce* (or its usual synonyms in other languages: in French *port de voix*, in English 'glide' or 'slur', and in German *Tragen der Töne*) was used in a number of different senses during the period 1750–1900, although all of these, except the English, contain the central meaning of 'carrying' the sound. In singing, string playing, and wind playing 'portamento' had two basic connotations: both implied a smooth connection of one sound with another, but this connection could be seen either simply as legato or as a linking of different notes by a more or less audible slide through the intervening pitches. 'Portamento' was sometimes employed in the context of keyboard instruments to mean the same as 'portato', for example by Brahms.[1] Other expressions, such as *Cercar della nota, messa di voce crescente*, or *messa di voce decrescente*, were used, in relation to vocal music, to describe specialized ways of connecting notes at different pitches; but as with so much terminology, the usage of these phrases by different authors is often inconsistent.

The effect of smoothly connecting sounds differs considerably from one medium to another. On bowed string instruments, a sharp distinction may be made between a perfect legato, which is easily achieved where notes can be played on one string or on adjacent strings without a change of left-hand position, and the use of special techniques to produce a sliding connection between notes when the left hand moves from one position to another; on most wind instruments legato may be obtained relatively easily, whereas an effective portamento is only possible in rather limited circumstances; in singing (as in trombone playing) a slight degree, at least, of audible connection, especially between notes at distant intervals, is a scarcely avoidable consequence of a true legato, though many writers made a distinction between portamento and legato in singing.

---

[1] *Briefwechsel*, vi. 146.

There is abundant evidence for the use of vocal portamento, in both the discreet and more obvious senses, during the Classical period. J. B. Lasser, in his rather conservative singing method of 1798, defined *portamento di voce* as 'when one lets the preceding note sound until the following one is enunciated, with modification of the strength and weakness of the notes themselves'.[2] Domenico Corri gave a similar definition of *portamento di voce*, which he regarded as 'the perfection of vocal music', but his wording explicitly incorporates the idea of an audible slide; he described it as 'the swelling and dying of the voice, the sliding and blending one note into another with delicacy and expression'; and he attributed much of the excellence of the great singers of the mid-eighteenth century to their fine use of this technique.[3] This combination of meanings is found in many nineteenth-century sources. J. A. Hamilton, for instance, defined it as 'The manner of sustaining and conducting the voice. A gliding from one note to another.'[4] Baillot also gave two ways of producing *ports de voix* on the violin, the first being simply a seamless legato and the second involving an audible slide.[5]

During the nineteenth century it became increasingly common to associate the term 'portamento' with a conspicuous slide, probably reflecting a growing tendency during the first two decades of the century for singers and string players to intensify the use of this technique as an expressive feature of their performance. A satirical article in the *Wiener allgemeine musikalische Zeitung* of 1813 observed: '*portamento* used to signify the gentle drawing together of two notes of different pitches. Nowadays it sometimes sounds like the song of dear little cats, which miaow rather than sing.'[6] In the 1820s Richard Mackenzie Bacon complained about what he regarded as the erroneous use of the term 'portamento' to describe 'a gliding of the voice from one [note] to the other'.[7] And in the early 1830s Nicola Vaccai was at pains to oppose not only abuse of the technique but also misuse of the word, saying: 'By Portamento must not be understood—as is often the case—the gliding (or dragging) of the voice through all the intermediate grades between one tone and another. On the contrary, it is the perfect connecting of two notes, each being confined strictly within its sound-limits.'[8] Yet by the middle of the century the association of the word 'portamento' with sliding was indissoluble, and Manuel García, in his influential *Traité complet de l'art du chant*, used *port de voix* and *con portamento* ('slur' in the English version[9]) to designate the technique of sliding audibly from one note to another, reserving the term 'legato' for the normal smooth connection between notes.

[2] *Vollständige Anleitung*, 154. [3] *The Singer's Preceptor*, 3.
[4] *Dictionary*, art. 'Portamento'. [5] *L'Art du violon*, 75–6. [6] Vol. i (1813), 531.
[7] Quoted without source reference by W. Crutchfield in *The New Grove Dictionary of Opera*, iii. 1070.
[8] *Metodo pratico di canto italiano per camera* (London, 1832), lesson xiii.
[9] *New Treatise*, 52 and elsewhere.

Whatever the words used to describe it, however, there is every reason to believe that portamento (henceforth the term will be used in the sense of an audible glide) already played a significant part in musical performance during the later decades of the eighteenth century. It seems particularly to have been cultivated by Italian singers and violinists. A writer in the *Allgemeine musikalische Zeitung* in 1814 observed that portamento (which he called *Durchziehen der Töne*) had been 'taken over from singing into instrumental music';[10] but only three years earlier Antonio Salieri had expressed an opposite opinion in the same journal, attributing the origin of portamento (at least in the exaggerated form to which he objected) to the violinist Antonio Lolli (*c*.1725–1802):

This laughable mannerism on the violin derived from a joke of the celebrated Lolli. When in his later years he was no longer master of the ravishing, magical energy through which he had formerly captivated the public, he sought, in order to gain acclaim for the concerts that he gave on his journeys, at least to make them laugh; thus in the last Allegro of his concerto he imitated now a parrot, now a dog, and now a cat. The Cat Concerto, as he himself called it, was relished by the public, and he therefore gave it often and to universal applause. Other violinists now copied the master's joke. Little by little the joke became a fashion (by which strangely not merely players but also singers allowed themselves to be carried away), became a method with the weaker and more foolish; and since the number of the latter is endless, so that false manner became little by little a sort of school from which a fine multitude of cats has proceeded to pain the ears of the listener, with the intention of delighting them, through playing and singing in this manner.[11]

From the reference to Lolli's 'later years' it seems that Salieri was referring to a development that had occurred during the previous twenty years; but there is no good reason to believe either that Lolli was the first practitioner of portamento, or that it had become a significant factor in violin playing or singing as recently as Salieri's statement implies. But Salieri's diatribe does suggest that portamento had begun to be used much more frequently towards the end of the eighteenth century and, probably, that it was being performed in a more conspicuous manner than formerly.

On bowed string instruments portamento is a natural outcome of position changing, and it had probably been employed to some extent as an artistic effect ever since violinists began to make regular use of shifting in the early eighteenth century. It is implied by a few fingerings in, for instance, Leopold Mozart's *Versuch einer gründlichen Violinschule* (Ex. 15.1: see also Ex. 14.22), where, however, such fingerings are generally avoided, and it appears to have been envisaged in a number of Haydn's string quartets (see below), where the fingerings evidently specify a particular effect. A comment in Burney's *General History* indicates that by the 1770s portamento in violin playing was already quite widespread; he observed that Geminiani 'was certainly mistaken in laying it down as a rule that "no two notes on the same string, in shifting, should

<hr>

[10] Vol. 16 (1814), 175–6.   [11] *Allgemeine musikalische Zeitung*, 13 (1811), 209.

Ex. 15.1. L. Mozart, *Versuch*, VIII, 3, §7

be played with the same finger"; as beautiful expressions and effects are produced by great players in shifting, suddenly from a low note to a high, with the
same finger on the same string'.[12] And in 1776 J. F. Reichardt wrote: 'Shifting
with a finger through various positions should be absolutely forbidden to the
orchestral player, although it is permissible from time to time for the solo
player.'[13] By the last quarter of the eighteenth century it had clearly become a
prominent feature in the techniques of some violinists.

In the eyes of many contemporaries, portamento seems to have been very
strongly associated with the Italian style of performance and in particular with
Italian and Italian-influenced musicians. A remarkable, if somewhat cryptic
passage in the preface to Michel Woldemar's *Grande méthode* suggests the
extent to which the practice had already taken root in Paris by the end of the
century, among both violinists and singers:

There were formerly three scales, that is to say, the diatonic, the chromatic, and the enharmonic. The diatonic is composed of five tones and two semitones. The chromatic is only
composed of semitones and the enharmonic of quarter-tones. There were three genres of
music: French, German, and Italian. The French and the German, although of a quite different style, formed their sounds from the diatonic scale, while the Italian was created, with
as much sensitivity as grace, by means of the chromatic or rather the enharmonic, which is
nothing more than a slur from one note into another through the inflexion of the voice.
This style, so touching, has triumphed over the other two in this century of enlightenment,
and Italian music, based on that of the Greeks, which they derived from the Egyptians, the
leading scholars of the world—this music so delicious and so touching has become the universal language of all musicians.[14]

Jean Jacques Rousseau in his dictionary of music (p. 270) informs us that there were only
five notes in Greek music and that it was St Gregory who increased the number to seven:
that the enharmonic style was the first of the three to be discovered and that Plutarch
reproached the musicians of his day for having abandoned it: if this philosopher returned
to Paris, he would witness its triumph since, despite the fact that it is not notated in musical works, it exists physically and makes itself felt in a palpable manner in all the diatonic
and chromatic slurs through the inflexion of the voice.

Mestrino caused the enharmonic style to be heard in Paris in an artful manner [*d'une
maniere savante*]; did Mestrino know that his slurs were of palpable enharmonics, or did he,

---

[12] *A General History of Music from the Earliest Ages to the Present Period* (London, 1776–89), ii. 992 n. n.

[13] *Ueber die Pflichten*, 35.

[14] This sentence is equally ungrammatical in the original: 'ce genre si touchant a triomphé des deux
autres dans ce siècle de lumières et la musique Italienne bazée sur celle des Grecs qui la reçurent des Egyptiens
les premiers savans du monde; cette musique si délicieuse et si touchante, est devenue la langue universelle
de tous les musiciens.'

like the Bourgeois Gentilhomme of Molière, speak prose without knowing it? That I do not know; but Voltaire was mistaken in saying, when talking about the supper of Charles VII with Agnès Sorel at the house of the compliant Bonneau, 'there was Italian music of the chromatic style' for it would have failed in its effect; the expression of tenderness belongs exclusively to the enharmonic style, and just as the trill comes to us from birds, I wager that this amorous scale comes from the cooing of tender turtle-doves.[15]

The mention of slurs that were 'of palpable enharmonics' seems to refer to a theoretical explanation of portamento as a series of quarter-tones (also adopted by Woldemar). But Woldemar's treatment of the 'enharmonic style' here and in his so-called *Méthode de violon par L. Mozart* makes clear beyond a shadow of doubt that he is referring to a true portamento. Later in the *Grande méthode* Woldemar gave an example of Mestrino's employment of portamento (Ex. 15.2) with the following explanation: 'One sees from the preceding example

Ex. 15.2. Woldemar, *Grande méthode*, 34

Du Couler a la MESTRINO d'un ton dans un autre au moyen de l'échelle enharmonique ou quarts de tons tous ces coulés se font du même doigt.

EXEMPLE

that Mestrino was only able to perform this piece by means of the enharmonic scale, that is to say, by quarter-tones, just as all these slides from one note to another are notated, and since these intervals are so small that the ear cannot distinguish them he made almost all of them with the same finger.'[16] In his *Méthode de violon* Woldemar's explanation was even more explicit, for he observed: 'The enharmonic genre may only be explained by the slur, for it is formed from immeasurable intervals, though to reduce them to a formula one divides them into quarter-tones.'[17]

By the date of Woldemar's treatise, the use of portamento by string players was widespread throughout Europe. Mestrino's début in Paris was in 1786 and he died in 1789, but, as already indicated, there is no reason to believe that either he or Lolli was the first violinist to make extensive use of portamento. Mestrino and Lolli may have been notable for making it a more prominent aspect of their style, but it was undoubtedly an integral part of the technique of many players of the time.

Despite the strictures of Reichardt and others it is also clear that string players were already beginning to use portamento in orchestral playing at the end of the eighteenth century. A reviewer of operas at the Magdeburg theatre in 1798 noted:

The theatre here supports 10 players of its own who all individually play splendidly, but on account of their dissimilar performance styles they do not form a good ensemble. This applies notably to the violinists.—So, for example, in a symphony I heard one of these players, instead of taking the third, D–F sharp, as two separate crotchets, slide from the D to the F sharp. Certainly the higher note is easier to find in this way, but does this sort of aid, which is over-used to the extent of nausea by the majority of violinists, belong in a piece where there are 3 or 4 players to a part? I have now noticed this embellishment, which is so disfiguring in tutti passages, in the orchestras of many places.[18]

The same reviewer also complained of the excessive and presumably unskilful use of portamento by the prima donna, Toscani, about whom he remarked that 'like the above-mentioned violinist' she 'constantly slid through the in-between notes on rising or falling fourths, fifths, or sixths, and since she carried on with this incessantly, with her in any case piping voice, a dreadful miaow developed out of what was supposed to be an Italian embellishment'.[19]

Salieri's condemnation of portamento confirms the spread of the practice to orchestral playing, for he observed:

This feeble and childish mannerism has, like an infectious disease, spread to some orchestral players and, what is most ridiculous, not merely to our courageous violinists, but also to violists and even double bass players. Because a tolerated evil always gets worse, such a mannerism, particularly in a full orchestra, must necessarily change a harmonious body into a collection of whining children and miaowing cats.[20]

---

[16] p. 34. [17] pp. 56–7. [18] *Allgemeine musikalische Zeitung*, 1 (1798–9), 461.
[19] Ibid. 463. [20] Cited in *Allgemeine musikalische Zeitung*, 13 (1811), 207.

And he went on to advise the directors of the Imperial Opera that any player who persisted in the habit should be dismissed from the orchestra.

Authorities such as Spohr in 1832 and Gassner in 1844[21] continued to maintain that portamento was not permissible in orchestral playing. Spohr instructed that the orchestral player should 'abstain from all superfluous appoggiaturas, turns, trills and the like, as well as all contrived position work, sliding from one note to another, changing the finger upon a note, in short from every thing appertaining to solo playing';[22] however, he appears to have envisaged portamento at times in his orchestral music, though only where he indicated it by the inclusion of fingering (Ex. 15.3). Meyerbeer, too, occasion-

Ex. 15.3.   Spohr, Fifth Symphony op. 102/ii

ally called explicitly for an orchestral portamento, as when he instructed in the score of *L'Étoile du nord* 'slide with the same finger' (*glissez avec le même doigt*).[23] But it seems highly likely that by the middle years of the century it was becoming an established and accepted practice in many orchestras. This was undoubtedly hastened and institutionalized by the proliferation of conservatoire training, which prepared violinists to be soloists (for whom portamento was an essential expressive device) even though their careers would mostly be spent as orchestral players. The frequent and prominent orchestral portamento that can be heard on some of the earliest orchestral recordings probably reflects a practice that had been established for at least half a century.

The use of portamento, even in solo playing, however, was strongly resisted for some time during the early nineteenth century. There were evidently many musicians whose views had been formed in the middle years of the eighteenth century, especially in Germany, who disliked either the introduction of portamento in unsuitable places, its too-frequent employment, or the manner of its execution (usually objecting that it was too slowly or intensely performed). Reichardt complained in 1805 that the 21-year-old Spohr produced a parody of Pierre Rode's manner by his 'constant sliding of the hand up and down on a string in order to give the notes the greatest possible connection and to melt them into one another, also presumably to inspire the string with the sighing sound of a passionate voice'.[24] And in 1808 a critic in Prague, after praising Spohr's ravishing performance in an Adagio, continued:

---

[21] *Dirigent und Ripienist* (Karlsruhe, 1844), 52–3.

[22] *Violin School*, 234.

[23] Full score (Paris, Brandus, 1854), 184.

[24] *Berlinische musikalische Zeitung*, 1 (1805), 95.

Yes, one could call him unsurpassed in this genre if he did not often disturb us in this enjoyment, and sometimes very unpleasantly, by a mannerism much too frequently employed, that is by sliding up and down with one and the same finger at all possible intervals, by an artificial miaow, as one might call it if that did not sound teasing.[25]

Salieri felt so infuriated by the extent to which portamento was being cultivated by singers and instrumentalists that he resumed his attack on the habit four years after his article of 1811.[26] And a decade later A. L. Crelle, a keyboard player, registered his objection to portamento by singers and violinists in terms that seem to propose its total abolition.[27]

Few writers, however, were quite so negative, and the tone of most complaints does not, on the whole, suggest that their authors necessarily regarded portamento, sensitively used, in the right proportion and in the correct circumstances, as an illegitimate technique. The comments of the reviewer from Magdeburg make it clear that it was the distortion of what was supposed to be an Italian embellishment that was objected to, rather than the embellishment itself; and Salieri's attacks on the practice must be seen in the light of other contemporary accounts, for instance that of the writer in 1814 who observed that it is an 'embellishment which is certainly pleasant in singing, if it is used with great moderation, with taste, and in the right places'.[28] Similar admonitions are encountered in virtually all nineteenth-century instruction books dealing with these techniques, for, like every expressive device, portamento was liable to abuse in the hands of less talented musicians. Notwithstanding periodic complaints about the over-use of portamento, there can be no doubt that by the middle decades of the nineteenth century it had become an orthodox and quite freely employed expressive resource, and until well into the twentieth century it remained, in its various forms, an integral aspect of vocal and instrumental technique.

Types of Portamento

There were basically two classes of portamento. The one involved gliding between notes sung to different syllables, or, on string instruments, played in separate bows, or, in the case of wind instruments, separately articulated. The other took place between two different pitches on the same syllable, between notes in the same bow, or between smoothly slurred notes. While the nature of vocal music or the technical exigencies of particular instruments played a part in determining the execution of the ornament, there were general similarities

---

[25] *Allgemeine musikalische Zeitung*, 10 (1807–8), 313.

[26] Eduard Hanslick, *Geschichte des Concertwesens in Wien* (Vienna, 1869), 233 n. 2.

[27] *Einiges*, 88.　　　　　　　　　　　　[28] *Allgemeine musikalische Zeitung*, 16 (1814), 175–6.

and close parallels between the varieties used in all cases. As a general rule instrumentalists seem to have taken vocal music as their starting-point.

Vocal Portamento on Notes between Different Syllables

Late eighteenth-century and early nineteenth-century treatments of portamento generally focused on the type for which the term *cercar la nota* or *cercar della nota* was sometimes used. In the 1780s it was discussed by Johann Carl Friedrich Rellstab and Domenico Corri. Rellstab, referring to the opening of Graun's aria 'Ihr weichgeschafne Seele' (Ex. 15.4(*a*)), commented that a good singer would use the *cercar la nota* on the rising minor third, and notated the ornament as a dotted rhythm with the short note anticipating the pitch of the following note. (Ex. 15.4(*b*))[29] Corri included it in the 'Explanation of the Graces' in his *Select Collection*, where it appears without a name, and again in his *The Singer's Preceptor* (1810), where he called it the 'anticipation grace'. In both cases he indicated it by a small note, but elucidated this by showing the same dotted rhythm as Rellstab. Here, as elsewhere, the rhythmic representation must not be taken too literally; the short note would almost certainly have been made much shorter in most instances. This is implied by many verbal descriptions of the execution of portamento, for instance, that of G. G. Ferrari in 1818: 'In carrying the voice from one note to another, the second must receive a slight intonation, previous to being articulated'.[30]

Ex. 15.4. Rellstab, *Versuch über die Vereinigung*, 37

In his earlier publication Corri illustrated only a rising form of this type of portamento, saying: 'As this has the peculiar property of uniting two notes of any intervals, in executing it, it is necessary to swell the note into the Grace, and the Grace must melt itself again into the note following'.[31] In the later tutor he illustrated both rising and falling forms (Ex. 15.5) and made the distinction: 'In

Ex. 15.5. D. Corri, *The Singer's Preceptor*, 32

---

[29] *Versuch über die Vereinigung der musikalischen und oratorischen Declamation* (Berlin, [1786]), 37.

[30] *Breve trattato di canto italiano* (London, 1818), cited by W. Crutchfield in 'Portamento', in *The New Grove Dictionary of Opera*, iii. 1070.

[31] *A Select Collection*, i. 8.

descending, drop the Grace into the note, and in ascending, swell the Note into the Grace'.[32]

Not all tutors from this period concurred precisely with the dynamic pattern proposed by Corri. J. F. Schubert considered that

> If afternotes [*Nachschläge*] of this kind are to produce the desired effect the main note should be strongly attacked and the afternote slurred very gently and weakly to the preceding note, particularly downwards. Only in vocal pieces of a fiery, vehement character would I now and then, upward, but never downwards, allow the afternote to have more accent than the main note.[33]

Fröhlich, on the other hand, who in the main poached his text directly from Schubert (including the above passage[34]), illustrated the *cercar della nota* both upwards and downwards with a *messa di voce* pattern (Ex. 15.6). He also observed: 'A portamento on a descending interval must be taken somewhat faster, as is marked by the little note at the fall of the octave, so that no howling instead of singing results and the unbearable drawling will be avoided. The more distant the interval, therefore, the faster it must be performed in descending.'[35] Later in the same treatise, where Schubert was cited more or less verbatim, this type of treatment was advocated for rising portamentos.

Ex. 15.6. Fröhlich, *Musikschule*, 36

Corri also gave an account of a related procedure where the portamento took place using the syllable of the second note (this he was to call the 'leaping grace' in *The Singer's Preceptor*). He observed in the *Select Collection* that this grace 'is to be taken softly, and to leap into the note rapidly',[36] and in the later publication added: 'the strength necessary to its execution must be regulated more or less according to the distance of the Intervals'[37] (see above, Ex. 13.38). As with the 'anticipation grace', the rhythmic representation must be regarded as approximate; it is clear that in most circumstances the grace-note would have been considerably shorter than a semiquaver.[38] One consequence of this is that, whereas with the 'anticipation grace' the portamento could be either rapid or drawn out, with the 'leaping grace' the portamento would seem almost invariably to have been executed rapidly, producing a quite different effect. This can be clearly heard on Patti's and Moreschi's recordings.[39]

---

[32] *The Singer's Preceptor*, 32.   [33] *Neue Singe-Schule*, 56.   [34] *Musikschule*, 58.
[35] Ibid. 36.   [36] Vol. i. 8.   [37] *The Singer's Preceptor*, 32.
[38] See Ch. 13 for a fuller citation of Corri's description of grace-note execution, in which he says that 'the more imperceptible they are, the more happy is the execution' (*A Select Collection*, i. 8).
[39] See Ch. 12.

Not only could the 'leaping grace' be used to connect the pitches of two notes directly, but, as pieces in the *Select Collection* indicate, it could also be used at the beginning of a phrase, in which case the grace-note occurred on another note of the harmony with which the main note was consonant; in the middle of a phrase, the grace-note would often be sounded at a different pitch from the preceding note (usually a tone or semitone above or below it), the essential factor being that the grace-note had to belong to the harmony of the note following it, with which it was connected (Ex. 15.7). With the 'anticipation grace', the anticipatory note seems always to have been at the pitch of the note it preceded, but it did not necessarily have to be consonant with the harmony of the note from which it took its value and to which it was tied. Ex. 15.8 illustrates some of the contexts in which Corri considered these techniques appropriate.

Ex. 15.7. D. Corri, *A Select Collection*: (*a*) vol. i. 3: Giordani (Hasse), *Artaserse*; (*b*) vol. i. 23: Gluck, *L'Olimpiade*; (*c*) vol. i. 42: Gluck, *Orfeo*

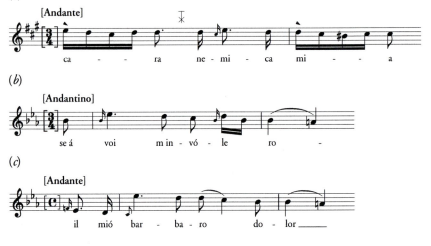

Ex. 15.8. D. Corri, *A Select Collection*: (*a*) vol. i. 17: Rauzzini, *L'ali d'amore*; (*b*) vol. i. 32: Giordani, *La marchesa Giardinera*; (*c*) vol. i. 42: Gluck, *Orfeo*

(*c*)

The extensively annotated pieces in Corri's *Select Collection* imply that the 'leaping grace' may have been more extensively used in the eighteenth century than the 'anticipation grace'; the latter occurs relatively seldom in these pieces, while the former is very frequently encountered. Corri's later publications, however, reverse this situation, suggesting, perhaps, that at the beginning of the nineteenth century the popularity of the 'leaping grace' was already diminishing in favour of the 'anticipation grace'. This is borne out by the expressed preferences of later writers. Vaccai in around 1832 described and illustrated these two forms of portamento in his *Metodo pratico di canto italiano per camera* (Ex. 15.9); he observed of the 'leaping grace', which he called portamento 'by posticipation', that 'This style is less usual than the first'.[40] Manuel García's treatise supports the notion that the 'anticipation grace' grew greatly in favour at the expense of the 'leaping grace' during the nineteenth century, at least in the opinion of the *cognoscenti*, to the extent that by the middle of the century the latter, though still used, had come to be regarded as being in dubious taste. García instructed: 'A slur placed between two notes, each having its syllable, is executed by carrying up the voice with the syllable of the first note; and not, as is frequently done with the syllable of the second. The second note ought to be heard twice—once on the first syllable, and again on its own—the passage [Ex. 15.10] will be correct as shown in A, and incorrect as shown in B.'[41] García gave another example to illustrate how 'Some singers, either from negligence or want of taste, slur the voice endlessly, either before or after notes';[42] this shows the types of 'leaping grace' approved of by Corri, though obviously used to excess in this instance (Ex. 15.11). Despite the disapproval of some nineteenth-

Ex. 15.9. Vaccai, *Metodo pratico*, lesson xiii

---

[40] Lesson xiii.   [41] *New Treatise*, 53.   [42] Ibid.

Ex. 15.10. García, *New Treatise*, 53

(A)

(B)

Ex. 15.11. García, *New Treatise*, 53

century authorities, the continued use of the 'leaping grace', in very much the sorts of context illustrated by Corri, is attested by its occurrences in Adelina Patti's 1905 recordings. As intimated in Chapter 12, it is surely not coincidental that she is one of the oldest female singers on record, and that this embellishment is very rare in, if not entirely absent from, the recordings of younger singers. Its pervasiveness in recordings made by the papal castrato Alessandro Moreschi in 1902–4, however, tempts one to see him as the direct, if somewhat unworthy heir of a school of singing that had been faithfully preserved among the castrati in Rome after they disappeared from the operatic stage at the beginning of the nineteenth century. (Meyerbeer's *Il crociato in Egitto* had been the last important opera to contain a major castrato role.)

Although composers only rarely indicated portamento explicitly, it seems likely that there is a connection between this technique and the occurrence of slurs over notes set to different syllables. Slurs over melismas in vocal music were not, during the eighteenth century and much of the nineteenth century, written as a matter of course. They were sometimes included to clarify the disposition of syllables and sometimes to indicate phrasing or breathing in long melismas, but many composers appear to have indicated them intermittently and haphazardly. However, where they are found between notes on different syllables it is always worth considering whether one of these types of portamento may have been intended. Such an interpretation seems probable in Ex. 15.12(*a*)–(*d*). In Ex. 15.12(*e*), Meyerbeer made his intention (which involved a

Ex. 15.12. (*a*) Rossini, *Semiramide*, no. 3, autograph (p. 120); (*b*) Spohr, *Jessonda*, no. 18; (*c*) Wagner, *Tristan und Isolde*, Act 2 sc. 2; (*d*) Meyerbeer, *Les Huguenots*, no. 3; (*e*)

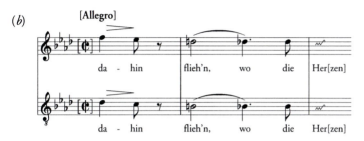

(*b*)

(*c*)

(*d*)

Meyerbeer, *Les Huguenots*, no. 24

(*e*)

(*a*)

'leaping grace' type of portamento) quite clear by the grace-note and the attached verbal instruction *portez la voix*. In 1858 Charles de Bériot specifically identified the slur between two syllables as a means of indicating a portamento of the 'anticipation grace' type, illustrating it with Ex. 15.13.

Ex. 15.13. Bériot, *Méthode*, 236

The song written thus   is interpreted thus

t'ap - pel - le   t'ap - pel - le

Vocal Portamento between Notes on the Same Syllable

The other type of portamento that seems to have been ubiquitous in late eighteenth-century and nineteenth-century singing, the simple connection produced by slurring the voice between two notes sharing the same syllable, was described by J. F. Schubert thus:

> There is yet another *cercar della nota* which is universal nowadays and is indeed very much misused by the majority of singers. It consists of a gentle, imperceptible drawing up or down of the voice from one note to another. It certainly cannot be done on the keyboard; on the violin it occurs when the player draws two different notes together with one finger on one string and at the same time melts them into each other. This gliding up and down of the voice is a real beauty of singing if it is well executed and brought in at the right place. Otherwise, however, it becomes disgusting and unbearable.[43]

This type of portamento was considered by Schubert to be particularly appropriate to use between successive semitones with a crescendo in a rising phrase and diminuendo in a falling one, but he warned: 'if this ornament [*Manier*] is not to become too strident the melting of one note into another should not happen too slowly.'[44] Schubert's description of this practice seems to connect it with the *messa di voce crescente* described in Lasser's *Vollständige Anleitung* of 1798, which occurred 'if one draws up the voice from a note to the note a semitone higher imperceptibly through all the commas until the second [note] is reached'.[45] When applied to descending semitones Lasser called this *messa di voce decrescente*.

Comparison with Fröhlich's treatment of the same subject in his *Musikschule* reveals that here, as elsewhere, Fröhlich copied much of his text word for word from Schubert, but there are some additions that suggest either that Fröhlich was a greater lover of portamento in general or that, as other accounts suggest, use of the device by singers and instrumentalists increased rapidly during the early years of the nineteenth century. Fröhlich repeated Schubert's comment about sliding a finger on the violin verbatim, except that he referred to the 'violin, viola, violoncello, etc.'; but he then went on to say:

[43] *Neue Singe-Schule*, 57.   [44] Ibid.; Fröhlich, *Musikschule*, 59.
[45] p. 154. A comma is a ninth of a tone.

Oboists, clarinettists, bassoonists can read about this in the article in the Flute Method [a later section of the *Musikschule*] and attempt to transfer it [portamento] to their instruments. Hornists, trombonists must, by dint of diligent study, try to make it as much like the singing voice as possible. But this is a matter for people who want to appear as up-to-date artists.[46]

But in singing Fröhlich cautioned that portamento was most appropriate in soprano voices, less good in tenor voices, and entirely to be avoided in bass voices. Like Lasser and Schubert he considered that rising or falling semitones were particularly apt to be embellished by a portamento and illustrated this with Ex. 15.14, in which the slanting lines were explained as signifying 'the melting together of the notes'.[47] Passages of this kind seem to have remained favourite places for portamento in the nineteenth century in singing, string playing, and wind playing.

Ex. 15.14. Schubert, *Neue Singe-Schule*, 57 (and Fröhlich, *Musikschule*, 59)

Another use for portamento suggested by Schubert was at fermatas, where he advised that 'the portamento can serve instead of another decoration, for example [Ex. 15.15]'.[48] His suggestion of using a line to indicate portamento between legato notes was not, however, taken up by composers in the nineteenth century.

Ex. 15.15. Schubert, *Neue Singe-Schule*, 59

Portamento in Wind Playing

Fröhlich was not alone in describing how wind instruments could attempt to imitate the vocal portamento. While it was scarcely possible for them effectively to make a portamento over larger intervals, a number of writers gave instructions for producing one, particularly on semitone intervals. Among those who discussed portamento on the flute were Adolph Bernard Fürstenau and the leading English flautist of the mid-nineteenth century, John Clinton. The latter observed:

[46] *Musikschule*, 58.   [47] Ibid. 59.   [48] *Neue Singe-Schule*, 59.

This ornament is effected by gradually drawing or sliding the fingers off the holes, instead of raising them in the usual manner; by this means is obtained, all the shades of sound between the notes, so that the performer may pass from one note to another, as it were, imperceptibly; it produces a pleasing effect when sparingly used. . . . The fingers must be drawn off the holes in a line towards the palm of the hand; the employment of the crescendo with the glide, heightens the effect; it may as well be observed, that this ornament is impracticable when the next note is made by opening a key, as from D♮ to Eb G♮ to Ab &c.

He then proceeded to give a table of 'the most effective glides and the best mode of fingering them'. The majority show the glide between semitones, some are between tones, and a small number are between larger intervals (Ex. 15.16).[49]

Portamento in String Playing

The various types of portamento employed by string players closely reflected the singer's portamento, though the nature of the instrument necessitated some differences. Dotzauer's *Méthode de violoncelle* of about 1825 gives a full description of the two basic methods of producing portamento between slurred notes on string instruments, in terms very similar to those used in many later methods. He gave the examples shown in Ex. 15.17. The first, involving a slide with a single finger to produce a continuous glide between two notes, is self-explanatory; of the others, he explained:

In example 2, the portamento [*Ziehen*] is introduced four times with different fingers. From B to G the first finger remains firmly down on the string during the slide approximately until E, and since the slide cannot continue from the E to the G the fourth finger must come down on the G so much the faster after this E. It is the same with the following C to G and C sharp to G; however, with the D to B one substitutes the third finger for the second during the slide: and it is the same with the next example from B to F. In examples 3 and 4 the rules already given are to be used. In the fourth example the third finger substitutes for the fourth and goes onto the A, and in the second bar the first finger slides from E downwards to B.[50]

In this type of portamento the aim seems to have been to give the impression that the glide continued all the way between the two notes. Spohr explained it thus in his 1832 *Violinschule*, in the context of one of the exercises, stressing that the prescribed method would prevent this sort of portamento from degenerating into 'a disagreeable whining':

in the 9th bar of the exercise, the first finger is moved upwards from E to B [Ex. 15.18(*a*)] and the fourth finger then falls at once on the second E: similarly in the 11th bar, the second finger is moved from E to B [Ex. 15.18(*b*)] at which instant the little finger falls on the upper B. This shifting, however, must be done so quickly, that the chasm or interstice between the small note and the highest (in the first example, a fourth, in the second an octave) shall be

---

[49] *A School or Practical Instruction Book*, 73.　　[50] *Méthode de violoncelle*, 46–7.

Ex. 15.16.   Clinton, *A School or Practical Instruction Book*, 73

ON THE GLIDE.

This ornament is effected by gradually drawing or sliding the fingers off the holes, instead, of raising them in the usual manner; by this means is obtained, all the shades of sound between the notes, so that the performer may pass from one note to another, as it were, imperceptibly; it produces a pleasing effect, when sparingly used. It is denoted by this mark ⌒. The fingers must be drawn off the holes in a line towards the palm of the hand; the employment of the crescendo with the glide, heightens the effect; it may as well be observed, that this ornament is impracticable when the next note is made by opening a key, as from D♮ to E♭ G♯ to A♭ &c.

The following example will point out the most effective glides, and the best mode of fingering them.

Clinton's Instructions.   (A&P. 5118.)

Ex. 15.17. Dotzauer, *Méthode de violoncelle*, 46

(*a*)

(*b*)

(*c*)

(*d*)

unobserved, and the ear cheated into the belief that the sliding finger has actually passed over the whole space from the lowest to the highest note.

But he went on to warn:

It is true that in opposition to the foregoing rule, many violinists are accustomed in such skips to slide with the finger employed for stopping the upper note and consequently to perform the above passages in the manner following: [Ex. 15.18(*c*)] But as the unpleasant whining before alluded to cannot then be possibly avoided, this mechanism must be rejected as faulty.[51]

---

[51] pp. 108–9. This passage has been misleadingly interpreted in Stowell, *Violin Technique*, 98.

Ex. 15.18. Spohr, *Violin School*: (*a*) p. 108; (*b*) p. 108; (*c*) p. 109

(*a*)

5th position

(*b*)

7th position

(*c*)

2nd, 5th position   3rd, 7th position

Spohr's *Violinschule* also includes equivalents of Corri's 'anticipation' and 'leaping' graces. The former occurs strikingly in his annotated version of Rode's Seventh Concerto, where Rode himself had not indicated any such connection;[52] and another good example can be found in the slow movement of Spohr's own Ninth Concerto (Ex. 15.19). In violin music a figure similar to the 'leaping grace' often occurs without any portamento (Ex. 15.20); this version of the ornament is frequently used on instruments that have more limited possibilities for portamento or, like the keyboard, none at all. But at times this, too,

Ex. 15.19. Spohr, *Violin School*, 214

Ex. 15.20. Spohr, *Violin School*, 167

---

[52] See Ex. 12.10, bar 68.

Ex. 15.21. Spohr, *Violin School*: (*a*) p. 208; (*b*) p. 216

(*a*)

(*b*)

was indicated by Spohr with a portamento fingering (Ex. 15.21). Portamento of this type was made even more explicit by Charles de Bériot, whose graphic markings demonstrate how they might have been expected to be executed faster or slower according to the musical context (Ex. 15.26 below).

A manner of executing portamento not discussed in Spohr's text, but implied in his annotated version of the Rode concerto, involved brushing the string with a finger during a descent to an open string (Ex. 15.31 below). Some violinists seem to have used this style of portamento habitually in the late nineteenth century, and Andreas Moser warned against using it, for instance, in the opening theme of the Andante of the Mendelssohn Violin Concerto at the place marked with an asterisk in Ex. 15.22, adding: 'In a very special case its use might be permissible when serving the purpose of a *nuance* in expression; but if it grows into a mannerism, it is to be condemned out and out.'[53]

Ex. 15.22. Mendelssohn, Violin Concerto, ii, in Joachim and Moser, *Violinschule*, iii.

Spohr's slightly older contemporary Baillot, a more direct heir of the Viotti school, had touched upon portamento in the 1803 *Méthode de violon*; he devoted more space to it in *L'Art du violon*, which was published two years after Spohr's *Violinschule*. In *L'Art du violon* Baillot described the basic types of portamento shown by Spohr, and also instructed that a descending portamento could be made by dragging the finger, 'not of the note one is playing but of that one is about to play, this finger scarcely brushing the semitone above the latter note' (Ex. 15.23).[54]

[53] Joachim and Moser, *Violinschule*, iii. 9.   [54] *L'Art du violon*, 77.

Ex. 15.23. Haydn String Quartet op. 33/2/ii, in Baillot, *L'Art du violon*, 77

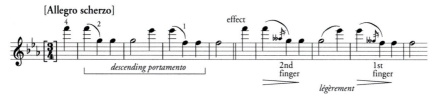

Later in the century it seems to have become a habit among French violinists to make portamento with something approaching the method by which, according to Spohr, 'an unpleasant whining' could hardly be avoided. Hermann Schröder, in 1887, having condemned the practice, added: 'Particularly in the French school, from which we have already acquired many good things in pleasant performance and in light handling of the bow, this perverted mannerism is often customary and beloved, but we ourselves absolutely cannot approve of it.'[55] Charles de Bériot's *Méthode de violon* of 1858 is particularly revealing because of the three signs Bériot devised to indicate the speed of the portamento (Ex. 15.24); he seems to recommend this French form of

Ex. 15.24. Bériot, *Méthode*, 237

---

[55] *Die Kunst des Violinspiels*, 33.

Ex. 15.25. Bériot, *Méthode*, 268

D Carry the sound with the little finger to the high A with vivacity and force

portamento in the annotated version of his Ninth Concerto (Ex. 15.25), though
it is not mentioned in his earlier discussion of the technique. Bériot also failed
to discuss or illustrate the 'leaping grace' type of portamento in the body of the
text, but several examples are graphically illustrated in his Ninth Concerto (Ex.
15.26).

Ex. 15.26. Bériot, *Méthode*, 272

Portamento in the Music of the Period

Bériot drew his examples of portamento initially from vocal music (which provided the basis for much of his treatment of violin playing) and emphasized the
vocal nature of the ornament. This was also stressed in the Joachim and Moser
Violinschule, where it was stated that 'As a means borrowed from the human
voice . . . the use and manner of executing the portamento must come naturally
under the same rules as those which hold good in vocal art'.[56] And, although
some uses of the device are specific to string music, it seems certain that
throughout the period of its use, the employment of portamento in string playing was largely analogous with that in singing. This is important for understanding how singers may have used it in various periods, for while in vocal
music there are often few clues as to where a portamento may have been introduced, the bowings and fingerings in string music are more revealing.

   While there can be no doubt about the extensive use of portamento by performers throughout the period, there is greater difficulty in determining how
much and in what sort of places composers themselves might have considered
it appropriate in their music. Nevertheless there are some persuasive notational
clues, as well as a considerable number of explicit indications. Haydn's own

---

[56] Vol. ii. 92.

fingerings in his op. 33 string quartets of 1781–2 indicate the use of violin portamento for special effects, and it may not be too fanciful to relate this use of it to his association with Nicola Mestrino, who was a member of the Esterházy establishment from 1780 to 1785. Woldemar's comments about Mestrino's employment of portamento (above) may give some idea of what Haydn had in mind when he wrote fingerings and other markings such as those in the trios of the menuettos in op. 33 no. 2 and later in op. 64 no. 6 (Ex. 15.27). In the latter there is an evident analogy with Corri's 'leaping grace'.

Ex. 15.27. Haydn: (*a*) String Quartet op. 33/2/ii; (*b*) String Quartet op. 64/6/iii

Few early nineteenth-century composers were as explicit as Meyerbeer, whose operas contain many clear instructions for the employment of vocal portamento (Ex. 15.28). What distinction, if any, he may have intended between *trainez la voix* and *portez la voix* (Ex. 15.12(*d*)) is uncertain. Wagner occasionally included instructions for portamento in his vocal parts. In *Der fliegende Holländer* he several times supplemented the vocal line with the words 'con portamento' or 'portamento' to indicate that whole phrases should be sung in this manner. One instance provides a close analogy with the *messa di voce*

Ex. 15.28. Meyerbeer, *Les Huguenots*, no. 10

trop heu - reux   de bra - ver   le tré - pas ___

Ex. 15.29. Wagner, *Der fliegende Holländer*, no. 29

Dies der Ver-dam - mnis Schreck-ge - bot,   dies der Ver-dam - mnis

decrescente (Ex. 15.29). (His use of slurs over notes on different syllables has already been illustrated above.)

Examples cited by Pierre Baillot of passages from his own music and that of Kreutzer and Rode 'fingered by the composer' provide some idea of how early nineteenth-century violinists of the Viotti school might have used portamento (Ex. 15.30). Spohr's performing version of Rode's A minor Concerto contains frequent instructions for portamento in fast movements (see Ex. 12.10) as well as slow ones (Ex. 15.31). Rode's portamento may also have influenced Beethoven in the composition of the Violin Sonata op. 96, which he wrote for Rode in 1812. The slurring as marked at bar 159 of the last movement can only be effectively managed if the violinist takes the c″ in sixth position on the A

Ex. 15.30. Examples in Baillot, *L'Art du violon*, 149: (*a*) Kreutzer, Violin Concerto in C; (*b*) Rode, Sonata no. 1; (*c*) Baillot, *Étude*

(*a*)

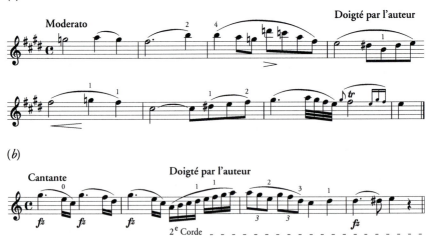

(*b*)

(*c*)

(2ᵉ Edition de la 1.ʳᵉ Méthode de Violon de Baillot. 50 Etudes sur la gamme. Ed. Ozi)

Ex. 15.31. Rode, Violin Concerto no. 7/ii, in Spohr, *Violinschule*, 195

string and the next note in first position on the D string, almost inevitably involving a portamento. This was the fingering suggested by Joseph Joachim in his Peters edition (Ex. 15.32). There may be a further hint of portamento in Beethoven's music in the fingering printed in the first edition of the String Quintet arrangement of the Piano Trio op. 1 no. 1, which was overseen, if not made, by the composer himself (Ex. 15.33). Another composer of the first half

Ex. 15.32. Beethoven, Violin Sonata op. 96/iv, Peters edition, fingered by Joachim

Ex. 15.33. Beethoven, String Quintet arranged from Piano Trio op. 1/3/ii

of the nineteenth century, Franz Berwald, who was himself a string player, frequently employed fingerings that suggest a fairly liberal use of portamento in his works for strings. In his Violin Concerto in C sharp minor (1820) there are examples corresponding with many of the different types of vocal portamento discussed by the theorists (Ex. 15.34). Mendelssohn did not provide many

Ex. 15.34. Berwald Violin Concerto in C sharp minor: (*a*) i; (*b*) ii; (*c*) iii

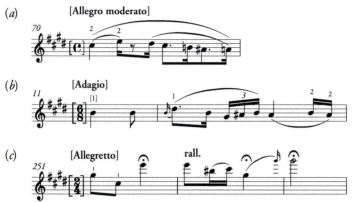

fingerings though he was a competent string player, but the copies of his string quartets fingered and bowed by his close friend and colleague Ferdinand David contain numerous indications for portamento (Ex. 15.35), and the fingerings included in his edition of the Violin Concerto are often suggestive of the same sort of effect (Ex. 15.36).[57]

Ex. 15.35. Mendelssohn, String Quartet op. 44/3/i, fingered by F. David

Ex. 15.36. Mendelssohn, Violin Concerto, ii, ed. F. David

The graphic signs adopted by Charles de Bériot in his *Méthode de violon* to indicate different speeds and intensities of portamento, which were referred to above, supply a particularly revealing key to the way in which he conceived of and would have employed it. The *Méthode* contains many examples of its application in his own and earlier music that clearly show the connection

[57] For extensive examples of David's portamento fingerings in his Beethoven editions, see Clive Brown, 'Ferdinand David's Editions of Beethoven', in Stowell, ed., *Performing Beethoven*, 117–49.

between expression and the manner in which the portamento might be applied (Ex. 15.37). The starting positions of some of the portamento signs, especially in the second and fourth examples, suggest that Bériot may sometimes have expected the portamento to begin at a lower pitch than the preceding note, in the manner of Corri's 'leaping grace', though he gave no explicit instructions to that effect. There is no evidence that what he indicates for the example from Mozart's G minor Quintet represents anything that Mozart might have envisaged, but it certainly resembles the effects that can still be heard on some recordings of the work from the first half of the twentieth century.

Ex. 15.37. Bériot, *Méthode*, 241

Ex. 15.37. *cont.*

Towards the end of the period we may also compare such notational clues with the sounds produced by leading performers of the later nineteenth century, some of whom were scarcely a generation younger than Bériot. Many examples of portamento in both singing and string playing are evident in the transcriptions given in Chapter 12; other interesting examples may be found in performances by violinists who were closely connected with major composers. Joachim recorded two of his arrangements of Brahms's Hungarian dances in 1903, and portamento plays a significant part in these. In the extract from the Hungarian Dance no. 2 (Ex. 15.38), given here with his own fingerings, he executed a very prominent portamento, slowly and with continuous bow pressure, in the penultimate bar. In the truncated version of Elgar's Violin Concerto, which Marie Hall recorded under the direction of the composer in 1916, there are many portamentos for both soloist and orchestra. The portamento implied by Elgar's fingering in the soloist's second bar in the Andante (Ex. 15.39) is performed very strikingly with a slow slide of the first finger up the G string. Interestingly, the same portamento, though still obvious, is much less promi-

Ex. 15.38. Brahms, Hungarian Dance no. 2, arranged by Joachim

Ex. 15.39. Elgar, Violin Concerto op. 61/ii

nent on Menuhin's 1932 recording with the composer, and in later recordings it is executed in an extremely discreet manner.

Virtually all the authors who discussed portamento in singing and in string playing stressed the danger of abusing it; but their notion of abuse is directly dependent on what they considered to be the norm. It is impossible from these writings to be absolutely certain how apparent or frequent the musicians of the Classical and Romantic periods expected portamento to be, yet there is every reason to believe that it was often meant to be a distinctly audible effect, not merely a by-product of singing distant intervals to the same syllable or shifting position on a single string. Even the authors of the most violent diatribes against its abuse were almost certainly quite happy to hear it tastefully and proportionately introduced, but here, as elsewhere, ideas of what was tasteful or proportionate will almost certainly have been very different from ours at all stages of the period.

16

PARALIPOMENA

✣

The Fermata

The fermata (corona, pause) could indicate a number of different things in the music of this period. Its functions were not generally distinguished by any graphic difference in the sign, though some composers adopted the practice of writing an elongated fermata over a passage of several notes where these were either to be embellished or performed *ad libitum* (see below). The various ways in which the sign might be used can be illustrated by a few theoretical discussions and practical examples.

C. P. E. Bach wrote:

At times one makes a fermata [*fermirt*] for expressive reasons, without anything being indicated. Apart from this, there are three circumstances in which these fermatas occur. One pauses either over the penultimate note, or over the last bass note, or over a rest after this bass note. To be correct this sign should always be indicated at the point at which one begins to make the fermata [*anfängt zu fermiren*] and, at best, once again at the end of the fermata.

Fermatas over rests occur mostly in Allegro, and are performed quite simply. The other two kinds are commonly found in slow and expressive [*affetuösen*] pieces, and must be embellished, or one would be guilty of naïvety. In any case, therefore, elaborate ornamentation can rather be left out in other parts of a piece than here.[1]

Türk, in his usual painstaking manner, discussed the contemporary usage of the sign, as it was known to him, in exhaustive detail. He observed that the sign could indicate a pause 'with or without arbitrary embellishment' or an elongated rest. The length of time for which a fermata should be held would be conditioned by 'whether one is performing alone or with others; whether the piece has a lively or sad character; whether the fermata is to be ornamented . . . or not,

---

[1] *Versuch,* i. II, 9, §§3–4.

etc.' Other things being equal, Türk recommended that in slow music it should be approximately twice its written length, but in fast tempo this would be too short; thus if it was a crotchet he recommended playing it four times its length, though with longer values he felt that twice the length should be enough. If the fermata were over a short pause in fast tempo, three or four crotchets' worth of rest would probably suffice, and if it were in slow tempo, twice the written length. He suggested that the rest after a fermata, whether it too had a fermata sign or not, would be lengthened. Commenting on the use of the sign to indicate a final cadenza, Türk observed that if one does not wish to make a cadenza, one holds the note 'a little and finishes with a trill approximately as long again as the written value requires'.[2] Where the sign was merely used to indicate the end of a piece or section, Türk called it an 'end-sign' (*Schlußzeichen*) and warned, particularly in songs with several verses or *da capo* pieces, against making an inappropriate pause (Ex. 16.1). He pointed out that many such signs could be misleading, and recommended that the only sure way to distinguish between end-signs and fermatas was to use the notation shown in Ex. 16.2(*a*) or (*b*), but not that in Ex. 16.2(*c*), since then 'a novice . . . might play on after a short delay, as now and then happens'; he instructed that: 'In such cases one plays the note that follows the end-sign each time without delaying the beat, and only in the last verse does the end-sign apply.'[3]

Ex. 16.1. Türk, *Klavierschule*, I, §85

Ex. 16.2. Türk, *Klavierschule*, I, §85

Türk later discussed the embellishment of fermatas, giving examples.[4] For those fermatas 'that come here and there, particularly in expressive pieces, where an appropriate embellishment can be of good effect', he proposed the following rules:

[2] *Klavierschule*, I, §83.   [3] Türk, *Klavierschule*, I, §85.   [4] Ibid. V, §§1 ff.

1. 'Each embellishment must be appropriate to the character of the piece.' (He warned against lively passages in a sad adagio.)
2. 'The embellishment ought, strictly speaking, only to be based on the given harmony.' (He conceded that 'in general one is not so exact about following this second rule. But one takes care to avoid actual modulations into other keys'.)
3. 'The embellishment ought not to be long; however, one is unrestricted in respect to the beat.'[5]

His examples offer varied treatment for given musical situations, of which Ex. 16.3 provides a representative selection.

Koch, too, regarded the embellishment of fermatas as optional, writing: 'In the performance of a solo part one has the freedom to decorate the sustained

Ex. 16.3. Türk, *Klavierschule*, V, §5

---

[5] Türk, *Klavierschule*, I, §4.

note of fermatas with arbitrary embellishments, or to make a transition from the fermata to the following phrase.'[6] And J. F. Schubert admitted a portamento alone as a substitute for the usual type of embellishment in certain cases (see Ex. 15. 15).

Domenico Corri, to judge by the examples included in his *Select Collection*, evidently felt that some degree of embellishment was necessary and offered his reader choices at these points in the music. The examples in his publications provide many interesting and useful models of appropriate embellishment. All of them conform to the often stated rule that embellished fermatas in arias should not exceed what is possible in a single breath. A couple of typical examples appear in Ex. 12.7. Very occasionally he seems to have felt that the context called for something more elaborate, as in the case of arias by Giordani and Sacchini (Ex. 16.4).

The Paris Conservatoire's *Principes élémentaires de musique* gave a particularly succinct account of how to recognize whether a fermata should be elongated or embellished or, in some cases, whether it implied neither type of treatment:

If the fermata is placed on a note, as in the following examples [Ex. 16.5(*a*)] it indicates that one should stop on this note and that one may pause there for as long as desired, but without introducing any embellishment or ornament. In this case the fermata is called a pause [*Point de Repos*]. One also calls it a pause when one employs the following style [Ex. 16.5(*b*)] In this case one may add some embellishments to the note on which the pause is placed. The fermata used in the following example is called a stopping point or suspending point [*point d'Arrêt, ou de suspension*] [Ex. 16.5(*c*)] In this circumstance one should certainly not prolong the note on which the fermata occurs, rather one should quit it crisply as soon as it is attacked.[7]

How widely this convention of the *point d'arrêt ou de suspension* was recognized by composers of the period is unclear, but it is certainly true to say that most modern performers in these circumstances would sustain the final note with the fermata rather than quitting it crisply. The *Principes* concluded by identifying the circumstances, recognizable by the harmonic context and the final trill, in which a fermata was used to indicate full cadenzas.

These instructions, which are almost certainly a good guide for early nineteenth-century French usage, may also be relevant to late eighteenth-century German usage. Haydn in op. 64 no. 2 uses what to all intents looks like a *point d'arrêt*, except that he includes the word 'tenuto', perhaps to counter a natural instinct of the players to quit the note too quickly (Ex. 16.6). On the other hand the addition of 'tenuto' might have been meant to warn the players not to make any embellishment. In op. 77 no. 1 there are two fermatas that may also be of this kind. In the case of the one at bar 42 of the Adagio, elongation certainly

---

[6] *Musikalisches Lexikon*, art. 'Fermate'. [7] Gossec et al., *Principes*, i. 45.

Ex. 16.4. D. Corri, *A Select Collection*: (*a*) vol. i. 4: Hasse, *Artaserse*, adapted by
Giordani; (*b*) vol. i. 74: Sacchini, *Creso*

(*a*)

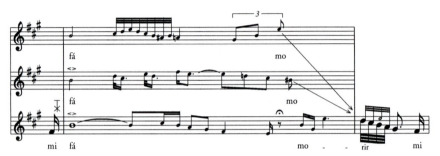

l'a - man – – – – – – – te   cor

(*b*)

Ex. 16.5. Gossec et al., *Principes*, i. 45

(*a*)

(*b*)

(c)

etc.

Ex. 16.6. Haydn, String Quartet op. 64/2/iv

seems out of the question (Ex. 16.7(*a*)); it would be more plausible in the presto Menuetto (Ex. 16. 7(*b*)), but whether this was intended is debatable.

It seems likely that a fermata sign may sometimes have been used simply for 'tenuto' (i.e. hold the note for its full value), with no implication of holding the note longer or affecting the tempo. Mozart, for instance, added such signs, twice, over a succession of notes in the finale of his E flat String Quartet K. 428, where they can scarcely imply anything else (Ex. 16.8), though the unusual form, with a stroke rather than a dot, suggests that his intention may have been to achieve an accented performance by means of a staccato stroke, but also to prevent the notes from being shortened. Another use of the fermata sign in late eighteenth-century and early nineteenth-century music, when it was written in

Ex. 16.7. Haydn, String Quartet op. 77/1: (*a*) ii; (*b*) iii

(*a*)

(*b*)

Ex. 16.8. Mozart, String Quartet K. 428/iv, Allegro vivace

a lengthened form, seems to have been to indicate that a group of notes in a vocal part should be sung without constraint of tempo (perhaps ritardando), and often with some degree of embellishment. In such cases it would frequently appear in the same form in the accompanying parts, to alert the instrumentalists to follow the singer (Ex. 16.9). Mozart's use of this type of fermata has been extensively discussed by, among others, Frederick Neumann, who gives a useful account of its probable treatment, vitiated only by the persistent representation, in his realizations, of pairs of notes on the same pitch without

Ex. 16.9. (*a*) Salieri, *Der Rauchfangkehrer*, Act III, no. 15; (*b*) Vogler, *Der Kaufmann von Smyrna*, no. 2, Hessische Landes- und Hochschulbibliothek, Darmstadt, mus. ms. 1090

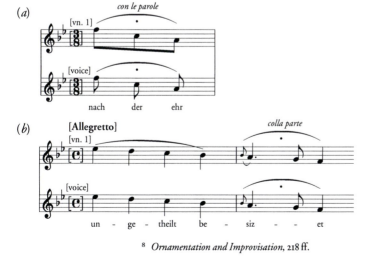

---

[8] *Ornamentation and Improvisation*, 218 ff.

Ex. 16.10. Weber, *Der Freischütz*, no. 13, autograph

any appoggiatura or similar embellishment.[8]

A good example of fermata embellishment supplied by the composer occurs in the autograph of Weber's *Der Freischütz*, in the insertion aria no. 13, where Weber wrote out an embellishment, apparently as an afterthought (Ex. 16.10). A little later in the nineteenth century Pierre Baillot gave the following description, which seems to be based fairly closely on that of the *Principes élémentaires de musique*. He categorized fermatas as:

1. a *point de repos* 'on which one adds nothing';
2. a *point de repos* (*point d'orgue*) 'after which one may make a little embellishment between the *point d'orgue* or *point de repos* and the note that follows';
3. a *point d'arrêt* or silence 'after which [*sic*] it is necessary to quit the note'.

Diverging from the *Principes*, however, he further observed:

One cannot recommend too much to remain on these *points d'arrêt* or *silences* all the time that is necessary for their effect. In order that the *silence* contrasts with the motion that precedes it, a certain length is required for it to be felt; reason will have it so, but sentiment does more; for it knows at the appropriate moment how to make eloquence felt: 'the genius of the musician subjects the entire universe to his art, it paints all pictures in sound and makes silence itself speak.' (J. J. Rousseau)[9]

---

[9] *L'Art du violon*, 165.

Ex. 16.11. (*a*) Baillot, *L'Art du violon*, 165; (*b*) Haydn, String Quartet op. 9/2/iii

(*a*)

(*b*)

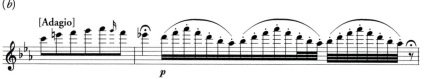

Baillot initially illustrated what he meant by his second type of fermata with an example from Haydn's String Quartet op. 9 no. 2 (Ex. 16.11(*a*)), where he provided a suitably restrained embellishment, presumably bearing in mind the much more florid one written in by the composer in the ornamented repetition of the melody (Ex. 16.11(*b*)). His encyclopaedic catalogue of *points d'orgue*, for which he provided sixteen pages of music examples, was organized under ten headings, though only the first two ('Suspensions or turns on the tonic' and 'Slightly extended *points d'orgue* or turns on the dominant to approach the final cadence') dealt with short embellished fermatas; the rest was concerned with more or less fully developed cadenzas.[10]

A. F. Häser, a slightly younger German contemporary of Baillot, wrote about the treatment of fermatas a few years later, observing that their decoration in solo playing or singing was frequent, but that they should not be embellished if they were there to express 'astonishment, expectation or exhaustion'. In singing he considered that the text should be the main guide, and that if the vowel were inappropriate for vocalizing, this might determine whether or not to include an embellishment.[11] Haydn Corri, however, gave instructions for modifying the vowel in such instances. García, too, referring both to the ornamentation of fermatas and to virtuoso figuration in general, observed that 'a singing master and pupil are at perfect liberty to add,—if the sense allows it,—one or other of the monosyllables, ah, no, si, either to increase the number of syllables or as a substitute for others'.[12]

Häser also gave five different ways of nuancing an unembellished fermata

---

[10] See Stowell, *Violin Technique*, 361 ff. for a selection of examples from Baillot's *L'Art du violon*.
[11] In Schilling, *Encyclopädie*, art. 'Fermate'. [12] *New Treatise*, 46.

Ex. 16.12. Häser, 'Fermate', in Schilling, *Encyclopädie*

1. $\overline{\overline{\mathbf{o}}}$ 2. $\overset{<}{\mathbf{o}}$ 3. $\overset{>}{\mathbf{o}}$ 4. $\overset{<>}{\mathbf{o}}$ 5. $\overset{><}{\mathbf{o}}$

(Ex. 16.12). He commented that those marked 1 and 2 were rare, that 3 was the most usual and that 4 was also not uncommon, while 5 was at least as rare as 1 and 2. His final observation reveals the growing expectation that the composer's intentions should be made more explicit and respected more closely, for he felt that although performers must rely upon their taste in deciding how to execute the fermata if the composer had not specified the manner of performance, it was necessary, in order to banish uncertainty, to mark anything except 3.[13]

Recitative

Recitative was one of the genres of music in which notation and performance were most sharply at odds with each other. The discrepancy was greatest in *recitativo secco*, which remained a current technique with Italian composers until almost the middle of the nineteenth century. *Recitativo accompagnato*, which in various modified forms, and without being specifically identified as such, can be found throughout the nineteenth century, was expected to be delivered more literally, but this did not exclude various freedoms and conventions that involved departure from the strict meaning of the notation.

There were various conflicting views about whether different manners of singing recitatives should be adopted in theatre, church, and concert-hall. Domenico Corri was among those who maintained that a distinction was necessary. He considered that in the sacred recitative 'A noble simplicity should govern throughout, corresponding with the sublime character of the words, in Church music, ornaments ought not to be used; every note should begin softly, and swell into a fine, well supported sound, decreasing it again in the same proportion.' The theatrical recitative he divided into two categories. Of the serious recitative he observed:

This should be graceful, dignified, imitation of speaking, delivered with emphatic expression, and accompanied with appropriate action; ornament very sparingly used, and such Recitative ought to be supported with strength and precision: in a soliloquy, or Instrumented Recitation, or where the words are intended to move the passions, a Performer should remember that the whole combination of gesture, look, and inflexion of voice, must contribute their various powers to convey the sentiment or feeling he would express.

Of the comic recitative he remarked: 'This differs from the serious only by

---

[13] Schilling, *Encyclopädie*, art. 'Fermate'.

requiring more free familiar delivery approaching still more nearly to speaking; yet in Compositions of this character there often occur passages that require energy and pathos of expression, equally as the Serious.' The concert recitative he regarded as including 'all other descriptions of Recitative', and he believed that it 'admits of more ornament than either of the preceding, as not being so narrative or requiring the accompaniment of action'.[14] Other authorities did not draw such clear distinctions or, in the case of Mancini, for instance, disagreed with the idea that church, theatre, and chamber recitative each automatically required a different style of performance.[15]

Most writers laid particular emphasis on the delivery of *secco* recitative in natural speech rhythms, and the importance of never being constrained by the notated rhythms. Schulz considered that

Recitative is distinguished from true song by the fact that a note should never, not even at perfect cadences, be sustained noticeably longer than it would be in declamation. . . . One can imagine the recitative as a brook that now flows gently, now rushes between stones, now plunges over cliffs. In the same recitative peaceful, merely narrative passages occur from time to time; a moment later, however, powerful and extremely pathetic passages.[16]

On the subject of ornamentation he remarked:

A singer of feeling does not fail, here and there, where the expression [*Affekt*] allows beauty, to introduce vibrations and drags [*Schwebungen und Ziehungen*: ?vibrato and portamento], also appoggiaturas (hardly trills), which however, look very silly on paper, and which no singer who is not a born and professional singer can well accomplish. For mediocre singers simple declamation, where one note is set to one syllable, makes a better effect.[17]

Koch shared the view that 'with respect to the duration of the individual syllables the recitative should be performed just like a speech', but he observed that this was by no means a universal practice, remarking:

In some regions of Germany the rural cantors and schoolmasters have the habit of performing the recitative in their church music in a measured tempo and teaching this manner to their singing pupils; by this means it acquires a modification that is wholly against its nature, and many passages in it get an extraordinary hardness and sound extremely nonsensical.[18]

Many of the same recommendations were made a generation later by A. F. Häser. He advised that in general there should be 'almost no ornamentation', but in accompanied recitative, perhaps recalling Schulz's view, he allowed that 'in very passionate passages, and also at the end, there can admittedly be exceptions, but it is advisable even in these instances to make use of portamento and *messa di voce*, and that sparingly, rather than over-elaborate coloratura'. With

---

[14] *The Singer's Preceptor*, 71.

[15] See W. Crutchfield, 'Voices' in Howard Mayer Brown, ed., *The New Grove Handbook of Performance Practice: Music after 1600* (London, 1989), 296.

[16] In Sulzer, *Allgemeine Theorie*, 2nd edn. iv. 5.   [17] Ibid. 11.

[18] *Musikalisches Lexikon*, art. 'Recitativ'.

respect to appoggiaturas, however, he was at pains to point out that recitative should not be sung strictly as written:

The recitatives of older composers and of most modern ones are so written that the individual notes, at least on the strong beats, mostly lie in the harmony. Since this sort of recitative, performed exactly as it is written, appears rather stiff and awkward, it is the responsibility of the singer, particularly on several identical notes following immediately after one another, to bring more flow into the melody by means of appoggiaturas and other small ornaments. It goes without saying that knowledge of harmony and declamation is necessary for this.[19]

Numerous treatises gave instructions for the proper application of appoggiaturas and other similar modifications in recitatives. There can be little doubt that in almost all cases where a pair of notes of the same pitch occur with a strong–weak placement, the singer would have been expected to modify the first of them. In most instances this would mean substituting a note a tone higher (Ex. 16.13); much more rarely the harmony note might be approached from below (Ex. 16.14). When the note preceding the pair on the same pitch was a fourth or fifth higher the first of the pair would usually be sung at the pitch of the higher note (Ex. 16.15). Most authorities were against the practice of embellishing so-called masculine endings, though J. A. Hiller allowed it.[20] His contemporary J. F. Schubert particularly condemned this practice on the grounds that 'the delivery thereby becomes dull, the flow of the text is pulled up and comes to a feeble conclusion'.[21] And Schulz similarly considered that

Ex. 16.13

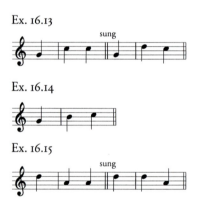

Ex. 16.14

Ex. 16.15

Ex. 16.16. Sulzer, *Allgemeine Theorie*, art. 'Recitativ'

[19] *Cäcilia*, 10 (1829), 154.
[21] *Neue Singe-Schule*, 142.

[20] *Anweisung zum musikalisch-zierlichen Gesang*, 101.
[22] In Sulzer, *Allgemeine Theorie*, 2nd edn. iv. 15.

this would be 'very halting and repugnant'.[22] In one circumstance, however, an appoggiatura on a masculine ending was seen as necessary: that was when the preceding note was a third higher, as illustrated by Schulz (Ex. 16.16).

The necessity to modify the text of recitatives in this manner, and indeed in many other subtle ways, was recognized throughout the nineteenth century and applied not only to earlier music but also to recitative-like passages in later nineteenth-century music. This remained especially true of Italian music and music in the Italian tradition. Lichtenthal's statement in 1826 that 'The Italian school made the appoggiatura so familiar to the singers that the composers found it unnecessary to write it in the recitatives'[23] was undoubtedly still valid for the next generation of musicians. The tradition remained so strong that composers could only be certain that appoggiaturas would not be added if they specified this clearly in the music. Thus Verdi in the 'Scena, terzetto e Tempesta' (no. 13) in *Rigoletto* instructed 'This recitative should be performed without the customary appoggiaturas.'

The addition of such appoggiaturas has been a matter of some controversy in the twentieth century. There was a tendency for many years to omit them, particularly in Germany, and deliver all recitatives exactly as they were notated. During the last quarter of the twentieth century it has been increasingly acknowledged that in virtually all cases of so-called 'blunt endings' appoggiaturas should be added not merely in recitatives but, in many instances, in arias.[24] The matter has not been uncontroversial, but the arguments of those who have claimed that the practice is not adequately supported by the evidence seem unconvincing. Seen in the light of the predominant late eighteenth-century and nineteenth-century attitude towards the relationship of notation and performance, it seems likelier that simply adding the conventional appoggiaturas would be erring on the side of caution, and that greater freedom and adventurousness in the rendition of recitative (within reasonable bounds) would be closer to the spirit of the period.

The Accompaniment of Recitative

In the early part of the period recitatives would normally have been accompanied by a keyboard instrument (organ in church music and harpsichord in theatre and chamber), sometimes with one or more melody instruments on the bass-line. By the last decades of the eighteenth century the harpsichord began to be superseded by the fortepiano in many places, though in others the harpsichord may have lingered on for a while after it had been abandoned for everything else.

---

[23] *Dizionario*, art. 'Appoggiatura'.

[24] Will Crutchfield, 'The Prosodic Appoggiatura in the Music of Mozart and his Contemporaries', *Journal of the American Musicological Society*, 42 (1989), 229–74.

By the end of the eighteenth century, direction of the opera was increasingly being entrusted to the violin rather than to the keyboard in many parts of Europe, and in some theatres this meant the total disappearance of the keyboard instrument from the pit. A writer in 1799 observed that 'If one wants to get rid of the harpsichord *qua* keyboard instrument, so one at the same time banishes its substitute, the pianoforte, and makes use of the violin to direct, as is now becoming ever more common.'[25] Coupled with this tendency was the practice of accompanying recitatives in the theatre with a cello or occasionally, strange as it may seem, with a violin. The same writer in the *Allgemeine musikalische Zeitung* observed:

> If one wants to attain these important goals by giving the chords on the violoncello, as in some places, or on the violin, as in others: so one has the disadvantage—leaving aside the question of whether the necessarily skilled men may well not be easy to find everywhere— that the chords on the former are too dull and transitory, and perform the necessary service neither for the singer nor hearer; the chords of the latter, however, sound too high and pointed, and repulsively offend the ear, particularly in the accompaniment of tenor and bass voices.[26]

The cello, nevertheless, seems to have been growing in favour as the principal accompaniment instrument for recitative at that time. Among the notable exponents of this practice were Johann Georg Christoph Schetky, whom the writer of the above article admitted to be highly effective at it, noting that he always gave the singers their note at the top of the arpeggiated chord.[27] Schetky's own *Practical and Progressive Lessons for the Violoncello* includes instructions for the accompaniment of recitative that confirm this account; it

Ex. 16.17. Schetky, *Practical and Progressive Lessons*, 38

not too quick

[25] *Allgemeine musikalische Zeitung*, 2 (1799), 17.   [26] Ibid. 18–19.   [27] 35.
[28] (London, 1811), 38.

advised: 'In Recitative the Violoncellist should fashion the Chords in such a manner that the highest note is the Singer's next one and should be struck as soon as the Singer has pronounced the last word viz. [Ex. 16.17].'[28]

In England the practice was continued by the cellist Robert Lindley, who was regularly partnered by Domenico Dragonetti on the double bass. This form of accompaniment, usually by a cellist alone, was widespread throughout Europe. Instructions for the performance of recitatives by cellists were given in the Paris Conservatoire's *Méthode de violoncelle* in 1804 and in Fröhlich's *Vollständige . . . Musikschule* (1810–11). In 1811 Gottfried Weber expressed his opinion that it was generally better to accompany recitative in this manner than with the fortepiano, because he considered that even the best fortepiano cannot sound good against an orchestra, and he suggested that if the cellist could not perform it from the figured bass the director should write it out.[29] He mentioned this type of accompaniment again, along with accompaniment of *secco* recitative by the piano, in 1831 as something that was employed from time to time in the Italian opera,[30] and it appears to have survived in Italy as late as the 1870s.[31] Mendelssohn employed something similar for his 1841 performance of Bach's *St Matthew Passion* in Leipzig; the Bodleian Library, Oxford, possesses a bass part in which the accompaniments for the recitatives are scored for double bass playing the basso continuo and two solo cellos playing chords to provide the harmony (the organ part in this performance material contains no music for the recitatives). Other examples of accompaniment of this kind occur in Meyerbeer's Parisian operas, in this case, with Meyerbeer's usual attention to detail, written out in full (Ex. 16.18).

There were several important aspects of the realization of the accompaniment of recitatives about which there was considerable confusion in the early nineteenth century. This undoubtedly resulted, to some extent, from the growing notion that there should be a closer correspondence between what composers wrote and what executants performed. Because composers were beginning to discard many of the old-established conventions, considerable doubt arose about how to interpret the notation in older music, and also about which convention a contemporary composer might have adopted. Significant differences of opinion and practice with respect to whether the accompanying chords should be sustained where so notated (i.e. as long notes) or cut short are revealed in articles published in the *Allgemeine musikalische Zeitung* in 1810 and 1811, which indicate that there was already uncertainty about what was intended in the recitatives of Haydn's *Die Schöpfung* within two years of the composer's death and only a decade after the work had been written. A correspondent remarked that Hasse and Graun intended that the notes should be played short (as they usually were), and that this was confirmed by the practice

[29] *Allgemeine musikalische Zeitung*, 13 (1811), 96–7.   [30] *Caecilia*, 12 (1831), 145 ff.
[31] See J. W. von Wasielewsky, *Das Violoncell und seine Geschichte* (Leipzig, 1889).

Ex. 16.18. Meyerbeer, *Les Huguenots*, no. 27

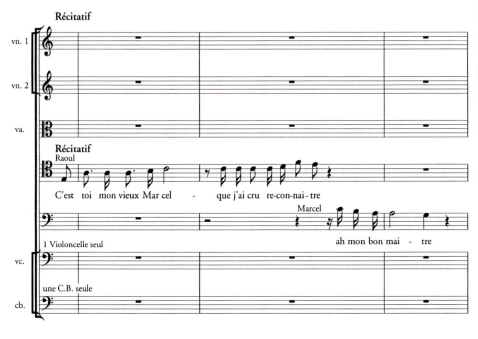

of the Dresden and Berlin orchestras, which they had trained; he added that Hiller, who was a pupil of Hasse, also did this in Leipzig. Only if Hasse wrote *ten.* (tenuto) did he require the bass notes to be sustained. On the other hand, he implied that orchestras in Italy, Vienna, and Munich sustained the notes. The writer also illuminated another doubt about the performance of recitative that seems to have arisen about that time: whether in a *secco* recitative any accompaniment other than the bass note was required. He concluded with a remark that reveals the rapidity with which many musical conventions were changing in the early nineteenth century. 'Certainly for a hundred years there has been no doubt about the best manner of accompanying recitative: however, it may well be possible that in the present revolutionary times one may also in this matter do and require the opposite of what was formerly recognized as good and correct.'[32] Gottfried Weber, responding to this the following year, suggested that, regarding the first query, it was necessary to be familiar with individual composers' practices, noting that some composers adopted the convention of always writing long notes, while others, for example his own teacher G. J. Vogler, wrote the notes as they wished them to be played. About the question of accompanying recitative only with a bass-line, he merely expressed astonishment that there should be any doubt, since Haydn would hardly have wasted time writing figures above the bass if he had not wanted a chordal accompaniment.[33]

There seems on the whole to have been a feeling in the early years of the nineteenth century that the accompaniment to *secco* recitative should be as simple and unobtrusive as possible. A Viennese writer in 1813 observed that 'far from marking this accompaniment in a brilliant fashion, it should be made scarcely noticeable, and should bring out the designed effect, with magical power, unnoticed'. However the writer added, perhaps supporting a Viennese tendency to hold on the bass notes: 'at times when the recitative is more passionately expressed and therefore takes on a more inward, moving character, a simple accompaniment in sustained notes may be used to effect'.[34] Gottfried Weber also took the view that the accompaniment should be unobtrusive and for this reason felt that figures were better than a written-out accompaniment.[35]

There was also some lack of consensus about the question of whether, when the entry of the voice coincided with the final note of the accompaniment (particularly in orchestrally accompanied recitative), or when the accompaniment was notated to begin at the same time as the singer's final note, the music should be performed literally as written or whether overlap should be avoided.

[32] *Allgemeine musikalische Zeitung,* 12 (1809–10), 974.
[33] Ibid. 13 (1811), 93–8.
[34] *Wiener allgemeine musikalische Zeitung,* 2 (1813), 14–15.   [35] *Caecilia,* 13 (1831), 145 ff.
[36] *Versuch,* XVII, 7, §59.

Quantz considered overlap to be not only proper, but also necessary in some instances.[36] Haydn, on the other hand, was quite specific about not performing such passages literally in the case of his 'Applausus' Cantata in 1768, for he instructed: 'In the accompanied recitatives you must observe that the accompaniment should not enter until the singer has quite finished his text, even though the score shows the contrary.'[37] Whether this indicates Haydn's awareness of conflicting opinion about this notation, or whether it merely shows his lack of confidence in the musical knowledge of the recipients of the cantata, is unclear.

It seems very probable that the practice outlined by Haydn was the normal

Ex. 16.19. D. Corri, *A Select Collection*, i. 3

N.B. In the Recitative this sign ≣ is used when the barr is lengthened, and the beginning of the Symphonies is precisely ascertained.

one, at least in Italian and Italian-influenced traditions. Domenico Corri, in the 1780s, was also quite specific about avoiding overlap, illustrating the relationship between notation and performance in such instances as in Ex. 16.19.

Once again Meyerbeer provides an illuminating perspective on the practice in the nineteenth century. His later operas, written for Paris, contain recitative-like passages where, on many occasions, he carefully warns the performers that the accompaniment should commence after the singer has finished (Ex. 16.20).

As an appendix to this matter, it is interesting to note that in much of Germany it quickly became customary to perform Mozart's Italian operas *Figaro* and *Don Giovanni* in German versions, in which the recitatives were replaced with spoken dialogue (as in Singspiel). This prevailed even in major centres until the middle of the century. In 1854, for instance, the *Neue Zeitschrift für Musik* reported that the recitatives in *Don Giovanni* had just been restored in Dresden.[38]

---

[37] See Landon, *Haydn at Eszterháza*, 146.   [38] Vol. 41 (1854), 113.

Ex. 16.20. Meyerbeer: (*a*) *Les Huguenots*, no. 22; (*b*) *Le Prophète*, no. 28 (supplément pour abréger le trio qui precède)
(*a*)

(*b*)

Arpeggiation

Various notations were used to indicate arpeggiation in the music of the period. These included the vertical wavy or curved line and the notation of the arpeggiation in small notes. Mozart, for instance, sometimes used the wavy line and sometimes the small notes: in his Violin Sonata K. 306 he used one form in the initial draft of the first movement (Ex. 16.21(*a*)) and the other in the final version (Ex. 16.21(*b*)). Other signs were used for specialized treatments of arpeggiation; for instance, as explained by Clementi and others,[39] where a grace-note or *acciaccatura* was required before one note of the arpeggio this might be indicated by a slanting line through the note to which the ornament should be added (Ex. 16.22).

Ex. 16.21. Mozart, Violin Sonata K. 306/i

(*a*)

(*b*)

---

[39] Clementi, *Introduction*, 9.

Ex. 16.22. Clementi, *Introduction*, 9

As with all such ornaments in this period, there is no reason to think that composers troubled to mark every place where they might have expected, or been happy to have heard arpeggiation, or that they specified every aspect of its performance. In fact, there is powerful evidence to suggest that in piano playing during the early part of the nineteenth century the arpeggiation of chords where they accompanied a melody, especially in slow movements, was almost ubiquitous.

Arpeggiation was recommended as an *ad libitum* expressive device by, among others, Philip Corri. Giving Ex. 16.23(*a*) he commented:

Observe that in the above Example, the longer notes only, are to be played appogiando; those that are equal are to be struck together, tho' not staccato; and the end of the tie must have the cadence or fall, that is; to be touched lightly.

But if on the contrary, all the chords are played appogiando, without distinction, the Time and Metre would be so confused and disguised that no air or melody could be discoverable, and therefore, it should be remember'd that where notes or chords are of equal length, in succession, they should all be played together.*

To prove what I have just asserted play the foregoing Example with all the notes appogiando and without emphasis—Judge then which is the most pleasing style; the 1st at No 1—monotonous without expression, the 2nd at No 2 with proper expression—or the 3rd as just directed, with an excess of expression.

The latter style is two [*sic*] often adopted by those who affect to play with Taste and who from ignorance of its effects, distort and disfigure the melody so hideously that no one can make it out; I therefore recommend the appogiando to be used cautiously and sparingly.

There are occasions where the appogiando may be used, altho' it be not for emphasis, for instance;—in a slow strain, the long chords are to be sustained, tho' there are many of the same quality, yet their harmony is better heard, and produces more effect by being touch'd appogiando, (As the Minims in the following Ex:) but then observe that the Crotchets that follow, being shorter, ought to be played together as a relief to the other style.—Example [Ex. 16.23(*b*)].

Further Examples, shewing that the appogiando should be used on the long chords; and also on shorter ones, where brilliancy is required to be given, touching them as nearly as possible together.—[Ex. 16.23(*c*)]

When the words 'con Espressione, con Anima, or Dolce etc.' are mark'd at a passage, it signifies that the appogiando must be particularly and often used, and made as long as possible.

   * [Corri's footnote] There is an exception which I shall next explain

Corri followed this with further examples from Cramer, Clementi, and Dussek, and then warned of some circumstances in which arpeggiation should generally be avoided, for instance, a succession of octaves, which 'must never be

Ex. 16.23. P. A. Corri, *L'anima di musica*, 75

(*a*)

[played:-]

(*b*)

(*c*)

played appogiando, but always together unless they are very long notes, or have emphasis'.[40] Where the arpeggiation occurred in livelier contexts, he included it among what he called the 'forcing or leaning Graces', instructing that it should 'always be played very swiftly with Emphasis and exactly with the Bass [Ex. 16.24]'.[41]

[40] *L'anima di musica*, 76–7.   [41] Ibid. 15.

Ex. 16.24. P. A. Corri, *L'anima di musica*, 15

The ubiquity of arpeggiation in piano playing in England during the early decades of the nineteenth century is suggested by a letter written by Samuel Wesley in 1829, in which he discussed the difference between playing the piano and playing the organ. He observed that pianists 'do not put down the Keys simultaneously *which on the Organ should always be done*, but one after another, beginning at the lowest note of the Base.'[42]

Thalberg in his *L'Art du chant appliqué au piano* considered the arpeggiation of chords, when accompanying a melody, to be a matter of course, observing: 'The chords that support a melody on the highest note should always be arpeggiated, but very tight, almost together [*presque plaqué*], and the melody note should be given more weight than the other notes of the chord.' He regarded this treatment as so natural that he introduced a sign ([) to indicate those chords that should not be arpeggiated; but this appears very infrequently in the volume.[43]

In 1839 Carl Czerny complained that 'Most players accustom themselves so much to Arpeggio chords, that they at last become quite unable to strike full chords or even double notes firmly and at once; though this latter way is the general rule, while the former constitutes the exception.'[44] He returned to the subject in 1846, expressing concern that 'those who exclusively devote themselves to the modern style of playing, are unable to perform a fugue properly'. And he attributed this largely to the fact that 'In the modern style, all passages in many parts are now invariably played in *arpeggio*; and so greatly is this the case, that many pianists have almost forgotten how to strike chords firmly.' Referring to a music example showing a succession of minim four- and five-part chords, he continued: 'Many otherwise really good players would not be able to perform the following passage *quite firm*; that is, to strike all the notes of each chord *exactly together*'. In fugue playing this was, for Czerny, self-evidently entirely inappropriate, though he conceded that 'in the free style of playing this may be often very well'.[45]

It is possible that many later nineteenth-century composers were more particular about indicating arpeggiation where it was required and would have

[42] British Library Add 31764, f.28. I am indebted to Dr Philip Olleson for kindly drawing my attention to this letter.

[43] Unpaginated [p. 2].   [44] *Piano Forte School*, iii. 55.

[45] *The Art of Playing the Ancient and Modern Piano Forte Works* (London, [1846]), 157.

been less happy to see it interpolated where it was not indicated. Yet Brahms was reported to have employed unwritten arpeggiation. After he gave the first performance of his D minor Piano Concerto in 1865 a critic complained about the 'incessant spreading of chords in the slower tempos'; and other contemporaries also mentioned this characteristic of Brahms's playing.[46] The continuation, into the early years of the twentieth century, of a tradition of liberally introducing unwritten arpeggiation in piano music, is abundantly documented in early recordings.[47]

The Variable Dot and Other Aspects of Rhythmic Flexibility

Many instances of the fluid relationship between the literal meaning of the musical notation, and the ways in which eighteenth- and nineteenth-century performers might have been expected to interpret it, have frequently been touched upon in the preceding chapters. Classical and Romantic notions of musical rhetoric undoubtedly excluded the idea that notated rhythms should, in general, be immune from expressive manipulation, though some may have been perceived to depend for their musical effect on a degree of strictness. Musical figures involving pairs of notes (with or without dots of prolongation) or figures with an upbeat were particularly prone to be modified in performance. Some of this modification might occur at the whim of the performer; but there were a number of circumstances in which particular types of rhythmic alteration appear to have been customary and others in which, by convention, composers employed misleading notation.

Pairs of notes were often performed unequally for much of the period under consideration, not so much as a matter of course, in the manner suggested by French theory or in Quantz's *Versuch*, but for particular expressive purposes. There are many examples in Domenico Corri's editions (see Ex. 12.7), and similar modifications of equal pairs were still common more than a century later, as can be heard in recordings by Joachim and Patti (see above, Ex. 12.12, 12.9, and below, Ex. 16.36). Other evidence of the manner in which rhythmic inequality might have been employed in performance can be found in a variety of documentary sources. It is interesting, for example, that when Spohr noted down in his diary how a singer in Milan performed a passage from Rossini's *L'Italiana in Algeri* in 1816, he notated dotted rhythms where Rossini had

---

[46] Review cited in Frithjof Haas, *Zwischen Brahms und Wagner: Der Dirgent Hermann Levi* (Zurich and Mainz, 1995), 106. See also Richard Hudson *Stolen Time: The History of Tempo Rubato* (Oxford, 1994), 333.

[47] Arpeggiation and extensive dislocation between the hands is abundant, for instance, on piano rolls by Saint-Säens (*b.* 1835), Carl Reinecke (*b.* 1824), and Theodor Leschetizky (*b.* 1830), available on CD Archiphon-106. See also Robert Philip, *Early Recording and Musical Style: Changing Tastes in Instrumental Performance 1900–1950* (Cambridge, 1992).

written equal pairs, presumably reflecting the performance he heard.[48] Where composers did write dotted rhythms, there were certain circumstances in which these were conventionally expected to be modified by either under-dotting (making triplets out of dotted figures) or over-dotting (making something like a double dot out of a single one).

Dotted Notes and Triplets

The question of whether a dotted rhythm was intended to be assimilated to a simultaneous triplet rhythm in another part was not uncontentious in the second half of the eighteenth century, as the move towards greater precision in notation began to gather pace. Many writers of instruction books in that period showed their awareness that composers were prone to notate the phrase shown in Ex. 16.25(*a*) as in Ex. 16.25(*b*), and some asserted unreservedly that

Ex. 16.25

(*a*)　♩ ♪
　　　＼3＿

(*b*)　♩. ♪

when triplets and dotted figures occurred together, the latter should be played with a triplet rhythm. This was stated in the first edition of Löhlein's *Clavier-Schule* in 1765,[49] but criticism by Agricola, who observed that 'this is true only in the utmost speed', led to amplification of the text of the 1773 edition of Löhlein's treatise, which contained the following observation: 'If triplets occur in fast tempo against dotted notes, they will be distributed as follows: [Ex. 16.26].[50] Otherwise the semiquaver must really be played, in accordance with its duration, after the last note of the triplet.'

Ex. 16.26.　Löhlein, *Clavier-Schule*, 2nd edn. (1773), 68

It seems very rarely indeed to have occurred to late eighteenth-century and early nineteenth-century composers to use the notation shown in Ex. 16.27, and it seems highly likely that on many occasions where they wrote a normal

Ex. 16.27

♩. ♪
　3

[48] *Louis Spohr Lebenserinnerungen*, i. 276.　　[49] p. 70.　　[50] 2nd edn., 68.

Ex. 16.28. Haydn, String Quartet op. 74/2/iv

dotted rhythm they would have expected assimilation. This is probably the case in passages such as Ex. 16.28, from the last movement of Haydn's String Quartet op. 74 no. 2, especially since this is a Presto, or in the first movement of op. 77 no. 1 (Ex. 16.29). But in the first movement of op. 74 no. 3 (Ex. 16.30),

Ex. 16.29. Haydn, String Quartet op. 77/li

Ex. 16.30. Haydn, String Quartet op. 74/3/i

assimilation was almost certainly not envisaged, and Haydn may, on the contrary, have expected over-dotting to emphasize the difference between the triplets and the dotted figure, especially since he marked the dotted motif to be played *sul' una corda* and probably saw it as a portamento of the 'anticipation grace' type. Assimilation of the dotted rhythm to a triplet was certainly intended by Haydn's pupil Pleyel in his 1787 Prussian quartets when, for instance, he gave the double stop shown in Ex. 16.31 to the cello in the first movement of the F major quartet in book 3.

Ex. 16.31. Pleyel Prussian Quartets, book 3/2/i

There are also instances in Beethoven's mature music where the dotted notation may have been meant to be assimilated to triplets (Ex. 16.32), but also many others where the notes were not intended to coincide exactly. Assimilation was clearly envisaged in many instances by Schubert, even in his last works, as the notation of passages in the piano part of *Winterreise* demonstrates (Ex. 16.33); but in his case, too, there are ambiguous situations where assimilation may not always be appropriate, for example in the first movement of the Piano Trio in B flat (Ex. 16.34).

Composers born in the nineteenth century were much less likely to adopt this type of ambiguous notation. Mendelssohn and Schumann, for instance, employed triplet notation in such circumstances, as did Berlioz and Brahms (Ex. 16.35). The examples from Berlioz and, especially, Brahms show these composers making a deliberate feature of the contrast between the triplet and

Ex. 16.32. Beethoven, String Quartet op. 59/2/ii

Ex. 16.33. Schubert, *Winterreise*: (*a*) 'Erstarrung'; (*b*) 'Wasserflut'

(*a*)

(*b*)

Ex. 16.34. Schubert, Piano Trio op. 99/i

the dotted figure. Not all nineteenth-century music in which a distinction between triplet figures and dotted figures seems intended, however, would appear to have been understood in that sense by contemporary performers. In 'Ah non credea', from the beginning of the finale of *La sonnambula*, Bellini employed a mixture of triplets and normal dotted figures over an accompaniment of almost continual triplets and even used the notation shown in Ex. 16.27 on a couple of occasions (not shown in the extract given in Ex. 16.36), but when Adelina Patti recorded the piece in 1905, as can be seen from the transcription of part of this recording in Ex. 16.36, she assimilated all the dotted

Ex. 16.35. (*a*) Mendelssohn, 'Italian' Symphony op. 90/iv; (*b*) Schumann, Second Symphony op. 61/ii; (*c*) Berlioz, *Romeo and Juliet* op. 17 pt. 2; (*d*) Brahms, Second Symphony op. 73/ii

(*a*)

(*b*)

(*c*)

Ex. 16.35. *cont.*

(*d*)

figures to the accompanying triplets, including not only figures of a dotted quaver and semiquaver, but also those of a dotted crotchet and quaver. It is also noteworthy that she several times sang the rhythm of Ex. 16.27 in places where Bellini notated a pair of equal quavers.[51] A similar disregard for the literal meaning of dotted figures can be demonstrated in at least one instance of an

[51] A complete transcription of this recording can be seen in Clive Brown, 'Notation and Meaning in Nineteenth-Century Music' [the title of the publication containing the papers of the Donizetti Conference, Venice, May 1997, including this one, is not yet known] (forthcoming).

Ex. 16.36. Bellini, *La sonnambula*, Act II Finale, 'Ah non credea' (bottom stave) and Adelina Patti's interpretation

important later nineteenth-century composer performing his own music. In Edvard Grieg's Humoresque op. 6 no. 2, which Grieg recorded in 1903, two bars of dotted quaver-semiquaver figures are followed by two bars of triplets with a similar melodic outline and the same bass line as the preceding bars; this pattern is then repeated a minor third lower (bb. 21–8). Grieg clearly plays the dotted figures in bb. 21–2 and 25–6 in triplet rhythm.

Over-Dotting

The question of whether dotted figures should be over-dotted was often addressed by theorists. Löhlein's *Clavier-Schule*[52] and *Anweisung zum*

[52] 2nd edn., 67.

Violinspielen positively required over-dotting in some circumstances. In the latter Löhlein stipulated: 'If there are many dotted figures in a sad and, in any case, moderate and pathetic melody, the rule of performance style demands that one lengthens the dot by half its worth and performs the following note that much shorter.'[53] In the practice pieces he repeated this instruction for an Adagio in F sharp minor and a Maestoso in D major, which he described as having a type of melody 'peculiar to marches'.[54] At the beginning of the nineteenth century J. F. Schubert recommended over-dotting in vocal music in the context of 'heavy and light performance style', noting:

in passionate passages the note with the dot will always be held longer than its value and the following note will be performed that much shorter. This applies also to passages of the following kind, where the rest takes the place of the dot. [Ex. 16.37] Here the rest will be sustained somewhat longer than its value, which will be taken from the following note.[55]

Ex. 16.37. J. F. Schubert, *Neue Singe-Schule*, 131

It was not uncommon for eighteenth-century composers to employ dots in a very imprecise manner. Examples of this may be found, for instance, in Clementi's music. In *La Chasse* op. 16 and the Sonata in F op. 26 he used a single dot to lengthen a note by less than half its value (Ex. 16.38). In the Sonata in

Ex. 16.38. Clementi: (*a*) *La Chasse* op. 16, 1st edn., p. 3; (*b*) Piano Sonata op. 26/iii
(*a*)

(*b*)

<hr>

[53] p. 30.   [54] *Anweisung zum Violinspielen*, 84.   [55] *Neue Singe-Schule*, 131.

G op. 40 no. 1 a dot lengths the note by two-thirds (Ex. 16.39), but in the second movement of op. 40 no. 1 a double dot is used for the same purpose (Ex. 16.40).

Ex. 16.39. Clementi, Piano Sonata op. 40/1/i

Ex. 16.40. Clementi, Piano Sonata op. 40/1/ii

Some eighteenth-century composers, however, including Mozart, were generally very precise about the difference between single dots and double dots, and in many cases they took trouble to indicate rests instead of dots (see Ex. 6.26). Yet it seems rather unlikely that in cases like the first section of Mozart's Adagio and Fugue, with its strong resemblance to the old French overture, Mozart would have expected a rhythmically precise performance of the dotted figures rather than an over-dotted one (Ex. 16.41).

An increasing number of later composers, from Beethoven onwards, seem to have differentiated carefully between various treatments of such figures. In the movement of the String Quartet op. 59 no. 2 cited above as an instance of where assimilation to triplets may have been intended, four different notations for dotted figures are employed with implications for rhythm and style of performance (Ex. 16.42). Such care over details might argue that everything should be performed as exactly as possible, and may be taken as an argument against the

Ex. 16.41. Mozart, Adagio and Fugue K. 546

Ex. 16.42. Beethoven, op. 59/2/ii

(*a*)

(*b*)

assimilation of the triplets. But in that period precise notation of this kind need not exclude a degree of freedom in performance. It may be legitimate to wonder how exact Beethoven might have expected the semiquavers in the second and third bars of Ex. 16.42(*b*) to be.

A number of nineteenth-century writers continued to recommend over-dotting in some cases, for instance the mathematician and musician August Crelle in 1823, though he pointed out that 'if the composer writes in a very correct manner one must play the passage just as it is written'.[56] About the same time Schubert made an interesting distinction in *Alfonso und Estrella* between his notation for orchestral instruments and for solo singers. The instruments have double dotted figures while the voices are left with single dots, but it seems highly unlikely that he did not intend them to perform them in the same manner; it looks as if he expected the singers to over-dot in this type of passage and spared himself the trouble of indicating this, but took the precaution of warning the orchestra (Ex. 16.43(*a*)). A similar instance occurs in his last completed opera, *Fierrabras* (Ex. 16.43(*b*)).

In Rossini, too, there is sometimes a lack of correspondence between the dotted rhythms of the accompaniment and those of the singer, for instance in the aria 'Ah si per voi già sento nuovo valor' from *Otello*, as illustrated by García,[57] which suggests an assumption that the singer would over-dot to match the orchestra. In similar pieces of a martial or majestic character it seems clear that the convention of over-dotting remained strong throughout the nineteenth century, especially in the Italian operatic repertoire. But it was not only in such genres of music, where composers conventionally left much in the way of detail to be supplied by the performer, that the practice persisted. Even a composer whose notation might be expected to have been particularly exact could, as late as the 1880s, call for performers to apply a degree of over-dotting to his music. According to Heinrich Porges, Wagner intervened at one point during a rehearsal of *Parsifal* (Ex. 16.44) to request: 'hold the quaver with the dot longer; the semiquaver can then be somewhat shorter—more to be effected through inner strength.'[58]

Early recordings demonstrate the widespread survival of the practice of over-dotting into the twentieth century. In the recording of Berlioz's overture *Carnaval romain* made by Nikisch and the Berlin Philharmonic orchestra in 1913 there is clear double-dotting of a single dotted figure in the cor anglais solo in bars 22 and 25 (Ex. 16.45). Whether all occurrences of this kind on early recordings would have met with the approval of the composer is a moot point, but it is surely not without significance that over-dotting can frequently be

[56] *Einiges*, 77.   [57] *New Treatise*, 50.

[58] Porges in the piano score which he used during rehearsals for the première of *Parsifal*, quoted in Martin Geck and Egon Voss, eds., *Richard Wagner: Sämtliche Werke*, xxx: *Dokumente zur Entstehung und erster Aufführung des Bühnenweihfestspiels Parsifal* (Mainz, 1970), 179.

Ex. 16.43. Schubert: (*a*) *Alfonso und Estrella*, no. 10; (*b*) *Fierrabras*, no. 6 (Scene xii)

heard on Elgar's own recordings of his music. The prevalence of this and other alterations of rhythmic detail in early recordings is amply documented by Robert Philip.[59] These recordings clearly reveal the change of attitude that has taken place during the course of the twentieth century with respect to the literal interpretation of musical notation.

[59] See *Early Recording and Musical Style*, and 'Traditional Habits of Performance in Early-Twentieth-Century Recordings of Beethoven', in Stowell, ed., *Performing Beethoven*, 198–9.

Ex. 16.44. Wagner, *Parsifal*, rehearsal number 74

Ex. 16.45. Berlioz, overture *Le Carnaval romain* op. 9

Heavy and Light Performance

These extremes of performance style and their intermediate stages were discussed by many German theorists in the late eighteenth century and early nineteenth century. The nomenclature of 'heavy and light' performance, and much of its systematized theory, seems to have derived from J. P. Kirnberger and J. A. P. Schulz, though the ideas dealt with under this heading by these and subsequent theorists were also alluded to in earlier texts.

In Kirnberger's *Die Kunst des reinen Satzes* there are many references to the role of metre in determining a heavier or lighter performance style; for instance: 'Longer note values are always performed with more weight and emphasis than shorter ones; consequently, a composition that is to be performed with weight and emphasis can only be notated with long note values, and another that is to be performed in a light and playful manner can only be notated with short note values.'[60]

These ideas were expounded more extensively by Schulz in Sulzer's *Allgemeine Theorie der schönen Künste* (1771–4), particularly in the article 'Vortrag', where he considered the 'appropriate lightness and heaviness of performance for the character and expression of the piece'. But his comments also indicate that theory was not entirely in line with the practice of the period:

A great part of the expression depends on this. A piece of grand and pathetic expression must be performed in the heaviest and most emphatic manner: this occurs if every note of it is firmly given and sustained, almost as if tenuta were written over it. In contrast, pieces of pleasant and gentle expression are performed more lightly; namely, every note is more lightly given and not sustained so firmly. A wholly merry or dance-like expression can only be obtained through the lightest performance. If this difference in performance is not observed a greater part of the expression is lost in many pieces; and yet it appears as if nowadays little attention is given to this anymore. It is certain that the practice of performing everything lightly and, as it were, playfully has so much gained the upper hand and even had a powerful effect on composition that people seem no longer to know about any grand and majestic expression in music. One composes for the church as for the theatre, because the true performance of good church music has been lost and no distinction is made between the performance of a church solo or an opera aria. . . . Unfortunate is the composer who really has a feeling for the grand and elevated and writes things that ought to be performed heavily; he will not find one in a hundred who knows how to enter into the simplicity of the melody and give due weight to every note.

Having proceeded to consider the role of metre in determining heaviness and lightness (metres with the longest note values being the heaviest and those with the shortest being the lightest), he continued:

In addition one must note from the character or coherence of the melody such places or phrases which ought to be particularly heavily or lightly performed; the expression will thereby be strengthened and the whole given a pleasant shading. Only in strict fugues and church pieces is this shading dispensed with, for it does not accord well with their dignity and elevation of expression. In such pieces every note, according to the metre, is given with equal firmness and emphasis. As a whole every metre will be more heavily performed in the church than in the chamber or theatre; also, the very light metres are not found in good church music.[61]

---

[60]   *The Art of Strict Musical Composition*, 384.   [61]   In Sulzer, *Allgemeine Theorie*, iv. 708–9.

Türk's treatment of the same subject in his *Klavierschule* shows his familiarity with Schulz's account; but he prefaced his discussion with an examination of staccato, portato, slurring (legato), and ties, since he considered that it was principally through the effective use of these means that heavy or light performance style could be achieved. He regarded a heavy performance style as one in which 'every note is firmly (emphatically) given and held to the full extent of the value of the note' and a light performance style as one in which 'one gives every note with less firmness (emphasis), and lifts the finger from the key somewhat earlier than the duration of the note specifies'. He felt it important, however, to remark that a heavy or light performance style had more to do with the sustaining or taking off of the notes than with strength or weakness:

For in certain cases, for example, an *Allegro vivo, scherzando, Vivace con allegrezza*, etc., the performance style must certainly be rather light, (short) but at the same time more or less strong; whereas on the other hand a piece of mournful character, for example an *Adagio mesto, con afflizzione*, etc. should certainly be slurred [legato] and consequently, so to speak, heavy, but nevertheless not exactly performed strongly. For all that, at any rate, heavy and strong go together in most cases.

He then observed that it was possible to determine whether performance style should be heavy or light:

1) from the character and purpose of a piece of music[,] 2) from the specified tempo, 3) from the metre, 4) from the note values, 5) from the way in which these are employed. In addition there is also the matter of national taste, the composer's style and that of the instrument for which a piece of music is written to be taken into consideration.

He further clarified the first point by referring the reader to §45, where he explained: 'pieces that are written to a serious end, e.g. fugues, well worked-out sonatas, religious odes and songs etc. require a far heavier style of performance than certain light-hearted divertimenti, humorous songs, lively dances and so on.'[62]

A somewhat later account of this subject, with the singer in mind, was given by J. F. Schubert, who, although showing his knowledge of earlier writers' views, contributed a number of different perspectives. He instructed:

Heavy performance style is distinguished from light in that the notes are firmly bound to each other, emphatic, and precisely held to the full extent of their value. In a light performance style, on the other hand, the notes are less sustained, less bound together, and are played shorter and with less firmness. Vocal pieces of a pathetic, serious, solemn, and elevated character must be performed with the greatest weight and emphasis. This genre is commonly given the direction grave, pomposo, maestoso, etc. Pieces with a pleasant, trifling, merry, and lively character require a light performance style. These are commonly headed Allegretto, scherzando, lusingando, etc. The metre also indicates a heavier or lighter performance style. In general one can assume the following rule. The greater the time units

[62] Ch. VI, §43.

[*Takttheile*] (beat divisions [*Glieder*]) in a piece, the heavier the performance style must be. . . .

A vocal piece with many dissonances demands a heavier performance style than one that consists of fewer dissonances and more consonant harmonies. Fugues, well worked out [contrapuntal] pieces of church music, require a heavy performance style throughout; in general the performance style in church is, regardless of the metre, heavier than in the chamber or the theatre—The contrapuntal [*gebunden*] (strict) style of writing demands a heavier performance style than the free [*frey*] (light, galant).* The manner or style of the composer is also to be considered in relation to a heavy or light performance style. Thus, for example, pieces by Mozart require, on the whole, a heavier performance style than those of Haydn. The vocal pieces of the latter must, on the other hand, be more heavily performed than those of Paisiello, Martin, etc. One also often finds that compositions of one and the same master must be differently performed with respect to weight or lightness. Thus, for example, Mozart's *Don Giovanni* requires (on the whole) a heavier performance style than *The Marriage of Figaro*. Salieri's *Axur* must be more heavily performed than *La cifra*.

*[Schubert's footnote] *gebundenen* = strict harmony etc.; *frey* = more licence, bold modulations, surprising entries.

One must also observe from the characteristics of the melody and from the meaning of the text which individual passages should be more heavily or lightly performed than others. A powerful unison, for example, always demands a heavier performance style in every type of musical composition as long as the composer has not deliberately specified the contrary. Dotted notes demand, for the most part, a heavier performance style, for example [Ex. 16.46][63] . . . Passagework and ornaments are, without exception, performed lightly.[64]

Ex. 16.46. J. F. Schubert, *Neue Singe-Schule*, 131

Hö - re   Her - rscher   der Wel - ten

Notions such as these were usually discussed under the general heading *Vortrag* (performance style) in late eighteenth- and early nineteenth-century treatises, but considerations of *Vortrag* in nineteenth-century writing changed significantly during the course of the century. Writers displayed less and less interest in drawing conclusions about performance style from the types of notes employed, the genre, the type of piece, or the musical context. It became almost an article of faith that, in a new era of individualism, each piece had its own unique demands that could only be indicated by specific instructions from the composer. Thus, in the *Musikalisches Conversations-Lexikon* of H. Mendel and A. Reissmann (1882) the entry for *Vortrag* was strikingly different from that in Sulzer's *Allgemeine Theorie* of just over a hundred years earlier.

[63] See above, 'Over-Dotting', for information on over-dotting, which Schubert includes at this point.
[64] *Neue Singe-Schule*, 130–1.

Mendel's *Lexikon* considered that performance style (*Vortrag*) 'requires two things above all: the most complete understanding of the notational signs [*Schriftzeichen*] employed by the creative artist, and the technical skill to execute, on the relevant musical instruments [*Musikorganen*], what they indicate'.[65] And the rest of the article concerned itself almost entirely with an explanation of signs and performance instructions.

Postscript

The change of attitude implied by these differences is profound. The onus for the performer had decisively shifted from one of determining in which of a number of different ways to interpret the notation, on the basis of general conventions of appropriate style, to one in which it was primarily necessary to know the precise meaning and intention behind the composer's symbols and instructions. The growing separation between composer and performer and the increasing definition of their roles as creative and interpretative artists were closely connected with this development. The concept of the great composer, which crystallized in the nineteenth-century view of the Viennese Classical masters, especially Beethoven, encouraged an unhistorical reverence for the literal meaning of their notation; the role of the performer was correspondingly circumscribed. Later nineteenth-century composers responded to this by greater precision and prescriptiveness in their scores, and by the beginning of the twentieth century such thoroughness had not only struck deep roots in France, Germany, and those parts of northern and central Europe where French or German influence predominated, but had also extended its sway over Italian composers. The evident detail in late nineteenth-century musical scores, however, can easily obscure the fundamental differences between what that music meant to its composers and their performing colleagues and what it means to musicians a century later, whose musical preconceptions have been moulded to a considerable extent by the exigencies of the recording studio. It was precisely those subtle aspects of performance, which were not and could not be written down, even at the end of the nineteenth century, that created the essential sound-world within which the composers of the age conceived their music. It may be true that we can safely ignore these details without detracting from the fundamental characteristics that give lasting and universal relevance to the best works of the past; yet awareness and knowledge of these matters, however speculative, may still offer a path towards deeper understanding of the music, especially for the performer.

Good taste is not an immutable quality; it is in a state of constant change. What was considered tasteful by eighteenth- and nineteenth-century

---

[65] xi. 212, art. 'Vortrag'.

musicians might seem to us unnatural or grotesque at first hearing, and they would doubtless have found the idioms of modern performance strange and probably unsatisfactory in many respects. Such considerations may prompt us to ponder whether we might not experiment with more radically different and audacious approaches to the performance of familiar repertoire, attempting to recapture something of the respectful but not excessively reverential attitudes that typified the finest performers of the Classical and Romantic periods, and seeking to develop a more finely tuned awareness of the different schools and stylistic traditions that were associated with particular composers and genres. By doing so we may be able to recapture some of the excitement of hearing great masterpieces for the first time, and we may also find that we begin to make discoveries about effectively performing music by less familiar composers of the period, which might in many cases help to rekindle the vitality that it was once felt to possess.

BIBLIOGRAPHY

❧

ABBIATI, FRANCO, *Giuseppe Verdi*, 4 vols. (Milan, 1959).

ADAM, JEAN LOUIS, *Méthode du piano du Conservatoire* (Paris, 1804).

ADAMS, JOHN S., *5000 Musical Terms* (Boston, 1851).

ADDISON, JOHN, *Singing Practically Treated in a Series of Instructions* (London, 1850).

AGRICOLA, JOHANN FRIEDRICH, *Anleitung zur Singkunst* (Berlin, 1757) (revised version of Tosi's *Opinioni*); trans. and ed. Julianne C. Baird as *Introduction to the Art of Singing by Johann Friedrich Agricola* (Cambridge, 1995).

ALBRECHT, HANS, ed., *Die Bedeutung der Zeichen Keil Strich und Punkt bei Mozart* (Kassel, 1957).

ALEXANDER, JAMES, *Complete Preceptor for the Flute* (London, [c.1821]).

Allgemeine musikalische Zeitung, ed. Johann Friedrich Rochlitz, Christian Gottfried Wilhelm Fink, Johann Christian Lobe, and others (Leipzig, Breitkopf & Härtel, 1789/9–1848).

Allgemeine Wiener Musik-Zeitung (from 1847 *Wiener allgemeine Musik-Zeitung*), ed. August Schmidt (1841–8).

ALONSO, LUIS, *Le Virtuose moderne* (Paris, [c.1880]).

ALTENBURG, JOHANN ERNST, *Versuch einer Anleitung zur heroisch-musikalischen Trompeter- und Paukenkunst* (Halle, 1795).

ANDERSCH, JOHANN DANIEL, *Musikalisches Wörterbuch* (Berlin, 1829).

ANDERSON, EMILY, trans. and ed., *The Letters of Beethoven* (London, 1961).

—— *The Letters of Mozart and his Family*, 2nd edn. (London, 1966).

ANON., *A Choice Collection of Lessons* (London, 1696); repr. with attribution to Purcell in *The Third Book of the Harpsichord Master* (London, 1702).

ANON., *New Instructions for Playing the Harpsichord, Pianoforte or Organ etc.* (London, [c.1790]).

ANON., *Reise nach Wien* (Hof, 1795).

ANON., *Instructions for the Violin by an Eminent Master* (London, [c.1795]).

ANON., *Violinschule oder Anweisung die Violine zu spielen von Leopold Mozart. Neue umgearbeitete und vermehrte Ausgabe* (Vienna, [c.1805]).

ANON., *Hints to Violin Players* (Edinburgh, [c.1880]).

ANON., *The Violin: How to Master it. By a Professional Player* (Edinburgh, [c.1880]).

ASIOLI, BONIFAZIO, *Principj elementari di musica* (Milan, 1809); trans. and ed. John Jousse as *A Compendious Musical Grammar in which the Theory of Music is Completely Developed, in a Series of familiar Dialogues written by Bonifacio Asioli* (London, [1825]).

AUER, LEOPOLD, *Violin Playing as I Teach it* (London, 1921).

AUHAGEN, WOLFGANG, 'Chronometrische Tempoangaben im 18. und 19. Jahrhundert', *Archiv für Musikwissenschaft*, 44 (1987), 40–57.

BACH, CARL PHILIPP EMANUEL, *Versuch über die wahre Art das Clavier zu spielen*, vol. i (Berlin, 1753, rev. 2nd edn. 1787), vol. ii (Berlin, 1762, rev. 2nd edn. 1797); fac. repr. of 1st edns., incl. revs. of 1787 as a separate section (Leipzig, 1787); trans. and ed. William J. Mitchell as *Essay on the True Art of Playing Keyboard Instruments* (New York, 1949).

BADURA-SKODA, PAUL, 'A Tie is a Tie is a Tie', *Early Music*, 16 (1988), 84.

BADURA-SKODA, EVA and PAUL, *Mozart-Interpretation* (Vienna and Stuttgart, 1957); trans. Leo Black as *Interpreting Mozart on the Keyboard* (London, 1962).

BAENSCH, OTTO, 'Zur Neunten Symphonie', in Adolf Sandberger, ed., *Neues Beethoven Jahrbuch* (Augsburg, 1925), 145 ff.

BAILLEUX, ANTOINE, *Méthode raisonné à apprendre le violon* (Paris, 1779).

BAILLOT, PIERRE MARIE FRANÇOIS DE SALES, RODE, PIERRE, and KREUTZER, RUDOLPHE, *Méthode de violon* (Paris, 1803).

—— LEVASSEUR, JEAN HENRI, CATEL, CHARLES-SIMON, and BAUDIOT, CHARLES-NICOLAS, *Méthode de violoncelle du Conservatoire* (Paris, 1804).

—— *L'Art du violon: Nouvelle méthode* (Paris, 1834).

BAYLY, ANSELM, *A Practical Treatise on Singing and Playing with Just Expression and Real Elegance* (London, 1771).

BECK, DAGMAR and HERRE, GRITA, 'Einige Zweifel an der Überlieferung der Konversationshefte', in Harry Goldschmidt, Karl-Heinz Köhler, and Konrad Niemann, eds., *Bericht über den Internationalen Beethoven-Kongress . . . 1977 in Berlin* (Leipzig, 1978).

BEMETZRIEDER, ANTON, *New Lessons for the Harpsichord* (London, 1783).

BÉRIOT, CHARLES DE, *Méthode de violon* (Mainz, [1858]): 1st edn. pub. with parallel Ger. and Fr. text; a later edn. (*c.*1880) issued with parallel Eng. and Fr. text (both have same layout and pagination).

BERLIOZ, HECTOR, *Grand traité d'instrumentation et d'orchestration modernes* op. 10 (Paris, 1843).

BRAHMS, JOHANNES, *Briefwechsel*, 16 vols. (Berlin, 1907–22).

BREMNER, ROBERT, 'Some Thoughts on the Performance of Concert Music', pub. as preface to J. G. C. Schetcky, *Six Quartettos for Two Violins, a Tenor, and Violoncello op. VI. To which are prefixed some thoughts on the performance of concert-music by the publisher* (London, R. Bremner, [1777]).

BROWN, CLIVE, 'Bowing Styles, Vibrato and Portamento in Nineteenth-Century Violin Playing', *Journal of the Royal Musical Association*, 113 (1988), 97–128.

—— 'Historical Performance, Metronome Marks and Tempo in Beethoven's Symphonies', *Early Music*, 19 (1991), 247 ff.

—— 'Dots and Strokes in Late 18th- and 19th-Century Music', *Early Music*, 21 (1993), 593–610.

—— 'String Playing Practices in the Classical Orchestra', *Basler Jahrbuch für historische Musikpraxis*, 17 (1993), 41–64.

—— 'Ferdinand David's Editions of Beethoven', in Stowell, ed., *Performing Beethoven*, 117–49.

—— 'Schubert's Tempo Conventions', in Brian Newbould, ed., *Schubert Studies* (Aldershot, Ashgate, 1998), 1–15.

BROWN, HOWARD MAYER, ed., *The New Grove Handbook of Performance Practice: Music after 1600* (London, 1989).

BURKHARD, JOHANN ANDREAS CHRISTIAN, *Neues vollständiges musikalisches Wörterbuch* (Ulm, 1832).

BURNEY, CHARLES, *A General History of Music from the Earliest Ages to the Present Period*, 4 vols. (London, 1776–89).

BUSBY, THOMAS, *A Complete Dictionary of Music* (London, 1806).

—— *A Dictionary of Three Thousand Musical Terms Ancient and Modern, Foreign and English including all that are to be found in the works of Bellini, Bertini, Chopin . . . Rossini, Spohr, Thalberg, and other composers of the present day. With descriptions of the various voices and instruments*, 3rd edn., rev. J. A. Hamilton (London, [1840]).

Cäcilia [from 1826, vol. 5, *Caecilia*]: *Eine Zeitschrift für die musikalische Welt*, ed. Gottfried Weber, 27 vols. (Mainz, Brussels, and Antwerp, Schott, 1824–48).

CALLCOTT, JOHN WALL, *A Musical Grammar* (London, 1806).

CAMBINI, GIUSEPPE MARIA, *Nouvelle méthode théorique et pratique pour le violon* (Paris, [*c*.1800]).

CAMPAGNOLI, BARTOLOMEO, *Nouvelle méthode de la mécanique du jeu de violon* (Leipzig, 1824).

CARTER, STEWART, 'The String Tremolo in the 17th Century', *Early Music*, 19 (1991), 43–58.

CARTIER, JEAN BAPTISTE, *L'Art du violon ou collection choisie dans les sonates des écoles italienne, françoise et allemande précédée d'un abrégée des principes pour cet instrument* (Paris, [1798]).

CASTIL-BLAZE, FRANÇOIS HENRI JOSEPH, *Dictionnaire de musique moderne* (Paris, 1821).

CASWELL, AUSTIN, 'Mme Cinti-Damoreau and the Embellishment of Italian Opera in Paris 1820–45', *Journal of the American Musicological Society*, 28 (1975), 459–92.

CHABRAN, CARLO FRANCESCO, *Compleat Instructions for the Spanish Guitar* (London, [*c*.1795]).

CHORLEY, HENRY FOTHERGILL, *Modern German Music* (London, [1854]).

CLEMENTI, MUZIO, *Introduction to the Art of Playing on the Pianoforte* (London, 1801); 11th edn. (1826).

CLINTON, JOHN, *A School or Practical Instruction Book for the Boehm Flute* (London, [*c*.1850]).

CONATI, MARCELLO, *Interviews and Encounters with Verdi*, trans. Richard Stokes (London, 1984).

CORRETTE, MICHEL, *L'École d'Orphée, méthode pour apprendre facilement à jouer du violon dans le goût françois et italien avec des principes de musique et beaucoup de leçons* op. 18 (Paris, 1738).

CORRI, DOMENICO, *A Select Collection*, 3 vols. (Edinburgh, [*c*.1782]).

—— *The Singer's Preceptor* (London, 1810).

CORRI, HAYDN, *The Delivery of Vocal Music* (London, 1823).

CORRI, PHILIP ANTHONY, *L'anima di musica* (London, 1810).

CRAMER, CARL FRIEDRICH, ed., *Magazin der Musik* (Hamburg, 1783–7).

CRELLE, AUGUST LUDWIG, *Einiges über musikalischen Ausdruck und Vortrag* (Belin, 1823).

CROME, ROBERT, *Fiddle, New Modell'd* (London, [*c*.1750]).

CROTCH, WILLIAM, 'Remarks on the Terms at Present Used in Music, for Regulating the Time', *Monthly Magazine*, 8 (1800), 941–3.

CRUTCHFIELD, WILL, 'The Prosodic Appoggiatura in the Music of Mozart and his Contemporaries', *Journal of the American Musicological Society*, 42 (1989), 229–74.

—— 'Voices', in Howard Mayer Brown, ed., *The New Grove Handbook of Performance Practice after 1600* (London, 1989).

CUDWORTH, CHARLES, 'The Meaning of "Vivace" in Eighteenth-Century England', *Fontes artis musicae*, 12 (1965), 194.

CZERNY, CARL, *Vollständige theoretisch-practische Pianoforte-Schule* op. 500, 3 vols. (Vienna, 1839); vol. iii, *Von dem Vortrage*, pub. in fac. (Wiesbaden, Breitkopf & Hartel, 1991); trans. as *Complete Theoretical and Practical Piano Forte School* op. 500, 3 vols. (London, [1839]).

—— *Chapter 1 to Czerny's Royal Pianoforte School. Being the Second Supplement by the Author* (London, [1846]).

—— *Die Kunst des Vortrags der älteren und neueren Klavierkompositionen* (vol. iv of *Vollständige . . . Pianoforte-Schule* op. 500) (Vienna, 1846); trans. John Bishop as *The Art of Playing the Ancient and Modern Piano Forte Works* (London, [1846]).

DADELSEN G. VON, ed., *Editionsrichtlinie musikalischer Denkmäler und Gesamtausgaben* (Kassel, 1967).

DAMERINI, A., 'Sei lettere inedite di Verdi a J. C. Farrarini', *Il pianoforte* (Aug.–Sept. 1926).

DANNELEY, J. F., *Dictionary of Music* (London, 1825).

DANNREUTHER, EDWARD, *Musical Ornamentation*, 2 vols. (London, 1893–5).

DASCHAUER, ANDREAS, *Kleines Handbuch der Musiklehre* (Kempton, 1801).

DAVID, FERDINAND, *Violinschule* (Leipzig, 1863).

—— ed., *Concert-Studien für die Violine. Eine Sammlung von Violin-Solo-Compositionen berühmter älterer Meister, zum Gebrauch beim Conservatorium der Musik in Leipzig*, 3 vols. (Leipzig, Bartholf Senf, n.d.).

DEAS, STUART, 'Beethoven's "Allegro assai"', *Music & Letters*, 31 (1950), 333.

DELUSSE, CHARLES, *L'Art de la flute traversière* (Paris, [c.1761]).

DIBDIN, CHARLES, *Music Epitomized: A School Book in which the Whole Science of Music is Completely Explained . . .* (London, 1808); 9th edn., rev. J. Jousse (London, [c.1820]).

DICKEY, BRUCE, 'Untersuchung zur historischen Auffassung des Vibratos auf Blasinstrumenten', *Basler Jahrbuch für historische Musikpraxis*, 2 (1978).

DOMMER, ARREY VON, *Musikalisches Lexicon auf Grundlage des Lexicon's von H. Ch.Koch* (Heidelberg, 1865): alternative title-page: *H. Ch. Koch's Musikalisches Lexicon. Zweite durchaus umgearbeitet und vermehrte Auflage von Arrey von Dommer*.

DONT, JACOB, *Zwölf Uebungen aus der Violinschule von L. Spohr mit Anmerkungen, Ergänzungen des Fingersatzes der Bogen-Stricharten und der Tonschattierungszeichen* (Vienna, 1874).

DOTZAUER, JUSTUS JOHANN FRIEDRICH, *Méthode de violoncelle/Violonzell-Schule* (Mainz, [c.1825]).

—— *Violoncell-Schule für den ersten Unterricht* op. 126 (Vienna, [c.1836]).

DUPORT JEAN LOUIS, *Essai sur le doigté du violoncelle et sur la conduite de l'archet* (Offenbach am Main, André, [c.1808]), with parallel Fr. and Ger. text.

EBERHARDT, SIEGFRIED, *Der beseelte Violin-Ton* (Dresden, 1910); trans. as *Violin Vibrato: Its Mastery and Artistic Uses* (New York, 1911).

EDWARDS, F. G., 'George P. Bridgetower and the "Kreutzer" Sonata', *Musical Times*, 49 (1908), 308.

EHRLICH, HEINRICH, 'Beim 84jährigen Verdi', *Deutsche Revue* (Stuttgart), 22/2 (1897), 325 ff.

ESCUDIER (frères), *Dictionnaire de musique théorique et historique* (Paris, 1854).

FÉTIS, FRANÇOIS-JOSEPH, *Traité élémentaire de musique* (Brussels, 1831–2).

—— and MOSCHELES, IGNAZ, *Méthode des méthodes de piano* (Paris, [*c*.1840]); trans. as *Complete System of Instruction for the Piano Forte* (London, [1841]).

FLEMING, J. M., *The Practical Violin School for Home Students* (London, 1886).

FLESCH, CARL, *Die Kunst des Violinspiels*, i (Berlin, 1923); trans. as *The Art of Violin Playing* (London, 1924).

—— *Mémoires* (London, 1957).

FOSTER, RONALD, *Vocal Success* (London, 1934).

FRÖHLICH, FRANZ JOSEPH, *Vollständige theoretisch-praktische Musikschule* (Bonn, 1810–11).

FULLER, DAVID, 'Notes inégales', *New Grove*, xiii. 420–7.

FULLER MAITLAND, J. A., 'Sostenuto', *Grove's Dictionary*, 3rd edn., ed. H. C. Colles (London, 1927).

FÜRSTENAU, ADOLF BERNARD, *Flöten-Schule* (Leipzig, [1826]).

GALEAZZI, FRANCESCO, *Elementi teorico-pratici di musica, con un saggio sopra l'arte di suonare il violino annalizzata, ed a dimostrabili principi ridotta*, 2 vols. (Rome, 1791–6).

GARCÍA, MANUEL PATRICIO RODRIGUEZ, *Traité complet de l'art du chant* i, (Paris, 1840) and ii (1847), rev. & trans. as *Garcia's New Treatise on the Art of Singing* (London, 1894).

GARDINER, WILLIAM, *The Music of Nature* (London, [1857]).

GASSNER, F. S., *Dirigent und Ripienist* (Karlsruhe, 1844).

GATHY, AUGUST, *Musikalisches Conversations-Lexikon* (Leipzig, 1835); 2nd edn. (Hamburg, 1840).

GECK, MARTIN, and VOSS, EGON, eds., *Richard Wagner: Sämtliche Werke*, xxx: *Dokumente zur Entstehung und ersten Aufführung des Bühnenweihfestspiels Parsifal* (Mainz, 1970).

GEHOT, JOSEPH, *A Treatise on the Theory and Practice of Music together with the Scales of Every Musical Instrument* (London, 1784).

GEIRINGER, KARL, *Joseph Haydn* (Potsdam, 1932).

GEMINIANI, FRANCESCO, *Rules for Playing in a True Taste* (London, 1748).

—— *The Art of Playing on the Violin* (London, 1751).

GERSTENBERG, WALTER, 'Authentische Tempi für Mozarts "Don Giovanni"?', *Mozart-Jahrbuch* (1960–1), 58–61.

GLEICH, CLEMENS VON, 'Original Tempo-Angaben bei Mendelssohn', in H. Herrtreich and H. Schneider, eds., *Festschrift Rudolf Elvers zum 60 Geburtstag* (Tutzing, 1985), 213 ff.

GOLLMICK, KARL, *Kritische Terminologie* (Frankfurt-am-Main, 1833).

—— *Handlexikon der Tonkunst* (Offenbach am Main, 1857).

GOSSEC, FRANÇOIS-JOSEPH, AGUS, JOSEPH, CATEL, CHARLES-SIMON, and CHERUBINI, LUIGI, *Principes élémentaires de musique arrêtés par les membres du Conservatoire, suivis de solfèges* (Paris, ?1798–1802).

GREULICH, CARL WILHELM, *Kleine practische Clavierschule zum Selbstunterricht* (Berlin, [*c*.1831]).

GRIMSON, SAMUEL B., and FORSYTH, CECIL, *Modern Violin-Playing* (New York, 1920).

GROVE, SIR GEORGE, ed., *A Dictionary of Music and Musicians* (London, 1879–89).

GUHR, CARL, *Ueber Paganini's Kunst die Violine zu spielen . . .* (Mainz, [1829]).

GUNN, JOHN, *The Art of Playing the German Flute* (London, [1793]).

GUTHMANN, FRIEDRICH, 'Ueber Abweichung vom Takte', *Allgemeine musikalische Zeitung*, 7 (1804–5), 347–9.

HABENECK, FRANÇOIS, *Méthode théorique et pratique de violon* (Paris, *c.*1840).

HAMILTON, JAMES ALEXANDER, *A Dictionary of Two Thousand Italian, French, German, English and other Musical Terms*, 4th edn. (London, 1837); rev. as *Hamilton's Dictionary of Musical Terms. New Edition . . . Enlarged* (London, [1882]).

HANSLICK, EDUARD, *Geschichte des Concertwesens in Wien* (Vienna, 1869).

HARDING, ROSAMOND E. M., *Origins of Musical Time and Expression* (London, 1938).

HARNONCOURT, NIKOLAUS, *Der musikalische Dialog* (Salzburg, 1984).

HAUPTMANN, MORITZ, *Die Natur der Harmonik und der Metrik* (Leipzig, 1853).

HERZ, HENRI, *Méthode complète de piano* op. 100 (Mainz and Anvers, 1838).

—— *A New and Complete Pianoforte School* (London [*c.*1838]).

—— *A Standard Modern Preceptor for the Pianoforte* (London, [*c.*1840]).

HICKMAN, ROGER, 'The Censored Publications of *The Art of Playing on the Violin* or Geminiani Unshaken', *Early Music*, 11 (1983), 71–6.

HILL, CECIL, *Ferdinand Ries: Briefe und Dokumente* (Bonn, 1982).

HILLER, JOHANN ADAM, *Sechs italienische Arien verschiedener Componisten* (Leipzig, 1778).

—— *Anweisung zum musikalisch-zierlichen Gesang* (Leipzig, 1780).

—— *Anweisung zum Violonspielen für Schulen und Selbstunterrichte* (Leipzig, 1792).

HOLDEN, JOHN, *An 'Essay' towards a Rational System of Music* (Glasgow, 1770).

HOULE, GEORGE, *Metre in Music 1600–1800* (Bloomington, Ind., and Indianapolis, 1987).

HUDSON, RICHARD, *Stolen Time: The History of Tempo Rubato* (Oxford, 1994).

HÜLLMANDEL, NICHOLAS-JOSEPH, *Principles of Music Chiefly Calculated for the Piano Forte or Harpsichord* (London, 1796).

HUMMEL, JOHANN NEPOMUK, *Ausführliche theoretisch-practische Anweisung zum Piano-Forte-Spiel*, 3 vols. (Vienna, 1828); trans. as *A Complete Theoretical and Practical Course of Instructions, on the Art of Playing the Piano Forte*, 3 vols. (London, [1828]).

JÄHNS, FRIEDRICH WILHELM, *Carl Maria von Weber in seinen Werken: Chronologisch-thematisches Verzeichniss seiner sämmtlichen Compositionen* (Berlin, 1871).

JAMES, W. N., *The Flutist's Catechism* (London, 1829).

JOACHIM, JOSEPH, and MOSER, ANDREAS, *Violinschule*, 3 vols. (Berlin, 1905).

JOUSSE, JOHN, *The Modern Violin Preceptor* (London, [*c.*1805]).

—— *The Theory and Practice of the Violin* (London, 1811).

—— see Asioli.

KALKBRENNER, FRÉDÉRIC, *Méthode pour apprendre le piano-forte à l'aide du guide mains* op. 108 (Paris, 1831); trans. as *Complete Course of Instruction for the Piano Forte* (London, [*c.*1835]).

KÄMPER, D., 'Zur Frage der Metronombezeichnungen Robert Schumanns', *Archiv für Musikwissenschaft*, 21 (1964), 141.

KIRNBERGER, JOHANN PHILIPP, *Die Kunst des reinen Satzes in der Musik*, i (Berlin and Königsberg, 1771), ii (Berlin and Königsberg, 1776–9); trans. David Beach and Jurgen Thym as *The Art of Strict Musical Composition* (New Haven, and London, 1982).

KLINDWORTH, KARL, 'Preface' and 'Explanatory Notes', in Mendelssohn's, *Lieder ohne Worte* (London, Novello, 1898).

KNECHT, JUSTIN HEINRICH, *Kleine theoretische Klavierschule für die ersten Anfänger* (Munich, [1799]).

—— *Knechts allgemeiner musikalischer Katechismus* (Biberach, 1803); 4th edn. (Freyburg, 1816).

KOCH, HEINRICH CHRISTOPH, *Versuch einer Anleitung zur Composition* (Rudolstadt und Leipzig, 1782–93).

—— *Musikalisches Lexikon* (Frankfurt-am-Main, 1802).

KOGEL, G. F., preface to Heinrich Marschner, *Hans Heiling*, full score, ed. Kögel (Leipzig, Peters, [*c.*1880]).

KOLLMANN, AUGUST FREDERIC CHRISTOPHER, *An Essay on Musical Harmony* (London, 1796).

KRAMER, RICHARD, 'Notes to Beethoven's Education', *Journal of the American Musicological Society*, 18 (1975), 75.

LANDON, H. C. ROBBINS, *Haydn at Eszterháza 1766–1790* (London, 1978).

LANZA, GESUALDO, *The Elements of Singing* (London, [1809]).

LASSER, J. B., *Vollständige Anleitung zur Singkunst* (Munich, 1798).

LAVIGNAC, ALBERT, and LAURENCIE, LIONEL DE LA, *Encyclopédie de la musique et dictionnaire du Conservatoire* (Paris, 1920–31).

LEE, DOUGLAS, 'Some Embellished Versions of Sonatas by Franz Benda', *Musical Quarterly*, 62 (1976), 58–71.

LICHTENTHAL, PIETRO, *Dizionario e bibliografia della musica* (Milan, 1826).

LINDSAY, THOMAS, *The Elements of Flute Playing* (London, [1828]).

LISZT, FRANZ, preface to *Liszts Symphonische Dichtungen für grosses Orchester*, 3 vols. (Leipzig, Breitkopf & Härtel, [1856]).

LOCKNER, LOUIS PAUL, *Fritz Kreisler* (London, 1951).

LÖHLEIN, GEORG SIMON, *Clavier-Schule, oder kurze und gründliche Anweisung zur Melodie und Harmonie, durchgehends mit practischen Beyspielen erkläret* (Leipzig and Züllichau, 1765); 2nd edn., *Georg Simon Löhleins Clavier-Schule . . .* (Leipzig and Züllichau, 1773); rev. and enlarged 5th edn., ed. Johann Georg Witthauer (Leipzig and Züllichau, 1791); 6th edn., *G. C. [sic] Löhlein's Klavierschule oder Anweisung zum Klavier- und Fortepiano-Spiel umgearbeitet und sehr vermehrt von A. E. Müller* (Jena, 1804): for the alternative title of 6th edn. see Müller below.

—— *Anweisung zum Violinspielen, mit pracktischen [sic] Beyspielen und zur Uebung mit vier und zwanzig kleinen Duetten erläutert* (Leipzig and Züllichau, 1774); 4th edn., rev. Johann Friedrich Reichardt (Leipzig and Züllichau, 1797).

LUSSY, MATHIS, *Traité de l'expression musicale: Accents, nuances et mouvements dans la musique vocale et instrumentale* (Paris, 1874); 6th edn. (Paris, 1892); trans. M. E. von Glehn as *Musical Expression* (London, [*c.*1885]).

—— *Le Rhythme musical, son origine, sa fonction et son accentuation* (Paris, 1883).

MACDONALD, HUGH JOHN, 'Two Peculiarities of Berlioz's Notation', *Music & Letters*, 50 (1969), 25–44.

—— 'Berlioz and the Metronome', in P. A. Bloom, ed., *Berlioz Studies* (Cambridge, 1992), 17–36.

MC KERRELL, J., *A Familiar Introduction to the First Principles of Music* (London, [*c.*1800]).

MACKINLAY, MALCOLM STERLING, *García the Centenarian and his Times* (Edinburgh, 1908).

MALIBRAN, ALEXANDRE, *Louis Spohr* (Frankfurt-am-Main, 1860).

MALLOCH, WILLIAM, 'Carl Czerny's Metronome Marks for Haydn and Mozart Symphonies', *Early Music*, 16 (1988), 72–81.

MANFREDINI, VINCENZO, *Regole armoniche o siene Precetti ragionate* (Venice, 1775).

MARPURG, FRIEDRICH WILHELM, *Anleitung zum Clavierspielen der schönen Ausübung der heutigen Zeit gemäss* (Berlin, 1755); 2nd edn. (Berlin, 1765; fac. New York, 1969).

—— *Kritische Briefe über die Tonkunst* (Berlin, 1760–4).

MARTIN, DAVID, 'An Early Metronome', *Early Music*, 16 (1988), 90–2.

MARTY, JEAN-PIERRE, *The Tempo Indications of Mozart* (New Haven and London, 1988).

MARX, ADOLF BERNHARD, *Allgemeine Musiklehre* (Leipzig, 1839); trans. A. H. Wehrhan as *A Universal School of Music* (London, 1853).

—— *Die Musik der neunzehnten Jahrhunderts und ihre Pflege: Methode der Musik* (Leipzig, 1855), trans. August Heinrich Wehrhan as *The Music of the Nineteenth Century and its Culture* (London, 1854).

MENDEL, HERMANN, and REISSMANN, AUGUST, *Musikalisches Conversations-Lexikon* (Berlin, 1882).

MIES, PAUL, *Textkritische Untersuchungen bei Beethoven* (Munich and Duisburg, 1957).

—— 'Die Artikulationzeichen Strich und Punkt bei Wolfgang Amadeus Mozart', *Die Musikforschung*, 11 (1958), 428.

—— 'Ueber ein besonderes Akzentzeichen bei Johannes Brahms', in Georg Reichert and Martin Just, eds., *Bericht über den internationalen musikwissenschaftlichen Kongress Kassel 1962* (Kassel, 1963), 215–17.

MILCHMEYER, JOHANN PETER, *Die wahre Art das Pianoforte zu spielen* (Dresden, 1797).

MOENS-HAENEN, GRETA, *Das Vibrato in der Musik des Barock* (Graz, 1988).

MORAZZONI, G., *Verdi: Lettere inedite* (Milan, 1929).

MOSCHELES, IGNAZ: see Fétis.

MOSER, ANDREAS, *Joseph Joachim*, trans. Lilla Durham (London, 1901).

—— *Violinschule*: see Joachim.

—— *Geschichte des Violinspiels* (Berlin, 1923).

MOZART, LEOPOLD, *Versuch einer gründlichen Violinschule* (Augsburg, 1756); 3rd edn. (Augsburg, 1787); trans. Editha Knocker as *A Treatise on the Fundamental Principles of Violin Playing*, 2nd edn. (Oxford, 1951): incl. the additions and changes in the 1787 edn. as well as the whole of the original text. See also Anon.

MÜLLER, AUGUST EBERHARDT, *A. E. Müller's Klavier- und Fortepiano Schule* (Jena, 1804) (expanded 6th edn. of Löhlein's *Klavierschule*).

—— *Elementarbuch für Flötenspieler* (Leipzig, [1815]).

MUNSTER, R., 'Authentische Tempi zu den sechs letzten Sinfonien W. A. Mozarts?', *Mozart-Jahrbuch 1962–3*, 185–99.

Neue Zeitschrift für Musik, ed. Robert Alexander Schumann, Franz Brendel, etc. (Leipzig, 1834–1928).

NEUMANN, FREDERICK, *Ornamentation in Baroque and Post-Baroque Music* (Princeton, 1978).

—— *Ornamentation and Improvisation in Mozart* (Princeton, 1986).

—— *New Essays on Performance Practice* (Ann Arbor, 1989).

—— 'Dots and Strokes in Mozart', *Early Music*, 21 (1993), 429–35.

The New Grove Dictionary of Music and Musicians, ed. Stanley Sadie (London, 1980).

The New Grove Dictionary of Opera, ed. Stanley Sadie (London, 1992).

NICHOLSON, CHARLES, *Complete Preceptor for the German Flute* (London, [c.1816]).

—— *Preceptive Lessons for the Flute* (London, 1821).

—— *A School for the Flute* (New York, 1836).

NISSEN, GEORG NIKOLAUS, *Wolfgang Amadeus Mozarts Biographie* (Leipzig, 1828).

NOVELLO, MARY, *Voice and Vocal Art* (London, 1856).

PASQUALI, NICCOLO, *The Art of Fingering the Harpsichord* (Edinburgh, [c.1760]).

PAUL, OSCAR, *Handlexikon der Tonkunst* (Leipzig, 1873).

PETRI, JOHANN SAMUEL, *Anleitung zur practischen Musik, vor neuangehende Sänger und Instrumentspieler*, 2nd edn. (Leipzig, 1782).

PHILIP, ROBERT, *Early Recording and Musical Style: Changing Tastes in Instrumental Performance 1900–1950* (Cambridge, 1992).

—— 'The Recordings of Edward Elgar (1857–1934): Authenticity and Performance Practice', *Early Music*, 12 (1984), 481–9.

PLATEN, EMIL, 'Zeitgenössische Hinweise zur Aufführungspraxis der letzten Streichquartette Beethovens', in Rudolf Klein, ed., *Beiträge '76–78: Beethoven Kolloquium 1977; Dokumentation und Aufführungspraxis* (Kassel, 1978), 100–7.

POLLINI, FRANCESCO, *Metodo per clavicembalo* (Milan, 1811).

PORGES, HEINRICH, *Die Bühnenproben zu der Bayreuther Festspielen des Jahres 1876* (Chemnitz and Leipzig, 1881–96); trans. Robert L. Jacobs as *Wagner Rehearsing the 'Ring'* Cambridge, 1983).

QUANTZ, JOHANN JOACHIM, *Versuch einer Anweisung die Flöte traversiere zu spielen* (Berlin, 1752); trans. Edward R. Reilly as *On Playing the Flute* (London, 1966).

REES, ABRAHAM, ed., *Cyclopaedia* (London, 1819).

REICHA, ANTON, *Cours de composition musicale*, trans. and ed. Carl Czerny as *Vollständiges Lehrbuch der musikalischen Composition* (with parallel Fr. and Ger. text), 4 vols. (Vienna, 1834).

REICHARDT, JOHANN FRIEDRICH, *Ueber die Pflichten des Ripien-Violinisten* (Berlin and Leipzig, 1776).

RELLSTAB, JOHANN CARL FRIEDRICH, *Versuch über die Vereinigung der musikalischen und oratorischen Declamation* (Berlin, [1786]).

RIBEIRO, ALVARO, SJ, ed., *The Letters of Charles Burney* (Oxford, 1991).

RIEMANN, CARL WILHELM JULIUS HUGO, *Musik-Lexikon* (Leipzig, 1882).

—— 'Der Ausdruck in der Musik', *Sammlung musikalische Vorträge*, i, no. 50 (Leipzig, 1883).

—— *Musikalische Dynamik und Agogik: Lehrbuch der musikalische Phrasierung* (Hamburg, 1884).

—— *New Pianoforte-School/Neue Klavierschule*, 12 pts. (London, [1897–1910]).

RIEPEL, JOSEPH, *Anfangsgründe zur musikalischen Setzkunst* (Regensburg etc., 1752–68).

—— *Gründliche Erklärung der Tonordnung* (Frankfurt-am-Main and Leipzig, 1757).

RIES, FERDINAND: see Wegeler.

RIGGS, ROBERT D., 'Articulation in Mozart's and Beethoven's Sonatas for Piano and Violin', dissertation (Harvard University, 1987).

ROMBERG, BERNHARD HEINRICH, *Méthode de violoncelle* (Berlin, 1840); trans. as *A Complete Theoretical and Practical School for the Violoncello* (London, 1840).

ROSENBLUM, SANDRA, *Performance Practices in Classic Piano Music* (Bloomington, Ind., and Indianapolis, 1988).

ROUSSEAU, JEAN JACQUES, *Dictionnaire de musique* (Paris, 1768).

ROTHSCHILD, FRITZ, *The Lost Tradition: Musical Performance in the Time of Mozart and Beethoven* (London, 1961).

RUDOLF, MAX, 'Ein Beitrag zur Geschichte der Temponahme bei Mozart', *Mozart-Jahrbuch* (1976–7), 204–24.

SAINT-SÄENS, CAMILLE, *Souvenirs* (Paris, 1900); trans. E. G. Rich as *Musical Memoires* (London, 1921).

SASLOV ISIDOR, 'Tempos in the String Quartets of Joseph Haydn', dissertation (Indiana University, 1969).

SAURET, EMILE, *Gradus ad Parnassum du violiniste* op. 36 (Leipzig, [*c.*1890]).

SCHEIBE, JOHANN ADOLF, *Ueber die musikalische Composition, erster Theil: Die Theorie der Melodie und Harmonie* (Leipzig, 1773).

SCHENK, ERICH, 'Zur Aufführungspraxis des Tremolo bei Gluck', in Joseph Schmidt-Görg, ed., *Anthony von Hoboken: Festschrift zum 75. Geburtstag* (Mainz, 1962).

SCHETKY, JOHANN GEORG CHRISTOPH, *Practical and Progressive Lessons for the Violoncello* (London, 1811).

SCHILLING, GUSTAV, ed., *Encyclopädie der gesammten musikalischen Wissenschaften* (Stuttgart, 1835–8).

SCHINDLER, ANTON, *Biographie von Ludwig van Beethoven* (Münster, 1840).

SCHÖNBERG, ARNOLD, Serenade op. 24 (Copenhagen and Leipzig, W. Hansen, 1924), preface.

SCHOTEL, B., 'Schumann and the Metronome', in A. Walker, ed., *Robert Schumann: The Man and his Music* (London, 1972); rev. 2nd edn. (1976).

SCHRÖDER, HERMANN, *Die Kunst des Violinspiels* (Cologne, 1887).

SCHUBART, CHRISTIAN DANIEL FRIEDRICH, *Ideen zu einer Ästhetik der Tonkunst* (Vienna, 1806).

SCHUBERT, FRANZ, Impromptus, ed. Hugo Riemann (Henry Litolff Verlag, n.d.).

SCHUBERT, JOHANN FRIEDRICH, *Neue Singe-Schule oder gründliche und vollständige Anweisung zur Singkunst* (Leipzig, [1804]).

SCHUBERT, LOUIS, *Violinschule nach modernen Principien* op. 50 (Brunswick, [1883]); trans. T. Baker as *Violin Method in Accordance with Modern Principles* (New York, n.d.).

ŠEVČÍK, OTAKAR, *Schule der Violine-technik* op. 1 (Leipzig, 1881).

—— *Schule der Bogentechnik* op. 2 (Leipzig, 1895).

SMART, SIR GEORGE, Papers, British Library Dept. of Manuscripts, Add. 41771–9.

SOMFAI, LASLO, 'How to Read and Understand Haydn's Notation in its Chronologically Changing Concepts', in Eva Badura-Skoda, ed., *Joseph Haydn: Bericht über den Internationalen Joseph Haydn Kongress, Wien . . . 1982* (Munich, 1986).

SPOHR, LOUIS, *Violinschule* (Vienna, [1832]); trans. John Bishop as *Louis Spohr's Celebrated Violin School* (London, [1843]).

—— *Louis Spohr's Autobiography* (London, 1865).

—— *Louis Spohr Lebenserinnerungen*, ed. F. Göthel (Tutzing, 1968).

STADLEN, PETER, 'Schindler's Beethoven Forgeries', *Musical Times*, 118 (1977), 551.

—— 'Schindler and the Conversation Books', *Soundings*, 7 (1978), 2–18.

STARKE, FRIEDRICH, *Wiener Pianoforte-Schule* (Vienna, 1819).

STEIBELT, DANIEL, *Méthode de piano* (Leipzig, [1809]).

STOWELL, ROBIN, *Violin Technique and Performance Practice in the Late-Eighteenth and Early-Nineteenth Centuries* (Cambridge, 1985).

—— ed., *Performing Beethoven* (Cambridge, 1994).

STRAETEN, EDMUND VAN DER, *The Romance of the Fiddle: The Origin of the Modern Virtuoso and the Adventures of his Ancestors* (London, 1911).

STRUNK, OLIVER, *Source Readings in Music History* (New York, 1952).

SULZER, JOHANN GEORG, ed., *Allgemeine Theorie der schönen Künste*, 2 vols. (Leipzig, 1771–4), 2nd rev. edn. (Leipzig, 1792–4): contains many articles on music by Johann

Peter Kirnberger and Johann Abraham Peter Schulz; the former wrote articles from A to R and the latter those from S to Z as well as assisting with and editing earlier articles.

TALSMA, WILLEM, *Wiedergeburt der Klassiker* (Innsbruck, 1980).

TANS UR, WILLIAM, *A New Musical Grammar: or The Harmonical Speculator, with Philosophical Demonstrations on the Nature of Sound* (London, 1746).

—— *A Musical Grammar and Dictionary or General Introduction to the Whole Art of Music* . . . (Stokesley, [*c.*1820]).

TARTINI, GIUSEPPI, *Traité des agréments de la musique*, ed. E. R. Jacobi (Celle and New York, 1961).

TAYLOR, FRANKLIN, articles 'Appoggiatura', 'Phrasing', 'Shake', and 'Tremolo', in Grove, *Dictionary.*

TEMPERLEY, NICHOLAS, 'Berlioz and the Slur', *Music & Letters*, 50 (1969), 388.

—— 'Haydn's Tempos in *The Creation*', *Early Music*, 19 (1991), 235–45.

THALBERG, SIGISMOND, *L'Art du chant appliqué au piano* (Paris, n.d.).

TOEPLITZ, URI, 'Über die Tempi in Mozarts Instrumentalmusik', *Mozart-Jahrbuch* (1986), 171–202.

TOFT, ROBERT, 'The Expressive Pause: Punctuation, Rests, and Breathing in England 1770–1850', *Performance Practice Review*, 7 (1994), 199–232.

TOSI, PIER FRANCESCO, *Opinioni de' cantori antici e moderni, o sieno Osservazioni sopra il canto figurato* (Bologna, 1723); trans. and ed. [J. E.] Galliard as *Observations on the Florid Song; or, Sentiments on the Ancient and Modern Singers* (London, 1742).

TROMLITZ, JOHANN GEORG, *Ausführlicher und gründlicher Unterricht die Flöte zu spielen* (Leipzig, 1791); trans. and ed. Ardal Powell as *The Virtuoso Flute-Player* (Cambridge, 1991).

TÜRK, DANIEL GOTTLOB, *Klavierschule oder Anweisung zum Klavierspielen für Lehrer und Lernende mit kritischen Anmerkungen* (Leipzig and Halle, 1789); 2nd enlarged edn. (Leipzig and Halle, 1802).

TURNER, E. O., 'Tempo Variation: With Examples from Elgar', *Music & Letters*, 19 (1938), 308–23.

VACCAI, NICOLA, *Metodo pratico di canto italiano per camera* (London, 1832).

VALENTINE, THOMAS, *Dictionary of Terms Used in Music*, 2nd edn. (London, 1824).

VOGLER, GEORG JOSEPH, *Kuhrpfälzische Tonschule* (Mannheim, 1778).

WACKENRODER, WILHELM HEINRICH, *Herzensergiessungen eines kunstliebenden Kloster- buders* (Berlin, 1797).

WAGNER, RICHARD, *Gesammelte Schriften und Dichtungen*, 10 vols., 2nd edn. (Leipzig, 1887–8); ed. and trans. William Ashton Ellis as *Richard Wagner's Prose Works*, 8 vols. (London, 1892–9).

WALKER, ERNEST, 'The Appoggiatura', *Music & Letters*, 5 (1924), 121–44.

WALTHER, JOHANN GOTTFRIED, *Musicalisches Lexicon* (Leipzig, 1732).

WASIELEWSKY, J. W. VON, *Das Violoncell und seine Geschichte* (Leipzig, 1889).

WATKIN, DAVID, 'Beethoven's Sonatas for Piano and Cello: Aspects of Technique and Performance', in Stowell, ed., *Performing Beethoven*, 89–116.

WEBER, GOTTFRIED, *Versuch einer geordneten Theorie der Tonsetzkunst* (Mainz, 1817–21); trans. J. F. Warner as *Theory of Musical Composition*, 2 vols. (London, 1846).

—— *Allgemeine Musiklehre zum Selbstunterricht für Lehre und Lernende* (Darmstadt, 1822).

WEGELER, FRANZ GERHARDT, and RIES, FERDINAND, *Biographische Notizen über Ludwig van Beethoven* (Koblenz, 1838).

WEIPPERT, JOHN ERHARDT, *The Pedal Harp Rotula, and New Instructions for that Instrument* (London, [*c.*1800]).

WEISS, CHARLES, *A New Methodical Instruction Book for the Flute* (London, [*c.*1821]).

Wiener allgemeine musikalische Zeitung, ed. Ignaz von Schönholz, 1 vol. (Vienna, 1813).

WILLIAMS, PETER, 'Two Case Studies in Performance Practice and the Details of Notation, I: J. S. Bach and 2/4 Time', *Early Music*, 21 (1993), 613–22.

WINRAM, J., *Violin Playing and Violin Adjustment* (Edinburgh and London, 1908).

WOLDEMAR, MICHEL, *Grande méthode ou étude élementaire pour le violon* (Paris, [*c.*1800]), 2nd edn. (Paris, [*c.*1800]).

—— ed., *Méthode de violon par L. Mozart redigée par Woldemar, élève de Lolli* (Paris, 1801).

WOLF, GEORG FRIEDRICH, *Kurzer aber deutlicher Unterricht im Klavierspiel* (Göttingen, 1783).

WOOD, SIR HENRY, *The Gentle Art of Singing* (Oxford, 1927).

WRAGG, J., *The Flute Preceptor* (London, *c.*1795).

ZASLAW, NEAL, 'Mozart's Tempo Conventions', *International Musicological Society Congress Report*, 11 (Copenhagen, 1972), 720–33.

—— 'The Compleat Orchestral Musician', *Early Music*, 7 (1979), 46–57.

—— 'The Orchestral Musician Compleated', *Early Music*, 8 (1980), 71.

INDEX

❦